European Environmental Law

Prof. Jan H. Jans & Dr. Hans H.B. Vedder

Third edition

Europa Law Publishing is a publishing company
specializing in European Union law, international trade
law, public international law, environmental law and
comparative national law.
For further information please contact Europa Law
Publishing via email: info@europalawpublishing.com
or visit our website at: www.europalawpublishing.com.

© Europa Law Publishing, Jans, Vedder, 2008

Typeset in Scala and Scala Sans, Graphic design by
G2K Designers, Groningen/Amsterdam

NUR 828
ISBN 978-90-76871-76-9 (hardback)
ISBN 978-90-76871-77-6 (paperback)

British Library Cataloguing-in-Publication Data
A catalogue record for this book is available from the
British Library

Preface

It is with great pleasure that I have accepted the offer of writing a preface to the third edition of this leading monograph on European environmental law. In cooperation with Dr. Vedder, this volume has now been completely updated and revised by Professor Jans, who is one of the foremost commentators on European environmental law.

In the past 30 years, the EU has adopted a substantial and diverse range of environmental measures aimed at improving the quality of the environment for European citizens and providing them with a high quality of life. This book provides an in-depth analysis of these measures and discusses important legal issues of European environmental law. What are the legal grounds for EC environmental policy and on what principles are directives and regulations based? To what extent do EC environmental directives preclude more stringent national environmental standards? What requirements has the Court of Justice imposed on the Member States implementing environmental directives? To what extent can European environmental law be relied upon and challenged before national courts and the Court of Justice? How do the Treaty rules on the internal market and undistorted competition co-exist with national environmental policy?

The book also addresses the important role played by the European Commission with respect to the implementation and enforcement of the law. Our environment can only be well protected if Member States properly transpose and apply the legislation they have signed up to. As Commissioner responsible for the environment, it is my duty to ensure that EU environmental legislation is implemented in full, with precision and on time. This is important because legislation which is not or incorrectly implemented will not achieve the desired effect for the environment. Although the responsibility for implementation of EU environmental law lies primarily with the Member States, it is an essential task for the Commission, as guardian of the Treaty, to check that the national measures adopted meet the requirements of the environmental directives they purport to transpose. Only when environmental legislation is properly implemented will it produce its desired effects: protecting and improving the quality of the environment and providing European citizens with the quality of life and the pleasant surroundings they deserve.

This book is indeed a very welcome contribution to the theory and practice of European environmental law.

Stavros Dimas
Brussels, November 2007

Acknowledgments

Many people contributed to this third edition of *European Environmental Law*, to all of whom we owe a debt of gratitude. In the first place, our colleagues at the Department of Administrative Law and Public Administration and the Department of European Law of the University of Groningen. They let us work on this book while, perhaps, they considered that more pressing university commitments should have taken priority instead.

We have benefited greatly from comments on the draft manuscript made by a number of colleagues. In particular we would like to mention Prof. Dr. Hanna Sevenster and Jos Janssen, Centre for Environmental Law, University of Amsterdam. We thank also those persons who have commented in the many book reviews on the second edition. We do hope that that their invaluable remarks are reflected in this edition.

Francisca Knoops assisted Jan Jans in gathering new case law and legislative developments which have occurred since the publication of the second edition in 2000. Her research assistance is highly appreciated. Hans Vedder would like to express his gratitude to Katharina Siebert for her work in sifting through several hundred amendments, new decisions, directives, regulations and footnotes. Most of all, his thanks go to his family for allowing him to continue working during the evenings and weekends.

Dr. Stavros Dimas, European Commissioner responsible for environmental policy was so kind to do us the honour in writing the preface to this third edition.

Finally, we would like to thank Janet Major for her work editing our English texts.

The book has been brought up to date to present new legislation, case law and literature as it stood on 1 September 2007. New developments after that date have only incidentally been taken into account.

As always, the authors will be pleased to receive any comments or suggestions readers may care to make.

The book is dedicated to future generations.

Jan Jans, Hans Vedder
Groningen/Appingedam, December 2007

Abbreviations

AB	Administratiefrechtelijke Beslissingen
ACP	African, Caribbean and Pacific (states which are party to the Lomé Convention)
ACEA	Association des constructeurs européens d'automobile
ALARA	As low as reasonable achievable
BAT(NEC)	Best available technology (not entailling excessive costs)
CAP	Common Agricultural Policy
CDM	Clean Development Mechanism
CEN	Comité Européen de Normalisation
CENELEC	Comité Européen de Normalisation Electrotechnique
CER	Certified Emissions Reduction
CITES	Convention on International Trade in Endangered Species of Wild Flora and Fauna
C.M.L.R.	Common Market Law Reports
CMLRev.	Common Market Law Review
COM	Communication of the European Commission
CO2	Carbon dioxide
DSD	Duales System Deutschland
DöV	Die öffentliche Verwaltung
DVBl.	Deutsches Verwaltungsblatt
EEAP	Energy Efficiency Action Plan
EIA	Environmental Impact Assessment
EINECS	European Inventory of Existing Chemical Substances
EAGGF	European Agricultural Guidance and Guarantee Fund
EAEC	European Atomic Energy Community (Euratom)
EEA	European Economic Area
ECA	European Chemicals Agency
ECJ	European Court of Justice
E(E)C	European (Economic) Community
ECR	European Court Reports
ECU	European Currency Unit
EELR	European Environmental Law Review
EFTA	European Free Trade Association
ECHR	Reports of Judgments and Decisions of the European Court of Human Rights
EFSA	European Food Safety Authority
EIA	Environmental Impact Assessment
ELR	European Law Review
ELV	End of Life Vehicles
EMAS	European eco-management and audit scheme
Env. L.R.	Environmental Law Reports
EP	European Parliament
EPER	European Pollutant Emission Register
EPL	European Public Law

ERDF	European Regional Development Fund
ERU	Emissions Reduction Unit
ESF	European Social Fund
ET	Emissions Trading
ETP	Eastern Tropical Pacific Ocean
EU	European Union
EUEB	European Union Eco-labeling Board
EuR	Europarecht
EWC	European Waste Catalogue
FAO	Food and Agriculture Organization
FEU	Treaty on the Functioning of the European Union
GATT	General Agreement on Tarrifs and Trade
GDB	Genossenschaft Deutscher Brunnen
GHS	Globally Harmonised System of Classification and Labelling of Chemicals
GLP	Good laboratory practice
GMM	Genetically modified micro-organism
GMO	Genetically modified organism
IBA	Inventory of Important Bird Areas in the European Community
ICRP	International Commission on Radiological Protection
IFCO	International Fruit Container Organization
ILM	International Legal Materials
ILO	International Labour Organization
IMO	International Maritime Organization
IMPEL	Network for the Implementation and Enforcement of Environmental Law
IPP	Integrated product policy
IPPC	Integrated Prevention and Pollution Control
IRLR	Industrial Relations Law Reports
ISO	International Standards Organisation
JEL	Journal of Environmental Law
JI	Joint Implementation
JWT	Journal of World Trade Law
LCA	Life cycle analysis
LIEI	Legal Issues of European/Economic Integration
LIFE	Financial Instrument for the Environment
LMO	Living modified organism
MARPOL	Convention on Maritime Pollution
MEP	Member of European Parliament
M&R	Tijdschrift voor Milieu en Recht
MR	Milieurechtspraak
MRL	Maximum Residue Levels
NAP	National allocation plan

NJ	Nederlandse Jurisprudentie
NJB	Nederlands Juristenblad
NVwZ	Neue Zeitschrift für Verwaltungsrecht
N.y.r.	Not yet reported
OECD	Organisation for Economic Co-operation and Development
OJ	Official Journal
OLAF	Office européen de lutte anti-fraude
PIC	Prior Informed Consent
PPM	Production and Processing Methods
PRTR	Pollutant Release and Transfer Register
REACH	Registration, Evaluation, Authorisation and Restriction of Chemicals
RECIEL	Review of European Community and International Environmental Law
ROHS	Restriction of certain hazardous substances
SAC	Special Area of Conservation
SCI	Site of Community Importance
SEA	Single European Act
SEA	Strategic Environmental Assessment
SEW	Sociaal-Economische Wetgeving
SME	Small and Medium-sized Enterprise
SOLAS	International Convention for the Safety of Life at Sea
SPA	Special Protection Area
TA	Technische Anleitung
TiO2	Titanium dioxide
TREM	Trade Related Environmental Measure
UNCLOS	United Nations Convention on the Law of the Sea
UNEP	United Nations Environment Programme
UNFCCC	United Nations Framework Convention on Climate Change
VAT	Value Added Tax
VOTOB	Vereniging van Onafhankelijke Tankopslag Bedrijven
WEEE	Waste Electrical and Electronic Equipment
WHO	World Health Organization
WTO	World Trade Organization
YEEL	Yearbook of European Environmental Law
YEL	Yearbook of European Law

CHAPTER I

Development and Principles

I The Development of European Environmental Law

The first phase

The development of European environmental law can be separated into a number of phases. The first phase began with the entry into force of the original version of the EEC Treaty on 1 January 1958 and continued up to 1972. This was the period during which the European institutions paid no specific attention to the development of an environment policy. Only incidentally were decisions taken which, in retrospect, could perhaps be regarded as environmental measures. For example, in 1967, Directive 67/548[1] relating to the classification, packaging and labelling of dangerous preparations, and, in 1970, Directive 70/157, relating to the permissible sound level and the exhaust system of motor vehicles.[2] Although these were primarily measures taken with a view to the attainment of the common market, environmental considerations undoubtedly played a part.

The second phase

In fact, the true starting signal for the development of a European environment policy was only given in 1972 when, at a European Council Summit meeting, it was declared that economic expansion, which is not an end in itself, must as a priority help to attenuate the disparities in living conditions. It was thought that it must result in an improved quality as well as an improved standard of life. Also, special attention should be paid to non-material values and wealth and to the protection of the environment so that progress could serve mankind. The European Council stressed the value of a European environment policy.[3] Therefore, they requested that the European institutions draw up an action program with a precise schedule before 31 July 1973. This Declaration marked the beginning of the second phase, which lasted until the entry into force of the Single European Act on 1 July 1987. In the Declaration of the Council of the European Communities and of the representatives of the Governments of the Member States meeting in the Council of 22 November 1973 on the programme of action of the European Communities on the environment, we read:

'Whereas in particular, in accordance with Article 2 of the Treaty, the task of the European Economic Community is to promote throughout the Community a harmonious development of economic activities and a continuous and balanced expansion, which cannot be imagined in the absence of an effective campaign to combat pollution and nuisance or of an improvement in the quality of life and the protection of the environment.'

---

[1] OJ 1967 L 196/1.

[2] OJ 1971 L 42/16.

[3] Bulletin EC 1972, No. 10.

Although the term 'environmental protection' was not as such found in the objectives enumerated in Articles 2 and 3 of the EEC Treaty in those days, this Declaration did in effect mean that, by an extensive interpretation of 'economic expansion', which is expressly included as an aim in Article 2 EC, environmental protection could become the subject of European decision-making. Henceforth, economic expansion was to be regarded not only in quantitative terms, but also qualitatively. Despite the Declaration, the extent of the competence of the EEC to effect a comprehensive environment policy remained a matter of controversy. Nevertheless, numerous directives and regulations have been adopted on almost every conceivable aspect of environment policy since 1971. One feature of this second phase was that policy which was specifically presented as European environment policy was developed on the basis of a treaty having no specific environmental competences.

In this second phase, decision-making in respect of European environment policy was based primarily on Articles 100 and 235 EEC (now Articles 94 and 308 EC). Examples of environmental measures dating from this period that were based exclusively on Article 100 EEC were:

· Directive 85/210 concerning the lead content of petrol;[4]
· Directive 73/404 relating to detergents;[5]
· Directive 78/1015 on the permissible sound level and exhaust system of motor cycles.[6]

Article 100 EEC could be used where differences in national environmental legislation had a detrimental effect on the common market. This practice was confirmed by the Court of Justice in Case 92/79, in a judgment in which the validity of Directive 75/716 relating to the maximum sulphur content of liquid fuels was raised.[7] In the words of the Court:

'It is by no means ruled out that provisions on the environment may be based upon Article 100 of the Treaty. Provisions which are made necessary by considerations relating to the environment and health may be a burden upon undertakings to which they apply and if there is no harmonization of national provisions on the matter, competition may be appreciably distorted.'

Most of the environmental legislation dating from the period before the Single European Act (1987) was based on both Article 100 and Article 235 EEC. Important examples include:

· Directive 76/464 on pollution caused by certain dangerous substances discharged into the aquatic environment of the Community;[8]

---

4   OJ 1985 L 96/25.
5   OJ 1973 L 347/51.
6   OJ 1978 L 349/21.
7   Case 92/79 Commission v. Italy [1980] ECR 1115.
8   OJ 1976 L 129/23.

- Directive 84/360 on the combating of air pollution from industrial plants;[9]
- Directive 82/501 on the major-accident hazards of certain industrial plants[10] and
- Directive 78/319 on toxic and dangerous waste.[11]

In practice, it was apparent that in the field of environmental protection there was a clear need for an additional legal basis besides the 'old' Article 100 EEC. After all, the objectives of Article 100 EEC, namely the abolishing of measures affecting the functioning of the common market, placed constraints on the use that could be made of that article as a legal basis for environment policy. On the principle that the powers extend only to what has been conferred by the Treaty, Article 100 EEC could not be employed where other or more far-reaching environmental measures had to be taken than were merely necessary for the proper functioning of the common market. Moreover, Article 3(h) EC still provides that the approximation of laws is only possible 'to the extent required for the proper functioning of the common market.'

To remedy this lacuna, the Council would generally invoke Article 235 EEC. This provision could be used 'if action by the Community should prove necessary to attain, in the course of the operation of the common market, one of the objectives of the Community and this Treaty has not provided the necessary powers'. It has already been noted that, by extensive interpretation of Article 2 EC, environmental protection was already considered an objective of the EC. This was confirmed by the Court of Justice in 1985 in the *ADBHU* case.[12]

> This case concerned the validity of a directive on the disposal of waste oils. It was contended that provisions imposing a system of permits on undertakings which disposed of waste oils and a system of zones within which such undertakings had to operate were incompatible with the principle of the free movement of goods. The directive in question was based on both Article 100 and Article 235 EEC. This joint legal basis was justified in the preamble to the directive as follows. On the one hand, it was pointed out that any disparity between the provisions on the disposal of waste oils in the various Member States could create unequal conditions of competition, thus necessitating the use of Article 100 EEC as the legal basis for approximation. On the other hand, the Council felt it necessary to accompany this approximation of laws by wider regulations so that one of the aims of the EC, protection of the environment, could be achieved. For this purpose, it invoked Article 235 EEC as an additional legal basis. The Court held as follows: 'In the first place it should be observed that the principle of freedom of trade is not to be viewed in absolute terms but is subject to certain limits justified by the objectives

---

9   OJ 1984 L 188/20.

10   OJ 1982 L 230/1.

11   OJ 1978 L 84/43.

12   Case 240/83 *ADBHU* [1985] ECR 531.

of general interest pursued by the Community provided that the rights in question are not substantively impaired. There is no reason to conclude that the directive has exceeded those limits. The directive must be seen in the perspective of environmental protection, which is one of the Community's essential objectives.'

The Court continued:

'It follows from the foregoing that the measures prescribed by the directive do not create barriers to intra-Community trade, and that in so far as such measures, in particular the requirement that permits must be obtained in advance, have a restrictive effect on the freedom of trade and of competition, they must nevertheless neither be discriminatory nor go beyond the inevitable restrictions which are justified by the pursuit of *the objective of environmental protection*, which is in the general interest. That being so, Articles 5 and 6 cannot be regarded as incompatible with the fundamental principles of Community law mentioned above.'[13]

The significance of this judgment was that the Court had for the first time recognised 'environmental protection' as one of the Community's essential objectives.[14] This meant that Article 235 EEC could be used not only as a supplementary legal basis to Article 100 EEC, but could *itself* form the legal basis for European environment policy. An example of a directive based solely on Article 235 EEC is the Wild Birds Directive.[15] Nevertheless, only a few measures have been based solely on Article 235 EEC, for example, Directive 82/884 on a limit value for lead in the air[16] and Recommendation 81/972 concerning the re-use of paper and the use of recycled paper.[17]

The third phase

The third phase in the development of a European environment policy commenced on 1 July 1987, the date on which the changes to the EEC Treaty brought about by the Single European Act came into force, and continued until the date the Treaty on European Union ('Maastricht') entered into force. Although the case law of the Court of Justice had specifically dealt with environmental protection before then, this phase was notable because, for the first time, the objectives of the environment policy were enshrined in the Treaty. The inclusion in the Treaty of provisions designed specifically to protect the environment, for example Articles 130r, 130s, 130t, 100a(3) and 100a(4) EEC,[18] confirmed the

---

[13] Emphasis added by the authors.

[14] This has been confirmed in more recent case law: Case 302/86 *Commission* v. *Denmark* [1988] ECR 4607, para. 8, Case C-213/96 *Outokumpu* [1998] ECR I-1777, para. 32 and Case C-176/03 *Commission* v. *Council* [2005] ECR I-7879.

[15] Directive 79/409 on the conservation of wild birds, OJ 1979 L 103/1.

[16] OJ 1982 L 378/15.

[17] OJ 1981 L 355/56.

[18] Now Articles 174, 175, 176, 95(3) and 95(4) EC.

Community's task in developing a European environment policy. The Treaty incorporated specific powers aimed at the protection of the environment.

In view of these express environmental powers, it was not surprising that the 'old' Article 235 EEC was in that period hardly ever invoked as a legal basis for environmental measures. The explicit environmental provisions of the Treaty made this unnecessary. Only in exceptional cases, such as Directive 93/76 to limit carbon dioxide emissions by improving energy efficiency,[19] might there be a need to base environmental measures on this 'catch all' provision.

The fourth phase

The fourth phase of European environmental law started with the entry into force on 1 November 1993 of the Treaty on European Union. In other words, the post-Maastricht phase. For the first time, the term 'environment' was actually referred to in the key Articles 2 and 3 of the EC Treaty, which set out the objectives and activities of the Community. Article 2 referred to 'the promotion, throughout the Community, of a harmonious and balanced development of economic activities, sustainable and non-inflationary growth respecting the environment', while Article 3(k) stated that one of the activities for attaining this was 'a policy in the sphere of the environment'.[20]

The formulation 'sustainable growth' in Article 2 EC was criticised as being a departure from the more usual formulation 'sustainable development'.[21] From the point of view of environmental protection, the concept of 'sustainable growth' seemed marginally weaker than that of 'sustainable development'. Be that as it may, the incorporation of an environmental objective was certainly of great political significance.

The fourth phase is also distinct in that, for the first time, decisions under the Title on the Environment could be taken by a qualified majority. A further striking change as a result of 'Maastricht' was the status given to the action programmes on the environment. The increased competences of the European Parliament in the adoption of these programmes should also be noted. These programmes could be adopted under what is known as the co-decision procedure, which meant the European Parliament could exercise a veto.

The fifth phase

The fifth phase is the post-Amsterdam and post-Nice phase. The Treaty of Amsterdam (1997) has introduced a number of interesting changes to the legal framework of European environmental policy. In the first place, the constitutional status of 'environmental protection' has been clarified. The text of Article

---

[19] OJ 1993 L 237/28. Now repealed by Directive 2006/32 on energy end-use efficiency and energy services; OJ 2006 L 114/64.

[20] Acknowledged by the Court in Case C-213/96 *Outokumpu Oy* [1998] ECR I-1801, para. 32.

[21] A reference to 'sustainable growth' in European secondary legislation can be found in the preamble of Directive 94/62 on packaging and packaging waste, OJ 1994 L 365/10: 'the reduction of waste is essential for the sustainable growth specifically called for by the Treaty on European Union'.

2 EC has been improved considerably. It now states that the Community shall have as its task promoting a harmonious, balanced and sustainable development of economic activities. This formulation is much more in line with internationally accepted practice in the environmental policy area.[22]

Sustainable development means the improvement of the standard of living and welfare of the relevant populations within the limits of the capacity of the ecosystems, by maintaining natural assets and their biological diversity for the benefit of present and future generations. In other words: to meet the needs of the present generation without compromising those of future generations.[23]

> The sustainable development strategy launched in 2001 by the Göteborg summit was composed of two main parts. The first proposed objectives and policy measures to tackle a number of key unsustainable trends, like combat climate change, ensure sustainable transport, address threats to public health, such as chemicals pollution, unsafe food and infectious diseases, manage natural resources more responsibly and stop biodiversity decline, combat poverty and social exclusion, and meet the challenge of an ageing population. The second part of the strategy called for a new approach to policy-making. The central instrument developed for this purpose was the obligation for the Commission to submit each new policy proposal to an Impact Assessment procedure.[24] More recently the EU reviewed its sustainable development strategy.[25]

Being more a guideline to policy action than a normative-legal concept, the political importance of this concept cannot be underestimated. Of course, the text is not entirely satisfactory, because there is still a link in Article 2 EC between the use of the terms 'sustainable development' and 'economic activities' and because we find a slightly different formulation in Article 2 of the Treaty on European Union.[26] Nevertheless, it must be said that as a whole the text really has improved.

As far as the constitutional status of environmental protection is concerned, there was however a second improvement. The Amsterdam Treaty not only

---

[22] See for a reference to the concept of 'sustainable development' in secondary legislation Article 9 of Directive 96/62 on ambient air quality assessment and management, OJ 1996 L 296/55.

[23] Presidency Conclusions European Council at Göteborg, 15 and 16 June 2001, point 19. At this summit the European Council declared sustainable development to be 'a fundamental objective under the Treaties.' Cf. also the 'classic' definition from the Brundtland report: 'Sustainable development is development that meets the needs of the present without compromising the ability of future generations to meet their own needs'; World Commission on Environment and Development, *Our Common Future* (Oxford 1987), at 8. See for a more in-depth treatment of the issue of sustainable development and European law, Lee (2005), chapter 2.

[24] Commission's Communication COM (2002) 276 of 5 June 2002 on Impact Assessment.

[25] The text of the Renewed Sustainable Development Strategy is published in the Annex to European Council DOC 10117/06, 9 June 2006.

[26] 'a balanced and sustainable development'.

speaks of sustainable development, in Article 2 EC, it also introduced as a task to promote 'a high level of protection and improvement of the quality of the environment'.[27] This 'high level of protection principle' will be dealt with more extensively in section 3.2 of this chapter. It is generally understood that within the objectives laid down in Article 2 EC, there is no hierarchy.[28]

A third improvement is the 'promotion' of the integration principle, Article 6 EC, according to which environmental protection requirements must be integrated into the definition and implementation of other Community policies, as a 'General Principle' of EC law. The legal consequences of this will be discussed in section 2 of this chapter.

With respect to the possibilities of derogation, after harmonisation, from internal market related measures by virtue of environmental protection requirements, it cannot be denied that the text introduced by the Amsterdam Treaty (Article 95(4) to (6) EC) is an improvement, not only from a substantive but also from a procedural point of view. The procedure will be discussed in detail in Chapter 3, section 6.

The provisions of the environmental paragraph, now Articles 174-176 in the EC Treaty, have not been changed by the Amsterdam Treaty in their material, their substantive meaning. Slight changes in the text of Article 175 EC however have been made by the Treaty of Nice (2001). A major change brought about by the Amsterdam Treaty however concerned the decision-making procedures. The co-decision procedure has become the standard decision-making procedure for environmental legislation. Although co-decision does not automatically lead to more environmentally friendly legislation, this change must nevertheless be welcomed. We have come a long way from decision-making by unanimity under the old Articles 100 and 235 EEC to majority voting and a strong role for the European Parliament under an explicit environment paragraph in the Treaty.

The next phase is now almost on us. After the collapse of the Constitutional Treaty[29] the Member States have agreed on a new text, the so called 'Reform Treaty'.[30] Before it can enter into force (2009?), the Reform Treaty must be ratified by all Member States according to the procedure of Article 48 EU. The Reform Treaty contains amendments to the EU Treaty and the EC Treaty. The Reform Treaty will rename the EC Treaty in 'Treaty on the Functioning of the European Union' (FEU) and will renumber some of its provisions.[31] The concept of *European Community* will be replaced throughout the treaties in *European Union*. Therefore, one can say that the European Union will replace and succeed the European Community after the Reform Treaty has entered into force.[32]

---

[27] Cf. also Article 3(3) EU after amendment by the Reform Treaty.

[28] Cf. Bär & Kraemer (1998) at 316.

[29] OJ 2004 C 310.

[30] We have made use of the text of the Reform Treaty in CIG 14/07, Brussels, 3 December 2007.

[31] For instance, the Articles 174-176 EC will be renumbered to Articles 191-193 FEU.

[32] The, limited, consequences of the Reform Treaty for European environmental policy will be discussed *infra*, in particular sections 2 and 3.1 of this chapter and in Chapter 2, sections 1-2.

2 General Principles of EC Law in Relation to Environmental Protection

The principle of specific competences

Why is it necessary to concern ourselves with the legal basis of European environment policy? Does it have any practical significance, apart from satisfying academic curiosity? The answer has to be: yes, it does! Establishing the legal basis of a proposed European measure on the environment is important for at least three reasons. In the first place because the institutions do not have the unlimited competences of the national legislators to take whatever measures they please. The institutions' powers extend only to what has been expressly conferred by treaty. As provided in Article 5 EC: 'The Community shall act within the limits of the powers conferred upon it by this Treaty and of the objectives assigned to it therein.'[33] In European law, acting without competence results in invalid measures.

Deciding the proper legal basis of a European environmental measure is thus in the first place important in order to determine the extent of the competence in the matter in question, and thus the validity of measures taken on the basis of this competence.

In the second place, deciding the legal basis is relevant for the decision-making procedure to be followed when adopting a particular environmental measure. In Chapter 2, we shall see that European law provides for various decision-making procedures in respect of environmental measures. Some decisions have to be taken using the co-decision procedure, others unanimously and yet others by a qualified majority. The role played by the various participants in the decision-making process (Commission, European Parliament and Council), and thus their means of influencing the environment policy, is different under each of these procedures. It is clear from the Court's case law that the choice of the correct legal basis depends on the 'main object' of the measure.[34] If the centre of gravity of a measure harmonising, for example, environmental product standards is the internal market, Article 95 EC is the appropriate legal basis. If the centre of gravity is protection of the environment, decision-making under Article 175 EC is appropriate.[35]

In the third place, the choice of legal basis affects the extent to which Member States are entitled to adopt more stringent environmental measures than the European standards agreed upon. This important point will be discussed in detail in Chapter 3, section 4.

The subsidiarity principle

The second paragraph of Article 5 EC refers to the principle of subsidiarity in general terms: 'In areas which do not fall within its exclusive competence, the

---

[33] Cf. also Article 5(2) EU after amendment by the Reform Treaty.

[34] Case C-155/91 *Commission* v. *Council* [1993] ECR I-939, Case C-187/93 *EP* v. *Council* [1994] ECR I-2857.

[35] See on this more in detail Chapter 2, section 4.

Community shall take action, in accordance with the principle of subsidiarity, only if and in so far as the objectives of the proposed action cannot be sufficiently achieved by the Member States and can therefore, by reason of the scale or effects of the proposed action, be better achieved by the Community.'[36]

The principle thus contains both a negative criterion (not sufficiently achieved by the Member States) and a positive one (better achieved by the Community) by which to judge European acts. According to the Amsterdam Treaty Protocol on the application of the principle of subsidiarity, European action must meet both criteria to be justified.[37] Any (proposed) legislation must be justified with regard to the principle. Legislation to date in general provides justification in this respect.[38] However, the references in the preamble of European environmental measures do have a somewhat 'standard' and therefore obligatory character.

> See for instance the reference to the subsidiarity principle in Directive 2004/101 establishing a scheme for greenhouse gas emission allowance trading, in respect of the Kyoto Protocol's project mechanisms. Point 19 of the preamble reads: 'Since the objective of the proposed action, namely the establishment of a link between the Kyoto project-based mechanisms and the Community scheme, cannot be sufficiently achieved by the Member States acting individually, and can therefore by reason of the scale and effects of this action be better achieved at Community level, the Community may adopt measures, in accordance with the principle of subsidiarity as set out in Article 5 of the Treaty. In accordance with the principle of proportionality, as set out in that Article, this Directive does not go beyond what is necessary in order to achieve that objective.'
>
> Or take the preamble (point 15) of Directive 2005/35 on ship-source pollution and on the introduction of penalties for infringements: 'Since the objectives of this Directive, namely the incorporation of the international ship-source pollution standards into Community law and the establishment of penalties – criminal or administrative – for violation of them in order to ensure a high level of safety and environmental protection in maritime transport, cannot be sufficiently achieved by the Member States and can therefore be better achieved at Community level, the Community may adopt measures, in accordance with the principle of subsidiarity as set out in Article 5 of the Treaty. In accordance with the principle of proportionality, as set out in that Article, this Directive does not go beyond what is necessary in order to achieve those objectives.'[39]

As far as the likely implications of the subsidiarity principle for environmental law are concerned, the following should be noted. In the first place, the Protocol states that action is justified where the issue under consideration has trans-

---

[36] Cf. also Article 5(3) EU after amendment by the Reform Treaty.

[37] Protocol on the Application of the Principles of Subsidiarity and Proportionality.

[38] OJ 2004 L 338/18.

[39] OJ 2005 L 255/11.

national aspects, which cannot be satisfactorily regulated by action by Member States.[40] This means that European action to prevent cross-border environmental effects satisfies the subsidiarity principle. In view of the territorial limitations of many national powers, unilateral action by Member States is clearly going to be less effective than concerted action where the source of pollution is situated abroad. This would, for example, apply to action to restrict all kinds of transfrontier environmental pollution of a regional (water and air pollution) or global (depletion of the ozone layer, greenhouse effect resulting from CO_2 emissions, maintenance of biodiversity) nature[41] or to the protection of wild fauna and flora.[42]

> As early as 1987 the Court held in Case 247/85 that the Wild Birds Directive is based on the assumption that the protection of wild birds is 'typically a transfrontier environment problem entailing common responsibilities for the Member States'.[43] The Habitats Directive[44] also stipulates that it is necessary to take measures at European level to conserve threatened habitats and species, as these form part of the Community's natural heritage and the threats to them are often of a transboundary nature. A further example is provided by Directive 91/676 on pollution caused by nitrates from agricultural sources.[45] Its preamble states that action at European level is necessary because pollution of water due to nitrates in one Member State can influence waters in other Member States. Other examples of directives in which the preamble refers to possible transfrontier effects are Directive 90/219 on genetically modified micro-organisms[46] and Directive 89/369 on the incineration of municipal waste.[47] One of the arguments supporting the conclusion by the EC of the Convention on the protection of the Alps was the cross-border nature of the ecological problems of the Alpine area.[48]

In general, therefore, action by the EU on transfrontier environmental matters would seem to pass the test of subsidiarity.

According to the Protocol, another important element of the application of the subsidiarity principle is whether action by Member States alone or lack

---

[40] See also Lee (2005) at 10.

[41] See for instance Directive 2001/81 on national emission ceilings for certain atmospheric pollutants, OJ 2001 L 309/22, point 13 of the preamble. It was stated that in accordance with the subsidiarity principle 'limitation of emissions of acidifying and eutrophying pollutants and ozone precursors, cannot be sufficiently achieved by the Member States because of the transboundary nature of the pollution'.

[42] Cf. however Lee (2005) at 12, who makes a distinction between physical spillovers (transnational pollution) and 'psychic' spillovers (protection of the EU's common heritage).

[43] Case 247/85 *Commission v. Belgium* [1987] ECR 3029.

[44] Directive 92/43 on the conservation of natural habitats, OJ 1992 L 206/7.

[45] OJ 1991 L 375/1.

[46] OJ 1990 L 117/1.

[47] OJ 1989 L 163/32.

[48] OJ 1996 L 61/32, concluded by Council Decision 96/191, OJ 1996 L 61/31.

of European action would conflict with the requirements of the Treaty, such as the need to correct distortion of competition or avoid restrictions on trade or strengthen economic and social cohesion.[49] As far as the environment is concerned, this could apply in the following situation, for instance. A purely national, product-oriented environmental policy could easily result in restrictions on the import and export of goods, which might harm the environment. Harmonisation of environmental product standards at a European level can ensure that effective environmental policy need not be at the expense of the operation and functioning of the internal market. As the scope of protection pursued by environmental product standards have immediate effects on trade, it is clear that these measures comply with the subsidiarity principle.[50]

More problematic from a subsidiarity point of view is its role in respect of emission and environmental quality standards.[51] On the one hand, it can be said that European standard setting tends to even out competitive differences and avoids 'a race to the bottom'.[52] On the other hand, it deprives Member States of the opportunity of maintaining 'healthy' policy competition. A reasonable balance could be attained here if European environmental rules were mainly cast in the mould of minimum harmonisation. This would allow the provision of a minimum level of protection throughout the EU, without depriving the Member States of the power to adopt more stringent standards for their own territory. Policy competition would then only be made impossible below the European minimum standard.

A third guideline for application of the subsidiarity principle is whether action at European level would produce clear benefits by reason of its scale or effects compared with action at the level of the Member States. Here, too, it could be said that the objective of attaining a certain minimum level of protection throughout the EU can only be achieved effectively by European legislation. The objectives set out in Article 174 EC imply this.

An examination of European environmental legislation in the light of the above guidelines would reveal that probably not one environmental directive or regulation would fail to pass the test. It should however be noted that the importance of the subsidiarity principle is above all political. The few judgments of the Court on the subject hardly give the impression that it would be quick to annul a Council decision for non-compliance with the principle of subsidiarity.[53]

---

49 Cf. Lee (2005) at 11.

50 Cf. Case C-377/98 *Netherlands v. EP and Council* [2000] ECR I-6229. The case concerned an application for annulment of Directive 98/44 on the legal protection of biotechnological inventions; OJ 1998 L 213/13.

51 Cf. also Faure (1998) and Revesz (2000).

52 Cf. Revesz (2000), Scott (2000) at 56, Lee (2005) at 11.

53 Cf. e.g. Case C-491/01 *British American Tobacco (Investments) and Imperial Tobacco* [2002] ECR I-11453 and Case C-377/98 *Netherlands v. EP and Council* [2000] ECR I-6229.

The principle of proportionality

The third paragraph of Article 5 EC continues: 'Any action by the Community shall not go beyond what is necessary to achieve the objectives of this Treaty.'[54] This is a statement of the principle of proportionality.[55] Here, too, the Protocol to the Treaty of Amsterdam provides several guidelines. All charges, both for the Community and for the national governments must be kept to a minimum and be proportionate to the proposed objective. The European legislature must choose measures, which leave the greatest degree of freedom for national decisions, and the national legal system should be respected. As much use as possible should be made of minimum standards, whereby Member States are free to lay down stricter national standards. Use of the directive is to be preferred above use of the regulation, and the framework directive is to be preferred above detailed measures. Non-binding instruments such as recommendations should be used wherever possible, as well as voluntary codes of conduct.[56]

> Examples of such voluntary codes can already be found in various environmental acts. Article 4 of Directive 91/676 on pollution caused by nitrates[57] provides that the Member States must establish codes of good agricultural practice, to be implemented by farmers on a voluntary basis. The purpose of these codes is to reduce the pollution of water caused by nitrates from agricultural sources. Another example is Regulation 1980/2000 on a revised Community Eco-label Award Scheme.[58] This regulation, which regulates a Community eco-label award scheme, operates on a wholly voluntary basis. Where a product meets the applicable environmental criteria, the Community eco-label may be used. What is remarkable here is that the various interest groups (industry, retailers, environmental organisations etc.) must be consulted for the purpose of defining the criteria that should apply. In the same vein is the Eco-audit Regulation 761/2001 (EMAS).[59] The eco-management and audit scheme is a management tool for companies and other organisations to evaluate, report and improve their environmental performance. Participation is completely voluntary.

A similar development is the growing interest in the use of voluntary environmental agreements.[60] Environmental agreements between public institutions and industry are increasingly used to implement environmental policies. A first

---

[54] Cf. also Article 5(4) EU after amendment by the Reform Treaty.

[55] Cf. in general on proportionality Jans et al. (2007), Chapter V, section 4.

[56] See Council Resolution on the drafting, implementation and enforcement of Community environmental law; OJ 1997 C 321/1. Cf. Winter (1996) and Verschuuren (2000).

[57] OJ 1991 L 375/1.

[58] OJ 2000 L 237/1. Cf. also the 'old' Regulation 880/92, OJ 1992 L 99/1.

[59] OJ 2001 L 114/1.

[60] See the Commission's Communication Environmental Agreements at Community Level; COM (2002) 412 final. Cf. Lee (2005) at 231-237.

example at the EU level was the 1998 agreement between the Commission and the European car industry (ACEA).[61] A more recent example concerns environmentally friendly plastic.[62] Agreements can also be used, under certain conditions, to implement provisions of environmental directives.[63]

The EU's environment policy can also be said to comply with the guidelines in terms of its use of the directive. From the start it has been customary to use the directive for action in the field of the environment. Regulations have been used in only a few cases, above all in those sectors where a more uniform regime is indeed necessary, for example, to implement international agreements or to regulate international trade. Examples are Regulations 338/97 on the protection of species of wild fauna and flora by regulating trade therein,[64] 348/81 on imports of whales and other cetacean products[65] and 1013/2006 on shipments of waste.[66] These all regulate the trade in certain goods or products with third countries. A more or less uniform regulation is required at the external frontier of the EU in order to avoid deflections of trade. In these cases, a regulation is a more appropriate instrument than a directive, because of its direct applicability. However, regulations are used not only to regulate international trade. They are also used when it is necessary to grant certain rights directly to manufacturers, importers or even particular companies, or to impose obligations on them. The element of uniformity and identical application of rules throughout the EU was also the primary reason to opt to use this instrument for the measures on the EC eco-label and eco-management and audit schemes.[67]

As far as the preference for minimum harmonisation expressed in the guidelines is concerned, minimum standards have regularly been utilised in European environmental law. The principle is even stated in so many words in the Treaty itself, in Article 176 EC.[68] In the vast majority of European environmental legislation, for example, the measures to combat water and air pollution, rules are laid down for the fixing of emission limit values, without going as far as complete harmonisation. There is in general no need for complete harmonisation.

It should be noted that the phenomenon of framework legislation can already be found in European environmental law, for example, in the EU Water Frame-

---

[61] See Commission Recommendation of 5 February 1999 on the reduction of CO_2 emissions from passenger cars; OJ 1999 L 40/49.

[62] Commission press release IP/05/170, 14 February 2005.

[63] Commission Recommendation 96/733 concerning environmental agreements implementing Community directives, OJ 1996 L 333/59 and Council Resolution on environmental agreements, OJ 1997 C 321/6. See for a more detailed discussion Chapter 4, section 2.4.

[64] Regulation 338/97, OJ 1997 L 61/1.

[65] OJ 1981 L 39/1.

[66] OJ 2006 L 190/1. Regulation 1013/2006 will repeal Regulation 259/93 (OJ 1993 L 30/1) with effect from 12 July 2007.

[67] Regulations 1980/2000, OJ 2000 L 237/1 and 761/2001, OJ 2001 L 114/1.

[68] See on this more in detail Chapter 3, section 5.

work Directive,[69] Directive 91/156 on waste[70] and Directive 96/62 on ambient air quality assessment and management.[71]

The case law of the Court shows that the Court is in principle willing to review European legislation in the light of the proportionality principle. In the *Standley* case, the Court considered the Nitrates Directive.[72] It was argued that this directive gave rise to disproportionate obligations on the part of farmers, so that it offended against the principle of proportionality. The Court was not impressed. After a careful study of the Nitrates Directive, it came to the conclusion:

> 'that the Directive contains flexible provisions enabling the Member States to observe the principle of proportionality in the application of the measures which they adopt. It is for the national courts to ensure that that principle is observed.' In general the Court, in its assessment of the proportionality of an EC measure, will apply the so called 'manifestly inappropriate' test: 'the legality of a measure adopted [...] can be affected only if the measure is manifestly inappropriate having regard to the objective which the competent institution is seeking to pursue'.[73]

The conclusion in *Standley* that the flexible provisions of the directive enables the Member States to observe the principle of proportionality will be applicable to most, if not all, European environmental legislation.

The integration principle

One of the most important principles of EC law of relevance for environmental protection is the integration principle stated in Article 6 EC:[74] 'Environmental protection requirements must be integrated into the definition and implementation of the Community policies and activities referred to in Article 3, in particular with a view to promoting sustainable development.'

---

[69] Directive 2000/60 establishing a framework for the Community action in the field of water policy ; OJ 2000 L 327.

[70] OJ 1991 L 78/32.

[71] OJ 1996 L 296/55.

[72] Case C-293/97 *Standley* [1999] ECR I-2603. Cf. also Case C-102/97 *Commission v. Germany* [1999] ECR I-5051, para. 42. The same approach can also be found in the Court's judgment in Case C-6/99 *Association Greenpeace France v. Ministère de l'Agriculture et de la Pêche* [2000] ECR I-1651, on the precautionary principle; See below section 3.2 of this chapter.

[73] Case 331/88 *Fedesa* [1990] ECR I-4023. Cf. also more recently Case C-189/01 *Jippes* [2001] ECR I-5689, para. 83 and Case C-27/00 *Omega Air a.o.* [2002] ECR I-2569, para. 72. In the latter case, concerning threshold levels for noise produced by airplanes, the Court did not find that the Council committed a manifest error of assessment even if alternative measures could have been taken which would have been economically less damaging. Cf. also, with respect to the Waste Oils Directive, Case C-15/03 *Commission v. Austria* [2005] ECR I-837, para. 38 in particular and Case C-92/03 *Commission v. Portugal* [2005] ECR I-867.

[74] Cf. Article 11 FEU after the entry into force of the Reform Treaty.

The importance of the integration principle is reaffirmed in the Sixth Environment Action Programme, which stipulates that 'integration of environmental concerns into other policies must be deepened' in order to move towards sustainable development.[75] This refers to what is known as external integration, in other words, the integration of environmental objectives in other policy sectors. The principle was introduced into the Treaty by the Single European Act. There it was provided that 'Environmental protection requirements shall be a component of the Community's other policies.' It is notable that the current version of the Treaty is worded more forcefully and refers explicitly to implementation of the Community policies. Moreover, the general formulation makes it clear that the operation of the integration principle extends to the entire EC Treaty. New is the introduction of the clause 'in particular with a view to promoting sustainable development.' This has given the concept of 'sustainable development' some legal 'weight' and therefore cannot be seen as merely stating a policy objective to be achieved.[76]

The first question which presents itself is what precisely has to be integrated. The Treaty refers to 'environmental protection requirements'. What should this be taken to mean? Certainly, it would seem to include the environment policy objectives of Article 174(1) EC. It also seems likely that it includes the principles referred to in Article 174(2) EC, such as the precautionary principle and the principle that preventive action should be taken. And finally integration of the environment policy aspects referred to in Article 174(3) EC should not *a priori* be excluded, though it is true that the Treaty does not state that these aspects have to be integrated, but only that they should be taken into account. This wide interpretation of the integration principle in effect leads to a general obligation on the European institutions to reach an integrated and balanced assessment of all the relevant environmental aspects when adopting other policy.

The next problem concerns the question of whether the integration principle implies that the EU's environment policy has been given some measure of priority over other European policy areas. Probably, it has not, at least if by priority it is meant that, in the event of a conflict with other policy areas, environment policy has a certain added value from a legal point of view.[77] The text of the Treaty does not support such a conclusion. The integration principle is designed to ensure that protection of the environment is at least taken into consideration, even when commercial policy is involved or when other decisions are being taken and have to be worked out in detail, for example in the fields of agricul-

---

[75] Decision 1600/2002 laying down the Sixth Community Environment Action Programme, OJ 2002 L 242. Cf. also Communication from the Commission 'A partnership for integration: a strategy for integrating the environment into EU policies', COM (1998) 333 and Commission working document 'Integrating environmental considerations into other policy areas – a stocktaking of the Cardiff process' COM (2004) 394.

[76] Cf. Bär & Kraemer (1998) at 316-318.

[77] See for a discussion of this issue Bär & Kraemer (1998) at 318-319.

ture, transport,[78] energy,[79] development aid,[80] trade and external relations,[81] internal market[82] and competition policy, regional policy, etc.[83] However, the manner in which potential conflicts between protection of the environment and, for example, the functioning of the internal market should be resolved cannot be inferred from the integration principle as such. Such conflicts should be resolved against the background of the body of case law established by the Court of Justice in respect of the principle of proportionality. If European legislation for the protection of the environment, which the Court has already designated as one of the essential EC objectives in the *ADBHU* case, results in restrictions of trade, this is regarded as permissible as long as the measures are not discriminatory and do not entail restrictions that go beyond what is strictly necessary for the protection of the environment.[84] The principle of proportionality may also prove a useful guide in relation to other areas of policy in which conflicts flowing from the integration principle are involved.

At the same time, it should be noted that when interpreting Article 33 EC, in the context of the common agricultural policy, the Court also has to weigh various objectives against each other. The institutions of the EC have wide discretionary powers when harmonising policy in relation to the various objectives contained in Article 33 EC (increasing productivity, ensuring a fair standard of living for the agricultural community, stabilising markets, assuring the stability of supplies and ensuring supplies reach consumers at reasonable prices). One or more of these objectives may (temporarily) be given priority, as long as the policy does not become so focused on a single objective that the attainment of other objectives is made impossible. This approach could also be employed in respect of the environment. It would then be arguable that, if a given objective could adequately be achieved in a variety of ways, the integration principle would entail a choice for the least environmentally harmful.

Now that the question of the priority has been addressed, the problem of the legal enforceability of the integration principle looms large. The following comments are called for. The Court's judgments clearly show that the contention that the integration principle is of no value whatsoever is not correct. For example, the principle fulfils an important function in the choice of the proper legal basis of environmental measures and has been used by the Court to justify 'environmental' legislation under legal bases other than Article 175 EC.

---

[78] Mahmoudi (2005).

[79] Dhondt (2005).

[80] Williams (2005).

[81] See Marín Durán & Morgera (2006).

[82] Cf. for instance with respect to the freedom to provide services the Services Directive, Directive 2006/123 on services in the internal market (OJ 2006 L 376/36), which states in its preamble at point 7: 'This Directive also takes into account other general interest objectives, including the protection of the environment'.

[83] Cf. Dhondt (2003) and Vedder (2003).

[84] Case 240/83 *ADBHU* [1985] ECR 531.

In the *Chernobyl I* case, the issue was whether Regulation 3955/87 on the conditions governing imports of agricultural products originating in third countries following the accident at the Chernobyl power station was rightly based on Article 113 (now Article 133) rather than Article 130s (now Article 175).[85] The Court held that the 'the principle whereby all Community measures must satisfy the requirements of environmental protection, implies that a Community measure cannot be part of Community action on environmental matters merely because it takes account of those requirements.' In the *TiO2* case,[86] the Court confirmed this.

A second legal consequence of the integration principle, closely connected with the above, is the following. The principle broadens the objectives of the other powers laid down in the Treaty and thus limits the role of the specific powers doctrine in environmental policy.

The *Chernobyl I* case and the *TiO2* case demonstrate that environmental objectives can be pursued in the context of the common commercial policy and its internal market policy. The principle has been used also in the interpretation of Directive 90/50 on public service contracts, leading to the conclusion that this does not exclude the possibility of using environmental criteria in identifying the economically most advantageous tender.[87] Without the integration principle, it is debatable to what extent environmental objectives, for example in connection with the approximation of laws for the attainment of the internal market, could be taken into account by the Council.

It was not without reason that most European environmental measures in the period prior to the Single European Act were based on a combination of the old Articles 100 and 235 EEC Treaty. The powers of approximation are limited in Article 3(h) 'to the extent required for the proper functioning of the common market'. And because the requirements of a properly functioning common market were not always and automatically synonymous with the requirements of environmental protection, it was necessary to invoke the additional legal basis supplied by Article 235 EEC. The integration principle makes such artificial devices unnecessary. Not only does it extend the objectives of the internal market policy and the common commercial policy, but environmental objectives can also be taken into account in other policy areas without the attributed powers doctrine interfering.

---

[85] Case C-62/88 *EP v. Council* [1990] ECR I-1527. In the *TiO2* case (Case C-300/89 *Commission v. Council* [1991] ECR I-2867), the Court confirmed this, stating: 'That principle implies that a Community measure cannot be covered by Article 130s [now Article 175 EC, authors] merely because it also pursues objectives of environmental protection.'

[86] Case C-300/89 *Commission v. Council* [1991] ECR I-2867.

[87] Case C-513/99 *Concordia Bus Finland* [2002] ECR I-7213, para. 57.

Thus in *Pinaud Wieger*, the Court held that the achievement of freedom to provide services in the transport sector can only be attained in an orderly fashion in the context of a common transport policy 'which takes into consideration the economic, social and ecological problems'.[88] And with respect to competition law, we argue that the impact on the environment must be taken into account in assessing whether agreements between undertakings violate Article 81 EC and is relevant to the Commission's when deciding whether or not to approve state aid under Article 87(3) EC.[89] Here, too, the environmental consequences can now be taken into account.[90]

Another aspect which is important when evaluating the legal status of the integration principle is whether the legitimacy of actions of the Council and Commission can be reviewed by the Court in the light of the principle. Can the validity of a directive or regulation, for example in the field of transport or agriculture, be questioned on the grounds that the decision has infringed the environmental objectives of the Treaty? In other words, the question as to the legal enforceability of the integration principle is in fact a question as to the legal significance of the objectives, principles and other aspects referred to in Article 174(1), (2) and (3) EC. It has already been noted that the present version of the principle has been formulated more forcefully than under the Single European Act. In principle, the review of European measures in the light of the environmental objectives should therefore be regarded as possible.

Indeed, in its judgment in the *Chernobyl I* case, the Court speaks in just such strong terms ('must satisfy the requirements of environmental protection'). In the *Betatti* case, in which the lawfulness of Ozone Regulation 3093/94 was disputed, the Court was also prepared to examine the compatibility of a measure with the environmental objectives and principles of the Treaty.[91] It observed that Article 174 EC 'sets a series of objectives, principles and criteria which the Community legislature must respect in implementing [Community environmental] policy.' However, it should be borne in mind that the institutions have wide discretionary powers as to how they shape the Community's environment policy, and will have to balance the relative importance of the environmental objectives and other Community objectives as they proceed. The Court expressed this in the following terms: 'However, in view of the need to strike a balance between certain of the objectives and principles mentioned in Article 130r and of the complexity of the implementation of those criteria, review by the Court must necessarily be limited to the question whether the Council, by adopting the Regulation, committed a

---

[88] Case C-17/90 *Pinaud Wieger* [1991] ECR I-5253. See also Case C-195/90 *Commission v. Germany* [1992] ECR I-3141.

[89] Cf. Community Guidelines on State aid for environmental protection, OJ 2001 C 37/3 containing a clear reference to the integration principle. See also Chapter 7 extensively.

[90] Cf. Chapter 7, section 7.3.3.

[91] Case C-341/95 *Gianni Bettati* [1998] ECR I-4355.

manifest error of appraisal regarding the conditions for the application of Article 130r of the Treaty.'

The conclusion that can be drawn from these judgments seems to be that only in very exceptional cases will a measure be susceptible to annulment (or being declared invalid) because certain environmental objectives seem not to have been taken sufficiently into account.[92] Another factor which will probably also have to be taken into account is that the degree to which measures are open to judicial review may differ depending on whether the objectives of Article 174(1) EC, the principles of Article 174(2) EC or the policy aspects of Article 174(3) EC are involved. As far as the latter are concerned, the Treaty states that the Community shall 'take account of' these aspects, which is not the same as observing them. Besides this, Article 174(2) EC states that the Community shall 'aim' at a high level of protection. The conclusion must surely be that the application of the integration principle is amenable to judicial review, but that the extent of that review is limited and may differ from one case to the next.

Perhaps more important than the possibility of relying on the principle before the Court of Justice is the following legal consequence. In our opinion, secondary European legislation can – and indeed must – be interpreted in the light of the environmental objectives of the Treaty, even outside the environmental field.

For example it has emerged as an important factor in justifying the application of the precautionary principle outside of the environmental sphere.[93]

Another example can be found in *Association Greenpeace France* v. *Ministère de l'Agriculture et de la Pêche* where the Court assessed if the precautionary principle was taken into account in Directive 99/220 on the deliberate release into the environment of genetically modified organisms.[94] Another example can be found in the *ARCO Chemie Nederland* case.[95] In that case, the Court of Justice ruled that the concept of 'waste', in view of the prevention and precautionary principle, cannot be interpreted restrictive. This is, as it were, a special form of the generally accepted method of interpreting European law so as to be compatible with the Treaty.[96] Furthermore, one could argue that the Treaty itself, for instance the provisions on the free movement of goods, has to be interpreted in the light of the

---

[92] See also the *Standley* case discussed above in the context of the proportionality principle; Case C-293/97 *Standley* [1999] ECR I-2603.

[93] In particular in relation to the protection of public health. See Joined Cases T-74, 76, 83, 85, 132, 137, 141/00 *Artegodan GmbH a.o.* v. *Commission* [2002] ECR II-4945, para. 183.

[94] Case C-6/99 *Association Greenpeace France* v. *Ministère de l'Agriculture et de la Pêche* [2000] ECR I-1651. The legal basis of the directive is Article 100a EEC.

[95] Joined Cases C-418/97 and C-419/97 *ARCO Chemie Nederland* [2000] ECR I-4475. See also Case C-270/03 *Commission* v. *Italy* [2005] ECR I-5233, para. 12.

[96] Case 172/82 *Inter-Huiles* [1983] ECR 555.

environmental objectives and principles mentioned in Article 175 EC.[97] In Chapter 6, we will see that the principle has been key in justifying recourse to the mandatory requirement relating to environmental protection to justify a directly discriminatory barrier to trade.[98]

Finally, we would like to refer to the Court's case law on the Waste Directive. It is settled case law that the concept of 'waste' cannot be interpreted restrictively in view of the environmental principles of Article 174 EC.[99]

A final question that should be discussed in connection with this principle is that of the possible consequences for Member States. In principle, in view of the fact that the text of the Treaty expressly refers to 'Community policies and activities', the integration principle should have no direct legal consequences for the Member States. Of course, there will be indirect effects, in the sense that the Council and the Commission will observe the principle in their legal acts, which are often addressed to the Member States. As these are often integrated regulations and directives, the Member States will also be required to observe a certain degree of integration. Also one could argue that where Member State exercise some discretion under a EU policy (e.g. the choice of trans European networks) the integration duty might apply directly to them.

On the other hand, it seems unlikely that the Member States will be bound by the environmental objectives and principles of the Treaty in areas that have not been harmonised, other than by the general obligation contained in Article 10 EC. They are not directly applicable.[100]

In the *Peralta* case, the lawfulness of Italian environmental legislation was disputed, *inter alia* because of alleged incompatibility with Article 130r (now Article 174) EC.[101] The Court rejected this claim and observed that this provision is confined to defining the general objectives of the European legislature in the matter of the environment. Responsibility for deciding what action is to be taken is conferred on the Council by Article 175. Moreover, Article 176 states that the protective measures adopted pursuant to Article 175 are not to prevent any Member State from maintaining or introducing more stringent protective measures compatible with the Treaty. Article 174 does not therefore preclude legislation of the kind in question in the main proceedings.

---

[97] See for instance Case C-209/98 *Sydhavnens Sten & Grus* [2000] ECR I-3743, para. 48.

[98] Case C-379/98 *PreussenElektra* [2001] ECR I-2099.

[99] Cf. for instance Case C-1/03 *Van de Walle a.o.* [2004] ECR I-7613, para. 45.

[100] Cf. Krämer (2007) at 6. This lack of direct applicability prompted the Avosetta group of European environmental lawyers to suggest adding the following provision in the EC Treaty: 'Subject to imperative reasons of overriding public interests significantly impairing the environment or human health shall be prohibited.' See for more details: www.avosetta.org.

[101] Case C-379/92 *Peralta* [1994] ECR I-3453.

In the same vein, we may point at the *Deponiezweckverband Eiterköpfe* case.[102] In that case, the Court decided that national measures that exceed the minimum level of protection of the Directive on the landfill of waste need not be reviewed in light of the principle of proportionality.

The scarce national case law on the subject also points in the same direction. In *Duddridge*, the English High Court held that the precautionary principle did not as such impose obligations on Member States.[103]

The integration principle is also reflected in the Charter of Fundamental Rights of the European Union.[104] Article 37 of the Charter contains a text similar, but not identical, to Article 6 EC: 'A high level of environmental protection and the improvement of the quality of the environment must be integrated into the policies of the Union and ensured in accordance with the principle of sustainable development.' A difference is, for instance, that Article 37 Charter only refers to EU 'policies' and not to EU 'activities'. Furthermore, Article 6 EC refers more broadly to 'environmental protection requirements', whilst the Charter requires only 'a high level of environmental protection and the improvement of the quality of the environment' to be integrated.

Fundamental rights and the environment

According to Article 6 EU, the EU shall respect fundamental rights, as guaranteed by the European Convention for the Protection of Human Rights and Fundamental Freedoms, as general principles of Community law.[105] It is well known that this provision is a codification of the case law of the Court of Justice.[106]

Although this is not the place to give a treatment of the case law of the European Court of Human Rights relevant to the protection of the environment, environmental issues nowadays do play a more important role than ever before.

The following *Öneryildiz* case is just to illustrate the importance of this case law.[107] Öneryıldız is a Turkish national who, along with twelve members of his family, was living in a shantytown of Hekimbaşı Ümraniye near Istanbul. This town was

---

[102] Case C-6/03 *Deponiezweckverband Eiterköpfe* [2005] ECR I-2753. See also Chapter 3, section 5.

[103] High Court, Queen's Bench Division (Smith L.J. & Farquharson L.J.) 3 October 1994, *R. v. Secretary of State for Trade & Industry*, ex parte *Duddridge & others* [1995] 3 C.M.L.R. 231. See also the judgment of the Dutch Den Haag District Court in the *Waterpakt* case, 24 November 1999 *Waterpakt* [2000] *MR* 1, which ruled in the same manner.

[104] OJ 2000 C 346/1. This charter was signed and proclaimed by the Presidents of the European Parliament, the Council and the Commission at the European Council meeting in Nice on 7 December 2000. After the entry into force of the Reform Treaty, according to the 'new' Article 6(1) EU, the provisions of the Charter 'shall have the same legal value as the Treaties'.

[105] Cf. Article 6(3) EU after amendment by the Reform Treaty.

[106] Case 29/69 *Stauder* [1969] ECR 419.

[107] ECHR 18 June 2002 *Öneryildiz v. Turkey* – 48939/99 [2002] ECHR 496.

nothing more than a collection of slums built on land surrounding a rubbish tip which had been used jointly by four district councils since the 1970s and was under the authority and responsibility of the main City Council of Istanbul. An expert report drawn up on 7 May 1991 at the request of the Üsküdar District Court drew the authorities' attention to the fact that no measure had been taken with regard to the tip in question to prevent a possible explosion of the methane gas being given off by the decomposing refuse. On 28 April 1993, a methane gas explosion occurred on the waste-collection site and the refuse erupting from the pile of waste buried eleven houses situated below it, including the one belonging to Öneryıldız, who lost nine members of his family. Criminal and administrative investigations were carried out into the case, following which the mayors of Ümraniye and Istanbul were brought before the courts. On 4 April 1996, the mayors in question were both convicted of 'negligence in the exercise of their duties' and sentenced to a fine of 160,000 Turkish liras (TRL) and the minimum three-month prison sentence provided for in Article 230 of the Criminal Code, which was, moreover, commuted to a fine. The court ordered a stay of execution of those fines.

Subsequently, the applicant lodged, on his own behalf and on the behalf of his three surviving children, an action for damages in the Istanbul Administrative Court against the authorities whom he deemed liable for the death of his relatives and the destruction of his property. In a judgment of 30 November 1995, the authorities were ordered to pay the applicant and his children TRL 100,000,000 in non-pecuniary damages and TRL 10,000,000 in pecuniary damages (the equivalent at the material time of approximately 2,077 and 208 euros respectively), the latter amount being limited to the destruction of household goods. The applicant complained, under Article 2 (right to life) of the ECHR, that the accident had occurred as a result of negligence on the part of the relevant authorities. He also complained of the deficiencies in the administrative and criminal proceedings instituted subsequently under Article 6 § 1 (right to a fair hearing within a reasonable time) and of Article 13 (right to an effective remedy). The Court held that there had been a violation of Article 2 (right to life) on account of the death of the applicant's relatives and the ineffectiveness of the judicial machinery; that there had been a violation of Article 1 of Protocol No. 1 (protection of property); and that there was no need to examine the applicant's other complaints.

From the case law of the European Court of Human Rights, it is clear that in particular Article 2 (protection of life), Articles 6 and 13 (access to court), Article 8 (privacy), Article 10 (freedom of expression) and Article 1 Protocol 1 (property) can be of some importance for the protection of the environment.[108]

Broadly speaking European environmental legislation probably meets the minimum requirements of the European Convention, with one possible excep-

---

[108] Cf. Daniel García San José, *Environmental protection and the European Convention on Human Rights* Council of Europe Publishing 2005.

tion[109] and that concerns the limited remedies available to third parties desiring to challenge decisions of the Commission affecting the environment. The arguments of the Court of Justice to the effect that these limited remedies do not violate Articles 6 and 13, in particular, of the European Convention are not very convincing.[110]

In this section, some reference is also necessary to the Charter of Fundamental Rights of the European Union.[111] We already mentioned Article 37 of the Charter containing a text similar to Article 6 EC. Although the Charter is, at present, as such not legally binding, the ECJ seems to be willing to acknowledge some sort of legal effect of the Charter in particular where a directive makes a reference to the Charter.[112] However, this will change after the Reform Treaty has entered into force. Article 6(1) of the new EU Treaty will read: 'The Union recognises the rights, freedoms and principles set out in the Charter of Fundamental Rights of 7 December 2000 [...], which shall have the same legal value as the Treaties.'[113]

> In few environmental directives we find a reference to the Charter. For instance in the preamble of Directive 2003/87 establishing a scheme for greenhouse gas emission allowance trading we read at point 27: 'This Directive respects the fundamental rights and observes the principles recognised in particular by the Charter of Fundamental Rights of the European Union.'[114]

---

[109] Cf. in a more general sense European Court of Human Rights 30 June 2005 *Bosphorus Airways* v. *Ireland* 45036/98 [2005] ECHR 440. The Court found that the protection of fundamental rights by EC law can be considered 'equivalent' to that of the Convention system.

[110] See on this extensively Chapter 5, section 4.

[111] OJ 2000 C 346/1.

[112] Case C-540/03 *EP* v. *Council* [2006] ECR I-5769, para. 38. See also Case T-377/00 *Philip Morris International* v. *Commission* [2003] ECR II-1, para. 122: 'Although this document does not have legally binding force, it does show the importance of the rights it sets out in the Community legal order.'

[113] See however for the 'special' position of Poland and the UK, Protocol 7 to the Reform Treaty 'On the Application of the Charter of Fundamental Rights to Poland and to the United Kingdom'.

[114] OJ 2003 L 275/32. See for another example Directive 2005/35 on ship-source pollution and on the introduction of penalties for infringements, OJ 2005 L 255/11. Point 16 of the preamble reads: 'This Directive fully respects the Charter of fundamental rights of the European Union; any person suspected of having committed an infringement must be guaranteed a fair and impartial hearing and the penalties must be proportional'. Cf. also the annulled Framework Decision 2005/667 to strengthen the criminal-law framework for the enforcement of the law against ship-source pollution (OJ 2005 L 255/164); Case C-440/05 *Commission* v. *Council*, judgment of 23 October 2007, n.y.r. in the ECR.

3 Article 174 EC[115]

3.1 The Objectives of European Environment Policy

The environmental objectives to be pursued by the EU are formulated in the first paragraph of Article 174 EC.[116] They are:
· preserving, protecting and improving the quality of the environment;
· protecting human health;
· prudent and rational utilisation of natural resources;
· promoting measures at international level to deal with regional or world-wide environmental problems.

Preserving, protecting and improving the quality of the environment
The first objective formulated in Article 174 EC is fairly general and inde-terminate. The term environment is given no further definition in the Treaty itself.[117] On the one hand, this is an advantage in that the objective is sufficiently flexible to be adapted to new developments and new needs for protection.[118] On the other hand, it is impossible to determine with absolute certainty from the Treaty itself what might be understood by a European environment policy. The following problems of interpretation present themselves in connection with the uncertain scope of these environmental objectives.

Does the objective also include protection of nature and landscape values? Having regard to the Habitats Directive, it seems quite clear that it does. The first consideration of the preamble to this directive states that the preservation, protection and improvement of the quality of the environment, 'including the conservation of natural habitats and of wild fauna and flora, are an essential objective of general interest pursued by the Community'. Even the care and accommodation of animals in zoos seem to be covered by this objective.[119] The Zoo Directive illustrates that to a certain extent 'animal welfare' is within the scope of application of Article 174 EC, albeit that animal welfare cannot be regarded a 'general principle of Community law'.[120] In general, however, animal welfare will find its regulatory basis in the Treaty provision on the Common Agricultural Policy (CAP); the Articles 32 *et seq.* EC.[121] It is also possible that

---

[115] Cf. the renumbered Article 191 FEU after the entry into force of the Reform Treaty.

[116] Although Article 174 EC defines the objectives to be pursued in the context of environmental policy, Article 175 EC constitutes the legal basis on which Community measures are adopted; Case C-284/95 *Safety Hi-Tech* [1998] ECR I-4301, para. 43.

[117] Cf. also the European Council's Declaration on the environmental imperative of 15 June 1990, Bulletin EC 1990 No. 6, at 16-20.

[118] Cf. Krämer (2007) at 2 who refers to an all-embracing concept.

[119] Cf. Directive 1999/ 22 relating to the keeping of wild animals in zoos, OJ 1999 L 94/24.

[120] Case C-189/01 *Jippes a.o.* [2001] ECR I-5689, paras. 71-79. See in general on animal welfare: the Amster-dam Treaty Protocol on protection and welfare of animals, OJ 1997 C 340/110. Cf. Krämer (2007) at 2-3.

[121] For instance Directive 1999/74 laying down minimum standards for the protection of laying hens, OJ 1999 L 203/53. See on CAP also Chapter 2, section 7.1.

certain aspects of animal welfare are integrated in secondary legislation. For instance, Article 4 (1)(b)(iii) of the Pesticide Directive 91/414 stipulates that a plant protection product is not authorised unless 'it does not cause unnecessary suffering and pain to vertebrates to be controlled'.[122]

Not only measures which result *directly* in the improvement of the environment fall under this objective, but also those which *result* in the improvement of the environment in a more indirect fashion fall within its scope.

> In the preamble to Directive 2003/4 on public access to environmental information, it is stated that 'increased public access to environmental information and the dissemination of such information contribute to a greater awareness of environmental matters, a free exchange of views, more effective participation by the public in environmental decision-making *and, eventually, to a better environment*.'[123] More generally, it is arguable that decision-making in respect of the non-substantive or procedural aspects of environmental legislation, such as issues of legal protection, authorisation procedures and even measures concerning the administrative organisation of the environment sector, is also within its compass.

A political 'hot potato' was dealt with by the Court in Case C-176/03 *Commission v. Council*.[124] The concerned the question to what extent, if any, Article 175 EC can or even must be used as legal basis to harmonise national criminal law. Based on Title VI of the EU Treaty, in particular, Articles 29 EU, 31(e) EU and 34(2)(b) EU the Council adopted Framework Decision 2003/80 on the protection of the environment through criminal law.[125] In essence, this framework decision laid down a number of environmental offences, in respect of which the Member States were required to introduce criminal penalties. The Commission challenged the Council's choice of Title VI EU as the legal basis for the framework decision. It submitted that the purpose and content of the latter are within the scope of the Community's powers on the environment, as they are stated in Articles 174 to 176 EC. The Court of Justice started its findings by pointing at Article 47 EU, which provides that nothing in the EU Treaty is to affect the EC Treaty and that it is the task of the Court to ensure that acts which, according to the Council, fall within the scope of Title VI of the EU Treaty do not encroach upon the powers conferred by the EC Treaty on the Community. The Court acknowledged that the framework decision did indeed entail partial harmonisation of the criminal laws of the Member States and that as a general rule, neither criminal law nor the rules of criminal procedure fall within the Community's competence. However, the Court followed by noting that this 'does not prevent the Community legislature, when the application of effective, proportionate and dissuasive criminal penalties by the competent national authorities is an

---

[122] Cf. Case T-229/04 *Sweden v. Commission*, judgment of 11 July 2007, n.y.r. in the ECR.

[123] OJ 2003 L 41/26, emphasis added by the authors. Cf. Lee (2005) at 69-73.

[124] Case C-176/03 *Commission v. Council* [2005] ECR I-7879. See on European environmental criminal law in general Comte (2005) and Comte & Krämer (2004).

[125] OJ 2003 L 29/55.

essential measure for combating serious environmental offences, from taking measures which relate to the criminal law of the Member States which it considers *necessary* in order to ensure that the rules which it lays down on environmental protection are fully effective.' [emphasis added] The framework decision had as its main purpose the protection of the environment (and not harmonising criminal law as such) and therefore could have been properly adopted on the basis of Article 175 EC.

> The Commission, in the aftermath of Case C-176/03, made a proposal for a Directive on the protection of the environment through criminal law.[126] The proposed directive establishes a minimum set of serious environmental offences that should be considered criminal throughout the EU when committed intentionally or with serious negligence. The scope of liability of legal persons is defined in detail. For offences committed under certain aggravating circumstances the minimum level of maximum sanctions for natural and legal persons is subject to approximation, too. It is in particular this part of the proposal, which goes well beyond the level of harmonisation of the annulled Framework Decision in Case C-176/03. In view of the ECJ judgment in Case C-440/05, to be discussed *infra*, it is questionnable whether the Council and European Parliament are competent to accept this proposal under Article 175(1) EC alone.

The judgment in Case C-176/03 was confirmed in Case C-440/05 *Commission v. Council*.[127] In that case the Commission was seeking annulment of Council Framework Decision 2005/667 to strengthen the criminal-law framework for the enforcement of the law against ship-source pollution.[128] However, the Court made it in that case perfectly clear that 'the determination of the type and level of the criminal penalties to be applied does not fall within the Community's sphere of competence'. In sum: whenever criminal penalties are essential for combating serious offences against the environment Article 175 EC provides for the correct legal basis to require Member States to introduce such penalties, but it does not provide a legal basis to determine the *type* and *level* of criminal penalties. This would require legislative measures under the Third Pillar of the EU Treaty. However, this debate on the use of correct legal basis for harmonising environmental criminal will become, more or less, obsolete after the entry into force of the Reform Treaty. In general, the 'depillarisation' undertaken by the Reform Treaty will cause that the 'ordinary legislative procedure' is applicable for both European environmental law as for European criminal law.

In the pre-Maastricht period, the territorial limitation of the environmental objectives was a matter for discussion. In other words, can the the European legislature act not so much to protect its own environment, but to preserve the environment outside the EU, to address global and regional environmental prob-

---

[126] COM (2007) 51 final.

[127] Judgment of 23 October 2007, n.y.r. in the ECR.

[128] OJ 2005 L 255/164.

lems, or even the environment of other states? Since 'Maastricht' this problem of interpretation has largely been resolved now the fourth objective of Article 174 EC explicitly includes 'promoting measures at international level to deal with regional or worldwide environmental problems.' This objective will be discussed in slightly more detail below.

An entirely different matter is the question whether the EU is entitled to concern itself with local and regional environmental problems. Would, for instance, the European legislature has a competence to maximise the allowed noise level caused by local bars and nightclubs? As Article 174 EC does not contain any such restriction, this must be regarded as a possibility.[129] Of course, the principle of subsidiarity would have to be taken into consideration here, which might require restraint in this respect. Article 2(3) of the Habitats Directive is relevant in this context. Protective measures taken pursuant to this directive must explicitly take account of 'regional and local characteristics.'

The last problem of interpretation that must be discussed concerns the formulation 'preserving, protecting and improving'. This is also broadly and flexibly worded. It affords possibilities to take environmental measures of a preservative, curative, repressive, precautionary and active nature. There is no question of a restriction to a certain type of measure.

> A reference to 'preserving, protecting and improving the quality of the environment' can, for example, be found in the preamble to Regulation 1367/2006 on the application of the provisions of the Aarhus Convention on Access to Information, Public Participation in Decision-making and Access to Justice in Environmental Matters to Community institutions and bodies and Directive 2006/7 concerning the management of bathing water quality.[130]

Protecting human health

The most important question of interpretation in respect of this objective is whether 'protecting *human* health' is a wider concept than protecting *public* health. The answer must be that it is. Protection of public health indicates measures required to protect the *collective* health interests of people in a given society. However, the wording of Article 174 EC makes action possible even when it is not so much a collective interest that is at stake as the interest of certain individuals or groups in society.[131] Of course, the principle of subsidiarity must be taken into account in such cases.

---

[129] Cf. however Case C-309/96 *Annibaldi* [1997] ECR I-7493 where the Court ruled that as the law stands at present, regional legislation, which establishes a nature and archaeological park in order to protect and enhance the value of the environment and the cultural heritage of the area concerned, applies to a situation which does not fall within the scope of Community law. The case concerned the authorities' refusal to grant Annibaldi permission to plant an orchard of 3 hectares within the perimeter of a regional park.

[130] OJ 2006 L 264/13 and OJ 2006/64/37.

[131] See for a reference to '*personal* health' point 2 of the preamble of Directive 2003/35 providing for public participation in respect of the drawing up of certain plans and programmes relating to the environment

It should be noted that the distinction between the two concepts has become somewhat blurred in the judgments of the Court of Justice, for example, in the *Fumicot* case, where the applicability of Article 30 EC to measures restricting the importation of plant protection products was at issue.[132] This provision does in fact talk of the protection of health and life of humans, animals or plants, and not of 'public health'. However, in its judgment (at paragraph 13), the Court equates the two concepts: 'In that respect, it is not disputed that the national rules in question are intended to protect public health and that they therefore come within the exception provided for in Article 36 [now Article 30, authors].'

A second problem of interpretation concerns the fact that the article only refers to human health. Does this therefore mean that the protection of animal health and flora and fauna must be regarded as lying outside the scope of the objective? On the other hand, it has been shown above that the protection of flora and fauna may be included within the first objective mentioned in Article 174 EC. The restriction of the second objective to the protection of human health does not therefore seem essential.

Various references to this objective can, for example, be found in Directive 2001/18 on the deliberate release into the environment of genetically modified organisms.[133] According to Article 1 of the Directive its objective is 'to protect human health and the environment'. A similar reference can be found in Article 1 of the new Bathing Water Directive.[134]

Prudent and rational utilisation of natural resources

It is understood that according to international law, states have the sovereign right to exploit their own resources pursuant to their own environmental and developmental policies.[135] It is also understood that to achieve sustainable development states should reduce and eliminate unsustainable patterns of production and consumption.[136] In the Sixth Environment Action Programme, a prudent use of natural resources has been acknowledged as a condition for sustainable development.[137] However, what precisely should be understood by 'natural resources' is not entirely clear.[138] From an international law point of view, Princi-

---

(OJ 2003 L 156/17): 'Community environmental legislation includes provisions for public authorities and other bodies to take decisions which may have a significant effect on the environment as well as on personal health and well-being'.

[132] Case 272/80 *Frans-Nederlandse Maatschappij voor Biologische Producten* [1981] ECR 3277.

[133] OJ 2001 L 106/1.

[134] Directive 2006/7 concerning the management of bathing water quality OJ 2006 L 64/37.

[135] Cf. Principle 2 of the so called Rio Declaration on Environment and Development.

[136] Principle 9 of the Rio Declaration.

[137] Decision 1600/2002, OJ 2002 L 242/1. Cf. also the reference in Article 21(f) EU after amendment by the Reform Treaty.

[138] Cf. the Communication from the Commission 'Thematic Strategy on the sustainable use of natural resources', COM (2005) 670 final.

ple 2 of the Declaration of the United Nations Conference on the Human Environment (the Stockholm Declaration)[139] may offer some assistance. Here natural resources are taken to mean: 'natural resources of the earth including the air, water, land, flora and fauna and especially representative samples of natural ecosystems [...]'. The following natural resources can assumed to be included: wood, minerals, water, oil, gas and chemical substances. Sevenster mentions the following policy items which might give some indication as to what might fall under the management of natural resources: nature conservation, soil protection, waste disposal (encouraging re-use), policy on urban areas, coastal areas and mountainous areas, disaster policy, water management, an environmentally friendly agricultural policy and energy-saving.[140] On the basis of the above, it can be concluded that this objective also has a wide scope.

> References to this objective can be found in e.g. Directive 91/676 on nitrates[141] (protection of living resources), in Regulation 2422/2001 on a Community energy efficiency labelling programme for office equipment[142] (rational use of energy), Directive 1999/94 relating to the availability of consumer information on fuel economy and CO_2 emissions in respect of the marketing of new passenger cars[143] and the Water Framework Directive (surface waters and groundwater).[144]

The inclusion of this objective in the Treaty at the time of the Single European Act was accompanied by the following declaration in the Final Act: 'The Conference confirms that the Community's activities in the sphere of the environment may not interfere with national policies regarding the exploitation of energy resources.'[145] In our opinion only limited value must be attached to this declaration. Firstly, because in legal terms such declarations derogate but little from the express text of the EC Treaty and, secondly, because it refers only to the *exploitation* and not the *use* of energy resources.

Regional or worldwide environmental problems
At the time of the Single European Act, the question of to what extent the environmental objectives were limited in a territorial sense was a matter of discussion. In the present version of the Treaty, it has at any rate become clear that Article 174 EC does in principle allow room for extraterritorial environmental objectives. By the inclusion of 'promoting measures at international level to

---

[139] *ILM* 1972, at 1416.

[140] Cf. Sevenster (1992) at 100. Cf. also Krämer (2007) at 14.

[141] OJ 1991 L 375/1.

[142] OJ 2001 L 332/1.

[143] OJ 1999 L 12/16.

[144] Directive 2000/60 establishing a framework for Community action in the field of water policy, OJ 2000 L 327/1. Cf. also Directive 2006/7 concerning the management of bathing water quality OJ 2006 L 64/37.

[145] Cf. in general Wägenbauer & Wainwright (1997).

deal with regional or worldwide environmental problems', existing practice has been confirmed.[146]

An important part of European environment policy is not concerned primarily with protecting the EU's own environment, but the environment outside the EU. The Sixth Environment Action Programme stresses the need for a positive and constructive role of the European Union in the protection of the global environment.[147] The carrying capacity of the global environment is even regarded as one of the Community's objectives to be pursued at the international level. The following legislative measures are examples of its concern and responsibility for the environment outside the EU:

- · Regulation 3254/91 prohibiting the introduction of pelts;[148]
- · Regulation 348/81 concerning the protection of whales;[149]
- · Directive 89/370 concerning the importation of skins of seal pups;[150]
- · the measures in Regulation 259/93 concerning the export of waste to countries outside the EC;[151]
- · Regulation 338/97 on the protection of species of wild fauna and flora by regulating trade therein;[152]
- · Regulation 2493/2000 on measures to promote the full integration of the environmental dimension in the development process of developing countries;[153]
- · Regulation 2494/2000 on measures to promote the conservation and sustainable management of tropical forests and other forests in developing countries.[154]

However, even some directives that are primarily designed to protect the EU environment contain references to 'the global environment' or the environment of 'third countries'.

For example, the overall objective of Directive 99/31 on the landfill of waste refers to measures to prevent negative effects on the environment, 'and on the global

---

[146] Cf. Krämer (2007) at 3. The Reform Treaty will amend this objective by adding 'and in particular combating climate change' at the end of the sentence. Cf. also Article 3(5) EU after the entry into force of the Reform Treaty: the Union 'shall contribute to [...] the sustainable development of the Earth'.

[147] Decision 1600/2002 laying down the Sixth Community Environment Action Programme, OJ 2002 L 242/1.

[148] OJ 1991 L 308/1.

[149] OJ 1981 L 39/1.

[150] OJ 1989 L 163/37.

[151] OJ 1993 L 30/1. Cf. the 'new' Regulation 1013/2006 on shipments of waste, OJ 2006 L 190/1. Regulation 1013/2006 will repeal Regulation 259/93 with effect from 12 July 2007.

[152] Regulation 338/97, OJ L 61/1.

[153] OJ 2000 L 288/1. This regulation also stresses that sustainable development in particular relies on the integration of the environmental dimension into the development process.

[154] OJ 2000 L 288/6.

environment, including the greenhouse effect'.[155] Another example is provided by Article 1 of Directive 94/62 on packaging and packaging waste.[156] The directive specifically aims to protect the environment of all Member States as well as of third countries.

In addition, the EC is a party to several multilateral conventions which have an extraterritorial objective, such as the 1985 Vienna Convention for the protection of the ozone layer and the 1987 Montreal Protocol, the 1989 Basel Convention on the control of transboundary movements of waste, the 1992 Framework Convention on Climate Change and subsequent Protocols[157] and the 1992 Convention on Biological Diversity.[158] All implementing measures of the EC are of course also directed to the global or extra-territorial objectives of the agreements.

Although there is ample practice of European legislative measures aiming to protect the environment outside the EU, the phrase 'regional or worldwide environmental problems' is still unclear in several respects. For example, is it intended to exclude unilateral measures? A large part of the EU's present extraterritorial environment policy has in fact been created by means of such measures. Nor is it clear whether, by referring only to 'regional or worldwide' problems, action to protect the environment of only one or a few third states is excluded. Take, for example, a prohibition on imports of tropical hardwood that has not been sustainably produced. It is highly debatable whether this would amount to a regional or worldwide environmental problem. In general, this kind of case will involve specific consequences for the environment in one state or a number of states.

For the time being, there is a lot to be said in favour of not interpreting Article 174 EC too narrowly. Nor should unilateral environmental measures or environmental measures directed at protecting the environment in only one state or a few states *a priori* be excluded, even though the problem of the international law constraints of such measures is at its most pronounced in this very case. Article 174 EC leaves room to seek to attain extraterritorial protective objectives, though this power should be interpreted in accordance with principles of public international law. Support for this view can be found both in the Treaty and in the case law of the Court of Justice.

With respect to the Treaty, we may point to Article 299 EC, which provides that the Treaty applies to the states named in the article. According to general

---

[155] Article 1 of Directive 1999/31, OJ 1999 L 182/1. Other measures aimed at reducing emissions causing global warming include, e.g., Directive 2003/87 establishing a scheme for greenhouse gas emission allowance trading within the Community, OJ 2003 L 275/32.

[156] See, for example, Directive 94/62 on packaging and packaging waste, OJ 1994 L 365/10. The directive aims to protect the environment of all Member States *as well as of third countries* (Art. 1).

[157] OJ 1994 L 33/13.

[158] OJ 1993 L 309/1.

principles of international law, this means that the Treaty in any event binds the parties with respect to the entire territory over which they are sovereign, unless the Treaty itself allows exceptions or applies special rules. As Article 299 EC does not contain any reference to the territory of the Member States, it cannot be regarded as limiting the territorial scope of the Treaty to territory which falls under the sovereignty (or full jurisdiction) of the Member States. The scope of the Treaty and other European law may indeed extend beyond that territory, to the extent international law allows the Member States to exercise a limited functional jurisdiction.

Directive 2001/81 on national emission ceilings for certain atmospheric pollutant provides a rare example of an environmental measure explicitly expanding its scope beyond the 'territory' of the Member States.[159] Article 2 states: 'This Directive covers emissions in the territory of the Member States *and their exclusive economic zones* from all sources of the pollutants referred to in Article 4 which arise as a result of human activities."[160] With respect to the Habitats Directive, we may also refer to an English High Court judgment applying that directive to the UK's Continental Shelf.[161]

Examples outside the environmental sector are the competence of Member States in respect of the Continental Shelf, the fishery zones and any exclusive economic zones. Being able to exercise such powers outside the direct territory of the EU Member States is conditional on the subject matter of the functional jurisdiction falling within the material sphere of operation of the relevant Treaty provisions, and on the provisions themselves not containing any restriction limiting the territorial sphere of operation to the territory of the Member States. This view finds support in the case law of the Court, and particularly in the *Kramer* case.[162] One of the matters at issue was to what extent the authority of the EC extended to fishing on the high seas. After the Court had established that the European legislature had internal competence to adopt measures for the conservation of the biological resources of the seas, it continued 'it follows [...] from the very nature of things that the rule-making authority of the Community *ratione materiae* also extends – in so far as the Member States have similar authority under public international law – to fishing on the high seas.' This judgment was confirmed by the Court in the *Drift-Net* case, in which a prohibition on the use for fishing of drift-nets longer than 2.5 km was held to be valid.[163] The validity of the measure was disputed on the grounds that the EC was not competent to take measures to preserve fish populations in the open sea. The Court dismissed this line of reasoning here, too.

---

[159] OJ 2001 L 309/22.

[160] Emphasis added.

[161] English High Court, Queen's Bench Division (Maurice Kay J) 5 November 1999 *Regina v. Secretary of State for Trade and Industry*, ex parte *Greenpeace* [2000] Env. L.R. 221. Cf. Case C-6/04 *Commission v. UK* [2005] ECR I-9017, para. 119.

[162] Joined Cases 3, 4 and 6/76 *Kramer* [1976] ECR 1279.

[163] Case C-405/92 *Etablissements Armand Mondiet v. Société Armement Islais* [1993] ECR I-6133.

A translation of the judgments in the *Kramer* and *Drift-Net* cases in terms of environmental law leads to the following conclusion. In so far as the Member States are competent under international law to protect the environment outside their own territories, the EC must also be regarded as being competent to take such measures, at least to the extent the subject matter of the measure falls within the scope of application of Article 174 EC. Action to protect the environment extraterritorially cannot therefore be regarded as being confined to international agreements or to those sectors where regional or global problems are at issue. The fourth indent of Article 174(1) EC should not be interpreted restrictively. In view of the transboundary nature of the environment, this follows – to quote the *Kramer* judgment – 'from the very nature of things'.[164] However, it should be remembered that extraterritorial environmental powers must be exercised in accordance with international law, including the provisions of the WTO.[165] In exercising its extraterritorial powers in respect of the environment, the EC has to act with regard to international law constraints. As has been stated, any interpretation of Article 174 EC, which would bring the EC into conflict with its obligations under international law, must be rejected.

3.2   The Principles of European Environment Policy

Article 174(2) EC sets out the principles on which European environment policy is based.[166] These are:
· the high level of protection principle;
· the precautionary principle;
· the prevention principle;
· the source principle;
· the polluter pays principle and
· the safeguard clause.

European environmental legislation will have to translate these principles into concrete obligations for the Member States. It will then be possible to interpret directives and regulations in the light of these principles. In this chapter, section 2, we have discussed in the context of the integration principle the question to

---

[164] English High Court, Queen's Bench Division (Maurice Kay J) 5 November 1999 *Regina* v. *Secretary of State for Trade and Industry*, ex parte *Greenpeace* [2000] Env. L.R. 221 which ruled, relying *inter alia* on the *Kramer* case that the Habitats Directive is also applicable outside the territorial waters of the UK.

[165] See in a general sense the Court's judgment in Case C-286/90 *Anklagemindigheden* v. *Poulsen and Diva Navigation* [1992] ECR I-6019. See also Article 9 of Directive 2005/35 on ship-source pollution and on the introduction of penalties for infringements: 'Member States shall apply the provisions of this Directive without any discrimination in form or in fact against foreign ships and in accordance with applicable international law, including Section 7 of Part XII of the 1982 United Nations Convention on the Law of the Sea [...].' Cf. Wiers (2002) and Montini (2005) with respect to the WTO.

[166] Cf. in general De Sadeleer (2005) and on the way national courts apply the European environmental principles Macrory (2004).

what extent these principles are legally enforceable. We concluded that only in very exceptional cases would a measure be susceptible to annulment because the environmental principles of Article 174(2) EC were not sufficiently taken into account.

High level of protection

Article 174(2) EC provides that a European environment policy shall aim at a high level of protection taking into account the diversity of situations in the various regions of the Community. This high level of protection principle is one of the most important substantive principles of European environment policy. It is stated at various places in the EC Treaty. It was the Treaty of Amsterdam which ensured that the principle was included in the general objectives of the EC Treaty. Under Article 2 EC, it is a task to promote 'a high level of protection and improvement of the quality of the environment'. Nevertheless, it should be quite clear that a high level of protection is not the same thing as the *highest* possible level of protection.[167]

As such, this 'high level of protection' principle is of course not new. The 'old' Article 100a(3) EEC, included in the Treaty by the Single European Act, provided that the Commission, in its internal market proposals in the field of environmental protection would take as a base a high level of protection. This proposal was criticised as being directed only at the Commission and that the Council, as the ultimate decision-making body, could depart from the Commission's proposals. It was also doubtful to what extent the obligation in the article was open to review by the courts. Suppose the Council were to have taken its decision in conformity with the Commission's proposal. Could it then have been argued before the courts that the decision was invalid if it did not take as a base a high level of protection? It seemed hardly conceivable. As amended by the Amsterdam Treaty the Article 95(3) EC now reads as follows:

> 'The Commission, in its proposals envisaged in paragraph 1 concerning health, safety, environmental protection and consumer protection, will take as a base a high level of protection, taking account in particular of any new development based on scientific facts. Within their respective powers, the European Parliament and the Council will also seek to achieve this objective.'

This provision makes it quite clear that the high level of protection principle is directed not only at the Commission, but also at the European Parliament and Council in their legislative capacity. However, the 'seek to achieve' formulation still makes it doubtful indeed whether this principle is subject to review in a

---

[167] Cf. Case C-284/95 *Safety Hi-Tech Srl* v. *S. & T. Srl* [1998] ECR I-4301, para. 49: 'whilst it is undisputed that Article 130r(2) of the Treaty requires Community policy in environmental matters to aim for a high level of protection, such a level of protection, to be compatible with that provision, does not necessarily have to be the highest that is technically possible.'

court of law to challenge the legality of the measures adopted by the Council.[168] Krämer however argues that where a Commission proposal is not based on high level of environmental protection, the European Parliament has right of action against the Commission under Article 230 EC. We fail to see however how a proposal of the Commission can be regarded as an 'act' in the meaning of Article 230 EC.[169]

That the enforceability of the principle is limited is also apparent from the text of Article 174(2) EC. European policy 'shall aim' at a high level of protection 'taking into account the diversity of situations in the various regions of the Community.' In fact this addition is totally unnecessary, as a similar formulation is also included in Article 174(3) EC, second indent. It is now stated twice.

> An explicit reference to this principle can, for instance, be found in Directive 96/61 concerning integrated pollution prevention and control, the so-called IPPC Directive.[170] Its aim is to achieve integrated prevention and control of pollution 'in order to achieve a high level of protection of the environment taken as a whole.' Other examples of legislation containing such references in their preambles include Regulation 1013/2006 on shipments of waste and Directive 2002/49 relating to the assessment and management of environmental noise.[171] Also the, current, Sixth Community Environment Action Programme contains various references to this principle.[172]

The precautionary principle[173]

Since 'Maastricht' the Treaty has stated that Community policy on the environment shall be based on the precautionary principle. This principle has its roots in what is described in German environmental law as the *Vorsorgeprinzip*.[174] This means that, if there is a strong suspicion that a certain activity may have environmentally harmful consequences, it is better to act before it is too late rather than wait until full scientific evidence is available which incontrovertibly shows the causal connection.[175] In other words, the principle of precaution may therefore justify action to prevent damage in some cases even though the causal link cannot be clearly established on the basis of available scientific

---

[168] Cf. Van Caltster & Deketelaere (1998) at 15 and Krämer (2007) at 11-12.

[169] Krämer (2007) at 13.

[170] OJ 1996 L 257/26.

[171] OJ 2006 L 190/1 and OJ 2002 L 189/12.

[172] Decision 1600/2002 laying down the Sixth Community Environment Action Programme, OJ 2002 L 242/1.

[173] Cf. in general, Trouwborst (2006), De Sadeleer (2006) and Lee (2005) at 97 *et seq.*

[174] Cf. Marr & Schwemer (2003).

[175] Cf. also Principle 15 of the Rio Declaration: 'In order to protect the environment, the precautionary approach shall be widely applied by States according to their capabilities. Where there are threats of serious or irreversible damage, lack of full scientific certainty shall not be used as a reason for postponing cost-effective measures to prevent environmental degradation.'

evidence.[176] Its objective is to avoid potential risks.[177] Or as some authors have put it: *in dubio pro natura*.[178] Another implication of the precautionary principle, at least according to the Commission, is that the EC has the right to establish the level of protection of the environment, human, animal and plant health, that it deems appropriate.[179]

According to the Commission guidelines the precautionary principle is all about 'risk-management', which does not mean that all risks must be reduced to zero. Judging what is an acceptable level of risk for society is a political responsibility. Where action is deemed necessary, measures based on the precautionary principle should be proportional to the chosen level of protection, non-discriminatory in their application, consistent with similar measures already taken, based on an examination of the potential benefits and costs of action or lack of action and subject to review in the light of new scientific data.

In the meantime, the precautionary principle has been applied by the Court of Justice in its case law. Where there is uncertainty as to the existence or extent of risks to human health, the *institutions* may take protective measures without having to wait until the reality and seriousness of those risks become fully apparent.[180] This case law show the consequences of the precautionary principle for the interpretation of the first sentence of Article 174(3) EC, which provides that in preparing its policy on the environment, the EC shall take account of 'available scientific and technical data'. In the 'old' days, this could easily have been used by the EC as a ground for not acting until there was absolute proof of the causes of certain undesirable environmental effects. Such an interpretation would now be at odds with the precautionary principle.

With respect to the Member States, the Court acknowledged the importance of the precautionary principle in applying so called 'safeguard clauses' in directives.[181]

With respect to the safeguard clause of Article 12(1) of Regulation 258/97,[182] the Court of Justice ruled that:[183]

---

[176] The Communication of the Commission Single Market and the Environment, COM (99) 263. Cf. Heyvaert (2006).

[177] Case T-229/04 *Sweden* v. *Commission*, judgment of 11 July 2007, n.y.r. in the ECR, para. 161.

[178] Backes & Verschuuren (1998) at 43.

[179] COM (2000) 1, containing Commission guidelines on how to apply the precautionary principle.

[180] Cf. Case C-157/96 *National Farmers' Union a.o.* [1998] ECR I-2211, para. 63 and Case C-180/96 *UK* v. *Commission* [1998] ECR I-2265, para. 99. Cf. also Joined Cases T-125/96 *Boehringer* [1999] ECR II-3427.

[181] See on safeguard clauses this chapter, section 3.2 in particular.

[182] Which reads: 'Where a Member State, as a result of new information or a reassessment of existing information, has detailed grounds for considering that the use of a food or a food ingredient complying with this regulation endangers human health or the environment, that Member State may either temporarily restrict or suspend the trade in and use of the food or food ingredient in question in its territory. It shall immediately inform the other Member States and the Commission thereof, giving the grounds for its decision.'

[183] Case C-236/01 *Monsanto* [2003] ECR I-8105.

'protective measures may be taken pursuant to Article 12 of Regulation No 258/97 interpreted in the light of the precautionary principle even if it proves impossible to carry out as full a risk assessment as possible in the particular circumstances of a given case because of the inadequate nature of the available scientific data [...].

Such measures presuppose, in particular, that the risk assessment available to the national authorities provides specific evidence which, without precluding scientific uncertainty, makes it possible reasonably to conclude on the basis of the most reliable scientific evidence available and the most recent results of international research that the implementation of those measures is necessary in order to avoid novel foods which pose potential risks to human health being offered on the market.'

Indeed, the inadequate nature of available scientific data does not preclude a Member State or the EC institutions from taking protective measures. However, the Court of Justice is not giving a *carte blanche* either in the sense that the burden of proof is reversed unreservedly.[184] Nor will mere hypothetical risks suffice for taking action.[185] Protective measures can be adopted only if a risk assessment has first carried out which is as complete as possible given the particular circumstances of the individual case, from which it is apparent that, in the light of the precautionary principle, the implementation of such measures is necessary in order to ensure that there is no danger for the human health and the environment.

The case law on safeguard clauses in directives is also relevant with respect to the application of Article 95(5) EC. This provision requires 'new scientific evidence' in order to accept Member States' introducing environmental legislation derogating from internal market measures. Article 95 EC should be interpreted in the light of the precautionary principle.[186] Of course, this does not mean that the precautionary principle implies that the conditions for application of that provision do not have to be met at all.[187] Finally, it is the authors' opinion that the Member States' powers under Article 30 EC and the 'rule of reason' must be interpreted in the same manner.[188]

---

[184] See, for instance, Case C-314/99 *Netherlands* v. *Commission* [2002] ECR I-5521, where the Court annulled Section 3 of the Annex to Commission Directive 1999/51 (tin, PCP and cadmium). The Commission acknowledged in that case that it did not possess sufficiently reliable scientific information for the measures taken.

[185] Case T-229/04 *Sweden* v. *Commission*, judgment of 11 July 2007, n.y.r. in the ECR, para. 161. This case concerned the annulment of Commission Directive 2003/112 to include paraquat as an active substance ex Article 5 of the Pesticide Directive 91/414.

[186] Cf. Commission Decision 1999/832, OJ 1999 L 329/25 (*Dutch creosote*). See also Chapter 3, section 6.

[187] Joined Cases T-366/03 and T-235/04 *Land Oberösterreich and Austria* v. *Commission* [2005] ECR II-4005, para. 71.

[188] See Chapter 6, section 5.3.

A fine example of the precautionary principle in secondary law can be found in Directive 98/81 on the contained use of genetically modified micro-organisms (GMMs).[189] Article 5(4) states that where there is doubt as to the appropriate classification of GMMs, the more stringent protective measures shall be applied unless sufficient evidence, in agreement with the competent authority, justifies the application of less stringent measures.

Another example can be found in Annex IV of Directive 96/61 (the IPPC Directive).[190] Annex IV contains considerations to be taken into account when determining best available techniques 'bearing in mind the likely costs and benefits of a measure and the principles of precaution and prevention'. One of the considerations is formulated as 'the need to prevent or reduce to a minimum the overall impact of the emissions on the environment and the risks to it'. With respect to definition of 'waste', it is also clear that this concept has to be interpreted in the light of the precautionary principle.[191]

With respect to the Habitats Directive, Article 6(3) must be mentioned. According to the first sentence of it, any plan or project not directly connected with or necessary to the management of the site but likely to have a significant effect thereon, either individually or in combination with other plans or projects, is to be subject to appropriate assessment of its implications for the site in view of the site's conservation objectives. The ECJ has held that the requirement for an appropriate assessment of the implications of a plan or project is thus conditional on its being likely to have a significant effect on the site. In the light, in particular, of the precautionary principle, such a risk exists if it cannot be excluded on the basis of objective information that the plan or project will have a significant effect on the site concerned.[192]

The prevention principle

European policy on the environment shall be based on the principle that preventive action should be taken. The principle of preventive action was included in the Treaty by the Single European Act. Put simply, prevention is

---

[189] OJ 1998 L 330/13. See also Article 1 of Regulation 1946/2003 on transboundary movements of genetically modified organisms, OJ 2003 L 287/1. Cf. also Case C-6/99 *Association Greenpeace France* v. *Ministère de l'Agriculture et de la Pêche* [2000] ECR I-1651, in which the French *Conseil d'Etat* asked the Court for a ruling on whether the precautionary principle permits national authorities to refuse market access for transgenic products, where the Commission has already approved the grant of such an authorisation. The Court said they could not, stating that observance of the precautionary principle was observed in Directive 90/220 itself.

[190] OJ 1996 L 257/26. See on this directive Chapter 8, section 5.

[191] E.g. Case C-9/00 *Palin Granit and Vehmassalon kansanterveystyön kuntayhtymän hallitus* [2002] ECR I-3533, paras. 22 and 23. See also Chapter 8, section 15.1.

[192] Case C-6/04 *Commission* v. *UK* [2005] ECR I-9017, para. 54. Cf. also Case C-127/02 *Landelijke Vereniging tot Behoud van de Waddenzee* [2004] ECR I-7405, para. 58. The Court ruled 'that the authorisation criterion laid down in the second sentence of Article 6(3) of the Habitats Directive integrates the precautionary principle'.

better than cure. The prevention principle allows action to be taken to protect the environment at an early stage. It is no longer primarily a question of repairing damage after it has occurred. Instead the principle calls for measures to be taken to prevent damage occurring at all.

> This is demonstrated by Directive 94/62 on packaging and packaging waste.[193] The directive makes it quite clear that the best means of preventing the creation of packaging waste is to reduce the overall volume of packaging. Article 9 of the directive requires Member States to ensure that packaging may be placed on the market only if it complies with all essential requirements defined by the directive. The prevention principle must not be confused with the precautionary principle, which is in essence more far-reaching (see above).[194]
> Pollution prevention is of course also the key word in the IPPC Directive.[195]

The Third Environmental Action Programme focused strongly on the prevention principle.[196] Prevention rather than cure was the central theme of this programme. According to the programme the following conditions must, *inter alia*, be met, if the prevention principle is to have full effect:
· the requisite knowledge and information must be improved and made readily available to decision-makers and all interested parties, including the public;[197]
· it is necessary to formulate and introduce procedures for judgment which will ensure that the appropriate facts are considered early in the decision-making processes relating to any activity likely to affect the environment significantly. The Environmental Impact Assessment (EIA) Directive should be noted in this connection.[198] The preamble to the EIA Directive, referring to the first three Environmental Action Programmes, states 'that

---

[193] OJ 1994 L 365/10.

[194] See for another example in the waste sector the 'Community Strategy for Waste Management' COM (96) 399 final. This states that, as regards the prevention principle, the following measures should be particularly developed promotion of clean technologies and products, reduction of the hazardousness of wastes, the establishment of technical standards and possibly EC-wide rules to limit the presence of certain dangerous substances in products, the promotion of reuse and recycling schemes, the appropriate use of economic instruments, eco-balances, eco-audit schemes, life-cycle analysis and actions on consumer information and education as well as the development of the eco-label system. Cf. also Joined Cases C-418/97 and C-419/97 *ARCO Chemie Nederland* [2000] ECR I-4475, paras. 39-40 in which the Court of Justice relied on the prevention principle to interpret the concept of 'waste' of the Waste Framework Directive. Cf. also Joined Cases C-175/98 and C-177/98 *Lirussi and Bizzaro* [1999] ECR I-6881, where the Court used the precautionary principle and the prevention principle to interpret certain aspects of Annex II of the Waste Framework Directive.

[195] Directive 96/61 concerning integrated pollution prevention and control, OJ 1996 L 257/26.

[196] OJ 1983 C 46/1.

[197] See, for example, Directive 2003/4 on public access to environmental information, OJ 2003 L 41/26.

[198] Directive 85/337, OJ 1985 L 175/40.

the best environment policy consists in preventing the creation of pollution or nuisances at source, rather than subsequently trying to counteract their effects'. For the same reason, account should be taken of the consequences of planning and decision-making processes for the environment at as early a stage as possible. Environmental impact assessment is an excellent example of an instrument in which the principle of prevention plays a vital role;

· the implementation of adopted measures must be monitored to ensure their correct application and their adaptation if circumstances or new knowledge should so require. Relevant in this respect are provisions in directives concerning the adaptation of technical standards to technical and scientific progress.[199]

Another example is Directive 80/68 on the protection of groundwater.[200] This directive imposes extensive monitoring and survey requirements on Member States. Before the competent authorities may grant an authorisation to discharge substances, a detailed investigation of the effects on the environment must have been carried out.

Finally, we can mention Regulation 842/2006 on certain fluorinated greenhouse gases which contains various references to the prevention and minimisation of emissions of fluorinated greenhouse gases.[201]

The source principle

European policy on the environment shall be based on the principle that environmental damage should as a priority be rectified at its source. According to the source principle, damage to the environment should preferably not be prevented by using end-of-pipe technology. This principle also implies a preference for emission standards rather than environmental quality standards, especially to deal with water and air pollution. Environmental directives requiring the Member States to reduce the emissions is not dependent on the general environmental situation of the region in which the emissions occur.[202] This preference becomes abundantly clear if the water quality legislation is examined.[203]

Other references to the source principle can be found in Directive 2002/96 on waste electrical and electronic equipment[204] (WEEE Directive) and in the EIA Directive 85/337.

---

[199] For example, Article 13 of the Sewage Sludge Directive 86/278, OJ 1986 L 181/6.

[200] OJ 1980 L 20/43.

[201] OJ 2006 L 161/1.

[202] Cf. Case C-364/03 *Commission v. Greece* [2005] ECR I-6159, para. 34 with respect to emissions of sulphur dioxide and nitrogen oxide under Directive 84/360,

[203] Directive 2006/11 on pollution caused by certain dangerous substances discharged into the aquatic environment of the Community; OJ 2006 L 64/52. See also Chapter 8, section 10.3.

[204] OJ 2002 L 37/24

The principle was given an unexpected dimension in the *Walloon Waste* case, where the Court of Justice applied it in determining to what extent Walloon measures restricting imports of foreign waste were discriminatory.[205] The Court held that the principle means that every region, municipality or other local authority must take those measures which are necessary to ensure the reception, processing and removal of its own waste. The waste must be disposed of as close as possible to the place of production in order to limit its transport as far as possible. Consequently, the Court held that, in view of the differences between the waste produced at various locations and the connection with the place of its production, the Walloon restrictions could not be considered discriminatory. In this case, the source principle was thus equated with what is known as the proximity principle in waste law.[206]

In the waste case *Sydhavnens Sten & Grus,* the Court seems to be willing to apply the source principle in a more direct manner.[207] In that case, the Court ruled that the source principle could not serve to justify *any* restriction on waste exports, but only when the waste in question is harmful to the environment. By implication the Court acknowledged that Member States are entitled to impose export restrictions on waste if this is necessary for the protection of the environment. Moreover, the concept of protection of the environment is to be interpreted in the light of the source principle.

The polluter pays principle

Action is based on the principle that the polluter should pay. This principle was one of the cornerstones of a European environment policy even before it was incorporated into the Treaty. It was referred to as a principle of Community environment policy in the First Action Programme on the Environment.[208] In simple terms: this is the principle that the costs of measures to deal with pollution should be borne by the polluter who causes the pollution.

The polluter pays principle is set out in a Communication from the Commission to the Council in 1975 regarding cost allocation and action by public authorities on environmental matters.[209] As far as we know, the 1975 communication is still the guiding principle for policy in that respect. The communication is not as such binding. The Council has however recommended that Member States conform to the principles contained in the communication. Both the communication and the recommendation were prompted by the consideration that the costs connected with the protection of the environment against pollution should be allocated according to the same principles throughout the EU.

This is, on the one hand, to avoid distortions of competition affecting trade, which would be incompatible with the proper functioning of the common

---

[205] Case C-2/90 *Commission v. Belgium* [1992] ECR I-4431.

[206] See Chapter 8, section 15. See also Case C-422/92 *Commission v. Germany* [1995] ECR I-1097.

[207] Case C-209/98 *Sydhavnens Sten & Grus* [2000] ECR I-3743, para. 48.

[208] OJ 1973 C 112/1. Cf. on the polluter pays principle in general Vandekerckhove (1994).

[209] OJ 1975 L 194/1.

market, and on the other, to further the aims set out in the First Action Programme on the environment. This programme is based on the principle that charging polluters the costs of action to combat the pollution they cause will encourage them to reduce that pollution and endeavour to find less polluting products or technologies. This would enable a more rational use to be made of scarce environmental resources. Apart from the use of charges, the principle can also be implemented by imposing environmental standards. Companies, which are required to observe environmental standards, will have to make various investments in their production process if they are to comply with the statutory standards. Setting standards in this way also helps ensure the polluter bears the cost of pollution.

The EU must therefore ensure, especially by laying down standards, environmental charges or creating a system of environmental liability,[210] that persons who are responsible for pollution in fact bear the cost. In other words, environmental protection should not in principle depend on policies which rely on grants of aid and place the burden of combating pollution on society. On the other hand, the polluter pays principle also seems to require that a European measure must avoid putting burdens on persons and undertakings for the elimination of pollution to which they have not contributed.[211]

The polluter pays principle is of particular relevance with respect to the Guidelines on state aid for environmental protection.[212] According to the Commission, the costs associated with protecting the environment should be internalised by firms just like other production costs. Aid control and environmental policy must, in the Commission's view, also support one another in ensuring stricter application of the polluter pays principle.[213]

> Several references to the polluter pays principle can be found in EC secondary legislation. Article 15 of Directive 75/442 on waste[214] states that, in accordance with the polluter pays principle, the cost of disposing of waste must be borne by:
> · the holder who has waste handled by a waste collector or by an undertaking authorised to carry out waste disposal activities or
> · the previous holders or the producer of the product from which the waste came.

---

[210] Cf. Directive 2004/35 on environmental liability with regard to the prevention and remedying of environmental damage, OJ 2004 L 143/56. Article 1 reads: 'The purpose of this Directive is to establish a framework of environmental liability based on the 'polluter-pays' principle, to prevent and remedy environmental damage.'

[211] Case C-293/97 *Standley* [1999] ECR I-2603.

[212] OJ 2001 C 37/3. See Chapter 7, section 7.3.

[213] See, for example, the Commission Decision in the *Cartiere del Garda* case, OJ 1993 L 273/51, where the Commission directly examined a national aid measure in the light of the polluter pays principle. In that case the Commission concluded that the proposed aid 'does not meet the polluter pays principle'. For a discussion of this case see Chapter 7, section 7.1.

[214] OJ 1975 L 194/47.

Article 14 of Directive 75/439 on the disposal of waste oils[215] provides that indemnities may be granted to collection and/or disposal undertakings for services rendered. These indemnities may be financed by a charge imposed on products, which after use are transformed into waste oils, or on waste oils. The financing of indemnities must be in accordance with the polluter pays principle (Article 15). According to the Court of Justice in the *ADBHU* case, provisions like these do not conflict with the Treaty rules on state aid.[216]

Outside environmental law, in view of the integration principle, a reference can be found in Directive 2006/38 on the charging of heavy goods vehicles for the use of certain infrastructures.[217] A fairer system of charging for the use of road infra-structure, for instance through the variation of tolls to take account of the environ-mental performance of vehicles, was felt necessary by the European legislature in order to encourage sustainable transport in the EU.

The safeguard clause

Harmonisation measures answering environmental protection requirements shall include, where appropriate, a safeguard clause allowing Member States to take provisional measures; for non-economic environmental reasons, subject to a European inspection procedure.

This clause is clearly of a different order from the above principles. It is deba-table whether its place in the Treaty, next to the true principles, is well chosen. The second paragraph of Article 174(2) EC provides that a directive or regulation may include a safeguard clause allowing Member States to take measures to protect the environment in cases of urgency.

In practice, there are many examples where this kind of safeguard clause is actu-ally embodied in the legislative act in question. For example, Article 11 of Direc-tive 91/414 concerning the placing of plant protection products on the market[218] provides that, where a Member State has valid reasons to consider that a product which is authorised under the directive constitutes a risk to human or animal health or the environment, it may provisionally restrict or prohibit the use and/or sale of that product on its territory.

Another example of such a safeguard clause can be found in Article 32 of the Biocides Directive: 'Where a Member State has valid reasons to consider that a biocidal product which it has authorised, registered or is bound to authorise or register pursuant to Articles 3 or 4, constitutes an unacceptable risk to human or animal health or the environment, it may provisionally restrict or prohibit the use or sale of that product on its territory. It shall immediately inform the Commission and the other Member States of such action and give reasons for its decision. A decision shall be taken on the matter within 90 days'.[219]

---

[215] OJ 1975 L 194/31.

[216] Case 240/83 *ADBHU* [1985] ECR 531. See also XXIVth Competition Report, point 388.

[217] OJ 2006 L 157/8.

[218] OJ 1991 L 230/1.

[219] Directive 98/8, OJ 1998 L 123/1.

Similar safeguard provisions can be found particularly in those environmental directives where there is a strong link with the functioning of the Internal Market. It is the authors' opinion that these safeguard clauses must be interpreted in line with the precautionary principle.[220]

3.3   The Policy Aspects to be Taken into Account

According to Article 174(3) EC the Community shall, in preparing its policy on the environment, take account of:
· available scientific and technical data;
· environmental conditions in the various regions of the Community;
· the potential benefits and costs of action or lack of action;
· the economic and social development of the Community as a whole and the balanced development of its regions.

By comparison with the formulation of, for instance, the integration principle in Article 6 EC ('must be integrated'), the language of this paragraph ('take account of') is much less forceful. Account shall be taken of the policy aspects referred to in it. The Treaty does not therefore prescribe observance of these criteria in all cases. It is true that inclusion of these policy aspects does not imply that the environmental objectives of Article 174(1) EC are in a legal sense subordinate to them. However, in practice, Member States will no doubt seize on them to delay environmental policies that do not suit them.

Available scientific and technical data

It is said that the function of this criterion under the Single European Act was to ensure the EC would only act when sufficient scientific data was available to prove that a given activity or product – for example, CFCs in aerosols – would have a harmful effect on the environment – in this case depletion of the ozone layer. As has already been shown in the discussion of the precautionary principle, a different interpretation would now seem more appropriate.[221] Indeed, all kinds of provisional, indicative and tentative scientific data may now be sufficient to require protective measures and action by the EC.

---

[220] See this chapter, section 3.1.

[221] See this chapter, section 3.1. See for an example of connecting the precautionary principle with this policy aspect: Annex II of Directive 2001/18 on the deliberate release into the environment of genetically modified organisms (OJ 2001 L 106/1). According to this annex the environmental risk assessment to be carried out prior to a release of GMOs should be carried out 'in accordance with the precautionary principle' 'in a scientifically sound and transparent manner based on available scientific and technical data'.

References to 'available scientific and technical data' can, *inter alia*, be found in the Bathing Water Directive and in the Water Framework Directive.[222] The Nitrates Directive, for instance, requires in Article 5 that the action programmes be established in respect of so-called 'vulnerable zones'. The action programmes shall take into account 'available scientific and technical data, mainly with reference to respective nitrogen contributions originating from agricultural and other sources'.[223]

The case law of the Court shows that decisions based on inadequate scientific and technical data can result in an annulment.[224]

Environmental conditions in the various regions

Application of this criterion entails a differentiated environmental policy based on the quality of the environment in a given region.

A good example can be found in the Nitrates Directive. The action programmes to be established in respect of vulnerable zones have to take into account 'environmental conditions in the relevant regions of the Member State concerned'. With respect to recovery of costs for water services the Water Framework Directive requires (Article 9) 'have regard to the social, environmental and economic effects of the recovery as well as the geographic and climatic conditions of the region or regions affected'.

This criterion may also give rise to the assumption that there is a preference for environmental quality objectives rather than emission limits. After all, the quality of the receiving environment would then determine the extent of emission of pollutants. However, from the point of view of the source principle, there is a preference for emission standards rather than environmental quality standards. It is up to the European legislature to consider in more depth the relative merits of these different aspects.

On the other hand, the criterion could also be applied differently. Additional protective measures might well be called for precisely in order to conserve those areas in which the environmental quality is high.

See, for example, the 'old' air quality directives of the 1980s.[225] These directives enable Member States to lay down more stringent air quality standards than those set out in the directives, for zones, which in the view of the Member State, require

---

[222] Directive 2006/7 concerning the management of bathing water quality, OJ 2006 L 64/37 and Directive 2000/60 establishing a framework for Community action in the field of water policy, OJ 2000 L 327/1.

[223] Directive 91/676 concerning the protection of waters against pollution caused by nitrates from agricultural sources, OJ 1991 L 375/1.

[224] E.g. Case C-3/00 *Denmark v. Commission* [2003] ECR I-2643. See also Chapter 3, section 6.

[225] See for instance Article 4(2) of Directive 85/203 on air quality standards for nitrogen dioxide (OJ 1985 L 87/1): 'In zones which the Member State concerned considers should be afforded special environmental protection, it may fix values which are generally lower than the guide values in Annex II'.

special protection from an environmental point of view. This approach has been followed in Article 9 of Directive 96/62 on ambient air quality assessment and management, according to which Member States shall draw up a list of zones and agglomerations in which the levels of pollutants are below the limit values.[226] They are required to maintain the levels of pollutants in these zones and agglomerations below the limit values and shall endeavour to preserve the best ambient air quality, compatible with sustainable development.

Potential benefits and costs

This criterion requires that the potential costs and benefits of action be assessed. Besides producing benefits for the environment, environmental action by the EC entails costs for Member States, in the sense of legislation, administrative organisation, enforcement, etc., and for private actors, such as industrial plants which cause pollution, and manufacturers and importers of goods and products which are harmful to the environment. Viewed in this way, the criterion could be seen as prompting application of the principle of proportionality, and thus adding little to what has already been provided in the third paragraph of Article 5 EC.

It is the authors' opinion that the concept of 'best *available* technology/techniques' is clearly related to this criterion.

An 'early' example of this can be found in Article 4 of Directive 84/360 on the combating of air pollution from industrial plants.[227] An authorisation may only be issued when the competent authority is satisfied that 'all appropriate preventive measures against air pollution have been taken, including application of the best available technology, provided that the application of such measures does not entail excessive costs'. The IPPC Directive also provides an example of this in its definition of the term 'best available techniques': '"Available" techniques shall mean those developed on a scale which allows implementation in the relevant industrial sector, under economically and technically viable conditions, *taking into consideration the costs and advantages*, whether or not the techniques are used or produced inside the Member State in question, as long as they are reasonably accessible to the operator'. [228]

A final example might be Euratom Directive 96/29 laying down basic safety standards for the protection of the health of workers and the general public against the dangers arising from ionizing radiation.[229] One of its basic general principles is the so called 'justification principle' according to which practices resulting in exposure

---

[226] OJ 1996 L 296/55.

[227] OJ 1984 L 188/20.

[228] Article 2(1) of Directive 96/61, OJ 1996 L 257/26, emphasis added. Reference to this definition can also be found in other environmental directives. E.g. Directive 2006/66 on batteries and accumulators and waste batteries and accumulators, OJ 2006 L 266/1, preamble point 17.

[229] OJ 1996 L 159/1.

to ionizing radiation are justified by their economic, social or other benefits in relation to the health detriment they may cause.

Further references to 'potential benefits and costs' can be found in the preamble of the Water Framework Directive and in the Council Resolution the drafting,
implementation and enforcement of Community environmental law.[230]

*Economic and social development of the Community as a whole and the balanced
development of its regions*

In fact this aspect is an elaboration of the more general principle contained
in Article 15 EC. Differentiated environmental policies may be adopted, whether
or not on a temporary basis, depending on the economic and social development
of certain regions. This opens – it goes without saying, in addition to the possibilities provided by the Treaty in the context of 'closer cooperation' under Article
11 EC – the possibility of a multi-speed environmental policy.

An example of such a multi-speed policy was given by Directive 88/609 on the
limitation of emissions of certain pollutants into the air from large combustion
plants.[231] Article 5 provided that Spain was temporarily entitled to apply less stringent emission standards than those normally laid down by the directive. This was
explained in the preamble to the directive by pointing out that Spain considered
it needed a particularly high amount of new generating capacity to allow for its
energy and industrial growth.

Another example can be found in Directive 94/62 on packaging and packaging
waste.[232] Article 6(7) provides that Greece, Ireland and Portugal may, because of
their specific situations, namely respectively the large number of small islands,
the presence of rural and mountain areas and the current low level of packaging
consumption, decide to:

a) attain, no later than 30 June 2001, lower targets than those fixed in paragraphs 1(a) and (c), but shall at least attain 25% for recovery or incineration at
waste incineration plants with energy recovery; b) postpone at the same time the
attainment of the targets in paragraphs 1(a) and c) to a later deadline which shall
not, however, be later than 31 December 2005; c) postpone the attainment of the
targets referred to in paragraphs 1(b), (d) and (e) until a date of their own choice
which shall not be later than 31 December 2011.

A further reference to this criterion can be found in the preamble of the Water
Framework Directive.[233]

---

[230] Directive 2000/60 establishing a framework for Community action in the field of water policy, OJ 2000
L 327/1; Resolution of 7 October 1997, OJ 1997 C 321.

[231] OJ 1988 L 336/1. The directive is repealed from 27 November 2002 by Directive 2001/80 on the limitation of emissions of certain pollutants into the air from large combustion plants, OJ 2001 L 309/1.

[232] As amended by Directive 2004/12 on packaging and packaging waste, OJ 2004 L 47/26.

[233] Directive 2000/60 establishing a framework for Community action in the field of water policy, OJ 2000
L 327/1.

Apart from giving certain Member States the power to derogate from European standards, the element of economic and social development can also be translated in terms of financial support by the EC for those Member States, which find it difficult to meet the standards required by a directive.

An example of this is the Habitats Directive 92/43.[234] Article 8 provides for a system of co-financing where measures to protect priority natural habitats and priority species would result in excessive financial burdens for some Member States.

Another example is provided by Article 175(5) EC. If the Council adopts an environmental measure based on Article 175(1) EC, which involves disproportionately high costs for the public authorities of a Member State, the Council can lay down appropriate provisions in the form of temporary derogations and/or financial support from the Community's Cohesion Fund (Article 161 EC).[235]

---

[234] OJ 1992 L 206/7.

[235] For a more detailed discussion of the phenomenon of the Community's environmental aid, see Chapter 7, section 7.4.

CHAPTER 2

Legal Basis

1 Article 175 EC[1]

The Treaty of Amsterdam has succeeded in less complex decision-making in the context of the Title on the Environment. After all, it reduced the number of decision-making procedures from four to three! The standard procedure is now, according to Article 175(1) EC, the co-decision procedure, as regulated in Article 251 EC:

> 'The Council, acting in accordance with the procedure referred to in Article 251 and after consulting the Economic and Social Committee and the Committee of the Regions, shall decide what action is to be taken by the Community in order to achieve the objectives referred to in Article 174.'

Under this procedure, the European Parliament is twice consulted on the measure proposed and has the ultimate power to prevent the adoption of a measure. Although co-decision does not automatically lead to more environmentally friendly legislation, the fact that the co-decision procedure is now the standard decision-making procedure must nevertheless be welcomed. We have come a long way from decision-making by unanimity under the 'old' Articles 100 EEC and 235 EEC to majority voting and a strong role for the European Parliament under an explicit environment paragraph in the EC Treaty. Perhaps even more important than the co-decision procedure as such is that there is now no longer a difference in the procedure between internal market legislation and purely environmental legislation. This means that time consuming inter-institutional battles fought before the Court of Justice concerning the choice of legal basis are less likely.[2]

The second paragraph of Article 175 EC states that by way of derogation from this procedure, and without prejudice to the provisions of Article 95 EC, the Council, acting unanimously on a proposal from the Commission and after consulting the European Parliament, the Economic and Social Committee and the Committee of the Regions, shall adopt:

a) provisions primarily of a fiscal nature;
b) measures affecting:
   · town and country planning,
   · quantitative management of water resources or affecting, directly or indirectly, the availability of those resources,
   · land use, with the exception of waste management;
c) measures significantly affecting a Member State's choice between different energy sources and the general structure of its energy supply.

Although Article 175(2) EC is hardly used in practice, its interpretation generates considerable problems. These include the following.

---

[1] Cf. the renumbered Article 192 FEU after the entry into force of the Reform Treaty.

[2] Like for instance in Case C-300/89 *Commission v. Council* [1991] ECR I-2867, Case C-70/88 *EP v. Council* [1991] ECR I-4529 and Case C-155/91 *Commission v. Council* [1993] ECR I-939.

Provisions primarily of a fiscal nature

In the first place, it should be noted that the Treaty does not provide for a definition of the term 'fiscal nature'. Arguably, this term should be interpreted in the same vein as the term 'fiscal provisions' in Article 95(2) EC.[3] The Court of Justice ruled in Case C-338/01 that fiscal provisions 'cover not only all areas of taxation, without drawing any distinction between the types of duties or taxes concerned, but also all aspects of taxation, whether material rules or procedural rules'.[4]

Taking this as a point of departure, it is the authors' opinion that measures such as the Commission proposal to introduce a tax on carbon dioxide emissions clearly fall within the scope of Article 175(2) EC.[5] This proposal is intended to achieve the harmonised introduction of a specific tax in the Member States, based on carbon dioxide emissions and the calorific value of several fuels. A harmonised approach is regarded by the Commission as necessary, on the one hand to ensure the free movement of the fuels subject to the tax and not to cause distortions of competition, and on the other to promote a rational use of energy. This is thus a measure of a fiscal nature designed to achieve certain environmental objectives. The present formulation of Article 175(2) EC could thus be interpreted in such a way that measures which concern the harmonisation of national taxes, but which ultimately aim to attain environmental objectives, could only be taken unanimously. Another problem with the interpretation is that it is not clear what should be understood by the addition *primarily*. Probably the term can be regarded purely as a contrast with *incidentally*. This does not mean that unanimity is therefore immediately required to adopt an environmental measure, which incidentally provides for a limited measure of tax harmonisation. When an environmental measure has only incidental fiscal effects, the primary decision-making rule contained in Article 175(1) EC applies. In other words, Article 175(2) EC does not intend to exclude any measure of tax harmonisation from the application of Article 175(1) EC.[6]

It is also not clear how Article 175(2) EC accords with Article 93 EC, which regulates the Council's power of harmonisation in respect of turnover taxes, excise duties and other forms of indirect taxation. Apparently Article 175(2) EC does not apply without prejudice to the provisions of Article 93 EC. For that to have been the case, Article 93 EC would have had to have been specifically excluded in the same way as it has been done with respect to Article 95 EC. This would mean that environmental measures primarily of a fiscal nature relating to the harmonisation of turnover taxes, excise duties and other forms of indirect taxation would have to be based on Article 175(2) EC and not on Article 93 EC. The specific rule of Article 175(2) EC would then have to be regarded as taking

---

[3] Article 95(2) EC states that Article 95(1) may not apply to 'fiscal provisions'.

[4] Case C-338/01 *Commission* v. *Council* [2004] ECR I-4829, para. 63.

[5] OJ 1992 C 196/92. The proposal is, formally speaking, still on the agenda, but is, to put it mildly, rather dormant.

[6] Applying, by analogy, the rule to be derived from Case C-36/98 *Spain* v. *Council* [2001] ECR I-779, para. 50.

precedence over the general rule contained in Article 93 EC.[7] Measures primarily of a fiscal nature with only incidental effects on environmental protection
should have Article 93 EC as its legal basis.[8] However, this is all of relative
practical importance as the decision-making procedure provided for in Article
175(2) EC is no different from that in Article 93 EC.[9] Both require unanimity.
However, an important difference remains the legal consequences Article 176
EC attaches to decisions adopted pursuant to Article 175 EC.[10]

*Measures affecting town and country planning, land use and quantitative manage-
ment of water resources*

The exceptions referred to in the second sentence of Article 175(2) EC are
also problematic. Measures 'affecting'[11] town and country planning are also
excepted from the co-decision procedure. However, is there then any power at all
to pursue an independent town and country planning policy under the title on
the environment? This does not follow from the objectives of Article 174(1) EC.
Nor will a comprehensive competence in the field of town and country planning
be found elsewhere in the Treaty. However, if such a power does not fall within
the scope of Article 174 EC, there is no need to except it. The current text of the
Treaty which speaks of 'affecting' rather then 'concerning' makes clear that the
mere fact that a measure which has consequences for the physical layout of the
territory of a Member State does not mean that it should be taken unanimously.
Otherwise, that would mean that any area-related environmental policy would
have to be adopted unanimously, whether within the framework of the protection of flora and fauna (Wild Birds and Habitats Directives), water quality policy
(designation of fishing and swimming areas) or the combating of air pollution
(zoning in connection with air quality policy). And what about measures in
connection with environmental impact assessment? The Court held that this
provision covers measures which, just like those based on Article 175(1) EC, are
intended to attain the objectives referred to in Article 174 EC, 'but which regulate the use of the territory of the Member States, such as measures relating to
regional, urban or rural management plans or the planning of various projects
concerning the infrastructure of a Member State'.[12] Once again we have to
conclude that, Article 175(2) EC does not intend to exclude any measure on town
and country planning from the application of Article 175(1) EC.[13]

---

7   The Court has consistently held that, where there is a specific legal basis, this should form the basis of
the measure to be adopted; Case C-271/94 *Parliament* v. *Council* [1996] ECR I-1689.

8   Cf. Directive 2003/96 restructuring the Community framework for the taxation of energy products and
electricity, OJ 2003 L 283/51.

9   Except for the fact that under Article 93 EC the Council is not required to consult the Committee of the
Regions.

10 See Chapter 3, section 5.

11 And not just 'concerning' like in the pre-Nice text of the provision!

12 Case C-36/98 *Spain* v. *Council* [2001] ECR I-779, para. 51.

13 Applying, by analogy, the rule to be derived from Case C-36/98 *Spain* v. *Council* [2001] ECR I-779, para.
50.

The same can be said with respect to the rule of unanimous decision-making in respect of measure affecting land use. Directive 96/82 on the control of major-accident hazards involving dangerous substances, the 'Seveso II' Directive provides an example.[14] According to Article 12 of the directive Member States are required to ensure that the objectives of preventing major accidents and limiting the consequences of such accidents are taken into account in their land-use policies. They shall pursue those objectives through controls on:
· the siting of new establishments;
· modifications to existing establishments;
· new developments such as transport links.

Member States are also required to ensure that their land-use policies take account of the need to maintain appropriate distances between establishments covered by the directive and residential areas, areas of public use and areas of particular natural sensitivity or interest. Although the effects on land use are clear, the directive was correctly adopted using the standard procedure and not the procedure of Article 175(2) EC.

An exception (to the exception of measures affecting land use) is made to the requirement of unanimity for waste management. In these cases the normal procedure contained in Article 175(1) EC applies again. This means that Directive 99/31 on the landfill of waste (or indeed any other measures designed to protect the soil against environmental hazards caused by waste) in *any* event fall within the scope of application of Article 175(1) EC. Directive 99/31 is therefore correctly based on Article 175(1) EC.[15]

The post-Nice text of Article 175(2) EC makes clear that only the *quantitative* aspects of management of water resources is subject to unanimity voting. In the pre-Nice text, the various language versions caused some confusion.[16] For instance, the Dutch text of the Treaty spoke of '*kwantitatief*' The Dutch text implied that only measures concerning the *quantity* of water are covered by the exception. However, the English text referred simply to 'management of water resources', the French to '*la gestion des ressources hydrauliques*' and the German to '*der Bewirtschaftung der Wasserressourcen*', in other words without the addition of 'quantitative'. The current text has remedied this.

Measures significantly affecting a Member State's choice between different energy sources

Thirdly, Article 175(2) EC excludes 'measures significantly affecting a Member State's choice between different energy sources and the general structure of its energy supply' from the standard procedure of Article 175(1) EC. The paragraph is particular problematic in respect of the interpretation of the term 'significantly affecting'.[17] First of all, the difference between 'measures affecting'

---

[14] OJ 1997 L 10/13.

[15] OJ 1999 L 182/1.

[16] Cf. Case C-36/98 *Spain v. Council* [2001] ECR I-779.

[17] Cf. also Frenz (1999).

(under b) and *'significantly* affecting' are obvious. The threshold 'significantly affecting' is clearly much higher than 'affecting'.

Take for example the Commission's proposal on the CO2 tax.[18] Does such a tax significantly affect the choice between various sources of energy or not? Or is it a measure primarily of a fiscal nature? Or is it one involving the harmonisation of indirect taxes? Another example is given by Directive 2001/80 on the limitation of emissions of certain pollutants into the air from large combustion plants.[19] This directive sets emission limit values for combustion plants designed for production of energy. The requirements of this directive (and its predecessor Directive 88/609) are so stringent that those Member States in which brown coal is used for power production face serious difficulties. The question which arises here is whether this directive 'significantly affects' a Member State's choice between the various sources of energy or not? Probably not as the directive was based on Article 175(1) EC.

The same can be argued about the measures to comply with the United Nations Framework Convention on Climate Change and subsequent Protocols. All implementing measures have Article 175(1) EC as their legal basis.

In any event, Directive 2006/32 on energy end-use efficiency and energy services was correctly based on Article 175(1) EC.[20] The purpose of this directive is to enhance the cost-effective improvement of energy end-use efficiency in the Member States by *inter alia* providing the necessary indicative targets as well as mechanisms, incentives and institutional, financial and legal frameworks to remove existing market barriers and imperfections that impede the efficient end use of energy.

These questions demonstrate that the interpretation of this category of measures, to which the requirement of unanimity ought to apply, will in practice give rise to the necessary problems.

The second subparagraph of Article 175(2) states that the Council may, acting unanimously, define on which of the matters discussed above decisions are to be taken by a qualified majority. In other words, measures to be established under Article 175(2) EC can, by means of self-delegation, stipulate that certain matters falling within its scope can be taken with a quality majority vote.

General action programmes
According to Article 175(3) EC the co-decision procedure also applies to the adoption of what the Treaty calls 'general action programmes setting out priority objectives to be attained'.[21] According to Article 175(3) EC, these action

---

[18] OJ 1992 C 196/92.

[19] OJ 2001 L 309/1.

[20] OJ 2006 L 114/64.

[21] Cf. the current Sixth Community Environment Action Programme, Decision 1600/2002, OJ 2002 L 242.

programmes are to be adopted 'in other areas'. But what other areas are in fact contemplated? Other areas than those referred to in paragraphs 1 and 2 of the article? This seems unlikely, as it would imply that action programmes are adopted for those environmental sectors which are not covered by paragraphs 1 and 2. But if that were so it would be hard to conceive of any example of an action programme that could still be adopted. The Reform Treaty will rectify this by simply deleting the words 'in other areas'.[22]

The second subparagraph of paragraph 3, which refers to the measures necessary for the implementation of the programmes which are to be adopted under the terms of paragraphs 1 and 2, also makes it clear that this cannot be the right interpretation. We shall have to assume that the drafters of the treaty were in error here, and the phrase 'in other areas' should perhaps be regarded as never having been written. It will therefore be assumed below that action programmes on the environment, which are adopted under the co-decision procedure, may cover the whole environmental spectrum. However, it would seem that only priority objectives can be set in these action programmes and that they cannot give rise to direct legal consequences for the Member States. This interpretation is supported by the second subparagraph of Article 175(3). Measures which are necessary for the implementation of these programmes must be based on paragraph 1 or 2 of Article 175 EC, depending on the subject matter. Obligations for Member States could then only be imposed by adopting the necessary measures of implementation (directives and regulations).

Criminal environmental law

In Chapter 1 we already discussed that whenever criminal penalties are *essential* for combating serious offences against the environment Article 175 EC provides for the correct legal basis and that the Council is not allowed to use its competences under Title VI of the EU Treaty.[23] However, this debate will become obsolete after the entry into force of the Reform Treaty, as the provisions on police and judicial cooperation in criminal matters of Title VI of the EU Treaty wille be integrated in the text of the FEU Treaty.

2 Articles 174-175 EC and External Relations

The EC is a participant in international legal affairs. Within that framework, the EC concludes environmental treaties, operates in international organisations which concern themselves with the environment and is otherwise actively involved with third countries in respect of environmental issues.

---

[22] The amended text will read: 'The measures necessary for the implementation of these programmes shall be adopted under the terms of paragraph 1 or 2, as the case may be.'

[23] See Chapter 1, section 3.1. Case C-176/03 *Commission v. Council* [2005] ECR I-7879 and Case C-440/05 *Commission v. Council*, judgment of 23 October 2007, n.y.r. in the ECR.

In its relations with third countries, the EC is of course required to respect its obligations under international law.[24]

Implied powers

Even before the entry into force of the Single European Act and the conferring of explicit external competence in what is now Article 174(4) EC, the EC had concluded environmental agreements with third countries. It derived this competence from a construction (*implied powers* doctrine), which has been developed by the Court of Justice, whereby internal competence can also be used in respect of external policy. The Court has determined that external competence can follow from internal competence in two cases. Firstly, where the EC has already implemented internal measures on the basis of that internal competence.[25]

> An application of the principle formulated in the case in respect of external environmental policy can be seen in Council Decision 81/462 on the conclusion of the Convention on Long-Range Transboundary Air Pollution.[26] This decision was based on Article 235 EEC. In the preamble, the Council states that the EC will participate in the implementation of the Convention 'by exercising its competence as resulting from the existing common rules as well as those acquired as a result of future acts adopted by the Council'. The competence, at least according to the Council, thus flows from the internal competence to lay down rules to prevent air pollution, in so far as this competence is or will in the future be exercised by means of internal legislation.

Alternatively, where the EC has not yet implemented internal rules, if the exercise of external powers is *necessary* to attain the objectives of the EC.[27]

> The declaration made by the EC in the Convention on Climate Change[28] is relevant in this context. The commitment set out in Article 4(2) of that convention to limit emissions of anthropogenic carbon dioxide will 'be fulfilled in the Community as a whole through action by the Community and its Member States, within the respective competence of each.' At the time the convention was concluded, there were no measures in force implementing the commitment. There was only a Commission proposal to introduce a tax on carbon dioxide emissions.[29] In other words, there was no internal legislation on which the competence to implement

---

[24] Case C-286/90 *Anklagemindigheden v. Poulsen and Diva Navigation* [1992] ECR I-6019 and Case C-341/95 *Gianni Bettati* [1998] ECR I-4355.

[25] Case 22/70 *ERTA* [1971] ECR 273.

[26] OJ 1981 L 171/11.

[27] Joined Cases 3, 4 and 6/76 *Kramer* [1976] ECR 1279 and Opinion 1/76 *Laying-up fund* [1977] ECR 754. Cf. also Case C-459/03 *Commission v. Ireland* [2006] ECR I-4635 (*MOX* case).

[28] OJ 1994 L 33/13.

[29] OJ 1992 C 196/92.

Article 4(2) could have been based. The conclusion must therefore be that the Council based its competence on Article 175(1), even though there was no internal legislation in place at the time. Thus the Court's conclusions in the *Kramer* case and Opinion 1/76 have implicitly been applied.

Explicit competences

Nowadays there is hardly any need to rely on the doctrine of *implied powers* to establish a competence in the area of external environmental relations, as we have now an explicit provision in the Treaty: Article 174(4) EC. The EC can enter into agreements in the area of environmental protection even if the specific matters covered by those agreements are not yet, or are only very partially, the subject of internal rules at European level.[30] Article 174(4), first subparagraph EC reads as follows:

> 'Within their respective spheres of competence, the Community and the Member States shall cooperate with third countries and with the competent international organisations. The arrangements for Community cooperation may be the subject of agreements between the Community and the third parties concerned, which shall be negotiated and concluded in accordance with Article 300.'

The material scope of the EC's external competence is determined in the same way as its internal competence, by the objectives contained in Article 174(1) EC and the principles referred to in Article 174(2) EC. In that sense, there are no additional legal difficulties involved in determining the material external competence in the field of the environment. Of course, for the EC to be able to conclude a treaty, it is not sufficient for it to be competent under European law. The other parties to the treaty must also make accession possible. A treaty on the environment will generally include a clause stating that accession is open not only to states, but also to 'regional economic integration organizations'.[31]

> Most recent important multilateral environmental conventions provide for the possibility of accession by the EC. The main exception to this rule remains the 1973 Washington Convention on International Trade in Endangered Species of Wild Fauna and Flora (CITES).[32] Accession by the EC has still not been made possible. The EC therefore applies the provisions of the Convention unilaterally by means of Regulation 338/97.[33]

---

[30] Case C-459/03 *Commission v. Ireland* [2006] ECR I-4635 (*MOX* case), para. 94 in particular.

[31] See, for example, Article 33 of the 1992 Rio de Janeiro Convention on Biological Diversity, OJ 1993 L 309/1.

[32] OJ 1982 L 384/7.

[33] OJ 1997 L 61/1.

Conventions that were concluded on the basis of the Title on the Environment in the Treaty include the following:

- the 1985 Vienna Convention for the Protection of the Ozone Layer and the 1987 Montreal Protocol on Substances that Deplete the Ozone Layer;[34]
- the 1989 Basel Convention on the Control of Transboundary Movements of Hazardous Wastes and Their Disposal;[35]
- the 1992 Rio de Janeiro Framework Convention on Climate Change;[36]
- the 1992 Rio de Janeiro Convention on Biological Diversity;[37]
- the 1991 Espoo Convention on Environmental Impact Assessment in a Transboundary Context;[38]
- the 1992 Helsinki Convention on the Transboundary Effects of Industrial Accidents;[39]
- the 1992 Helsinki Convention on the Protection and Use of Transboundary Watercourses International Lakes;[40]
- the United Nations Convention on the Law of the Sea (UNCLOS);[41]
- the 1998 Aarhus Convention on access to information, public participation in decision-making and access to justice in environmental matters.[42]

Division of powers

The competences of the EU on environmental protection must be regarded, also in the words of the Reform Treaty, as a 'shared competence'.[43] A shared competence implies that the EC and the Member States may legislate and adopt legally binding acts in that area. However, the Member States shall exercise their

---

[34] OJ 1988 L 297/10 and OJ 1988 L 297/21, concluded by Council Decision 88/540, OJ 1988 L 297/8.

[35] OJ 1993 L 39/3, concluded by Council Decision 93/98, OJ 1993 L 39/1.

[36] OJ 1994 L 33/13, concluded by Council Decision 94/69, OJ 1994 L 33/11. See also the subsequent Kyoto Protocol, OJ 2002 L 130/1.

[37] OJ 1993 L 309/3, concluded by Council Decision 93/626, OJ 1993 L 309/1. Cf. also the Cartagena protocol on biosafety to the convention on biological diversity, OJ 2002 L 201/50.

[38] Bull. EC 1/2-1991. Signed on 26 February 1991. Ratified on 26 June 1997.

[39] OJ 1998 L 326/6, concluded by Council Decision 96/685, OJ 1998 L 326/1.

[40] OJ 1995 L 186/44, concluded by Council Decision 95/308, OJ 1995 L 186/42.

[41] 16 years after it was signed, the EC became a party to UNCLOS. The Convention contains several provisions on the protection of the environment, in particular Articles 145 to 147 and Part II (Articles 192 to 237). Decision 98/392 concerning the conclusion by the EC of the United Nations Convention of 10 December 1982 on the Law of the Sea and the Agreement of 28 July 1994 relating to the implementation of Part XI thereof, OJ 1998 L 179. The decision is based on the combined articles 37, 133 and 175(1) EC.

[42] OJ 2005 L 124/4, concluded by Council Decision 2005/370, OJ 2005 L 124/1.

[43] Cf. Articles 2(2) and 4 FEU after amendment by the Reform Treaty. Cf. also Case C-114/01 *AvestaPolarit Chrome* [2003] ECR I-8725, para. 56, making it quite clear that at the present stage environmental policy cannot be regarded an exclusive competence and Case C-459/03 *Commission v. Ireland* [2006] ECR I-4635 (*MOX* case), para. 92, with respect to the external competences of the EC in regard to the protection of the (marine) environment. Cf. on the *MOX* case, Lavranos (2006). See also Lee (2005) at 10. Cf. in general on the multi-level aspects of environmental administration in the EU, Winter (2005).

competence only to the extent that the EC has not exercised, or has decided to cease exercising, its competence.[44] In view of this, some attention should be paid to the second subparagraph of Article 174(4) EC. It reads: 'The previous subparagraph shall be without prejudice to Member States' competence to negotiate in international bodies and conclude international agreements.' This provision has been inserted by the Single European Act and has caused confusion since then. This formulation is open to the risk that it can be interpreted in such a way that Member States might still be able to negotiate international conventions on the environment, even though the EC had already adopted internal legislation. Such an interpretation is contrary to the case law of the Court of Justice and in particular to its judgment in the *ERTA* case.[45] However, a Declaration was added in the Final Act of the Single European Act to the effect that this paragraph does not affect the principles resulting from the judgment handed down by the Court of Justice in the *ERTA* case.

This was no doubt intended to remove any doubt that the fact that the Treaty currently gives the EC express competence to conclude treaties on the environment does not therefore necessarily imply that it is exclusive. But having said that, it is reasonable to ask when does a competence to conclude an environmental treaty become exclusive? First of all it should be said that, like common commercial policy measures, measures with regard to fishing resources are also within the exclusive competence of the EC. In the Declaration concerning the competence of the EC with respect to matters governed by UNCLOS,[46] the EC points out that:

'its Member States have transferred competence to it with regard to the conservation and management of sea fishing resources. Hence in this field it is for the Community to adopt the relevant rules and regulations (which are enforced by the Member States) and, within its competence, to enter into external undertakings with third States or competent international organisations.'

However, this process of transferring competence to the EC is not always entirely clear. After all, 'the scope and the exercise of such Community competence are, by their nature, subject to continuous development'.[47] In the *ERTA* case, the Court held that the EC's implied external authority is exclusive where competence in internal matters has been transferred from the Member States to the EC.[48] Whether or not the EC's external competence is exclusive thus depends on the extent of the measures the European institutions have taken

---

[44] See also Chapter 3, sections 2 and 3 in particular.

[45] Case 22/70 *ERTA* [1971] ECR 273.

[46] Declaration concerning the competence of the EC with respect to matters governed by UNCLOS, OJ 1998 L 179/3.

[47] Declaration concerning the competence of the EC with respect to matters governed by UNCLOS, OJ 1998 L 179/3.

[48] Case 22/70 *ERTA* [1971] ECR 273.

internally or externally. If the EC has laid down internal rules, the Member States no longer have the right, acting outside the framework of those common rules, to undertake obligations which would affect those rules. Again quoting the Declaration concerning the competence of the EC with respect to matters governed by UNCLOS:

> 'with regard to the provisions on maritime transport, safety of shipping and the prevention of marine pollution [...] the Community has exclusive competence only to the extent that such provisions of the Convention or legal instruments adopted in implementation thereof affect common rules established by the Community.'

Particularly in the case of total harmonisation, there will be a transfer of internal competence resulting in exclusive external competence.[49] The Member States will no longer have any competence of their own. Any treaty concluded by the Member States will affect the internal rules implementing total harmonisation.

However, a large part of European environment policy consists not of total harmonisation but of minimum standards, whereby Member States are expressly permitted to take more stringent environmental measures than provided for in the acts in question.[50] It is arguable that, to the extent that European law leaves the Member States competent to adopt more stringent environmental standards than the European standards, there can hardly be any question of wholly exclusive external EC competence in respect of the environment. As far as the adoption in an international context of such environmental minimum standards is concerned, there can be no question of exclusive competence.

> Suppose a convention was under consideration which would lay down more stringent emission standards to prevent air pollution (discharges of no more than 2 mg of the hazardous substance) than those contained in an internal directive (no more than 5 mg). The fact that a Member State agreed to the more stringent standard in an international context would in no way prevent compliance with the European standard. Compliance with the more stringent international standard would necessarily imply compliance with the European standard in this respect. Nor would it be problematic if the convention were to lay down a less stringent standard (discharges of no more than 5 mg) than the European standard (no more than 2 mg). As long as it is clear that the standards laid down in the convention must also be regarded as minimum standards, Member States would be able to continue to apply the more stringent European standard.

The mere fact that the European environmental standard may come under pressure as a result of the less stringent international standard is not sufficient to

---

[49] See Opinion 1/94 *WTO* [1994] ECR I-5267, in particular para. 96. See also Opinion 2/91 [1993] ECR I-1061 (*ILO-convention no. 170*).

[50] See, for example Article 176 EC, which will be discussed in detail in Chapter 3, section 5.

make it a matter for exclusive EC competence. The Court confirmed this view in Opinion 2/91.[51] Only if the convention on the environment were to prevent the more stringent European environmental standard being applied would there be a problem. However, in that case, there would be no question of minimum harmonisation. Conclusion of such a convention, in fact intended to amend internal legislation on the environment, would seem an exclusive matter for the EC.

Thus, in the case of minimum harmonisation, there can be no question of exclusive external EC competence. In that case competence resides in the EC and the Member States jointly, and conclusion of such a convention on the environment should be effected in the form of a mixed agreement, in other words, one to which both the EC and the Member States are party. An illustration of this can be found in the Declaration concerning the competence of the EC with respect to matters governed by UNCLOS,[52] which states:

'When Community rules exist but are not affected, in particular in cases of Community provisions establishing only minimum standards, the Member States have competence, without prejudice to the competence of the Community to act in this field.'[53]

Mixed agreements[54]

It is clear from Opinion 2/91 that when a convention falls partly within the competence of the Member States and partly within that of the EC, it can be implemented only by means of 'close association between the institutions of the Community and the Member States both in the process of negotiation and conclusion and in the fulfilment of the obligations entered into.' The practice of concluding treaties in the field of the environment accords with this principle: the Member States have been parties to virtually all the conventions on the environment concluded by the EC.

The conclusion of mixed agreements requires that certain matters must be regulated as regards the relationship between the EC and its Member States on the one hand, and the other parties to the convention on the other. Thus multilateral conventions in particular generally contain a provision on the exercise of voting rights under the treaty.

For example, Article 31(2) of the Convention on Biological Diversity[55] provides that regional economic integration organisations, in matters within their competence, shall exercise their right to vote with a number of votes equal to the number of their member states which are parties to the convention. However, the EC may

---

[51] Opinion 2/91 [1993] ECR I-1061 (*ILO-convention no. 170*).

[52] OJ 1998 L 179/3-134.

[53] Emphasis added by the authors.

[54] Cf. Lavranos (2002), 48-49 in particular.

[55] OJ 1993 L 309/1.

not exercise its right to vote if the Member States exercise theirs, and vice versa. Similar provisions can be found in other conventions on the environment.[56]

Another problem with regard to mixed environmental agreements concerns the extent to which the EC and its Member States are bound by them vis-à-vis the other contracting parties. After all, mixed agreements are concluded because neither the EC nor the Member States has exclusive competence. To what extent does this internal division of powers affect the legal position of the other parties? Is the EC only bound as far as third countries are concerned in respect of those provisions which fall within its competence? To overcome these problems, most recent multilateral treaties on the environment contain specific provisions on the matter.

> Again, the Convention on Biological Diversity provides an example. Article 34(2) of the convention provides that, if the EC becomes a party to the convention without any of the Member States being a party, it shall be bound by all the obligations under the convention. If one or more of the Member States should be a party to the convention, the EC and its Member States must decide on their respective responsibilities under the convention. To that end they must declare the extent of their competence to the other parties to the convention (Article 34(3)). Similar provisions can be found in other conventions on the environment.[57]

However, in most cases, closer study of such declarations only reveals the contours of the internal delineation of competence. Thus the Declaration by the EC regarding the extent of its competence in the context of the Convention on Biological Diversity reads:[58]

> 'In accordance with the relevant provisions of the Treaty establishing the European Economic Community, the Community alongside its Member States has competence to take actions aiming at the protection of the environment.
>   In relation to the matters covered by the Convention, the Community has adopted several legal instruments, both as part of its environment policy and in the framework of other sectoral policies, the most relevant of which are listed below: [...]'

Following which twelve directives and regulations are mentioned, including the Directive on Wild Birds[59] and the Habitats Directive.[60] It cannot be inferred from this Declaration how the precise division of competence between the EC and its Member States, with specific reference to the individual provisions of the convention, is regulated. Nor are the similar declarations in most other multilat-

---

[56] See, for example, Article 24(2) of the Basel Convention, OJ 1993 L 39/23.

[57] See, for example, Articles 22(2) and (3) of the Basel Convention, OJ 1993 L 39/23.

[58] OJ 1993 L 309/1.

[59] OJ 1979 L 103/1, later amended.

[60] OJ 1992 L 206/7.

eral environmental conventions models of clarity and precision.[61] The advantage to the EC and its Member States is that they are still able to operate with some degree of flexibility. The disadvantage of such an imprecise declaration to the other parties is, however, that it is not always clear which party they can call to account for performance of the obligations under the Convention.

3 Article 95 EC[62]

Article 95 EC provides that the Council, acting in accordance with the co-decision procedure, shall adopt the measures for the approximation of national legislation 'which have as their objective the establishment and functioning of the internal market.' It will be clear that many measures which can be characterised as environmental measures may also have a significant impact on the establishment of the internal market. This is recognised in the Treaty. The provisions of Article 95(3) EC, by which the Commission, in its proposals on, *inter alia*, environmental protection, will take as a base a high level of protection, indicates that at any rate certain environmental measures fall within the scope of Article 95 EC. The Court also held that whenever the conditions for recourse to Article 95 EC as a legal basis are fulfilled, the European legislature cannot be prevented from relying on that legal basis on the ground that 'public health protection' is a decisive factor in the choices to be made. It is the authors' opinion that, in view of Article 95(3) EC, the same can be said with respect to 'environmental protection'.

Thus it could be said that the harmonisation of the conditions under which certain environmentally harmful products are placed on the market is important for attaining the free movement of goods. After all, as long as the environmental product standard rules continue to differ in the various Member States, there can be no question of the free movement of environmentally hazardous goods. Harmonisation of the conditions under which such products are allowed to be placed on the market and/or used will thus often fall within the scope of Article 95 EC.[63] However, many other environmental measures may also relate to the

---

[61] Cf. with respect to UNCLOS, Case C-459/03 *Commission* v. *Ireland* [2006] ECR I-4635 (*MOX* case), para. 105 *et seq.* where the ECJ ruled that within the specific context of that Convention the Declaration of Community competence confirms that a transfer of areas of shared competence, in particular in regard to the prevention of marine pollution, took place within the framework of the Convention, subject only to the *existence* of EC rules.

[62] The Reform Treaty will reverse the order of Articles 94 and 95 EC. Article 94 EC shall be renumbered Article 115 FEU and Article 95 EC shall be renumbered Article 114 FEU.

[63] But not always as is shown by the *Chernobyl II* case; Case C-70/88 *EP* v. *Council* [1991] ECR I-4529. Regulation 3954/87 laid down maximum permitted levels of radioactive contamination of foodstuffs and feeding-stuffs. Products with too high a level of contamination may not be placed on the market. The Court held that the regulation was designed to protect the general public and that as a result the regulation falls outside the scope of Article 100a (now Article 95).

functioning of the internal market. In general one could say that any national rule concerning production conditions has an effect on competition and may therefore be subject to decision-making under Article 95 EC. This has been acknowledged by the Court of Justice. In the *TiO2* case concerning emission limit values, the Court of Justice, referring to its judgment in Case 92/79[64] observed:

> 'Action intended to approximate national rules concerning production conditions in a given industrial sector with the aim of eliminating distortions of competition in that sector is conducive to the attainment of the internal market and thus falls within the scope of Article 100a, a provision which is particularly appropriate to the attainment of the internal market.' The Court held that the content of Directive 89/428 on the reduction of pollution caused by waste from the titanium dioxide industry[65] fell within the scope of Article 100a EEC. The directive contains rules prohibiting or requiring the reduction of the discharge of waste and lays down timetables for the implementation of the various provisions. An unusual feature of this case was of course that the directive applied to a specific industry. The Court referred to this in its judgment.

The question which accordingly arises is to what extent environmental measures which have a more diffuse effect on the competitive position of companies could in principle fall within the scope of this article. In its judgment in the *Waste Framework Directive* case on the validity of Directive 91/156 on waste,[66] the Court acknowledged that the obligation contained in Article 4 of that directive – under which Member States are required to take the necessary measures to ensure that waste is recovered or disposed of without endangering human health and without harming the environment – can have a *certain* harmonising effect.[67] However, the mere fact that the internal market is *concerned* was insufficient to cause Article 95 EC to apply. It therefore seems that this case can be used to show that a measure does not fall within the scope of Article 95, if the effect of attaining market integration is only incidental.

It is reasonable to conclude that the scope of Article 95 EC is in principle more than sufficient to serve as a basis for measures approximating national laws on environmental product standards and for environmental measures which regulate conditions of production and remove distortions of competition in a particular industry. In those cases it could be argued that the primary objective of the measure is related to 'the establishment or functioning of the internal market'. For more general environmental measures, which rather than

---

[64] Case 92/79 *Commission v. Italy* [1980] ECR 1115, discussed in Chapter 1, section 1.

[65] OJ 1989 L 201/56.

[66] OJ 1991 L 78/32.

[67] Case C-155/91 *Commission v. Council* [1993] ECR I-939. The Court's approach in the *Waste Framework Directive* case has been confirmed in its judgment concerning the legal basis of Regulation 259/93 (Basel Regulation), Case C-187/93 *EP v. Council* [1994] ECR I-2857.

having a *specific* effect on the competitive position of companies have a more *diffuse* effect, it can be concluded from the case law that when the effects are of an incidental nature, the measure falls outside the scope of Article 95 EC and should therefore be based on Article 175 EC.

Examples of environmental measures the Council has based on Article 95 EC and its 'predecessor' the 'old' Article 100a EEC are:

- Directive 90/220 on the deliberate release into the environment of genetically modified organisms;[68]
- the 'old' and 'new' Batteries Directive;[69]
- Directive 92/112 on procedures for harmonizing the programmes for the reduction and eventual elimination of pollution caused by waste from the titanium dioxide industry;[70]
- Directive 94/62 on packaging and packaging waste;[71]
- the Biocides Directive;[72]
- Directive 2006/40 relating to emissions from air conditioning systems in motor vehicles;[73]
- Regulation 1907/2006 on the Registration, Evaluation and Authorisation of Chemicals (REACH).[74]

These are indeed measures in which the preamble states that European action is needed on the one hand because the laws in force in the Member States may constitute a barrier to trade or result in unfair conditions of competition and on the other because measures are necessary from the point of view of protecting the environment.

4 Article 175 EC or Article 95 EC?

It is settled case law that the choice of the legal basis for a European measure must be based on objective factors which are amenable to judicial review and include in particular the aim and content of the measure.[75] In other words, the European legislature is not free to choose a legal basis as he sees fit. With respect to the use of Article 175 or Article 95 EC (or any other legal basis), it is important to look for the 'centre of gravity' of the measure. Or in the words of the Court of Justice:

---

[68] OJ 1990 L 117/15, later amended.

[69] Directive 91/157, OJ 1991 L 78/38, repealed by Directive 2006/66, OJ 2006 L 266/1.

[70] OJ 1992 L 409/11.

[71] OJ 1994 L 365/10.

[72] Directive 98/8, OJ 1998 L 123/1.

[73] OJ 2006 L 161/12.

[74] OJ 2006 L 396/1; See on this regulation Chapter 8, section 13.1.

[75] Case 45/86 *Commission* v. *Council* [1987] ECR 1493, para. 11; Case C-300/89 *Commission* v. *Council* (*TiO2*) [1991] ECR I-2867, para. 10; Case C-268/94 *Portugal* v. *Council* [1996] ECR I-6177, para. 22; and Case C-176/03 *Commission* v. *Council* [2005] ECR I-7879, para. 45.

'If examination of a Community measure reveals that it pursues a twofold purpose or that it has a twofold component and if one of those is identifiable as the main or predominant purpose or component, whereas the other is merely incidental, the act must be based on a single legal basis, namely that required by the main or predominant purpose or component'.[76]

The fact that a measure pursues an environmental objective does not necessarily imply that Article 175 EC is the correct legal basis.[77] The main rule is: a single legal basis, either Article 175 EC or Article 95 EC. And indeed, it is clear from the practice of the past few years that environmental directives and regulations are based either on Article 175 or Article 95 EC. Exceptionally, if on the other hand it is established that the act simultaneously pursues a number of objectives or has several components that are indissociably linked, without one being secondary and indirect in relation to the other, such an act will have to be founded on both legal bases, the Court followed in Case C-178/03. This is provided that the procedures laid down for each legal basis are not incompatible with each other and the use of two legal bases does not undermine the rights of the Parliament.[78] Where different decision-making procedures are combined, their modalities must also be combined. In practice this means that the 'more demanding' of the procedures must be adhered to plus any additional requirements of the less demanding procedure.

Recent practice shows a few examples of environmental measures which have a dual legal basis. Take for instance Regulation 842/2006 on certain fluorinated greenhouse gases.[79] According to the EU legislature, it is the primary objective of the regulation to reduce the emissions of the fluorinated greenhouse gases covered by the Kyoto Protocol and thus to protect the environment and that therefore the legal base should be Article 175(1) EC. Nevertheless, the legislature felt it appropriate to take measures on the basis of Article 95 EC to harmonise requirements on the use of fluorinated greenhouse gases and the marketing and labeling of products and equipment containing fluorinated greenhouse gases.

This example demonstrates that the combination of the decision-making procedures of Article 95 EC and Article 175(1) EC is clearly possible. Both provide for use of the co-decision procedure. However, when combined, the Committee of the Regions must be consulted. Furthermore, the measure in question must

---

[76] Case C-178/03 Commission v. EP and Council [2006] ECR I-107, para. 42.

[77] E.g. Case C-377/98 Netherlands v. EP and Council [2000] ECR I-6229. The case concerned an application for annulment of Directive 98/44 on the legal protection of biotechnological inventions; OJ 1998 L 213/13.

[78] Case C-178/03 Commission v. EP and Council [2006] ECR I-107, para 59. But see already Case C-300/89 Commission v. Council (TiO2) [1991] ECR I-2867.

[79] OJ 2006 L 161/1. See for another example Directive 2006/66 on batteries and accumulators and waste batteries and accumulators, OJ 2006 L 266/1.

address the problem of more stringent national measures. As far as the measure is based upon Article 175 EC, Article 176 EC is applicable. As far as provisions are based upon Article 95 EC and Member States want to derogate from them by taking more stricter environmental standards, the procedure and the conditions of Article 95(4-6) EC have to be followed.[80]

> An elegant solution to the problems caused by the differences between the two can be found, e.g. in Article 14 of Regulation 842/2006. This example makes it quite clear than the differences between Article 176 EC and Article 95(4-6) EC do not make the decision-making procedures of Article 175 EC and Article 95 EC incompatible. Article 14 reads: 'Without prejudice to Article 9(3), Member States may maintain or introduce more stringent protective measures in accordance with the procedures laid down in Article 95 of the Treaty, in relation to Articles 7, 8 and 9 of this Regulation, or Article 176 of the Treaty in relation to other Articles of this Regulation.'

Whether the decision-making procedure of Article 95 EC can be combined with Article 175(2) EC is not entirely clear. In fact this would mean that the Council would have to act unanimously during the co-decision procedure. The Treaty does contain examples of this, for example in Article 151(5) EC, and the combination is not, as such, impossible. The European Parliament retains its veto in all cases. However, it is questionable whether the prerogatives of the Parliament would not be essentially impaired *during* the procedure. After all, it could be argued that, given that the Court of Justice considers a unanimity requirement to be incompatible with the cooperation procedure,[81] this would apply *a fortiori* in respect of the co-decision procedure.

With respect to the combination of the decision-making procedures of Article 133 EC and Article 175(1) EC the Court ruled in Case C-178/03 that they are not incompatible.[82]

5   Article 133 EC[83]

Where environmental product standards are applied to direct imports from third countries, the question arises as to how this is compatible with the EC's competence in respect of the common commercial policy, as conferred by Article 133 EC. This question is relevant in at least two respects:
· the decision-making procedure for measures implementing the common commercial policy is different from the procedures in respect of European environment policy and

---

[80] Cf. on Articles 176 EC and 95(4-6) EC and their differences, Chapter 3, sections 5 and 6 in particular.

[81] Case C-300/89 *Commission v. Council* [1991] ECR I-2867.

[82] Case C-178/03 *Commission v. EP and Council* [2006] ECR I-107, paras. 58-59.

[83] After entry into force of the Reform Treaty, Article 207 FEU.

· the EC's powers in respect of the common commercial policy are in principle *exclusive*, meaning that national measures are, in principle *ultra vires*.[84]

An important question, therefore, is to what extent an external environment policy – if it also affects trade with third countries – must be regarded as common commercial policy within the meaning of Article 133 EC. For years there has been a conflict between the institutions, in particular the Council and the Commission, as to the extent of the EC's competence in respect of the common commercial policy. The Commission prefers to take a more *objective* and *instrumental* approach to the interpretation of the article. This implies that all the common commercial policy measures listed (not exhaustively) in Article 133 EC, whether unilateral or by international agreement, as well as all related measures, fall within the competence of the EC, irrespective of the purpose for which the measures are applied. According to the Commission, measures regulating international trade often pursue a wide range of different objectives, but this does not mean that they must be adopted on the basis of the various Treaty provisions relating to those objectives. Thus, in the environmental sector, the Commission has regarded measures implementing a system of import and export licences in the trade in endangered species of wild fauna and flora and a system of notification on the import of certain dangerous chemicals as common commercial policy measures.[85]

In contrast with the *instrumental* doctrine pursued by the Commission is the more *subjective* approach taken by the Council, looking to the content of a measure to identify its objectives. In this view, it is the objectives of an intended measure that are paramount. If these are not common commercial policy objectives, but are rather prompted by considerations of development policy or environmental protection, they cannot be based on Article 133 EC. Normal common commercial policy measures, for instance containing a system of import and export licences, were based by the Council on Article 175 EC or on Article 308 EC, where the purpose of the measure was the protection of species of wild fauna and flora or the environment.[86] Only in exceptional cases has it based measures on the common commercial policy provision in the Treaty, for example Regulation 3254/91 prohibiting the use of certain kinds of traps,[87] which it based both on Article 113 (now Article 133) and on Article 130s (now Article 175).

---

[84] Cf. for instance Case C-173/05 *Commission v. Italy*, judgment of 21 June 2007, n.y.r. in the ECR, where the Court declared that an environmental tax levied on Algerian methane gas violates a.o. Article 133 EC.

[85] See, for example, the proposal of the Commission to implement the CITES Convention, OJ 1980 C 243/16 and the proposal of the Commission for the Whales Regulation, OJ 1980 C 121/5.

[86] See for instance the CITES-Regulation 3626/82, OJ 1982 L 384/1 (and its successor Regulation 338/97, OJ 1997 L 61/1) and Regulation 304/2003 concerning the export and import of dangerous chemicals, OJ 2003 L 63/1.

[87] OJ 1991 L 308/1.

However, the preamble to the regulation offers no clue as to why Article 113 (now Article 133) was used in this case.

The Court of Justice handed down a number of important judgments concerning the borderline between environmental protection and common commercial policy. The first case to be discussed is the *Chernobyl I* case.[88]

> This case concerned uniform rules on the conditions under which agricultural products from third countries, which could be radioactively contaminated, could be imported into the EC. In its judgment, the Court held that such a measure comes under the exclusive common commercial policy competence of the EC and not within the sphere of operation of the environmental Title of the Treaty. After recalling its consistent case law[89] that in the context of the organisation of the powers of the EC the choice of the legal basis for a measure must be based on objective factors which are amenable to judicial review, the Court went on to examine the objectives of the contested regulation. The preamble to the regulation stated that 'the Community must continue to ensure that agricultural products and processed agricultural products intended for human consumption and likely to be contaminated are introduced into the Community only according to common arrangements' and that those 'common arrangements should safeguard the health of consumers, maintain, without having unduly adverse effects on trade between the Community and third countries, the unified nature of the market and prevent deflections of trade'. According to the Court the regulation established uniform rules regarding the conditions under which agricultural products likely to be contaminated may be imported into the Community from non-member countries: 'It follows that, according to its objectives and its content, as they appear from the very terms of the regulation, the regulation is intended to regulate trade between the Community and non-member countries; accordingly it comes within the common commercial policy within the meaning of Article 113 [now Article 133, authors] of the EEC Treaty.'

The Court stated that the fact that maximum permitted levels of radioactive contamination are fixed in response to a concern to protect public health and that the protection of public health is also one of the objectives of EC action in environmental matters likewise cannot remove the contested regulation from the sphere of the common commercial policy. According to the Court, Articles 174 and 175 EC are intended to confer powers on the EC to undertake specific action on environmental matters. However, those articles leave intact the powers held by the EC under other provisions of the Treaty, even if the measures to be taken under the latter provisions pursue at the same time any of the objectives of environmental protection. The Court went on to refer specifically to the integration principle.

---

[88] Case C-62/88 *EP* v. *Council* [1990] ECR I-1527.

[89] Case 45/86 *Commission* v. *Council* [1987] ECR 1493.

This judgment makes it clear that common commercial policy measures which at the same time pursue environmental objectives may fall within the sphere of operation of Article 133 EC. If a measure, according to its objective and its content, is intended to regulate trade with countries outside the EC, it is a common commercial policy measure, even if it includes provisions concerning environmental protection. However, it will have to be determined in each individual case whether a measure, according to its objective and its content, is intended to regulate trade between the EC and third countries.

The second case to be discussed is the Court's judgment in de *Cartagena Protocol* case.[90] In the context of the Convention on Biological Diversity, the parties to that convention negotiated a protocol on biosafety, specifically focusing on transboundary movement, of any living modified organism (LMO) resulting from modern biotechnology that may have adverse effect on the conservation and sustainable use of biological diversity, setting out for consideration, in particular, appropriate procedure for advance informed agreement (the so called Cartagena Protocol). The Commission and the Council had different views on the correct legal basis to conclude the protocol. While the Commission's proposal was based on Articles 133 EC and 174(4) EC, the Council argued that the protocol should be concluded on the basis of Article 175(1) EC alone. On request of the Commission, the Court gave an Opinion pursuant to Article 300(6) EC and ruled that a single use of Article 175(1) EC is the appropriate legal basis for conclusion of the Protocol on behalf of the EC.

> The Court started its reasoning by recapitulating its settled case law 'that the choice of the legal basis for a measure, including one adopted in order to conclude an international agreement, does not follow from its author's conviction alone, but must rest on objective factors which are amenable to judicial review. Those factors include in particular the aim and the content of the measure'. This was followed by a reformulation of the *centre of gravity* doctrine: 'If examination of a Community measure reveals that it pursues a twofold purpose or that it has a twofold component and if one is identifiable as the main or predominant purpose or component, whereas the other is merely incidental, the measure must be founded on a single legal basis, namely that required by the main or predominant purpose or component'. The key question therefore is, whether the protocol constitutes an agreement principally concerning environmental protection which is liable to have incidental effects on trade in LMOs, or whether, conversely, it is principally an agreement concerning international trade policy which incidentally takes account of certain environmental requirements. After a close examination of the Cartagena Protocol the Court concludes that 'the Protocol is, in the light of its context, its aim and its content, an instrument intended essentially to improve biosafety and not to promote, facilitate or govern trade.'

---

90   Opinion 2/00 [2001] ECR I-9713.

The importance of Opinion 2/00 is in particular that, with respect to the delimination of powers between common commercial policy and environmental protection, the Court for the first time applied the *centre of gravity* doctrine. In view of the *Chernobyl I* case, one could take the position that as soon as measures intend to regulate trade (whatever objectives environmental, human health, agricultural, etc. are pursued) they fall within the scope of Article 133 EC. In view of the *Chernobyl I* case, the Commission argued in Opinion 2/00 that the fact that provisions governing international trade in certain products pursue objectives which are not primarily commercial cannot have the effect of excluding the EC's exclusive competence and justifying recourse to, in the case of environmental objectives, Article 175 EC. By applying the *centre of gravity* doctrine, the Court showed that this interpretation of the *Chernobyl I* case can no longer be maintained.

The third case we would like to mention is the *Energy Star Agreement* case.[91] In 1992 the United States Environmental Protection Agency (the EPA) set up a voluntary labeling programme for office equipment, called the Energy Star Program. The programme, which enjoyed a high level of manufacturer participation, encouraged the vast majority of manufacturers to introduce energy-saving features and raised consumer awareness of the energy losses of office equipment in stand-by mode. After observing that the Energy Star requirements were becoming the standard worldwide, the Commission decided that, rather than developing a separate labelling programme for energy-efficient office equipment in the EU, the better course was to introduce the Energy Star Program there. On 1 July 1999 the Commission submitted to the Council, for the purpose of concluding an agreement between the United States and the EC (the Energy Star Agreement), a proposal for a decision based on Article 133 EC. On 14 May 2001 the Council, by Decision 2001/469, approved the Energy Star Agreement on behalf of the EC on the basis of Article 175(1) EC. Accordingly, it was signed in Washington on 19 December 2000. The Commission, however, was of the opinion that Decision 2001/469 should have been adopted on the basis of Article 133 EC, on the ground that the Energy Star Agreement seeks to facilitate trade and brought an action for annulment under Article 230 EC. The Court concluded that 'the Energy Star Agreement simultaneously pursue a commercial-policy objective and an environmental-protection objective.' However, the commercial-policy objective pursued by the agreement had to be regarded as predominant, so that the decision approving the agreement should have been based on Article 133 EC:

'It is clear from the terms in which the Energy Star Agreement is couched, in particular from Articles I and V, that the Energy Star labelling program is essentially intended to enable manufacturers to use, in accordance with a procedure for the mutual recognition of registrations, a common logo to identify for consumers certain products complying with a common set of energy-efficiency specifications

---

91 Case C-281/01 *Commission* v. *Council* [2002] ECR I-12049. See also Chapter 8, section 7.1.

which they intend to sell on the American and Community markets. An instrument having a direct impact on trade in office equipment is therefore involved.

It is true that in the long term, depending on how manufacturers and consumers in fact behave, the programme should have a positive environmental effect as a result of the reduction in energy consumption which it should achieve. However, that is merely an indirect and distant effect, in contrast to the effect on trade in office equipment which is direct and immediate.'[92]

It seems that the *direct* and *immediate* effects on trade were decisive for the Court to rule that the Energy Star Agreement fell within the scope of Article 133 EC. This case also makes clear that, although the ultimate goal of the Energy Star logo is to persuade producers to manufacture (and consumers to buy) products with a reduced energy consumption, this does not mean that Agreement concerning the use of such a logo makes the agreement an environmental agreement.

Finally, the *Rotterdam Convention* case on the Prior Informed Consent (PIC) Procedure for certain hazardous chemicals and pesticides in international trade should be mentioned.[93] According to Article 1 of the Rotterdam Convention, its objective is 'to promote shared responsibility and cooperative efforts among Parties in the international trade of certain hazardous chemicals in order to protect human health and the environment from potential harm and to contribute to their environmentally sound use'. Article 5 of the Convention established a procedure for the exchange of information concerning actions taken by the parties in order to ban or severely restrict the use of a chemical product on their territory, while Article 12 of the Convention imposed on the same parties an obligation to send an export notification to the importing party where a banned or severely restricted chemical is exported from their territory and which also calls on the latter party formally to acknowledge receipt of that notification. Those provisions are intended, in essence, to ensure that no party, in particular a developing country, is confronted with imports of hazardous chemicals without first having had an opportunity to take the requisite precautions to protect human health and the environment. The proposal of the Commission to approve the convention was based on Article 133 EC, but the Council took its decision exclusively on Article 175 EC. The Court found that the decision approving that Convention should have been based on the combined legal bases of Articles 133 EC and 175(1) EC. The Court held that it cannot be denied that the protection of human health and the environment was the most important concern in the mind of the signatories of the Convention. However, that alone does not justify Article 175 EC as a single legal basis, as the Court found that the commercial component of the Convention is not 'purely incidental':

---

[92] Paras. 40 and 41 of the judgment.

[93] Case C-94/03 *Commission v. Council* [2006] ECR I-1. See also Chapter 8, section 13.4.

'A reading of the provisions of the Convention and, more particularly, of its articles concerning the PIC procedure, prompts the conclusion that the Convention also contains rules governing trade in hazardous chemicals and having *direct* and *immediate* effects on such trade' [emphasis added]. [...] 'it must therefore be concluded that the Convention includes, both as regards the aims pursued and its contents, two indissociably linked components, neither of which can be regarded as secondary or indirect as compared with the other, one falling within the scope of the common commercial policy and the other within that of protection of human health and the environment. In accordance with the case-law cited in paragraph 36 of the present judgment, the decision approving that Convention on behalf of the Community should therefore have been based on the two corresponding legal bases, namely, in this case, Articles 133 EC and 175(1) EC, in conjunction with the relevant provisions of Article 300 EC.'

6 'Comitology' and Environmental Legislation

Not unimportant in practical terms are the 'Comitology' procedures.[94] Under Article 202 EC, it is for the Commission to implement legislation at European level. In practice, each legislative instrument specifies the scope of the implementing powers conferred on the Commission by the Council. In this context, the Treaty provides for the Commission to be assisted by committees (advisory, management or regulatory), in accordance with a procedure known as 'comitology'. Relations between the Commission and the committees are based on models set out in a Council Decision, the so-called Comitology Decision.[95] The decision contains, in Article 2, criteria with respect to the choice of procedural methods for the adoption of the implementing measures. Although the criteria laid down in Article 2 are not binding, where the European legislature departs from those criteria in the choice of a committee procedure, it must give reasons for its choice.[96]

In general a directive will contain a reference to the applicable procedure to be followed.[97]

---

[94] See for a more in-depth treatment of the issue Lee (2005) at 85 *et seq.*

[95] Council Decision 1999/468 laying down the procedures for the exercise of implementing powers conferred on the Commission, OJ 1999 L 184/23, as amended by Decision 2006/512, OJ 2006 L 200/11.

[96] Cf. Case C-378/00 *Commission* v. *EP and Council* [2003] ECR I-937, in respect to the implementation of the Financial Instrument for the Environment (LIFE) and Case C-122/04 *Commission* v. *EP and Council* [2006] ECR I-2001, in respect to the implementation of the Forest Focus programme.

[97] E.g. Article 9 of Directive 2006/118 on the protection of groundwater against pollution and deterioration, OJ 2006 L 372/19.

7 Other Incidental Legal Bases

7.1 The Provisions on the Common Agricultural Policy

Under Article 33 EC (Article 39 FEU) the objectives of the common agricultural policy (CAP) are: to increase agricultural productivity; to ensure a fair standard of living for the agricultural community; to stabilise markets; to assure the availability of supplies; and to ensure that supplies reach consumers at reasonable prices. In view of the integration principle, it is still strange that the text of Article 33 EC does not contain any reference whatsoever to the environmental objectives or to sustainable development, even though it is generally acknowledged that the CAP can be a major source of environmental damage.[98] Furthermore, there are strong links between agriculture and bio-diversity, genetic resources, genetically modified organisms, climate change, soil protection, pesticides, forestry, nitrates and water pollution. Environmental considerations have played a role in some measures which have been adopted, even if only in part, within the context of the common agricultural policy.[99] Important measures which have been taken in this context concern:

- Directive 91/414 concerning the placing of plant protection products on the market;[100]
- Regulation 2092/91 on organic production of agricultural products and indications referring thereto on agricultural products and foodstuffs;[101]
- Regulation 2152/2003 concerning monitoring of forests and environmental interactions in the Community (Forest Focus);[102]
- Regulation 2158/92 on protection of the Community's forests against fire.[103]

Similarly, at the international level, the EC is a party to the Agreement on the International Dolphin Conservation Programme.[104]

As far as the relationship between the provisions on CAP and the environment paragraph in the Treaty is concerned, the *Hormones* case is of particular interest.[105] In that judgment the Court of Justice stated that:

---

[98] Cf. 'Strategy for integrating the environmental dimension into the CAP' adopted at European Council in Helsinki (December 1999).

[99] See for a detailed study of the application of the integration principle in CAP, Dhondt (2003).

[100] OJ 1991 L 230/1, later amended.

[101] OJ 1991 L 198/1. See also Regulation 1804/1999 supplementing Regulation 2092/91 on organic production of agricultural products and indications referring thereto on agricultural products and foodstuffs to include livestock production, OJ 1999 L 222/1.

[102] OJ 2003 L 324/1.

[103] OJ 1992 L 217/3. Implemented by Commission Regulation 1727/1999, OJ 1999 L 203/41.

[104] Decision 1999/337 on the signature by the EC of the Agreement on the International Dolphin Conservation Programme, OJ 1999 L 132.

[105] Case 68/86 *UK* v. *Council* [1988] ECR 855.

'Article 43 [now Article 37, authors] of the Treaty is the appropriate legal basis for any legislation concerning the production and marketing of agricultural products listed in Annex II to the Treaty which contributes to the achievement of one or more of the objectives of the common agricultural policy set out in Article 39 [now Article 33, authors] of the Treaty. There is no need to have recourse to Article 100 [now Article 94, authors] of the Treaty where such legislation involves the harmonisation of provisions of national law in that field.'

In this connection, Barents came to the conclusion that the EC powers in respect of the common agricultural policy and the common transport policy are indivisible and include everything necessary for the management of these sectors: the attainment of free movement, price intervention measures, external relations, as well as flanking measures, such as elements of social policy relating specifically to these sectors.[106] He concluded that the provisions on CAP (and the same holds for the provisions on transport policy) have priority over all provisions conferring competence in so far as the measures in question concern agricultural products or transport services, and are designed to attain the specific objectives of these sectoral policies. In these cases there is neither room nor need for an additional legal basis in either Article 95 or Article 175 EC.

As far as the relationship between Article 37 EC and Article 175 EC is concerned, in the *Drift-Net* case[107] the Court of Justice stated that Regulation 345/92,[108] which prohibited the use of drift-nets, was rightly based on Article 43 (now Article 37 EC) since its principal objective was the protection of marine resources. The integration principle implies that a European measure cannot be part of EC action on environmental matters merely because it takes account of environmental requirements.

However, the theory of the 'indivisibility' of the CAP may require rethinking in view of the Court's judgment in Case C-164/97.[109] The case concerned an action brought by the European Parliament for the annulment, first, of Regulation 307/97 on the protection of the Community's forests against atmospheric pollution and, second, Regulation 308/97 on protection of the Community's forests against fire.[110] The regulations, whose purpose was to extend for a further five years the duration of EC schemes to increase the protection of forests against, respectively, atmospheric pollution and fire, were adopted on the basis of Article 37 EC. The Parliament maintained that they were adopted on an inappropriate legal basis, so that its prerogatives in respect of the procedure involving its participation in the drafting of legislation were undermined. In its view both regulations should have been based on Article 175 EC. The Court ruled that:

---

[106] Barents (1993) at 15.

[107] Case C-405/92 *Etablissements Armand Mondiet v. Société Armement Islais* [1993] ECR I-6133.

[108] OJ 1992 L 42/15.

[109] Joined Cases C-164/97 and C-165/97 *EP v. Council* [1999] ECR I-1139.

[110] OJ 1997 L 51/9 and OJ 1997 L 51/11.

'Although the measures referred to in the regulations may have certain positive repercussions on the functioning of agriculture, those indirect consequences are incidental to the primary aim of the Community schemes for the protection of forests, which are intended to ensure that the natural heritage represented by forest ecosystems is conserved and turned to account, and does not merely consider their utility to agriculture. Measures to defend the forest environment against the risks of destruction and degradation associated with fires and atmospheric pollution inherently form part of the environmental action for which Community competence is founded on Article 130s [now Article 175, authors] of the Treaty.'

The Court added:

'With more particular reference to the common agricultural policy and the Community environmental policy, there is nothing in the case-law to indicate that, in principle, one should take precedence over the other. It makes clear that a Community measure cannot be part of Community action on environmental matters merely because it takes account of requirements of protection referred to in Article 130r(2) [now Article 174(2), authors] of the EC Treaty'.

This seems to indicate that the Court has dissociated itself from the doctrine of the indivisibility of the CAP. Indeed, the *Huber* case, indicates that the 'principle of gravity' doctrine is also applicable with respect to delimit the agricultural competences from those under the environment paragraph.[111] The case involved the correct legal basis of Regulation 2078/92 on agricultural production methods compatible with the requirements of the protection of the environment and the maintenance of the countryside.[112] The regulation had as its legal basis Articles 36 and 37 EC. The Court ruled that it was clear from the regulation that the main purpose was to regulate the production of agricultural products. Promoting more environmentally friendly forms of production was considered by the Court as 'certainly a genuine objective, but an ancillary one, of the common agricultural policy'. The judgment in *Huber* seems to suggest that the Court will accept Article 175 EC as legal basis for those agri-environmental measures which do as their main purpose the protection of the environment.

7.2   The Provisions on the Common Transport Policy

The second sector in which the Treaty refers to a common policy is transport. In the same way as with agriculture, environmental considerations play a part in transport policy.[113] Council measures on transport, based

---

[111] Case C-336/00 *Huber* [2002] ECR I-7699.

[112] OJ 1992 L 215/85.

[113] Cf. Dhondt (2003) and Rodi (2006).

at least partly on Articles 70-80 EC (Articles 90-100 FEU), and where environmental considerations figure are:

· Regulation 1592/2002 on common rules in the field of civil aviation and establishing a European Aviation Safety Agency;[114]
· Directive 92/6 on the installation and use of speed limitation devices for certain categories of motor vehicles within the Community;[115]
· Directive 89/629 on the limitation of noise emissions from subsonic aircraft;[116]
· Directive 2005/35 on ship-source pollution and on the introduction of penalties for infringements.[117]

To a certain extent environment-related transport measures will be established on other Treaty provisions, in particular Article 95 EC. Measures harmonising motor vehicle emissions (Directives 98/69 and 1999/96) or environmental fuel quality specifications for petrol and diesel (Directive 98/70) have their legal basis in Article 95 EC.

7.3 Harmonisation of Indirect Taxes

These days a great deal is said about making more frequent use of market-oriented instruments for the pursuit of environmental policy. Financial instruments should be used to attain certain environmental objectives. One of the means at the disposal of the Member States is indirect taxation. As will be seen in Chapter 6, section 3, where Article 90 EC is discussed, Member States may use environmental criteria to justify tax differentiation. Put briefly, the Treaty allows the possibility of taxing products that cause more environmental pollution more than those that cause less. However, it will be clear that, if Member States introduce varying differentiations based on environmental considerations, this will have a negative impact on the operation of the internal market. Thus Article 93 EC (Article 113 FEU) offers the Council a legal basis on which to adopt provisions for the harmonisation of legislation concerning turnover taxes, excise duties and other forms of indirect taxation. The more popular the national authorities find the use of financial instruments to protect the environment, the more frequently the Council will be required to use its powers under Article 93 EC.[118] It should be noted that Article 93 EC does not provide a basis for a truly European environmental tax in the sense of an environmental tax introduced by the EC and for the EC. The only basis for such a tax is found in Article 175(2) EC, and would, in any case, require an extensive interpretation of the provision.

---

[114] OJ 2002 L 240/1, later amended.

[115] OJ 1992 L 57/27.

[116] OJ 1989 L 363/27, later amended.

[117] OJ 2005 L 255/11.

[118] See in general Commission Communication 'Tax policy in the European Union – Priorities for the years ahead', COM (2001) 260 final, OJ 2001 C 284/6.

Up to now Article 93 EC has played only a modest role in the field of the environment. The Commission has, for example, based its proposal for a directive introducing a tax on carbon dioxide emissions and energy on Articles 99 and 130s (now Articles 93 and 175 EC).[119] One of the considerations stated in the preamble is that a number of Member States have already introduced or are planning to introduce taxes on carbon dioxide emissions and the use of energy, and that a harmonised approach is therefore needed to ensure the functioning of the internal market.

As a fine example of environment-related tax harmonisation, Directive 2003/96 has to be mentioned.[120] According to the Council, the proper functioning of the internal market required minimum levels of taxation to be laid down for most energy products, including electricity, natural gas and coal. The Council acknowledged that, in view of the integration principle, environmental protection requirements had to be integrated in the directive.

7.4   Research and Technological Development

Articles 163-173 EC (Articles 179-190 FEU) provide for powers in the field of research and technological development. Their objective is strengthening the scientific and technological bases of European industry and encouraging it to become more competitive at international level, while promoting all the research activities deemed necessary by virtue of other Chapters of the Treaty.

The Sixth Framework Programme of the European Community for research, technological development and demonstration activities addresses thematic priorities, of which one is concerned with sustainable development, global change and ecosystems.[121] According to Article 5, the framework programme is to be implemented through a number of specific programmes.[122] With respect to programmes adopted under Article 175 EC we have to mention in particular the SAVE, ALTENER, STEER and COOPENER programmes.[123]

7.5   Nuclear Energy and Basic Safety Standards

The most significant environmentally relevant legal bases outside the EC Treaty are to be found in the Euratom Treaty. Chapter 3 of Title II of that Treaty in particular deserves mention here. Articles 30 to 39 require that basic standards be laid down for the protection of the health of workers and the

---

[119] OJ 1992 C 196/92.

[120] Directive 2003/96 restructuring the Community framework for the taxation of energy products and electricity, OJ 2003 L 283/51. See on this directive also Chapter 6, section 4.

[121] Decision 1513/2002 concerning the Sixth Framework Programme of the European Community for research, technological development and demonstration activities (2002-2006), OJ 2002 L 232/1.

[122] See for instance Council Decision 2002/834, OJ 2002 L 232/1.

[123] Decision 1230/2003 adopting a multiannual programme for action in the field of energy 'Intelligent Energy – Europe' (2003 – 2006); OJ 2003 L 176/29.

general public against the dangers arising from ionizing radiation.[124] According to Article 30 the expression 'basic standards' means:
· maximum permissible doses compatible with adequate safety;
· maximum permissible levels of exposure and contamination;
· the fundamental principles governing the health surveillance of workers.

The Council has based various decisions on Articles 31 and 32 Euratom for the purpose of attaining these objectives.[125] These decisions relate to radiation from permanent plants, radioactive products, cross-border transport of radioactive waste and products contaminated with radiation. The case law shows that if the Council's measures, according to their objectives and their content, are designed to protect the general public and workers against the dangers of radioactivity, they will fall within the scope of application of Article 31 Euratom.

> In the *Chernobyl I* case, the European Parliament tried to restrict the scope of Article 31 Euratom to measures concerning protection against primary radiation, in other words, radiation released directly from a nuclear plant or resulting from the handling of fissile materials.[126] In the view of the European Parliament, Article 31 Euratom did not relate to so-called secondary radiation, that is, radiation emanating from contaminated products and other incidental consequences of primary radiation. The Court rejected this restricted interpretation: 'There is no support in the relevant legislation for that restrictive interpretation which cannot therefore be accepted. The indications are rather that the purpose of the articles referred to is to ensure the consistent and effective protection of the health of the general public against the dangers arising from ionizing radiations, whatever their source and whatever the categories of persons exposed to such radiations.'

The only real restriction on the scope of application of the article is to be found in its objectives. Advocate General Van Gerven properly concluded that Article 31 Euratom cannot be used as a legal basis for the adoption of measures relating to the establishment and functioning of the internal market. Thus the question arises as to what extent measures of the Council, based exclusively on Article 31 Euratom, may contain provisions which limit the freedom of Member States to enact more stringent measures than those actually provided for in the measures in question.[127]

Although current legal practice assumes that Articles 31 and 32 Euratom have a wide sphere of application, there is some uncertainty as to what kind of

---

[124] See Directive 96/29 laying down basic safety standards for the protection of the health of workers and the general public against the dangers arising from ionizing radiation, OJ 1996 L 159/1 and Commission Communication concerning the implementation of Council Directive 96/29/Euratom, OJ L 133/3. See further Chapter 8, section 16.1.

[125] See Chapter 8, section 16.

[126] Case C-70/88 *EP* v. *Council* [1991] ECR I-4529.

[127] This will be discussed in more detail in Chapter 3, section 4.2.

measure does fall within their scope and what does not, especially in relation to the sphere of application of the EC Treaty.

In the *Chernobyl II* case, the European Parliament petitioned the Court for the annulment of Regulation 3954/87 laying down maximum permitted levels of radioactive contamination of foodstuffs and feedingstuffs following a nuclear accident or other case of radiological emergency.[128] This regulation is based on Article 31 Euratom. The European Parliament contested that, in view of its effects on the internal market, it should have been based on Article 100a EEC. Relevant to this problem of demarcation is Article 305 EC, which provides that the provisions of the Treaty 'shall not derogate from' those of the Euratom Treaty. This provision therefore implies that if Article 31 Euratom provides an adequate legal basis for a given measure, Article 95 EC cannot apply, even if it could be shown that Article 95 EC would in principle be appropriate. In his Opinion in the case, Advocate General Van Gerven rightly concluded that the European Parliament's appeal would have to succeed in two cases:
   · if Article 31 Euratom could not in any event have been used;
   · if the regulation ought to have been based both on Article 31 Euratom and on Article 95 EC. This would be the case if the regulation, in addition to the objectives of Article 31 Euratom, pursued aims and laid down rules which could not be based on Article 31, but rather concerned the establishment and functioning of the internal market.
   The Court noted that, according to the preamble, the aim of the regulation was to provide for the establishment of basic standards for the protection of the health of the general public and workers. As far as its content is concerned, the regulation lays down maximum permitted levels of radioactive contamination of foodstuffs and feedingstuffs. If these levels are exceeded, the product may not be placed on the market. However, this does not justify the conclusion that the regulation is also a harmonisation measure within the meaning of Article 95 EC. The Court stated that the prohibition of marketing is only one condition for the effectiveness of the application of the maximum permitted levels. The regulation therefore has only an incidental effect of harmonising the conditions for the free movement of goods within the EU, inasmuch as, by means of the adoption of uniform protective measures, it avoids the need for trade in foodstuffs and feedingstuffs which have undergone radioactive contamination to be made the subject of unilateral national measures.

Another problem is to what extent a distinction should be made, as far as it concerns the question of EC competences, between the protection of the health of the general public and the safety of *sources* of ionising radiation.

With respect to the conclusion by the EC of the Convention on Nuclear Safety, the Council argued that that no article of the Euratom Treaty bestowed on the EC

---

[128] Case C-70/88 *EP* v. *Council* [1991] ECR I-4529. See Chapter 8, section 16.2.

the competence to regulate the opening and operation of nuclear facilities. That competence was retained by the Member States. The EC has competence only as regards protection of the general public. The Court ruled however 'it is not appropriate, in order to define the EC's competences, to draw an artificial distinction between the protection of the health of the general public and the safety of sources of ionising radiation'.[129]

---

[129] Case C-29/99 *Commission* v. *Council* [2002] ECR I-11221, para. 82.

CHAPTER 3

Harmonisation

1 General Remarks

The dual objective of many European environmental measures has been referred to more than once in the previous chapters. On the one hand, it is aimed at attaining European environmental objectives (Article 174 EC), but on the other it can be aimed at integration and the establishment and proper functioning of the internal market (Article 95 EC). This dual objective is also very relevant as regards the degree of freedom Member States enjoy to pursue national policies in fields in which European legislation already exists. To what extent may the Member States, following harmonisation, adopt additional or even more stringent environmental standards than the European standards. Are they entitled to adopt less stringent standards? And, if so, under what conditions? These questions will be addressed in this chapter.

The instrument most frequently used in the harmonisation of national environmental provisions is the directive. A directive shall be binding, as to the result to be achieved, upon each Member State to which it is addressed, though it is left to the national authorities to choose form and methods (Article 249 EC). Directives, including environmental directives, thus impose on Member States an obligation to achieve a particular result. This they have to implement and incorporate into national law within the time set by the directive. An important feature is that the national legislature has in principle to act within the limits set by the directive. Thus, once national environmental laws have been harmonised, the extent to which the Member States are still free to pursue policies of their own depends primarily on the content of the directive. It is therefore important to examine the various methods of harmonisation more closely, at least in so far as they are relevant to environmental policy. This means examining the mechanisms of total harmonisation on the one hand, and minimum harmonisation on the other.

In addition the question will be addressed as to what extent Member States are free to pursue additional national environmental policies outside the system of harmonisation legislation or to derogate from EU environmental measures. Articles 95(4) and 176 EC in particular will be discussed.

2 The Scope of Harmonisation

It has been pointed out in Chapter 2 that in the area of environmental protection competences are 'shared' between the EU and the Member States. Until national laws have been harmonised, Member States are completely free to pursue any environmental policy of their own, under the condition that it complies with the relevant provisions of the Treaty, such as *inter alia* the provisions on the free movement of goods. However, once a matter has been regulated by an environmental directive, the Member States competencies are first of all dependent on the content of the directive concerned. One of the consequences of exhaustive harmonisation is that Member States may no longer have recourse to the provisions of Article 30 EC or the 'rule of reason',[1] for example to justify environmental measures restricting imports or exports. In other words: recourse to Article 30 EC or the rule of reason is not possible where European directives provide for harmonisation of the measures necessary to achieve the specific objective which would be furthered by reliance upon Article 30 EC or the rule of reason.[2]

Harmonisation and the scope of the European measures

However, it must be noted that the legal consequences of harmonisation only come into play if the directive was actually intended to regulate the matter in question. Anything outside the scope of the directive remains within the competence of the Member States. Outside the scope of the directive their competence is, once again, limited only by primary European law. This means that if a matter falls outside the scope of a harmonisation measure, it is irrelevant whether Article 95(4-6) EC or Article 176 EC are applicable.[3] Where there is no European standard, there can be no question of 'more stringent' national environmental rules. There can thus be no question of a requirement, under Article 95(4-6) EC or Article 176 EC, to notify national legislation, which is outside the scope of a harmonisation directive.

What is crucial is whether a directive applies in a given field. However, it is not always easy to determine whether a national environmental standard is or is not within the scope of a directive. If a national standard falls within the sphere of application of a directive, then the European legislative framework in principle given by that directive or regulation is said to be 'exhaustive'.

> Thus the Court of Justice observed in the *Compassion in World Farming* case that with respect to Directive 91/629 'the Community legislature laid down exhaustively common minimum standards'.[4] As a result it was impossible to rely on Article 30 EC to justify the British legislation in question. After all, the European legislative framework for that national policy was given by the directive. This approach was also clearly stated by the Court of Justice in the *Red Grouse* case.[5] The Dutch Supreme Court referred to the Court of Justice for a preliminary ruling a question on the interpretation of what are now Articles 28 and 30 EC. That

---

[1] See Chapter 6, sections 3.5 and 3.6.

[2] See Case C-473/98 *Kemikalieninspektionen v. Toolex Alpha AB* [2000] ECR I-5681, para. 25 and Case C-324/99 *DaimlerChrysler* [2001] ECR I-9897, paras. 41-43. In the latter case the Court ruled that the so-called Basel Regulation 259/93 regulates shipments of waste in a harmonised manner and that accordingly, any national measure relating to shipments of waste must be assessed in the light of the provisions of the Regulation and not of Articles 28-30 EC.

[3] Cf. Case C-127/97 *Burstein* [1998] ECR I-6005. See on Articles 95(4-6) and 176 EC sections 5 and 6 of this chapter.

[4] Case C-1/96 *Compassion in World Farming* [1998] ECR I-1251.

[5] Case C-169/89 *Gourmetterie v.d. Burg* [1990] ECR I-2143.

question arose in criminal proceedings instituted against a trader in foodstuffs, Gourmetterie Van den Burg. The Supreme Court questioned the compatibility of Article 7 of the Dutch Vogelwet, containing a prohibition on the marketing of red grouse on the domestic market, with Article 30 EC: 'With regard to Article 36 [now Article 30, authors] the Court has consistently held that a directive providing for full harmonisation of national legislation deprives a Member State of recourse to that article.' The Court held that, in view of the fact that the Wild Birds Directive 'has [...] regulated exhaustively the Member States' powers with regard to the conservation of wild birds', compatibility with Article 36 [now Article 30] was not at issue. The Court then proceeded to consider whether the prohibition contained in Article 7 of the *Vogelwet* was in conformity with the directive.

On the other hand the *Radlberger* case illustrates that as regards the reuse of packaging, Article 5 of Directive 94/62 on packaging and packaging waste does no more than allow the Member States to encourage, in conformity with the Treaty, systems for the reuse of packaging that can be reused in an environmentally sound manner. In view of the fact that the directive did not exhaustively harmonised this, the Court went on to discuss the German rules on deposit and return obligations for non-reusable packaging on the basis of the Treaty provisions relating to the free movement of goods.[6]

Once it has been established that a directive (exhaustively) regulates a matter, it can be determined what degree of harmonisation the directive provides for, for example minimum harmonisation or total harmonisation. This is crucial as regards the extent to which Member States may derogate from the measure. It is important to note that exhaustive regulation is not the same thing as total harmonisation. It is easy to confuse this distinction, particularly as the Court on occasion refers to 'exhaustive harmonisation' as 'full harmonisation'[7] and 'total harmonisation' as 'comprehensive',[8] 'complete'[9] or 'exhaustive harmonisation'.[10] There is perhaps some consolation in the thought that it is not the Court's task to write textbooks!

It is not always easy to say what falls within and what falls outside the scope of a directive. The first thing that has to be determined is the personal, territorial and substantive scope of the directive.

A good example can be found in comparing the 'old' Batteries Directive 91/157 with the new Batteries Directive 2006/66.[11] The 'old' directive provided for harmonisation of national laws in respect of levels of mercury contained by batteries and

---

[6]   Case C-309/02 *Radlberger Getränkegesellschaft and S. Spitz* [2004] ECR I-11763.

[7]   Cf. Case C-169/89 *Gourmetterie v.d. Burg* [1990] ECR I-2143.

[8]   Cf. Case C-2/90 *Commission v. Belgium* [1992] ECR I-4431 on Directive 84/631.

[9]   Case C-422/92 *Commission v. Germany* [1992] ECR I-1097, once again on Directive 84/631! Cf. also Case C-318/98 *Fornasar* [2000] ECR I-4785, para. 46.

[10] Case 278/85 *Commission v. Denmark* [1987] ECR 4069.

[11] Directive 91/157, OJ 1991 L 78/38, repealed by Directive 2006/66, OJ 2006 L 266/1.

accumulators, which are placed on the market. However, it applied only to batteries and accumulators expressly listed in Appendix I of the directive. Those which are not on the list were therefore excluded from the scope of application of the directive. Member States were thus entirely free to determine the mercury content of such batteries and accumulators, though of course subject to the provisions of Articles 28 and 30 EC. The substantive scope of new directive however is much broader. Article 2 of it states that the directive 'shall apply to all types of batteries and accumulators, regardless of their shape, volume, weight, material composition or use.'

An example, which shows that it is not always an easy matter in practice to determine the extent to which an environmental directive has regulated a particular subject matter, is provided by the *Improsol* case.[12]

This case concerned the extent to which Dutch plant protection legislation was compatible *inter alia* with Directive 79/117 prohibiting the placing on the market and use of plant-protection products containing certain active substances.[13] Because the substances contained by the product Improsol were not prohibited by the directive, the importer concluded that this implied that Improsol had to be allowed under the directive. The Court held otherwise: 'However, the prohibition imposed by Directive 79/117/EEC of marketing and using plant-protection products containing certain active substances applies only, by virtue of Article 3 thereof, to the substances listed in the annex. Directive 79/117/EEC does not therefore pursue complete harmonization of national rules concerning the marketing and use of plant-protection products.' And went on to discuss the compatibility of the Dutch legislation with Article 30 EC.

A broadly similar case, but then in the waste sector, was the *Balsamo* case.[14]

The Mayor of Balsamo prohibited the supply to consumers of non-biodegradable bags and other containers in which to carry away their purchases. Various manufacturers of plastic bags argued that this decision was in breach of Directive 75/442 on waste. The Court stated: 'It must be borne in mind that the purpose of Directive 75/442 is to harmonize the legislation of the various Member States regarding the disposal of waste in order on the one hand to avoid barriers to intra-Community trade and inequality of conditions of competition resulting from disparities between such provisions and on the other to contribute to the attainment of Community objectives concerning protection of health and the environment. It does not prohibit the sale or use of any product whatsoever, but nor can

---

[12] Case 125/88 *Nijman* [1989] ECR 3533. In the same vein Case 94/83 *Albert Heijn* [1984] ECR 3263 and Joined Cases C-54/94 and C-74/94 *Stanghellini and Cacchiarelli* [1995] ECR I-391.

[13] OJ 1979 L 33/36.

[14] Case 380/87 *Balsamo* [1989] ECR 2491.

it be inferred that it prevents Member States from imposing such prohibitions in order to protect the environment.

There is no basis in the wording of the directive for a different interpretation, and in any case any different interpretation would conflict with its objectives. As is apparent from Article 3, the directive is intended *inter alia* to encourage national measures likely to prevent the production of waste. Limitation or prohibition of the sale or use of products such as non-biodegradable containers is conducive to the attainment of that objective.'

Also interesting in this respect is the *Toolex* case.[15] In that case the Court ruled that Directive 67/548 relating to the classification, packaging and labelling of dangerous substances covers a very clearly defined field, namely the notification, classification, packaging and labelling of dangerous substances. As regards the use of such substances, the classification directive merely requires that their packaging bear safety recommendations designed to inform the general public of the particular care that should be taken when handling the substance in question. Therefore, it does not harmonise the conditions under which dangerous substances may be marketed or used, which are the very matters that fall within the purview of national legislation.

The last case we want to mention in this respect is the *Burstein* case.[16] There the question was raised whether the limit values established by Directive 76/769 relating to restrictions on the marketing and use of certain dangerous substances and preparations were applicable only to PCP, its salts and esters and to preparations produced from those substances, or also to products treated with those substances or preparations. The Court decided that they were not, so that was a matter the Member States were free to regulate.

Apart from the necessity of determining the substantive scope of application of a directive, it is in the second place important to examine its objectives. If European rules do exist, but do not relate to environmental requirements, the directive will not affect the competence of Member States to take additional protective measures. As the Court held in the *Holdijk* case, European law will not in principle prevent a Member State from introducing or maintaining national rules if these are designed to achieve different aims from the European rules.[17] Of course, the opposite may also apply. An environmental directive will not prevent Member States from regulating other, non-environmental, aspects. This is generally clear from the formulation of a so-called 'free movement' or 'market access' clause.[18]

---

[15] Case C-473/98 *Kemikalieninspektionen* v. *Toolex Alpha AB* [2000] ECR I-5681.

[16] Case C-127/97 *Burstein* [1998] ECR I-6005.

[17] Joined Cases 141-143/81 *Holdijk* [1982] ECR 1299.

[18] See, more extensively, this chapter, section 4.

For example, Article 18 of Directive 99/45 provides that 'Member States may not prohibit, restrict or impede the placing on the market of preparations because of their classification, packaging, labelling or safety data sheets if such preparations comply with the provisions laid down in this Directive'.[19] Or take as an example Article 6 of the Batteries Directive 2006/66: 'Member States shall not, *on the grounds dealt with in this Directive*, impede, prohibit, or restrict the placing on the market in their territory of batteries and accumulators that meet the requirements of this Directive.' [emphasis added] These formulations indicate that the legal consequences of harmonisation do not extend beyond the objectives of the directive in question. A clear example in the case law of the Court of Justice can be found in the *Geharo* case.[20] The case concerned criminal proceedings brought before the Dutch Supreme Court against Geharo for having stocked toys with a cadmium content greater than the maximum content permitted under Dutch law (Article 2(1) of the Decree relating to cadmium). This Decree aimed at implementing Directive 76/769 as amended, *inter alia*, by Directive 91/338 relating to restrictions on the marketing and use of certain dangerous substances and preparations.[21] Geharo argued that it complied with the so-called Safety of Toys Directive 88/378 which contains also specific standards concerning cadmium.[22] The Court had a close look at both directives. Although both directives contained rules on cadmium, the objectives of the directives differ. According to the Court, Directive 88/378 seeks to protect the user of a toy against the risks connected with the chemical properties of the product at the time of use, whereas Directive 91/338 is part of a policy which seeks to protect the general population against the dispersion of cadmium into the environment. The Court concluded: 'Having regard to the different content and the different objectives of those standards, the application to toys covered by Directive 88/378 of a limit in the amount of cadmium, such as that laid down by Directive 91/338, is not incompatible with the application to the same toys of the limit in bioavailability laid down by Directive 88/378'. Therefore, Geharo had to comply with the Dutch Decree relating to cadmium.

But even if a directive is intended to achieve environmental objectives, this does not mean that Member States will be prevented from acting at all. It may be that the directive harmonises different aspects of the matter in question from those that are regulated by the national laws.

An example of this is provided by the decision of the UK House of Lords in the *London Lorries* case.[23] The case concerned a London Council byelaw which prohibited lorries from driving through certain London boroughs during the night. The

---

[19] OJ 1999 L 200/1.

[20] Case C-9/04 *Geharo* [2005] ECR I-8525.

[21] OJ 1991 L 186/59.

[22] OJ 1988 L 187/1.

[23] House of Lords 24 July 1991 *Regina v. London Boroughs Transport Committee;* ex parte *Freight Transport Association Ltd. a.o.* [1992] 1 C.M.L.R. 5.

purpose of the byelaw was to reduce the noise nuisance caused by the lorries. The problem was that there were two directives governing the permitted noise levels of lorries. One related to the requirements on the braking systems of lorries,[24] and the other to the maximum permissible sound levels of exhaust systems.[25] Both directives contained a free movement clause, to the effect that if vehicles met the requirements of the directive, Member states were no longer entitled to take restrictive measures: 'No Member State may, on grounds relating to the permissible sound level and the exhaust system, refuse of prohibit the sale, registration, entry into service or use of any vehicle in which the sound level and the exhaust system satisfy the requirements of Annex I.' That one of the aims of the directives was to prevent noise nuisance seems evident. Nevertheless, the House of Lords held that there was no question of infringement of the directives, as they were not intended to regulate local traffic and the consequent noise nuisance. The directives did not therefore prohibit local authorities from taking certain measures to prevent noise nuisance at a local level. The House of Lords' judgment was not uncontroversial at the time, and it has been pointed out that the matter should perhaps have been referred to the Court for a preliminary ruling.[26]

It has already been shown above several times that if a given subject matter falls outside the scope of a directive, the Member States are still competent to take the necessary national measures. It must however be stressed that the sole fact that a particular matter is not specifically addressed by a directive does not imply that it therefore falls outside the directive's scope of application. There might have been what could be called 'implied harmonisation'.

An example of just such a form of implied harmonisation is provided by the *Inter-Huiles* case.[27] This case concerned the extent to which a Member State could employ policy instruments other than those provided for in the directive in question. The validity of French restrictions on the export of waste oils was disputed. The French Government maintained that the disputed legislation satisfied an economic requirement, since only the collection of all waste oils would be sufficient to ensure the profitability of undertakings approved for the disposal of waste oils and, therefore, the achievement of the aims of the directive. However, the Court held: 'That argument cannot be accepted. Articles 13 and 14 of the directive provide that, by way of compensation for the obligations imposed on the undertakings for the implementation of Article 5, Member States may, without placing restrictions on exports, grant to such undertakings "indemnities" financed in accordance with the principle of "polluter pays".'

---

[24] Directive 71/320, the Brakes Directive, OJ 1971 L 202/37, later amended.

[25] Directive 70/157, the Sound Level Directive, OJ 1970 L 42/16, amended many times since then.

[26] Cf. the *London Lorries* case with Commission Decision 98/523, OJ 1998 L 1998 L 233/25. The case concerned Swedish noise-related restrictions affecting access to Karlstadt airport.

[27] Case 172/82 *Inter-Huiles* [1983] ECR 555.

As the directive provided for financial instruments with which the objectives of the Waste Oils Directive[28] could be achieved, the French export prohibitions could not be accepted. Nevertheless, this does not justify the conclusion that application of different instruments from those envisaged by a directive is never possible. This will depend on the objectives, content and system of the directive.

The above shows that it is very important to determine precisely what a directive is intended to harmonise. There can only be harmonisation to the extent a particular subject matter actually does fall within the scope of the directive. When deciding whether or not this is the case, it is important to examine what products are covered by the directive, to what extent the directive is also intended to harmonise environmental objectives, what these environmental objectives are, and what instruments are applied in the directive.

3 Total Harmonisation

3.1 General Remarks

Harmonisation is said to be *full* or *total* when a directive is intended to provide for a more or less uniform European standard in a particular field, from which it is no longer possible to derogate. In principle this kind of directive excludes both more stringent and less stringent national rules. Of course, such a directive may itself provide exhaustively for derogation.

An example where total harmonisation was at issue is the *VAG Sverige AB* case.[29] Swedish legislation required that vehicles meet Swedish exhaust emission requirements before they could be registered. However, Directive 70/156 provides for total harmonisation of the rules on exhaust emissions and noise. The Court ruled that a Member State may refuse to register a vehicle with a valid EC type-approval certificate only if it finds that the vehicle is a serious risk to road safety. In this case the Swedish refusal to register was linked to considerations of protection of the environment. As a result the Court held the Swedish legislation to be in breach of the directive.

Total harmonisation is found above all in those fields of environmental policy where there is a definite relationship with the free movement of goods. In particular, the Council makes use of total harmonisation in legislation to harmonise product standards, as it is the only way to ensure the free movement of the goods in question. This means that total harmonisation is encountered particularly frequently in environmental measures based on Article 95 EC.

---

[28] OJ 1975 L 194/31, later amended.

[29] Case C-329/95 *VAG Sverige AB* [1997] ECR I-2675.

3.2 Derogation Precluded

Total harmonisation precludes any derogation other than that allowed by the directive itself. This applies both to derogation allowing less stringent national requirements and to derogation providing for more stringent national requirements. Directives which are intended to implement total harmonisation can often, but not always, be recognised by the inclusion of a 'free movement clause'. This is a clause which provides that if a given (environmentally harmful) product or substance meets the requirements laid down by the directive, it may not be refused access to the common market.

> See, for example, once again Article 6 of Directive 2006/66 on batteries and accumulators and waste batteries and accumulators:[30] 'Member States shall not, on the grounds dealt with in this Directive, impede, prohibit, or restrict the placing on the market in their territory of batteries and accumulators that meet the requirements of this Directive.'

The justification for such a provision is that directives which harmonise product standards are designed not only to protect the environment, but also to achieve a properly functioning internal market. As long as the national rules on batteries and accumulators have not been harmonised, there is the danger of disparities between the various national systems. A given battery may be allowed in one country, but not in another. However, if – as is the case in Directive 2006/66 – conditions have been laid down under which batteries to which the directive applies may be marketed (thus implementing the directive's environmental objectives), the inclusion of a free movement clause will prevent Member States imposing their own stricter requirements. The *quid pro quo* of such a clause is of course that products that do not meet the requirements of the directive are not placed on the market or are withdrawn from it.[31]

> Another example is provided by the *Ratti* case.[32] In its consideration of Italian requirements in respect of solvents, which differed from those contained in the relevant directive, the Court held: 'The combined effect of Articles 3 to 8 of Directive No 73/173 is that only solvents which "comply with the provisions of this directive and the annex thereto" may be placed on the market and that Member States are not entitled to maintain, parallel with the rules laid down by the said directive for imports, different rules for the domestic market. Thus it is a consequence of the system introduced by Directive No 73/173 that a Member State may not introduce into its national legislation conditions which are more restrictive

---

[30] OJ 2006 L 66/1.

[31] E.g. Article 6(2) of Directive 2006/66: 'Member States shall take the necessary measures to ensure that batteries or accumulators that do not meet the requirements of this Directive are not placed on the market or are withdrawn from it.'

[32] Case 148/78 *Ratti* [1979] ECR 1629.

than those laid down in the directive in question, or which are even more detailed or in any event different, as regards the classification, packaging and labelling of solvents and that this prohibition on the imposition of restrictions not provided for applies both to the direct marketing of the products on the home market and to imported products.'

The judgment of the Court in Case 278/85, dealing with Denmark's failure to fulfil its obligations under one of the directives on dangerous substances, will serve to illustrate the contention that total harmonisation imposes constraints on the freedom of Member States to pursue policies of their own.[33]

The case involved Directive 79/831, the sixth amendment to Directive 67/548, which contained rules for the marketing of 'new' substances as well as rules on 'old' substances, in other words, substances which had been placed on the market before the directive entered into force (on 18 September 1981).[34] The core of the directive was the requirement in Article 6 that notification be given of 'new substances'. Any manufacturer or importer into the EU was required to submit a notification to the competent national authority at the latest 45 days before the substance was placed on the market. This notification had to include, *inter alia*, a technical dossier supplying the information necessary for evaluating the foreseeable risks for man and the environment. As regards 'old' substances, however, the directive required the Commission to draw up an inventory of such substances, on the basis in particular of information provided by the Member States. According to the directive the obligation to notify did not apply to old substances until six months after the publication of the inventory and, six months after publication of the inventory, to substances which appear in that inventory. However, the relevant Danish legislation contained the provision that a chemical substance should be regarded as new if it had not been placed on the market or imported into Denmark as a chemical substance or constituent of a chemical product before 1 October 1980. The Commission complained that, in adopting that provision, the Danish Government departed from the directive by fixing a date prior to 18 September 1981 and by thus imposing an obligation to notify even substances placed on the market before 18 September 1981. Thus the compulsory notification would have applied to a wider group of substances and products than provided for by the directive. In its judgment the Court noted that the directive was designed to attain two objectives: the protection of the population and the environment and the elimination of obstacles to trade in dangerous substances. It went on to point out that the date provided for in the directive (18 September 1981) was meant to be the date from which both objectives, in particular the measures concerning the obligation to notify new substances, were to take effect. It follows, held the Court, that the European legislature had laid down exhaustive rules on this point and that

---

[33] Case 278/85 *Commission v. Denmark* [1987] ECR 4069.

[34] See Chapter 8, section 13.2.

it had not left the Member States any scope to introduce earlier or later dates in their rules adopted to implement the directive.

Total harmonisation is not only employed in the field of environmental *product* standards. For example, Directive 84/631[35] on the transfrontier shipment of hazardous waste contained a complete regulation of the way in which Member States were entitled to intervene in respect of the import and export of dangerous substances. It provided for an extensive system of notification and objections, which meant that national authorities have the option of raising objections and therefore prohibiting a particular transfer of dangerous waste (as opposed to transfers of such waste in general) in order to overcome problems relating to the protection of human health and the environment. The Court regarded this detailed regulation as a comprehensive system, whereby the system did not imply that the Member States had the power to prohibit transfers of waste generally.[36] What was remarkable was that the directive did not contain similar measures in respect of waste that was not regarded as hazardous. It would therefore, in principle, have been quite possible to introduce a general, more global restriction on imports of non-hazardous waste. This seems contradictory, but in fact it is not. Once national laws have been harmonised, there is no need for additional national regulations to protect the environment, as this aim has been achieved at European level, provided at least that the directive is not intended to implement minimum harmonisation. If there has been no harmonisation, Member States will still feel the need to adopt measures to protect the environment until the European institutions have taken legislative action in that respect.

Another example can be found in Directive 94/62 on packaging and packaging waste.[37] Article 6 of the directive requires Member States to attain targets pertaining to the recovery and recycling of packaging waste. No later than five years from the date by which the directive must be implemented in national law, between 50% as a minimum and 65% as a maximum by weight of the packaging waste must be recovered. Within this general target, and with the same time limit, between 25% as a minimum and 45% as a maximum by weight of the totality of packaging materials contained in packaging waste must be recycled with a minimum of 15% by weight for each packaging material. Member States are only

---

[35] Now replaced by Regulation 259/93, OJ 1993 L 30/1, later amended. Cf. the 'new' Regulation 1013/2006 on shipments of waste, OJ 2006 L 190/1. Regulation 1013/2006 has repealed Regulation 259/93 with effect from 12 July 2007.

[36] Case C-2/90 *Commission* v. *Belgium* [1992] ECR I-4431. Cf. also the *Dusseldorp* case where the Court ruled, with respect to Regulation 259/93, that the principles of self-sufficiency and proximity cannot be applied to waste for recovery, Case C-203/96 *Dusseldorp* [1998] ECR I-4075.

[37] OJ 1994 L 365/10.

permitted to go beyond these targets if they meet the conditions and comply with the procedure set out in Article 6(6) of the directive.[38]

4 Minimum Harmonisation

4.1 General Remarks

As far as European environmental law is concerned, minimum harmonisation can be defined as a form of European legislation which leaves Member States competent to adopt more stringent environmental standards than the European ones. It is often used in fields in which differences in national standards affect the functioning of the internal market less than do differences in product standards. This applies, for example, to measures to protect the quality of water and air, flora, fauna, and to measures in respect of waste, protection against radiation, etc. In this sense, European emission standards and quality standards can all be regarded as minimum standards. There is less need for absolute uniformity in these areas. Differences in emission and quality standards do not detract from the free movement of goods. They can however affect conditions of the competitive position of businesses. Some degree of harmonisation is therefore necessary, if only to prevent Member States using flawed environmental legislation as an instrument of industrial policy. It is not strictly necessary to place constraints on the Member States' competence to take more stringent measures, though it cannot be entirely ruled out. Market forces will probably ensure that national legislators do not get too much out of line with those in other Member States, as this would be to the detriment of their own industries. This is another example of the difference between stricter emission standards and quality objectives on the one hand and stricter product standards on the other. As more stringent national product standards are likely above all to affect foreign manufacturers and products, it is not surprising that minimum harmonisation is used much less frequently as a means of regulation in this area.

Environmental directives which implement minimum harmonisation could always be easily recognised by their 'minimum harmonisation clause'. They regularly contained a provision similar to the following: 'Member States may, at any time, fix values more stringent than those laid down in this Directive.'[39] Such provisions were especially frequent in environmental directives setting European quality standards for air and water. Environmental quality standards are standards laid down with legally binding force which prescribe the levels of pollution or nuisance that may not be exceeded in a given environment or part of an environment. Similar provisions are also to be found where emission standards are harmonised: these are standards which set the levels of pollut-

---

[38] This procedure is to a certain extent similar to the Article 95(4) procedure. See section 6 below.

[39] Article 5 of Directive 85/203 on air quality standards for nitrogen dioxide, OJ 1985 L 87/1, later amended.

ants or nuisances not to be exceeded in emissions from fixed installations.[40] Member States may require compliance with emission limit values and time limits for implementation which are more stringent than those set out in the directive itself. Court of Justice case law seems to require that the consequences of such additional requirements are consistent with the objective pursued by the directive.[41] These examples demonstrate that a large part of European law implements a form of minimum harmonisation, whereby minimum standards are adopted which Member States are required at the very least to meet (except where they apply special safeguard clauses). In other words, a minimum level is set in the legislation on environmental protection.

However, even where a directive contains such a minimum harmonisation clause, close attention must be paid to the context within which the directive was adopted. This was demonstrated by the Court of Justice in the *Red Grouse* case.[42]

> In this case the Dutch Government invoked a provision of the Wild Birds Direc-
> tive,[43] which provided that Member States were allowed to adopt stricter measures
> to protect birds than those provided for under the directive (Article 14). The direc-
> tive provided *inter alia* that red grouse could be hunted within the Member State
> in which they occurred (the UK). After interpreting the directive, the Court reached
> the conclusion that only the United Kingdom was competent to adopt stricter
> measures to protect the bird in question, and that other Member States were not:
> 'It follows from the foregoing that Article 14 of the directive does not empower a
> Member State to afford a given species which is neither migratory nor endangered
> stricter protection, by means of a prohibition on importation and marketing, than
> that provided for by the legislation of the Member State on whose territory the
> bird in question occurs, where such legislation is in conformity with the provisions
> of Directive 79/409.'

A good example of minimum harmonisation combined with a form of total harmonisation is provided by Article 16 of Directive 80/778 relating to the qual- ity of water intended for human consumption.[44] Member States may lay down more stringent provisions than those provided for in the directive, but may not prohibit or impede the marketing of foodstuffs on grounds relating to the qual- ity of the water used where the quality of such water meets the requirements of the directive.

---

[40] See, for example, Article 4(3) of Directive 88/609 on the limitation of emissions of certain pollutants into the air from large combustion plants, OJ 1988 L 336/1, later amended.

[41] Cf. Case C-232/97 *Nederhoff* [1999] ECR I-6385, para. 58. See also Case C-6/03 *Deponiezweckverband Eiterköpfe* [2005] ECR I-2753. In section 5 of this chapter we will deal more extensively with Case C-6/03.

[42] Case C-169/89 *Gourmetterie v.d. Burg* [1990] ECR I-2143.

[43] OJ 1979 L 103/1, later amended.

[44] OJ 1980 L 229/11, later amended.

Today, environmental directives are unlikely to contain a minimum harmonisation clause. Indeed, it is not unknown for such a clause to be removed from an 'old' environmental directive when it is amended.[45] This is because the principle that European protective measures lay down a minimum standard which can be enhanced by the Member States has now been incorporated into Article 176 EC.[46]

4.2 Minimum Standards and the Euratom Treaty

The 'basic standards' referred to in Article 30 *et seq.* of the Euratom Treaty must also be regarded as minimum standards. The Court has held thus in Case C-376/90.[47]

In that case the Commission brought an action for a declaration that, by failing to take the steps necessary to implement Article 10(2) of Directive 80/836 on health protection against the dangers of ionizing radiation,[48] Belgium had failed to fulfil its obligations under the directive. The Commission considered that Article 10(2) did not authorize Member States to fix different dose limits from those laid down in that provision, even if they were stricter. The Belgian Government argued that the dose limits laid down in the directive represented the minimum level of protection that Member States were obliged to ensure and that they were free to set stricter limits if they considered it desirable to do so. The Commission relied *inter alia* on Article 2(b) of the Euratom Treaty, which provides that the Community must establish 'uniform safety standards'. This would seem to indicate that Member States were not entitled to set stricter national standards. The Court rejected this argument. The standards laid down in the directive were based on the recommendations of the International Commission on Radiological Protection (ICRP), according to which the dose limits represented the dose levels whose consequences for the health of persons regularly exposed to ionizing radiation were at the limit of what was tolerable and that the choice of dose limits necessarily included assessments which might vary according to the companies concerned. There was no indication in the directive that the European legislature had adopted a different position from that of the ICRP in relation to dose limits, and that it did

---

[45] See for instance Directive 97/11 amending Directive 85/337 on the assessment of the effects of certain public and private projects on the environment, OJ 1997 L 73/5, which deleted the minimum harmonisation clause in Article 13 of Directive 85/337.

[46] See below, section 5. See however Article 9 of Directive 2006/11 (OJ 2006 L 64/52) on pollution caused by certain dangerous substances discharged into the aquatic environment of the Community: 'Where appropriate, one or more Member States may individually or jointly take more stringent measures than those provided for under this Directive.'

[47] Case C-376/90 *Commission v. Belgium* [1992] ECR I-6153.

[48] OJ 1980 L 246/1, later amended. Now replaced by Directive 96/29, OJ 1996 L 159/1. See on this directive Chapter 8, section 16.1.

not leave Member States any discretion to provide for a higher standard of protection than that laid down in the directive.

The conclusion that can be drawn from this judgment in respect of the legal status of the present dose limits contained in the directive must therefore be that this is a case of minimum harmonisation. Member States are thus entitled to set stricter standards than those laid down in the directive.

4.3   Minimum Harmonisation and Article 95 EC

Whenever the European legislature takes a measure under Article 95 EC, for instance laying down environmental product standards, one must assume that such a measure is intended to eliminate obstacles to trade resulting from the existence of divergent national rules in the field directly affecting the establishment and functioning of the internal market. With respect to Directive 76/769 relating to restrictions on the marketing and use of certain dangerous substances and preparations, the Court ruled that it 'thus follows from its legal basis as well as from its recitals that Directive 76/769 aims to eliminate obstacles to trade within the internal market in the substances'.[49] And with respect to the submission, i.e. from the Dutch Government, that this directive merely brings about minimum harmonisation and therefore permits the Member States to lay down additional conditions, the Court answered:

> 'the objective of Directive 76/769 would not be attainable if the Member States were free to widen the obligations provided for therein. The provisions of that directive have exhaustive character and the retention or adoption by the Member States of measures other than those laid down by the directive is incompatible with its objective [...]'.

From this judgment we can learn that minimum harmonisation is not the normal *habitus* of an 'Article 95' directive. Because such a directive is primarily aimed at removing obstacles to trade and the internal market, most of these directives will contain total harmonisation. However, this triggers the question whether environmental measures which are based on Article 95 EC (or on the 'old' Article 100a) can implement minimum harmonisation at all. Or is this *legally* impossible, in view of the functioning of the internal market? According to Advocate General Geelhoed, the objective of the unity and functioning of the common market does not accord with the view that an 'Article 95 directive' only provides for minimum harmonisation.[50]

The Court's view on this issue does not seem crystal clear. Its rulings on the Product Liability Directive are open for different interpretation and there-

---

[49] Case C-281/03 *Cindu Chemicals* [2005] ECR I-8069.

[50] Cf. his Opinion concerning the Product Liability Directive in Case C-52/00 *Commission v. France* and Case C-183/00 *González Sánchez* v. *Medicina Asturiana SA* [2001] ECR I-3827 en I-3901, para. 50.

fore some confusion.[51] This could also explain why the Commission, in its proposal for the Batteries Directive 2006/66, opted for the combined legal basis of Articles 175 and 95 EC.[52] According to the Commission, these two articles of the Treaty set different conditions as regards the right of Member States to maintain or introduce more stringent protective measures. As a consequence, the Commission felt necessary to specify the legal basis for each part of the proposal. Article 95 EC should be the appropriate legal basis to harmonise the laws of the Member States as regards product requirements (like a mercury ban and labelling requirements). This legal basis was felt appropriate by the Commission 'since the disparities between the laws of the Member States on product requirements could create barriers to trade and distort competition in the Community and thus have a direct impact on the establishment and functioning of the internal market.' On the other hand, the Commission found it more appropriate that harmonisation measures to prevent or reduce the generation of spent batteries and accumulators and to prevent or reduce the negative environmental impacts of the metals used in them, are based on Article 175 EC: '[T]hese measures, which aim to provide a high level of environmental protection, should not prevent Member States from adopting more stringent measures on their national territory.' Arguably, the Commission was under the impression that Article 95 EC cannot be used to serve as a legal basis for the minimum harmonisation of environmental product standards. However, it is the authors' opinion that it is not the legal basis as such which determines whether or not minimum harmonisation is being implemented, but the content of the measure in question. In sum, in the event that product standards were harmonised on the basis of Article 95 EC, there is no reason to rule out minimum harmonisation altogether.

It is clear however that when the European legislature harmonises environmental product standards by way of minimum harmonisation, this should be accompanied with a market access clause.[53]

> A good example can be found in Directive 94/62 on packaging and packaging waste.[54] On the one hand Article 11 requires Member States to ensure that the sum of concentration levels of lead, cadmium, mercury and hexavalent chromium present in packaging or packaging components shall not exceed certain levels, the use of 'shall not exceed' indicating minimum harmonisation. On the other hand Article 18 provides that Member States shall not impede the placing on the market of their territory of packaging which satisfies the provisions of this directive, thus precluding the application of more stringent standards to imported products.

---

[51] Case C-52/00 *Commission v. France* and Case C-183/00 *González Sánchez v. Medicina Asturiana SA* [2001] ECR I-3827 and I-3901.

[52] COM (2003) 723, at point 9.

[53] See Case C-376/98 *Germany and EP v. Council* [2000] ECR I-8419.

[54] OJ 1994 L 365/10.

In any case, it is clear from the example of the TiO2 Directive,[55] which was based on Article 100a [now Article 95], that the measures this directive contains to control *emissions* must specifically be seen as a form of minimum harmonisation, whereby Member States are permitted to require stricter standards. One of the recitals in the preamble to the directive deals expressly with this. Minimum harmonisation and Article 95 EC need not therefore be regarded as mutually exclusive.

5   Article 176 EC[56]

The practice of minimum harmonisation as a means of attaining environmental objectives has now been enshrined in Article 176 EC: 'The protective measures adopted pursuant to Article 175 shall not prevent any Member State from maintaining or introducing more stringent protective measures. Such measures must be compatible with this Treaty. They shall be notified to the Commission.'

Although there is no hard empirical data on the use of Article 176 EC by the Member State, the impression is that Member States hardly make any use of their powers.[57] Therefore, the impact of Article 176 EC on national law making should not be overestimated. One of the reasons for this could be that, in view of the express text of the article, it relates only to more stringent national measures adopted pursuant to Article 175 EC. Case law of the Court of Justice seems to require that the consequences of taking more stringent measures are consistent with the objective pursued by the directive.[58] In the *Deponiezweckverband* case the Court ruled that Article 176 EC makes provision for and authorises the minimum requirements laid down by a EC measure to be exceeded 'to the extent that a measure of domestic law pursues the same objectives as' the European measure. We assume that by this the Court means to say not only that when national legislation pursues other objectives than those of the directive, this legislation cannot be considered to be a more far-reaching measure of protection, but also that such legislation is not allowed. If not, this would lead to the absurd consequence that stricter measures that do not pursue the same objectives as the directive, would be allowed, but would not need to be reported to the Commission (because they are not stricter measures in the sense of Article 176 EC).

In any event, Article 176 EC does not confer competence on Member States to adopt *less* stringent protective measures.[59] Nor can Article 176 EC be used to

---

[55] Directive 92/112, OJ 1992 L 409/11.

[56] Cf. Article 193 FEU after the entry into force of the Reform Treaty.

[57] Cf. Pagh (2005).

[58] Cf. Case C-232/97 *Nederhoff* [1999] ECR I-6385, para. 58. Cf. Case C-6/03 *Deponiezweckverband Eiterköpfe* [2005] ECR I-2753, para. 58. Cf. also Krämer (2007) at 127.

[59] To adopt less stringent standards Member States will have to rely on a specific clause in the directive/ regulation. See e.g. Article 18(1) of Batteries Directive 2006/66 (OJ 2006 L 266/1) according to which

adopt protective measures in connection with European environmental legislation which has not been adopted pursuant to Article 175 EC, but pursuant to other provisions of the Treaty like Articles 95, 133 or 37 EC.

What are 'more stringent' measures?

The question is whether it is at all necessary to rely on Article 176 EC (and thus to have to report the more stringent measures on the basis of Article 176 EC to the Commission) if the European measure itself leaves room, implicitly or explicitly, for more stringent national measures. In other words, does 'more stringent protective measures' concern national standards that go beyond what the EC measure allows, or stricter measures than EC law requires from the Member States? The Court clarified the issue in the *Deponiezweckverband* case.[60]

Deponiezweckverband Eiterköpfe concerned the compatibility with European law of German legislation on waste. The Deponiezweckverband is an association of administrative districts, for the purpose of waste disposal, in the region of Koblenz, and operates the central landfill site Eiterköpfe. This association sought a permit from the *Land* Rheinland-Pfalz to fill, after 31 May 2005, two landfill cells site with waste that had been treated by mechanical processes only. The *Land* Rheinland-Pfalz argued that the *Verordnung über die umweltverträgliche Ablagerung von Siedlungsabfällen* (Regulation on the environmentally sound deposit of municipal waste) does not allow this. This regulation was adopted for the purpose of transposing the directive on the landfill of waste[61] into domestic German law. The *Verwaltungsgericht* (Administrative Court) Koblenz, before which the Deponiezweckverband had brought a dispute, had doubts as to whether the national legislation was compatible with Article 5(1) and (2) of the directive. According to Article 5(1) of the directive, the Member States must develop a national strategy to decrease the amount of biodegradable waste which is transferred to the landfill sites. And according to the same provision this strategy must ensure that the amount of waste which is to be transferred to landfill sites is decreased before specific dates and by specific percentages. The German implementing legislation contains more 'stringent' environmental rules than the directive (tighter time-limits; higher percentages). The legal basis of the directive is Article 175 EC, which means that Article 176 EC also applies. Nevertheless, the *Verwaltungsgericht* wished to know whether the directive would preclude the more stringent German implementing legislation. The Court ruled in paras. 31 and 32: 'Under Article 5(1) of the directive, the Member States are to set up national strategies in order to reduce the amount of biodegradable waste going to landfills. Under the same provision, those national strategies must include measures to achieve the targets fixed in Article 5(2) of the directive. The last-mentioned provi-

---

Member States may exempt producers which place very small quantities of batteries or accumulators on the national market, from some requirements of the directive.

[60] Case C-6/03 *Deponiezweckverband Eiterköpfe* [2005] ECR I-2753.

[61] OJ 1999 L 182/1.

sion states that those national strategies must provide that the amount of waste going to landfill should be reduced by certain percentages before certain fixed dates. The wording and broad logic of those provisions make it clearly apparent that they set a minimum reduction to be achieved by the Member States and they do not preclude the adopting by the latter of more stringent measures.

It follows that *Article 176 EC and the Directive* allow the Member States to introduce more stringent protection measures that go beyond the minimum requirements fixed by the Directive [...].' [emphasis added]

The Court thus put an end to an ambiguity concerning the concept 'more stringent protective measures'. Whenever the national rules are stricter than those required by a European measure, Article 176 EC is applicable. National legislation concerning situations falling outside the scope of a European measure is, of course, not to be considered as 'more stringent protective measures'. In our view, the same would apply when the stricter national legislation finds its legal basis in 'Article 176-type' provisions in the directives concerned. Finally, there does not appear to be any reason why this conclusion would not apply to those cases where the stricter national measure is not legally based on *explicit* provisions in the Treaty or secondary law, but where the power to take more stringent measures follows *implicitly* from secondary law; i.e. directives for which it must be concluded from the wording – with terms such as 'at least', 'maximum', 'at most' – that they aim at minimum harmonisation.

More stringent protective measures must be compatible with the Treaty

More stringent protective measures must be compatible with the Treaty. This means in particular that the requirements of the free movement of goods[62], the rules on competition and the provisions on taxation must be observed in national environmental rules.[63] Article 176 EC does indicate that Member States may still have some freedom to pursue national policies after the adoption of European measures, of course, under the same rules as if there had been no harmonisation, but Article 176 EC most definitely does not give Member States a licence to act in contravention of the provisions of Articles 28-30 EC, or to fail to meet their commitments to the EU in other respects, for instance secondary legislation.

A good example of this can be found in the *Dusseldorp* case.[64] The case concerned the question whether the principles of self-sufficiency and proximity could be applied to shipments of waste for recovery, given that Regulation 259/93 only provided for this in respect of waste for disposal. After noting that Regulation

---

[62] Case C-389/96 *Aher-Waggon GmbH* [1998] ECR I-4473, provides an example where the Court tested more stringent German legislation to combat disturbances from air-traffic noise for compatibility with Article 28 EC.

[63] And, arguably, the rules of the WTO; Cf. Scott (2000) at 40-41.

[64] Case C-203/96 *Dusseldorp* [1998] ECR I-4075.

259/93 was based on Article 130t EC, the precursor of Article 176, the Court observed: 'It is therefore necessary to consider whether, in accordance with that provision, measures such as those adopted in the Long-term Plan for the application of the principles of self-sufficiency and proximity to waste for recovery are compatible with Article 34 of the Treaty [now Article 29, authors].'

After ruling that the Dutch measures were not thus compatible, the Court continued:

'It must therefore be concluded that the object and effect of application of the principles of self-sufficiency and proximity to waste for recovery, such as oil filters, is to restrict exports of that waste and is not justified, in circumstances such as those in the present case, by an imperative requirement relating to protection of the environment or the desire to protect the health and life of humans in accordance with Article 36 [now Article 30, authors] of the Treaty. A Member State cannot therefore rely on Article 130t [now Article 176, authors] of the Treaty in order to apply the principles of self-sufficiency and proximity to such waste.'

More stringent measures and the proportionality principle

When Member States fulfil *obligations* laid down in minimum directives, there is no doubt that they are obliged to take account of the proportionality principle when doing so – this is evident from the case law of the Court.[65] But, are they also obliged to respect the principle of proportionality when they make use of their *competence* to take stricter national measures?

Although the proportionality principle is enshrined in Article 5(3) of the EC Treaty, the Court made clear in the *Deponiezweckverband* case that the more stringent national legislation adopted does not have to be reviewed in the light of the EU principle of proportionality.[66] The paragraphs 61-64 relating to this are quoted here:

'It is clear from the broad logic of Article 176 EC that, in adopting stricter measures, Member States still exercise powers governed by Community law, given that such measures must in any case be compatible with the Treaty. Nevertheless, it falls to the Member States to define the extent of the protection to be achieved.

In that context, in so far as it is a matter of ensuring that the minimum requirements laid down by the Directive are enforced, the Community principle of proportionality demands that measures of domestic law should be appropriate and necessary in relation to the objectives pursued.

---

[65] Case C-293/97 *Standley* [1999] ECR I-2603.

[66] Case C-6/03 *Deponiezweckverband Eiterköpfe* [2005] ECR I-2753. See also Case C-2/97 *Società italiana petroli* [1998] ECR I-8597, which also demonstrates that the principle of proportionality does not play a role in the review of more stringent national measures if such measures do not form an obstacle to free movement.

In contrast, and inasmuch as other provisions of the Treaty are not involved, that principle is no longer applicable so far as concerns more stringent protective measures of domestic law adopted by virtue of Article 176 EC and going beyond the minimum requirements laid down by the Directive.

As a result, the reply to the second question has to be that the Community-law principle of proportionality is not applicable so far as concerns more stringent protective measures of domestic law adopted by virtue of Article 176 EC and going beyond the minimum requirements laid down by a Community directive in the sphere of the environment, inasmuch as other provisions of the Treaty are not involved.'

This conclusion – more stringent national legislation adopted on the basis of Article 176 EC does not have to be reviewed in the light of the principle of proportionality – is not only relevant for the interpretation of Article 176 EC, but seems to us also to be significant for all other cases of minimum harmonisation.

Article 176 EC and total harmonisation?

These observations lead us to a possible third restriction on the use of Article 176 EC. Can the article be invoked by a Member State to justify its taking more stringent protective measures, even where the matter in question is totally harmonised by European legislation? In other words, can the content of secondary European environmental legislation as such prevent Member States invoking Article 176 EC?[67]

Let us present the following example to illustrate the importance and practical relevance of this question. According to Article 16(3) of Directive 2003/87 establishing a scheme for greenhouse gas emission allowance trading within the EU 'Member States shall ensure that any operator who does not surrender sufficient allowances by 30 April of each year to cover its emissions during the preceding year shall be held liable for the payment of an excess emissions penalty. The excess emissions penalty shall be €100 for each ton of carbon dioxide equivalent emitted by that installation for which the operator has not surrendered allowances'.[68] The penalty is fixed by the directive on €100 for each ton of carbon dioxide emitted. Would the Member States, in view of their powers under Article 176 EC, be allowed to apply a penalty of say €150 for each ton emitted?

Legal writers differ on the subject. The prevailing view is that Member States can *always* adopt more stringent measures following harmonisation under Article 175 EC.[69] A strong argument in favour of this view is that the Treaty at all times takes precedence over secondary legislation. If the Treaty states that stricter measures are allowed, this competence cannot then be restricted by

---

[67] Cf. Krämer (2007) at 127 *et seq.*

[68] OJ 2003 L 275/32.

[69] Cf. Winter (1998), Winter (2000) 666.

a legal instrument of a lower order. Another strong argument is that Article 176 EC has no significance unless that interpretation is allowed.[70] After all, only where there is total harmonisation does the question of more stringent measures arise. A third argument is that environmental directives based on Article 175 EC are aimed at achieving the environmental objectives of Article 174(1) and based on the environmental principles of Article 174(2). If an environmental directive were to preclude Member States from taking more stringent measures, this would not be covered by those objectives and principles. In other words, if the Council were indeed to limit the Member States power to derogate from environmental standards, the only legal basis for this could be Article 95 EC. Environmental directives based on Article 175 EC necessarily leave Member States the option of applying stricter standards.

Another view, also taken by the present authors, is the following. If a measure based on Article 175 EC expressly provides that Member States shall not adopt certain protective measures, a Member State cannot then invoke Article 176 EC to justify adopting such a measure after all. This argument is based on the fact that Article 176 EC must be considered a codification of legislative practice before the Single European Act. As stated above, minimum harmonisation clauses were frequently included in directives on the environment prior to the entry into force of the Single European Act. On the other hand, total harmonisation was possible then, under the 'old' Articles 100 and 235 (now Articles 94 and 308). The inclusion of Article 176 EC by the Single European Act was designed solely to give the practice of using minimum harmonisation clauses a basis in the Treaty, without thereby implicitly making total harmonisation impossible. This view implies that the inclusion of Article 176 in the Treaty was not really intended to have legal consequences. According to this interpretation, Article 176 EC merely expresses the principle that, in general, decision-making under Article 175 EC takes the shape of minimum harmonisation, but does not limit the Council's power, by way of 'self-binding', of setting total harmonising standards. In other words it is up to the Council to decide to what extent Member States are allowed to adopt more stringent standards than those set in a directive.

Another argument against the use of Article 176 EC to derogate from provisions in environmental directives and regulations providing for total harmonisation is the following. If this were not the case then, where a directive explicitly limited the Member States' power to adopt more stringent measures, Article 176 EC would give a Member State the power unilaterally and without any control *ex ante* from the Commission to disregard standards set by the Council. This seems strange, particularly in view of the procedure set out in paragraphs 4 to 6 of Article 95. In *Dusseldorp* the Court was asked to give its opinion on this issue. The parties were totally divided on the point, as is clear from the following quote from the judgment:

---

[70] Cf. Winter (1998), Winter (2000) 666.

'According to Dusseldorp and the Commission, the Regulation brought about full harmonisation of the rules on shipments of waste between Member States, so that in principle the latter can object to such shipments only on the basis of that Regulation. Furthermore, Article 130t [now Article 176, authors] of the Treaty permits Member States to adopt rules only if they are compatible with, *inter alia*, Article 30 [now Article 28, authors] *et seq.* of the Treaty. They maintain that the Long-term Plan contains measures having equivalent effect to quantitative restrictions on export prohibited by Article 34 [now Article 29, authors] of the Treaty, which are not justified either by imperative requirements relating to the protection of the environment or under Article 36 [now Article 30, authors] of the EC Treaty.

According to the Netherlands Government, it can be concluded from the wording and the general scheme of the Regulation and from Article 130t [now Article 176, authors] of the Treaty that the measures adopted pursuant to Article 130s [now Article 175, authors] constitute minimum harmonisation. In those circumstances, there is nothing to prevent Member States from seeking to achieve a higher level of protection on the basis of Article 130t [now Article 176, authors]. Furthermore, the Plan is not contrary to the Treaty and, in particular, does not contain any prohibition on export.

In the alternative, the Netherlands Government submits that, if the Long-term Plan does contain a prohibition on export for the purposes of Article 34 [now Article 29, authors], that prohibition is justified under Article 36 [now Article 30, authors] of the Treaty by the pursuit of the best method of disposal of waste and by the need for continuity of disposal, which are intended to protect the health and life of humans.'

The Court expressly did not address the question of whether Article 176 EC could be relied on in the event of total harmonisation. Indeed, in his Opinion, Advocate General Jacobs advised the Court not to. In his view this was unnecessary in this case as the policy rules of the Netherlands Government would not withstand the test of Articles 29 and 30 EC anyway. The fact that the Court proceeded to examine the compatibility of the measures with Articles 29 and 30 EC without considering whether it was possible to apply Article 176 EC suggests that the Court did not, *a priori*, regard this as impossible.[71] On the other hand, it could also be argued that the Court did not yet want to rule on the matter in this case.

In a judgment rendered after *Dusseldorp,* the Court seems to have settled this doctrinal dispute. In the *Fornasar* case the Court, referring to Article 176 EC, stated in very broad terms that 'it must be observed that the European rules do not seek to effect complete harmonisation in the area of the environment'.[72] And as a consequence the Court ruled that the Hazardous Waste Directive 91/689 does not prevent the Member States from classifying as hazardous waste other

---

[71] Winter (2000) 666, who argues that the Court in *Dusseldorp* has implicitly accepted the use of Article 176 EC in the context of total harmonisation.

[72] Case C-318/98 *Fornasar* [2000] ECR I-4785, para. 46.

than that featuring on the list of hazardous waste laid down by Decision 94/904 (the so called Hazardous Waste Liste), and thus from adopting more stringent protective measures in order to prohibit the abandonment, dumping or uncontrolled disposal of such waste.[73]

However, the discussion can be re-opened again in view of the judgment in *Deponiezweckverband*. As appears from paragraph 61 of *Deponiezweckverband*, that when the Member States take more stringent environmental measures, they are exercising a competence which 'is governed' by EC law. This seems not unimportant. After all, if Article 176 EC is considered to contain an obligation for the European legislature to adopt minimum rules, thus, would they not have the competence to restrict the Member States in adopting or maintaining stricter environmental rules? How would this be tenable in light of the Court's considerations quoted above: how can the competence of the Member States to take more stringent environmental measures be 'governed' by European law, if the European legislature is not granted such competences?

Article 176 EC and local and regional authorities

A problem of an entirely different order is posed by the possible application of Article 176 EC in the relations between the central government of a Member State and its local or regional authorities. Can such a local authority, relying on Article 176 EC, apply stricter protective measures than allowed by the central government, thus ignoring any restrictions imposed by that government? The answer to this question will depend on the legal relations Article 176 EC was intended to regulate. It seems clear that Article 176 EC was drafted to allow Member States to take stricter protective measures in their relations with the EU. It was designed to regulate relations between the Member States and the EU, and not those between central government and local government. Local authorities should not therefore be permitted to invoke Article 176 EC in support of stricter protective measures than those laid down by a central government. It goes without saying that a local or regional authority may invoke Article 176 EC in respect of the EU where what is involved is the application of environmental law within their competence.[74] As long as the national laws allow this, there is no problem at all.

Notification under Article 176 EC

The final point that must be discussed in connection with Article 176 EC concerns the requirement that Member States must notify the Commission of stricter protective measures. Unlike notification in the context of Article 95 EC, there is no standstill requirement here and non-notification will not preclude application of national rules in the national legal order.[75] Questions as

---

[73] See also Chapter 8, section 15.2.

[74] The same applies *mutatis mutandis* with respect to the derogation procedure of Article 95(4-6) EC, cf. Case T-366/03 and T-235/04 *Land Oberösterreich und Österreich v. Commission* [2005] ECR-II-4005.

[75] Cf. Scott (2000) at 39.

to whether or not national rules can be applied before notification and whether or not the obligations are directly effective are therefore not at issue. On the other hand, the Commission will be able to institute proceedings for violation of the Treaty. Finally, if Article 176 EC is interpreted literally, the requirement to notify the Commission applies not only to stricter measures adopted *after* a directive has come into force, but also to *existing* provisions laying down stricter standards.

6   Derogation ex Article 95 EC[76]

Paragraphs 4 and 5 of Article 95 EC read as follows: '4. If, after the adoption by the Council or by the Commission of a harmonisation measure, a Member State deems it necessary to maintain national provisions on grounds of major needs referred to in Article 30, or relating to the protection of the environment or the working environment, it shall notify the Commission of these provisions as well as the grounds for maintaining them. 5. Moreover, without prejudice to paragraph 4, if, after the adoption by the Council or by the Commission of a harmonisation measure, a Member State deems it necessary to introduce national provisions based on new scientific evidence relating to the protection of the environment or the working environment on grounds of a problem specific to that Member State arising after the adoption of the harmonisation measure, it shall notify the Commission of the envisaged provisions as well as the grounds for introducing them'.

The Court of Justice has held that the procedure of Article 95 EC allows a Member State to *maintain*[77] (para. 4) or to *introduce* (para. 5) national rules derogating from a harmonisation measure taken in the framework of the internal market.[78] Article 95(4-5) EC provides an exception to the principles of uniform application of European law and the unity of the market and therefore must be strictly interpreted. It is for the Member State which invokes Article 95(4-5) EC to prove that the conditions for application of those provisions have been met.[79]

However, it hardly seems tenable that Article 95(4-5) EC must be invoked in all cases where a Member State desires to take more stringent protective measures. Article 95(4-5) EC aims at approving or rejecting national measures

---

[76]   The Reform Treaty will reverse the order of Articles 94 and 95 EC. Article 94 EC shall be renumbered Article 115 FEU and Article 95 EC shall be renumbered Article 114 FEU.

[77]   In general national provisions which, at the moment of adoption of the measure, exist only in draft will have to be examined under Article 95(5) EC. See for exception to that rule, Commission Decision 2002/884, OJ 2002 L 308/30.

[78]   Case C-41/93 *France* v. *Commission* [1994] ECR I-1829.

[79]   Case T-366/03 *Land Oberösterreich and Austria* v. *Commission* [2005] ECR II-4005, para. 63 and Case C-3/00 *Denmark* v. *Commission* [2003] ECR I-2643, para. 84. Cf. also Case T-182/06 *Netherlands* v. *Commission*, judgment of 27 June 2007, n.y.r. in the ECR, para. 50.

that *derogate* from a harmonisation measure. Where the harmonisation measure itself leaves room for such measures, it is not necessary to invoke these paragraphs, because in that case there is no *derogation* from the European measures. It appears from the case law of the Court of Justice that when more stringent national measures are still within the range laid down by the internal market directives, they are permitted without there being the necessity to use the procedures provided for in the fourth and fifth paragraphs of Article 95 EC.[80] National provisions that are falling outside the scope of a harmonisation directive will not be assessed under this procedure either.[81] Notification of such national measures should be declared inadmissable by the Commission.[82]

In view of the judgment of *Deponiezweckverband*, discussed above, the somewhat paradoxical result is that more stringent measures based on Article 176 EC must be reported to the Commission, but more stringent measures that fall within a European measure based on Article 95 EC do not have to be reported.

The two paragraphs of Article 95, paragraph 4 in respect of *maintaining* existing national provisions and paragraph 5 in respect of *introducing* new provisions, make it clear that it is permitted to introduce new and to maintain existing national legislation which derogates from European harmonisation measures. Article 95(4-5) must be interpreted in the sense that any Member State, irrespective of how it voted in Council, can in principle be allowed to rely on the derogation procedure.[83]

More stringent or less stringent national standards?

As has been demonstrated above, Article 176 EC allows Member States to take more stringent protective measures. In view of the wording 'more stringent protective measures', we ruled out that Member States are able to invoke the article to avoid meeting European standards implying a higher degree of protection than they regard as necessary. The article permits a more stringent national environment policy, not one that is less stringent. However, Article 95(4-5) EC does not contain this phrase. Does this therefore imply that a Member State may invoke Article 95(4-5) EC if it believes that the level of harmonisation sought by the Council is too high? There are two arguments against this view.

In the first place, Article 95(3) EC provides that the Commission, in its proposals concerning environmental protection and pertaining to the establishing and functioning of the internal market, will take as a base a high level

---

[80] Case C-11/92 *Gallaher*, para. 43.

[81] Cf. Case T-234/04 *Netherlands* v. *Commission*, judgment of 8 November 2007, n.y.r.

[82] E.g. Commission Decision 2002/65 OJ L 25/47.

[83] Under the old version of the Treaty, it was not altogether clear whether a Member State, wanting to rely on Article 100a(4), had to vote against (or at least not vote in favour of) a directive or regulation it wanted to derogate from. The text suggested this, because it referred to the Council having voted by a qualified majority. As a result, Member States were confronted with a dilemma: voting against a measure could mean that no measure would be adopted at all; voting in favour would mean losing the possibility of relying on Article 100a(4) in the future.

of protection. Allowing Member States to derogate from this high level would contravene the aim of the article. In the second place, the text of Article 95(4-5) EC does not contain anything to support this, either. It would be hard to imagine how a less stringent national provision could be 'necessary' for the protection of the environment. On the other hand, it is not inconceivable that a Member State might invoke one of the *other* exceptions referred to in Article 95 EC and so fails to fulfil an obligation in an environmental directive. In short, Article 95(4-5) EC can only be applied to justify national measures which aim to achieve a greater degree of protection than does a harmonisation measure which has been adopted by the Council. The only, somewhat theoretical, exception to this rule might be where application of a less stringent environmental standard could be offset by improvements in other sectors of the environment. The following might serve as an example. Suppose that a directive imposes emission limit values for the discharge of substances in air or water. Suppose also that certain discharges could be avoided altogether by means of a new production process. This would, however, entail minor infringements of the emission limit values laid down by the directive. If it were assumed, for the purpose of the example, that these minor infringements were more than offset in environmental terms by the other benefits, a derogation based on Article 95(4-5) EC might be possible.

Introducing national provisions

Although the *introduction* of legislation is indeed covered by Article 95(5) EC, the cumulative[84] conditions under which this is possible are not altogether clear. First of all, paragraph 5 requires that Member States must prove that there is 'new scientific evidence' justifying their behaviour. *New* evidence requires that the scientific evidence on which the request is based was not available at the time of adoption of the directive in question.[85] However, it is not quite clear whether 'new' must be understood as evidence produced and/or published after the adoption of the European measure only, or that it also includes 'older' evidence but which has not been taken into account by the European institutions during the decision-making procedure.

> In a case concerning emissions of particulate matter by diesel powered vehicles, the Dutch Government produced recent scientific studies to show that susceptible population groups are subject to higher health risks associated with particulate matter.[86] Although the Commission noted that the environmental and health effects related to particulate matter concentrations were already known to a certain extent before the adoption of Directive 98/69, it did accept the studies as *new* evidence. Since the adoption of the directive, a large number of new epidemiological studies on many aspects of exposure and health effects of particulate

---

[84] Case C-512/99 *Germany* v. *Commission* [2003] ECR I-845 (*German man-made mineral fibres*), para. 81.

[85] Case C-3/00 *Denmark* v. *Commission* [2003] ECR I-2643, para. 56 *et seq.*

[86] Commission Decision 2006/372, OJ 2006 L 142/16.

matter have been completed which led the World Health Organisation to produce updates of its air quality guidelines.

Watertight proof should not be necessary, as this clause must be interpreted in the light of the precautionary principle.[87] However, a mere policy change would not seem sufficient.[88] Secondly, paragraph 5 requires that this evidence relate to the protection of the environment or the working environment. The 'public policy' grounds of Article 30 EC are omitted. This clearly restricts the Member States options to derogate from European standards in the area of chemicals, dangerous substances, biocides and so on. This of course seems odd, particularly given that the 'public policy' grounds can be used for maintaining existing national standards. Introducing new national standards is therefore more difficult than maintaining existing ones. The reason for this has been explained by the Court in the *German Man-made Mineral Fibres* case:[89]

'The difference between the two cases provided for in Article 95 EC is that, in the first, the national provisions predated the harmonisation measure. They were therefore known to the Community legislature but it could not or did not seek to be guided by them for the purpose of harmonisation. It was therefore considered acceptable for the Member State to request that its own rules remain in force. To that end, the EC Treaty requires that such national provisions must be justified on grounds of the major needs referred to in Article 30 EC or relating to the protection of the environment or the working environment. By contrast, in the second case, the adoption of new national legislation is more likely to jeopardize harmonisation. The Community institutions could not, by definition, have taken account of the national text when drawing up the harmonisation measure. In that case, the requirements referred to in Article 30 EC are not taken into account and only grounds relating to protection of the environment or the working environment are accepted, on condition that the Member State provides new scientific evidence and that the need to introduce new national provisions results from a problem specific to the Member State concerned arising after the adoption of the harmonisation measure.'

We are not completely convinced by this line of reasoning, particularly not by looking at it from a non-discrimination point of view. This imbalance in the Treaty, and sanctioned by the Court, could result in a certain national measure being allowed in one Member State (as existing national legislation covered by

---

[87] See point 104 of Decision 1999/832, OJ 1999 L 329/25 (*Dutch creosote*). See on the precautionary principle also Chapter 1, section 3.1.

[88] The precautionary principle does not imply that either; Cf. Case C-3/00 *Denmark* v. *Commission* [2003] ECR I-2643, para. 103: 'a Member State cannot unilaterally invoke the precautionary principle in order to maintain derogating national provisions. In an area where Member State legislation has been harmonised, it is for the Community legislature to apply the precautionary principle.'

[89] Case C-512/99 *Germany* v. *Commission* [2003] ECR I-845 (*German man-made mineral fibres*), para. 41.

an Article 30 EC ground) but not in another (because it was being introduced there). However, this problem can be solved, to a certain extent, if we either interpret 'the protection of the environment' to include 'the protection of health and life of humans, animals or plants' mentioned in Article 30 EC[90] or interpret it in light of the more broadly formulated objectives of Article 174 EC. 'Environment' in Article 174 EC does include the protection of human health. It remains to be seen if the Court is willing to embark on this line of reasoning.

A problem specific to that Member State and Article 95(5) EC
Under Article 95(5) EC, the Member State must show that the new national measures are necessary to tackle a problem that is specific to that Member State, for instance, because of its high population density, highly concentrated infrastructure, special geological, metrological or geomorfological circumstances, etc. In other words, there have to be circumstances specific to that Member State justifying the more stringent environmental measures. This means that a simple statement: 'we want stricter environmental legislation', would not be sufficient. The *Land Oberösterreich* case made this quite clear.[91]

> The case concerned a notification under Article 95(5) EC of a draft law of the *Land Oberösterreich* (Province of Upper Austria in Austria) banning genetic engineering altogether. The decision of the Commission rejecting Austria's request for derogation was challenged at the Court of First Instance under Article 230 EC. The Court upheld the Commission's decision in view of Austria's failure to establish that the territory of the *Land Oberösterreich* contained 'unusual or unique ecosystems that required separate risk assessments from those conducted for Austria as a whole or in other similar areas of Europe.' Consequently, the Court held that the arguments by which the applicants have disputed the findings made by the Commission on the condition relating to the existence of a problem specific to the notifying Member State had to be rejected.

In the *Dutch Diesel Engine* case, the Court of First instance further clarified this requirement.[92] It argued that it is not possible to rely on Article 95(3) 'in order to deal with a general environmental danger in the Community':

> 'Any problem which arises in terms which are on the whole comparable throughout the Member States and which lends itself, therefore, to harmonised solutions at Community level is general in nature and is, consequently, not specific within the meaning of Article 95(5) EC.'

---

[90] This does not however seem very logical. Article 95(4) uses the term 'environment' in addition to the grounds mentioned in Article 30 EC. This shows that the two concepts are – at least in the context of Article 95 EC – not identical.

[91] Case T-366/03 and T-235/04 *Land Oberösterreich und Österreich* v. *Commission* [2005] ECR II-4005; Judgment upheld by the ECJ on 13 September 2007 in Case C-439/05P and C-454/05P, n.y.r. in the ECR.

[92] Case T-182/06 *Netherlands* v. *Commission*, judgment of 27 June 2007, n.y.r. in the ECR.

[...]

'It is therefore necessary, in order correctly to interpret Article 95(5) EC, to envisage the requirement of national specificity of a problem essentially from the angle of the aptness or inaptness of the harmonisation of the applicable Community rules to confront adequately the difficulties encountered locally, since the established inaptness of those rules justifies the introduction of national measures.'

In other words, the justification for Member State action lies in the fact that, due to the local nature of the problem, a solution at European level is unsuitable to resolve the problem established.

However, this requirement does not necessarily mean that a Member State would be precluded from taking more stringent measures simply because the same problem occurred elsewhere also. In the *Dutch Diesel Engine* case, the Dutch Government complained that the Commission made the grant of the derogation requested subject to the requirement that the air quality problem relied upon in support of its request affects the Netherlands exclusively. After stating, as a matter of principle, 'for a problem to be specific to a Member State within the meaning of the relevant provision, it is not necessary that it is the result of an environmental danger within that State alone', the CFI found that the Commission did not apply such an exclusivity test and rejected the Netherlands government as lacking any factual basis.[93] Indeed, specific does not mean exclusive.

A problem specific to that Member State and Article 95(4) EC

This criterion cannot be found, at least not explicitly, in the text regarding existing national legislation and this seems to imply another imbalance. However, there is a point in saying that this condition must be met with respect to Article 95(4) EC as well. When national environmental legislation has been harmonised, the presumption must be that the level of protection resulting from harmonisation is adequate.[94] If Member States want to derogate from a directive, either by introducing new legislation or by maintaining existing stricter standards, they have to show that this is justified on grounds specific to that Member State.[95]

However, in the *Danish Foodstuffs* case, the Court decided 'that neither the wording of Article 95(4) EC nor the broad logic of that article as a whole entails a requirement that the applicant Member State prove that maintaining the national provisions which it notifies to the Commission is justified by a problem specific to that Member State.'[96] Exit, the 'specific ground' criterion one might

---

[93] Case T-182/06 *Netherlands v. Commission*, judgment of 27 June 2007, n.y.r. in the ECR, paras. 65 and 72 in particular.

[94] The famous *Inter-Huiles* case seems to point in the same direction. Case 172/82 *Inter-Huiles* [1983] ECR 555.

[95] Cf. Case C-389/96 *Aher-Waggon GmbH* [1998] ECR I-4473.

[96] Case C-3/00 *Denmark v. Commission* [2003] ECR I-2643, para. 59. Analogous considerations apply to the requirement for new scientific evidence, para. 62 of the judgment.

presume? Wrong, as the Court in the next paragraph of the same judgment acknowledges, 'when a problem specific to the applicant Member State in fact exists, that circumstance can be *highly relevant* in guiding the Commission as to whether to approve or reject the notified national provisions. It is a factor which, in the present case, the Commission should have taken into account when it adopted its decision.' [emphasis added] In other words, Article 95(4) EC does not make approval of the Commission conditional of the existence of a problem specific to that Member State, but it is 'highly relevant'. And because the Commission considered the possible existence of a situation specific to Denmark merely as a useful element in assessing what decision to adopt and not as a condition of approval the decision of the Commission was upheld. With all respect to the Court of Justice, but it looks as if the Court is playing with words in particular if we have look at the decision of the Commission itself.[97] At point 32 of the decision we read that '[I]n the light of the information supplied by Denmark, the Commission also examined whether sulphites constituted a particular health problem for the Danish population as compared with the populations of the other Member States.' This was followed by: 'Consequently, the information available to the Commission has not made it possible to conclude that the Danish population is in a specific situation compared with the populations of other Member States, notably its immediate neighbours, as regards this question of allergies related to sulphites' and concluded 'that the Danish measures, though based on public health considerations, are still not justified by the need to protect public health.' In other words, the Commission was looking for specific circumstances in Denmark, could not find them and concluded that the derogating measures could not be justified for reasons of public health protection. So it may be the case that *de jure* the 'specific ground' criterion is not being applied with respect to Article 95(4) EC; the Commission does apply this criterion *de facto*[98] and the Court has accepted this.

The role of the Commission under Article 95(6) EC
        Article 95(6) EC reads as follows: 'The Commission shall, within six months of the notifications as referred to in paragraphs 4 and 5, approve or reject[99]

---

[97] OJ 1999 L 329/1.

[98] See also the Commission Decision approving stricter Dutch legislation on creosote in the light of the specific geographic situation of the Netherlands. Decision 1999/832, OJ 1999 L 329/25 (*Dutch creosote*). Cf. also one of the more recent Dutch creosote cases: Commission Decision 2002/884, OJ 2002 L 308/30, point 66 in particular. Similar observations can be made with respect to submitting scientific evidence. Although only required under Article 95(5) EC, a Member State is well advised to submit relevant and convincing scientific evidence with its notification. Otherwise, Member State will run the risk of not convincing the Commission of the necessity of the derogating measures. Cf. for instance Commission Decision 2003/829 (*German azodyes*). OJ 2003 L 311/46, point 47 in particular.

[99] Practice shows that the Commission can approve a notification with conditions, for instance a temporeral one in the Austrian cadmium decision; Decision 2002/366, OJ 2002 L 132/65. Imposing conditions can even be necessary in order to avoid a conflict with the proportionality principle.

the national provisions involved after having verified whether or not they are a means of arbitrary discrimination or a disguised restriction on trade between Member States and whether or not they shall constitute an obstacle to the functioning of the internal market. In the absence of a decision by the Commission within this period, the national provisions referred to in paragraphs 4 and 5 shall be deemed to have been approved. When justified by the complexity of the matter and in the absence of danger for human health, the Commission may notify the Member State concerned that the period referred to in this paragraph may be extended for a further period of up to six months.' Given the procedural framework, the Commission normally has to limit itself to examining the relevance of the elements, which are submitted by the requesting Member State, without having itself to seek possible reasons or justifications. The responsibility of proving that the national measures are justified lies with the Member State making the request.[100]

Two further issues have to be discussed in this context. The first concerns the grounds the Commission must take into account in its assessment. The second concerns the legal consequences of notification.

Article 95(6) EC states the conditions which must be met before the Commission is allowed to approve national derogating measures, In addition to the familiar[101] conditions of 'no arbitrary discrimination' and 'no disguised restriction to trade', another condition is that there should be 'no obstacle to the functioning of the internal market'. Such an the assessment is a matter for the Commission, and the Court will not, in an application for annulment, substitute its assessment for that of the Commission.[102]

'No arbitrary discrimination' is interpreted by the Commission as meaning that no different treatment should be give to similar situations, nor similar treatment to different situations.[103] According to the Commission the 'no disguised restriction to trade' provision is intended to prevent the restrictions based on the criteria of paragraph 4 being applied for inappropriate reasons, and in reality constituting economic measures introduced to impede the import of products from other Member States in order to protect indirectly national production.[104] In other words: is there a real and genuine concern for the protection of human health and the environment or not?

According to the Commission the condition 'no obstacle to the functioning of the internal market' cannot be interpreted in such a way that it prohibits the approval of any national measure likely to affect the establishment of the

---

[100] Case T-366/03 *Land Oberösterreich and Austria v. Commission* [2005] ECR II-4005, para. 63 and Case C-3/00 *Denmark v. Commission* [2003] ECR I-2643, para. 84. Cf. also Case T-182/06 *Netherlands v. Commission*, judgment of 27 June 2007, n.y.r. in the ECR, para. 50.

[101] See Article 30 EC.

[102] Case C-3/00 *Denmark v. Commission* [2003] ECR I-2643, para. 125.

[103] Decision 1999/832, OJ 1999 L 329/25 (*Dutch creosote*).

[104] Decision 1999/832, OJ 1999 L 329/25 and Decision 2002/59, OJ 2002 L 23/37 (*Dutch creosote II*). See also Chapter 6, section 6.

internal market.[105] In fact, any national measure derogating from a harmonisation measure aiming at the establishment and operation of the internal market, constitutes in substance a measure that is likely to affect the internal market. This of course raises the interesting question of what the condition does mean? The first series of Commission decisions applying this clause give the impression that the Commission interprets it as a special application of the proportionality principle. In the *Dutch Creosote* case the Commission stated that the concept of obstacle to the functioning of the internal market 'has to be understood as a disproportionate effect in relation to the pursued objective.'[106] The Commission went on to discuss the possible effects of the Dutch legislation on production, sales and trade of creosote. In this case the Dutch legislation met the Commission requirements. This way of applying the proportionality principle seems to differ in two respects from the manner in which it is normally applied in the context of the assessment of national measures affecting the free movement of goods.[107] First, it includes effects on the market other than barriers to trade and, second, the effects on the internal market are weighed in the same basket as the environmental objectives pursued (proportionality *stricto sensu*).[108]

The conclusion seems to be that the 'no obstacle' clause has a meaning of its own. The decisions of the Commission show that the Commission has been given a fairly wide discretionary power to block derogating national standards even if the national measures are justified from an environmental point of view and even if there is no arbitrary discrimination or disguised restriction to trade. In assessing the national measures the Commission can take into account any effect on the internal market and has therefore been given a power to balance, rather intensive, different objectives and interests going well beyond the standard way of applying the proportionality principle.

As far as the consequences of notification are concerned, the first thing to note is that the Commission must take a decision within six months of notification, failing which the measures are deemed to have been approved. However, the text does not state what the consequences are of non-notification. Two judgments of the Court of Justice relating to the 'old' Article 100a(4) must be mentioned in this respect, the *PCP* case[109] and the *Kortas* case.[110]

---

[105] Decision 1999/832, OJ 1999 L 329/25.

[106] Decision 1999/832, OJ 1999 L 329/25. More recent decisions confirm this. See e.g. Commission Decision 2006/372, OJ 2006 L 142/16.

[107] In other words, is the measure 'suitable and necessary', see point 105 in the Dutch Creosote Decision 1999/832, OJ 1999 L 329/25. See on the proportionality principle in the context of Articles 28-30 EC, Chapter 6, section 5.5.

[108] Cf. for instance Decision 94/783, OJ 1994 L 316/43 (*German PCP*). See on the concept of proportionality *stricto sensu*, also Chapter 6, section 5.5.

[109] Case C-41/93 *France* v. *Commission* [1994] ECR I-1829.

[110] Case C-319/97 *Kortas* [1999] ECR I-3143.

In the *PCP* case, Germany had invoked Article 100a(4) to justify national provisions prohibiting pentachlorophenol (PCP), which were stricter than those provided for in the PCP directive.[111] The Commission decided to approve the German provisions on the grounds that Germany had voted against the directive, that it had notified the Commission of the provisions, that the German provisions were already in force before the directive was adopted and that they were not discriminatory, as they applied without distinction to both national and imported products.[112] France appealed against the Commission's decision to the Court of Justice. The Court held that the Commission's decision must be annulled, because it did not satisfy the obligation to state reasons.

Two points to note are that, in the first place, the Court regarded the Commission's decision to approve or reject national legislation as a decision, which is amenable to an action for annulment under Article 230 EC.[113] Secondly, the legal consequence of the Commission's decision is plain: 'A Member State is not, therefore, authorized to apply the national provisions notified by it until after it has obtained a decision from the Commission confirming them.'

Until the national provisions have been approved, a standstill requirement applies. In the *Kortas* case, the Court went a step further.[114] The interesting thing about *Kortas* is that the Commission had not responded to Sweden's notification for several years. In its judgment the Court referred to the text of Article 100a(4) and concluded that the aim of the procedure is to ensure that no Member State applied national rules derogating from the harmonised legislation without obtaining due confirmation from the Commission. Referring to the *PCP* case, the Court observed that harmonisation measures would be rendered ineffective if Member States retained the right unilaterally to apply national rules derogating from those measures. A Member State is not, therefore, authorised to apply the national provisions notified by it until after it has obtained a decision from the Commission approving them.

Although Article 95(6) EC provides for a time limit within which the Commission must have taken a decision, failing which national provisions will be deemed to have been approved, *Kortas* does have more general implications. From the judgment in *Kortas*, it can be implied that national legislation cannot be applied once the deadline allowed for transposition of the directive in question had expired, unless the Commission has given its approval.

---

[111] Directive 91/173, OJ 1991 L 85/34.

[112] OJ 1992 C 334/8.

[113] See however Case T-234/04 *Netherlands* v. *Commission*, judgment of 8 November 2007, n.y.r. in the ECR. A Member State cannot on the basis of Article 95(4) EC request the Commission to take a decision on the extent of harmonisation under a Community directive and/or on the compatibility of national legislation with such a directive. Any position adopted by the Commission pertaining such a request is not capable of being the subject of an application for annulment.

[114] See on this case Sevenster (2000) at 296-298.

Based on the combined effect of the *PCP* and *Kortas* cases, Sevenster has concluded that after expiry of the implementation period Member States must refrain from applying any legislation that has been notified to the Commission without receiving its approval, and that the same applies to new legislation that has been notified but not received approval, even before expiry of the implementation deadline.[115] It should be added that the same applies to legislation which has not been notified, but which should have been under Article 95(4-6) EC.

7 Inherent Competence to Derogate?

An entirely different question arises if there is an inherent general competence in European law for Member States to derogate from environmental standards in directives, even where the directive does not provide for such a competence and neither Article 95(4-6) EC nor Article 176 EC are applicable.

In principle, obligations entered into within the framework of an environmental directive have to be fulfilled. Member States have no freedom to derogate from the level of protection required by a directive beyond the provisions of the directive itself. It is thus European law which determines whether, and if so to what extent, Member States may depart from common levels of protection. Many environmental directives contain safeguard clauses allowing Member States to derogate temporarily from the requirements of the directive.[116]

That the competence of the Member States to derogate from the requirements of a directive is indeed determined by European law was demonstrated in Case 228/87.[117]

Directive 80/778 relating to the quality of water intended for human consumption[118] sets a maximum value of 0.1 microgram per litre of atrazine. In proceedings initiated by the Turin magistrate to determine the possible criminal liability of the Italian Government for not prohibiting the use of water intended for human consumption in which a limit of 0.1 microgram per litre of atrazine was exceeded, the court requested a preliminary ruling from the Court of Justice as to the possible competence of a Member State to derogate from the limit. The directive contains three provisions, Articles 9, 10 and 20, which provide for derogations. The Court held, with appropriate severity: 'Derogations from the directive are permitted only under the conditions provided for in Articles 9, 10 and 20 thereof. These provisions must be interpreted strictly.'

---

[115] Sevenster (2000) at 308.

[116] See on this Chapter 1, section 3.2.

[117] Case 228/87 *Preiore di Torino* v. *Persons unknown* [1988] ECR 5099.

[118] OJ 1980 L 229/11, later amended.

The next question to be addressed is whether derogations from the requirements of a directive can be accepted, which are not provided for by the directive
in question. The case law of the Court of Justice does indeed contain indications
that this might be the case under certain circumstances.

In the *Leybucht* case, German dredging, filling and dyke-building operations in the Leybucht area were at issue.[119] Germany had designated the area a
protected area under Article 4 of the Wild Birds Directive.[120] According to Article
4(4) of the directive, Germany had to take appropriate steps to avoid pollution or
deterioration of habitats or any disturbances affecting the birds. The dyke-rein-
forcement work would result in a reduction in the size of the special protection
area. The Court had to address several questions of principle which may also be
relevant to other cases.

In the first place, the question is whether – and if so, under what conditions
– the Member States are authorised to reduce the size of a special protection
area and to what extent other interests may be taken into account. The Court
observed that a reduction in the geographical extent of a protected area was not
expressly envisaged by the terms of the directive.

Does this mean that Member States are now stuck forever with a decision
to designate a special protection area? Has it thereby become impossible to
review such a decision, even in the light of changed insights and circumstances?
From the point of view both of environmental interests and of other interests
that might be affected, this would not seem reasonable. The Court stated that,
though Member States do have a certain discretion with regard to the choice of
the territories most suitable for classification as a special protection area, they
do not have the same discretion in modifying or reducing the extent of those
areas.[121] If that were not so, the Member States could unilaterally escape from
the obligations imposed on them by Article 4(4) of the directive. Only 'exceptional grounds' will serve to justify an alteration in the extent of the protected
area. It could also be that review or alteration of the terms of the decision might
be permitted if the conditions on which it was decided to make the designation no longer applied. This might be the case if external events had altered the
nature of the area to such an extent that they could no longer be considered the
'most suitable territories'. It is clear that the mere fact that a Member State had
altered its policies will not be sufficient ground to justify reviewing or changing the decision. The emphasis the Court placed on preventing Member States
from escaping unilaterally from European obligations, confirms this. Thus, if
Member States wish to give themselves such powers, they will have to include
them explicitly in the directive.

In the second place, the Court addressed the question as to what interests
could be regarded as exceptional grounds which might justify a decision to
modify a classification. It is worth noting that the Court expressly rejected the

---

[119] Case C-57/89 *Commission v. Germany* [1991] ECR I-883.

[120] OJ 1979 L 103/1, later amended.

[121] See on this more in detail Chapter 8, section 17.1.

view that the economic and recreational requirements referred to in Article 2 of the directive could be regarded as such. Article 2 does not constitute an autonomous derogation from the general system of protection established by the directive. It contains a widely formulated obligation to maintain the level of population of wild birds. In fulfilling this obligation, Member States may take account of economic and recreational requirements.

The Court held that those 'exceptional grounds' must correspond to a general interest which is superior to the general interest represented by the ecological objective of the directive. In this case the Court held that the danger of flooding and the protection of the coast constitute sufficiently serious reasons to justify the dyke works and the strengthening of coastal structures as long as those measures are confined to a strict minimum and involve only the smallest possible reduction of the special protection area. Economic considerations, for example to ensure that fishing vessels had access to the harbour, were not however acceptable.

The more general conclusion that can be drawn from this judgment seems to be that even in cases where a directive does not provide for derogations from its requirements, there is apparently an inherent competence to derogate in those cases where higher interests are involved than those the directive is designed to protect. In each individual case it will have to be considered which higher interests are acceptable in European law. In addition, this judgment seems to imply that economic and recreational interests cannot necessarily be regarded as falling under this inherent competence.

Finally, there is a third point of interest in the judgment. That is the introduction of the concept of 'offsetting ecological benefits'. After the Court had noted that securing access to the fishing harbour of Greetsiel could not be regarded as a superior interest, it reflected that the work in question might also have positive ecological effects. The ecological disadvantages would be offset by the formation of new salt meadows of ecological importance. The Court was thus applying the principle of 'offsetting ecological benefits' as a condition under which a Member State might derogate from the obligations contained in Article 4(4) of the directive. The question is however if, and to what extent, this principle is generally applicable to European environmental law. More recent case law seems to suggest that it is not. In a case concerning the implementation in Austria of the Waste Directive, the Court ruled that the directive 'cannot be interpreted as meaning that the Member States are released from adopting transposing measures where they consider that their national provisions are better than the European provisions concerned and that the national provisions are therefore better able to ensure that the objective pursued by the directive is achieved.'[122] We will have to wait on further case law to clarify this issue.

---

[122] Case C-194/01 *Commission v. Austria* [2004] ECR I-4579, para. 39. See also Case C-103/02 *Commission v. Italy* [2004] ECR I-9127, para. 33. Cf. on this issue also Pagh (2005) at 8-9.

Laying down environmental standards in directives therefore has an important stabilizing function. They prevent unilateral steps by Member States in derogation from the required level of protection – this is prevented by the pre-emptive effect of European environmental law. Derogation is possible where:
- · the Commission has approved national legislation according to Article 95(6) EC, or
- · the directive in question allows it, or
- · interests superior to the environmental interest are involved, or ecological benefits are offset.

European environmental law differs from national environmental law in this respect. If a national parliament decides to lower its environmental standards, it is competent to do so. All that is required is that the national laws and policies are altered in accordance with new ideas and policy considerations and according to the relevant national decision-making procedures.

Implementation and Enforcement

1   The Duty to Transpose Environmental Directives into National Law

Obligations under directives are generally formulated as instructions to the Member States. For example, Article 4(1) of Directive 2006/66 on batteries and accumulators and waste batteries and accumulators stipulates the following:

'1. Without prejudice to Directive 2000/53/EC, Member States shall prohibit the placing on the market of:

a) all batteries or accumulators, whether or not incorporated into appliances, that contain more than 0,0005% of mercury by weight; and

b) portable batteries or accumulators, including those incorporated into appliances, that contain more than 0,002% of cadmium by weight.'[1]

Such obligations have to be transposed into the national legal system, within the time limits[2] set by the directive. To that end a directive will contain a provision like 'Member States shall bring into force the laws, regulations and administrative provisions necessary to comply with this Directive by 1 March 2007 and forthwith inform the Commission thereof. When Member States adopt those provisions, they shall contain a reference to this Directive or be accompanied by such a reference on the occasion of their official publication. Member States shall determine how such reference is to be made.'

It is true that the third paragraph of Article 249 EC (Article 288 FEU) provides that a directive shall be binding, as to the result to be achieved, upon each Member State to which it is addressed, but shall leave to the national authorities the choice of form and methods. However, this power has been severely curtailed by judgments of the Court of Justice in connection with Article 10 EC. This provides that Member States shall take all appropriate measures, whether general or particular, to ensure fulfilment of their European obligations. As early as the *Royer* case the Court had held that the freedom left to the Member States by Article 249 EC as to the choice of forms and methods of implementation of directives does not affect their obligation to choose the most appropriate forms and methods.[3] But the Court has also repeatedly held that the transposition of a directive into national law does not necessarily require the provisions of the directive to be enacted in precisely the same words in a specific express legal provision.[4] Here the Court is respecting the freedom left to the Member States by Article 249 EC. The competence to choose the most appropriate forms and methods implies that a general legal context may be sufficient if it actually ensures the full application of the directive in a sufficiently clear and precise manner. In the *Traen* case the Court stated that the exercise of a discre-

---

[1]   OJ 2006 L 266/1.

[2]   Cf. on possible extensions of time limits Case C-236/99 *Commission v. Belgium* [2000] ECR I-5657.

[3]   Case 48/75 *Royer* [1976] ECR 497.

[4]   Case C-339/87 *Commission v. Netherlands* [1990] ECR I-851.

tionary power is qualified only by the requirement that the objectives of the directive, namely the protection of human health and of the environment, must be complied with.[5]

This fine balance between the freedom left to Member States in implementing directives and the constraints imposed on them emerges clearly in the Declaration on the Implementation of Community Law which was annexed to the Final Act of the Treaty on European Union at Maastricht. On the one hand it was recognised that it must be for each Member State to determine how the provisions of EC law can best be enforced in the light of its own particular institutions. On the other hand, this must be in compliance with Article 249 EC. Moreover it was considered essential that the measures taken by the different Member States should be applied with the same effectiveness and rigour as in the application of their national law. The need for balance is similarly expressed in the Amsterdam Protocol on the Application of the Principles of Subsidiarity and Proportionality, which states: 'While respecting Community law, care should be taken to respect well established national arrangements and the organisation and working of Member States' legal systems.'

In several judgments relating to the Wild Birds Directive, the Court has added the requirement that the precision of transposition is of particular importance. This requirement is generally expressed in words such as the following:

'However, a faithful transposition becomes particularly important in a case such as this in which the management of the common heritage is entrusted to the Member States in their respective territories.'[6]

'The directive is based on the consideration that effective bird protection, and in particular protection of migratory species, is typically a transfrontier environment problem entailing common responsibilities for the Member States.'[7]

Thus as far as the transposition of the Wild Birds Directive is concerned, and the same could also be said of the Habitats Directive,[8] the Court seems to take a very strict view of the adequacy of national implementing legislation.

These judgments may also be important for the way other 'transboundary' provisions in environmental directives are implemented, in particular for the many provisions on conducting consultations, providing information etc. where

---

[5] Joined Cases 372-374/85 *Traen* [1987] ECR 2141.

[6] Case 252/85 *Commission v. France* [1988] ECR 2243.

[7] Case 262/85 *Commission v. Italy* [1987] ECR 3073.

[8] Case C-6/04 *Commission v. UK* [2005] ECR I-9017, para. 25: 'that threatened habitats and species form part of the European Community's natural heritage and that the threats to them are often of a transboundary nature, so that the adoption of conservation measures is a common responsibility of all Member States. Consequently [...], faithful transposition becomes particularly important in an instance such as the present one, where management of the common heritage is entrusted to the Member States in their respective territories.'

transboundary environmental effects are involved.[9] Even without explicit reference to the Wild Birds Directive, it is clear from its judgments that the Court
also attaches great importance to the proper transposition of such obligations
into national law.[10]

Thus Member States retain the freedom to adapt the content of a directive to
their national systems of environmental law, and in doing so may utilise their
own legal instruments, legal terminology and division of public law powers.
As long as an environmental directive is transposed fully and accurately into
national law within the deadlines set by the directive, the legal relations it covers
are governed by the national measures taken to implement it. Nevertheless, until
the deadline has expired, the Member State to which the directive is addressed
must refrain from taking any measures liable seriously to compromise the result
prescribed.[11]

From a legal point of view, once national implementing legislation has
entered into force, the directive is, in general,[12] no longer of interest. Only where
that legislation gives rise to problems of interpretation will it be necessary to
consult the directive.

2   Aspects of Transposition

2.1   Must Every Provision be Transposed?

European legislative practice shows that there may be great
differences in the types of obligations which directives impose on the Member
States and therefore in the results which must be achieved.[13] A question that has
to be answered before discussing what requirements national implementing
legislation should be required to fulfil is whether every provision of an environmental directive has to be transposed into national legislation. An examination
of various environmental directives shows that they contain many different
kinds of provisions. Essential for understanding the Court's case law on the
Member States' duty to transpose provisions of environmental directives into
binding national law is that it is applicable to all provisions 'intended to create
rights and obligations for individuals'.[14] This case law, to be discussed more
exhaustively below, also shows that the Court interprets the concept of 'rights
and obligations' in a fairly broad and flexible manner.

---

9   Cf. Case C-365/93 *Commission* v. *Greece* [1995] ECR I-499, concerning the implementation of directives
     intended to accord rights to nationals of other Member States.

10   Case C-186/91 *Commission* v. *Belgium* [1993] ECR I-851.

11   Case C-129/96 *Inter-Environnement Wallonie ASBL* v. *Waals Gewest* [1997] ECR I-7411. This case will be
     discussed more extensively in Chapter 5, section 2.1.

12   See however Case C-62/00 *Marks & Spencer* [2002] ECR I-6325.

13   Case C-60/01 *Commission* v. *France* [2002] ECR I-5679, para. 25.

14   Case C-361/88 *Commission* v. *Germany* [1991] ECR I-2567.

So what provisions do have to be transposed into national law and what provisions do not? In the first place, some provisions are not directed at the Member States, but at the Council or the Commission. For example, the Commission can be required to review the implementation of the European measure and to produce implementation reports and/or feasibility studies.[15] By their very nature, such provisions, which are not addressed to the Member States, do not require transposition into national law by the Member States.

In the second place there are provisions which concern exclusively the relations between the Member States and the European institutions, in particular the Commission. This category includes all kinds of obligations for the Member States to provide the Commission with information, such as the obligation to notify the Commission of the texts of implementing legislation, or to send the Commission brief factual reports or situation reports. Of course, the Member States must fulfil the obligations contained in such provisions. In other words, they must send the Commission required reports and provide it with the required information. Rights and obligations for individuals are not at issue here.[16] However, there is no need to have these kind of provisions transposed into national law.

> This conclusion is supported by the case law of the Court.[17] For instance, Article 12(1) of the Wild Birds Directive 79/409 requires the Member States to draw up every three years a report on the implementation of national provisions taken under that directive and forward it to the Commission so that it can check that the directive has been complied with by the Member States. According to the Court, that provision concerns only the relations between those Member States and the Commission.[18]

Of course, the above categories do not contain the most essential elements of a directive. The core of a directive is formed by the concrete and specific provisions. And in the case of environmental directives, these are specific substantive and operational provisions directed at the objectives[19] of environmental protec-

---

[15] E.g. Article 14 of the 'new' Shellfish Water Directive: '[...] The Commission shall publish a Community report on the implementation of this Directive within nine months of receiving the reports from the Member States'; Directive 2006/113 on the quality required of shellfish waters, OJ 2006 L 376/14.

[16] Cf. Case 380/87 *Balsamo* [1989] ECR 2491 in respect of the Member States' obligation to notify the Commission of draft rules on waste disposal under Article 3 of Directive 75/442.

[17] E.g. Case C-58/89 *Commission v. Germany* [1991] ECR I-4983, Case C-296/01 *Commission v. France* [2003] ECR I-13909, para. 92 and 35.

[18] Case C-72/02 *Commission v. Portugal* [2003] ECR I-6597, paras. 19 and 20.

[19] Provisions of directives which merely specify the particular objectives the directive seeks to achieve – like Article 1 of the Water Framework Directive 2000/60 – do not require transposition; Case C-32/05 *Commission v. Luxembourg* [2006] ECR I-11323, para. 44. According to Article 1, its purpose is 'to establish a framework for the protection of inland surface waters, transitional waters, coastal waters and groundwater'. On the other hand, we would argue that definitions in the directive of key legal concepts

tion and/or market integration. In general these provisions will be designed to regulate more than simply the legal relations between the Member States and the European institutions. Environmental directives are bound to have some measure of external impact and are designed to regulate relations between individuals and between individuals and the state. In other words, they will generally be intended to create rights and obligations for individuals. Rights are granted to those who are confronted with the effects of pollution while obligations are imposed on those who cause it. Such provisions must be fulfilled not only *in fact*, but also *in law*. In other words, they must be given a legal basis and transposed into national law. There is in fact only one reason why an environmental directive containing rights and obligations for individuals should not result in further national legislative activity, and that is where national law already fully meet the requirements of the directive in every respect.

The judgments of the Court indicate that rights for individuals are readily implied. Thus procedural rules may contain rights and obligations for individuals.[20] Case C-131/88 involved the procedural obligations under Articles 7 to 11 and 13 of Directive 80/68 on the protection of groundwater against pollution caused by certain dangerous substances.[21] Article 7 requires prior investigations of the hydrogeological conditions of the area concerned before authorisations are issued and Articles 8 to 11 and 13 impose further conditions on the issue of authorisations. The Court held that the procedural provisions of the directive are intended to create rights and obligations for individuals. In Case C-361/88, in interpreting the European air quality standards, the Court also took a broad view of the question of when an individual's rights are at stake.[22] It pointed out that the obligation imposed on Member States in Article 2 of Directive 80/779 on air quality limit values and guide values for sulphur dioxide and suspended particulates was imposed 'in order to protect human health in particular', and that it therefore implies rights for individuals.

A final example in this context is the judgment in Case C-186/91, where the Court rejected the Belgian argument that the obligation to hold transboundary consultations contained in Article 11 of Directive 85/203 on air quality standards for nitrogen dioxide did not contain rights for individuals and therefore did not require incorporation into national law.[23]

(like 'waste' or 'surface waters') do require transposition, in view of legal certainty. See on the latter point also Krämer (2007) at 420-421.

[20] Case C-131/88 *Commission v. Germany* [1991] ECR I-825.

[21] The 'old' Groundwater Directive will be repealed from 21 December 2013 by the Water Framework Directive 2000/60 (OJ 2000 L 327/1).

[22] Case C-361/88 *Commission v. Germany* [1991] ECR I-2567. Cf. also Case C-13/90 *Commission v. France* [1991] ECR I-4327, Case C-14/90 *Commission v. France* [1991] ECR I-4331, Case C-64/90 *Commission v. France* [1991] ECR I-4335 and Case C-58/89 *Commission v. Germany* [1991] ECR I-4983.

[23] Case C-186/91 *Commission v. Belgium* [1993] ECR I-851.

More recent examples in the case law of the Court of Justice concern the way France implemented the Incineration Directives 89/369 and 89/429.[24] The Court ruled that both directives require legislative measures to be adopted at the national level and compliance with those measures is to be the subject of judicial or administrative review. It stated that Directives 89/369 and 89/429 impose on the Member States obligations, formulated in clear and unequivocal terms, to achieve a certain result, in order that their incineration plants meet detailed and precise requirements within the stated time-limits and rejected the French Government's assertions that it is sufficient for a Member State to take all reasonably practicable measures.

Generally, the natural choice will be transposition of the material and operational requirements of directives into national law. And where a directive prohibits certain activities, such as the marketing of environmentally harmful products which do not meet the requirements of the directive or emissions of certain pollutants, legislation is perhaps the only possible solution.

Other directives provide that the Member States are to take the necessary measures to ensure that certain objectives formulated in general and unquantifiable terms are attained, whilst leaving the Member States some discretion as to the nature of the measures to be taken. An example of this can be found in the San Rocco case.[25]

This case involved the enforcement of Article 4 of the Framework Waste Directive, according to which Member States are required to take the necessary measures to ensure that waste is disposed of without endangering human health and without harming the environment.[26] The Commission accused the Italian Government of having failed to take measures to repair the ecological situation in the San Rocco valley. As far as the alleged infringement of Article 4 of the directive was concerned, the Court observed that even though this provision does not say anything about the actual content of the measures to be taken, it is nevertheless binding on the Member States in respect of the objective to be achieved, albeit that they are allowed some measure of discretion in assessing the need for such measures.

A more recent example is provided in Case C-32/05.[27] The Commission argued that the directive requires Member States to adopt both general and specific measures in order to render their national legal system compatible with the objectives laid down under the directive. With respect to the general measures to be taken, the Commission was of the opinion that the directive obliges Member States to adopt 'framework legislation' for water. However, the Court relying on its San Rocco judgment, ruled that Member States are not under a duty to adopt such

---

[24] Case C-60/01 Commission v. France [2002] ECR I-5679.

[25] Case C-365/97 Commission v. Italy [1999] ECR I-7773 and more recently Case C-135/05 Commission v. Italy, judgment of 26 April 2007, n.y.r. in the ECR. See on this case law also Chapter 8, section 15.

[26] OJ 1975 L 194/47, later amended by Directive 91/156, OJ 1991 L 377/48.

[27] Case C-32/05 Commission v. Luxembourg [2006] ECR I-11323, para. 34.

framework legislation in order to implement its provisions correctly: 'It is true [...] that adopting framework legislation may be an appropriate, or more straightforward, method of implementing the directive, since it may provide the competent authorities with clear legal bases, in a single document, for drawing up the various measures laid down by the directive as regards water and whose implementation is to be spread over a period of time. The adoption of such framework legislation may also facilitate the work of the Commission, which has to ensure that the obligations imposed on Member States by the directive are complied with.

Nevertheless, adopting framework legislation is not the only way in which Member States may ensure that the directive is fully applied and provide for an organised and coherent system for complying with the objectives laid down under the directive.

Had the European legislature intended to require Member States to adopt framework legislation in their national legal systems in order to implement the directive, it would have been open to it to insert a provision to that effect in the text of the directive. It did not do so.'

Also difficult are those cases where the directive actually requires something to be done, such as the establishment of collecting systems for urban wastewater[28] or the drawing up of waste management plans.[29] Although such directives require the Member States to obtain very precise and specific results after a certain period, they do not seem to require legislative measures to be adopted at national level.

The *Blackpool* case should be mentioned in this respect.[30] In this case the United Kingdom was held to have failed to take all the necessary measures to ensure that the quality of bathing water in the bathing areas in Blackpool and adjacent to Formby and Southport conformed to the limit values set in accordance with Directive 76/160 on bathing water. The Court observed that it was clear from Article 4(1) of the directive that the Member States are to take all necessary measures to ensure that, within 10 years following the notification of the directive, bathing water conforms to the limit values set in accordance with Article 3 of the directive. The provision requires a particular result to be achieved, but not necessarily by way of adopting legislative measures.

A final category which could be distinguished includes those provisions referred to in section 1 above, which relate to transboundary environmental issues. As has been said earlier, the Court attaches great importance to the precision of their transposition in national legislative measures by the Member States.

---

[28] Article 3 of Directive 91/271 concerning urban waste water treatment, OJ 1991 L 135/40, as amended.

[29] Cf. Article 7 of the 'new' Waste Directive Directive 2006/12 (OJ 2006 L 114/9).

[30] Case C-56/90 *Commission v. UK* [1993] ECR I-4109, paras. 42-44. See also Case C-268/00 *Commission v. Netherlands* [2002] ECR I-2995, paras. 12 to 14, Case C-198/97 *Commission v. Germany* [1999] ECR I-3257, para. 35, and Case C-307/98 *Commission v. Belgium* [2000] ECR I-3933, paras. 48 and 49.

2.2 Legally Binding Rules

In essence, the case law of the Court means that provisions of a directive containing rights and obligations for individuals has to be transposed into binding provisions of national law, in a manner which fully satisfies the requirements of clarity and legal certainty, and affords interested parties recourse to the courts. It is important that the result intended by the directive is ensured not only in *fact*, but also in *law*.[31]

An example of the terms in which the Court frames these requirements is the following, from the judgment in Case C-415/01 concerning the way Belgium had implemented the Wild Birds Directive.[32] The case was about the question whether the maps used in Belgium demarcating special protection areas were legally binding. The Court outlined that: 'according to consistent case-law, the provisions of directives must be implemented with *unquestionable* binding force, and the specificity, precision and clarity necessary to satisfy the requirements of legal certainty [...]. The principle of legal certainty requires appropriate publicity for the national measures adopted pursuant to Community rules in such a way as to enable the persons concerned by such measures to ascertain the scope of their rights and obligations in the particular area governed by Community law' [emphasis added]. With regard to those maps the Court ruled that they must be invested with binding force. If not, the boundaries of SPAs could be challenged at any time.

And in Case C-32/05 concerning the way Luxembourg implemented the Water Framework Directive 2000/60, the Court ruled: '[...] the Court has repeatedly held that it is not always necessary formally to enact the requirements of a directive in a specific express legal provision, since the general legal context may be sufficient for implementation of a directive, depending on its content. In particular, the existence of general principles of constitutional or administrative law may render superfluous transposition by specific legislative or regulatory measures provided, however, that those principles actually ensure the full application of the directive by the national authorities and that, where the relevant provision of the directive seeks to create rights for individuals, the legal situation arising from those principles is sufficiently precise and clear and that the persons concerned are put in a

---

[31] Cf. Case C-83/97 *Commission* v. *Germany* [1997] ECR I-7191 on the implementation of the Habitats Directive. Germany did not deny that it had not adopted all the measures necessary for implementation of the directive. It stated, however, that since the passing of the deadline for transportation, the directive had been directly applied by the competent authorities and existing national provisions have been interpreted in accordance with European law. The Court: 'Since the directive has not been transposed into national law by the Federal Republic of Germany within the prescribed period, the action brought by the Commission must be held to be well founded.'

[32] Case C-415/01 *Commission* v. *Belgium* [2003] ECR I-2081, para. 21. Cf. also Case C-159/99 *Commission* v. *Italy* [2001] ECR I-4007, para. 32 and Case C-225/97 *Commission* v. *France* [1999] ECR I-3011, para. 37.

position to know the full extent of their rights and, where appropriate, to be able to rely on them before the national courts'.[33]

Legislation is an instrument of implementation of environmental directives which meets this requirement as regards its binding nature.[34] Or, as the Court put it in Case C-339/87, in respect of the use of ministerial rules adopted pursuant to the Dutch *Jachtwet* (Hunting Act), the rules are 'published in the Nederlandse *Staatscourant* (Dutch official gazette), are of a general nature and capable of creating rights and obligations for individuals.'[35] Thus provisions of directives which require transposition cannot in principle be transposed by means of rules which are not legally binding. This means that, generally speaking, directives have to be transposed by means of legislation adopted by the central government or by other administrative authorities. It would not, for example, be acceptable to implement a directive using plans which were not strictly binding.

> Dutch *Indicatieve Meerjaren Programma's* (Prospective Multiennial Programmes) clearly fall under that category, as the Court held in Case 96/81, as such a programme is 'nothing more than a set of guidelines for those responsible for the supervision of water quality and had no legally binding force.'[36] This implies that if a measure is only effective in respect of a Member State's internal authorities, this will be insufficient to create rights and obligations for individuals.[37]

Another element is that the national measures must ensure a complete and full transposition. In the *German TA Luft* cases, which will be discussed more in detail below, the Court had to decide on the way Germany implemented air quality standards. The area of application of the air quality standards in Germany was limited to industrial plants for which a licence was required, within the meaning of the German legislation on protection against pollution. The Commission argued that the nuisance created by sulphur dioxide may originate elsewhere than in the plant subject to a requirement of authorisation, for example in a high density of road traffic, private heating systems or pollution from another State. The Court accepted these arguments: 'The general nature of the directive cannot be satisfied by a transposition confined to certain sources of

---

[33] Case C-32/05 *Commission* v. *Luxembourg* [2006] ECR I-11323, para. 34. Cf. also Case C-361/88 *Commission* v. *Germany* [1991] ECR I-2567 where the Court ruled in the event a directive intends to create obligations for individuals, transposition of European legislation into a provision whose binding nature is undeniable is also necessary in order that all those whose activities are liable to give rise to nuisances may ascertain precisely the obligations to which they are subject.

[34] Draft legislation will, of course, not suffice: Case C-65/00 *Commission* v. *Italy* [2002] ECR I-1795.

[35] Case C-339/87 *Commission* v. *Netherlands* [1990] ECR I-851.

[36] Case 96/81 *Commission* v. *Netherlands* [1982] ECR 1791.

[37] Other environmental cases where the Court was not satisfied with the binding force of the implementing measures include Case C-239/03 *Commission* v. *France* [2004] ECR I-9325.

the exceeding of the limit values which it lays down and to certain measures to be adopted by the administrative authorities.'

These judgments indicate that when quality standards are transposed, it is not sufficient to link the standards to activities for which an authorisation is required. It is also required that provisions be adopted which are binding in respect of the other activities which might cause air pollution.[38] The same could be said in respect of the implementation of emission limit values. Polluters who do not require authorisation must also in one way or another be obliged to comply with European standards. A full implementation must be guaranteed.

However, it can be implied that binding national legislation to implement an environmental directive may refer to standards, which are not as such binding,[39] for example, those of private standards organisations such as ISO, CEN and CENELEC. In that case the legislation containing the reference would have to make it clear that the standards have binding force in this particular context.

2.3 Transposition by Means of Administrative Circulars

An important question is to what extent a national government may make use of circulars, policy rules and other instruments which are binding only on the administration itself and have no effect in respect of third parties. Relevant cases in this respect are the *German TA Luft* cases,[40] the *French Air Quality* cases[41] and Case C-58/89[42] in the field of water quality. The Court had great difficulty with the manner in which France and Germany had transposed the European air quality limit values and guide values for sulphur dioxide and suspended particulates and the limit values for lead in the air into their national legal systems.

In the *TA Luft* cases, the manner of transposition of European air quality directives by Germany was at issue. The air quality standards prescribed by the directives had been transposed by means of the *Technische Anleitung zur Reinhaltung der Luft (TA Luft)*. There was no clear indication in German legal writing and case law as to the precise legal nature of the instrument. In the first place, the Court pointed out that the obligation to prescribe limit values not to be exceeded is imposed in order to protect human health in particular. It implies, therefore, that whenever the exceeding of the limit values could endanger human health, the

---

[38] See also with respect requirements to the quality of water intended for human consumption Case C-316/00 *Commission v. Ireland* [2002] ECR I-10527, para. 49. The Court required Ireland to impose 'direct duties' on water distribution companies to comply with the provisions of the directive concerned.

[39] Case 208/85 *Commission v. Germany* [1987] ECR 4045. Directive 79/831, OJ 1979 L 259/10.

[40] Case C-361/88 *Commission v. Germany* [1991] ECR I-2567 and Case C-59/89 *Commission v. Germany* [1991] ECR I-2607.

[41] Case C-13/90 *Commission v. France* [1991] ECR I-4327, Case C-14/90 *Commission v. France* [1991] ECR I-4331 and Case C-64/90 *Commission v. France* [1991] ECR I-4335.

[42] Case C-58/89 *Commission v. Germany* [1991] ECR I-4983.

CHAPTER 4   IMPLEMENTATION AND ENFORCEMENT

persons concerned must be in a position to rely on mandatory rules in order to be able to assert their rights. Furthermore, the fixing of limit values in a provision whose binding nature is undeniable is also necessary in order that all those whose activities are liable to give rise to nuisances may ascertain precisely the obligations to which they are subject. In view of the differences in German case law, as to the extent to which such technical circulars are recognised as binding, the Court took the view that the *TA Luft* did not meet these criteria: 'It must be stated that, in the particular case of the technical circular 'air', the Federal Republic of Germany has not pointed to any national judicial decision explicitly recognising that that circular, apart from being binding on the administration, has direct effect vis-à-vis third parties. It cannot be claimed, therefore, that individuals are in a position to know with certainty the full extent of their rights in order to rely on them, where appropriate, before the national courts or that those whose activities are liable to give rise to nuisances are adequately informed of the extent of their obligations.'

Environmental quality standards are established to protect the health of man and are in that sense intended to create rights for individuals. Transposition by means of binding provisions is therefore essential. Rules which are binding only on the administration and do not have any direct effect in respect of third parties do not meet the criteria. Nor do circulars which are binding only on the administrative hierarchy but nowhere else and which do not contain obligations for polluters.[43] The *French Air Quality* cases confirm the *German TA Luft* decisions.[44] Any person whose activities may cause pollution must be able to know precisely what obligations he has.

In sum: rules which bind only the administrative authorities but otherwise neither have binding effect nor are enforceable are not adequate as transposition instruments. The mere fact that they have been published does not detract from this. Similarly, circulars which only have binding force within the administrative hierarchy but not otherwise and which do not impose obligations on polluters are also inadequate as a means of implementing European environmental directives.[45]

---

[43] Cf. also Case C-95/92 *Commission* v. *Italy* [1993] ECR I-3119. This case concerned the implementation by Italy of Euratom Directive 84/466 (repealed by Directive 97/43, OJ 1997 L 180/22). Here the Court held that implementation by means of circulars, which have never been officially published and were subject to amendment by the Italian administration at will, only made recommendations which had no binding force. The Court reiterated its standpoint that Member States must implement directives in a manner which fully meets the requirement of legal certainty and must consequently transpose their terms into national law as binding provisions.

[44] Case C-13/90 *Commission* v. *France* [1991] ECR I-4327.

[45] See for instance Case C-262/95 *Commission* v. *Germany* [1996] ECR I-5729. Cf. also Case C-315/98 *Commission* v. *Italy* [1999] ECR I-8001, para. 10.

2.4 Transposition by Means of Environmental Agreements

An environmental agreement is a voluntary agreement between the administrative authorities and industry in which the realisation of certain environmental objectives is agreed in a given field, generally in relation to a particular substance or a particular product. The way the Court of Justice has stressed the importance of the legally binding nature of implementing measures and the guarantee that the obligations imposed by a directive are fully implemented raises the question whether the Court will approve the use of such environmental agreements.[46]

A possible exception to the basic rule is where the directive itself provides for implementation by means of a voluntary agreement.[47]

Article 27 of the Batteries Directive gives us an example of the use of voluntary agreements as an instrument to implement, albeit some and not all, provisions of the directive.[48] Article 27 of Directive 2006/66 states: '1. Provided that the objectives set out in this Directive are achieved, Member States may transpose the provisions set out in Articles 8, 15 and 20 by means of agreements between the competent authorities and economic operators concerned. Such agreements shall meet the following requirements:
a) they shall be enforceable;
b) they must specify objectives with the corresponding deadlines;
c) they must be published in the national official journal or an official document equally accessible to the public and transmitted to the Commission.
2. The results achieved must be monitored regularly, and reported to the competent authorities and the Commission, and made available to the public under the conditions set out in the agreement.
3. The competent authorities shall ensure that the progress made under such agreements is examined.
4. In cases of non-compliance with the agreements, Member States shall implement the relevant provisions of this Directive by legislative, regulatory or administrative measures.'

---

[46] This might be otherwise if such a voluntary agreement was accompanied by binding public law measures, such as the Dutch *algemeen verbindend verklaring*, an instrument by which the applicability of a collective agreement is extended to cover an entire industry. The judgment of the Court in Case 215/83 indicates that this might be the case. Case 215/83 *Commission* v. *Belgium* [1985] ECR 1055.

[47] This would seem to have been confirmed with respect to the repealed Directive 85/339 on containers of liquids for human consumption by the Court's judgment in Case C-255/93 *Commission* v. *France* [1994] ECR I-4949.

[48] OJ 2006 L 266/1. See for other examples Article 22(3a) of Directive 94/62 as amended by Directive 2004/12 on packaging and packaging waste, OJ 2004 L 47/26; Article 17(3) of Directive 2002/96 on waste electrical and electronic equipment, OJ 2003 L 37/24 and Article 10(3) of Directive 2000/53 on end-of-life vehicles, OJ 2000 L 269/34.

The example provided in the Batteries Directive is very much in line with Commission Recommendation 96/733 concerning environmental agreements implementing European directives.[49] The Commission, followed by the Council, has announced that it wants to promote the use environmental agreements as a policy instrument to achieve environmental objectives. It has provided guidelines for the use of such agreements as a means of implementing European directives in the field of the environment and stated them in fairly uncompromising terms. Agreements should in all cases:

- take the form of a contract, enforceable either under civil or under public law;
- specify quantified objectives and indicate intermediary objectives with the corresponding deadlines;
- be published in the national Official Journal or as an official document equally accessible to the public;
- provide for the monitoring of the results achieved, for a regular reporting to the competent authorities and for appropriate information to the public;
- be open to all partners who wish to meet the conditions of the agreement.

Agreements should, where appropriate:

- establish effective arrangements for the collection, evaluation and verification of the results achieved;
- require the participating companies to make available the information regarding the implementation of the agreement to any third person under the same conditions applying to public authorities under Council Directive 90/313[50] on the freedom of access to information on the environment;
- establish dissuasive sanctions such as fines, penalties or the withdrawal of a permit, in case of non-compliance.

There would seem to be little difference between environmental agreements and 'normal' legislation once all these conditions have been met. Nevertheless, we believe it is right that the conditions should be so stringent. It could be argued that Article 249(3) EC not only deals with the manner in which Member States implement directives, but also imposes constraints on the legislative competence of the Council. Or do the principles of legal certainty and legal protection not apply where the Council specifies the choice of implementation instruments in directives on the environment? Presumably they do.

---

49 Commission Recommendation 96/733 concerning environmental agreements implementing Community directives, OJ 1996 L 333/59 and Council Resolution on environmental agreements, OJ 1997 C 321/6.

50 See now however Directive 2003/4 on public access to environmental information and repealing Council Directive 90/313/EEC, OJ 2003 L 41/26.

As yet the Court has not ruled explicitly on whether environmental agreements are an acceptable instrument of implementation.[51] It seems questionable that they can be used to implement those provisions of environmental directives which require – in the words of the Court – implementation with *unquestionable* binding force.[52] On the other hand, it is arguable that they might under certain conditions be used. Not only the conditions mentioned by Commission in its Recommendation 96/733 must be met. It is the authors' opinion that such an agreement would also have to be enforceable before the courts, applicable to the entire sector targeted (including newcomers on the market!) be entered into for an indefinite period and not be unilaterally terminable by the industry concerned. It would also have to provide for guarantees of legal protection for third parties, if the directive was intended to create rights for third parties. But even where all these criteria have been met, the directive would itself – like the Batteries Directive – have to allow sufficient room for implementation by environmental agreement.

2.5 Implementation by Compliance in Fact

A defence frequently employed by national governments during infringement procedures is that no measures have been adopted *in practice* which are in breach of the directive in question. This defence occurs in two kinds of situation. The first is where implementing legislation does exist, but the administrative powers granted under that legislation are too wide in comparison with the underlying directive. The second is where the particular practice that is prohibited by the directive does not occur in that Member State, and there would thus seem no reason to pass legislation.

If the national implementing provisions allow the administrative body in question too much discretion, the directive may well prove not to have been properly implemented. This area is fraught with problems.

An example is the judgment of the Court in Case 291/84, concerning the manner in which the Netherlands had implemented Directive 80/68 on the protection of groundwater.[53] Article 6 concerns artificial recharges of groundwater, which are subject to a special authorisation issued by the Member States on a case-by-case basis and on condition that there is no risk of polluting the groundwater. Accord-

---

[51] An indication that they might be acceptable can be implied from Case C-340/96 *Commission* v. *UK* [1999] ECR I-2023. On the other hand in Case C-96/98 *Commission* v. *France* [2001] ECR I-779, para. 26, the Court held that the agri-environmental measures concerned (in fact contracts concluded between the State and farmers which are designed to develop environmentally conscious farming methods), were 'voluntary and purely hortatory' in nature in nature and therefore not capable of supplementing effectively the protection regime for the classified special conservation areas for wild birds.

[52] Case C-415/01 *Commission* v. *Belgium* [2003] ECR I-2081, para. 21.

[53] Case 291/84 *Commission* v. *Netherlands* [1987] ECR 3483. The 'old' Groundwater Directive will be repealed from 21 December 2013 by the Water Framework Directive 2000/60 (OJ 2000 L 327/1).

ing to the Commission, that second condition was not included in Netherlands legislation. Article 14 of the *Grondwaterwet* (Law on groundwater) merely provided that the authorisation may be issued on terms such as to ensure the proper management of groundwater, and thus leaves the national authorities issuing the authorisation greater latitude than is permitted by the directive. The Netherlands Government contended that as a matter of policy such authorisation was granted only when there was no danger of pollution. However, the Court accepted the Commission's argument: 'As the Commission maintains, the possibility under the Netherlands legislation of making authorization conditional on proper groundwater management cannot be held to satisfy the requirement that the risk of groundwater pollution must be examined when an authorization is issued under Article 6 of the directive. Article 6 of Directive 80/68/EEC has therefore not been transposed into national law with sufficient precision.'

If a statutory provision leaves the national authorities too much discretionary power, it cannot successfully be argued that the obligations contained in a directive have been implemented by legislation. In that case implementation is only effected when an authorisation is issued under the legislation. The Court will not accept this.[54] Therefore, the conclusion is clear. If the legislation implementing the directive grants too much administrative freedom, this cannot be compensated by bringing the practice of issuing authorisations into line with the requirements of the directive.[55] Further legislative action is required.

Case C-339/87 concerning the implementation of the Wild Birds Directive in the Dutch legal system is also illustrative of the second kind of situation referred to above. Under Article 5(c) of the Wild Birds Directive, Member States are required to take measures prohibiting taking birds' eggs in the wild and keeping them, even if empty. Under the provisions of the Dutch *Jachtwet* it was permitted to seek, collect or possess the eggs of the wood pigeon, the carrion crow, the jackdaw, the jay and the magpie. The Dutch Government argued that in fact eggs of these species were not sought or collected in the Netherlands and that legislation was therefore unnecessary. The Court rejected this defence: 'The fact that a number of activities incompatible with the prohibitions contained in the directive are

---

[54] Another example is Case C-339/87 concerning the implementation of the Wild Birds Directive in the Dutch legal system; Case C-339/87 *Commission* v. *Netherlands* [1990] ECR I-851. The Court, in its consideration of the Dutch *Jachtwet* (Hunting Act), expressly stated that '[T]he explanation that the requirements as to protection set out in Article 9 of the directive are observed in fact by ministerial practice with regard to the use of hunting permits cannot be accepted, since [...] mere administrative practices, which by their nature may be changed at will by the authorities, cannot be regarded as constituting proper compliance with the obligation on Member States to which a directive is addressed.'

[55] Cf. also Case C-392/99 *Commission* v. *Portugal* [2003] ECR I-3373, para. 79 *et seq.* on the permitting conditions of the Waste Oils Directive. The Court speaks of 'implementation of the requisite measures must constitute a *sine qua non* for issue of the permit', leaving no doubt about the required clearness of the implementing legislation.

unknown in a particular Member State cannot justify the absence of appropriate legal provisions. In order to secure the full implementation of directives in law and not only in fact, Member States must establish a specific legal framework in the area in question.'

In other words, it is important not only that an activity that is prohibited by directive does not occur in *fact*, but also that it *may not occur in law*. This is not mere legal formalism on the part of the Court. It is a requirement of legal certainty. In the case in question, the Advocate General considered that a Member State would only be relieved of its obligation to implement the provisions of the directive if the practices in question could not occur on its territory. In that case national legislation would not be required.

In Case C-290/89 it is apparent that the Commission has adopted this view.[56] This case concerned the defective implementation by Belgium of Directives 75/440 and 79/869 concerning the quality and methods of measurement of surface water intended for the abstraction of drinking water in the Member States.[57] The Commission accepted the Belgian position that no measure of transposition was required for the Brussels Region since there is no surface water in that region intended for the production of drinking water. Although the Court did not explicitly consider the matter, it is clear from the operative part of the judgment that Belgium was only held to have failed to fulfil its obligations under the Treaty because it had not taken the measures necessary to implement the directives in the Flemish and Walloon Regions. No reference was made to the Brussels Region.
    The fact that there is no titanium dioxide industry on Portuguese territory does of course not mean that Portugal is not required to submit to the Commission a report on the implementation of the TiO2 Directive. According the Court, Portugal must indicate that fact in its report, which it may not dispense with under any circumstances.[58]

This seems a sensible solution. If a situation cannot in fact occur, there is no need for legislative measures.

This applies, for example, to the Netherlands in respect of implementation of Article 4(2) of Directive 91/271 concerning urban waste water management.[59] This provides for measures in respect of discharges to waters situated in high mountain regions (over 1500 m above sea level). As the highest point in the Netherlands is only 300 m above sea level, this provision is totally irrelevant in the Netherlands. The difference between this provision and the ones in Article 5 of the Wild Birds Directive discussed above is clear. Seeking and collecting certain eggs

---

[56] Case C-290/89 *Commission v. Belgium* [1991] ECR I-2851.

[57] Both directives will be repealed by the Water Framework Directive by 22 December 2007.

[58] Case C-435/99 *Commission v. Portugal* [2000] ECR I-11179.

[59] OJ 1991 L 135/40.

may not occur in the Netherlands now but it cannot be ruled out that this might change in the future. The practice referred to in the Urban Waste Water Directive not only does not occur, but also could not occur. That is why the Netherlands does have to implement the provisions of the former, but not of the latter, directive.

Legal writers have severely criticised the Court's strict approach as being unduly formalist. This criticism is not really justified. If the Court were not to adopt such a strict approach to the formal side of implementation, it would become impossible for the Commission to exercise any kind of effective control on compliance with directives inside the Member States. After all, the Commission would then be unable to rely on national laws, but would have to take on the actual control of compliance. In view of the limited size of the Commission apparatus and its extremely limited investigative powers within the territory of the Member States, such *de facto* control can hardly be regarded as a realistic proposition. In terms of the European legal order it is therefore of great importance that obligations imposed by directives are properly transposed into national laws. In this light the Court's case law should be regarded not as unduly formalistic, but as providing legal certainty in European environmental law.

2.6   Use of Different Wording in National Legislation

It has been stated above that incorporation of a directive into national law does not necessarily require the formal repetition of its rules word for word in an express, specific, statutory provision. Depending on its content a general legal context may be satisfactory, provided that it effectively ensures full application of the directive in a way which is sufficiently clear and precise so that, if the directive aims to create rights for individuals, they will be able to ascertain the full extent of their rights and to rely on them before the national courts, if necessary.[60] One of the reasons for a national legislature not to adopt the definitions from a directive word for word is to avoid causing confusion. There is no need to adopt the definitions contained in a directive if the national store of concepts is wide enough to include the concepts used in the directive. However, if the national legislature chooses not to adopt the provisions of a directive formally and word for word, or if it takes the view that the existing legal framework is adequate to satisfy the requirements of the directive, there is a danger that the national concepts will not provide a seamless fit with those used in the directive. There may be some slight divergence between the obligations set out in the directive and the requirements of the national provisions. In other words there will be a greater danger that implementation is not complete.

---

[60]   Case C-190/90 *Commission v. Netherlands* [1992] ECR I-3265.

Case 412/85 is interesting in this connection.[61] The case concerned a provision in the German *Bundesnaturschutzgesetz*. Paragraph 22(3) allowed a departure from the prohibitions in respect of bird protection where the acts take place in the course of 'the normal use of the land for agricultural, forestry or fishing purposes'. According to Article 5 of the Wild Birds Directive, Member States are required to prohibit deliberate killing or capture and deliberate destruction of nests and eggs. Unintentional acts are not prohibited by the directive. The German Government argued that the derogations provided for in Paragraph 22(3) presuppose the absence of any intentional acts. The activities defined by Paragraph 22(3), such as the normal use of land, could never be regarded as constituting a deliberate failure to protect birds, because actions performed with the intention of killing, capturing, disturbing, keeping or selling wild birds cannot be described as forming part of normal agricultural, forestry or fishing activities. The Court was not prepared to accept this interpretation. It held that Paragraph 22(3) does not provide a precise indication of the extent to which damage to the environment is permitted. The concept of the normal use of the land and the concept of an unintentional infringement of the provisions for the protection of birds belong to two different legal planes. Since the German legislation does not define the concept of 'normal use', unintentional damage to the life and habitat of birds is not excluded from the scope of Paragraph 22 (3) of the *Bundesnaturschutzgesetz* in so far as such damage is necessary in the course of the normal use of the land. Thus the German Government's attempt to translate the concept of 'unintentional infringement' using the national concept of 'the normal use of the land' foundered. The Court held that these were not equivalent, and that German law therefore conflicted with the provisions of the Wild Birds Directive.

Another example of Court of Justice case law relates to the implementation of Article 9 of the same directive. Under this provision Member States are permitted to derogate from the provisions on bird protection contained in Articles 5 to 8 of the directive for various reasons. For example, 'to prevent serious damage to crops, livestock, forests, fisheries and water'. The question is to what extent the concept of 'serious damage' has to be incorporated into the national legal systems. In Case 247/85 the Commission argued that it was essential that the expression should be used in the Belgian legislation, but the Belgian Government disputed this.[62] The Court stated: 'In this regard it must be noted that the aim of this provision of the directive is not to prevent the threat of minor damage. The fact that a certain degree of damage is required for this derogation from the general system of protection accords with the degree of protection sought by the directive.

It must, however, be noted that the Commission has not proved that the concept of 'damage' in the Belgian rules is not interpreted and applied in the same way as the concept of 'serious damage' in the third indent of Article 9(1)(a) of the directive. This part of the complaint cannot therefore be upheld.'

---

[61] Case 412/85 *Commission v. Germany* [1987] ECR 3503.

[62] Case 247/85 *Commission v. Belgium* [1987] ECR 3029.

In other words, literal transposition is not necessary, as long as the provision is interpreted and applied as intended in the directive.

This judgment was confirmed several months later in Case 236/85 concerning the manner in which the Wild Birds Directive had been implemented in Dutch law.[63] Article 2 of the Dutch *Vogelwet*, which allows derogations from the bird protection regulations, did not contain the term 'serious damage'. The Netherlands Government claimed that the exceptions from the provisions regarding the protection of birds relate only to certain species which do indeed cause serious damage, so that the requirements of Article 9 of the directive were satisfied. The Court, referring to its judgment in Case 247/85, concluded that the Commission had not made any submissions that might establish that the Netherlands legislation attributed to the permitted derogations greater scope than is given to them by the directive as so interpreted. It therefore followed that the Commission's complaint could not be upheld.

However, sometimes the Court is stricter. Another issue which was raised in the same case was whether a further requirement of Article 9 of the directive had to be literally transposed. Derogation under Article 9 is allowed only 'where there is no other satisfactory solution'. The Court observed:

'As regards Article 20 of the *Vogelwet*, it must be stated that the exception to the protection of birds which it contains is likewise not founded on any of the criteria laid down in Article 9 of the directive. Moreover, Article 20 of the *Vogelwet* takes no account of the fact that any derogation is conditional upon there being no other satisfactory solution. The fact that administrative practice in the Netherlands appears to be in conformity with the criteria laid down in Article 9 of the directive – a situation which, moreover, the Commission acknowledges – is not sufficient to ensure adequate transposition of the directive into national law.'

This judgment illustrates the point that the Court does not always explain why one provision of a directive should be incorporated into national law and another not.

An example of a much more global approach to the question of whether obligations under a directive have been properly implemented can be found, e.g. in the *Post-Seveso* case.[64]

The Commission argued that the Netherlands had not fully implemented Article 3 of the Post-Seveso Directive. Article 3 of the directive provided that Member States must adopt the provisions necessary to ensure that, in the case of any of the industrial activities specified, the manufacturer is obliged to take all the measures necessary to prevent major accidents and to limit their consequences

---

[63] Case 236/85 *Commission v. Netherlands* [1987] ECR 3989.

[64] Case C-190/90 *Commission v. Netherlands* [1992] ECR I-3265.

for man and the environment. The Court observed that, like the directive, all the national legislation to which the Dutch Government referred, has the objective of the adoption of specific, effective measures for preventing major accidents and any consequences they may have outside the establishment. It is worth noting that in this case the Court seems to attach great importance to the concurrence of the objectives of the directive and the national environmental legislation. Reference was made to all the national legislation which served to implement Article 3. This would indeed seem to indicate a more global approach to the question of whether a Member State has properly implemented a directive, whereby the Court would not examine to what extent each specific national regulation contributed to implementation.

The above examples show that it will generally be acceptable for a Member State not to adopt provisions and concepts in a directive literally, but that it will then run the risk that it will not properly have fulfilled its obligations under the directive. The Court is stricter in some cases than in other, apparently similar, cases. Bearing in mind the unpredictability of the Court, if a national legislature wishes to apply its own national concepts when implementing a directive, it is advised to operate with extreme care and precision.

2.7   Implementation by Local or Regional Authorities

As the Court has frequently stated, each Member State is free to attribute or delegate powers to its public authorities as it considers fit[65] and to implement directives by means of measures adopted by regional or local authorities. That division of powers does not however release it from the obligation to ensure that the provisions of the directive are properly implemented in national law.[66] It is thus irrelevant in European law whether a directive is implemented by the central government by means of legal rules which are universally applicable within its territory, or by local or regional authorities such as the German *Länder*, the Dutch *provincieën*, the *Comunidades Autónomas* in Spain[67], or the Belgian *Gewesten*. European law makes only one condition. The Member State must ensure that European environmental law is adopted and applied throughout its territory in accordance with the provisions of the directive.[68]

---

[65] Only occasionally does a directive try to limit national discretion in this respect. See for instance Article 3 of Directive 96/62 on ambient air quality assessment and management (OJ 1996 L 296/55): 'For the implementation of this Directive, the Member States shall designate *at the appropriate levels* the competent authorities and bodies responsible for [...]'. Emphasis added. Cf. Case C-417/99 *Commission* v. *Spain* [2001] ECR I-6015.

[66] Joined Cases 227-230/85 *Commission* v. *Belgium* [1988] ECR 1, Case C-225/96 *Commission* v. *Italy* [1997] ECR I-6887 and Case C-236/99 *Commission* v. *Belgium* [2000] ECR I-5657.

[67] Cf. Case C-474/99 *Commission* v. *Spain* [2002] ECR I-5293, with respect to the implementation of the EIA Directive.

[68] Cf. Case C-260/93 *Commission* v. *Belgium* [1994] ECR I-1611 and also Case C-225/96 *Commission* v. *Italy* [1997] ECR I-687, where it was shown that only 11 of Italy's 20 regions had made a designation of shell-

The Commission has indeed occasionally attempted to restrict decentralisation it has considered to be too extreme. According to Article 5 of the 'old' Waste Directive, Member States had to designate the competent authority or authorities to be responsible 'in a given zone' for organizing waste disposal operations. These will generally be regional or local authorities. The Court had already stated in the *Traen* case that this provision does not lay down any restrictive criteria concerning the choice of competent authorities to be responsible for the planning, organisation, authorisation and supervision of waste disposal operations.[69]

In later proceedings the Commission argued that a Member State, to avoid excessive fragmentation of the relevant powers, must not allocate these powers to an excessive number of local authorities.[70] This argument also seemed to appeal to Advocate General Jacobs. Though it is true that the Member States are competent to designate the competent authorities, this competence is limited by the need to ensure respect for the aims of the directive, namely, the protection of human health and the environment. In his opinion, Member States should not therefore divide responsibility for designating the competent authorities to such an extent that the achievement of these aims is jeopardised. The Court did not refer to these remarks at all, but relied on the express text of the directive, which allowed the issue of authorisations by local and regional authorities.

If it were decided that a directive was to be implemented by autonomous measures on the part of local authorities, it would be necessary for the national legislatures to make provision for the event the local authorities should fail to fulfil the obligations under European law.

In Case C-237/90, Germany was held to have failed to comply with its obligations under the now repealed Directive 80/778 relating to the quality of water intended for human consumption.[71] According to Article 10(1), the competent national authorities could, in the event of emergencies, allow the maximum admissible concentration to be exceeded. Article 10(3) provided that Member States which have recourse to this derogation shall immediately inform the Commission

---

fish waters, covering little more than 50% of the national territory. See also Case C-365/97 *Commission v. Italy* [1999] ECR I-7773, para. 69, where the Court ruled that the fact that Italy had failed to fulfil its obligation under Framework Waste Directive only in the San Rocco valley, cannot have a bearing on any finding of an infringement. Cf. also Case C-292/99 *Commission* v. *France* [2002] ECR I-4097, where the Court ruled 'a failure to fulfil the obligation to draw up waste management plans must be regarded as serious, even if the failure relates to only a very small part of a Member State's territory, such as a single department [...], or a single area within a valley'.

[69] Joined Cases 372-374/85 *Traen* [1987] ECR 2141. See now Article 6 of the 'new' Waste Directive: 'Member States shall establish or designate the competent authority or authorities to be responsible for implementing this Directive.'

[70] Case C-359/88 *Zanetti* [1990] ECR I-1509.

[71] Case C-237/90 *Commission* v. *Germany* [1992] ECR I-5973. Cf. now Directive 98/83 on the quality of water intended for human consumption, OJ 1998 L 330/32.

thereof, stating the reasons for and probable duration of such derogation. In Germany, application of this derogation was delegated to the *Länder*. Germany was held to have failed to meet its obligations because it had not ensured its national laws contained provisions to require the *Länder* to notify the central government of such derogations, so that it in turn could comply with its obligation to notify the Commission. The Court took a similar judgment in Case C-301/95.[72] The case concerned the manner in which Germany had transposed the EIA Directive. The directive was implemented partly at federal level and partly at the level of the *Länder*. The Court ruled that all of the national provisions, including those of the *Länder*, had to be communicated to the Commission. In this respect it was irrelevant that federal law takes precedence over regional provisions.

Regional implementation has also given rise to problems in Belgium. For example, waste management legislation there has been delegated to the regional authorities. Meanwhile the central government does not have the power to require the regional authorities to implement European legislation on waste, or to take alternative measures if the regional authorities fail to fulfil their obligations. In Joined Cases 227 to 230/85, this omission did not prevent the Court finding the State of Belgium had failed to meet its obligations under the directives on waste.[73] The Court has consistently held that a Member State may not plead provisions, practices or circumstances existing in its internal legal system in order to justify a failure to comply with its obligations under European law.[74]

3 Transposition of Environmental Regulations?

A regulation is the appropriate legal instrument where precise requirements must be imposed directly on the parties concerned, which are to be implemented at the same time and in the same manner throughout the EU. In spite of the fact that regulations are, according to Article 249(1) EC, directly applicable in the Member States and thus do not generally have be transposed into the national legal systems to be effective, national authorities may nevertheless have to issue rules, particularly in the areas of enforcement and the designation of competent public authorities. The problem of which national implementing instrument to choose is therefore also relevant where European environmental law is enacted by regulation.

---

[72] Case C-301/95 *Commission v. Germany* [1998] ECR I-6135.

[73] Joined Cases 227-230/85 *Commission v. Belgium* [1988] ECR 1.

[74] Cf. also Case C-71/97 *Commission v. Spain* [1998] ECR I-5991, Case C-274/98 *Commission v. Spain* [2000] ECR I-2823 and Case C-297/95 *Commission v. Germany* [1996] ECR I-6739.

A good example was Regulation 259/93 on the supervision and control of ship-ments of waste.[75] The regulation contained numerous provisions which had to be worked out by the Member States. Thus Member States had to take appropriate legal action to prohibit and punish illegal shipments (Article 26(5)) and to require that financial guarantees are provided (Article 27(3)) and they also had to make all kinds of organisational arrangements. Where details of important provisions in a regulation are left to be worked out by the Member States, the dividing line between directives and regulations becomes very hard to draw. It is therefore not surprising that Regulation 259/93 entered 'into force' on the third day following its publication in the Official Journal of the EC, but that it did not became applicable 15 months after publication (Article 44). In fact this gave the Member States 15 months to produce the necessary 'implementing' legislation.

Because substantive law does not have to be incorporated into the national legal systems in order to implement a regulation, the following consequence should be noted. The legal consequences of annulment of an environmental regulation are generally much more far-reaching than in the case of a directive.[76] Suppose, for example, that the Court had held in the *Basel Regulation* case[77] that Regula-tion 259/93 must be regarded as invalid. In that case there would be no provi-sions left which could be applied and enforced at a national level, as there would be with a directive. The annulment of the TiO2 Directive in the *TiO2* case[78] did not mean that national implementing measures could no longer be applied. In so far as these measures were in conformity with the rules of European law (and national law!), they could be applied without any problem. The danger of a legal vacuum at the national level in the event of the annulment of a European regula-tion on the environment is therefore all the greater.

An important difference between regulations and directives is that regulations may have direct legal consequences for individuals. Environmental directives, on the other hand, cannot impose obligations on individuals unless there are national rules implementing them. In other words, they have no 'direct horizon-tal effect'.[79] Environmental regulations do, in principle. Once a regulation has entered into force (or, as the case may be, from the date on which it has to be applied), it directly binds individuals. It is therefore very important to determine whether a provision of European law must be regarded as a provision in a direc-tive or one in a regulation. Generally this will not be a problem, as the Council's decision will clearly indicate whether a measure is a directive or a regulation.

---

75 OJ 1993 L 30/1, later amended. Cf. Article 50 of the 'new' Regulation 1013/2006 on shipments of waste, OJ 2006 L 190/1. Regulation 1013/2006 repealed Regulation 259/93 with effect from 12 July 2007.

76 Cf. in general on invalid directives Vandamme (2005).

77 Case C-187/93 *EP* v. *Council* [1994] ECR I-2857.

78 Case C-300/89 *Commission* v. *Council* [1991] ECR I-2867.

79 See Chapter 5, section 2.1.2.

However, it is sometimes less easy to determine the legal nature of a European environmental provision.

> Take, for example, Article 16 of Regulation 304/2003 concerning the export and import of dangerous chemicals.[80] Dangerous chemicals which are intended for export are made subject to the measures on packaging and labelling established pursuant to Directive 67/548.[81] In fact Article 16 of the regulation is here extending the scope of application of the directive. It is not clear whether this extension has the characteristics of a directive or of a regulation. As has been stated, the distinction is important for the purpose of establishing whether the measure has direct horizontal effect.

4 Enforcement of European Environmental Law

4.1 General Remarks

The mere transposition of environmental directives into national law is, of course, not enough. The obligations they contain have first to be applied and then enforced. This is primarily, but certainly not exclusively, a responsibility of the Member States. Article 175(4) EC states in so many words that the Member States shall implement the environment policy.[82] However, the Court has held in connection with Article 10 EC that, to the extent that environmental directives and regulations do not provide for specific enforcement obligations, national enforcement measures must be proportionate, effective and preventive.[83] Furthermore, national rules dealing with infringements of European environmental standards should not be less favourable than those governing infringements of national environment rules. Except for Article 10 EC, many of the environmental measures taken by the European legislature contain a general obligation in this respect. Therefore, enforcement of European environmental law can be characterised as a shared responsibility.[84]

> For instance Article 8 of Directive 2005/35 on ship-source pollution and on the introduction of penalties for infringements states: '1. Member States shall take the necessary measures to ensure that infringements within the meaning of Article 4 are subject to effective, proportionate and dissuasive penalties, which may include criminal or administrative penalties.

---

[80] OJ 1992 L 251/13, later amended.

[81] OJ 2003 L 63/1.

[82] Or as the Court has held in the *San Rocco* case: 'it is primarily for the national authorities to conduct the necessary on-the-spot investigations'; Case C-365/97 *Commission v. Italy* [1999] ECR I-7773, para. 85.

[83] Case C-186/98 *Nunes en de Matos* [1999] ECR I-4883.

[84] See also Recommendation of the European Parliament and of the Council providing for minimum criteria for environmental inspections in the Member States, OJ 2001 L 118/41.

2. Each Member State shall take the measures necessary to ensure that the penalties referred to in paragraph 1 apply to any person who is found responsible for an infringement within the meaning of Article 4.'

In the absence of concrete and specific provisions, it is in the first place for Member States to determine how the factual situation must be brought in line with the legally desired situation. The manner in which European environmental law is enforced by the Member States is however under Commission control. Inadequate enforcement, once again in law and in fact, may be a reason for the Commission to initiate proceedings under Article 226 EC (Article 258 FEU).[85] It should be noted that the Commission does not have any formal competence to ensure compliance with European environmental legislation on the territory of the Member States. Only occasionally is the Commission given some investigative competences in secondary legislation. This is for example the case in Article 20 of Regulation 2037/2000 on substances that deplete the ozone layer.[86]

On a voluntary basis Member States sometimes allow Commission officials in their territory for inspection. For instance, in 1998, Commission officials went on a mission to Zakinthos (Greece) to verify whether any measures for the protection, required by the Habitats Directive, of the sea turtle *Caretta caretta* had in fact been implemented. In the course of the mission, they visited the beaches at Laganas, Kalamaki, Sekania, Dafni and Gerakas, the places where that species lays its eggs.[87]

European environmental measures sometimes contain provisions which require a certain type of enforcement by the Member States. In many cases the requirements are couched in fairly general terms in the sense that Member States must take appropriate legal or administrative action in case of infringement of the provisions of the directive or regulation.[88] In other cases the requirements are more detailed, as in Article 17 of Directive 90/219 on the contained use of genetically modified micro-organisms, which provides that Member States shall ensure that the competent authority organises inspections and other control measures to ensure compliance with the directive.[89]

---

[85] Cf. for instance the unpublished judgment in Case C-317/02 *Commission v. Ireland*, judgment of 18 November 2004. The Court ruled that Member States are required to ensure that the appropriate measures are taken, including administrative action or criminal proceedings, against those persons who have failed to comply with European rules.

[86] OJ 2000 L 244/1, as amended. See Article 20(4) of the regulation in particular: 'Subject to the agreement of the Commission and of the competent authority of the Member State within the territory of which the investigations are to be made, the officials of the Commission shall assist the officials of that authority in the performance of their duties.'

[87] Case C-103/00 *Commission v. Greece* [2002] ECR I-1147.

[88] For example Article 21 of the Regulation 2037/2000 on substances that deplete the ozone layer, OJ 2000 L 244/1: 'Member States shall determine the necessary penalties applicable to breaches of this Regulation. The penalties shall be effective, proportionate and dissuasive.'

[89] OJ 1990 L 117/1, later amended. See also Article 18(2) of the Seveso II Directive 96/82. It states that the competent authorities are required to organise an inspection system which can either consist of a

We could also point at the obligation contained in Article 13(1) of the Waste Oils Directive under which undertakings shall be inspected periodically by the Member States, particularly as regards their compliance with the conditions of their permits. The case law of the Court of Justice shows that the implementing national legislation must 'ensure that the undertakings concerned are in fact inspected periodically'.[90] Or take Article 4(9) of the Waste Incineration Directive: 'If an incineration or co-incineration plant does not comply with the conditions of the permit, in particular with the emission limit values for air and water, the competent authority shall take action to enforce compliance.'[91] This provision surely implies a duty for the authorities to shut down a plant, if necessary, when the emission limit values are exceeded by the undertaking.

Only occasionally does an environmental legislative measure contain an obligation to ensure criminal enforcement.[92] Member States are quick to regard such requirements as an incursion on their own competence.

An exception was Article 26(5) of Regulation 259/93, under which the Member States had to take appropriate legal action 'to prohibit and punish' illegal traffic of waste.[93] Another example is provided by Directive 2005/35 on ship-source pollution and on the introduction of penalties for infringements.[94] According to Article 4 of the directive: 'Member States shall ensure that ship-source discharges of polluting substances into any of the areas referred to in Article 3(1) are regarded as infringements if committed with intent, recklessly or by serious negligence. These infringements are regarded as criminal offences by, and in the circumstances provided for in, Framework Decision 2005/667/JHA supplementing this Directive.' And in Article 18 of the same directive: '1. Member States shall take the necessary measures to ensure that infringements within the meaning of Article 4 are subject to effective, proportionate and dissuasive penalties, which may include criminal or administrative penalties. 2. Each Member State shall take the measures necessary to ensure that the penalties referred to in paragraph 1 apply to any person who is found responsible for an infringement within the meaning of Article 4.'

---

systematic appraisal of each establishment or of at least one on-site inspection per year.

[90] Case C-392/99 *Commission* v. *Portugal* [2003] ECR I-3373, para. 168.

[91] Directive 2000/76 on the incineration of waste, OJ 2000 L 332/91.

[92] Cf. more general on the efforts of the EU harmonising environmental criminal law our observations in Chapter 1, section 3.

[93] OJ 1993 L 30/1, later amended. Cf. however now Article 50 of the 'new' Regulation 1013/2006 on shipments of waste, OJ 2006 L 190/1. It speaks more generally on 'penalties' that 'must be effective, proportionate and dissuasive'. Regulation 1013/2006 has repealed Regulation 259/93 with effect from 12 July 2007.

[94] OJ 2005/ L 255/11. See also the annullment of Council Framework Decision 2005/667 to strengthen the criminal-law framework for the enforcement of the law against ship-source pollution (OJ 2005 L 255/164) by the ECJ in Case C-440/05 *Commission* v. *Council*, judgment of 23 October 2007, n.y.r. in the ECR.

It will be clear that the differences between environmental directives as regards the action to be taken to enforce them are still great. Even ignoring the fact that some directives contain no provisions on enforcement at all, it seems there can be no question of a coherent European enforcement policy yet.

At a more practical level, we must note the importance of the IMPEL network. Since its inception in 1992, the informal EU Network for the Implementation and Enforcement of Environmental Law (IMPEL), consisting of European regulators and inspectors concerned with the implementation and enforcement of environmental law, has been a key instrument in discussing the practical application and enforcement of existing legislation.[95]

Enforcement in law and in fact

It was stated above that directives have to be implemented not only in fact, but also in law. Conversely, even where a directive is adequately transposed into national law, but the national provisions are not effectively enforced, this will not suffice either. Or in the words of the Court, with respect to the Waste Incineration Directive: 'Accordingly, a Member State will comply with its obligations under Directive 89/369 and thus achieve the result prescribed therein only if, in addition to the correct implementation of the provisions of that directive into domestic law, the incineration plants located in its territory have in actual fact been commissioned and operate in accordance with the requirements of the provisions of Directive 89/369'.[96]

> The first time this was confirmed, at least in the environment sector, was in Case C-42/89, in which the Court held that Belgium had failed to fulfil its obligations under the Treaty because the supply of drinking water to the city of Verviers did not in fact meet the required standards.[97] Furthermore, in the *Großkrotzenburg* case, the Court rejected Germany's claim that, under Article 226 EC, the Commission is not entitled to bring an action, in respect of failure in a specific case.[98]
>
> Another case which is relevant in this connection is Case C-361/88 concerning the absence of appropriate measures for securing observance of air quality limit values (sulphur dioxide).[99] Article 3(1) of Directive 80/779 required the Member States to take appropriate measures to ensure that as from 1 April 1983 the concentrations of sulphur dioxide in the atmosphere are not greater than the limit values given in the directive. As far as the legal situation in Germany was concerned, the Court concluded: 'There are, therefore, no general and mandatory

---

[95] See http://ec.europa.eu/environment/impel/index.htm.

[96] Case C-139/00 *Commission v. Spain* [2002] ECR I-6407. Directive 89/369 is repealed by the 'new' Waste Incineration Directive 2000/76.

[97] Case C-42/89 *Commission v. Belgium* [1990] ECR I-2821.

[98] Case C-431/92 *Commission v. Germany* [1995] ECR I-2189.

[99] Case C-361/88 *Commission v. Germany* [1991] ECR I-2567. Directive 80/779 is no longer valid since 1 January 2005.

rules under which the administrative authorities are required to adopt measures in all the cases where the limit values of the directive are likely to be exceeded.'

This indicates that Member States are required not merely to do their best to enforce standards contained in a directive, but to produce the desired result.

An example of a Court of Justice judgment where a Member State was held to have failed to implement a directive *in fact* is the *Blackpool* case.[100] In this case the United Kingdom was held to have failed to take all the necessary measures to ensure that the quality of bathing water in the bathing areas in Blackpool and adjacent to Formby and Southport conformed to the limit values set in accordance with the Bathing Water Directive.[101] The main argument of the UK Government was that it had taken 'all practicable steps' to meet the limit values. The Court rejected this argument, observing that it was clear from Article 4(1) of the directive that the Member States are to take all necessary measures to ensure that, within 10 years following the notification of the directive, bathing water conforms to the limit values set in accordance with Article 3 of the directive. It added that this period is longer than that laid down for the implementation of the directive, namely two years from the date of notification (Article 12(1)), in order to enable the Member States to comply with this requirement. The only derogations from the obligation contained in Article 4(1) are those provided for in Articles 4(3), 5(2) and 8. The Court reached the following conclusion: 'It follows that the directive requires the Member States to take steps to ensure that certain results are attained, and, apart from those derogations, they cannot rely on particular circumstances to justify a failure to fulfil that obligation. Consequently, the United Kingdom's argument that it took all practicable steps cannot afford a further ground, in addition to the derogations expressly permitted, justifying the failure to fulfil the obligation to bring the waters at issue into conformity at least with the annex to the directive.' The operative part of the judgment makes it quite clear. The Court declared that, 'by failing to take all the necessary measures to ensure that the quality of the bathing water in Blackpool and of those adjacent to Southport conforms to the limit values set in accordance with Article 3 of Council Directive 76/160/EEC [...] the United Kingdom has failed to fulfil its obligations under the EEC Treaty.' In other words, there is nothing for it but to ensure that the bathing water conforms to the limit values set in the directive.[102]

---

[100] Case C-56/90 *Commission v. UK* [1993] ECR I-4109. Cf. also Case C-427/00 *Commission v. UK* [2001] ECR I-8535.

[101] See for the consolidated version of the Bathing Water Directive, Directive 2006/7 concerning the management of bathing water quality and repealing Directive 76/160/EEC, OJ 2006 L 64/37.

[102] This strict approach is also apparent in a case concerning the failure in parts of Germany to comply with the standards in the Bathing Water Directive, Case C-198/97 *Commission v. Germany* [1999] ECR I-3257: 'Contrary to what the German Government claims, it is not sufficient to take all reasonably practicable measures: the Directive requires the Member States to take all necessary measures to ensure that bathing waters conform to the limit values set therein, within a period which is longer than that laid down

The Court ruled that Member States must, in order to secure the full implementation of directives in law and not only in fact, establish a specific legal framework in the area in question. In the case of the mechanism of undertakings which was at issue in these proceedings, the Court held that this had not been achieved.

'[The Act] authorises the Secretary of State to accept an undertaking on the sole condition that it contains such measures as it appears to him for the time being to be appropriate for the company to take in order to secure or facilitate compliance with the standards in question. The Act thus does not specify the matters to be covered by the undertakings, in particular the parameters to be observed in respect of derogations, the programme of work to be carried out and the time within which it must be completed, and, where appropriate, the information to be given to the population groups concerned.'

This judgment makes it clear that a statutory system which allows the government to tolerate infringements of a directive is incompatible with European law.[103]

It is not entirely clear to what extent the Court has adopted a more flexible approach for the Member States in the *San Rocco* case, already mentioned above in this chapter.[104] This case involved the enforcement of Article 4 of the 'old' Framework Waste Directive, according to which Member States were required to take the necessary measures to ensure that waste is disposed of without endangering human health and without harming the environment. The Commission accused the Italian Government of having failed to take measures to repair the ecological situation in the San Rocco valley. As far as the alleged infringement of Article 4 of the directive was concerned, the Court observed that even though this provision did not say anything about the actual content of the measures to be taken, it was nevertheless binding on the Member States in respect of the

---

for transposition of the Directive, in order to enable the Member States to satisfy such a requirement [...]. The Directive therefore requires the Member States to ensure that certain results are achieved and, apart from the derogations provided for, does not allow them to rely on particular circumstances to justify a failure to fulfil that obligation.' See also, with respect to the Bathing Water Directive case C-268/00 *Commission* v. *Netherlands* [2002] ECR I-2995, para. 12: 'the Directive is not to be understood as meaning that the Member States need only *endeavour* to adopt all reasonably feasible measures. On the contrary, that provision imposes upon Member States an *obligation to achieve a particular result*'. Emphasis added by the authors.

[103] Cf. also, outside the field of environmental law, Case C-265/95 *Commission* v. *France* [1997] ECR I-6959. See on the possible role of this judgment on Member States' duties to enforce environmental law Temmink (2000) at 77-80.

[104] Case C-365/97 *Commission* v. *Italy* [1999] ECR I-7773. Cf. for a similar case, and confirming *San Rocco*, concerning an illegal waste site in Greece, Case C-420/02 *Commission* v. *Greece* [2004] ECR I-11175. See also Chapter 8, section 15.

objective to be achieved, albeit that they were allowed some measure of discretion in assessing the need for such measures. However, the Court went on, where a factual situation is not consistent with the objectives set out in Article 4 it cannot in principle be concluded from this that the Member State in question has necessarily failed to fulfil its obligation to comply with Article 4. Continuation of such a factual situation, particularly where this results in a significant deterioration of the environment during a prolonged period without the competent authorities intervening, may however indicate that the Member State has exceeded the limits of its discretion. In other words, the key element is not the actual violation of the environmental objectives but the failure of the competent authorities to respond adequately.

This judgment seems to imply that the mere fact that the factual situation is not in accordance with the directive does not in itself mean that the Member State is infringing its environmental obligations. It should be noted however that the obligation in Article 4 of the Waste Framework Directive was framed in very general terms and this may have been the reason the Court adopted this more flexible approach. Be that as it may, these judgments underline the fact that not only failure properly to transpose a directive into national law may cause the Court to hold that a Member State has failed to fulfil its obligations, but also a factual infringement of European standards.

General practices of non-compliance

Finally, we have to note that according to the judgment of the European Court of Justice in Case C-494/01 (*Commission* v. *Ireland*) on 12 specific factual infringements of the Waste Framework Directive, the Court ruled that 'in principle nothing prevents the Commission from seeking in parallel a finding that provisions of a directive have not been complied with by reason of the conduct of a Member State's authorities with regard to particular specifically identified situations and a finding that those provisions have not been complied with because its authorities have adopted a general practice contrary thereto, which the particular situations illustrate where appropriate.'[105] In other words, the Commission is entitled to deduct from a series of *individual* infringements, that there is a 'general practice' of non-compliance and non-enforcement. This implies that the Commission is not only entitled to demand that these individual infringements of the directive are remedied, but also that the public authorities in question change, more fundamentally and structurally, their enforcement policies.[106] To qualify as a general practice of non-compliance it must be, to some degree, of a consistent and general nature and must not be geographically confined to only a part of the territory of the Member State in question.[107]

---

[105] Case C-494/01 *Commission* v. *Ireland* [2005] ECR I-3331, para. 27 in particular.

[106] Cf. Wennerås (2007) at 252 *et seq.*

[107] Case C-441/02 *Commission* v. *Germany* [2006] ECR I-3449, para. 50, and on the criterium of 'geographically confined' Case C-248/05 *Commission* v. *Ireland*, judgment of 25 October 2007, n.y.r. in the ECR, para. 115.

5 Supervision by the Commission

Under Article 211 EC, the Commission is charged with ensuring that the provisions of the Treaty and the measures taken by the institutions pursuant to the Treaty are applied.[108] This means the Commission has been given primary responsibility for monitoring the application of European law in the Member States.[109] Even so, the full formal and substantive application of the law, as has been demonstrated in the previous section of this chapter, in the first place is a matter for the Member States.

This is apparent from Article 10 EC, under which Member States must take all appropriate measures to ensure fulfilment of their European law obligations and from the first sentence of Article 175(4) EC, which requires the Member States to finance and implement the environment policy. Moreover it is clear from the use of the directive as an instrument of European environment policy that it is the Member States which are primarily responsible for implementation. In addition to the Commission's role in monitoring compliance with European law, it should not be ruled out for the future that the European Environment Agency will play an increasingly important part in this respect. Figures on the Commission's monitoring of the application of European law are to be found in the annual reports on that subject.[110]

5.1 The Treaty Infringement Procedure

The most important instrument at the Commission's disposal is the procedure laid down in Article 226 EC (Article 258 FEU). This provides that the Commission may bring a matter before the Court of Justice if it considers that a Member State has failed to fulfil an obligation under the Treaty. Nevertheless, in terms of monitoring application of the law, the Commission only avails itself of this formal power as a last resort. The Court long ago established that private persons cannot compel the Commission to initiate infringement proceedings, nor do they have legal recourse against decisions of the Commission not to commence proceedings, or to discontinue or stay proceedings that have been instituted.[111]

The Commission distinguishes 3 different types of infringement proceedings:
1) non-communication cases, for failure to adopt and communicate national implementing measures;
2) non-conformity cases, where Member State transposition measures do not conform to the requirements of the directive;

---

[108] Cf. for a critical comment on the Commission's role in enforcement, Macrory (2005A).

[109] See Seventh Annual Survey on the Implementation and Enforcement of Community Environmental Law 2005, SEC (2006) 1143. See also Lee (2005) at 51.

[110] See e.g. XXIIIrd Report on monitoring the application of Community law, COM (2006) 416.

[111] Case 48/65 *Lütticke* [1966] ECR 19.

3) bad application cases, where a Member State, through action or inaction, fails to comply with EU environmental law requirements other than the requirements to adopt and communicate correct implementing legislation.[112]

The Article 226 procedure gives the Commission extensive powers in its relations with the Member States.

Thus, in Case C-422/92, Germany disputed the Commission's admissibility in a proceeding for infringement of, the now repealed, Directive 84/631 on the supervision and control within the EC of the transfrontier shipment of hazardous waste.[113] The Commission brought its action long after the publication of the contested national provisions and did so at a time when developments in European policy and law on the environment were such as could give the impression that there was no longer any expectation that such action would be brought. The Court, however, argued that it is not necessary for the Commission to have a specific interest in bringing an action in order to commence proceedings under Article 226 EC: 'Article 169 [now Article 226 EC, authors] is not intended to protect the Commission's own rights but provides one of the means by which the Commission ensures that the Member States give effect to the provisions of the Treaty and the provisions adopted under the Treaty by the institutions.'

The Court continued by observing that:

'It is true, and somewhat surprising, that the Commission brought its action more than six years after the entry into force of the basic German legislation on the shipment of waste, and did so at a time when the Community had in fact changed its policy in that field along the same lines as those followed by that legislation. As the Advocate General points out at paragraphs 18 and 79 of his Opinion, it is relevant to ask why the Commission thought that it was under an obligation to commence and pursue the present action in such circumstances.'

However, in the light of the settled case law that the Commission is not obliged to act within a specified period, the Court came to the conclusion that the Commission is entitled to decide, in its discretion, on what date it may be appropriate to bring an action. And it is not for the Court to review the exercise of that discretion.

The application of European environmental law is the subject of many and regular contacts of a less formal nature between the Commission and the Member States. For example, after approval of a directive by the Council, the Commission writes an official letter to the Member States notifying them of the direc-

---

[112] Detailed data can be found in the annual survey of the Commission on the Implementation and Enforcement of Community Environmental Law. See e.g. SEC (2006) 1143 for data on the year 2005.

[113] Case C-422/92 *Commission v. Germany* [1995] ECR I-1097.

tive and the time limits within which national law must have been adjusted to comply with the directive. About three months before expiry of the time limit for incorporation into national law, the Commission writes a second letter to those Member States which have not yet informed the Commission that the necessary adjustments have been made. As the Member States are twice reminded by the Commission of their obligations, a practice has evolved whereby the Commission will automatically initiate Article 226 proceedings after expiry of the time limit if a Member State has not informed it that the necessary measures have been taken. The complaint addresses the formal aspect of failure to notify the Commission. Later proceedings may deal with the substance of the case.

Member States are required to give such notification, either under a specific provision of the directive in question, or pursuant to Article 10 EC.[114] The Commission requires the Member States to specify in detail the provisions of national law in which each article and clause of the directive is incorporated, for example in a synoptic table.[115] Directive 91/692 standardizing and rationalizing reports on the implementation of certain directives relating to the environment is also relevant in this context.[116] This provision should lead to greater uniformity in the Member States' reports, and thus enable the Commission to carry out more effective control.

In order to ensure effective implementation, the Commission also makes use of a wide range of non-legal instruments, for instance by producing so-called interpretation and guidance documents.[117] Better implementation is also promoted through multilateral contacts with Member States in expert groups and committees to discuss implementation issues. Such meetings are held in the chemicals, air, nature and waste sectors, but are more rare in the fields of noise and water.[118]

As indicated above, the Article 226 procedure is a final resort as regards the enforcement of European law. There are three stages in this procedure:

1) a letter of formal notice from the Commission;
2) a reasoned opinion from the Commission and
3) referral to the Court of Justice.

---

[114] See also Chapter 8, section 2.1.

[115] OJ 1991 C 338/1, Annex C, section 8. Where the directive is implemented by regional authorities, this can cause severe problems, see Case C-474/99 *Commission v. Spain* [2002] ECR I-5293, with respect to the implementation of the EIA Directive.

[116] OJ 1991 L 377/48. Cf. on its limited success, Wennerås (2006) at 198. See also Commission Decision 94/741 concerning questionnaires for Member States reports on the implementation of certain Directives in the waste sector, OJ 1994 L 296/42 and Commission Decision 97/622, OJ 1997 L 256/13.

[117] Cf. Commission Communication on better monitoring of the application of Community law; COM (2002) 725 final.

[118] Some directives even provide for technical committees to be established, for instance the ORNIS Committee under Article 16 of the Wild Birds Directive, the Habitats Committee under Article 20 of the Habitats Directive and the standing Committee on Biocidal Products established by Article 28 of the Biocides Directive 98/8.

In 2005, the Commission issued 141 reasoned opinions on the basis of Article 226 of the EC Treaty and brought 42 cases against Member States before the Court of Justice.[119]

The content of the letter of formal notice, though not bound by any formality, is important for the further procedure.[120] This is because the Court has decided that the scope of an application under Article 226 EC is delimited by the pre-litigation procedure.[121] The Commission is not permitted to introduce new grounds and pleas in law, either in its reasoned opinion or before the Court. Member States usually have two months to reply to the formal notice. If the response is not satisfactory, the Commission may decide to issue a reasoned opinion in which it details the alleged infringement and sets a new time limit. Should the Member State still fail to comply within the time limit, the Commission may refer the matter to the Court. In order to prove that the transposition of a directive is insufficient or inadequate, it is not necessary to establish the actual effects of the legislation transposing it into national law: it is the wording of the legislation itself which harbours the insufficiencies or defects of transposition.[122] In principle it is for the Commission to prove a Treaty infringement, but if the Member State does not provide any indications to the contrary, the Court will deem that the Commission has proved the alleged infringement.[123]

One of the problems with respect to infringement proceedings is the length of the procedure and that, in view of Article 242 EC (Article 278 FEU), actions brought before the Court of Justice do not have a suspensory effect. Recently however, the Commission seems to be willing to petition to the Court for suspension orders, where a Member State is violating its obligations under environmental directives. Two, more or less successful, actions must be mentioned. In Case C-503/06R, the President of the Court ordered the suspension of a regional Italian act on hunting and in Case C-193/07R, the Polish government

---

[119] Seventh Annual Survey on the Implementation and Enforcement of Community Environmental Law 2005, SEC (2006) 1143, at 6.

[120] See on the confidentiality of documents related to infringement proceedings Case T-105/95 *WWF UK v. Commission* [1997] ECR II-313 and Case T-191/99 *Petrie a.o. v. Commission* [2001] ECR II-3677. Cf. Krämer (2003A). See also Article 4(2) Regulation 1049/2001 regarding public access to European Parliament, Council and Commission documents, OJ 2001 L 145/43.

[121] Case C-52/90 *Commission v. Denmark* [1992] ECR I-2187.

[122] Case C-392/96 *Commission v. Ireland* [1999] ECR I-5901.

[123] Cf. Case C-365/97 *Commission v. Italy* [1999] ECR I-7773. The case concerned an infringement of the Waste Directive. See also Case C-494/01 *Commission v. Ireland* [2005] ECR I-3331, para. 41: 'It is the Commission's responsibility to place before the Court the information needed to enable the Court to establish that the obligation has not been fulfilled, and in so doing the Commission may not rely on any presumption'. With regard more specifically to the EIA Directive, the Court held in Case C-117/02 *Commission v. Portugal* [2004] ECR I-5517, para. 85, that the Commission must furnish at least some evidence of the effects that the disputed project in question is likely to have on the environment.

was ordered not to proceed with a reforestation project as this would be in violation of the Habitat Directive.[124]

A successful action results in a judgment in which the Court declares that the Member State has failed to fulfil its obligations under the Treaty. Article 228 EC provides that if the Court of Justice finds that a Member State has failed to fulfil an obligation under the Treaty, the State shall be required to take the necessary measures to comply with the judgment of the Court.[125]

Imposing financial sanctions on a Member State

Since the Treaty of Maastricht the Court has been able to impose a lump sum and/or[126] penalty payment on a Member State that has failed to implement a judgment establishing an infringement.[127] Although the decision on the imposition of the sanctions lies with the Court of Justice, which has full jurisdiction in this area, the Commission plays a determining role in so far as it is responsible for initiating the Article 228 procedure and bringing the case before the Court of Justice with a proposal[128] for the application of a lump sum and/or penalty payment of a specific amount. In the meantime, the Commission has published some guidelines on how to apply financial sanctions.[129] According to the Commission the fixing of sanctions should be based on three fundamental criteria:

· the seriousness of the infringement;
· its duration;
· the need to ensure that the penalty itself is a deterrent to further infringements.

From the point of view of the effectiveness of the sanction, the Commission regards that it is important to fix amounts that are appropriate in order to ensure their *deterrent* effect. In the meantime the Commission has brought the first environment-related cases of this nature before the Court.[130]

---

[124] Case C-503/06R *Commission* v. *Italy*, orders of 19 December 2006 and 27 February 2007, n.y.r. in the ECR and Case C-193/07R *Commission* v. *Poland*, orders of 18 April and 18 July 2007, n.y.r. in the ECR.

[125] And the failure to comply with this can lead to another Treaty infringement procedure; Cf. Case C-291/93 *Commission* v. *Italy* [1994] ECR I-859. Cf. Article 260 FEU.

[126] The judgment in case C-304/02 *Commission* v. *France* [2005] ECR I-6263, confirmed that the two kinds of financial sanction (penalty and lump sum) can apply cumulatively for the same infringement. According to the Commission a combined sanction should be the rule, although the Commission does not exclude the possibility, in very specific cases, of recourse to the lump sum alone; Cf. Commission Communication Application of Article 228 of the EC Treaty, SEC (2005) 1658 final, at 3.

[127] In Chapter 5, section 2.3 we will discuss the question of Member State liability for failing to comply with its obligations under the so called *Francovich* doctrine.

[128] This proposal 'cannot bind the Court and merely constitute a useful point of reference'; Case C-278/01 *Commission* v. *Spain* [2003] ECR I-14141, para. 41.

[129] Cf. Commission Communication Application of Article 228 of the EC Treaty, SEC (2005) 1658 final.

[130] Case C-387/97 *Commission* v. *Greece* [2000] ECR I-5047 and Case C-278/01 *Commission* v. *Spain* [2003] ECR I-14141.

In Case C-387/97, the Commission had requested that Greece be ordered to pay a penalty as long as it fails to take the necessary measures to ensure that toxic waste in the area around Chanià is disposed of without endangering human health and without harming the environment. The Court had already found in 1992 that Greece had failed to fulfil its obligations in this matter.[131] The Court agreed with the Commission and ordered Greece to pay a penalty of €20,000 per day as long as it failed to take the necessary measures. In particular the Court took into account that the failure to comply with the obligations resulting from the Framework Waste Directive could, by the very nature of that obligation, endanger human health directly and harm the environment and therefore had to be regarded as particularly serious.

Case C-278/01 concerned the failure of Spain to comply with the Bathing Water Directive. The Court ordered Spain to pay to the Commission a penalty payment of €624,150 per year and per 1% of bathing areas in Spanish inshore waters which have been found not to conform to the limit values laid down under the directive for the year in question, as from the time when the quality of bathing water achieved in the first bathing season following delivery of this judgment is ascertained until the year in which the judgment in *Commission v. Spain* is fully complied with.

In both cases the Court affirmed the importance of the proportionality principle and that therefore a penalty payment should be appropriate to the circumstances and proportionate both to the breach found and to the ability to pay of the Member State concerned. According to the Court in Case C-278/01, there may be infringement situations, for instance concerning quality standards for bathing water set by the directive, where, as the Court noted, 'it is particularly difficult for the Member States to achieve complete implementation', and where 'it is conceivable that the defendant Member State might manage significantly to increase the extent of its implementation of the Directive but not to implement it fully in the short term'. In those circumstances, the Court ruled, 'a penalty which does not take account of the progress which a Member State may have made in complying with its obligations is neither appropriate to the circumstances nor proportionate to the breach which has been found'.

The Commission acknowledged that it might be justified to provide for the suspension of a penalty. For instance, a Member State found against for having allowed an important nature site to deteriorate as a result of land drainage may carry out infrastructure works aimed at restoring the hydrological conditions that are ecologically necessary. A period of monitoring may be needed to determine whether the works have succeeded in remedying the harm done.[132]

In fixing the amount of the penalty, the importance of the European rules breached and the impact of the infringement on general and particular interests

---

[131] Case C-45/91 *Commission v. Greece* [1992] ECR I-2509.

[132] Commission Communication Application of Article 228 of the EC Treaty, SEC (2005) 1658 final, at 5.

will be taken into account. '[S]erious or irreparable damage to human health or the environment' is explicitly mentioned by the Commission as such a factor.

5.2   Informal Complaints to the Commission

As has been noted, the Commission's decision whether or not to initiate Article 226 proceedings, or to terminate a proceeding that has already been started, is not open to review by the Court. Neither private individuals, local residents or environmental organisations can compel the Commission to initiate infringement proceedings.[133] However, a complaints procedure has been developed in practice, which, though having no basis in the Treaty, is nevertheless beginning to exhibit some degree of formalisation.[134] A standard form for complaints to be submitted to the European Commission for failure by a Member State to comply with European law is available at the EU's website.[135]

The Commission pursues an active policy involving private citizens in its monitoring duties. Each letter mentioning an alleged infringement of European law is filed in a special register of complaints. There are no formal requirements. The only requirement to be admissible is that the complaint has to relate to an infringement of European law by a Member State. Complainants are notified of inclusion in the complaints register and the Commission requests the Member State in question to supply the necessary information. The Commission does not, in principle, have formal powers of inspection of its own in the territories of the Member states, as it does in competition law. Officials of the Commission do, however, after consultation with and with the consent of the Member State in question, visit sites to apprise themselves of the situation there. Only occasionally has a Member State refused such a visit.[136] If necessary, the Commission can see that it obtains expert reports and has other evidence submitted. After the facts have emerged, the Commission takes a decision on the procedure to be followed, generally within one year of the complaint being lodged. The complainant is notified of this.

The Commission receives many complaints in the field of the environment. In 2005 the Commission registered 279 new complaints alleging breaches of European environmental law.[137] The number of complaints indicates that there

---

[133] Not to be confused with complaints under Regulation 1367/2006 on the application of the provisions of the Aarhus Convention on Access to Information, Public Participation in Decision-making and Access to Justice in Environmental Matters to Community institutions and bodies (OJ 2006 L 264/13). See on this regulation Chapter 5, section 4.2.

[134] Commission Communication on relations with the complainant in respect of infringements of Community law, COM (2002) 141 final.

[135] However, complainants are not obliged to use this form. A complaint submitted by ordinary letter is also admissible.

[136] Krämer (1993), at 405.

[137] Annex to the XXIIIrd Report on monitoring the application of Community law, COM (2006) 416, Situation in the different sectors, SEC (2006) 999, at 23.

is a need in the Member States for legal protection against infringements of European environment law. It is debatable whether the present centralisation of legal protection through an unofficial complaints procedure and the infringement procedure is desirable in the long term. Many complaints concern local or regional environmental problems. An additional factor is that proper scrutiny demands detailed knowledge of the case in point, but the Commission is geographically remote and lacks both the powers and the ability to conduct investigations, having no resources to carry out inspections in the environmental field. This is why the Commission concentrates its efforts on dealing with problems of conformity, though without neglecting cases which reveal questions of principle or horizontal questions.[138] Clearly the complaints procedure does not remove the need for legal protection in the event of an incidental wrong application of European environmental law. Partly with a view to the principle of subsidiarity, it would be appropriate to create a system of legal protection, particularly for interested third parties, in the Member States themselves. However, access to the courts for third parties, including environmental organisations, is not available so easily and cheaply in some other Member States as it is in, for example, the Netherlands. Although some environmental directives also contain provisions requiring Member States to provide recourse to the courts,[139] there is as yet no question of an integrated approach. The number of complaints still received in Brussels does however show the urgent need for legal protection in European environment law.

---

[138] Cf. Sixteenth Annual Report on monitoring the application of community law (1998), OJ 1999 C 354/1, at 10.

[139] See Chapter 5, section 2.1.

Legal Protection

1 General Remarks

According to Article 6(1) EU, the European Union is founded on the principles of liberty, democracy, respect for human rights and fundamental freedoms, and the *rule of law*.[1] With respect to the EC Treaty we may point at Article 220 EC, which states that the Court of Justice and the Court of First Instance[2], each within its jurisdiction, shall ensure that *the law* is observed in the interpretation and application of this Treaty. In its case law the Court of Justice has repeatedly held that the European Union is a community based on the rule of law.[3] The Court has also stated many times that individuals are entitled to effective judicial protection of the rights they derive from the European legal order, and that the right to such protection is one of the general principles of law stemming from the constitutional traditions common to the Member States.[4]

This is not the place to discuss exhaustively all aspects of the *rule of law* and its significance to the European legal order. However as far as European environmental law is concerned, one aspect deserves our attention in particular, and that is the question of access to court and legal protection of individuals in case they feel that their 'environmental' rights have been infringed. This chapter will discuss their position at national level before national courts, as well as at European level before the Court of Justice and the Court of First Instance.

2 Legal Protection before National Courts

European environmental law is applied before national courts by means of three different mechanisms: through the direct effect of European environmental law, through the requirement that national courts interpret national law in conformity with European environmental law (consistent interpretation) and via the doctrine of state liability for infringements of European environmental law. It should be noted from the outset that in a number of respects the doctrine of state liability differs fundamentally from the mechanisms of direct effect and consistent interpretation. It is a feature of EC law that national organs of the state are required to apply EC rules when they make, interpret and apply national rules. In other words, direct effect and consistent interpretation play a part from the very start whenever these organs are making, interpreting or applying national law. By contrast, state liability is a means which enables individuals to obtain compensation, in retrospect, for damage that has arisen as a result of the improper application of EC law.

---

[1] Cf. Article 2 EU after amendment by the Reform Treaty.

[2] The 'General Court' in the terminology of the Reform Treaty.

[3] Cf. Case C-50/00P *Unión de Pequeños Agricultores* v. *Council* [2002] ECR I-6677, para. 38.

[4] E.g. Case 222/84 *Johnston* [1986] ECR 1651, para. 18, and Case C-424/99 *Commission* v. *Austria* [2001] ECR I-9285, para. 45.

2.1 The Direct Effect of EC Environmental Law[5]

General remarks

The Court of Justice established the foundations for its case law on the direct effect of EC environmental law in 1963, in *Van Gend & Loos*.[6] The Court ruled that EC law, apart from legislation by Member States, can confer rights on individuals, which are capable of being enforced before the national courts. Since then the Court has developed a number of conditions for EC law to have direct effect. These are:

- the provision must establish a clear obligation on the part of Member States;
- the obligation must be unconditional;
- the obligation must not be dependent on further implementing measures by the institutions of the Community or the Member States;
- the Member States must not be left with any discretion in the implementation of the obligation.

Over the course of time the initial rather restrictive criteria have been significantly relaxed. In the Court's current case law these criteria are summarised as follows: provisions of EC law are directly effective if they are unconditional and sufficiently precise.[7] A provision is unconditional where it is not subject, in its implementation or effects, to the taking of any measure either by the European institutions or by the Member States. Moreover, a provision is sufficiently precise to be relied on by an individual and applied by a court where the obligations which it imposes are set out in unequivocal terms.

The most important condition which follows from the Court's case law is that discretionary powers in the implementation of a provision of EC law will prevent it from having direct effect. Examples are provisions allowing a certain degree of freedom of choice or ones that leave the exercise of powers to the discretion of the public authorities. In such cases powers can be relied upon only if they have been exercised. This will apply only if fulfillment of the obligation is conditional upon the implementing measures, and the discretion in question is 'real'. However, vagueness or imprecision in a provision of EC law need not be an obstacle to its having direct effect.

The way the Court has extended the concept of direct effect in recent years justifies the assertion that the crucial criterion is whether a provision provides a court with sufficient guidance to be able to apply it without exceeding the limits of its judicial powers. Viewed thus, a provision of EC law is directly effective if a national court can apply it without encroaching on the jurisdiction of national or European authorities. This implies that, even when Member States enjoy some discretion, some measures can have direct effect. After all, no power is ever

---

[5] This section builds upon Jans et al. (2007), Chapter III.

[6] Case 26/62 *Van Gend & Loos* [1963] ECR 1.

[7] Case C-236/92 *Comitato di coordinamento per la difesa della Cava* v. *Regione Lombardia* [1994] ECR I-485.

totally unfettered; the rule of law implies that the exercise of State competence is conditioned by legal rules. In many cases a provision of EC law which confers discretionary powers will at the same time establish the conditions for their exercise. The case law of the Court, the *Kraaijeveld* case in particular, also offers indications that the doctrine of the direct effect of EC law is developing in that direction.[8]

> *Kraaijeveld* concerned, among other things, the question to what extent certain works involving dykes should be subject to a prior environmental impact assessment under the EIA Directive. Article 2(1) of the directive lays down the general obligation that 'projects likely to have significant effects on the environment' are to be subject to an assessment. This general obligation is further specified in Article 4(1) in combination with Annex I of the directive, which states the projects for which an assessment is always required. There is no question of a discretion here. However, Article 4(2) in combination with Annex II clearly gives the national legislature more freedom when implementing the directive. So much so that the Dutch *Raad van State* (Council of State) denied its direct effect.[9] This was because it allows the national legislature to establish the criteria and/or thresholds necessary to determine whether or not a project is to be subject to an assessment. In the Netherlands, works involving dykes (among the projects listed in Annex II), were subject to an assessment if the dyke was 5 km or more in length, with a cross-section of at least 250 square metres. The Court of Justice concluded that Article 4(2) did allow Member States 'a certain discretion', namely to fix specifications, thresholds and criteria. However, it went on to say that this discretion was itself limited, namely by the obligation set out in Article 2(1) that projects likely to have significant effects on the environment are to be subject to an impact assessment. The national court was instructed to examine whether the legislature had remained within the limits of its discretion, and thus to review the national legislation in the light of the directive.
>
> In *Landelijke Vereniging tot Behoud van de Waddenzee*,[10] the Court extended this approach. Where the national court was required in *Kraaijeveld* to examine whether the *national legislature* had remained within the limits of discretion allowed by the directive, in this case it became clear that even where there is no implementing legislation, the decisions of an *administrative authority* must also remain within those limits, and that the national courts must examine whether or not this is the case. This case concerned Article 6(2-3) Habitats Directive.

What the Court in fact did in cases like *Kraaijeveld* and *Waddenzee* was to acknowledge that individuals may also rely on provisions that allow discretion (in this case the freedom to make exceptions in certain cases). The national court must then examine whether the *national legislature* has stayed within the

---

[8]   Case C-72/95 *Kraaijeveld* [1996] ECR I-5403. See also Case C-287/98 *Linster* [2000] ECR I-6917.

[9]   Dutch *Raad van State* 3 August 1993 [1994] AB 287.

[10] Case C-127/02 *Landelijke Vereniging tot Behoud van de Waddenzee* [2004] ECR I-7405, para. 65.

limits of the law when exercising its powers. In the literature this type of direct effect is referred to as 'legality review'.[11] We however agree with Prechal who notes that there is no need to distinguish legality review as a separate category.[12]

In summary, then, a provision of EC law can be said to have direct effect if it can be applied by the national courts, acting within their judicial powers. It is the responsibility of the courts to ensure that the national legislature and administrative authorities, when acting within the sphere of operation of EC law, abide by their EC law obligations and do not exceed any discretion they may have. As far as environmental law is concerned, the direct effect of primary EC law has been accepted by the Court in respect of, *inter alia*, Articles 25, 28, 29, 30, 81, 82, 88(3) and 90 of the EC Treaty. The validity of national environmental law which is incompatible with these provisions may be challenged before the national courts.

Direct effect and individual rights

In its case law the Court uses various formulations to describe the implications of direct effect. On the one hand, the Court observes that directly effective provisions of EC law can confer rights on private individuals which the national courts have to uphold, and, on the other hand, that a directly effective provision of EC law can be invoked before a national court. Both formulations stress the role of the national courts in enforcing direct effect. The second, more neutral formulation is to be preferred. The formulation that focuses on 'rights of individuals' is misleading, as it gives the impression that only those provisions of EC law are directly effective which confer, to a greater or lesser extent, rights on individuals. It is the authors' view that 'rights of individuals' should be seen in a procedural rather than a substantive light. Individual rights stem from Member States' obligations. In other words it is necessary to distinguish the concept of direct effect from the question of whether EC law creates rights for individuals.[13] Direct effect is concerned with the quality of the EC law provision being relied on. Has it been formulated so as to be 'unconditional and sufficiently precise', or not? Either way, this does not necessarily imply a substantive entitlement. Where the Court refers to direct effect in terms of creating 'rights for individuals' the Court is, in our view, acknowledging a procedural right, namely the right to rely on that provision before the national courts. Viewed thus, direct effect and the conferring of rights on individuals are distinct concepts. Nevertheless, it must be admitted that other scholars argue that substantive rights are indeed a prerequisite for direct effect.[14]

This doctrinal issue is of particular relevance in the field of environmental law. As Prechal & Hancher rightly noted, environmental law is different from

---

[11] See for an overview of the literature: Prechal (2005), at 234 *et seq.*

[12] Prechal (2005), 234-241.

[13] Cf. also Case C-431/92 *Commission v. Germany* [1995] ECR I-2189.

[14] Cf. for a more comprehensive treatment of relevant case law and literature: Prechal (2005), Chapter 6.

other areas of law.[15] The diffuse interests which environmental law represents cannot easily be captured in the language of individual rights. It is the authors' view that individuals wanting to rely on an environmental directive do not have to show, as a condition of EC law, that their substantive rights under the directive have been affected. This means that they can also rely on those provisions which do not as such confer rights on individuals, but are 'unconditional and sufficiently precise'. Any other view would imply that 'pure' environmental protection provisions could not be relied upon in national courts. Implicitly the Court seems to have accepted our view in its *Großkrotzenburg* and *Kraaijeveld* judgments.[16] Especially in the *Kraaijeveld* case it was quite clear that Kraaijeveld was affected in his business interests. Nevertheless it was, albeit again implicitly, accepted that he could rely on the EIA Directive, even though its objective is to prevent significant harm to the environment. On the other hand, there is national environment-related case law which seems to endorse a different view. Some argue that, as a matter of EC law, individuals can only rely on directly effective provisions of EC law if these provisions are meant to confer rights on individuals.[17]

The importance of national procedural law

The way in which a directly effective provision can be invoked in the national legal system and the form in which this occurs depend largely on national law. According to the established case law of the Court of Justice, it is for the national legal order of each Member State to designate the competent courts and to lay down the procedural rules for proceedings designed to ensure the protection of the rights which individuals acquire through the direct effect of EC law.[18] Hence, private individuals are first and foremost dependent on the legal procedures established by national law. The form in which the direct effect of a provision of EC law can be invoked is therefore primarily[19] determined by national law. Invoking a directly effective provision in interlocutory proceedings before a civil court will produce a different result from the result produced in administra-

---

[15] Prechal & Hancher (2002) at 109.

[16] Case C-431/92 *Commission v. Germany* [1995] ECR I-2189 and Case C-72/95 *Kraaijeveld* [1996] ECR I-5403.

[17] See for instance Advocate General Kokott in the *Waddenzee* case; Case C-127/02 *Landelijke Vereniging tot Behoud van de Waddenzee* [2004] ECR I-7405, points 142-144 of her Opinion. She argued that Article 6(2) and (3) of the Habitats Directive did not establish 'individual rights' and that accordingly individuals may rely on these provisions only in so far as avenues of legal redress are available to them under *national* law. In view of the judgment of the Court in that case, it must assumed that the Court did not agree with her. Cf. also the Dutch District Court 's-Gravenhage 24 November 1999 *Waterpakt* [2000] *MR* 1.

[18] Case 45/76 *Comet* [1976] ECR 2043 and Case 265/78 *Ferwerda* [1980] ECR 617.

[19] Unless the directive has dealt with the issue. For instance, it must assumed that 'any natural or legal person' whose rights under Directive 2003/4 on public access to environmental information (OJ 2003 L 41/26) are violated has standing in national courts.

tive or criminal proceedings. Because national procedural law also varies from one country to the next (e.g. differences in time limits for appeal,[20] standing requirements[21], access to legal aid, intensity of judicial review,[22] court costs etc.), comparable proceedings may produce very different outcomes. Moreover, it is not always easy to determine whether or not a rule of national procedural law can be applied.

The following example in relation to the EIA Directive may illustrate this. What, for example, should the national court do where the competent authority has granted an environmental permit for a project for which an environmental impact statement was required under the directive. German administrative courts equate the absence or defectiveness of an EIA with other procedural errors. According to some English[23] and German[24] courts, procedural errors do not in themselves entitle those affected by a project to have the permit set aside or annulled. The permit will only be annulled where the error was obvious and influenced the outcome of the decision. At the other end of the spectrum is the Dutch *Raad van State*, which considers that any violation of the obligation to submit an EIA will result in the annulment of the underlying permit. The question whether the lack of an EIA would have resulted in a materially different decision is irrelevant in the Dutch context and is not examined by the courts.[25] A third approach can be found in the judgment of the Swedish Supreme Administrative Court regarding the cessation of the right to operate the Barsebäck nuclear power reactor.[26] With respect to a possible minor procedural defect (the failure to provide a non-technical summary)

---

[20] Cf. English Court of Appeal 12 April 2000 *Regina* v. *North West Leicestershire Country Council, East Midlands International Airport Ltd.*, ex parte *Moses* [2000] Env. L.R. 443. Reasonable time limits have been upheld as being compatible with the requirements of EC law; Case C-188/95 *Fantask* [1997] ECR I-6783. In the *Fantask* case the Court more or less retracted from its earlier judgment in Case C-208/90 *Emmott* [1991] ECR I-4269.

[21] Cf. on standing in transboundary environmental disputes Macrory & Turner (2002).

[22] Case C-120/97 *Upjohn Ltd.* [1999] ECR I-223. Once again: unless the directive has dealt with the issue specifically. For instance, national courts have to review 'the procedural and substantive legality' of the decisions, acts or failure to act of national authorities under the Liability Directive (OJ 2004 L 143/56, Article 13).

[23] English Court of Appeal 12 February 1998 *Berkeley* v. *Secretary of State for the Environment* [1999] 1 C.M.L.R. 945. Cf. also English Court of Appeal 12 April 2000 *Regina* v. *North West Leicestershire Country Council, East Midlands International Airport Ltd.*, ex parte *Moses* [2000] Env. L.R. 443. See however UK House of Lords 6 July 2000 *Berkeley* v. *Secretary of State for the Environment* [2000] UKHL 36. According to the House of Lords, a court exercising its discretion to uphold a planning permission which has been granted contrary to the provisions of the EIA Directive, would seem to conflict with Article 10 EC.

[24] Cf. German *Bundesverwaltungsgericht* 23 February 1994 [1994] *DVBl.* 763. Cf. also German *Bundesverwaltungsgericht* 17 February 1997 [1997] *Natur und Recht* 305. See Ladeur and Prelle (2002).

[25] See Jans & de Jong (2002).

[26] Judgment of the Swedish Supreme Administrative Court on 16 June 1999, case no. 1424-1998, 2397-1998 and 2939-1998, RÅ 1999 ref. 76.

the Swedish Court ruled: 'Should the examination show that while there have been deficiencies in relation to what the directive requires, these deficiencies have not been so extensive so that they evidently lack importance for the Government's decision [...]. In this situation [...] the Government decision [...] shall not be revoked on the basis of lack of compliance with the directive.' [...] 'Taking this into consideration, it is evident in the view of the Supreme Administrative Court that a publication of a non-technical summary would not have contributed anything new to the matter and that accordingly the defect that can be considered as having existed in relation to the requirements of the directive lacked significance for the Government decision'.

However, it is not altogether clear how this divergent national case law relates to the judgments of the Court of Justice in *Kraaijeveld* and *Bozen*. In both cases the Court ruled that if the Member States have exceeded their discretion under the EIA Directive, the national provisions must be set aside. Furthermore, 'it is for the authorities of the Member State, according to their relevant powers, to take all the general or particular measures necessary to ensure that projects are examined in order to determine whether they are likely to have significant effects on the environment and, if so, to ensure that they are subject to an impact assessment'.[27] Dutch case law seems to be more in line with these judgments than the German and English.

2.1.1   Direct Effect of Provisions in Environmental Directives

Apart from the direct effect of provisions of primary EC law, the possibility of invoking the provisions of an environmental directive is particularly important in the sphere of the environment. After all, directives have to be transposed into national legislation and the question therefore arises what the legal significance is of an environmental directive in the national legal orders where it has not been implemented, or not within the requisite time limit, or otherwise incorrectly.

It is important to note that individuals can rely upon directly effective provisions of a directive only *after* expiry of the period for transposition. This is because Member States must be given the time to bring their legislation into line with the requirements of the directive. In the *Inter-Environnement* judgment, however, the Court of Justice introduced an important nuance.[28] Having acknowledged the basic rule that Member States cannot be faulted for not having transposed a directive into their internal legal order before expiry of the transposition period, it went on to observe that it followed from Article 10 EC in

---

[27] Case C-72/95 *Kraaijeveld* [1996] ECR I-5403, para. 61 and Case C-435/97 *World Wildlife Fund* v. *Autonome Provinz* [1999] ECR I-5613, para. 70.

[28] Case C-129/96 *Inter-Environnement* [1997] ECR I-7411. See also, more recent, Case C-422/05 *Commission* v. *Belgium*, judgment of 14 June 2007, n.y.r. in the ECR, on noise-related operating restrictions at Belgium airports.

conjunction with Article 249 EC 'that during that period they must refrain from taking any measures liable seriously to compromise the result prescribed.' The question however remains whether this obligation is directly effective.[29]

> The Dutch *Raad van State* (Council of State) has applied this rule – and therefore seems to have accepted that it is directly effective – in many cases involving the Habitats Directive.[30] It observed that the principle of Community loyalty meant that, in a case like the one before it, Member States and their national authorities must refrain from activities which could seriously jeopardise the result prescribed by the directive during the period between the transmission of a list as referred to in Article 4(1) of the directive and adoption of the list by the Commission. As the government had not taken this into account in its decision-making, the decision was annulled for lack of due care in its preparation. By examining whether the government had acted in conformity with its obligations under Article 10 EC, the Dutch *Raad van State* followed the example of the highest German administrative court, which had also carried out a similar *Inter-Environnement* test in relation to the same provision of the Habitats Directive.[31]
>
> In *Stichting Zuid-Hollandse Milieufederatie*, the Court applied this doctrine to the interpretation of Article 16 of the Biocides Directive.[32] After having ruled that the words 'continue to apply its current system or practice of placing biocidal products on the market' in Article 16(1) the directive are not to be interpreted as constituting a standstill obligation, the Court continued by stating that the Member States' right to amend their systems for the authorisation of biocidal products cannot be regarded as unlimited either. During the implementation period they must refrain from taking any measures liable seriously to compromise the result prescribed by the directive.

Clearly, it is impossible to examine here the many environmental directives, each containing numerous provisions, in order to ascertain their direct effect. A general approach will suffice. Various categories of provisions will be discussed. In this respect we will not only rely on the case law of the Court specifically dealing with direct effect, but also on the Court's judgments in infringement proceedings under Article 226 EC. Although the Court of Justice stated in the *Großkrotzenburg* case that an obligation flowing directly from a directive is 'quite separate' from the question of whether individuals may rely on provisions of an unimplemented directive[33], we agree with Prechal who notes that if the Court of

---

[29] The judgment in *Rieser*, Case C-157/02 [2004] ECR I-1477, paras. 66-69 seems to suggest that this obligation is not directly effective. Cf. also Case C-212/04 *Adeneler a.o.* [2006] ECR I-6057.

[30] E.g. Dutch *Raad van State* 11 July 2001 [2001] MR 38.

[31] German *Bundesverwaltungsgericht* 19 May 1998 [1998] NVwZ (*Ostsee-autobahn*), 961 and German *Bundesverwaltungsgericht* 27 January 2000 BVerwGE 110, 302, 308 (*Hildesheimer Ortsumgehung*).

[32] Case C-316/04 *Stichting Zuid-Hollandse Milieufederatie* [2005] ECR I-9759.

[33] Case C-431/92 *Commission v. Germany* [1995] ECR I-2189, para. 26. Cf. Case C-365/97 *Commission v. Italy* [1999] ECR I-7773 (*San Rocco*), para. 63.

Justice is able to examine in infringement proceedings whether a Member State has remained within the limits of a directive, there are no fundamental reasons why a national court could not do the same.[34]

Direct effect of product standards

Environmental directives laying down precise and detailed conditions to which products harmful to the environment must conform before being placed on the market will normally be directly effective, as is illustrated by the Court's judgment in *Ratti*.[35]

> Directive 73/173 contains detailed provisions regarding the packaging and labelling of solvents.[36] However, Italian legislation imposed additional conditions and required publication of certain information not required by the directive. Ratti was prosecuted for an infringement of the Italian legislation, even though he had acted in compliance with the provisions of the directive. The Court held: 'It follows that a national court requested by a person who has complied with the provisions of a directive not to apply a national provision incompatible with the directive not incorporated into the internal legal order of a defaulting Member State, must uphold that request if the obligation in question is unconditional and sufficiently precise.'
>
> Ratti was acquitted because the provisions of the directive could indeed be considered unconditional and sufficiently precise. In the light of this judgment, product standards such as those contained in the Batteries Directive[37] must be regarded as producing direct effect. Article 4 of this directive requires Member States to prohibit the placing on the market of a) all batteries or accumulators, whether or not incorporated into appliances, that contain more than 0.0005% of mercury by weight; and b) portable batteries or accumulators, including those incorporated into appliances, that contain more than 0.002% of cadmium by weight. National provisions which are not of the required stringency but specify a value of, say, 0.05% may be challenged by invoking the directive. The standards of '0.0005% of mercury by weight' and '0.002% of cadmium by weight' are of course sufficiently precise and unconditional.

The reverse is also true, and a more stringent product standard may also be challenged. In that case the directive must contain a 'free movement' clause, as it did in the *Ratti* case. The Batteries Directive does contain such a clause: 'Member States shall not, on the grounds dealt with in this Directive, impede, prohibit, or restrict the placing on the market in their territory of batteries and accumulators that meet the requirements of this Directive' (Article 6). As is

---

[34] Prechal (2005) at 313. Cf. also Wennerås (2007) at 30.

[35] Case 148/78 *Ratti* [1979] ECR 1629.

[36] OJ 1973 L 189/7.

[37] Directive 2006/66 on batteries and accumulators and waste batteries and accumulators, OJ 2006 L 266/1.

confirmed by, for example, the *Ratti* case, such a clause produces direct effect. A more stringent national provision would be incompatible with such a provision, unless the Commission has approved these more stringent measures under Article 95(4-6) EC.[38]

Direct effect and emission limit values and environmental quality standards

In Chapter 3 it was noted that most European environmental legislation can be characterised as effecting 'minimum harmonisation'.[39] Directives lay down minimum standards of protection, though more stringent national standards are allowed. This applies in particular to emission standards and environmental quality objectives. Does the fact that a directive allows the Member States to adopt more stringent environmental standards imply that the minimum standards of the directive do not produce direct effect? For instance, Directive 2000/76[40] lays down a number of emission limit values to waste incineration plants. It is quite clear that these emission limit values are directly effective in as far as the directive establishes sufficiently precise numerical minimum standards.[41] In the present example, measures which allowed emissions exceeding the standards of the directive would be in breach of the directive and could be challenged on the basis of the emission limit values laid down in the directive. However, national measures containing a more stringent standard could not be challenged under the directive, since in that case no provision of the directive would have been breached.

Provisions requiring further implementation

Environmental directives requiring further national or European implementation lack the necessary 'unconditionality' and therefore do not have direct effect. It has been noted in literature that environmental directives have become increasingly vague, open-ended and conditional.[42] There is indeed a shift, in particular in the area of water and air pollution, from exact numerical emission standards and quality limit values to an increased reliance on environmental framework directives requiring further implementation. Wennerås states that this trend of more flexible lawmaking may provide cost-efficiency benefits, but it

---

[38] See more extensively Chapter 3, section 6.

[39] See Article 176 EC and, for example, Case C-376/90 *Commission* v. *Belgium* [1992] ECR I-6153.

[40] OJ 2000 L 332/91.

[41] Cf. on the direct effect of minimum standards outside EC environmental law: Joined Cases C-6/90 and C-9/90 *Francovich* [1991] ECR I-5357. See for an opposite view the Opinion of Advocate General Elmer in *Arcaro*, Case C-168/95 *Criminal proceedings against Arcaro* [1996] ECR I-4705, who seems to suggest that minimum emission standards do not have direct effect in view of the 'substantial discretion' for the national authorities. His view is clearly untenable, as it would mean – in view of Article 176 EC – that almost all European environmental legislation based on Article 175 EC lacks direct effect.

[42] Somsen (2003). Cf. on this trend of 'proceduralisation' also Lee (2005) 166 *et seq.*

does so at the expense of the direct effect of environmental directives and effective enforcement of EC environmental law.[43]

In this respect the IPPC Directive can illustrate the above. Instead of fixing, directly effective, emission standards in the directive itself, Article 9(4), delegates that to the Member States. They are required to set emission standards, which 'shall be based on the best available techniques, without prescribing the use of any technique or specific technology, but taking into account the technical characteristics of the installation concerned, its geographical location and the local environmental conditions.' The flexible nature of this provision provides a strong argument against it being directly effective. However, the Dutch *Raad van State* decided that the obligation to apply the best available techniques, also in view of the definition of BAT in Article 2 in combination with Annex IV, is sufficiently precise to be directly effective in the *Kraaijeveld* sense of the doctrine.[44]

Another question concerns the possible direct effect of broadly formulated provisions setting out the general scope of the directive. Arguably, they are not. Thus in the *Lombardia Waste* case the Court decided that Article 4 of the 'old' Waste Directive, although binding,[45] is not directly effective.[46]

That provision stated in general terms that Member States should take the necessary measures to ensure that waste is disposed of without endangering human health and without harming the environment. According to the Court this provision did not meet the conditions for it to have direct effect. It must be regarded as a framework provision: 'Article 4 [...] indicates a programme to be followed and sets out the objectives which the Member States must observe in their performance of the more specific obligations imposed on them by Articles 5 to 11 of the directive concerning planning, supervision and monitoring of waste disposal operations.' The Court therefore concluded that: 'The provision at issue must be regarded as defining the framework for the action to be taken by the Member States regarding the treatment of waste and not as requiring, in itself, the adoption of specific measures or a particular method of waste disposal. It is therefore neither unconditional nor sufficiently precise and thus is not capable of conferring rights on which individuals may rely as against the State.'[47]

---

[43] Wennerås (2007) at 43-44.

[44] Dutch *Raad van State* 13 November 2002 [2003] *M&R* 39.

[45] Case C-365/97 *Commission* v. *Italy* [1999] ECR I-7773 (*San Rocco*).

[46] Case C-236/92 *Comitato di coordinamento per la difesa della Cava* v. *Regione Lombardia* [1994] ECR I-485. Cf. Holder (1996).

[47] Cf. also Case C-60/01 *Commission* v. *France* [2002] ECR I-5679, were the Court makes a distinction between provisions 'formulated in general and unquantifiable terms' like in *Lombardia Waste* and provisions which require 'require the Member States to obtain very precise and specific results after a certain period' like the *Blackpool* case.

Such framework provisions are a regular feature of European environmental law. They are those provisions which set out the general aim of an environmental directive. Another example is Article 1 of the Water Framework Directive 2000/60. According to Article 1, its purpose is 'to establish a framework for the protection of inland surface waters, transitional waters, coastal waters and groundwater'. According to the Court of Justice, provisions of directives, which merely specify the particular objectives the directive seeks to achieve, do not require transposition.[48] It is the authors' opinion that such provisions will in general not be directly effective either. Hence these general obligations cannot be invoked independently before national courts.

> In the Netherlands the courts have had to decide on a number of questions arising in connection with the possible direct effect of Article 1(1) of Directive 78/176.[49] This provision provides: 'The aim of this Directive is the prevention and progressive reduction, with a view to its elimination, of pollution caused by waste from the titanium dioxide industry.' This general requirement is then worked out in more detail in a number of operative provisions. The Dutch court was asked to clarify whether, apart from the operative provisions of the directive, Article 1(1) should be afforded independent significance and, if so, whether it was directly effective. A number of environmental interest groups interpreted this provision as a 'standstill' requirement, in the light of which the Dutch licensing system could be reviewed. It was decided that the provision could not be invoked before a Dutch court.[50] In the light of the Court of Justice judgment in the *Lombardia Waste* case[51] this judgment would seem to be correct.

Derogation clauses and direct effect
The following construction is regularly found in environmental directives. Often Member States are required to fulfil a certain obligation, while at the same the directive provides for derogations from these obligations, provided certain conditions are met.

> A good example from Dutch case law is the judgment of the *Raad van State* (Council of State) concerning the creation in Dutch legislation of an exemption from the requirement to carry out an environmental impact assessment. Under the EIA Directive, certain precisely defined projects are subject to an environmental impact assessment. This requirement, laid down in Article 4(1) of the directive, is unconditional and sufficiently precise, albeit that Article 2(3) gives the Member States a power to exempt specific projects in exceptional cases. In this case, the primary rule is the obligation to carry out an environmental impact assessment; the secondary rule gives a power to grant exemptions. Does the discretion given

---

[48] Case C-32/05 *Commission v. Luxembourg* [2006] ECR I-11323, para. 44.

[49] OJ 1978 L 54/19.

[50] Decision of the Dutch Crown 13 May 1985 *Dutch TiO2* [1986] M&R, 90-94.

[51] Case C-236/92 *Comitato di coordinamento per la difesa della Cava v. Regione Lombardia* [1994] ECR I-485.

by the secondary rule stand in the way of the direct effect of the primary rule?
According to the *Raad van State* in *Rosmalen-Geffen*, it does not:[52] 'The Council
of State notes that Article 2(1) read together with Article 4(1) and the Annex I
mentioned there precisely defines when there is an obligation to carry out an
environmental impact assessment. It is true that Article 2(3) of the directive gives
Member States a certain discretion to grant exemptions from this obligation, but
this discretion is limited to exceptional cases, and for specific projects. Given the
above, it is our view that Articles 2(1) and 2(3) read together with Article 4(1) of the
directive are directly effective provisions in the context of the EEC Treaty.'

The direct effect of such a provision resides in the limitations it imposes on the
exercise by a public authority of a particular competence. These limitations are
subject to judicial control and therefore have direct effect. The power to derogate
as such, in other words, whether or not actually to use the power, is not directly
effective. As far as the direct effect of these limitations is concerned, the following should also be borne in mind. If the principal provision is directly effective,
but the power of derogation is not, this may produce results which run counter
to the objective and the intention of the directive.[53]

From the case law of the Court it appears that, where a directive contains
both provisions which are directly effective and provisions which are not,
an individual can invoke directly effective provisions which, owing to their
particular subject matter, are capable of being severed from the general body of
provisions and applied separately.[54] By extension it can be concluded that directly
effective provisions contained in environmental directives cannot be invoked if
they are not capable of being severed from the general body of provisions.

The following may serve as an example. Article 3(1) of Directive 2003/4 on public
access to environmental information[55] states that Member States shall make
available environmental information held by or for them to any applicant at his
request and without his having to state an interest. This provision is sufficiently
precise and unconditionally formulated to produce direct effect. Article 4 of the
directive gives Member States the power to refuse such a request for information
where it affects, *inter alia*, public security or commercial and industrial confidentiality. Article 4 confers a discretionary power and does not impose an obligation
on the Member State. There is therefore no question of direct effect in the sense
that Member States are allowed to refuse a request for information relating to, for

---

[52] Dutch *Raad van State* 11 November 1991, *Rosmalen-Geffen* [1992] AB 50.

[53] Cf. also C-53/02 *Commune de Braine-le-Château a.o.* [2004] ECR I-3251, para. 43 in particular. The Court
ruled that a failure to draw up waste management plans does not imply that individual permits can no
longer be issued, as this would result in the implementation of other provisions of the Waste Directive
being unduly delayed, to the detriment of achieving the objectives pursued by the directive.

[54] Case 8/81 *Becker* [1982] ECR 53. Confirmed for environmental law in Case C-346/97 *Braathens Sverige
AB* [1999] ECR I-3419. See on this case section 4 of Chapter 6.

[55] OJ 2003 L 41/26.

example, commercial and industrial confidentiality. Does this mean that if Article 4 of the directive has not been implemented correctly, all information relating to the environment must be made available as a consequence of the direct effect of Article 3(1)? All these questions presumably have to be answered in the light of *Becker*.[56] When is a provision, in view of the context in which it has been placed, capable of being separated from the general body of provisions in the directive concerned? This will require a close examination of the effects the direct effect of a single provision have and whether these effects coincide with the objective and scope of the directive. In the case of Directive 2003/4, it could be argued that a general obligation to provide information on the environment goes too far and would produce results which are in conflict with the general context of the directive. Public authorities should be given the opportunity to consider in each individual case whether any of the grounds for derogation apply. Denying the public authorities this margin of discretion is in conflict with the objective of the directive. In that case the direct effect of the directive can only be invoked when information is refused on grounds other than those contained in Article 4 of the directive.

Clearly wrong is Justice Tucker's view in *Wychavon District Council* v. *Secretary of State for the Environment and Velcourt Ltd*.[57] With respect to the direct effect of the EIA Directive, he held 'it is unnecessary for me to analyse each Article in the Directive in turn in order to determine whether it is unconditional or uncertain. It will suffice if in respect of any Article which offends against the principle it is identified'. He then identified a number of provisions in the directive which did not meet the threshold of 'unconditional and sufficiently precise' and held as a consequence that the EIA Directive was incapable of having direct effect.

Direct effect and licensing/permitting/authorisation requirements

Many directives contain licensing, permitting or authorisation requirements. Examples can be found in European waste, water pollution and air pollution directives in particular.

For instance, Article 4(1) of the Waste Incineration Directive 2000/76 states that 'no incineration or co-incineration plant shall operate without a permit to carry out these activities'.[58] Or take Article 4 of Directive 2006/11 on pollution caused by certain dangerous substances discharged into the aquatic environment of the Community which requires that, with respect to so called 'List 1' substances, 'all discharges into the waters [...] which are liable to contain any such substance, shall require prior authorisation by the competent authority of the Member State concerned'.[59]

---

[56] Case 8/81 *Becker* [1982] ECR 53. Cf. also Case C-365/98 *Brinkmann Tabakfabriken* [2000] ECR I-4619.

[57] English High Court, Queen's Bench Division, 16 December 1993 [1994] 2 Env. LR 239. Cf. on this case Davies (2004) at 105.

[58] OJ 2000 L 332/91.

[59] OJ 2006 L 64/52.

Of course, it could be that the competent national authorities have discretion in issuing authorisations under directives like the ones mentioned above. However, the prohibition on discharges without prior authorisation is as such clear, precise and unconditional and therefore directly effective, so that any interested party may rely on it before the national courts in an action to halt discharges which are not authorised in accordance with the procedure and criteria which it prescribes.[60]

Similar remarks can be made with respect to Article 2(1) of the EIA Directive according to which an environmental impact assessment must be carried out before the competent authority gives consent to a developer to proceed with a project which is likely to have significant effects on the environment. In the *Wells* case the Court of Justice ruled that an individual may rely on Article 2(1) of the EIA Directive before a national court.[61]

Enforcement measures with direct effect

It follows from the case law of the Court that obligations arising from environmental directives should be considered obligations to attain certain results rather than merely requiring the Member States to take all practicable steps.[62] An individual will primarily be interested in whether or not he or she, by invoking the directive, can force public authorities to take certain measures which will result in compliance with the standards contained in the directive. In general, national law provides a wide range of instruments which public authorities can use to attain the appropriate level of environmental protection. Thus, a plant producing excessive emissions of dangerous substances can be closed down, subject to criminal sanctions, etc. The question here is to what extent an individual can rely upon the direct effect of environmental directives relating to enforcement mechanisms where the Member State has failed to comply with the standards set out in the directive.

It must be assumed that Member States enjoy considerable discretion, at least in respect of the question *how* standards contained in environmental directives are enforced, within the limits of Article 10 EC (effective, preventive, non-discriminatory and proportional). As a result of this discretion, an individual does not have a right (i.e. there is no direct effect) to demand specific enforcement action, unless this has been expressly provided for in the directive itself. Some directives do indeed prescribe in detail the inspection, supervision and other enforcement mechanisms. Whether this is the case will have to be examined from one directive to the next. If a directive does contain directly effective enforcement provisions they have to be applied.

---

[60] Cf. Case C-213/03 *Pêcheurs de l'étang de Berre* [2004] ECR I-7357, para. 42 in particular.

[61] Case C-201/02 *Wells* [2004] ECR I-723, para. 61. Cf. well before *Wells* at national level, English High Court, Queen's Bench Division (McCullough J) 26 October 1990 *Twyford Parish Council a.o. v. Secretary of State for the Environment and another* [1992] 1 C.M.L.R. 276.

[62] Case C-56/90 *Commission v. UK* [1993] ECR I-4109.

Take for instance Article 4(9) of the Waste Incineration Directive: 'If an incineration or co-incineration plant does not comply with the conditions of the permit, in particular with the emission limit values for air and water, the competent authority shall take action to enforce compliance.'[63] This provision clearly implies a duty for the authorities to shut down a plant, if necessary, when the emission limit values are exceeded by the undertaking.

Another example of such a provision is Article 5(4) of Directive 2006/11.[64] This directive requires national authorities to establish emission standards in authorisations to prevent water pollution. The provision states: 'Should the emission standards not be complied with, the competent authority in the Member State concerned shall take all appropriate steps to ensure that the conditions of authorisation are fulfilled and, if necessary, that the discharge is prohibited.' This provision implies that it is not permitted to tolerate discharges which violate the emission standards contained in the directive.

Most interesting are the enforcement obligations in Article 4(5) of Directive 1999/22 relating to the keeping of wild animals in zoos.[65] It states: 'If the zoo is not licensed in accordance with this Directive or the licensing conditions are not met, the zoo or part thereof:

a) shall be closed to the public by the competent authority; and/or

b) shall comply with appropriate requirements imposed by the competent authority to ensure that the licensing conditions are met.

Should these requirements not be complied with within an appropriate period to be determined by the competent authorities but not exceeding two years, the competent authority shall withdraw or modify the licence and close the zoo or part thereof.'

However, in the absence of concrete and specific provisions, it is primarily for the Member States to determine how the factual situation must be brought into line with the legal situation, although it appears from the relevant case law that the Court can subject this decision to rigorous review.[66] Where discretionary powers exist this presumably rules out the direct effect of the obligation to enforce European values. As regards the latter, it is worth noting the conclusion of Advocate General Mischo in the German *TA Luft* cases.[67] In his opinion Member States do enjoy discretion as to the choice concerning the measures which are necessary to enforce air quality standards. The European institutions

---

[63] Directive 2000/76 on the incineration of waste, OJ 2000 L 332/91.

[64] Directive 2006/11 on pollution caused by certain dangerous substances discharged into the aquatic environment of the Community, OJ 2006 L 64/52.

[65] OJ 1999 L 94/24.

[66] Cf. Case C-365/97 *Commission v. Italy* [1999] ECR I-7773 (*San Rocco*). See also outside the field of environmental law cases 68/88 *Commission v. Greece* [1989] ECR 2965, 326/88 *Hansen* [1990] ECR I-2911 and C-287/91 *Commission v. Italy* [1992] ECR I-3315.

[67] Case C-361/88 *Commission v. Germany* [1991] ECR I-2567 and Case C-59/89 *Commission v. Germany* [1991] ECR I-2607.

would only be able to challenge the approaches adopted by Member States if it appeared from the facts that these were not capable of achieving the intended goals. As long as the factual and legal situations have not been brought into line it must be assumed that, even though the obligations imposed by a directive have not been fulfilled, individuals do not always have the right to invoke the directive by insisting that specific enforcement measures are taken by the public authorities.

The designation of special protection areas

Another type of obligation arising out of environmental directives requiring further implementation and therefore apparently lacking direct effect, are provisions requiring Member States to designate geographical areas to which special protection measures will then apply. An example is the classification of special bird protection areas under the Wild Birds Directive. For protected species of birds, Article 4(1) requires Member States to 'classify in particular the most suitable territories in number and size as special protection areas for the conservation of these species, taking into account their protection requirements in the geographical sea and land area where this directive applies'.[68] Failure to classify special protection areas while protected species of birds and migrating birds do occur in the territory of the Member State, constitutes a clear breach of the directive. This may result in the Commission initiating an infringement procedure under Article 226 EC.

> In Case C-334/89, Italy was brought before the Court of Justice because it had not classified any special protection areas.[69] The Court held: 'The Italian Government has not, either during or before the proceedings before the Court, reported any special conservation measures adopted by it at national level of the species listed in that annex. Nor has it made any claim to the effect that none of the species in question occurs in Italian territory. Accordingly, it should have established special protection areas and adopted special conservation measures in respect of the species present on its territory.' The Court ruled that Italy had failed to fulfil its obligations under the Treaty.

From this case it can be concluded that there is an obligation to classify special protection areas when specific species of birds occur in the territory of the Member State. A much more difficult question is whether, in a specific case, the directive also creates an obligation to classify a certain clearly identified area as a special protection area. From the early case law of the Court it appeared that Member States have some margin of discretion in the classification of special protection areas.

---

[68] See on this more in detail Chapter 8, section 10.1.2.

[69] Case C-334/89 *Commission v. Italy* [1991] ECR I-93.

In the *Leybucht* case the question was to what extent the Member States are entitled to reduce or modify the geographical size of a special protection area.[70] The
Court observed that the Member states 'do have a certain discretion with regard
to the choice of the territories which are most suitable for classification as special
protection areas pursuant to Article 4(1) of the directive.'

On the basis of this judgment, the conclusion has been drawn that where the
Member States do have a certain discretion, it would be difficult to establish
an obligation to classify a particular area. This would only be otherwise if the
discretion were restricted by the Member State itself, for example because the
area in question had been given protected status on the basis of other, national
or international, law. That a Member State's discretion could indeed be more
limited than is suggested in the *Leybucht* case is evident from later judgments.

Thus in Case C-3/96 the Commission argued that the Netherlands had wrongly
failed to designate a number of specifically named areas as special protection
areas.[71] The Court, while acknowledging that the Member States have a certain
margin of discretion in the choice of SPAs, stated that the classification of those
areas is nevertheless subject to certain ornithological criteria. It follows, the Court
continued, that the Member States' margin of discretion in choosing the most
suitable territories for classification as SPAs does not concern the appropriateness
of classifying as SPAs the territories which appear the most suitable according
to ornithological criteria, but only the application of those criteria for identifying
the most suitable territories for conservation of the species listed in the directive.
Member States are obliged to classify as SPAs all the sites which, applying ornithological criteria, appear to be the most suitable for conservation of the species
in question, the Court concluded.

Although this case concerned a Treaty infringement procedure in which the
question of direct effect was not as such at issue, the judgment is nevertheless
pertinent. If the Court has restricted a Member State's discretion to designate SPAs to such an extent that this could amount to a concrete obligation to
designate a specific area, it is hard to see why that obligation should not also be
directly effective.[72] Furthermore, it must be assumed that also the obligations
in directives in relation to these special protection areas can be directly effective as well and that therefore these obligations are not conditional upon prior
designation. In the *Santoña marshes* case, for instance the Court ruled that the
obligations ex Article 4(4) of the Wild Birds Directive to take appropriate steps
to avoid pollution or deterioration of special protection areas are applicable to

---

[70] Case C-57/89 *Commission v. Germany* [1991] ECR I-883.

[71] Case C-3/96 *Commission v. Netherlands* [1998] ECR I-3031. Cf. also Case C-166/97 *Commission v. France*
[1999] ECR I-1719 and Case C-355/90 *Commission v. Spain* [1993] ECR I-4221 (*Santoña marshes*).

[72] Cf. Prechal (2005) 313.

the *Santoña marshes*, although they were not designated as such.[73] With respect to the possible direct effect of the protective measures required by the Habitats Directive, the *Dragaggi* case must be mentioned.[74] The Court ruled that the protective measures prescribed in Article 6(2) to (4) of the directive are required only as regards sites which are placed on the list of sites selected as sites of Community importance. This rules out any direct effect of these provisions with respect to habitats erroneously not being designated.[75]

Other environmental directives contain similar obligations to designate special protection areas, for example, the Bathing Water Directive,[76] the Water Framework Directive[77] and Nitrates Directive.[78] For these directives too, it will have to be determined in each individual case whether the criteria in the directive in question require that a particular area is classified or not.

As regards the Bathing Water Directive, existing case law points to similar conclusions to those in the cases on the Wild Birds Directive discussed above. Under this directive bathing water in bathing areas is supposed to satisfy minimum standards. In the *Blackpool* case, one of the questions addressed was which waters had to be considered as bathing areas within the meaning of the directive.[79] The Court pointed out that the directive defines the term 'bathing water' as all running or still fresh waters, or parts thereof, and sea water in which bathing is not prohibited and is traditionally practised by a large number of bathers. The United Kingdom contended that it was not clear whether Blackpool and Southport fell within the scope of the directive. Here, too, the Member State appears to have little real discretion. It could be inferred from the presence of changing huts, toilets, markers and lifeguards that certain areas fell within the scope of the directive and that its quality objectives therefore had to be adhered to.

Similar conclusions can be drawn with respect to the duty to designate 'vulnerable zones' under the Nitrates Directive. Although the Member States have a 'wide discretion' to identify those vulnerable zones, France was nevertheless in violation because it did not designate the Seine bay under the directive.[80]

---

[73] Case C-355/90 *Commission v. Spain* [1993] ECR I-4221.

[74] Case C-117/03 *Dragaggi a.o.* [2005] ECR I-167, para. 25.

[75] See however C-244/05 *Bund Naturschutz in Bayern a.o.* [2006] ECR I-8445, where the Court ruled that the Member States are required to take all the measures necessary to avoid interventions which incur the risk of seriously compromising the ecological characteristics of the sites which appear on the national list transmitted to the Commission. See also Chapter 8, section 17.2.

[76] OJ 2006 L 64/37.

[77] OJ 2000 L 327/1.

[78] OJ 1991 L 375/1.

[79] Case C-56/90 *Commission v. UK* [1993] ECR I-4109.

[80] Case C-258/00 *Commission v. France* [2002] ECR I-5959. Similar rulings have been rendered to other Member States as well. Cf. e.g. with respect to Spain's failure to designate the Rambla de Mojácar as a vulnerable zone Case C-416/02 *Commission v. Spain* [2005] ECR I-7487.

However, if the Member States do not have a genuine obligation to determine the areas to which stringent environmental quality standards apply, there can be no question of direct effect. For example, certain air quality directives allow Member States to classify areas to which more stringent air quality standards apply.[81] Such areas are classified if 'the Member State concerned considers' these zones should be afforded special environmental protection. Where a provision of a directive does not impose an obligation on the Member States, such provision is clearly not directly effective.

Direct effect of procedural rules

Procedural rules do not always give individuals rights which they may enforce before the national courts. That was made clear by the Court in the *Balsamo* case.[82]

Article 3(2) of the 'old' Waste Directive required Member States to inform the Commission in good time of any draft rules concerning, *inter alia*, the use of products which might be a source of technical difficulties as regards disposal or lead to excessive disposal costs.[83] The Italian Government did not notify the Commission of a decision of the Mayor of Cinisello Balsamo prohibiting the supply to consumers of non-biodegradable bags. The competent Italian court submitted several questions to the Court of Justice. One of the questions was whether Article 3(2) of the directive gave individuals a right which they could enforce before the national courts in order to obtain the annulment or suspension of national rules falling within the scope of that provision on the ground that those rules were adopted without having previously been communicated to the Commission. According to the Court, Article 3(2) was intended to ensure that the Commission is informed of any plans for national measures regarding waste disposal so that it can consider whether harmonising legislation is called for and whether the draft rules submitted to it are compatible with EC law. The Court held that neither the wording nor the purpose of the provision in question provides any support for the view that failure by the Member States to give prior notice to the Commission in itself renders unlawful the rules thus adopted. The Court concluded that Article 3(2) of the directive concerned relations between the Member States and the Commission and did not give rise to any right for individuals which might be infringed by

---

[81] E.g. Article 4(2) of Directive 85/203 on air quality standards for nitrogen dioxide, OJ 1985 L 87/1.

[82] Case 380/87 *Balsamo* [1989] ECR 2491.

[83] See now also Article 3(2) of the new Waste Directive 2006/12 (OJ 2006 L 114/9): 'Except where Directive 98/34/EC of the European Parliament and of the Council of 22 June 1998 laying down a procedure for the provision of information in the field of technical standards and regulations applies, Member States shall inform the Commission of any measures they intend to take to achieve the aims set out in paragraph 1. [...]'. Also in view of Case C-159/00 *Sapod Audic* [2002] ECR I-5031, para. 61-63, it is the authors' opinion that this new text does not in any way affect the substance of the reasoning underlying the *Balsamo* judgment.

a Member State's breach of its obligation to inform the Commission in advance of draft rules.[84]

In view of the *CIA Security* case law we cannot agree with Wennerås, who states that the notification requirement of Article 2(3) of the EIA Directive is directly effective.[85] That provision enables Member States, in exceptional cases, to exempt a specific project in whole or in part from the provisions of the directive. However, Member States must inform the Commission.

However, it is evident from another judgment of the Court that *procedural* rules can contain rights and obligations for private individuals.[86]

This case was *inter alia* about the formal obligations flowing from Articles 7 to 11 and Article 13 of the 'old' Ground Water Directive (80/68).[87] Article 7 requires prior examination of the hydrogeological conditions and Articles 8 to 11 and Article 13 impose further requirements on the issuing of authorisations. The authorisations may not be issued until it has been checked that the ground water, and in particular its quality, will undergo the requisite surveillance (Article 8). That is why Articles 9 and 10 of the directive lay down the information to be specified in the authorisations. The authorisations may be granted for a limited period only, and are to be reviewed at least every four years (Article 11). Moreover, the directive requires the Member States to monitor compliance with the conditions laid down in the authorisations and the effects of discharges on groundwater (Article 13). According to the Court, it must be observed that the procedural provisions of the directive lay down, in order to guarantee effective protection of groundwater, precise and detailed rules 'which are intended to create rights and obligations for individuals'. In particular this judgment shows that the term 'rights and obligations' should be understood not only to include the rights and obligations of individuals, but far more in terms of 'having an interest in' or 'being affected by'. The conclusion must therefore be that in such cases the Member State must offer interested parties adequate legal protection against breaches of obligations imposed by directives.

Direct effect of provisions in environmental treaties concluded by the EC

It has been acknowledged by the Court that provisions of international treaties concluded by the EC could be directly effective, when these provisions contain clear and precise obligations which are not subject, in their implementation or effects, to the adoption of any subsequent measures.[88] This doctrine has

---

[84] See Dutch *Raad van State* 16 June 1995 [1995] *M&R* 93, applying the '*Balsamo* doctrine' on the duty to notify national legislation under Article 2(3) of the EIA Directive.

[85] Wennerås (2007) at 54.

[86] Case C-131/88 *Commission v. Germany* [1991] ECR I-825.

[87] OJ 1980 L 20/43. The 'old' Groundwater Directive will be repealed from 21 December 2013 by the Water Framework Directive 2000/60 (OJ 2000 L 327/1).

[88] Case 12/86 *Demirel* [1987] ECR 3719, para. 14.

been applied with respect to for the first time in the *Pêcheurs de l'étang de Berre* case.[89] The case involved, *inter alia*, Article 6(3) of the Protocol for the Protection of the Mediterranean Sea against Pollution from Land-based Sources.[90]

> Under Article 6(1) and (3) of the Protocol provides: '1. The Parties shall strictly limit pollution from land-based sources in the Protocol Area by substances or sources listed in Annex II to this Protocol. [...] 3. Discharges shall be strictly subject to the issue, by the competent national authorities, of an authorisation taking due account of the provisions of Annex III [...].' The Court ruled that that provision clearly, precisely and unconditionally lays down the obligation for Member States to subject discharges of the substances listed in Annex II to the Protocol to the issue by the competent national authorities of an authorisation taking due account of the provisions of Annex III. In view of the Court, the fact that the national authorities have discretion in issuing authorisations under the criteria set out in Annex III in no way diminishes the clear, precise and unconditional nature of the prohibition on discharges without prior authorisation and that finding is also supported by the purpose and nature of the Protocol. In conclusion the Court ruled that the provision has direct effect, so that any interested party is entitled to rely on it before the national courts.

But even if an international environmental treaty concluded by the EC contains no directly effective provisions, in the sense that they can be relied on by individuals directly before the national courts, that fact does not preclude review by the ECJ of compliance with the obligations incumbent on the EC as a party to that agreement, for instance in application for annulment under Article 230 EC.[91] However, provisions of the WTO agreements are not in principle among the rules in the light of which the Court is to review the lawfulness of measures adopted by the European institutions.[92]

Direct effect of the environmental principles of Article 174(2) EC?

In Chapter 1, section 2, we argued on the basis of the case law of the Court of Justice that the environmental principles do not as such impose obligations on Member States. *A fortiori*, they are not directly effective vis-à-vis the Member States either. However, a recent judgment of the Court of Justice outside environmental law could change things in the future.[93] In the *Mangold* case, the Court concluded that 'the principle of non-discrimination on grounds of age

---

[89] Case C-213/03 *Pêcheurs de l'étang de Berre* [2004] ECR I-7357.

[90] Approved by Council Decision 83/101, OJ 1983 L 67/1.

[91] See in general, Case C-162/96 *Racke* [1998] ECR I-3655, paras. 45, 47 and 51. In Case C-377/98 *Netherlands* v. *EP and Council* [2000] ECR I-6229 the Court seemed willing to review Directive 98/44 on the legal protection of biotechnological inventions (OJ 1998 L 213/13) in the light of the EC's obligations under the Convention on Biological Diversity.

[92] See for instance Case C-27/00 *Omega Air a.o.* [2002] ECR I-2569.

[93] Case C-144/04 *Mangold* [2005] ECR I-9981.

must [...] be regarded as a general principle of Community law' and that it is the responsibility of the national court, hearing a dispute involving the principle of non-discrimination in respect of age, to provide, in a case within its jurisdiction, the legal protection which individuals derive from the rules of EC law and to ensure that those rules are fully effective, setting aside any provision of national law which may conflict with that law. It remains to be seen if, and to what extent, this case law is capable of being applied by analogy to the environmental principles of Article 174(2) EC.

2.1.2   Absence of Horizontal Direct Effect of Directives

Directives do not produce horizontal or third-party effect in the sense that, in the absence of national implementing measures, they directly result in obligations for private individuals.[94] Under Article 249(3) EC, directives are addressed to Member States and hence oblige the Member States to take the necessary steps. They therefore only have vertical direct effect. In principle therefore, direct effect cannot be invoked to establish a breach of a provision of a directive in relations between individuals. In the *Traen* case the Court was very explicit in deciding that provisions of the Waste Directive 'do not directly impose obligations upon persons or undertakings.'[95] Or, to give another clear example, it is out of the question that the obligations for the operator under the Environmental Liability Directive to take preventive and/or remedial measures can be enforced without national implementing legislation.[96] This doctrine has been applied consistently in national courts.

In the Dutch *Drenthe Crows* case, the issue was to what extent an environmental directive, in this case the Wild Birds Directive,[97] can impose obligations on private individuals.[98] A hunting association had called its members to hunt crows on a certain day. Dutch hunting laws allowed crow hunting even though the birds were in principle protected under the directive. An environmental interest group argued that the hunters were acting unlawfully because they were acting in breach of the directive. The judge in the case dismissed the application, observing that the directive created obligations for Member States, namely to adapt the national

---

[94] Case 152/84 *Marshall* I [1986] ECR 737. Regulations however do have horizontal effect. In view of the ECJ judgment in Case C-253/00 *Muñoz* [2002] ECR I-7289, it must be assumed that in national law a tort claim must be available to enforce environmental standards laid down in the regulation. Cf. on the relevance of the *Muñoz* case for environmental law Betlem (2005).

[95] Joined Cases 372-374/85 *Traen* [1987] ECR 2141.

[96] Directive 2004/35 on environmental liability with regard to the prevention and remedying of environmental damage, OJ 2004 L 143/56, in particular Articles 4 and 5. The question whether the obligation for public authorities take the necessary action vis-a-vis the operator is directly effective will be discussed below.

[97] OJ 1979 L 103/1, later amended.

[98] Dutch District Court Assen 11 April 1989 *Drenthe Crows* [1989] M&R 372-374.

legislation. However, he added that, in legal relations between individuals, it would be going too far to accept that they should act as if the laws had already been adapted.

Another example is provided by the judgment of a Dutch court in interlocutory proceedings in which the Belgian firm of Cockerill Sambre was taken to court by several environmental interest groups in connection with discharges into the River Maas.[99] One of the arguments was that the discharges of so-called 'PACs' in particular were in breach of Directive 76/464.[100] The applicants alleged that Cockerill had abused the failure by the Belgian Government to comply with its obligations under the directive. The court dismissed the application, observing that the directive addresses the Member States, and therefore does not have the effect of binding individuals directly.

In short, an individual can invoke a directive vis-à-vis national authorities, but not vis-à-vis another individual. This position is wholly in line with the case law of the Court of Justice. Individuals do not therefore act unlawfully when they act in breach of standards set by environmental directives, if these standards have not been transposed into national legislation.

Directly effective provisions of a directive will therefore normally only be invoked in respect of an 'emanation of the state'. It is important to note that the term 'emanation of the state' must be interpreted in a broad sense. As was observed in *Foster* v. *British Gas,* provisions of a directive having direct effect may 'in any event' be relied on against a body, whatever its legal form, 'which has been made responsible, pursuant to a measure adopted by the State for providing a public service under the control of the State and has for that purpose special powers beyond those which result from the normal rules applicable in relations between individuals.'[101] Regional gas, water[102] and electricity companies, but probably also certain waste disposal companies may, depending on the circumstances fall within this broad definition.

Inverse direct effect[103]

Apart from lacking horizontal effect, a directive *a fortiori* also lacks 'inverse direct effect'.[104] In other words, a public authority cannot invoke a directive against an individual and thereby require him to act in conformity with the directive, where the obligations contained in the directive have not yet been implemented in the national legal order. If the Member State is at fault, this

---

99 Dutch District Court Maastricht 3 February 1993 *Cockerill Sambre* [1993] MR 17.

100 Now repealed by Directive 2006/11 on pollution caused by certain dangerous substances discharged into the aquatic environment of the Community, OJ 2006 L 64/52.

101 Case C-188/89 *Foster* v. *British Gas* [1990] ECR 3343.

102 See English High Court 25 August 1994 *Griffin* v. *South West Water Services Ltd* [1995] IRLR 15.

103 The notion 'inverse direct effect' was introduced by the Court in Case C-201/02 *Wells* [2004] ECR I-723, para. 58.

104 Case 14/86 *Pretore di Salò* v. *Persons unknown* [1987] ECR 2545, in particular para. 19.

cannot be held against the individual (principle of 'estoppel'). The State must be prevented from taking advantage of its own failure to comply with EC law.

> The following example will serve to clarify what the consequences of this doctrine could be in the environmental law field. Suppose that a new directive requires Member States to introduce an energy-eco tax. Would the state be entitled to apply this directive and charge a tax on energy, even though the directive had not yet been implemented in the national legislation? The answer has to be that it could not. If the Member State has not fulfilled its obligations, it may not rely on the directive against an individual.

Horizontal side-effects of vertical direct effect

It has been explained above that the horizontal effect of environmental directives has been rejected by the Court of Justice. This does not mean that environmental directives which have not been properly implemented produce no horizontal legal effects between individuals at all. An environmental directive can give rise to obligations in a more indirect way. If the competent authorities grant a permit which is in conflict with a directive, an appeal by an interested third party will result in its annulment. Acts which were allowed by the permit before are no longer allowed once it has been annulled. This has obvious consequences in the sphere of civil liability. In this roundabout way, horizontal effects may after all arise.

There are other ways in which environmental directives can produce indirect horizontal effects. Thus, where an interested third party invokes a directly effective provision of an environmental directive, for example in an appeal against the grant of an environmental permit, a successful appeal would mean that the permit-holder would be placed in a less favourable position, because his permit would be void. There is nothing special about this, because a permit which contravenes national environmental law can be annulled. The Court of Justice addressed this problem in the *Wells* case.[105]

> This case concerned a dispute between Mrs Wells and the Secretary of State for Transport, Local Government and the Regions concerning the grant of a new consent for mining operations at Conygar Quarry without an environmental impact assessment having first been carried out. In 1947 an 'old mining permission' had been granted for Conygar Quarry under the Town and Country Planning (General Interim Development) Order 1946. Conygar Quarry was divided into two sections, of slightly more than 7.5 hectares each, separated by a road on which Mrs Wells' house was situated. Mrs Wells had bought her house in 1984, that is to say 37 years after the permission had been granted, but at a time when the Quarry had long since been dormant. The site was recognised to be environmentally extremely sensitive. The area in or adjacent to which the quarry lay was subject to

---

[105] Case C-201/02 *Wells* [2004] ECR I-723. And confirmed in Case C-127/02 *Landelijke Vereniging tot Behoud van de Waddenzee* [2004] ECR I-7405.

several designations of nature and environmental conservation importance. At the beginning of 1991, the owners of Conygar Quarry had applied to the competent Mineral Planning Authority (MPA) for registration of the old mining permission under the Planning and Compensation Act 1991. Registration was granted by a decision of 24 August 1992, which stated that no development could lawfully be carried out unless and until an application for the determination of new planning conditions had been made to the MPA and finally determined (the registration decision). The owners of Conygar Quarry had therefore applied to the competent MPA for determination of new planning conditions. As the MPA, by decision of 22 December 1994, had imposed more stringent conditions than those submitted by the owners of Conygar Quarry, the latter exercised their right of appeal to the Secretary of State. By decision of 25 June 1997, the Secretary of State imposed 54 planning conditions, leaving some matters to be decided by the competent MPA. Those matters were approved by the competent MPA by decision of 8 July 1999. Neither the Secretary of State nor the competent MPA had examined whether it was necessary to carry out an environmental impact assessment pursuant to Directive 85/337.

According to the United Kingdom Government, acceptance that an individual was entitled to invoke Directive 85/337 would amount to inverse direct effect. The Court of Justice rejected this: 'mere adverse repercussions on the rights of third parties, even if the repercussions are certain, do not justify preventing an individual from invoking the provisions of a directive against the Member State concerned'. These adverse repercussions, the Court stated in paragraph 58, were 'not directly linked' to the performance of any obligation which would fall on the quarry owners under the directive. They were 'the consequence of the belated performance of [the Member State's] obligations.'

This case demonstrates that, where a third party successfully invokes the direct effect of the directive, this may put the permit holder at a disadvantage. However, it is impossible to regard this as an unacceptable form of horizontal effect: 'mere adverse repercussions on the rights of third parties' do not constitute inverse direct effect. The effects for the permit holder have to be seen as flowing from the rights which the third party has obtained under the directive vis-à-vis the competent authorities and are not 'directly linked'[106] with obligations of the permit holder. The adverse consequences of direct effect for the permit holder do not stem from the directive, but from the fact that the authorities have failed to fulfil their obligations under it. If the directive had been correctly implemented, the authorities would not have granted the authorisation in the first place. In so far as the additional burden results from the authorities' failure to fulfil their obligations under the directive vis-à-vis other individuals, this cannot be regarded as horizontal effect. However, whenever the obligations

---

[106] Case C-201/02 *Wells* [2004] ECR I-723, para. 56. This paragraph of the judgment is however lacking in Case C-127/02 *Landelijke Vereniging tot Behoud van de Waddenzee* [2004] ECR I-7405. Cf. on this Verschuuren (2005) and Lee (2005) at 63-64.

of the authorities are *directly linked* with obligations of individuals stemming from the (non-implemented) directive, this would amount to inverse direct effect.

> As an example for the latter we could point to the Liability Directive.[107] According to Article 5(1) of the directive an operator shall, in case of an imminent threat of environmental damage occurring, take the necessary preventive measures without delay. Article 12 states that natural or legal persons shall be entitled to request the competent authority to take action under this directive. In our view the obligations for public authorities under Article 12 are directly linked with the obligations of individuals, like the one in Article 5(1). This seems to exclude, under the *Wells* doctrine, that third parties can rely on the Liability Directive vis-à-vis public authorities to enforce the obligations of Article 5(1). As this would create, in absence of national implementing legislation, a direct obligation for individuals.

Although the Court's judgments in *Wells* and *Waddenzee* seem to be in line with the general case law of the Court of Justice, further case law needs to be awaited in order to establish a clear line between 'mere adverse consequences' and creating obligations for individuals.

2.1.3 Consequences of Direct Effect: Integral Application of EC Law

The Court repeatedly held that under the principle of cooperation in good faith laid down in Article 10 EC, the Member States are required to nullify the unlawful consequences of a breach of EC law.[108] Such an obligation is owed, within the sphere of its competence, by every organ of the Member State concerned.[109] In the *Simmenthal II* case the Court of Justice explained the implications of direct effect in combination with the principle of supremacy.[110] In a case within its jurisdiction, every national court must apply EC law in its entirety and protect the rights which it confers on individuals and must accordingly set aside any provision of national law which may conflict with it, whether prior or subsequent to the European rule. The consequences are thus twofold:

1) EC law must be applied in its entirety and
2) any provision of national law which is in conflict with it must be set aside.

In other decisions, it has also drawn attention to the implications of direct effect for authorities other than the judiciary. In *Fratelli Costanzo* the Court decided that all national administrative authorities, including regional and local authori-

---

[107] OJ 2004 L 143/56. See on this directive also Chapter 8, section 8. Cf. also Wennerås (2007) at 49.

[108] Case 6/60 *Humblet* [1960] ECR 559, at 569, and Joined Cases C-6/90 and C-9/90 *Francovich* [1991] ECR I-5357, para. 36.

[109] Case C-8/88 *Germany v. Commission* [1990] ECR I-2321, para. 13.

[110] Case 106/77 *Simmenthal* [1978] ECR 629.

ties, are under an obligation to apply directly effective provisions of EC law.[111] The *Costanzo* case is of great significance for national environmental law, in view of the competences regional and local authorities have in applying (implemented) environmental law. The case illustrates that regional and local authorities have an *independent* responsibility to ensure the fulfilment of EC law obligations. Regional and local authorities cannot 'hide' behind national legislation if this legislation is contrary to European rules. If necessary, they must independently set aside national legislation if its application would cause them to act in breach of directly effective provisions of EC law.

> A good example from Dutch administrative law is a judgment of the *Raad van State* (Council of State) in a case involving Directive 2000/53 (end-of-life vehicles). The *Raad van State* required the provincial authorities, in their decision-making, to take account of whether the legislation adopted in implementation of Directive 2000/53 was consistent with Article 29 EC. By simply assuming that the implementing legislation adopted by central government was lawful, the provincial authorities had acted without due care. It is hard to imagine a clearer illustration of local and regional authorities' own responsibility.[112]

In Dutch environmental law however, we still encounter problems on how exactly this *Costanzo* doctrine should be applied in practice.

> The problems can be illustrated by referring to two judgments of the Dutch *Raad van State* relating to Article 3(4) of Directive 76/464 on pollution caused by certain dangerous substances discharged into the aquatic environment of the Community.[113] According to the *Raad van State*, this provision is directly effective in the national legal order. Authorisations to emit substances on the 'black list' which had been issued for an unlimited period were therefore contrary to Article 3(4) of the directive and were consequently revoked.[114] However, in a subsequent case where a public authority applied the rule in *Costanzo* and issued an authorisation for a limited period of time, the *Raad van State* annulled the decision, arguing that this would imply the horizontal direct effect of a directive not properly transposed into national law.

---

[111] Case 103/88 *Fratelli Costanzo* [1989] ECR 1839.

[112] Dutch *Raad van State* 26 November 2003 [2004] M&R 39.

[113] Directive 76/464 is repealed by Directive 2006/11 on pollution caused by certain dangerous substances discharged into the aquatic environment of the Community, OJ 2006 L 64/52.

[114] Dutch *Raad van State* 23 October 2002 [2003] M&R 4 and 5. The cases are also mentioned in Annex VI, Application of Community law by national courts: a survey. Twentieth annual report on monitoring the application of Community law (2002), COM (2003) 669. Recently similar problems occurred with respect to the duty to apply Article 6 (3) of the Habitat Directive, Dutch *Raad van State* 7 December 2005 [2006] M&R 19.

Depending on the proceedings, reliance on a directly effective provision of EC law can lead to full or partial annulment of the decision taken by the competent authority, to an award of damages, or to any other order the national court is capable of imposing on the public authorities under national law. As far as environmental law is concerned the problem of direct effect will primarily arise in public law disputes before the various administrative courts. Where the competent authorities take concrete decisions, for example by granting, withdrawing or changing environmental permits, it will generally be the courts with jurisdiction over such matters that will be competent to decide disputes. Where directly effective provisions of EC law are at issue, this may result in the national law or decree in question being ignored or annulled.

In some Member States, in cases concerning actions based on the unlawfulness of acts by the State resulting from its failure to fulfil obligations under an environmental directive, the competent courts will be the civil courts. In principle this can lead to the award of damages, an injunction, etc. Dutch civil courts, for instance, have accepted that breaches of directly effective provisions of environmental directives by public authorities are unlawful.

When the direct effect of EC law is invoked in criminal proceedings, this will often involve a situation in which the national law prohibits something which ought not to have been prohibited according to a directive. Defendants who successfully invoke EC law will be acquitted, as the charges will not constitute a criminal offence. In such cases the national provision on which the charges were based will be set aside or held inapplicable.

> The *Ratti* case provides a clear example of this.[115] Similarly, in the *Red Grouse* case regarding the infringement of certain prohibitions in the Dutch *Vogelwet* concerning the sale of species threatened with extinction, the Court decided that these prohibitions were at variance with the Treaty.[116] In this case a restaurant in The Hague had sold red grouse, a protected bird under the *Vogelwet*. The owner argued that he had bought the birds in the United Kingdom, where the species is not protected. The Court held that the Dutch prohibitions breached the rules on the free movement of goods. Here, too, the decision of the Court resulted in acquittal in the criminal proceedings before the national court.[117]

Integral application of directives, protection of the rights of individuals and non-application of conflicting national laws are thus the most important legal consequences of the direct effect of directives. But what does this mean for environmental law in practice? What precisely has to be applied in its entirety? The answer to these questions depends on what exactly the environmental directive requires. In each instance it has to be borne in mind that the basis for direct effect resides in the obligations the directive imposes on the Member

---

[115] Case 148/78 *Ratti* [1979] ECR 1629.

[116] Case C-169/89 *Gourmetterie v.d. Burg* [1990] ECR I-2143.

[117] Dutch *Hoge Raad* 20 November 1990 *Gourmetterie v.d. Burg* [1991] NJ 241.

States. Thus each provision of each directive has to be examined to determine what obligations it imposes. This implies also that if a directive provides for various options out of which the Member States may choose, direct effect, in the *Kraaijeveld* meaning, does not require the national court to take the place of the national legislature on which alone it is incumbent to choose the option which it deems appropriate. The fact that directly effective provisions of environmental directives have to be applied in their entirety therefore implies a wide diversity of application modalities.

In the case of directives laying down product standards, which generally aim for total harmonisation, direct effect implies that a product which satisfies the environmental requirements contained in the directive must be allowed on the market, whereas a product which does not meet the requirements must be refused. Or, as was held in the *Braathens* case, which concerned a Swedish energy tax incompatible with Directive 92/81, individuals were entitled to rely on the directive to oppose the taxation.[118]

In environmental directives involving minimum harmonisation, for example directives concerning the quality of water and air, direct effect resides in the limits the directive establishes in respect of the maximum level of pollution. In such cases it is these minimum limits that must be applied. Application of directly effective emission standards or quality standards prevents the lawful application of national environmental law which is not sufficiently stringent in the light of European environmental standards.

In the derogation clauses described above, for example the exemptions from the obligation to carry out an environmental impact assessment, direct effect resides in the limitations of these powers of exemption. This means that the power of derogation as such is not subject to judicial control, but only the extent to which the authorities have remained within the limits allowed by the directive. The significance of this remark becomes apparent if a closer look is taken at the powers of exemption contained in the EIA Directive.

> Above it was stated that the powers of exemption contained in Dutch EIA legislation were too wide by comparison with Article 2(3) of the directive. In proceedings before the competent Dutch court the Dutch exemption provisions were set aside on the ground that they were incompatible with the directly effective provision in the directive.[119] Consequently, the power to grant exemptions conferred by Dutch law could no longer be applied and all such projects had to be made subject to an EIA. In a situation like this the question arises whether the competent authorities can directly invoke the powers of exemption contained in the directive. If this is a case of direct effect, it could be argued that this provision should be applied. This need not, however, follow from the direct effect of Article 2(3) of the EIA Directive for the following reasons. The directive does not impose an obligation to grant an exemption when an exceptional case arises. It merely creates the power to do so.

[118] Case C-346/97 *Braathens Sverige AB* [1999] ECR I-3419. See on this case also section 4 of Chapter 6.

[119] Dutch *Raad van State* 11 November 1991 *Rosmalen/Geffen* [1992] AB 50.

It does not give holders of a planning permit a right to be exempted. The question whether an exemption should be granted or not is not addressed by the directive. The directive has no direct effect in this respect. Direct effect, and hence the obligation for Member States, resides in the limitation of the use of these powers to exceptional cases. In other words, the directive requires Member States to limit the exercise of their powers of exemption to exceptional cases. This limitation has direct effect and should be applied in the sense of *Fratelli Costanzo*.[120] Nothing more is meant by application than 'fulfilling obligations'. In view of the fact that the directive does not provide for an obligation to grant an exemption when an exceptional case occurs, a secretary of state or minister cannot directly invoke the directive. Such a form of 'application' of environmental law would amount to what has been referred to above as 'inverse vertical direct effect'. It would be the State which invoked an unimplemented provision of a directive as against an individual and not the other way round as is usually the case where direct vertical effect is concerned.

It must therefore be concluded that the obligations under a directive and the rights it aims to protect must be determined in each individual case. However, it will generally not be easy to determine what obligations the directive imposes and what rights it aims to protect. The conclusion must therefore be that the extent to which the national authorities can apply unimplemented provisions depends on what obligations the directive imposes and what rights of individuals it aims to protect. This requires careful examination by the national courts in each case and for each directive.

2.2   The Doctrine of Consistent Interpretation[121]

In the event of a conflict between national law and a directive, the national courts are required to interpret the national law as far as possible in conformity with the directive. In *Marleasing*, the Court observed:

'In applying national law, whether the provisions in question were adopted before or after the directive, the national court called upon to interpret it is required to do so, as far as possible, in the light of the wording and the purpose of the directive in order to achieve the result pursued by the latter and thereby comply with the third paragraph of Article 189 [now Article 249, authors] EC.'[122]

In *Pfeiffer* the Court further specified this requirement by stating that 'if the application of interpretative methods recognised by national law enables, in certain circumstances, a provision of domestic law to be construed in such a way as to avoid conflict with another rule of domestic law or the scope of that provi-

---

[120] Case 103/88 *Fratelli Costanzo* [1989] ECR 1839.

[121] This section builds upon Jans et al. (2007), Chapter IV.

[122] Case C-106/89 *Marleasing* [1990] ECR I-4135.

sion to be restricted to that end by applying it only in so far as it is compatible with the rule concerned, the national court is bound to use those methods in order to achieve the result sought by the directive.'[123] The qualification *as far as possible* indicates that the requirement is not unlimited. In *Kolpinghuis* the Court of Justice observed that the obligation to interpret national law in the light of EU law is limited 'by the general principles of law and in particular the principle of legal certainty'.[124]

> Consider the following example: in a given Member State, national rules expli-
> citly permit discharges of certain substances into surface water, even though the
> relevant directive requires Member States to prohibit such discharges. In this kind
> of situation, individuals consulting the national rules are surely entitled to assume
> that they 'mean what they say'.

In such a case, consistent interpretation would imply a *contra legem* interpreta-tion of national law. In *Pupino* the Court of Justice has explicitly ruled that inter-pretation *contra* the law should be rejected and made clear that national admin-istrative courts are not in fact required to interpret national rules in this way.[125]

Consistent interpretation must thus be regarded as a means of ensuring a national court does not take a decision which is incompatible with EC law. It follows from the Court's case law that the duty of national courts to interpret national law in the light of EC law applies not only to relations between the State and the individual, but also to relations between individuals.[126] In such cases, some indirect horizontal effects would seem to be recognised.[127]

It should be noted that interpretation in this way does not release the Member State from its obligation to ensure that proper implementing legisla-tion is put in place. Nor does the presence of direct effect release the Member State from its obligation to implement a directive.[128] The Court has on several occasions rejected the argument put forward by Member States that direct effect guarantees that an interested party, at least in his relation to the State, will get what he is entitled to anyway. Directives that have not been properly imple-mented cause uncertainty as to the legal position of those to whom they apply. This is why the Court insists on full and correct implementation. Courts can be said to interpret national law in conformity with a directive when they construe national provisions in a way which is different from the normal manner of interpretation and where a 'normal' interpretation would have produced a result which was at odds with the directive. This manner of interpretation is therefore

---

[123] Joined Cases C-397/01 to C-403/01 *Pfeiffer* [2004] ECR I-8835, para. 116.

[124] Case 80/86 *Kolpinghuis* [1987] ECR 3969, para. 13.

[125] Case C-105/03 *Pupino* [2005] ECR I-5285, para. 47.

[126] Case C-106/89 *Marleasing* [1990] ECR I-4135.

[127] See the Opinion of Advocate General Darmon in Case C-236/92 *Comitato di coordinamento per la difesa della Cava v. Regione Lombardia* [1994] ECR I-485, para. 28.

[128] Case C-208/90 *Emmott* [1991] ECR I-4269, in particular para. 20.

in many ways artificial and irregular and serves only as a makeshift for poor implementation. Full and correct implementation is necessary to put an end to legal uncertainty.

Consistent interpretation of private environmental law

The significance of this doctrine for private environmental law is illustrated in the *Cockerill Sambre* case referred to above.[129] Although there was no question of the emission limit values laid down in Directive 76/464[130] having true horizontal direct effect, the question nevertheless arose to what extent interpretation in the light of the directive might have given rise to an obligation for Cockerill Sambre to comply with the limit values. It should be remembered that since *Marleasing* the national courts are obliged to interpret national law 'as far as possible' in conformity with the directive. Although opinions may differ as to the precise meaning of the phrase, national law must presumably be sufficiently flexible to allow such an interpretation. If express environmental legislation had existed which would have allowed Cockerill Sambre to carry out certain environmentally harmful activities, this rule of interpretation would have been of little use. After all, the national courts can hardly change something which is expressly permitted into something which is prohibited. *Contra legem* interpretation is not required.[131] This would conflict with the requirement of legal certainty. Similarly, where a polluter acts in accordance with an authorisation which has been recently and validly granted, it would seem hard to defend the position that it is unlawful to act in accordance with its conditions because the limit values of the directive have been exceeded. This despite the fact that in some Member States, like the Netherlands, liability law does not automatically preclude an action for damages, even if the defendant has acted in conformity with the permit. In this type of case, direct action against the authorised discharge would be unlikely to succeed and interested third parties would be well advised to challenge any acts or decisions of the authorities by invoking the (vertical) direct effect of the limit values.

Under EC law direct action at the national level against an authorised polluter would only seem possible in a national legal situation which is open to multiple interpretations. In such a case the polluter could be required to act in accordance with the provisions and standards contained in a directive by interpreting the national law in conformity with the directive. In particular it could be argued that the 'duty of care', a central concept of liability law in many national legal systems, should be interpreted in the light of the limit values contained in the directive. The violation of limit values (or other obligations) contained in environmental directives which have not been implemented would constitute a breach of the duty of care, and hence be unlawful. As has already

---

[129] Dutch District Court Maastricht 3 February 1993 *Cockerill Sambre* [1993] MR 17.

[130] Now repealed by Directive 2006/11 on pollution caused by certain dangerous substances discharged into the aquatic environment of the Community, OJ 2006 L 64/52.

[131] Case C-105/03 *Pupino* [2005] ECR I-5285, para. 47.

been observed, this would only be practicable if the courts have sufficient leeway to apply this rule of interpretation.

Consistent interpretation of criminal environmental law

Interpreting national criminal environmental law in this manner will obviously have to be approached even more cautiously than is the case with private and administrative law.[132] After all, it might result in an act becoming an offence which would not have been if the directive had not existed. As the Court of Justice has recognised, the principle that penal provisions may not have retroactive effect is one which is common to all the legal orders of the Member States.[133] It is incompatible with the requirement of legal certainty. The significance for the environment sector was made clear in the *Arcaro* case.[134]

> In this case the Court answered several question referred to it by the Pretura di Vicenza in connection with criminal proceedings before that court. Arcaro was suspected of having discharged cadmium into surface water in contravention of Italian rules on the subject. These rules were designed to implement a number of European directives concerning industrial discharges of dangerous substances into water. Under the Italian legislation only new plant was required to obtain an authorisation and not existing plant such as Arcaro's. This was in breach of the directive, the Court ruled, as it makes any discharge, irrespective of the date on which the plant from which it comes commenced operation, subject to the issue of a prior authorisation. The Court also confirmed that a directive may not by itself create obligations for an individual and that a provision of a directive may not therefore be relied upon as such against such a person. Referring to earlier judgments, it observed that this case law seeks to prevent a Member State from taking advantage of its own failure to comply with EC law. Consequently, a directive cannot, of itself and independently of a national law adopted by a Member State for its implementation, have the effect of determining or aggravating the liability in criminal law of persons who act in contravention of the provisions of that directive. A public authority may not therefore rely on the directive against an individual. The Pretura was still keen to know whether there were any means available to it which would enable it to apply the Italian legislation, despite the fact that the directive had not been fully transposed. Could the rules be interpreted otherwise than in the light of the directive? The Court replied in the following terms: 'the obligation of the national court to refer to the content of the directive when interpreting the relevant rules of its own national law reaches a limit where such an interpretation leads to the imposition on an individual of an obligation laid down by a directive which has not been transposed or, more especially, where it has the effect of determining or aggravating, on the basis of the directive and in

---

[132] Case C-105/03 *Pupino* [2005] ECR I-5285, para. 47.

[133] Case 63/83 *Kent Kirk* [1984] ECR 2689.

[134] Case C-168/95 *Arcaro* [1996] ECR I-4705.

the absence of a law enacted for its implementation, the liability in criminal law of persons who act in contravention of that directive's provisions.'

In other words, the national court's obligation to apply the law in such a way as to achieve the result intended by a directive may not be taken so far that it would cause or compound an individual's criminal liability for failing to comply with provisions of a directive which have not been properly transposed.[135]

Consistent interpretation of public environmental law

In the Netherlands the doctrine of consistent interpretation has frequently been applied with respect to implementing legislation which has been formulated too broadly in the light of the relevant directive. An example is the judgment of the Dutch *Raad van State* in the *ATM* case.[136]

> This case concerned the relationship between the then section 10.36a of the Dutch Environmental Protection Act (*Wet milieubeheer*) and the second paragraph of Article 4(6) of Directive 84/631[137], as it then was, concerning transfrontier shipments of hazardous waste. The problem was that, under the Dutch statute, the export of waste could be prohibited if that might jeopardise the implementation of plans and programmes prepared by the Dutch environment minister for the disposal of hazardous waste. The directive only regarded an export ban as permitted if this 'would adversely affect the implementation of a plan prepared pursuant to Article 12 of Directive 78/319/EEC or Article 6 of Directive 76/403/EEC'. The national court compared the two provisions and concluded that the Dutch legislation was drafted too broadly and allowed an obstruction of exports on grounds that were not consistent with those of the directive. It referred to a defect in the Dutch legislation regarding the implementation of the applicable EC law. In this case it decided to interpret the domestic legislation in the light of the European rules: the defect in the Dutch Act could 'given its nature and extent, be resolved by interpreting this part of the section in the light of the wording and purpose of the applicable directives.'
>
> Another example in Dutch environmental case law can be found in a judgment of the Council of State on Directive 2001/18 on the deliberate release into the environment of genetically modified organisms.[138] This directive had not been transposed precise enough into Dutch law, in particular with respect to the transposition of the precautionary principle. Under the Environmentally Dangerous Substances Act (*Wet milieugevaarlijke stoffen*) authorisation had been granted for small-scale trials with flowering genetically modified rape. Pursuant to the second

---

[135] Case 80/86 *Kolpinghuis* [1987] ECR 3969. Cf. also Joined Cases C-387/02, C-391/02 and C-403/02 *Berlusconi* [2004] ECR I-3565, paras. 74 *et seq.*

[136] Dutch *Raad van State* 15 December 1994 [1996] AB 29.

[137] Repealed by Regulation 259/93 on the supervision and control of shipments of waste within, into and out of the European Community (Basel Regulation), OJ 1993 L 30/1.

[138] Dutch *Raad van State* 28 June 2004 [2004] M&R 104.

paragraph of section 26 of the Act, the authorisation could only be refused 'in the interest of the protection of man and the environment'. According to the court this statutory framework provided sufficient basis for the court to interpret in the light of the directive. The obligations set out in the directive, including the precautionary principle and the duty to carry out a specific environmental risk assessment in accordance with the criteria of Annex II of the directive, were 'read into' the national law.

An interesting example from German law is the following. Under § 4 bs. 1 Satz 2 *Umweltinformationsgesetz* German administrative authorities have a certain discretion (*freies Ermessen*) as to whether they supply environmental information requested by a citizen by sending copies, or by allowing the citizen to inspect the documents on site. The *Bundesverwaltungsgericht* ruled that this discretion must be interpreted in the light of the objective of the directive on freedom of access to information on the environment.[139] In this specific case it meant that the administrative body had to send the copies requested even though this was significantly more burdensome than allowing their inspection.

In England the judgment in *R* v. *Secretary of State for the Environment*, ex parte *Greenpeace* is worthwhile mentioning.[140] The case concerned the British Nuclear Fuels Ltd. nuclear waste reprocessing plant at Sellafield. According to the 'justification principle' of Article 6 of the directive 'every activity resulting in an exposure to ionising radiation shall be justified by the advantages which it produces'. The High Court acknowledged that the Radioactive Substances Act 1993 had to be interpreted in the light of Article 6 of the directive.[141]

Where the domestic court interprets the domestic rules so as to give full effect to European rules, it is using the 'superior' rule of EU law in order to be able to apply national law properly.

2.3   The Significance of *Francovich* for Environmental Law[142]

In the *Francovich* case the Court of Justice ruled that Member States are obliged to make good the losses and damage caused to individuals by breaches of EC law for which they can be held responsible.[143] The doctrine devel-

---

[139] BverwGE 102, 282, 286. See on this directive, Chapter 8, section 14.

[140] [1994] 4 All ER 352. Cf. on this case Davies (2004) at 107.

[141] Interestingly, in a Dutch case the Council of State relied on the doctrine of direct effect in order to apply the justification principle of Article 6 of the Directive; Dutch *Raad van State* 27 March 1991 [1991] AB 537.

[142] This section builds upon Jans et al. (2007), Chapter VIII. The national case law discussed in this chapter is largely taken from the various Annual Reports of the Commission on monitoring the application of EC law, and the *Francovich* Follow-up website www.eel.nl, Dossiers / Links (Applications by national courts), edited by Gerrit Betlem, Carmen Pérez González, Marie-Pierre Granger and Birgit Schoißwohl.

[143] Joined Cases C-6/90 and C-9/90 *Francovich* [1991] ECR I-5357.

oped in *Francovich* has been refined and elaborated in later cases.[144] Member States can be held responsible for legislative, executive or factual acts. The Court has based this liability on Article 10 EC. Individuals who have suffered damage have a right to reparation where three conditions are met:
- the rule of law infringed must have been intended to confer rights on individuals;
- the breach must be sufficiently serious;
- and there must be a direct causal link between the breach of the obligation resting on the state and the damage sustained by the injured parties.

In developing its case law on the non-contractual liability of the Member States, the Court has had regard to its case law on liability under Article 288 EC. According to the Court's judgment in *Bergaderm*, the liability regimes for the EU institutions and the Member States are founded on the same basis.[145]

Liability applies in respect of whatever organ of the State was responsible for the breach.[146] In terms of environmental law, this means that local and regional authorities must also ensure that they do not act in breach of EC law when applying national environmental rules.[147] This can give rise to problems, especially when such local or regional authorities are applying 'superior' national environmental rules in good faith. The question of who to hold liable, the State or the local or regional authority, is not easily answered. On the one hand it is the State which is the cause of the problem – it should have ensured the legislation was in order – but on the other hand local and regional authorities have a responsibility of their own, as is clear from the judgment in *Fratelli Costanzo*.[148] In principle, it could be argued that any person suffering loss or damage as a result of the application of legislation which is not in conformity with EC law can hold both the State and the local or regional authority in question liable.[149] The question which then arises, as to the relationship between the State and the local or regional authority, is a matter for national law.[150]

It is on the basis of the rules of national law of liability that the State must make reparation for the consequences of loss and damage caused. The procedural rules governing this EC-inspired state liability are hence governed by national law. National liability law, including its procedural rules, therefore serve as a 'vehicle' for a remedy of state liability based on EC law. However, national provisions which are more restrictive than the conditions formulated

---

[144] Joined Cases C-46/93 and C-48/93 *Brasserie du pêcheur and Factortame* [1996] ECR I-1029 and Joined Cases C-178/94, C-179/94, C-188/94, C-189/94 and C-190/94, *Dillenkofer a.o.* [1996] ECR I-4845.

[145] Cf. Case C-352/98P *Bergaderm* [2000] ECR I-5291, para. 41.

[146] Joined Cases C-46/93 and C-48/93 *Brasserie du pêcheur and Factortame* [1996] ECR I-1029, in particular para. 32. Cf. Wennerås (2004).

[147] Cf. Case C-302/97 *Konle* [1999] ECR I-3099.

[148] Case 103/88 *Fratelli Costanzo* [1989] ECR 1839.

[149] Cf. Case C-424/97 *Haim II* [2000] ECR I-5123.

[150] Cf. Case C-302/97 *Konle* [1999] ECR I-3099.

in *Francovich* must be ignored.[151] Since it is not a requirement for reparation that provisions have direct effect, breaches of provisions which lack direct effect may also give rise to liability. Below the various conditions for state liability and the manner in which they are applied in respect of European environmental law will be considered.

2.3.1 The Breach Must be Sufficiently Serious

In the context of the obligation to implement European environmental law, a breach will be sufficiently serious if:
- a Member State has failed to take legislative measures, for instance to implement an environmental directive, unless the Member State was entitled to assume that its legislation was already satisfactory;
- a Member State has taken legislative measures, but not the right ones, while it could have known that the measures it had taken were not satisfactory.

In cases other than those where a Member State is required to implement European environmental law, legislative activities of a Member State would initially have been regarded as involving a sufficiently serious breach if it could be concluded that the Member State could not, in good faith, believe that its action was compatible with EC law. Since *Bergaderm*, it must be assumed that the crucial element in relation to legislative acts is how broad the Member State's discretion is.[152] If the Member State has only considerably reduced or even no discretion, the mere infringement of EC law is sufficient. If it does have a real choice, the decisive test is whether there has been a manifest and grave disregard of the limits of that discretion.[153]

If the Member State has no discretion, as in respect of time limits for implementation (which must be met regardless), a mere breach will at the same time constitute a sufficiently serious breach. If there is discretion, application of the system developed by the Court of Justice amounts in practice to little more than a test of whether the Member State could reasonably have arrived at the assumption that the decision or act was compatible with EC law.

2.3.2 Conferring Rights on Individuals

As regards the condition that the rule infringed must be intended to create rights for individuals, the following remarks must be made. Firstly, the question of whether a rule of EC law implies 'rights for individuals' is not only relevant in relation to the liability of Member States for infringements. As has been demonstrated in Chapter 4, the Court of Justice also uses

---

[151] Cf. Case C-177/88 *Dekker* [1990] ECR I-3941.

[152] Cf. Case C-5/94 *Hedley Lomas* [1996] ECR 2553 and Case C-352/98P *Bergaderm* [2000] ECR I-5291.

[153] Case C-352/98P *Bergaderm* [2000] ECR I-5291, para. 43. Cf. on discretion Hilson (2005).

the concept 'rights for individuals' in order to determine which provisions from directives must be transposed into national law. Thus it emerges from the case law of the Court, in the context of infringement proceedings brought against a Member State for failure to transpose a directive, that the Court is fairly willing to accept that a directive creates 'rights for individuals'. All kinds of obligations in environmental directives have been held create 'rights for individuals', even where the scope of the protection afforded by these directives is very broad.[154]

> The following example may help to clarify this. In Case C-186/91, the Belgian Government argued that the obligation set out in Article 11 of Directive 85/203 on air quality standards for nitrogen dioxide, requiring Member States to hold transboundary consultations, did not confer rights on individuals and therefore did not require incorporation into national law; the Court rejected this argument.[155]

However, it hardly seems tenable to argue that the mere infringement of a procedural obligation to hold transboundary consultations could result in individuals being able to hold a Member State liable. This example makes it clear that a provision of a directive that has to be transposed into national law because it creates 'rights for individuals' does not necessarily have to be qualified as 'conferring rights on individuals' in terms of state liability.[156]

Secondly, complex problems concerning 'rights for individuals' were also discussed in section 2.1 of this chapter in relation to direct effect. In *Brasserie du Pêcheur*, concerning the infringement of the directly effective Article 28 and 43 EC, the Court stated that these provisions 'have direct effect in the sense that they confer on individuals rights upon which they are entitled to rely directly before the national courts. Breach of such provisions may give rise to reparation.' The question is whether the Court intended to say that directly effective provisions by definition create rights for individuals which are relevant in the context of the case law on liability. This seems highly doubtful, particularly in the light of the judgment in *Peter Paul*.[157] However, some authors still argue that '[...], infringements of Community provisions that are directly effective satisfy the first condition for state liability'.[158]

In summary, even though the case law is not entirely clear on the matter, it must be assumed that the Court of Justice does not always apply the concept 'rights for individuals' consistently. In other words, the term may have one

---

[154] E.g. Case C-361/88 *Commission v. Germany* [1991] ECR I-2567.

[155] Case C-186/91 *Commission v. Belgium* [1993] ECR I-851.

[156] See for an opposite view Wennerås (2007) at 152. In the authors' view, it is also unlikely that the mere infringement by a Member State of its obligation to notify the Commission under Article 176 EC will give rise to state liability.

[157] Case C-222/02 *Peter Paul a.o. v. Germany* [2004] ECR I-9425.

[158] Wennerås (2007) at 152.

meaning in the context of direct effect and another in the context of state liability and yet another in relation to the transposition of directives.[159]

Thirdly, it is the authors' opinion that this condition may be expected to cause some particular problems inside the field of European environmental law. The point is that most of European environmental law does not *specifically* aims to protect the rights of individuals, but is intended to protect 'the public and/or the environment in general'. For instance, can one really say that the Habitats and Wild Birds Directives are intended to confer rights on individuals? This will be discussed in the next paragraph more extensively.

Also, but not specifically

From the case law of the Court of Justice, in particular from its judgment in *Peter Paul*, we must assume that it is not sufficient if the rule that had been infringed *also* protected the interests of the claimant, but that the rule infringed should *specifically* have the objective to protect individuals.[160] This case law amounts to introducing a rather strict *Schutznorm* requirement into European state liability law. However, the case law of the Court of Justice does not seem to be consistent in all respects. Take, for example, the directly effective obligations under the EIA Directive. Under this directive, an environmental impact assessment must have been carried out before consent is given for certain projects likely to have significant effects on the environment. From the case law of the Court of Justice it is clear that interested third parties may rely on these provisions before the national courts.[161] However, it cannot be said that the directive gives third parties a right to have an environmental impact assessment carried out. They are only affected indirectly by the obligations of the state. Nevertheless, in *Wells*, the Court of Justice stated, albeit in an *obiter*, that a Member State may be liable for a breach of the obligation not to grant a consent before an environmental impact assessment has been carried out.[162] Apparently it found that this was a provision 'intended to confer rights on individuals'. Be this as it may, a *Schutznorm* requirement can be found in most national laws on (state) liability. It is therefore not surprising that national courts have also applied a similar strict *Schutznorm* requirement.

In the first place, the Dutch *Gerechtshof Den Haag* (The Hague appeal court) in a judgment concerning Article 5 in combination with Annex III of the Nitrates Directive (91/676) must be mentioned.[163] Under this provision, Member States must establish and implement action programmes to reduce and prevent pollution caused by nitrates. The measures to be included in the action programmes must

---

[159] Cf. Prechal (2005), 97-111.

[160] Case C-222/02 *Peter Paul a.o. v. Germany* [2004] ECR I-9425. See for an opposite view Wennerås (2007) 154-155.

[161] Case C-201/02 *Wells* [2004] ECR I-723, para. 66.

[162] Case C-201/02 *Wells* [2004] ECR I-723, para. 66.

[163] Dutch *Gerechtshof* Den Haag 27 October 2005 (*Waterpakt*) [2006] M&R 4.

ensure that the amount of livestock manure applied to the land each year does not exceed 170 kg per hectare. In the view of the *Gerechtshof* these provisions were not intended to confer rights on individuals on the basis of which individuals could hold the state liable for the cost of purifying ground and surface water, or the cost of alternative drinking water. It held that the directive did not lay down the obligation to guarantee a particular quality of water, upon which individuals could base quality entitlements as against the state. This judgment seems to be at odds with a judgment of the French *Tribunal administratif* (administrative court) at Rennes.[164] In 1995, the *Tribunal d'instance* (district court) at Guincamp had ordered the Société Suez Lyonnaise des Eaux to pay compensation to 176 subscribers of its drinking water distribution network on account of the excessive nitrate content of the water it distributed. The Société accordingly brought proceedings before the *Tribunal administratif* to obtain compensation for the state's late transposition of Article 5 of Directive 91/676. The *Tribunal* accepted this argument and concluded that the state was liable.

In the second place we refer to an English judgment in *Bowden* v. *South West Water and Another*, where a mussel fisherman claimed that he had been driven out of business because his fishing waters had been classified under a directive and because of pollution of the waters.[165] The fisherman pleaded the breach of the Bathing Waters Directive, the Shellfish Waters Directive and the Urban Waste Water Directive. The Court of Appeal formulated the test to be applied as follows: 'The question is whether the provision was adopted in order to protect the interests of the person who claims to be entitled to a right under the directive [...].' The High Court judge who heard the case, whose conclusion was followed by the Court of Appeal, noted that the plaintiff's claim was as a fisherman and observed that neither the Bathing Waters Directive nor the Urban Waste Water Directive was intended to confer rights on mussel fisherman: 'There is nothing in either which could possibly be said to entail the grant of rights to shell-fisherman, or which would enable the content of any such a right to be identified. They are concerned with different subject matter. Of course, improvements in water quality for bathers, and in treatment standards of waste water, may assist other interest groups, but that is not enough to give them a right of action.' As regards the Shellfish Directives, the Court of Appeal agreed with the High Court judge that they were at least related to the plaintiff's activities and that it could be said that if there was a failure by the United Kingdom to implement or to comply with the requirements of those directives it could have contributed to the loss of the plaintiff's fishing grounds. However, if there was a breach, it would be a breach of an obligation owed to the public in general and there was nothing to tie such a

---

[164] French *Tribunal administratif Rennes*, 2 May 2001, *Société Suez Lyonnaise des Eaux*, req. No 97182. Reported in the Nineteenth annual report on monitoring the application of Community law; COM (2002) 324.

[165] English High Court, 17 December 1997, *Bowden* v. *South West Water and Another* [1998] 3 C.M.L.R. 330 and Court of Appeal, 15 December 1998, [1999] 3 C.M.L.R. 180. Cf. on this case Lee (2005) at 65.

breach to specific rights of individuals or which would enable the content of such a right to be ascertained. Accordingly, there was no basis for a claim for damages.

This judgment in *Bowden* v. *South West Water and Another* is particularly interesting because the court adopted the position that where the rule infringed aims to protect 'the public in general', it could not give rise to a successful claim for damages. If this position were correct, it would mean that infringements by the state of, for example, environmental (air and water) quality standards could not give rise to liability.

2.3.3 Direct Causal Link

At present there is no question of a clearly developed European doctrine of causality. The Court refers to the requirement of a direct causal link. But though it is a matter for the national courts to decide whether there is a direct causal link, it is not clear to what extent causality may be interpreted according to national law. It is therefore not clear what exactly this requirement entails. Nor is it clear to what specific problems this may give rise in relation to environmental law. Nevertheless, the following is worth considering. It is possible that in certain cases parties directly affected might be able to obtain compensation for loss or damage resulting from incorrect implementation. Suppose the authorities have granted a permit on the basis of national legislation which has not yet been adapted to conform with the directive. The permit may be revoked and ultimately the applicant will have to comply with the more stringent requirements. This may well involve additional investment in the production process. It seems likely that these costs, necessary to comply with the more stringent European standard, are not open to compensation. This is because they would have been incurred anyway if the directive had been correctly implemented and it would run counter to the polluter pays principle. On the other hand, costs which have been incurred by an individual relying in good faith on the correctness of national environmental law may qualify for compensation. Certain development costs might, for example, fall in this category.

Another potential problem is the compensation of damage to the environment. To what extent can environmental damage qualify for compensation where a Member State has, for instance, failed to designate special protection areas for birds? And who would be entitled to claim the damage? Or would this example fail by virtue of the simple fact that the standard breached must create rights for individuals?[166]

Francovich shows that an action for damages against the State is possible. However, it is unclear to what extent this embraces reparation for environmental damage other than mere pecuniary damage.[167] Future case law will have to clarify the situation. Moreover, an injunction or other court order will generally

---

[166] Cf. also the Commission's White Paper on Environmental Liability, COM (2000) 66.

[167] Cf. Wennerås (2007) at 156.

prove more useful to interested third parties than damages. To what extent can Francovich accommodate these needs? Probably it should not be interpreted too narrowly. *Francovich* after all concerned the detrimental financial consequences of the State's failure to act. As a matter of principle, there appear to be few objections against extending the remedies available to adversely affected individuals if this means that the effect of directives in Member States is strengthened. The significance of this would be that a breach of a provision of an environmental directive which lacked direct effect could also be challenged in court.

3 Legal Protection Before the Court of Justice

3.1 Legal Protection under Article 230 EC

Finally, it is important to devote some attention to another aspect of judicial protection. The protection of individuals against breaches of EC environmental law by public authorities of the Member States or by other individuals, through the doctrines of direct effect, consistent interpretation and state liability, is largely effected through national procedures. However, where an individual objects to the very substance of EC environmental law, there are few means of obtaining a remedy at national level. Even if the validity of an environmental directive could be challenged before a national court, under EC law the national court is not competent to pronounce on its validity.[168] In that case the national court will avail itself of the preliminary ruling procedure set out in Article 234 EC and refer the matter to the Court of Justice. The Treaty does not offer individuals any form of direct legal protection in such a case.

Neither will an action for annulment under Article 230 EC offer a solution. Actions for the annulment of *directives* or *regulations* brought by individuals will certainly be declared inadmissible.[169] However, actions by individuals against *decisions* of the Council or the Commission are admissible in Article 230 proceedings. Although the implementation of EC environmental law is largely a matter for the Member States, the Commission can increasingly be seen to possess powers to take decisions in the field of or related to the environment. Sometimes these powers are conferred by the Treaty, in other cases by secondary legislation.

An example where the Commission derives its powers from the Treaty is provided by the provisions relating to state aid (Articles 87 and 88 EC). These articles are also relevant for the assessment of national aid for the protection of the environ-

---

[168] Case 314/85 *Foto-Frost* [1987] ECR 4199.

[169] Case T-475/93 *Buralux* v. *Council* [1994] ECR 3229 and Case C-209/94P *Buralux* v. *Council* [1996] ECR I-615. However, national courts are allowed to refer to the Court of Justice under Article 234 EC for a ruling on the validity of such measures; See for instance Case C-27/00 *Omega Air a.o.* [2002] ECR I-2569.

ment. They give the Commission the power to approve national environmental aids, not to approve them or to make aid subject to certain conditions, and other, more procedural decisions can also be taken.[170]

Another example is provided by the Treaty provisions on competition law (Articles 81 and 82 EC). In practice, it has become clear that certain practices of undertakings, even when they concern environmental protection, can conflict with Treaty provisions. Here, too, the Commission has the power to take decisions.[171]

As far as the Commission's powers under secondary legislation are concerned, particular reference is made to Regulation 2037/2000 on substances that deplete the ozone layer.[172] This provides that a license issued by the Commission is required for the release into free circulation in the EU of certain ozone depleting substances (Article 6). The powers of the Commission under Directive 2001/18 on the deliberate release into the environment of genetically modified organisms provide for another example.[173] Or take the powers of the Commission to allow (or not to allow) access to environmental information in documents under Regulation 1049/2001.[174] Finally, it should be noted that the Commission also has powers to finance projects in the context of the European Regional Development Fund, the European Social Fund and the Cohesion Fund.[175] As provided in Article 17 of Regulation 1083/2006, the objectives of the Funds shall be pursued in the framework of sustainable development and the Community promotion of the goal of protecting and improving the environment as set out in Article 6 of the Treaty. Here, too, the need may be felt for judicial protection against decisions by the Commission which take insufficient account of European environmental law.

In any event, persons to whom decisions of the Commission with an environmental impact are addressed may in any event appeal under Article 230 EC. Such an appeal must be lodged with the Court of First Instance. In the examples mentioned above, it is sometimes the Member State to which the decision is addressed. It is the Member State which is given the option of granting aid for the protection of the environment or not and it is the Member State which can be considered the beneficiary of Structural Fund projects. However, in the case of the Ozone Regulation, it is the importer who should be considered the applicant and the person addressed.[176] In the case of decisions based on the provisions of Articles 81 and 82 EC the undertakings concerned should be regarded as the persons addressed.

---

[170] See Chapter 7, section 7.

[171] See on this issue Chapter 7, sections 3 and 4 in particular.

[172] OJ 2000 L 244/1, as amended.

[173] OJ 2001 L 106/1, as amended.

[174] OJ 2001 L 145/43.

[175] Regulation 1083/2006 laying down general provisions on the European Regional Development Fund, the European Social Fund and the Cohesion Fund, OJ 2006 L 210/25.

[176] Admissibility is no problem whatsoever: cf. Case T-336/94 *Efisol* [1996] ECR II-1343.

In addition to the persons to whom a Commission decision is addressed, third parties may also be admissible in Article 230 proceedings, if the decision is of 'direct and individual concern' to them. The case law – the so-called *Plaumann* doctrine[177] – on this point can briefly be summarised as follows: a third party is admissible if he is affected by the decision in a manner which distinguishes him from others. While the EC was more or less exclusively aimed at market integration, this criterion was sufficient. Where an importer, exporter or other market participant was affected in his particular private interests, the criterion of direct and individual concern would distinguish him from all other market participants. This means that where an 'environmental decision' of the Commission affects a market participant in his private market interests, there will often be no problem as regards admissibility.

A case in point is the judgment of the Court of First Instance in *Waterleiding Maatschappij 'Noord-West Brabant' NV* v. *Commission*.[178] The case involved a decision of the Commission not to open formal procedures under the state aid rules of the Treaty against certain environment-related tax relief in Dutch law. With respect to some of the tax relief the Court found that they directly affected the structure of the market in which the applicant operated and therefore affected its competitive position on that market. The applicant therefore had to be regarded as directly and individually concerned by the contested decision of the Commission.

The judgment of the Court in Case C-295/92 points in the same direction.[179] This case concerned the intention of the Dutch parliament to adapt taxes on fossil fuels in such a way that the energy content and the carbon content would each count for half. The measure contained a number of exemptions, including one for large-scale industrial users. The measure had been notified to the Commission as state aid within the meaning of Article 87(1) EC. The Commission considered the measure compatible with the common market. The Dutch Agricultural Association (*Landbouwschap*) considered the exemption for large-scale industrial users unlawful and lodged an appeal. There was a background of many years of discussion about the price of gas for the glasshouse sector. The Court of Justice declared the Association inadmissible, because the aid in question would only benefit a group of large industrial undertakings, which were not in competition with either the Association or the glasshouse farmers it represented. According to the Court, the interests of the Association would not be affected in any way whether the Commission decision was upheld or annulled. *A contrario*, it could be inferred from this that if an interested third party is in direct competition and the interests of the third party have been affected by a decision, an appeal would be admissi-

---

[177] Case 25/62 *Plaumann* v. *Commission* [1963] ECR 95, 107. This case law is still very much alive: Case C-50/00P *Unión de Pequeños Agricultores* v. *Council* [2002] ECR I-6677 and Case C-263/02P *Commission* v. *Jégo-Quéré* [2004] ECR I-3425. See also Case T-94/04 *EEB a.o.* v. *Commission* [2005] ECR II-4919. Cf. Lee (2005) at 139 *et seq.*

[178] Case T-188/95 *Waterleiding Maatschappij 'Noord-West Brabant' NV* v. *Commission* [1998] ECR II-3713.

[179] Case C-295/92 *Landbouwschap* v. *Commission* [1992] ECR I-5003.

ble. In the light of this case law, the legal protection of this category of interested parties would probably cause few problems. The most important condition is that there must be a competitive relationship between the party ultimately benefiting from the decision and the party lodging the appeal.

Matters are different however when the decision of the Commission is of a general and normative character, like its decisions on national plans for the allocation of greenhouse gas emission allowances. An operator of an installation subject to compulsory emissions trading, cannot claim to be individually concerned by these decisions when the decision, addressed to a Member State, affects all undertakings subject to compulsory emission trading in more or less the same way.[180]

Much more complicated is the admissibility of individuals who object to a Commission decision on environmental grounds. Here there are no *private* or *specific* interests at issue but, on the contrary, the *public interest*. The case law mentioned above, which required that a person's interests be specifically affected cannot, almost by definition, fulfil a distinguishing function here. After all, the key feature of the public interest is that it is universal, applicable to all. If the criterion of 'direct and individual concern' is applied with full force this must inevitably produce the paradoxical result that the more serious the infringement (the harm to the environment) and the wider the group potentially affected the less is the likelihood that the criterion can be met.[181] The judgments of the Court of First Instance and the Court of Justice in the *Greenpeace* case discussed below show that both these courts have fallen into this paradoxical trap.[182] The leading case on the admissibility of interested third parties trying to annul decisions affecting the environment is the *Greenpeace* case.

This case concerned two power stations on the Canary Islands, for which no environmental impact assessment had been prepared. Greenpeace had appealed against a judgment of the Court of First Instance.[183] That Court had declared Greenpeace's action seeking annulment of a Commission decision to pay the Spanish Government ECU 12 million from the European Regional Development Fund for the construction of the two power stations inadmissible. The Court of First Instance had reached this decision referring to the settled case law of the Court of Justice according to which persons other than the addressees may claim that a decision is of direct concern to them only if that decision affects them by reason of certain attributes which are peculiar to them, or by reason of factual

---

[180] Case T-28/07 *Fels-Werke a.o.* v. *Commission*, judgment of 11 September 2007, n.y.r. in the ECR.

[181] Cf. Winter (1999).

[182] Case C-321/95P *Greenpeace* v. *Commission* [1998] ECR I-1651. See also, in the same vein, Case T-219/95R *Danielsson* [1995] ECR II-3051 and Case T-142/03 *Fost Plus* v. *Commission* [2005] ECR II-589.

[183] Case T-585/93 *Greenpeace* v. *Commission* [1995] ECR II-2205. Cf. also Case T-117/94 *Associazione Agricoltori della Provincia di Rovigo a.o.* v. *Commission* [1995] ECR II-455 and Case C-142/95P *Associazione Agricoltori della Provincia di Rovigo a.o.* v. *Commission* [1996] ECR I-6669.

circumstances which differentiate them from all other persons and thereby distinguish them individually in the same way as the person addressed. The Court of First Instance observed that whilst this case law concerned essentially cases involving economic interests, the essential criterion which it applied remained applicable whatever the nature, economic or otherwise, of the applicants' interests which were affected.

Accordingly, the Court of First Instance held that the criterion proposed by the applicants for appraising their *locus standi*, namely the existence of harm suffered or to be suffered, was not in itself sufficient to confer *locus standi* on an applicant. This was because such harm might affect, in a general abstract way, a large number of persons who could not be determined in advance in such a way as to distinguish them individually just like the addressee of a decision, as required under the settled case law mentioned above.

There was thus no question of a special regime of *locus standi* in respect of environmental decisions, reflecting the public function of the environment. In this regard the Court of First Instance held that the status of a 'normal' interested third party, such as a 'local resident', 'fisherman' or 'farmer' or of persons concerned by the impact which the building of two power stations might have on local tourism, on the health of Canary Island residents and on the environment did not differ from that of all the people living or pursuing an activity in the areas concerned and that the applicants thus could not be affected by the contested decision otherwise than in the same manner as any other local resident, fisherman, farmer or tourist who was, or might be in the future, in the same situation.

As far as the *locus standi* of the organisation Greenpeace was concerned, the Court of First Instance observed that an association formed for the protection of the collective interests of a category of persons could not be considered to be directly and individually concerned, for the purposes of the fourth paragraph of Article 230 EC, by a measure affecting the general interests of that category, and was therefore not entitled to bring an action for annulment where its members could not do so individually.

On appeal the Court of Justice upheld the judgment of the Court of First Instance. It did however consider the argument that the Court of First Instance had failed to take account of the nature and specific characteristics of the environmental interests underpinning the action. It emphasised that it was the decision to build the two power stations in question which was liable to affect the environmental rights arising under the EIA Directive that the appellants sought to invoke. The contested decision, which concerned the Commision's financing of those power stations, could affect those rights only indirectly. As regards the appellants' argument that if they were denied *locus standi* before the Court of Justice, the rights which they derive from the EIA Directive would have no effective judicial protection at all, the Court noted that Greenpeace had also brought proceedings before the national courts challenging the administrative authorisations issued concerning the construction of those power stations. The Court of Justice added that although the subject-matter of those proceedings and of the action brought before the Court of First Instance was different, both actions were based on the same rights afforded to individuals by the EIA Directive, so that those rights were fully protected by the national courts which could refer a question to the Court of Justice for a preliminary ruling. This case law has been severely criticised, and in our opinion rightly.[184]

In summary the conclusion seems justified that third parties can rely on little judicial protection against environmental decisions taken by the European institutions. In fact it seems that the ECJ is applying a double standard here. While Member States are required to offer legal protection where rights and obligations under environmental directives are breached, the standard seems to be applied far less strictly to acts and omissions of the EC itself. Furthermore, in these judgments the Court has failed adequately to appreciate that the old remedies, designed to protect private interests, are inadequate to protect public goods, such as the environment. As long as the Court fails to acknowledge this in its case law, the somber conclusion must be that legal protection against European decisions having significant environmental effects is seriously flawed.

It remains to be seen to what extent the amendment of Article 230(4) envisaged by the Reform Treaty[185] will improve the situation as far as it concerns environmental decisions. The Reform Treaty intends to introduce the following text: 'Any natural or legal person may, under the conditions laid down in the first and second paragraphs, institute proceedings against an act addressed to that person or which is of direct and individual concern to him or her, and against a regulatory act which is of direct concern to him or her and does not entail implementing measures'.

3.2 Regulation 1367/2006[186]

On 25 June 1998 the EC signed the Convention on Access to Information, Public Participation in Decision-making and Access to Justice in Environmental Matters (the 'Aarhus Convention') and was approved by Council Decision in 2005.[187] Provisions of EC law should therefore be consistent with the Aarhus Convention. In view of the remarks made in section 3 of this chapter, it was not a big surprise that the EC felt it necessary to improve access to justice in environmental matters as far as it concerns acts of the European institutions. Article 9(3) of the Aarhus Convention requires access to judicial or other review procedures for challenging acts and omissions by private persons and public authorities which contravene provisions of law relating to the environment. Reg-

---

[184] Cf. Ward (2000) at 154-156.

[185] Renumbered as Article 263(4) FEU.

[186] Regulation 1367/2006 on the application of the provisions of the Aarhus Convention on Access to Information, Public Participation in Decision-making and Access to Justice in Environmental Matters to Community institutions and bodies, OJ 2006 L 264/13. This section builds upon Jans (2006).

[187] Council Decision 2005/370, OJ 2005 L 124/1.

ulation 1367/2006 on the application of the provisions of the Aarhus Convention on Access to Information, Public Participation in Decision-making and Access to Justice in Environmental Matters to Community institutions and bodies (the 'Aarhus Regulation') is to ensure that European law is in sync with the Aarhus Convention. Therefore, let us have a look at its provisions.

The internal review procedure

According to Article 10(1) of the regulation, the internal review procedure is open to allow challenges to an 'administrative act' and omissions to take such an act. The concept of an 'administrative act' is defined in Article 2(1)(g) of the regulation as meaning: 'any measure of individual scope under environmental law, taken by a Community institution or body, and having legally binding and external effects'. The word 'individual' makes clear that only 'decisions' and alike are subject to the internal review procedure. Directives and regulations they are all excluded.

Furthermore, Article 2(2) of the regulation makes it clear that not even all decisions are subject to the internal review procedure. Excluded are also measures taken by a institution or body in its capacity as an administrative review body, such as under:

a) Articles 81, 82, 86 and 87 EC (competition rules);
b) Articles 226 and 228 EC (infringement proceedings);
c) Article 195 EC (Ombudsman proceedings);
d) Article 280 EC (OLAF proceedings).

The use of the words 'such as' clearly indicate the non-exhaustive character of the list, which of course triggers the question of what is meant by 'its capacity as an administrative review body'. It is in particular questionable to see the Commission's decisions in the area of competition law on the same footing as its role in infringement proceedings. Can one really say that, in the area of competition law, the Commission is acting in an administrative review capacity? In our view the Commission is only exercising decision-making competences like in any other area where it possesses decision-making authority. What makes a decision of the Commission applying competition rules in individual cases so significantly different from any other decision it can take? One could even ask if it is necessary at all to exclude decisions related to the application of the competition rules. The regulation restricts the internal review procedure to administrative acts 'under environmental law'. When we look at the definition of 'environmental law' in Article 2(1)(f) of the regulation we notice the following: 'Community legislation which, irrespective of its legal basis, contributes to the pursuit of the objectives of Community policy on the environment as set out in the Treaty: preserving, protecting and improving the quality of the environment, protecting human health, the prudent and rational utilisation of natural resources, and promoting measures at international level to deal with regional or worldwide environmental problems.' Can one really say that the Treaty rules on competition law contribute to the pursuit of the environmental objectives of the EC? And what about the rules on structural funds, agriculture, fisheries, industrial policy, development aid, etc. etc. Of course, one could say that, according to the integration principle of Article 6 EC all Community policies should contribute to the pursuit of the environmental objectives of the Treaty. But, in that interpretation the clause 'under environmental law' becomes meaningless at all. If it was not the intention to significantly restrict the scope of the internal review procedure, why on earth did the European legislature include in Article 10(1) the term 'under environmental law'? And why did it exclude *expressis verbis* its role under the infringement proceedings? Is it not standard case law[188] of the ECJ that those decisions do not have any legally binding and external effect and would therefore already be excluded, if one looks at the definition in Article 2(1)(g) of the regulation?

Article 10(1) opens the internal review procedure to challenge acts of a 'Community institution or body'. Article 2(1)(c) gives the following definition of the phrase: 'any public institution, body, office or agency established by, or on the basis of, the Treaty except when acting in a judicial or legislative capacity. However, the provisions under Title II shall apply to Community institutions or bodies acting in a legislative capacity.' On the one hand, this definition is very broad indeed, as it does not limit the review procedure to the 'traditional' institutions mentioned in Article 7 EC. Any 'organ' of the EU will be covered by this. But the limitation to non-judicial and non-legislative capacity is less clear. Probably, activities of the Commission in infringement-proceedings – Article 226 EC Treaty – must be regarded as 'judicial', but that is already excluded in Article 2(2) of the proposed regulation. And as far as directives and regulations are concerned, they are excluded because of the requirement in Article 2(1)(g) of 'individual' measures. There would also be some sense in excluding general state aid schemes. The Commission's decision to approve general state aid has a more normative character than approving individual state aid and could therefore being labelled 'legislative' in nature.[189] But, any state aid decision has already been excluded in Article 2(2) of the regulation. It does not make sense to exclude the same decision twice, so once again, what does 'except when it acts in a judicial or legislative capacity' really mean?

Standard of review

The internal review procedure was, according to the Commission's proposal (Article 9(1)), related to 'a breach of environmental law'. Environmental law was defined in Article 2(1)(g) of the proposal and 'means any Community legislation which has as its objective the protection or the improvement of the environment including human health and the protection or the rational use of natural resources.' That sounded very nice and broad indeed. The problem was of course

---

[188] E.g. Case 48/65 *Lütticke* v. *Commission* [1966] ECR 19.

[189] For instance, would a party be entitled for internal review of the Commission's decision not to approve Italian state aid in Case T-176/01 *Ferriere Nord SpA* [2004] ECR II-3931.

that most of European environmental law does not contain any such obligation at all for the European institutions. Instead, the more specific and concrete
environmental standards – in directives and regulations – are directed to the
Member States. Of course, the institutions are bound by the general environmental principles in Article 174(2) EC[190] and their obligation under the integration principle of Article 6 EC to integrate these principles 'into the definition
and implementation of the Community policies and activities'. But we also know
how much latitude the ECJ leave to the institutions in meeting their obligations
under the Treaty and that the intensity of judicial review exercise by the ECJ is
rather low.[191] And we could not assume that the institution, under the text of
the Commission's proposal was required in the internal review procedure to
exercise not just a 'marginal' or 'discretionary' review, but a 'full' or 'merits'
review. The text was not clear on that either. So the Commission's proposal
raised the pertinent question of what are the legal standards in order to assess
if the institutions have breached environmental law or not and how intense
should this review be? Surprisingly, the already lamentable text of the Commission's proposal was even worsened. In the regulation any reference to a standard of review is omitted! Article 10 of the regulation just states the entitlement
to an internal review procedure, without mentioning the applicable standards
for such a review. Therefore, it is now completely unclear when a request for
internal review is substantiated of not. This makes the duty for the institution to
'consider any such request' an empty shell. And it makes the right of the institution not to consider a request if the request is 'clearly unsubstantiated' a *carte
blanche* to disregard any request.

Broadening the scope of Article 230 EC?
As the saying goes, 'The proof of the pudding is in the eating'. So does
the regulation indeed bring about an improvement in the legal protection of
interested parties seeking judicial review of acts of the European institutions
breaching environmental principles?
As a preliminary remark, we must notice that in the Commission's proposal
object of the proceedings before the ECJ is not the initial 'administrative act' but
the decision in response of the request for internal review. According to Article
11 of the Commission's proposal it was for the qualified entity to challenge the
substantive and procedural legality of that decision. But once again the text was
unclear on what are the environmental standards to be applied by the ECJ.
Once again, the European legislature managed to deteriorate the text
significantly. Article 12(1) of the regulation now reads: 'The non-governmental
organisation which made the request for internal review pursuant to Article 10
may institute proceedings before the Court of Justice in accordance with the
relevant provisions of the Treaty.' Indeed, 'may institute proceedings', but is the

---

[190] Case C-284/95 *Safety High Tech* [1998] ECR I-4301 and Case C-341/95 *Gianni Bettati* [1998] ECR I-4355,
   para. 34.
[191] Case C-341/95 *Gianni Bettati* [1998] ECR I-4355, para. 35. Cf. Winter (2004).

original administrative act challenged or the decision of the institution taken in the internal review procedure? Although one may assume that it one has to challenge the decision taken in review, the current text is not clear at all.[192] By the way, this lack of clarity can trigger some rather awkward procedural complications. It is (is it?) conceivable that the initial decision is challenged directly at the Court under Article 230 EC by those who are 'directly and individually'[193] concerned, whilst, at the same time the act is being reviewed according to Article 10 of the regulation. It is also not quite clear to what extent parties with opposite interests can participate in this review procedure[194] and what constraints the principle of legal certainty will bring about.

Even more serious, though, is our second observation. According to the Commission's proposal qualified entities could institute proceedings before the ECJ 'in accordance' with Article 230(4) EC. The problem with that was of course that this provision still requires that the applicant must be 'direct and individually' concerned by the decision.

And what did the European legislature do in the final text of the regulation? It replaced 'in accordance with Article 230(4) EC Treaty' with 'in accordance with the relevant provisions of the EC Treaty'. However, the problem does not disappear by not addressing the problem. So the question still remains: how can secondary EC legislation broaden the scope of Article 230(4) EC Treaty? In view of the case law of the Court of Justice we do have serious doubts that the regulation will improve *locus standi* of third parties under Article 230(4) EC.

Our view is that the regulation creates an internal review procedure. However, the scope of the internal review procedure is severely limited. Only (some) individual decisions are subject to it and the procedure is only accessible for non-governmental organisations. Furthermore, the regulation lacks any substantive standard to be applied in the internal review procedure. Furthermore, it is highly unlikely that the regulation will be capable of broadening the scope of Article 230(4) EC beyond the current case law of the ECJ.[195] At best, the ECJ will accept actions of non-governmental organisations for annulments of decisions taken during the internal review procedure, but only in so far such an action seeks to safeguard the prerogatives of qualified entity in such an internal

---

[192] According to Wennerås (2007) at 238 the written reply is the subject matter for judicial review. His main argument is that the regulation apparently aims to align with Regulation 1049/2001 regarding public access to European Parliament, Council and Commission documents (OJ 2001 L 145/43).

[193] For instance by individuals not having access to the internal review procedure.

[194] Our guess is that they cannot participate. In any case, the regulation should have addressed this point.

[195] This is supported by the ruling of the CFI in Case T-94/04 *EEB a.o.* v. *Commission* [2005] ECR II-4919. In that case the European Environmental Bureau tried to rely on the proposal for the Aarhus Regulation to have access to the CFI under Article 230 EC in order to challenge Commission Directive 2003/112 to include paraquat as an active substance. The CFI ruled: 'The Court notes, first, that the principles governing the hierarchy of norms [...] preclude secondary legislation from conferring standing on individuals who do not meet the requirements of the fourth paragraph of Article 230 EC. A fortiori the same holds true for the statement of reasons of a proposal for secondary legislation.'

review procedure:[196] has there been a fair hearing of the complaints and other due process type of arguments? But we are afraid that the Court will leave at that and that we need, even after the entry into force of the Reform Treaty, a change of the text of Article 230(4) EC (then Article 263(4) FEU) to improve *locus standi* for third parties.

---

[196] See for parallel case law: Case C-70/88 *EP* v. *Council* [1990] ECR I-2041, para. 27.

CHAPTER 6

Free Movement of Goods

1   General Remarks

The preceding five chapters have discussed in some depth the contours of European environmental law as reflected in directives and regulations on the environment, and the consequences for the Member States. It has been demonstrated that the limits within which Member States may develop national environmental policy are primarily defined by such European secondary legislation. The first questions that have to be addressed, when endeavouring to establish what freedom the Member States do have when adopting national protective measures, are whether the field is already covered by European legislation, what the content of that legislation is and to what extent it leaves room for extensions, derogations, etc.[1]

Even though there is European legislation in almost every conceivable field of environmental policy, there are still major parts of environmental law which have not been harmonised. It must indeed be assumed, in the light of the principle of subsidiarity and of the provisions of Article 176 EC, that certain areas of national environmental law will never fully be harmonised. In these areas the Member States retain primary responsibility for the content of their environmental legislation. Only the restrictions flowing from European primary law – in particular the EC Treaty – limit them. This chapter will examine the extent to which the provisions on the free movement of goods, Articles 23 to 31 EC, are relevant.[2]

There is another reason for considering these provisions, as the Court of Justice held in the *Inter-Huiles* case, which is that the European institutions are themselves also bound by these rules.[3] This means, for example, that the Council may not in its legislative capacity adopt measures which are incompatible with Articles 28-30 EC (Articles 34-36 FEU). However, the European institutions may have a greater degree of discretionary power as regards the manner and form of legislation than do the Member States in implementing it.[4] In order that European secondary legislation should not be incompatible with the Treaty, it must as far as possible be interpreted in the light of the Treaty.[5]

Article 28 EC however does not have horizontal effect. In *Sapod Audic* the Court ruled that a contractual obligation to affix the 'Green Dot logo' to products cannot be regarded as a barrier to trade for the purposes of Article 28 EC 'since it was not imposed by a Member State but agreed between individuals'.[6] Having

---

[1] See Chapter 3, sections 2 and 3 in particular.

[2] Cf. the renumbered Articles 28-37 FEU after the entry into force of the Reform Treaty.

[3] Case 172/82 *Inter-Huiles* [1983] ECR 555. Confirmed in Case C-341/95 *Gianni Bettati* [1998] ECR I-4355, para. 61: 'It is settled law that the prohibition of quantitative restrictions and of all measures having equivalent effect applies not only to national measures but also to measures adopted by the Community institutions'.

[4] Cf. in general Mortelmans (2002).

[5] Case C-128/89 *Commission v. Italy* [1990] ECR 3239.

[6] Case C-159/00 *Sapod Audic* [2002] ECR I-5031, para. 74.

said this, we have to take into account that according to the ruling in *Schmidberger*, the states have to take a certain responsibility for actions of individuals affecting the Treaty rules on goods.[7]

2 Environmental Charges and Article 25 EC[8]

Article 25 EC prohibits customs duties and all charges having equivalent effect on trading between the Member States. Since all 'genuine' customs duties on inter-state trading have been abolished since 1 January 1970, only charges having equivalent effect are now of any practical significance. In Case 24/68, the Court of Justice defined the extent of the prohibition as follows:[9]

'Any pecuniary charge, however small and whatever its designation and mode of application, which is imposed unilaterally on domestic or foreign goods by reason of the fact that they cross a frontier, and which is not a customs duty in the strict sense, constitutes a charge having equivalent effect within the meaning of Articles 9, 12, 13 and 16 [now Article 25 EC, authors] EC, even if it is not imposed for the benefit of the State, is not discriminatory or protective in effect and if the product on which the charge is imposed is not in competition with any domestic product.'

A tax levied by the local municipality of Carrara on marble excavated in the territory of the municipality on its transportation across the boundaries of the municipal territory therefore constitutes a charge having effect equivalent to a customs duty.[10] Also the German legislation establishing a solidarity fund for the return of waste and requiring exporters of waste to contribute to the fund, including those exporting to other Member States, was to be considered a charge in the meaning of Article 25 EC.[11]

There are no derogations from the prohibition. Customs duties and charges having equivalent effect are prohibited regardless of the purpose for which they were introduced and the destination of the revenue from them. Unlike non-tariff restrictions, such charges cannot be justified by pleading protection of the environment or protection of the health of humans, animals or plants. This does not mean that any environmental charge levied on an imported product must necessarily be incompatible with European law.

---

[7] Case C-112/00 *Schmidberger* [2003] ECR I-5659. This case will be discussed more in depth in section 5.1 of this chapter. See also Case C-265/95 *Commission v. France* [1997] ECR I-6959, discussed in Chapter 4, section 4.1.

[8] See in general also Commission Communication on environmental taxes and charges in the Single Market, OJ 1997 C 224/6. Cf. Article 30 FEU.

[9] Case 24/68 *Commission v. Italy* [1969] ECR 193.

[10] Case C-72/03 *Carbonati Apuani* [2004] ECR I-8027.

[11] Case C-389/00 *Commission v. Germany* [2003] ECR I-2001. Cf. also Case C-173/05 *Commission v. Italy*, judgment of 21 June 2007, n.y.r. in the ECR on an environmental tax on gas pipelines installed in the Sicilian Region.

Certain charges are not regarded as charges having equivalent effect and are thus not prohibited as such. Thus the Court has allowed, *inter alia*, a recompense for a service actually rendered to an importer.[12] However, this exception has hardly any relevance in the field of environmental law. Where certain controls are necessary from the point of view of protection of the environment or of health, for example, tests for the presence of chemical residues on products, they will be regarded as necessary in the public interest and not as services rendered to an individual importer.[13] In that case, the Court held that the costs must be borne out of state funds. It could be added that the mere fact that certain environmental tests may be allowed on the basis of Articles 28 to 30 EC does not imply that a charge to cover the cost will also be allowed.

More relevant from a practical point of view is that charges which form part of a general system of domestic taxation must not be regarded as a charge having equivalent effect. If a charge does form part of such a system, it is not assessed in the light of Article 25 EC but in the light of Article 90 EC.[14] This is important because, as will be shown below, Article 90 EC allows Member States much more freedom than Article 25 EC.

The main criterion for distinguishing between the scope of application of Article 25 EC and that of Article 90 EC is that charges having equivalent effect are in principle levied only on imported products or, in the case of a levy on exports, on domestic goods, whereas Article 90 EC applies to charges levied on both domestic and foreign goods.

One rather special case is where an environmental charge within the general system of internal taxation applying systematically to domestic and imported products, according to the same criteria, can nevertheless constitute a charge having an effect equivalent to customs duty on imports, when such contribution is intended exclusively to support activities which specifically benefit the taxed domestic product.[15] The taxed product and the favoured national product must be identical, and the tax burden on the domestic product must be fully compensated. These conditions will not easily be met.

---

[12] Case 133/82 *Commission v. Luxembourg* [1983] ECR 1669. See also Case C-72/03 *Carbonati Apuani* [2004] ECR I-8027, para. 32, where the Court stresses the existence of a direct link between the tax at issue and the services provided for the operators on which the tax is imposed. Using the charge or tax to improve the environment will in general not satisfy this requirement. Cf. also Case C-389/00 *Commission v. Germany* [2003] ECR I-2001. The compulsory export charge did not confer on exporters of waste 'any specific or definite benefit'. That finding was supported by the fact that the charge as determined solely according to the type and quantity of the waste to be shipped. There was thus nothing given in return for any service actually provided to them, either as a category of operators or in an individual capacity, the Court argued.

[13] By analogy with Joined Cases C-277/91, C-318/91 and C-319/91 *Ligur Carni* [1993] ECR I-6621.

[14] Cf. Commission Communication on environmental taxes and charges in the Single Market, OJ 1997 C 224/6 at 6.

[15] Case 77/72 *Capolongo* [1973] ECR 611.

Consider the following, fictitious example. A charge is levied on certain environmentally harmful products, both imported and domestic products. This would normally be regarded as a tax within the meaning of Article 90 EC, and not as a charge having equivalent effect. This would only be otherwise if the proceeds of the charge were used exclusively to finance activities to promote sales of the domestic product.

In that case only the imported product would in fact be taxed, and the tax might be regarded as a charge having equivalent effect within the meaning of Article 90 EC. If, however, the proceeds were used for a more general publicity campaign to promote environmentally friendly behaviour, there could be no question of there being such a charge. Domestic manufacturers would no longer be fully compensated, nor would there be a direct relation between the product taxed and the recipient of the proceeds. In that case the charge would have to be assessed in the light of Article 90 EC.

From these conditions it is evident that national legislators must have regard to the manner in which the proceeds of environmental charges are applied. Financial bonuses to national enterprises may make such a charge incompatible with the Treaty provisions prohibiting customs duties and charges having equivalent effect.

3 Article 90 EC[16]

According to Article 90(1) EC, Member States are prohibited from imposing on the products of other Member States any internal taxation of any kind in excess of that imposed on similar domestic products. The Member States are moreover prohibited from imposing on the products of other Member States any internal taxation of such a nature as to afford indirect protection to other, domestic, products (Article 90(2) EC).

The aim of Article 90 EC is to guarantee the fiscally neutral position of imported products as compared with domestic production. The simple fact that a product crosses a border may not lead to a difference in fiscal treatment. However, the Article 90 prohibition does not affect environmental taxes which hit domestic products harder than imported products.[17] In the *Outokumpu Oy* for instance the Court ruled that the fact that electricity of domestic origin is in some cases taxed more heavily than imported electricity is immaterial in this connection since, in order to ascertain whether the system in question is compatible with Article 90 EC, the tax burden imposed on imported electricity must be compared with the lowest tax burden imposed on electricity of domestic origin.[18] This *reverse* discrimination is in principle outside the scope of the EC Treaty.

---

[16] Cf. the renumbered Article 110 FEU after the entry into force of the Reform Treaty.

[17] Case 86/78 *Peureux* [1979] ECR 897.

[18] Case C-213/96 *Outokumpu Oy* [1998] ECR I-1801, para. 36

In view of the manner in which the Court has regarded all kinds of parafiscal charges as taxes to which Article 90 EC applies, it may be assumed that environmental taxes will also fall within its scope of application. This applies above all to those taxes whose primary function is the financing of certain measures, such as water purification installations, rather than the promotion of environmentally friendly behaviour.

Regulatory charges, by contrast, are expressly designed to discourage environmentally harmful behaviour, for example by taxing certain emissions or the use of certain raw materials. Behaving in an environmentally friendly manner thus becomes relatively cheaper, which will supposedly encourage polluters to move in the right direction. In the past it has been argued that such charges, not being 'taxes', fall outside the scope of Article 90 EC. This seems unlikely, particularly in the light of the *Outokumpu Oy* case, to be discussed below.[19] In any case, the dividing line between regulatory charges and those intended as a source of finance is hard to draw. In practice the latter also usually have significant regulatory effects. On the other hand, some regulatory charges may also be used to finance a particular environmental policy. For the purposes of this chapter all environmental charges will be regarded as taxes within the meaning of Article 90 EC, whether regulatory or not.[20]

For sake of completeness we must note that under special circumstances a national tax or charge can neither be reviewed in the light of Article 90 EC or Article 25 EC. The Danish Law on registration duty on motor provided for the levy of a charge, ('registration duty'), on new motor vehicles. Because there is no domestic car industry the charge was in fact imposed solely on imported new vehicles. However, this does not mean that the charge had to be characterised as a charge having equivalent effect since the charge was part of a general system of internal taxation. On the other hand, Article 90 EC cannot be invoked where there is no similar or competing domestic production. Under those circumstances the Court will examine the charge in the light of Article 28 EC.[21]

Similar products

In assessing the compatibility of a tax with Article 90 EC, the tax on an imported product must be compared with the tax on the equivalent domestic product. The first question to be answered is whether the products are similar, in which case the first paragraph of Article 90 EC applies, or competitive, in which case the second paragraph applies. It should be noted that the Court has not always made a clear distinction between the two paragraphs, and in cases of doubt has preferred to apply the second paragraph.

When assessing whether the products are similar within the meaning of Article 90(1) EC, the following specific problem arises, particularly in respect of regulatory charges. Such charges are imposed in order to encourage people

---

[19]   Case C-213/96 *Outokumpu Oy* [1998] ECR I-1801

[20]   Cf. Case C-213/96 *Outokumpu Oy* [1998] ECR I-1801.

[21]   Case C-383/01 *De Danske Bilimportører* [2003] ECR I-6065.

to purchase products which cause less environmental harm. It may be asked whether a difference in terms of environmental features (degree of harm caused during production, use or disposal) is sufficient to make a product dissimilar. Is a car fitted with a catalytic converter similar to one that is not? Is timber that has been produced sustainably similar to timber that has not? Are batteries that can be re-used similar to those that can only be used once?[22]

As yet the Court has not had to decide on this specific issue. However, the Court gives a broad interpretation of the term 'similar' in the sense of the first paragraph.[23] The comparison is not based on the products being completely identical, but on their having similar characteristics and meeting the same needs from the point of view of consumers. If this approach is applied to the environment sector, either of two arguments is possible. On the one hand it could be said, for example, that both a car that is fitted with a catalytic converter and one that is not serve the same transport needs of the consumer and are thus similar. On the other hand it could be argued that a car without a catalytic converter does not meet the needs of the environmentally conscious consumer and could not therefore be regarded as a true alternative. Indeed this distinction is made in Regulation 1980/2000 on a revised Community eco-label award scheme, under which eco-labels can be awarded for products with the same function but with different ecological properties.[24] In any case, it would be hard to deny that the two types of product bear a certain competitive relationship with each other. From the case law, it can be deduced that when it is difficult to make a demarcation, the Court tends to judge the factual situation under the second paragraph of Article 90 EC. This provision requires that a Member State's internal taxation must not have the effect of protecting domestic products. In the assessment of this aspect, not only the actual situation but also the potential market for foreign products, if no protectionist measures were involved, should be taken into consideration. It is also necessary to take into account how the revenue from the levy is used. The Court has ruled that when the revenue from a levy is used to partly offset the burden borne by domestic products, the charge constitutes discriminatory taxation within the meaning of Article 90 EC.[25]

Neutrality of tax burdens

The tax burden on the imported and domestic products should be neutral and should not impede or hinder the importation. The non-discrimination should be evident in tariffs, tax basis, exemptions, means of payment, etc. Not

---

[22] Cf. Commission Communication on environmental taxes and charges in the Single Market, COM (97) 9 final at 9.

[23] Cf. Case C-221/06 *Stadtgemeinde Frohnleiten*, judgment of 8 November 2007, n.y.r. in the ECR, were the Court refused to apply the 'loose' discrimination test from the *Walloon Waste* case (Case C-2/90 *Commission v. Belgium* [1992] ECR I-4431; see below, section 5 of this chapter) to Article 90(1) EC.

[24] Regulation 1980/2000 on a revised Community eco-label award scheme, OJ 2000 L 237/1. See on this Regulation Chapter 8, section 7.1.

[25] Case C-17/91 *Georges Lornoy* [1992] ECR I-6523.

only is there a range of case law on this issue, but also specifically for the environment sector, notably the *Italian Oil* case.[26] Under Italian legislation, regenerated waste petroleum products received certain tax advantages. The objective of the Italian law was to stimulate recycling of used oil. The preferential taxes were however not applicable to imported oil. The first question addressed by the Court was whether Article 90 EC allows any differentiation at all of taxes on broadly defined product groups in this type of case. The Court observed that it was clear:

> 'that at the present stage of the development of Community law and in the absence of any unification or harmonization of the relevant provisions, Community law does not prohibit Member States from granting tax advantages, in the form of exemption from or reduction of duties, to certain products or to certain classes of producers. The Treaty does not therefore forbid, as far as domestic tax laws are concerned, the taxation at differential rates of products which may serve the same economic ends, especially if, as in the case of regenerated mineral oils, it appears that the cost of production, objectively speaking, differs considerably from that of oils of primary distillation.'

Although the Court did not say so in as many words, this would seem to imply that environmental considerations – in this case a measure to promote the recycling of waste – could be a legitimate social or economic reason for applying differential taxation. The next question the Court had to address was whether these tax advantages could be granted exclusively to the domestic products. The Court held that they could not:

> 'On the other hand pursuant to the first paragraph of Article 95 [now Article 90 EC, authors] the tax advantages in question must also be granted without any discrimination to products from the other Member States which satisfy the same conditions as the domestic products which qualify for the exemptions or reductions allowed by national law.'

In the *Outokumpu Oy* case the Court was given the opportunity to confirm its position in the *Italian Oil* case.[27] The Court indicated that Member States may apply different rates of duty to electricity, according to its manner of production. A lower rate for electricity produced by water power – as opposed to electricity produced by conventional means – is permitted, provided this rate also applies to imported electricity. The Court ruled that:

> 'Community law does not restrict the freedom of each Member State to establish a tax system which differentiates between certain products, even products which are similar within the meaning of the first paragraph of Article 95 [now Article 90 EC, authors] EC, on the basis of objective criteria, such as the nature of the raw materials used or the production processes employed. Such differentiation

---

[26] Case 21/79 *Commission* v. *Italy* [1980] ECR 1.

[27] Case C-213/96 *Outokumpu Oy* [1998] ECR I-1801.

is compatible with Community law, however, only if it pursues objectives which are themselves compatible with the requirements of the Treaty and its secondary legislation'.[28]

Following these cases there can be no doubt that environmental considerations can be regarded as a legitimate reason for applying differential taxation. Furthermore, Article 90 EC would not appear to give the EC a right to judge whether a levy in a Member State is excessively high in relation to its environmental objective.[29] However, differential taxation may not lead to any form of discrimination, direct or indirect, against imports from other Member States or any form of protection of competing domestic products[30] and any tax advantage granted to domestic products must also be granted without any discrimination to products from the other Member States which satisfy the same conditions as the domestic products which qualify for the exemptions or reductions allowed by national law.[31] As soon as the discriminatory character of national legislation has been established, there is no room to justify the measure for reasons of environmental protection.[32]

In summary, differential taxation based on the environmental characteristics of products is allowed, provided the differentiation also applies to imported products and any other form of discrimination or protectionism is avoided.[33]

4 The Impact of Tax Harmonisation

The consequences of harmonisation for national legislation have been discussed in some detail in Chapter 3. Nevertheless, a few brief observations on the impact of harmonisation on national environmental taxes remains to be made.[34] In the context of completion of the internal market, important steps have been made in harmonising the rates of VAT and customs duties. Directive 77/388 sets out narrow margins within which the Member States may set their VAT rates.[35] Differential taxation on environmental grounds is virtually ruled out as far as VAT is concerned. It is true that the harmonised VAT rates are minimum rates, but any increase must apply to all products. In

---

[28] Case C-213/96 *Outokumpu Oy* [1998] ECR I-1801, para. 30.

[29] This seems to follow from Case C-132/88 *Commission v. Greece* [1990] ECR 1567, para. 17.

[30] Case C-213/96 *Outokumpu Oy* [1998] ECR I-1801.

[31] Case 21/79 *Commission v. Italy* [1980] ECR 1 and more recently Case C-313/05 *Brzeziński* [2007] ECR I-519, with respect to Polish excise duties on second-hand vehicles.

[32] Case C-313/05 *Brzeziński* [2007] ECR I-519, para. 39.

[33] Cf. Commission Communication on environmental taxes and charges in the Single Market, OJ 1997 C 224/6 at 7-8.

[34] See Commission Communication on environmental taxes and charges in the Single Market, OJ 1997 C 224/6 at 9-11.

[35] OJ 1997 L 145/1, as amended.

other words, goods that have been sustainably produced may not be taxed at a lower rate than those that have not.

Directive 92/12 on excise duties[36] leaves more latitude for a differential system of environmental charges. It explicitly permits Member States to impose taxes on products other than those covered by the directive. However, Article 3(3) requires that these taxes should not give rise to border-crossing formalities in trade between Member States. This requirement may well prove a serious obstacle to practical implementation. The 'border', traditionally the place where imports are subjected to the national tax systems, here ceases to perform this function.[37] Other means will have to be found in national tax laws to actually impose taxes on goods, including imports.

Other limitations on national environment policy can be found in Directive 2003/96 on taxation of energy products and electricity.[38] This directive extended the existing European system of minimum rates, which under Directive 92/81 was confined to mineral oils, to coal, natural gas and electricity. Under Directive 1999/96, the levels of taxation applied by the Member States may not be lower than the minimum rates set in the directive. According to Article 14 of the directive, exempt from taxation are *inter alia* energy products and electricity used to produce electricity and electricity used to maintain the ability to produce electricity. However, Member States may, for reasons of environmental policy, subject these products to taxation. And under Article 15 of the directive Member States may apply total or partial exemptions or reductions in the level of taxation to, *inter alia*, energy products used under fiscal control in the field of pilot projects for the technological development of more environmentally-friendly products or in relation to fuels from renewable sources; biofuels; forms of energy which are of solar, wind, tidal or geothermal origin, or from biomass or waste. Finally, Article 19 of the directive allows for further exemptions or reductions 'for specific policy considerations'. These further reductions or exemptions need to be approved, on a proposal of the Commission, by a unanimous decision of the Council.[39] In its decisions the Council should ensure, in accordance with the integration principle, that its decisions are in line with the environmental policy of the EC. The following decision taken by the Council under Article 19 of Directive 2003/96 illustrates the importance of the integration principle in this respect.

---

[36] OJ 1992 L 76/1.

[37] See for instance Case C-313/05 *Brzeziński* [2007] ECR I-519, paras. 42-53, with respect to certain requirements relating to Polish excise duties on second-hand vehicles.

[38] Directive 92/81 was repealed by Council Directive 2003/96 restructuring the Community framework for the taxation of energy products and electricity, OJ 2003 L 283/51.

[39] To the extent that an approved exemption/reduction constitutes State aid, the normal rules apply and it should be notified to the Commission in accordance with Regulation 659/1999 laying down detailed rules for the application of Article 93 EC.

The United Kingdom applied for a derogation allowing them to continue to apply an exemption from their climate change levy (CCL) for low-value solid fuel. According to the Council, a tax exemption would support the use of low-value solid fuel for energy production instead of landfilling it. While energy use is preferable to landfilling from an environmental policy point of view, the polluter-pays principle would lead to the application of a lower rate of tax to such low-value solid fuel. The Council therefore decided that a complete exemption could be acceptable as a temporary measure only and should therefore be time-limited.[40]

Another example, under the predecessor of Directive 2003/96 Article 8(4) of Directive 92/81, can be found in Council Decision 2002/550 authorising the United Kingdom to apply a differentiated rate of excise duty to fuels containing biodiesel.[41] Production costs of biodiesel exceed those of conventional diesel, and its retail price would therefore be uncompetitive without a duty reduction. The requested duty reduction was intended to offset the additional production costs and it should enable biodiesel to be sold at a similar pump price to conventional diesel. As the requested reduction was considered to be in line with the policy of developing the biofuel sector and in the interests of protecting the environment, the Council approved.

In view of its existing international obligations as well as the maintaining of the competitive position of European companies, Article 14 of Directive 2003/96 continues to exempt from taxation energy products supplied for air and sea navigation and sea navigation.[42] Under Directive 92/81 the Court ruled in the *Braathens* case that as this directive provided for a mandatory exemption for all public air navigation, and held that to allow a Member State to levy another indirect tax on that use would render the exemption entirely ineffective.[43] It remains to be seen to what extent this case law is expected to be applied by analogy. In particular the second paragraph of Article 14 of Directive 2003/96[44] could imply some room for Member States to introduce a 'kerosene-tax' unilaterally.

Finally there are directives like Directive 93/59, 1999/96 and 98/69, concerning polluting emissions from motor vehicles,[45] which contain specific frameworks for fiscal incentives related to the environmental performance of vehicles.

---

[40] Decision 2005/153, OJ 2005 L 51/17.

[41] OJ 2002 L 180/20.

[42] National law implementing this provision cannot be regarded Sate aid in the meaning of Article 92 EC; Case T-351/02 *Deutsche Bahn AG v. Commission* [2006] ECR II-1047.

[43] Case C-346/97 *Braathens Sverige AB* [1999] ECR I-3419. This case concerned an energy tax on various products, including kerosene used during domestic flights in Sweden.

[44] It reads: 'Member States may limit the scope of the exemptions provided for in paragraph 1(b) and (c) to international and intra-Community transport. In addition, where a Member State has entered into a bilateral agreement with another Member State, it may also waive the exemptions provided for in paragraph 1(b) and (c). In such cases, Member States may apply a level of taxation below the minimum level set out in this Directive.'

[45] OJ 1993 L 186/21; OJ 1999 L 44/1; OJ 1998 L 350/1.

5 Non-tariff Restrictions and Protection of the Environment

General remarks

In order to guarantee unobstructed movement of goods between the Member States, Article 28 EC prohibits national authorities from imposing quantitative import restrictions on the import of goods from other Member States, and all measures having equivalent effect. Article 29 EC contains a similar prohibition with respect to exports. Article 30 EC lists a number of exceptions to these two prohibitions.[46] In addition, the Court of Justice has formulated a number of supplementary grounds justifying barriers to imports of goods ('rule of reason' or *Cassis de Dijon* exception).[47] It is up to the national authorities to prove that the conditions allowing these exceptions have been met.

One of the consequences of harmonisation is that whenever a national measure has been the subject of *exhaustive* harmonisation at European level it must be assessed in the light of the provisions of the harmonising measure and not those of the Treaty concerning the free movement of goods or one of the other market freedoms.[48] After harmonisation the directive, or in some cases the regulation, provide the context for review of the national legislation.[49] It should however be noted that European environmental legislation is also required to be compatible with Articles 28 to 30 EC.[50]

All products?

The applicability of the rules on the free movement of goods has been at issue in several cases concerning waste. Thus, in the *Walloon Waste* case the Belgian Government contended that waste cannot be considered as goods within the meaning of Article 28 EC.[51] The Belgian Government added that the operations for disposing of waste are covered by the provisions of the Treaty relating to the freedom to supply services. It was argued that waste, in particular waste which cannot be recycled or re-used, did not have an intrinsic commercial value and could not therefore be sold. In itself this argument is not without merit. It could be argued that the disposal of waste, which has a negative economic value, is not primarily a commercial transaction directed at the purchasing of waste, but above all an act which is by way of being a service, namely the removal of waste. Although the practical significance of this distinction is limited – the rules and exceptions applying to the freedom to provide services are quite simi-

---

[46] See below, section 5.3.

[47] See below, section 5.4.

[48] See for a detailed discussion Chapter 3, section 2.

[49] Leading cases in this respect are: Case C-37/92 *Vanacker and Lesage* [1993] ECR I-4947 and Case C-324/99 *DaimlerChrysler* [2001] ECR I-9897.

[50] Case 172/82 *Inter-Huiles* [1983] ECR 555, para. 12. It should be noted that in this respect the Court seems to allow the institutions a wider margin of discretion than the Member States; Cf. Temmink (2000) at 71.

[51] Case C-2/90 *Commission* v. *Belgium* [1992] ECR I-4431.

lar to those applying to goods[52] – the Court made it clear that there is no room for application of the treaty provisions on services:

> 'In reply to these arguments it is sufficient to point out that objects which are transported over a frontier in order to give rise to commercial transactions are subject to Article 30 [now Article 28 EC, authors], irrespective of the nature of those transactions.'

Equally, the Court rejected a distinction based on the difference between recyclable and non-recyclable waste. It reasoned that, from a practical point of view, serious difficulties would arise, especially with respect to border control, if such a distinction was made. Such a distinction would also be based on uncertain characteristics – which, because of technical developments and the profitability of reused waste, could be changed in time. Because of these factors, the Court found that all waste should be treated as a 'good' under Article 28 EC.

In short, what is crucial for determining whether or not goods should be regarded as being subject to Article 28 EC is whether they may be the object of a commercial transaction. This is also true of waste, even though it has negative value. As a result, waste is subject to the rules on the free movement of goods. This decision shows that measures which hinder intra-EU trade in waste are not covered by the rules on the freedom to provide services.[53]

5.1 The Scope of Application of Article 28 EC

The Dassonville *formula*
One of the most important restrictions on national, but also on EU, environment policy is the prohibition of measures having an effect equivalent to quantitative restrictions on imports and exports. A large number of national environmental measures are in principle covered by the definition given in the *Dassonville* case of a measure having equivalent effect to a restriction on imports.[54] There the Court defined such measures as national measures 'which are capable of hindering, directly or indirectly, actually or potentially, intra-Community trade.' Any measure which may in the slightest way be a restriction in this sense is covered by the prohibition in Article 28 EC. These include not only measures affecting imports, such as import bans, import permits, tests and samples of goods which may be harmful to the environment, but also 'measures applicable without distinction'. In other words measures which are applicable both to imports and to domestic products, like for example, regu-

---

[52] Case C-76/90 *Säger* [1991] ECR I-4221. See also the Services Directive, Directive 2006/123 on services in the internal market (OJ 2006 L 376/36). The protection of the environment is regarded as one of the 'overriding reasons relating to the public interest' which may be relied upon by Member States to restrict access to or exercise of a service activity in their territory.

[53] The decision was implicitly confirmed in the *Vanacker* case; Case C-37/92 *Vanacker* [1993] ECR I-4947.

[54] Case 8/74 *Dassonville* [1974] ECR 837.

lations on safety, packaging and labelling, quality requirements etc. Regulations which, in the event of disparities between the legislation in the Member States, are clearly capable of hindering intra-EU trade. According to the judgment of the Court of Justice in the *Cassis de Dijon* case, products lawfully produced and marketed in one of the Member States must be granted market access in other Member States.[55] It should also be noted that in accordance with the settled case law of the Court of Justice, Article 28 EC is applicable without distinction to products originating in the EU and to those which have been put into free circulation in any of the Member States, irrespective of the actual origin of those products.[56]

The case law of the Court of Justice contains several examples of environmental measures which have been regarded as 'measures having equivalent effect'.

> In the *Improsol* case the Court held that a prohibition, enforced by penalties in criminal law, of selling, storing or using any plant-protection product not authorised by a national law is capable of affecting imports from other Member States where the same product is admitted wholly or in part and thus of constituting a barrier to intra-EU trade.[57] Such rules therefore constitute a measure having an effect equivalent to a quantitative restriction. Similar, a general prohibition on the industrial use of trichloroethylene constitutes also a 'measure having equivalent effect'.[58]
>
> In the *Danish Bottles* case a system requiring manufacturers and importers to market beer and soft drinks only in re-usable containers, which must be approved by a National Agency for the Protection of the Environment, was held to be subject to Article 28 EC.[59] The requirement implied a prohibition against the marketing of goods in containers other than ones which were returnable. The import of foreign beer and soft drinks which were legitimately marketed in other Member States, but did not meet the requirements of the country of importation, was thus not possible. Furthermore, the fact of having to establish a system for the return of containers meant that foreign manufacturers would be obliged to incur relatively high transport costs.
>
> Labelling requirements quite clearly fall under the scope of Article 28 EC. The Court ruled that Italy, by subjecting manganese alkaline batteries containing less than 0.0005% mercury by weight to a marking scheme which requires, in particu-

---

[55] Case 120/78 *Rewe-Zentral AG* [1979] ECR 649.

[56] Case C-131/93 *Commission v. Germany* [1994] ECR I-3303, para. 10.

[57] Case 125/88 *Nijman* [1989] ECR 3533. Cf. also Case C-293/94 *Brandsma* [1996] ECR I-3159 and Case C-400/96 *Harpegnies* [1998] ECR I-5121. In the same vein, more recently, Case C-443/02 *Schreiber* [2004] ECR I-7275.

[58] Case C-473/98 *Kemikalieninspektionen v. Toolex Alpha AB* [2000] ECR I-5681.

[59] Case 302/86 *Commission v. Denmark* [1988] ECR 4607. See also on German rules concerning deposit and return obligations for non-reusable packaging Case C-309/02 *Radlberger Getränkegesellschaft and S. Spitz* [2004] ECR I-11763 and Case C-463/01 *Commission v. Germany* [2004] ECR I-11705.

lar, an indication as to the presence of heavy metals, failed to fulfil its obligations under Article 28 EC.[60]

A Dutch measure which fell foul of Article 28 EC was one prohibiting the importation and keeping of red grouse. The Court held in the *Red Grouse* case that this could not be justified in respect of a bird which does not occur in the territory of the legislating Member State, but is found in another Member State (the United Kingdom) where it may be lawfully hunted.[61]

In the *Balsamo* case it was argued that the Mayor of Cinisello Balsamo's prohibition of the supply to customers of non-biodegradable bags in which to carry away their purchases was incompatible with Article 28 EC.[62] However, the Court was not required to give a preliminary ruling on this point, as the national court had not submitted a question on the matter. Since such a prohibition virtually amounts to a total prohibition on the sale of non-biodegradable bags, it should probably be regarded as falling within the scope of Article 28 EC.

A prohibition on the disposal of foreign waste also falls under the scope of application of Article 28 EC, as is clear from the judgment in the *Walloon Waste* case.[63]

From the *Bluhme* case it is clear that legislation prohibiting the keeping of a certain type of bee on the Danish island of Læsø constituted a restriction within the meaning of Article 28 EC.[64]

In *Aher-Waggon* the Court found that national legislation making the first registration in national territory of aircraft previously registered in a Member State conditional upon compliance with stricter noise standards than those laid down by an EC directive restricted intra-EU trade.[65]

In *Schmidberger* Article 28 EC was applicable with respect to a decision of a local authority in Austria not to prohibit a demonstration by environmental protesters which resulted in the complete closure of the Brenner motorway for almost 30 hours.[66] The decision not to intervene is capable of restricting intra-EU trade in goods and, in the words of the Court 'must, therefore, be regarded as constituting a measure of equivalent effect to a quantitative restriction which is, in principle, incompatible with the Community law'.

German legislation requiring electricity supply undertakings to purchase electricity produced from renewable energy sources at minimum prices was considered, in the *PreussenElektra* case, to be an import restriction.[67] Indeed, the German

---

[60] Case C-143/03 *Commission v. Italy*, unpublished judgment of 14 October 2004.

[61] Case C-169/89 *Gourmetterie v.d. Burg* [1990] ECR I-2143.

[62] Case 380/87 *Balsamo* [1989] ECR 2491.

[63] Case C-2/90 *Commission v. Belgium* [1992] ECR I-4431.

[64] Case C-67/97 *Bluhme* [1998] ECR I-8033. Cf. however the Dutch *Raad van State*, which ruled that a national prohibition on the keeping of squirrels is not covered by Article 28 or 29 EC; 18 June 1998 [1999] M&R 12. In the light of the *Bluhme* ruling this would not seem correct.

[65] Case C-389/96 *Aher-Waggon* [1998] ECR I-4473.

[66] Case C-112/00 *Schmidberger* [2003] ECR I-5659.

[67] Case C-379/98 *PreussenElektra* [2001] ECR I-2099.

Stromeinspeisungsgesetz limits the possibility of importing the same product by preventing those undertakings from obtaining supplies in respect of part of their needs from traders situated in other Member States.

All these judgments demonstrate that if national environmental legislation in one way or another concerns or affects the trade in goods, it is likely to be subject to the provisions of Article 28 EC. This does not mean that such measures will necessarily be prohibited, but it does mean they will have to be justified in the light of one of the exemptions to the article.

No de minimis

As the Court decided in the *Peralta* case, legislation is not incompatible with Article 28 EC where its purpose is not to regulate trade in goods with other Member States and the restrictive effects which it might have on the free movement of goods are too *uncertain* and *indirect* for the obligation which it lays down to be regarded as being of a nature to hinder trade between Member States.[68]

The case concerned an Italian law which prohibited any vessel from discharging harmful substances into the sea. However some caution is advised here, as the uncertain and indirect restrictions referred to in *Peralta* are pertinent to the causal connection required between a measure and its consequences, but say nothing about the extent of those restrictions.

Another relevant case in this connection is *Bluhme*, which concerned Danish legislation prohibiting the keeping on the Danish island of Læsø of bees other than a certain sort.[69] Denmark argued that as the legislation applied to only 0.3% of its territory, it fell outside the scope of Article 28 EC. The Court rejected this argument, implicitly following the view taken by Advocate General Fennelly that a distinction had to be made between the 'scale' and the 'remoteness' of the effect on the movement of goods. The fact that the scale of the effects was limited did not imply that the measures were excluded from the scope of Article 28 EC.

In other words, Article 28 EC does not contain a *de minimis* rule.[70]

The Keck *formula*

In the *Keck* case, the Court made a significant distinction as to what measures must be deemed to hinder trade:[71]

'However, contrary to what has previously been decided, the application to products from other Member States of national provisions restricting or prohibiting certain selling arrangements is not such as to hinder directly of indirectly, actually

---

[68] Case C-379/92 *Peralta* [1994] ECR I-3453.

[69] Case C-67/97 *Bluhme* [1998] ECR I-8033.

[70] Cf. on the issue of remoteness and the *de minimis* rule Oliver (1999) at 788-793.

[71] Joined Cases C-267/91 and C-268/91 *Keck* [1993] ECR I-6097.

or potentially, trade between Member States within the meaning of the *Dassonville* judgment [...] provided that those provisions apply to all affected traders operating within the national territory and provided that they affect in the same manner, in law and in fact, the marketing of domestic products and of those from other Member States.

If national regulations satisfy the criterion given in the *Keck* case, there is no need further to review the national measure in the light of the exemptions allowed by Article 30 EC or the rule of reason, nor of the principle of proportionality. It cannot yet be said what the consequences of this judgment for environmental law will be, particularly in the field of product policy. In general however, it can safely be said that import bans (or restrictions) on 'dangerous' products, import licensing systems and national environmental product standards will continue to be considered a restriction on trade.[72] In *Bluhme* the Court made it quite clear that the Danish legislation prohibiting the keeping of bees 'concerns the intrinsic characteristics of the bees' and could not therefore be considered a 'selling arrangement'.[73]

A possible example which might be regarded as falling under the *Keck* doctrine would be a measure whereby pesticides could be sold only on prescription, or only to certain persons. The same might apply to a ban on advertising certain environmentally harmful products.[74] Such measures might now be regarded as lawful without further review or justification.

Trade restrictions within a Member State

Another question regarding the scope of Article 28 (and 29) EC is to what extent the prohibition extends to trade restrictions *within* a Member State. For instance, in terms of environmental law, is Article 28 EC applicable to regional waste bans within a country or not.[75] According to the settled case law of the Court, Article 28 EC does not apply to such internal trade restrictions.[76] For instance, in the *RI.SAN* case, concerning the organisation of a local solid urban waste collection service the Court stated that the free movement rules do not apply in a situation in which all the facts are confined to within a single Member State.[77] This case law is completely in line with the text of Article 28 EC. The text of Article 28 EC, and the same can be said with respect to Articles 23, 25 and 29 EC, seems crystal clear indeed. The articles prohibit restrictions 'between

---

[72] Cf. Temmink (2000) at 74.

[73] Case C-67/97 *Bluhme* [1998] ECR I-8033, para. 21.

[74] Cf. Joined Cases 34, 35 and 36/95 *De Agostini* [1997] ECR I-3843, paras. 21 and 31.

[75] National case law on this issue is somewhat scarce, although there is a judgment of the Dutch *Raad van State* in which it refused to apply Article 28 EC with respect to inter-provincial restrictions on the import of waste; Dutch *Raad van State* 24 December 1998 [1999] AB 153. See on this judgment Temmink (2000) at 85-87.

[76] For example Case 314/81 *Waterkeyn* [1982] ECR 4337.

[77] Case C-108/98 *RI.SAN* [1999] ECR I-5219.

Member States' only. The problem however was that the case law of the Court of Justice on customs duties and charges having equivalent effect gave support for a more wider interpretation.[78]

It seems however that the case law of the Court is changing bit by bit and that the doctrine on the non-applicability of Article 28 EC in 'internal situations' is due for overhaul.

> In the *Pistre* case the Court apparently did consider Article 28 EC applicable in a case without any clear cross-border implications.[79] The Court stated in so many words that Article 28 EC 'cannot be considered inapplicable simply because all the facts of the specific case before the national court are confined to a single Member State.'[80] More important than *Pistre* seems the more recent judgment of the Court in *Jersey Potatoes*.[81] The case concerned a restriction on the export of potatoes from Jersey to the UK. Exports to 'other' Member States were not covered by the prohibition. However, the Court did find Article 29 EC applicable because there is nothing to rule out the possibility that ultimately this 'internal trade restriction' could have a negative effect on trade with other Member States as well.

From these judgments it looks more likely that the prohibitions of Article 28 (and 29) EC will be capable of being applied in so called 'internal situations' and that the test of the existence of a cross-border implication in a particular case has been eased by recent case law.

5.2   The Scope of Application of Article 29 EC

Restrictions on exports are prohibited by Article 29 EC. Although the prohibition is framed in identical terms to Article 28 EC, the Court has adopted a different approach to the interpretation of this article.[82] Not just any restriction is covered by Article 29 EC, only those national measures which have as their specific object or effect the restriction of patterns of exports and thereby the establishment of a difference in treatment between the domestic trade of a Member State and its export trade, in such a way as to provide a special advantage for national products or for the domestic market of the State in question.[83] Unlike Article 28 EC, 'measures applicable without distinction' are not within the scope of application of Article 29 EC. This means that non-discriminatory measures which restrict exports do not require further justification by the Member States; they are simply allowed.

---

[78]   Cf. Case C-163/90 *Legros* [1992] ECR I-4625, Case C-363/93 *Lancry* [1994] ECR I-3957, Case C-485/93 *Simitzi* [1995] ECR I-2655 and Case C-72/03 *Carbonati Apuani* [2004] ECR I-8027.

[79]   Case C-321/94 *Pistre* [1994] ECR I-2343. Cf. Oliver (1999) at 786.

[80]   Cf. Jarvis (1997) at 15.

[81]   Case C-293/02 *Jersey Produce Marketing Organisation* [2005] ECR I-9543.

[82]   See for a critique Oliver (1999) at 799-803.

[83]   Case 172/82 *Inter-Huiles* [1983] ECR 555.

In this light, the judgment of the Swedish Supreme Administrative Court in the *Barsebäck* case seems correct.[84] The circumstance alone that the export share of nuclear power electricity that is produced at the Barsebäck station is stated as being higher than at the other nuclear power stations is not a ground for considering that the decision of the Swedish Government to dismantle it is in violation of Article 29 EC.

Another example of a measure which is not covered by Article 29 EC is the following. Suppose that, in order to limit the amount of waste produced, a national legislature were to prohibit the use of certain substances in the manufacture of a particular product. Such a measure would have the effect of restricting the export of that product to other Member States which do not have similar legislation. However, as the measure is non-discriminatory, it would not be prohibited under Article 29 EC. Nevertheless, as it would probably also operate to restrict imports, it would still have to stand up to review in the light of Article 28 EC. Thus, to determine the scope of Article 29 EC, it is crucial to examine whether or not a measure discriminates in favour of a Member State's domestic trade.

In the *Vanacker* case,[85] which will be discussed in greater detail below, the Court confirmed its judgment in the *Inter-Huiles* case[86] and held that a prohibition on the export of waste oils was in breach of the rules on the free movement of goods. The scope of Article 29 EC has been examined by the Court in several cases in the context of national protective measures.

In the *Inter-Huiles* case, the question at issue was whether the French system of regulation of waste oils was in accordance with European law. The core of the French legislation was the requirement that waste oils should be delivered to approved disposal undertakings. It was not disputed that the French legislation prohibited, by implication, the export of waste oils to foreign countries, including other Member States. The French Government contended that their legislation was justified in the light of Article 5 of Directive 75/439.[87] However, having discussed the directive, the Court reached the conclusion that the directive does not automatically authorise the Member States to establish barriers to exports. It continued: 'That conclusion is reinforced by Article 34 [now Article 29 EC, authors] of the EEC Treaty, which prohibits all measures having an effect equivalent to quantitative restrictions on exports. As the Court has repeatedly held, the prohibition concerns all national measures which have as their specific object or effect the restriction of patterns of exports and thereby the establishment of a difference

---

[84] Judgment of the Swedish Supreme Administrative Court on 16 June 1999, case no. 1424-1998, 2397-1998 and 2939-1998, RÅ 1999 ref. 76, regarding the cessation of the right to operate the Barsebäck 1 nuclear power reactor.

[85] Case C-37/92 *Vanacker* [1993] ECR I-4947. Cf. also Case C-203/96 *Dusseldorp* [1998] ECR I-4075, to be discussed more in detail below.

[86] Case 172/82 *Inter-Huiles* [1983] ECR 555.

[87] OJ 1975 L 194/23, later amended.

in treatment between the domestic trade of a Member State and its export trade, in such a way as to provide a special advantage for national products or for the domestic market of the State in question. Consequently, provisions which contravene those rules are also contrary to Article 34 [now Article 29 EC, authors] EC.'

The requirement that certain goods and/or products should only be delivered to domestic companies in fact means that the export of those products is prohibited.[88] Such requirements are thus covered by the prohibition contained in Article 29 EC.[89]

> In the *Dusseldorp* case, rules prohibiting the export of oil filters unless their processing abroad was superior to that in the Netherlands was held incompatible with Article 29 EC: 'It is plain that the object and effect of such a provision is to restrict exports and to provide a particular advantage for national production.'[90]

Once it has been established that a measure is within the scope of application of Article 29 EC, it must then be examined to what extent the measure may nevertheless prove to be a justified restriction on the free movement of goods.

5.3   Exceptions under Article 30 EC

General remarks
To the extent that national environmental legislation falls within the scope of the prohibitions contained in Articles 28 and 29 EC, the question arises whether this means that all this legislation must be set aside as being incompatible with European rules. This is not the case. Article 30 EC provides that restrictions on trade may be justified if they are necessary for the protection of health and life of humans, animals or plants and do not constitute a means of arbitrary discrimination or a disguised restriction on trade between Member States.

The burden of proving that the criteria for application of Article 30 EC have been met (and the same holds for application of the *rule of reason*) lies primarily with the Member State wishing to rely on Article 30 EC.[91] It should be noted however that Article 30 EC must be interpreted in the light of the precautionary

---

[88] Cf. also Case C-209/98 *Sydhavnens Sten & Grus* [2000] ECR I-3743, para. 37.

[89] This approach is confirmed in the *Vanacker* case, Case C-37/92 *Vanacker* [1993] ECR I-4947. A similar approach is found in the *Nertsvoederfabriek* case, Case 118/86 *Nertsvoederfabriek* [1987] ECR 3883.

[90] Case C-203/96 *Dusseldorp* [1998] ECR I-4075.

[91] Cf. Case 251/78 *Denkavit Futtermittel* v. *Minister für Ernährung Landwirtschaft und Forsten* [1979] ECR 3369, para. 24. See also Advocate General Fennelly in the *Bluhme* case: 'In order to benefit from the application of Article 36 [now Article 30 EC, authors] of the Treaty, it is for a Member State to prove that a national measure is effective in attaining its protective objective'; Case C-67/97 *Bluhme* [1998] ECR I-8033.

principle of Article 174(2) EC.[92] In other words, it would not seem necessary in every case that there should be unambiguous scientific evidence that the product or substance in question is harmful.[93] Protective measures are permissible if there is a strong suspicion that the substance in question poses a health threat.

Protection of health and life of humans, animals or plants

Although the Court repeatedly held that 'the health and life of humans rank foremost among the property or interests protected by Article 30 of the Treaty'[94] and that it is for the Member States to decide at what level they wish to set the protection of the life and health of humans,[95] the early case law of the Court of Justice has clearly shown that the scope of Article 30 EC, as an exception to a fundamental Treaty provision, had to be interpreted narrowly. As the protection of the environment is not included in the exhaustive list of exceptions contained in Article 30 EC, a restriction on imports or exports to protect the environment, without there being a real and actual threat to health and life of humans, animals or plants, was not capable of being justified by Article 30 EC.

Import prohibitions of non-harmful wastes, which do not directly threaten life or health, cannot be justified on the grounds of Article 30 EC, as was made clear in the Court's judgment in the *Walloon Waste* case: 'So far as the environment is concerned, it should be observed that waste has a special characteristic. The accumulation of waste, even before it becomes a health hazard, constitutes a threat to the environment because of the limited capacity of each region or locality for receiving it.'[96] This case clearly makes a distinction between protecting the environment and protecting health.

The same strict approach employed in the *Walloon Waste* case can also be found in the *Dusseldorp* case.[97] The Dutch Government argued that their export restrictions for oil filters could be justified under Article 30 EC. The Court did not

---

[92] Cf. Case C-463/01 *Commission* v. *Germany* [2004] ECR I-11705, para. 74: 'the precautionary principle and the principle that preventive action should be taken, laid down in Article 174(2) EC, confer on the Member States a discretion in the interests of environment policy'.

[93] Cf. the Communication of the Commission Single Market and the Environment, COM (99) 263. Cf. also Case C-473/98 *Kemikalieninspektionen* v. *Toolex Alpha AB* [2000] ECR I-5681, para. 45. See also Case C-121/00 *Hahn* [2002] ECR I-9193, para. 38: 'in so far as there are uncertainties at the present state of scientific research, it is for the Member States, within the limits imposed by the Treaty, to decide what degree of protection they wish to assure and, in particular, the stringency of the checks to be carried out'.

[94] See for instance Case C-473/98 *Kemikalieninspektionen* v. *Toolex Alpha AB* [2000] ECR I-5681, para. 38.

[95] For instance Case 272/80 *Frans-Nederlandse Maatschappij voor Biologische Producten* [1981] ECR 3277 and Case 125/88 *Nijman* [1989] ECR 3533. Confirmed in Case C-293/94 *Brandsma* [1996] ECR I-3159, para. 11 and Case C-400/96 *Harpegnies* [1998] ECR I-5121, para. 33.

[96] Case C-2/90 *Commission* v. *Belgium* [1992] ECR I-4431.

[97] Case C-203/96 *Dusseldorp* [1998] ECR I-4075, para. 46. Cf. Case C-209/98 *Sydhavnens Sten & Grus* [2000] ECR I-3743, para. 45.

agree: 'Such a justification would be relevant if the processing of oil filters in other Member States and their shipment over a greater distance as a result of their being exported posed a threat to the health and life of humans. The documents before the Court do not, however, show that to be the case. On the one hand, the Netherlands Government itself conceded that the processing of filters in Germany was comparable to that performed by AVR Chemie. On the other, it has not been established that the shipment of the oil filters posed a threat to the environment or to the life and health of humans.'

In line with this narrow and strict interpretation is the case law from the Court of Justice that an important criterion for application of Article 30 EC is that there must be a *real* and *actual* danger threatening life or public health. In particular national legislation restricting the placing on the market of plant protection products, pesticides, biocides and other dangerous substances could benefit from the exception of Article 30 EC.[98]

One example is the *Fumicot* case, in which the Frans-Nederlandse Maatschappij voor Biologische Producten, a plant protection manufacturer, was fined in the Netherlands for an offence under Article 2(1) of the 1962 Dutch *Bestrijdingsmiddelenwet* (Law relating to plant protection products), which prohibits the sale, storage or use as a plant protection product of a product which has not been approved.[99] The company concerned had imported, sold or supplied in the Netherlands a quantity of a plant protection product called 'Fumicot Fumispore'. That product had already been lawfully marketed in France but had not received the approval which is required in the Netherlands in accordance with the Bestrijdingsmiddelenwet. The company contended that the system of approval was incompatible with Articles 28 and 30 EC: 'It should be noted that, at the time of the alleged offences, there were no common or harmonised rules relating to the production or marketing of plant protection products. In the absence of harmonisation, it was therefore for the Member States to decide what degree of protection of the health and life of humans they intended to assure and in particular how strict the checks to be carried out were to be [...], having regard however to the fact that their freedom of action is itself restricted by the Treaty. In that respect, it is not disputed that the national rules in question are intended to protect public health and that they therefore come within the exception provided for by Article 36 [now Article 30 EC, authors]. The measures of control applied by the Netherlands authorities, in particular as regards the approval of the product, may not therefore be challenged in principle.'[100]

---

[98] Case 94/83 *Albert Heijn* [1984] ECR 3263 and Case 54/85 *Mirepoix* [1986] ECR 1067.

[99] Case 272/80 *Frans-Nederlandse Maatschappij voor Biologische Producten* [1981] ECR 3277.

[100] This judgment was confirmed in the *Improsol* case, Case 125/88 *Nijman* [1989] ECR 3533. Cf. also Case C-400/96 *Harpegnies* [1998] ECR I-5121. Cf. also Case C-293/94 *Brandsma* [1996] ECR I-3159.

From these judgments it appeared that the Court made a rather strict distinction between 'environmental protection' on the one hand and 'the protection of health and life of humans, animals or plants' on the other.[101] In view of this restrictive approach, it was doubtful whether measures not addressing a demonstrable direct interest to health and life of humans, animals or plants were covered by Article 30 EC.

However, in the light of more recent case law it should not be ruled out that the Court now approves a wider interpretation of Article 30 EC.

> In the *Bluhme* case the Court observed that measures to preserve an indigenous animal population with distinct characteristics contribute to the maintenance of biodiversity by protecting the population concerned against extinction, 'or, even in the absence of such risk, on account of a scientific or other interest in preserving the pure population at the location concerned'. By so doing, they are aimed at protecting the life of those animals and are capable of being justified under Article 30 EC.[102] And in *PreussenElektra*, discussed above, the Court ruled that promoting the use of renewable energy sources for producing electricity 'is useful for protecting the environment in so far as it contributes to the reduction in emissions of greenhouse gases' and 'is also designed to protect the health and life of humans, animals and plants'.[103] It remains to be seen to what extent this wider interpretation of Article 30 EC will be pursued in future cases as well.

Finally, it should be noted that, as far as animals and plants are concerned, not only species that are threatened with extinction or are extremely rare or uncommon qualify for protection. In principle, protection extends to all species of animals and plants.[104]

Arbitrary discrimination and disguised restrictions

According to the second sentence of Article 30 EC, national measures may not constitute a means of arbitrary discrimination or a disguised restriction on trade between Member States. The Court has not systematically addressed the question of what is and what is not a disguised restriction or an arbitrary discrimination. It could even be debated, in view of the requirement of the proportionality principle,[105] whether the second sentence adds anything at all. The most meaningful interpretation of the sentence is probably the following. Its wording indicates that it is possible, in principle, for domestic and foreign goods to be treated differently under Article 30 EC. In other words, the addition

---

[101] There were however some cases where the Court seemed to apply a wider interpretation of Article 30 EC. See for instance Case 125/88 *Nijman* [1989] ECR 3533 and Case C-389/96 *Aher-Waggon* [1998] ECR I-4473, para. 19.

[102] Case C-67/97 *Bluhme* [1998] ECR I-8033.

[103] Case C-379/98 *PreussenElektra* [2001] ECR I-2099.

[104] See also Advocate General Van Gerven in Case C-169/89 *Gourmetterie v.d. Burg* [1990] ECR I-2143.

[105] See on this principle more in detail section 5.5 of this chapter.

that there may be no arbitrary discrimination could be taken to mean that any difference must be based on grounds capable of objective justification.

> Take the case where a Member State desired to restrict the import of certain dangerous substances, by introducing a system of import permits. This would be an arbitrary discrimination, if the domestic manufacture and marketing of the same substances was not subject to any restrictions. Any such measure in respect of foreign goods would have to be accompanied by corresponding, but not necessary identical, protective measures in respect of domestic goods.

Trading rules might constitute a disguised restriction on trade, if their restrictive effect is not limited to what is necessary to protect the interest referred to by the rules.[106] The dividing line between this requirement and the proportionality principle is not a sharp one.

> An example from the environmental case law of the Court, where the term disguised restriction was discussed, is the *Fumicot* case referred to above.[107] After the Court had noted that, in the absence of harmonisation, it was for the Member States to decide what degree of protection of the health and life of humans they intended to assure, the Court continued: 'However, that leaves open the question whether the detailed procedures governing approvals, as indicated by the national court, may possibly constitute a disguised restriction, within the meaning of the last sentence of Article 36 [now Article 30 EC, authors], on trade between Member States, in view, on the one hand, of the dangerous nature of the product and, on the other hand, of the fact that it has been the subject of a procedure for approval in the Member State where is has been lawfully marketed. Whilst a Member State is free to require a product of the type in question, which has already received approval in another Member State, to undergo a fresh procedure of examination and approval, the authorities of the Member States are nevertheless required to assist in bringing about a relaxation of the controls existing in intra-EU trade. It follows that they are not entitled unnecessarily to require technical or chemical analyses or laboratory tests where those analyses and tests have already been carried out in another Member State and their results are available to those authorities, or may at their request be placed at their disposal.'

5.4   The *Rule of Reason* and Environmental Protection

Apart from Article 30 EC, the Court's case law provides another means of considering certain trade restrictive measures admissible. In the *Cassis de Dijon* judgment and in subsequent cases it was decided that, in the absence of common rules, obstacles to free movement within the EU resulting from disparities between the national laws must be accepted, in so far as such rules,

---

[106] See Advocate General Van Gerven in Joined Cases C-1/90 and C-176/90 *Aragonesa* [1991] ECR I-4151.

[107] Case 272/80 *Frans-Nederlandse Maatschappij voor Biologische Producten* [1981] ECR 3277.

applicable to domestic and imported products without distinction, may be recognised as being necessary in order to satisfy 'mandatory requirements' recognised by European law.[108] This is known as the 'rule of reason' exception. In that case the Court referred to public health, the fairness of commercial transactions and the defence of the consumer as examples of such mandatory requirements.

In the *Danish Bottles* case the Court added 'protection of the environment'[109] to this list.[110] In that case Danish legislation only allowed the marketing of beer and soft drinks if returnable containers were used and if the importer or manufacturer set up an approved system to ensure the collection and return of such containers. As a result the Danish market was virtually closed to foreign manufacturers of beer and soft drinks. The Commission decided to bring an action against Denmark for infringement of the Treaty. Recognizing that protection of the environment could justify a restriction of the free movement of goods, it contended that alternatives were available which would restrict trade less while still protecting the environment. In a key passage the Court held:

> '[...] that the protection of the environment is one of the Community's essential objectives, which may as such justify certain limitations of the principle of the free movement of goods. That view is moreover confirmed by the Single European Act. In view of the foregoing, it must therefore be stated that the protection of the environment is a mandatory requirement which may limit the application of Article 30 [now Article 28 EC, authors] EC.'

In the light of the Court's earlier judgment on the status of environmental protection in the European legal order, this judgment was hardly surprising. It took the Court remarkably few words to establish that protection of the environment could justify import restrictions. This statement of principle was later confirmed in the *Walloon Waste* case.[111]

Environmental protection is clearly a more comprehensive concept than protection of health and life of humans, animals or plants, even if nowadays the Court seems to interpret Article 30 EC less strict than it used to.[112] The deposit-and-return system in the *Danish Bottles* case could probably not have been justified under Article 30 EC. The interests at stake – prevention of litter, energy conservation, promotion of re-use etc. – seem less easily encompassed by Article 30 EC. The material scope of the rule of reason is still wider and thus offers the Member States more latitude to take protective measures.

---

[108] Case 120/78 *Rewe-Zentral AG* [1979] ECR 649.

[109] Which has to be interpreted in the light of the principles mentioned in Article 174(2); Cf. Case C-209/98 *Sydhavnens Sten & Grus* [2000] ECR I-3743, para. 48.

[110] Case 302/86 *Commission v. Denmark* [1988] ECR 4607.

[111] Case C-2/90 *Commission v. Belgium* [1992] ECR I-4431.

[112] See our remarks with respect to Article 30 EC in this chapter, section 5.3 above.

Article 30 EC or a mandatory requirement?

It could be asked to what extent a national import restriction for environmental reasons should be regarded as a ground for justification in the sense of Article 30 EC, or as a 'mandatory requirement' in the sense of *Cassis de Dijon*[113] and the *Danish Bottles*[114] judgments? As the material scope of the rule of reason is wider and offers the Member States more leeway to take protective measures one could even argue that there is hardly any need to rely on Article 30 EC if the rule of reason is available to the Member States.

However, on the basis of older case law the rule of reason seemed more limited than Article 30 EC in a different respect. In principle, Article 30 EC allows an exemption for national measures which relate in particular to imported products only. In other words, it offers some room for 'measures applicable *with* distinction'. Such specific import restrictions may not, however, constitute an arbitrary discrimination. And prohibition of the importation of a harmful product will constitute an arbitrary discrimination if no restriction whatever is imposed on the domestic use of that product. It is not arbitrary however, if there is a valid and objective reason why the imported product is to be treated differently. In other words under Article 30 EC *differentiation* is allowed, but *discrimination* is not.

As far as the rule of reason is concerned, the measure in question had to be applied without distinction to domestic and foreign products. It was well-established case law that the rule of reason doctrine could not be relied on to justify national measures which were not applicable to domestic products and imported products *without* distinction.[115] This meant that national protective measures which might be justified on environmental grounds, but do not fall within the more limited scope of Article 30 EC, are only allowed if they can be regarded as measures applicable without distinction.

However, the judgment in the *Walloon Waste* case was the first case which caused some confusion as to the degree to which a measure must be applicable without distinction for the rule of reason to apply.[116]

In that case, the lawfulness of a Walloon prohibition on the disposal of foreign waste was at issue. The Commission argued that these mandatory requirements of environmental protection could not be relied on to allow the Walloon restrictions. The Commission insisted that the measures at issue discriminated against waste coming from other Member States though that waste was no more harmful than that produced in Wallonia. The same line of reasoning was developed by Advocate General Jacobs in his Opinion. In the Advocate General's view, there was 'plainly' discrimination between foreign and Belgian waste and therefore the ruling

---

[113] Case 120/78 *Rewe-Zentral AG* [1979] ECR 649.

[114] Case 302/86 *Commission* v. *Denmark* [1988] ECR 4607.

[115] See for instance, Joined Cases C-1/90 and C-176/90 *Aragonesa de Publicidad Exterior and Publivía* [1991] ECR I-4151, para. 13.

[116] Case C-2/90 *Commission* v. *Belgium* [1992] ECR I-4431.

of the Court in the Danish Bottles case could not serve as a precedent.[117] The Court of Justice first confirmed that the 'mandatory requirements are to be taken into account only with regard to measures which apply to national and imported products without distinction. However, in order to determine whether the obstacle in question is discriminatory, the particular type of waste must be taken into account. The principle that environmental damage should as a priority be rectified at source – a principle laid down by Article 174(2) EC for action by the EC relating to the environment – means that it is for each region, commune or other local entity to take appropriate measures to receive, process and dispose of its own waste. Consequently waste should be disposed of as close as possible to the place where it is produced. It then observed that this principle is in conformity with the principles of self-sufficiency and proximity set out in the Basel Convention. The Court therefore concluded that, having regard to the differences between waste produced in one place and that in another and its connection with the place where it is produced, the Belgian measures could not be considered to be discriminatory.

What is interesting is, in the first place, that the Court has *de facto* equated the fact that a measure applies without distinction to the absence of discrimination. By thus equating the two, the Court has made the test of whether or not a measure applies without distinction a test of whether or not it is discriminatory. The relevance of this discussion could be that, for a national measure to benefit from the rule of reason exception, it no longer has to be framed as a measure applicable without distinction. Apparently, differential measures can also be excepted using the rule of reason, as long as there is an objective justification. More recent case law indeed seems to suggest that the criterion 'measure applicable without distinction' is no longer a hard and fast rule in the case law of the Court of Justice.

For example, it could be argued that the German rules in *Aher-Waggon* do indeed adversely affect foreign aircraft in particular, and it could also be argued that the Danish bee regulations in *Bluhme* are in essentially distinctly applicable measures.[118] The most clear example of an environmental case where the Court applied a rule of reason test, albeit not explicitly, with respect to a distinctly applicable measure is *PreussenElektra*.[119] The German rules clearly favoured domestic 'green energy' producing undertakings and it is hard to see those rules as being indistinctly applicable. It is the authors' opinion that the Court in that case applied the rule of reason and not Article 30 EC. The dictum of the judgment, where the Court ruled that the German measures 'are not incompatible' with Article 28 EC shows that the Court is not applying the exception of Article 30 EC. In that case the dictum of the judgment would entail something like '...is justified by Article 30 EC' or 'Article 30 EC does not preclude....'.

---

[117] Case 302/86 *Commission v. Denmark* [1988] ECR 4607.

[118] Case C-389/96 *Aher-Waggon* [1998] ECR I-4473 and Case C-67/97 *Bluhme* [1998] ECR I-8033.

[119] Case C-379/98 *PreussenElektra* [2001] ECR I-2099.

Finally, we should mention Case C-320/03.[120] That case involved regional Austrian legislation prohibiting lorries of more than 7.5 tons, carrying certain goods, from being driven on a section of the A12 motorway in the Inn valley. This legislation had clearly discriminatory elements as the prohibition affected the international transit of goods – carried out as to more than 80% by non-Austrian undertakings – in particular. Nevertheless, the Court ruled – subject to the proportionality principle – that now the Austrian legislation was adopted in order to ensure the quality of ambient air the measure can be justified on 'environmental protection grounds'.

Taken together with indications in the Court's case law outside the field of the environment that the rule of reason will be applied where measures do make a distinction,[121] it cannot be ruled out that the relevance of the distinction between Article 30 interests and rule of reason exceptions has ceased to exist. May be it is time that the Court will rule on this explicitly.[122]

The rule of reason *and export restrictions*

Above it was stated that Article 29 EC applies only to discriminatory restrictions on exports. Measures applicable without distinction which have a restrictive effect on exports are therefore outside the scope of this provision. This means that there is no need to apply the rule of reason as far as Article 29 EC is concerned. There is thus no need for further review in the light of the requirement of the proportionality principle.

Under the 'old' rule that the rule of reason cannot be applied with respect to distinctly applicable measures, export restrictions which are within the scope of application of Article 29 EC may be justified only on the grounds contained in Article 30 EC.

However, it was suggested above that the case law of the Court on the distinction between Article 30 interests and rule of reason exceptions is becoming blurred. And that there are indications that protection of the environment can also be relied on to justify measures other than those 'applicable without distinction'. If our interpretation of the direction the law is taking is correct, it is hard to understand why 'protection of the environment' should not be relied on to justify (necessarily distinctly applicable) measures falling under the scope of Article 29 EC.

---

[120] Case C-320/03 *Commission v. Austria* [2005] ECR I-9871.

[121] Case C-385/99 *Müller-Fauré and van Riet* [2003] ECR I-4509, C-34/95 *De Agostini* [1997] ECR I-3843 and Case C-388/95 *Belgium v. Spain* [2000] ECR I-3123. Cf. on the shifting of the Court's case law in this respect Oliver (1999) at 804-806.

[122] The Court has been invited to do so by Advocate General Jacobs in the *PreussenElektra* case; See point 229 of his Opinion. Cf. also the Opinion of Advocate General Geelhoed in Case C-320/03 *Commission v. Austria* [2005] ECR I-9871, point 106 of his Opinion.

A paragraph from the *Dusseldorp* judgment will illustrate this. In that case the Dutch Government had argued that a ban on the export of oil filters was justified by the imperative requirement of protection of the environment. Unlike Advocate General Jacobs, the Court apparently did not want to dismiss the possibility of applying Article 29 in this way out of hand: 'It must therefore be concluded that the object and effect of application of the principles of self-sufficiency and proximity to waste for recovery, such as oil filters, is to restrict exports of that waste and is not justified, in circumstances such as those in the present case, *by an imperative requirement relating to protection of the environment* or the desire to protect the health and life of humans in accordance with Article 36 [now Article 30 EC, authors] EC.'[123]

However, in *Sten & Grus* the Court ruled 'that the protection of the environment cannot serve to justify any restriction on exports'.[124] This seems to have settled the case. On the other hand, the quoted phrase should be read in context of the facts of the case. The Court was quite clear that the waste in *Sten & Grus* was non-hazardous and intended for recovery and that nothing has been put forward to the Court to show that there is a danger to the health and life of humans, animals or plants. As some commentators rightly put it, this leaves open the possibility that a restriction on exports might be justifiable for environmental reasons if the waste in question would cause environmental damage.[125]

If our interpretation is correct, the Court has significantly extended the possibilities of imposing restrictions on the free movement of goods based on environmental considerations. Some caution must nevertheless be exercised in interpreting this paragraph thus. However, in view of the extremely cautious wording of the paragraph, the conclusion might also be drawn that the Court simply did not want to rule on this point. We shall have to await further developments.

5.5 Other Aspects for the Application of the Exceptions

Non-economic purposes only

It is established case law of the Court that Article 30 EC and the rule of reason may only be used for non-economic purposes. It should not be ruled out that in some cases a particular measure, even though its primary function is protection of health or the environment, will also aim to achieve a certain economic objective. This is particularly true of export restrictions in the waste sector. One of the reasons for Member States to prohibit the export of waste is to ensure that their own national waste disposal installations can operate profitably. There is always the danger that, as a result of the export of large quantities of waste, the capacity of national disposal installations will be greater than the demand for waste disposal. This can result in under-utilised national

---

[123] Emphasis added by the authors. Cf. the case note of Notaro in [1999] *CMLRev.* 1317-1319.

[124] Case C-209/98 *Sydhavnens Sten & Grus* [2000] ECR I-3743, paras. 48.

[125] Davies (2004) at 208 and Notaro (2000) at 310-311.

waste disposal capacity, driving up prices of waste disposal, and creating even more waste exports. To avoid this, some Member States want to restrict the export of waste, improving the supply for their own national disposal installations.

> The question which arises here is whether the economic profitability of waste disposal installations falls within the scope of Article 30 EC. The judgments of the Court, particularly in the *Inter-Huiles*, *Nertsvoederfabriek* and *Dusseldorp* cases, show that this poses its own problems.[126] The *Inter-Huiles* case concerned French legislation, according to which all waste oil must be delivered to officially authorised waste oil collectors. The French Government argued that the disputed legislation satisfied an economic requirement, since only the collection of all waste oils is sufficient to ensure the profitability of undertakings approved for the disposal of waste oils. The Court did not accept that argument: 'Articles 13 and 14 of the directive provide that, by way of compensation for the obligations imposed on the undertakings for the implementation of Article 5, Member States may, without placing restrictions on exports, grant such undertakings "indemnities" financed in accordance with the principle of "polluter pays".'

It is impossible to draw any too far-reaching conclusions from this. In this particular case the argument that the measure was necessary to ensure the profitability of waste disposal installations was rejected because the directive itself provided for other instruments to protect this interest. The judgment cannot be seen as implying a general preference for financial incentives rather than non-tariff instruments.

> Another relevant Court judgment can be found in the *Nertsvoederfabriek* case. A Dutch law required poultry offal to be delivered only to licensed rendering plants. This law implied a prohibition of exports. The Netherlands Government argued that the law was essential in order to maintain the overall effectiveness of the system. As the Court acknowledged, referring to an earlier judgment: 'The mere fact that national provisions, justified by objective circumstances corresponding to the needs of the interests referred to therein, enable other objectives of an economic nature to be achieved as well, does not exclude the application of Article 36 [now Article 30 EC, authors]. That applies with greater force where the objective of an economic nature necessarily enables the objective relating to health to be attained.'

In this case the implied prohibition of exports could not be maintained, because another condition was not met. The Court held that it does not appear necessary to prohibit the exportation of poultry offal, provided that the conditions relating

---

[126] Case 172/82 *Inter-Huiles* [1983] ECR 555, Case C-203/96 *Dusseldorp* [1998] ECR I-4075 and Case 118/86 *Nertsvoederfabriek* [1987] ECR 3883.

to health laid down by those provisions are satisfied with respect to removal and transport on national territory.

In the *Dusseldorp* case the Court explicitly rejected the Dutch Government's argument concerning the profitability of waste processing plant. The Netherlands had argued that the measures in question were necessary to provide the Dutch waste company with sufficient waste to be able to operate profitably, and to ensure that it received a sufficient supply of oil filters for use as fuel. In the absence of sufficient supply, the company would have been obliged to use a less environmentally friendly fuel. The Court responded as follows:

> 'Even if the national measure in question could be justified by reasons relating to the protection of the environment, it is sufficient to point out that the arguments put forward by the Netherlands Government, concerning the profitability of the national undertaking AVR Chemie and the costs incurred by it, are of an economic nature. The Court has held that aims of a purely economic nature cannot justify barriers to the fundamental principle of the free movement of goods'.

It is worth noting that the Court did not desire to link the profitability test with an underlying environmental objective. Surely it could be argued that, ultimately, the export ban was not designed to ensure AVR's profitability, but that it was a prerequisite to achieving certain environmental goals (adequate waste disposal). There are other judgments where the Court has indeed considered the underlying aims.[127]

In the light of all this case law, the conclusion must be that Article 30 EC and the rule of reason do not seem to allow Member States to restrict the export of waste to ensure the profitability of their national waste disposal installations. More general, the condition that Article 30 EC and the rule of reason may only be used for non-economic purposes can pose a serious obstacle for the Member States. However, Article 86(2) EC may be used to do just this.[128]

The proportionality principle

It is clear from the judgments of the Court that national measures restricting the free movement of goods, but which are in principle capable of being justified under Article 30 EC or the rule of reason, must be compatible with the proportionality principle. This principle involves two or possibly three different aspects, which are discussed below.

In the first place the national measure must be *suitable* actually to protect the interest to be protected. In the environment field this means there must be a causal link between the measure and the protection of the environment. It is hardly surprising that this hurdle rarely proves difficult to cross. After all, why should a Member State desiring to protect a particular interest not adopt

---

[127] For example, Case C-324/93 *Evans Medical* [1995] ECR I-563, Case 118/86 *Nertsvoederfabriek* [1987] ECR 3883 and, on waste disposal (!), Case C-209/98 *Sydhavnens Sten & Grus* [2000] ECR I-3743.

[128] Cf. Chapter 7, section 6.2.

an effective measure? Nevertheless, this criterion does give the Court a means of acting against measures which are presented as necessary for the protection of the environment, but are essentially protectionist. The measure taken or proposed must be appropriate actually to protect the interest that requires protection and to avert the danger to the health of humans, animals or plants. A national measure is certainly not allowed if it does not, or could not, have the desired effect.

The causal link between the measure and the environmental objective which is required should be demonstrated by the Member States by reference to relevant science. However the precautionary principle may in some cases justify a measure even where the causal link cannot be clearly established on the basis of the scientific evidence available.[129] It is not entirely clear how strict the Court is in respect of the required causal link. Is it sufficient that the measure has some positive effect on the interest to be protected, or must more be required?

> In the *Red Grouse* case, Advocate General Van Gerven discussed the question whether the Dutch prohibition of imports would actually have a positive effect on the protection of the species outside the Netherlands.[130] His reply was affirmative: 'There is a possibility that the prohibition of imports into the Netherlands may reduce demand for dead birds of the species in question from the United Kingdom and thereby exert a positive influence on the population of that species in the Member State in which it occurs; in other words, there may to some extent be a causal connection between the measure in question and the objective pursued.'

'Positive influence' and 'to some extent a causal connection' were thus sufficient, in his view, to regard the measure as acceptable in this respect.

In the *Danish Bottles* case the Court was particularly concerned to assess whether the measure could be regarded as necessary.[131] The Court examined the connection between the mandatory deposit-and-return system and the attainment of environmental objectives:

> 'First of all, as regards the obligation to establish a deposit-and-return system for empty containers, it must be observed that this requirement is an indispensable element of a system intended to ensure the re-use of containers and therefore appears necessary to achieve the aims pursued by the contested rules.'

The causal connection is not always explicitly examined, as it was in this case. In most cases the causal relation is so obvious and unproblematic that the Court does not need to examine it explicitly.

---

[129] Cf. Case C-473/98 *Kemikalieninspektionen v. Toolex Alpha AB* [2000] ECR I-5681, paras. 41-45.

[130] Case C-169/89 *Gourmetterie v.d. Burg* [1990] ECR I-2143.

[131] Case 302/86 *Commission v. Denmark* [1988] ECR 4607.

Secondly, a measure must be *necessary* in the sense that it restricts trade as little as possible; there must be no measures less restrictive, but adequate, available. Possible alternative national instruments will first be assessed in the light of the question: would they or would they not protect the interest similar[132] or equally effective? If the answer is that they would, the question must then be addressed which of these instruments would entail the least negative effects for market integration. This also implies that the mere fact that other Member States have less strict rules or have chosen a different system of protection, does not necessarily mean that the proportionality principle has been violated.[133]

> In the *Danish Bottles* case the Court expressed the necessity requirement as follows: 'Such rules must also be proportionate to the aim in view. If a Member State has a choice between various measures for achieving the same aim, it should choose the means which least restricts the free movements of goods.' And, referring to its judgment in the *ADBHU* case: 'Measures adopted to protect the environment must not "go beyond the inevitable restrictions which are justified by the pursuit of the objective of environmental protection".'[134]

The Court then proceeded to review the compatibility of the mandatory system of collection and return of containers with the principle of proportionality it had thereby formulated. Having observed, as regards the obligation to establish a deposit-and-return system for empty containers, that this requirement was an indispensable element of a system intended to insure the re-use of containers and therefore appeared necessary to achieve the aim pursued, it concluded: 'That being so, the restrictions which it imposes on the free movement of goods cannot be regarded as disproportionate.' Here the causal connection was examined simultaneously with the test of proportionality.

> In the *Crayfish* case, the German Government fell foul of the Court's review of a measure in the light of the necessity test.[135] According to the Federal Law on the Protection of Nature (*Bundesnaturschutzgesetz*) the importation of live crayfish for commercial purposes is in principle prohibited. However, the competent public authority may, on application, derogate from that prohibition where the application of the law would, contrary to the legislator's intention, lead to excessive hardship. The German Government argued that the import restrictions were needed for the effective protection of native species of crayfish against disease and the risks of faunal distortion. The Commission submitted that this objective could have been achieved by measures having less restrictive effects on intra-EU trade. For example, instead of simply prohibiting imports of all species of live fresh-

---

[132] Cf. Case C-297/05 *Commission v. Netherlands*, judgment of 20 September 2007, n.y.r. in the ECR, para. 79.

[133] Cf. Case C-227/02 *EU Wood Trading* [2004] ECR I-11957, paras. 51-52.

[134] Case 240/83 *ADBHU* [1985] ECR 531.

[135] Case C-131/93 *Commission v. Germany* [1994] ECR I-3303.

water crayfish, Germany could have confined itself to making consignments of crayfish from other Member States or already in free circulation in the EU subject to health checks and only carrying out checks by sample if such consignments were accompanied by a health certificate issued by the competent authorities of the dispatching Member State certifying that the product in question presented no risk to health, or instead confined itself to regulating the marketing of crayfish in its territory, in particular by subjecting to authorisation only the restocking of national waters with species likely to be carrying the disease and restricting release of animals in the wild and restocking areas in which native species are to be found. The Court of Justice agreed with the Commission: 'However, the Federal Government has not convincingly shown that such measures, involving less serious restrictions for intra-Community trade, were incapable of effectively protecting the interests pleaded.' In view of the *Crayfish* case one could argue that there exist a presumption against total bans.

In *Toolex* however the Court was more lenient towards Swedish legislation which laid down a general prohibition on the use of trichloroethylene for industrial purposes and established a system of individual exemptions, granted subject to conditions.[136] In particular the Court accepted the so called 'substitution principle' according to which an exemption is granted only on the condition that no safer replacement product is available and provided that the applicant continues to seek alternative solutions which are less harmful to public health and the environment.

The more general conclusion that can be drawn from these judgments is that *general prohibitions* on imports of goods and products which will be harmful to the environment or pose a threat to health will not easily pass the proportionality test. Most of the time, the Court lays the burden of proof on the Member States. They must be able to show convincingly that the less stringent alternatives suggested by for instance the Commission are not adequate to protect the environment or health equally effectively. By implication, Member States are also under a duty to examine carefully the possibility of using measures less restrictive.[137] In other words, Member States who did not even contemplate the possibility of taking less restrictive measures *ex ante* will fail this part of the proportionality test already at the beginning.

In the area of national legislation on pesticides and biocides we come across the following, very specific, application of the necessity test. Although the Court allowed restrictions on the marketing of such products and held that Member State are free to require such products which have already received approval in another Member State to undergo a fresh procedure of examination and approval, the proportionality principle requires:

'that technical or chemical analyses or laboratory tests are not unnecessarily required when the same analyses and tests have already been carried out in that

<hr>

[136] Case C-473/98 *Kemikalieninspektionen* v. *Toolex Alpha AB* [2000] ECR I-5681.

[137] Case C-320/03 *Commission* v. *Austria* [2005] ECR I-9871, para. 87.

other Member State and their results are available to the competent authorities of the importing Member State or can, at their request, be made available to them.'[138]

Some authors argue that there is a third criterion to the application of the principle of proportionality. Would a measure be disproportionate if the obstacles resulting for intra-EU trade were not proportionate to the object intended or the result achieved (proportionality *stricto sensu*)? The problem will become clear if placed against the background of the Court's considerations in the *Danish Bottles* case.[139]

> The different arguments put forward in the case are both interesting and of practical relevance. The Commission considered that it follows from the principle of proportionality that the level of protection should not be fixed exaggeratedly high and that other solutions should be accepted even if they are a little less effective in assuring the aim pursued.[140] By implication, this means that interests such as the environment and public health must be weighed in the same balance as the interest of free movement of goods. The United Kingdom supported this view. Protection of the environment is indeed one of the important objectives of the EC, but it does not follow that every measure adopted for the protection of the environment is *prima facie* justified and that it only remains to examine whether the same results could be achieved by alternative means. The effect of such a view would be that measures to eliminate all forms of pollution would always be justified, since it would be obvious that very often similarly effective results could not be obtained by other means: 'It is submitted that there must be a point beyond which measures for the protection of the environment can no longer be regarded as fulfilling one of the Community's essential objectives and that a balance between protection of the environment and the free movement of goods must be sought in accordance with the case law of the Court.' Advocate General Slynn expressed a similar view: 'There has to be a balancing of interests between the free movement of goods and environmental protection, even if in achieving the balance the high standard of the protection sought has to be reduced. The level of protection sought must be a reasonable level.'

Advocate General Van Gerven took more or less the same view in the *Red Grouse* case.[141] In his view, two tests of proportionality ought to be carried out in connection with Article 30 EC. He referred to the first of these as the criterion of the least restrictive alternative. Together, review in the light of this criterion and

---

[138] Case C-400/96 *Harpegnies* [1998] ECR I-5121, para. 36.

[139] Case 302/86 *Commission v. Denmark* [1988] ECR 4607.

[140] See however Commission Decision 98/523, OJ 1998 L 233/25 concerning certain noise-related restrictions affecting air carriers' access to the new Karlstad airport in Sweden. According to the Commission the proportionality principle requires merely 'an *adequate* level of protection against aircraft noise', para. 38 of the decision.

[141] Case C-169/89 *Gourmetterie v.d. Burg* [1990] ECR I-2143.

examination of the causal connection between the measure adopted and attainment of the aim pursued constituted the requirement of necessity. In addition, in his view, another test of proportionality was required. A measure which has a causal connection with the objective it pursues, and to which there is no less restrictive alternative, must subsequently be assessed in the light of the criterion of proportionality between the obstacle introduced and the objective pursued and/or the result actually achieved thereby. As a result of the application of that criterion, a Member State may be obliged to dispense with the measure in question or resign itself to a less effective one, where the restrictive effect of the first measure is disproportionate so far as the free movement of goods is concerned to the objective pursued by the measure or to the result actually achieved thereby. In other words, a measure taken to protect the life and health of humans, animals and plants may lose its lawfulness if its contribution to the protective aim is too little in the light of its restrictive effect on trade, even if there are no less restrictive measures available. In this view, proportionality implies that the interests named in Article 30 EC should be weighed against the free movement of goods. Van Gerven invoked the Court's decision in the *Danish Bottles* case to support his view.[142] The Court's considerations with respect to the requirement that only approved containers should be used do indeed seem to support this view:

> 'It is undoubtedly true that the existing system for returning approved containers ensures a maximum rate of re-use and therefore a *very considerable degree of protection of the environment* since empty containers can be returned to any retailer of beverages. Non-approved containers, on the other hand, can be returned only to the retailer who sold the beverages, since it is impossible to set up such a comprehensive system for those containers as well. Nevertheless, the system for returning non-approved containers *is capable of protecting the environment* and, as far as imports are concerned, affects only limited quantities of beverages compared with the quantity of beverages consumed in Denmark owing to the restrictive effect which the requirement that containers should be returnable has on imports.'

There is much to be said for applying the principle of proportionality only in the form of the suitability and necessity tests. This view receives support from considerations of the Court that, in the absence of common or harmonised rules on health and/or the environment, it was for the Member States to decide upon the level at which they wished to protect the health and life of animals, and the

---

[142] Case 302/86 *Commission* v. *Denmark* [1988] ECR 4607. See also, outside environmental law, where the Court seemed to have applied the proportionality *stricto sensu* test: Case C-169/91 *Council of the City of Stoke-on-Trent and Norwich City Council* v. *B & Q Plc* [1992] ECR I-6635 and Case C-112/00 *Schmidberger* [2003] ECR I-5659, para. 81. Cf. also Case C-413/99 *Baumbast* 2002 ECR I-7091.

environment.[143] The precautionary principle also points in this direction. In its guidelines on the precautionary principle the Commission argues that the EC has the right to establish the level of protection of the environment, human, animal and plant health that it deems appropriate.[144] If the EC is entitled to set its own level of protection, in particular vis-à-vis the other WTO members, it is hard to see how this right can be denied the Member States.

Other reasons for restricting the application of the proportionality principle are of a more 'constitutional' nature. The third variant (proportionality *stricto sensu*) is problematic, as it requires a weighing of interests, normally reserved for the legislature. The proper functioning of the internal market must be balanced against protection of the environment. This is not simply a matter of a proper separation of the functions of the judiciary and the legislature. In the European context, application of the proportionality principle also impinges on the division of powers between the EC and its Member States. After all, application of Article 30 EC, the rule of reason, etc. is by definition[145] only at issue where the European legislature has not yet taken any action. A weighing of interests in the context of the proportionality principle therefore implies that the courts must first decide on the level of protection in the EC and then balance this against the interest of market integration. This, moreover, in a situation in which the European legislature has not yet proved able to adopt legislation on the matter. This fact leads us to conclude that the courts should apply this variant of the proportionality principle with extreme caution.

This does not, of course, mean that all kinds of trade restrictions may now be introduced in the guise of environmental protection. In the first place, the 'no arbitrary discrimination and no disguised restriction on trade' tests can be applied to avoid this. At the same time the Court may require a degree of causal connection between the national measure and the environmental aim pursued. Such an assessment may be appropriate to measures which only indirectly and without any close connection produce a positive effect on the environment. But where an environmental interest is at stake which needs protection and the national measure in question is indeed capable of providing it, the lawfulness of the measure should not be capable of being questioned merely because the free movement of goods is seriously restricted.

Proportionality after minimum harmonisation?

In Chapter 3, section 4 with respect to minimum harmonisation we have noted that whenever Member States exercise their discretion by taking more stringent national environmental standards, this is made subject to an important condition. More stringent measures are permitted inasmuch as other provisions of the Treaty are not involved. Should the more stringent measures

---

[143] See Case C-131/93 *Commission v. Germany* [1994] ECR I-3303, para. 16, and Case 272/80 *Frans-Nederlandse Maatschappij voor Biologische Producten* [1981] ECR 3277, para. 12. Cf. Krämer (2007) at 106-110.

[144] Communication from the Commission on the precautionary principle; COM (2000) 1 final.

[145] See for a detailed discussion Chapter 3, section 2.

come into conflict with the Treaty prohibitions regarding the internal market, for instance, then a review of proportionality is in fact carried out; this occurs as part of the examination whether the national measures are justified. An example from the case law is the judgment of the Court of Justice in *Aher-Waggon*.[146]

In 1992, Aher-Waggon bought a propeller-driven Piper PA 28-140 aircraft in Denmark which had been registered in that State since 1974. Subsequently, it requested the German *Bundesamt* to register the aircraft in Germany. This request was refused, on the ground that the aircraft exceeded the noise limits permitted in Germany. The aircraft did comply with the relevant European standard (73 dB(A)), however, with a sound level of 72.2 dB(A), it exceeded the German thresholds (69 dB(A)). Aher-Waggon was unsuccessful in its action before the *Verwaltungsgericht* (Administrative Court) and on appeal. In an application for review on a point of law (*Revision*) before the *Bundesverwaltungsgericht*, Aher-Waggon held that the refusal to register the aircraft in Germany was a breach of European law. It based this on the fact that aircraft of the same type and sound level that were already registered in Germany retained their registration.

The Court first determined that the directive only laid down minimum requirements, and thus allowed the Member States to adopt stricter noise limits.[147] Here, however, the possibility of applying the principle of proportionality is not excluded. The reason is that in this case the stricter limits have a negative effect on the free movement of goods, and should in principle be considered measures having equivalent effect under Article 28 EC. The question that then arises is what influence the minimum level of protection laid down in the directive has, or should have, on the manner in which the proportionality principle is applied. We would argue that in such cases a stricter review on the basis of the proportionality principle is appropriate. After all, from the moment there is a directive with minimum standards, these standards must be considered to offer an adequate or even 'a high level of protection'. Otherwise the directive itself might be considered to fail the 'suitability' test and infringe the principle of proportionality! But, if the standards of the directive provide an adequate level of protection, how can stricter national measures be *necessary*? Surely it must be assumed that a Member State infringes the principle of proportionality when in fact there is nothing to protect. Member States may in principle be allowed to determine the desired level of protection, but obviously there must be something to protect. This aspect, in particular, could be reviewed more intensively by the Court in cases of European minimum standards.

So, what is the best way of dealing with the review – in light of the principle of proportionality – of stricter national measures that involve a breach of one of

---

[146] Case C-389/96 *Aher-Waggon* [1998] ECR I-4473. Cf. also Case C-510/99 *Tridon* [2001] ECR I-7777, where stricter national rules in the area of endangered species of animals and plants were reviewed in the light of the rules on free movement of goods.

[147] Case C-389/96 *Aher-Waggon* [1998] ECR I-4437.

the free movement provisions of the EC Treaty? As mentioned, in such cases a more intensive review in light of the principle of proportionality seems appropriate, precisely because account must be taken of the level of protection already realised by the relevant directive.[148] In order to demonstrate the necessity of the national measures, the Member State will usually have to demonstrate why the protection offered by the directive does not offer a solution in its specific case. In other words, is there such an exceptional situation that the Member State feels it must disregard the level of protection of the directive, and adopt more stringent measures? In such cases, therefore, we would advocate a similar proportionality review to that laid down by the EC Treaty in the framework of Article 95(5) EC for national measures derogating from harmonisation measures. This is notwithstanding the fact that it may be questioned whether the Court actually does carry out a more intensive proportionality review in these kinds of cases.[149]

Diagonal proportionality?

A problem which has likewise not been solved in the Court's interpretation of the principle of proportionality is the extent to which the principle should be applied *diagonally*, in other words across Treaty provisions. What this means can be illustrated as follows. It has been noted above that where national authorities impose justified trade restrictions, they should in any event choose the least restrictive policy instrument. A system of authorisations is to be preferred above a total prohibition; an obligation to give notification above a system of authorisations. However, these examples concern instruments which have been applied within the context of a particular Treaty provision (or group of provisions). Diagonal proportionality assumes that it is important that there should be no 'less restrictive alternative' not only in the light of Articles 28 to 30 EC, but also in the light of the other Treaty provisions. Thus, in the case of a non-tariff restriction, in the light of Article 90 or Articles 87 and 88 EC. In other words, a given non-tariff restriction might conflict with the proportionality principle, even if there were no less restrictive non-tariff instrument, where there was an appropriate tariff instrument which would produce a less restrictive effect. Diagonal proportionality presupposes that public authorities examine a wide range of potential alternatives each time they wish to use certain restrictive policy instruments. It is not clear from the case law of the Court of Justice whether, and if so to what extent, the principle of proportionality operates in this way.

---

[148] See also, but then in the framework of Article 95 EC [then Article 100a EC, authors], Advocate General Tesauro: 'The control entrusted to the Community institutions by Article 100a(4), on the other hand, seems necessarily to be inspired by more stringent criteria than those underlying the provisions of Article 36 [now Article 30 EC], in that there is no possibility of not taking account of the standards of protection already laid down by the harmonization rules'; Case C-41/93 *France* v. *Commission* [1994] ECR I-1829, para. 6 of his Opinion.

[149] Neither in *Aher-Wagonn*, nor in *Tridon* did the Court clarify whether it carried out a more intensive review of proportionality than normal.

The transfrontier application of the exceptions

To what extent can Member States justify trade restrictions by invoking the grounds for justification formulated in the *Cassis de Dijon*[150] and *Danish Bottles*[151] cases, where it is not their own protective interests which are at stake, but those of other states or Member States, or even global environmental interests? In other words, to what extent can Article 30 EC and the rule of reason be applied 'transfrontier'.

Obviously, many environmental interests are of a transfrontier nature. In many cases, protection of the environment can no longer be regarded as a strictly national matter. The transfrontier nature of the environment has been acknowledged by the European legislature, for example in the many directives that have been enacted in which the Member States undertake obligations to prevent and control transfrontier pollution. It would be in contradiction of this if the lawfulness of national measures implying trade restrictions were again to be sharply divided into national categories. In this connection, Article 174(1) EC, fourth indent, is relevant, where dealing with regional or worldwide environmental problems is defined as a Community environmental objective. This demonstrates that responsibility for the environment is not tied to strict national boundaries.

On the one hand it could be argued that the grounds for justification should be interpreted strictly and that only measures to protect the interests of the Member State in question are covered. In this view Member States should 'mind their own business'. This was the view taken by Advocate General Trabucchi. Article 30 EC allows every State the right to protect exclusively its own national interests, he stated in his Opinion in *Dassonville*.[152] He elaborated this view in the *Kramer* case.[153] Talking of the spirit and purpose of this exempting clause, he referred to 'the genuinely unilateral character', confined to a particular State, which results from the fact that the interest for which Article 30 EC provides protection is essentially national and internal to the State. In his view, this particular function of Article 30 EC resisted a broader interpretation. He was, however, prepared to make an exception for those interests which, though not strictly national interests, could be regarded, by their nature, as common to all the Member States and which should therefore be regarded as Community interests. The interest involved in the *Kramer* case was the protection of fishery resources.

The Court seems to have endorsed Trabucchi's view on the use of Article 30 EC to protect the common interests of the Member States or even the world community as such in the *PreussenElektra* case.[154] The Court ruled that promoting the use of renewable energy sources for producing electricity 'is useful for

---

[150] Case 120/78 *Rewe-Zentral AG* [1979] ECR 649.

[151] Case 302/86 *Commission* v. *Denmark* [1988] ECR 4607.

[152] Case 8/74 *Dassonville* [1974] ECR 837.

[153] Joined Cases 3, 4 and 6/76 *Kramer* [1976] ECR 1279.

[154] Case C-379/98 *PreussenElektra* [2001] ECR I-2099.

protecting the environment in so far as it contributes to the reduction in emissions of greenhouse gases'. It also referred explicitly, in accepting the German rules, to United Nations Framework Convention on Climate Change and the Kyoto Protocol.

Arguably the same can be said with respect to the application of Article 30 EC in cases related to the protection of endangered or migratory species and protected habitats. In Chapter 3 we have discussed the case law of the Court of Justice regarding the implementation of the Wild Birds and Habitats directives. In view of the Court's opinion that those directives concern typically 'a transfrontier environment problem entailing common responsibilities for the Member States',[155] we must assume that Member States must also be allowed to rely on Article 30 EC to protect their common heritage. In his Opinion in the *Red Grouse* case, Advocate General Van Gerven argued that the transfrontier nature of the protection of birds was such that he considered it sufficient to assume that a Member State could rely on the concern for animal life in another Member State to justify a restriction on the free movement of goods.[156]

> That case concerned a prohibition on keeping or selling birds, including red grouse, under Article 7 of the Dutch *Vogelwet* (Law on Birds). The Netherlands *Hoge Raad* had referred the matter to the Court for a preliminary ruling on whether such a prohibition was justified under Article 30 EC. In principle, like the Commission and the Netherlands Government, Van Gerven regarded transfrontier application as possible, though he felt that the proportionality principle must be assessed even more stringent in such cases. He assumed that a Member State would adopt a restrictive measure 'having regard to the requirements of mutual confidence under the legislation of other Member States, where the measure adopted relates primarily to an interest located in those States.'

The Court might have given further clarification of the possibilities of transfrontier application of Article 30 EC in this case but it did not.[157] It observed that the Court had consistently held that a directive providing for full harmonisation of national legislation deprives a Member State of recourse to Article 30 EC. After discussing the directive in question, the Court concluded that the directive did regulate exhaustively the Member States' powers with regard to the conservation of wild birds. Member States are not authorised to adopt stricter protective measures in respect of a species of bird which does not occur in the territory of the legislating Member State but is found in another Member State where it may lawfully be hunted under the terms of the directive and under the legislation of that other State, and which is neither migratory nor endangered within the meaning of the directive. In other words, the directive's regulation of the conservation of wild birds, not being migratory birds nor birds threatened with

---

[155] E.g. Case 262/85 *Commission v. Italy* [1987] ECR 3073 and Case C-6/04 *Commission v. UK* [2005] ECR I-9017.

[156] Case C-169/89 *Gourmetterie v.d. Burg* [1990] ECR I-2143.

[157] Case C-169/89 *Gourmetterie v.d. Burg* [1990] ECR I-2143.

extinction, is exhaustive for those Member States where the birds in question do not normally occur. Application of Article 30 EC is therefore not at issue. The Court's approach is thus not clear on this point. At best it could be argued that the distinction made by the Court between migratory birds and endangered birds does not entirely rule out the transfrontier application of Article 30 EC.

With respect to endangered species, the *Tridon* case, is also of particular interest.[158] The case concerned French stricter measures than those laid down by the CITES Regulation. According to the French Government, the protection of captive born and bred specimens was necessary because the breeding of those species for commercial purposes could have marked negative effects on the conservation in the natural state of the species concerned. Such breeding would enable a real market to be created. To meet the demand created by such a market, there would be a great temptation to collect birds or eggs in their natural habitat. In *Tridon* the Court seemed to have accepted the French plea, subject to the proportionality principle only.

When 'common responsibilities' are absent, the extra-territorial application of Article 30 EC seems more problematic. Old and new case law of the Court of Justice is not clear in this respect.

> The *Inter-Huiles* case may offer some indication that the Court takes a wider view of the territorial extent of grounds which will justify trade restrictions.[159] In that case the French Government refused to allow the import of waste oil in part because it feared environmental damage in Belgium. The Court, considering the French Government's argument that the rules in question were justified by the need to protect the environment, stated: 'That argument cannot be accepted. Clearly, the environment is protected just as effectively when the oils are sold to an authorized disposal or regenerating undertaking of another Member State as when they are disposed of in the Member State of origin.'

This could be taken to imply that, if the interest invoked by the state of origin was not already adequately protected in the receiving state, protective measures might be justified. This is however somewhat speculative. Although the *Inter-Huiles* case could be said to provide some support for the transfrontier application of Article 30 EC, the *Nertsvoederfabriek* case does not.[160] That case concerned a prohibition on the exportation of poultry offal. This could not be justified on the grounds of public health, because 'it does not appear necessary to prohibit the exportation of poultry offal, provided that the conditions relating to health laid down by those provisions are satisfied with respect to removal and transport on national territory.' Protection of foreign territory is apparently exclusively a matter for the foreign state.

---

[158] Case C-510/99 *Tridon* [2001] ECR I-7777.

[159] Case 172/82 *Inter-Huiles* [1983] ECR 555.

[160] Case 118/86 *Nertsvoederfabriek* [1987] ECR 3883.

More recent are the following cases. Advocate General Léger discussed the issue of extraterritorial application at length in *Hedley Lomas* and *Compassion in World Farming*.[161] In his view a Member State can rely on Article 30 EC only to ensure protection of an interest safeguarded by that provision within its own national territory. However, the Court again refused to answer the question whether extraterritorial application of Article 30 EC was possible.[162] In *Compassion in World Farming* it repeated its position in *Hedley Lomas* and *Red Grouse* that recourse to Article 30 EC is no longer possible where European directives provide for harmonisation of the measures necessary to achieve the specific objective which would be furthered by reliance upon that provision.[163] However, it may be possible to detect a shift in the Court's position in *Dusseldorp*, a case in which Dutch restrictions on the export of oil filters were held incompatible with Article 176 EC in the light of Articles 29 and 30 EC. The Dutch Government argued that the restrictions could be justified under Article 30 as concerning the protection of the health and life of humans. The Court did not agree, stating: 'Such a justification would be relevant if the processing of oil filters in other Member States and their shipment over a greater distance as a result of their being exported posed a threat to the health and life of humans.'[164] The interesting thing is, of course, that this observation, placed in the context of the possible justification of an export ban, might imply that Member States were also entitled to restrict the free movement of goods, even if the threat was to the health and life of persons in other Member States. Let it suffice to note that, again, the Court has not explicitly ruled on this form of extraterritorial application of Article 30 EC and we shall have to await further developments on this point, too.

In our view transfrontier application of Article 30 EC and the rule of reason should in principle be possible in particular where common interests are at state. However, Member States must bear in mind that the protection of health and/or the environment in other states is primarily the responsibility of those states. It could be added that this primary responsibility will tend to blur the greater the transfrontier, and thus common, nature of the interest to be protected.

There is an additional problem in respect of states outside the EU. Free movement of goods also applies to products coming from third countries which are in free circulation in Member States, according to Article 23(2) EC. Applying Article 30 EC more widely than allowed under the WTO rules is thus problematic. This should therefore be taken into account where Article 30 EC is applied transfrontier.[165]

---

[161] Case C-5/94 *Hedley Lomas* [1996] ECR I-2553 and Case C-1/96 *Compassion in World Farming* [1998] ECR I-1251.

[162] Case C-5/94 *Hedley Lomas* [1996] ECR I-2553.

[163] Case C-1/96 *Compassion in World Farming* [1998] ECR I-1251.

[164] And repeated in Case C-209/98 *Sydhavnens Sten & Grus* [2000] ECR I-3743, para. 45. Cf. Davies (2004) at 214.

[165] Cf. on this issue Wiers (2002).

CHAPTER 7

Environment and Competition

1   General Remarks

In the first chapter we have seen that one of the fundamentals of European environmental policy is the 'polluter pays' principle. When fully applied, this principle means that the negative effects of production and consumption are translated into costs. This is called the internalisation of environmental costs. This internalisation allows the price mechanism to perform its signaling function.[1] More polluting products will become more expensive, and as a result there will be less consumption of these environmentally unfriendly products. This in turn will encourage more environmentally friendly production as well as research and development of more environmentally friendly production methods and products, thus putting the economy on a structurally less polluting path and leading to sustainable development.[2]

From the point of view of environmental protection, some competitive pressure is therefore necessary, as this pushes firms most effectively to minimise their environmental costs and thus reduce environmental pressure.

However, the polluter pays principle is by no means fully applied at the present time. Because adequate standards do not exist, some environmental costs are still not, or only partially, reflected in the price. Moreover, some environmental effects are partially internalised in some jurisdictions whereas other impacts on the environment may not be internalised and other jurisdictions may not apply the 'polluter pays' principle at all. In those cases there will be a distortion of the level playing field. Consider for example the situation in which the environmental effects of steel production have been internalised in one Member State while the environmental impact of the production of other metals has not been translated into costs. The result will be that steel production in one Member State will be more expensive compared to steel production in other Member States. Furthermore, the production of aluminum, which may be just as polluting, will be relatively cheaper. As a result, measures that internalise environmental costs in one Member State will not come about, as no government would willfully put its own industry out of business. The only way to make such a scheme palatable to both the people suffering from the pollution and the industry would be compensate the industry for the extra costs arising from the internalisation. However, such compensation may very well constitute state aid within the meaning of Article 87 EC. This is just one example of an internalisation of environmental costs leading to a distortion of the level playing field which in turn leads to a distortion or restriction of competition covered by the competition provisions in the EC Treaty.

The competition rules in the EC Treaty have two addressees: undertakings and Member States. Undertakings, a term that roughly translates into business enterprises, may conclude environmental agreements or they may abuse a domi-

---

[1]   XXIInd Competition Report, point 77 and XXIIIrd Competition Report, point 164.

[2]   XXIIIrd Competition Report, point 164.

nant market position for environmental reasons. Such practices fall within the compass of Articles 81 and 82 EC.

Member States may also restrict or distort competition for environmental purposes, as the example above shows. They may grant exclusive rights on environmental grounds, which would make Article 86 EC applicable or they could grant state aids, in which case Article 87 EC is relevant. The relation between environmental protection and Articles 81, 82, 86 and 87 EC will be examined below. However, first the fundamentals of competition law will be examined for their relation with environmental protection. The confines of this book make it impossible to give a complete overview of EC competition law. For this the reader is referred to other works.[3]

2　The Fundamentals of EC Competition Law

2.1　Market Definition

Determining whether a restriction or distortion of competition takes place requires a definition of the relevant market first.[4] The relevant market consists of a relevant product market and the relevant geographical market. Basically, the product market consists of all products that are substitutable or interchangeable from the perspective of the consumer and the producer.[5] This substitutability is determined by various practicalities such as the price, intended use for certain groups of consumers or rules to which the treatment of certain waste is subject.[6] Furthermore, environmental considerations may also play a role in defining the relevant product market. If, for example, consumers are willing to pay 10% more for organic vegetables, this would point at organic fruit constituting a separate product market with only limited substitutability from non-organic fruit. Similar considerations may also be relevant in defining the geographical market. In the *CECED* case the Commission found that the percentage of energy inefficient washing machines was higher in the UK and the southern Member States compared to the other Member States.[7] This could point to the fact that consumers in certain Member States did not consider energy efficiency of washing machines as important, which could make these states a separate geographical market.

---

[3]　See, for example, Jones & Sufrin (2004), Whish (2003).

[4]　See for example, Case 27/76 *UBC* v. *Commission (United Brands)* [1978] ECR 207, para. 10.

[5]　See for more details: Commission Notice on the Definition of the Relevant Market, OJ 1997 C 372/5.

[6]　Case C-209/98 *Sydhavnens* [2000] ECR I-3743, para. 61.

[7]　Decision 2000/475 *CECED*, OJ 2000 L 187/47, para. 17.

2.2 Undertaking

EC competition law applies only to undertakings. An undertaking has been defined as an entity engaged in an economic activity.[8] This raises the question to what extent environmental activities constitute economic activities. In *Diego Calì*, the Court was confronted with an Italian entity, SEPG, that was responsible for environmental protection in the port of Genoa.[9] According to Calì, SEPG was an undertaking that had abused its dominant position when it presented him with the bill for preventive environmental surveillance activities while no pollution whatsoever had occurred. According to the Court the preventive environmental surveillance constituted a task in the public interest which forms part of the essential functions of the State as regards protection of the environment in maritime areas.[10] It is important to note that the Court expressly distinguished between *preventive* surveillance and *curative* environmental services (which would be used once actual pollution had occurred). The latter would probably constitute an economic activity, whereas it is indeed very difficult to envisage a market for or competition in preventive environmental surveillance. Finally, experiences with the liberalisation of markets have shown that competition is indeed possible in areas of the economy that were previously thought to be domain of public service obligations and state intervention. As a result of the internalisation of environmental costs, environmental protection may indeed increasingly constitute an economic activity.

3 Article 81 EC[11]

3.1 Why Environmental Agreements exist and Restrict Competition

In a nutshell Article 81(1) EC prohibits coordination between undertakings that have as the object or effect to distort or restrict competition. This prohibition may be declared inapplicable on the basis of the third paragraph in case the agreement has certain positive effects that are considered more important than the restriction of competition. Before the details and elements of Article 81 are examined we will first establish why Article 81 EC is relevant in the environmental sphere.

Above it was shown how an internalisation of environmental costs may lead to a distortion of the level playing field that may in turn result in a reaction that falls under EC competition law. The same can happen with so-called

---

[8] Case C-41/90 *Höfner and Elser v. Macrotron* [1991] ECR I-1979, para. 21.

[9] Case C-343/95 *Diego Calì & Figli v. SEPG* [1997] ECR I-1547.

[10] Case C-343/95 *Diego Calì & Figli v. SEPG* [1997] ECR I-1547, para. 22.

[11] Cf. the renumbered Article 101 FEU after the entry into force of the Reform Treaty.

environmental agreements. This term is used to describe agreements between undertakings in order to protect the environment. These agreements may be purely voluntary, because companies realise that the environment is increasingly becoming a sales point, or they may be the result of government intervention. The ACEA environmental agreement, for example, was concluded among the European car manufacturers in order to avoid European legislation on this topic.[12] Environmental agreements may also be the result of legislation. The WEEE Directive, for example, explicitly envisages collective action from the industry as part of its implementation.[13]

So when a group of companies decides to collectively organise the collection and recycling of waste products, in order to meet the producer responsibility under the WEEE-Directive,[14] this will entail costs. In a competitive business environment all the parties will want to minimise their actual costs. Thus in order to prevent free riding, the situation where one or more companies do not make the actual investments themselves, but take a free ride on the investments of others, the companies will want to include some obligations in the environmental agreement. These obligations may restrict competition. They could relate to the passing on of the costs of the collection and recycling.[15] They could also concern the fixing of the price charged for the use of a collective take back and recycling system.[16] Finally, in the *CECED* case the restriction of competition took the form of a restriction of production, since the agreement prohibited the parties from manufacturing or importing energy inefficient washing machines. Again, this clause in the agreement was necessary because there is a demand for energy inefficient washing machines and in a stagnant market,[17] no company will willfully give up a business opportunity unless it is certain that its competitors will do the same.

3.2 Article 81(1) EC

Given that they want to prevent free riding, most environmental agreements will be in writing and signed by the parties. Alternatively, they will take the form of a decision of an industry association, an association of undertakings in Article 81 terminology. This hardly leads to questions concerning the applicability of Article 81(1) EC. Most competition problems with environmental agreements are the result of so-called horizontal agreements, i.e. agreements between competing undertakings in the same stage of produc-

---

[12] See press release IP/06/1134, where the Commission threatens to come with legislation should the agreement not lead to the results.

[13] Directive 2002/96, OJ 2002 L 37/24, notably recital 20 and Article 8(3) and 5(2)(c).

[14] See further Chapter 7, section 15.5

[15] This occurred in the Dutch *Wit en Bruingoed* case; see Vedder (2003) at 376 *et seq.*

[16] This was one of the restrictions in the *FKS* case; see Vedder (2003) at 383 *et seq.*

[17] Decision 2000/475 *CECED*, OJ 2000 L 187/47, para. 31.

tion, be it manufacture, distribution, retail or disposal. Examples of this kind of agreement in the field of the environment are:

- agreements in the sphere of *research and development* with a view to developing more environmentally friendly products, production processes or methods of disposal. See, for example, the *BBC Brown Boveri* case, concerning cooperation in developing sodium-sulphur high-performance batteries intended primarily for use in electrically driven vehicles. This was considered to restrict competition because the parties could no longer conclude research and development agreements with third parties in this field;[18]
- agreements that set up collective systems for waste collection, sorting and treatment. Pursuant to the Packaging Waste Directive, the packaging industry in most Member States has opted for collective systems to organise the collection and treatment of packaging waste. Examples are: the *Duales System Deutschland (DSD)*,[19] *Eco-emballages*,[20] *ARA/ARGEV/ARO*.[21] These systems allow companies that use packaging to pay a fee and then a green dot on their products, showing that the packaging will normally be sorted and can be recycled.[22] Competition concerns in these cases essentially involve exclusivities that have a foreclosure effect. Participating companies should be free to exit such green dot systems or joint a green dot system for only a part of their packaging waste. Furthermore, the companies that collect or treat the packaging waste on behalf of the green dot organisation should be free to decide how they market the processed waste;[23]
- agreements to protect the environment, for example to use the same environmentally friendly production processes, or not to use or manufacture certain harmful substances. An example may be the system created by the International Fruit Container Organization (IFCO) promoting re-usable plastic crates for the transport of fresh fruit and vegetables[24] or agreements between water bottlers to standardize bottles so as to enable them to comply with legislation requiring these bottles to be re-usable if a system for their recycling did not exist.[25]

---

[18] Decision 88/541 *BBC Brown Boveri*, OJ 1988 L 301/68.

[19] Decision 2001/837 *DSD* (Article 81), OJ 2001 L 319/1, This decision was unsuccessfully appealed in Case T-289/01 *Duales System Deutschland v. Commission*, judgment of 24 May 2007, n.y.r. in the ECR.

[20] Decision 2001/663 *Eco-Emballages*, OJ 2001 L 233/37.

[21] Decision 2004/208 *ARA/ARGEV/ARO*, OJ 2004 L 75/59.

[22] XXIIIrd Competition Report, point 168.

[23] See also Pons (2001).

[24] XXIIIrd Competition Report, point 168.

[25] XXIIIrd Competition Report, points 169 and 240.

The above examples show the diversity of competition problems arising from environmental agreements. For an agreement to be caught by Article 81(1) EC a number of further requirements needs to be fulfilled.

The most obvious requirement is that the agreement must entail a restriction of competition. Case law has specified this in that a restriction must be qualitatively or qualitatively appreciable. With quantitative appreciability the market share of the parties to the agreement is the guiding criterion. In its *de minimis* notice the Commission has set out that a horizontal agreement will appreciably restrict competition if the market share of the parties exceeds 10%.[26] In determining qualitative appreciability the substance of the agreement has to be analysed with regard to the question of to what extent the parties are still free to decide for themselves what their actions on the market will be. Both approaches to appreciability can be found in the Guidelines on Horizontal Agreements, which contain a chapter devoted to environmental agreements and Article 81 EC.[27]

In the Horizontals Guidelines the Commission distinguishes three categories of environmental agreements on the basis of the appreciability of the effects of a certain agreement on competition.[28] Agreements that do not directly limit the technical solutions open to parties and impose on the parties only loosely defined industry-wide targets will not appreciably restrict competition irrespective of the market share of the parties. The ACEA Agreement that imposes a general energy efficiency target on the European car manufacturers without limiting the means by which this target is to be achieved is an example of this type of agreement.[29] Needless to say, the environmental effectiveness of such agreements can be doubted. Agreements that do have a direct effect on the parties' choice of means to achieve environmental objectives or that influence marketing decisions, production processes or products may fall under Article 81(1) EC dependent on the market share of the parties. This is the reasoning that has been used in the *CECED* case, where the agreement involved a reduction of output in the form of restriction to market energy inefficient washing machines.[30] Finally, the Commission is of the opinion that environmental agreements that 'serve as a tool to engage in a disguised cartel' almost always fall under the prohibition. In this regard the Commission points to environmental agreements that involve price fixing or market sharing. An example of this type of case is the *VOTOB* case that involved tank storage undertakings in the Netherlands, which had agreed to impose a uniform environmental surcharge upon their consumers, in order to recoup the costs of environmental investments.[31]

---

[26] Commission Notice on Agreements of Minor Importance (*De Minimis*), OJ 2001C 368/13.

[27] OJ 2001 C 3/2, Chapter 7, hereafter Horizontals Guidelines.

[28] Horizontals Guidelines, sections 7.3.1.1 – 7.3.1.3.

[29] See further Vedder (2003) at 142.

[30] Decision 2000/475 CECED, OJ 2000 L 187/47.

[31] XXIInd Competition Report, point 177-186, see further Vedder (2003) at 157.

Apart from non-appreciability, environmental agreements can also be outside the scope of Article 81(1) EC on the basis of the *rule of reason* or because they benefit from a so-called state action defence.

Whether or not there is a rule of reason is uncertain, partly because of gnomic and contradictory judgments by the CFI and ECJ, and partly because of the Babel-like confusion between legal writers. In a nutshell, the rule of reason boils down to a balancing of pro-competitive and anti-competitive effects within Article 81(1) EC. Even though the European Courts have never explicitly recognised the existence of such a thing, the ECJ has certain employed reasoning that can best be characterised as a rule of reason. Furthermore the Commission appears also to use a rule of reason analysis where it states that agreements which give rise to genuine market creation, for instance recycling agreements, will not generally restrict competition, provided that the parties would not be capable of conducting the activities in isolation, whilst other alternatives and/or competitors do not exist.[32]

It must however be pointed out that this is a balancing of 'genuine market creation' (as a pro-competitive effect) with anti-competitive effects. This does not allow for environmental concerns to be balanced with anti-competitive effects. With the *Wouters* case this may be different. This case involved a restriction of competition for members of the bar that served the good functioning of their profession. In *Wouters* the Court balanced the restriction of competition with these public interest-related positive effects within the framework of Article 81(1) EC.[33] As a result, it would also seem possible to balance environmental effects with restrictions of competition as part of the first paragraph of Article 81 EC.[34] The integration principle laid down in Article 6 EC lends further support for this.

The 'state action defence' is available for so-called compulsory cartels. This refers to environmental agreements that have been forced upon the parties by public authorities.[35] Given the often close relation between government regulation and environmental agreements, it is conceivable that an environmental agreement is the result of 'conduct [that] was unilaterally imposed upon them by the national authorities through the exercise of irresistible pressures, such as, for example, the threat to adopt State measures likely to cause them to sustain substantial losses'.[36]

---

[32] Horizontals Guidelines, point 187.

[33] Case C-309/99 *Wouters* [2002] ECR I-1577, paras. 97-110. See further paras. 99-107 of the Opinion of Advocate General Léger.

[34] See further Vedder (2003) at 145 *et seq.*

[35] See for an application outside the environmental context: Case C-198/01 *CIF* [2003] ECR I-8055.

[36] Case T-387/94 *Asia Motor France* v. *Commission* [1996] ECR II-961, para. 65. In Joined Cases C-359/95P and C-379/95P *Commission and France* v. *Ladbroke* [1997] ECR I-6265, the ECJ employed a more stringent test.

Even if an environmental agreement is covered by the prohibition of Article 81(1) EC this does not mean that there is no room whatever for environmental protection in competition law. Such an interpretation would be contrary to the integration principle laid down in Article 6 EC, under which environmental protection requirements must be integrated into the definition and implementation of the Community's policies and activities. 'Competition must therefore, as much as any other Community policy, take account of environmental considerations'.[37] These environmental considerations could also be taken into account in the application of Article 81(3) EC.

3.3   Article 81(3) EC

On the basis of Article 81(3) EC, in connection with Regulation 1/2003,[38] the prohibition of Article 81(1) EC may be declared inapplicable by the Commission, Member State competition authorities and national judges. This can only happen if the following conditions are met:

- · the agreement contributes to improving the production or distribution of goods or to promoting technical or economic progress;
- · it allows consumers a fair share of the resulting benefit;
- · the restriction of competition is indispensable to the attainment of the benefits;
- · competition is not eliminated in respect of a substantial part of the products in question.

Concerning the application of the integration principle of Article 6 EC in connection with Article 81(3) EC, two consequences are worth noting. In the first place it can be said that, under the integration principle, environmental protection aims should play a part in the normal criteria that have to be taken into account in assessing an agreement on the basis of Article 81(3) EC. The degree to which Article 81(3) EC allows this will be discussed below. In the second place it is legitimate to ask whether Article 81(3) EC could be applied if this would have serious environmental effects. In principle it could be argued that this would be inconsistent with the integration principle.[39] Such negative environmental effects would certainly have to be taken into account, but this does not mean that the applicability of Article 81(3) EC is ruled out completely. These effects should be taken into account and carefully balanced against the other interests involved. Following the entry into force of Regulation 1/2003 an interesting question is to what extent national judges are bound by the integration principle. Article 6 EC does not have any particular addressees, but is confined to 'the Community activities and policies referred to in Article 3

---

[37] XXIIIrd Competition Report, point 162.

[38] OJ 2003 L1/1.

[39] Cf. Vedder (2003) at 185 *et seq.*

EC'. The question therefore is to what extent national judges directly applying Community law are in fact defining and implementing Community policies and activities. The Court's case law that characterises national judges as decentralised Community judges when they apply directly effective Community law probably indicates an affirmative answer to this question.

3.3.1   Promoting Technical or Economic Progress

The question at issue here is whether – and to what extent – environmental protection can be regarded as 'technical or economic progress'. Even without an integration principle, environmental improvements can be seen as technical improvements for the simple reason that such products are technically more advanced. These technical/environmental improvements may relate to a relatively 'clean' production process, an environmentally friendly use of a product, or a less polluting form of disposal. The so-called life-cycle approach is a central feature of both national and European[40] product policy. The presence of the integration principle only strengthens this, as is evidenced by the Commission's decision-making practice, where even prior to the introduction of the integration principle, environmental considerations were taken into account. In the 1983 *Carbon Gas Technologie* decision, concerning a cooperation agreement for the purpose of developing a combined pressure gasification process using run-of-mine coal, the fact that the Commission regarded the process as 'less harmful to the environment' was one of the arguments for deciding that the prohibition on competition contributes to the promotion of technical and economic progress.[41] The Commission also found that environmental improvements contributed to technical and economic progress in *BBC Brown Boveri*,[42] *Assurpol*,[43] and *Ford/Volkswagen*.[44] In *ARA/ARGEV/ARO*, however, Article 81(3) EC was applied to an environmental agreement on primarily economic grounds.[45]

Much more interesting is the *CECED* case where the environmental improvements were not just taken into account, but in fact constituted the technical and economic progress by themselves.[46] Partly in line with its reasoning in the Horizontals Guidelines, the Commission first translates the environmental benefits into an economic benefit.[47] In *CECED* this meant that the phasing out of energy inefficient washing machines resulted in avoided carbon dioxide emissions and thus avoided costs. Moreover, the Commission also calculated

---

[40] E.g. Regulation 1980/2000 on a revised Community eco-label award scheme, OJ 2000 L 237/1.

[41] Decision 83/669 *Carbon Gas Technologie*, OJ 1983 L 376/17.

[42] Decision 88/541 *BBC Brown Boveri*, OJ 1988 L 301/68.

[43] Decision 92/96 *Assurpol*, OJ 1992 L 37/16.

[44] Decision 93/49 *Ford/Volkswagen*, OJ 1993 L 20/14, see further Vedder (2003) at 163.

[45] Decision 2004/208 *ARA/ARGEV/ARO*, OJ 2004 L 75/59, notably para. 270.

[46] Decision 2000/475 *CECED*, OJ 2000 L 187/47.

[47] Horizontals Guidelines, paras. 193 and 194, see for a discussion Vedder (2003) at 164.

individual economic benefits in *CECED* when it considered that the average consumer would recoup the higher purchasing costs within 6 to 40 months because of the reduced energy usage.

3.3.2 Allowing Consumers a Fair Share

On the basis of the first requirement, discussed above, the environmental and economic benefits of the agreement have been established. The second requirement of Article 81(3) EC ensures that these benefits flowing from an environmental agreement are passed on to consumers. It should be noted that in the light of the integration principle the term consumer should be interpreted widely. It should be taken to include third parties who benefit from the positive effects, in terms of reduced environmental pressure, of the environmental agreements, or even the society as a whole.[48] With true environmental benefits, this should not be a problem, as all consumers invariably benefit from better protection of the environment. However, improved quality of the environment will often also mean that prices are higher. In this case the higher price must be balanced with the environmental or economic benefit, for example in the form of lower running costs that will result in the initial investment being recouped.[49]

> Furthermore, in its decision in the *KSB/Goulds/Lowara/ITT* case, concerning an agreement for the joint research, development and production of a single-stage, single-flow radial centrifugal pump, the energy conservation and the fact that the fluids handled by the water pumps are not polluted were regarded as environmentally beneficial and thus as constituting an improvement in operating characteristics.[50] The agreement would therefore also benefit consumers.
>
> The decision in the *Assurpol* case referred to above is also relevant. The Commission regarded the fact that victims of environmental damage can be compensated and the environment repaired as a benefit for consumers.

One of the clearest decisions given by the Commission in this respect is that concerning a set of agreements between chemical companies of the Exxon and Shell Groups related to establishing, financing, constructing, managing and operating a production joint venture.[51] The principal aim of the joint plant is production of linear low-density polyethylene. Reduction in the use of raw materials and of plastic waste and the avoidance of environmental risks involved in transport will be perceived 'as beneficial by many consumers at a time when the limitation of natural resources and threats to the environment are of increasing public concern.'

---

[48] Vedder (2003) at 170.

[49] Decision 2000/475 *CECED*, OJ 2000 L 187/47, para. 52.

[50] OJ 1991 L 19/25.

[51] OJ 1994 L 144/20.

3.3.3   Restrictions Must be Indispensable

From the text of Article 81(3) EC, and as the Commission explicitly stated in its XXIInd Competition Report, point 77, it is clear that the restrictions of competition must be *indispensable* to the alleged ecologic benefits. An objective evaluation of these benefits must be supported with a cost-effectiveness analysis showing that alternative means of attaining the expected environmental benefits would be more economically or financially costly, under reasonable assumptions.[52]

In its XXIIIrd Competition Report the Commission reaffirmed that it will examine carefully all agreements between companies to see if they are indispensable to attain the environmental objectives.

> In respect of the *Spa Monopole/GDB* case[53] the Commission noted that it will be particularly vigilant to ensure that such agreements do not foreclose market entry to outsiders and that where membership of the system is necessary for market access because there is no viable alternative, then this membership will be given on non-discriminatory terms. Other cases concerning collective waste management systems set up by industry foreclosure proved similarly important, with the Commission focusing on the duration of exclusive contracts.[54]
>
> In *CECED* the Commission investigated whether the environmental objectives could be achieved using alternative means. According to the Commission possible alternative means such as setting an industry-wide target, informing the consumers and or eco-labeling would not deliver the same benefits.[55]

With regard to those environmental agreements characterised by the Commission as disguised cartels, the indispensability requirement may be very difficult to fulfil. For example, environmental agreements, which contain uniform fees, charged irrespective of individual costs for e.g. waste collection, are highly suspect. Such an agreement would more or less amount to a price cartel. Moreover, price cartels are always prohibited, because their purpose is to pass on the cost rather than to protect the environment. It does not, therefore, matter that a price agreement is disguised as an environmental agreement.

> Relevant in this connection is the *VOTOB* case.[56] The association, Vereniging van Onafhankelijke Tankopslag Bedrijven (VOTOB), groups six undertakings offering tank storage facilities (land tanks) in the Netherlands. They decided to increase prices charged to their customers by a uniform, fixed amount. This 'environmental

---

[52]   Horizontals Guidelines, point 196.

[53]   XXIIIrd Competition Report, point 240.

[54]   E.g. Decision 2004/208 *ARA/ARGEV/ARO*, OJ 2004 L 75/59, para. 277

[55]   Decision 2000/475 *CECED*, OJ 2000 L 187/47, paras. 59-63.

[56]   XXIIrd Competition Report, points 177-186.

charge' was to cover the costs of investment required to reduce vapour emissions from members' storage tanks. The Commission objected to this charge as being incompatible with Article 81 EC for three reasons.

Firstly, the environmental charge was fixed. All members of VOTOB were to apply it regardless of their own considerations. When a price or an element of it is fixed, competition on that price element is excluded. By fixing the charge members of VOTOB have less incentive to make investments as cheaply and efficiently as possible. Secondly, it was a uniform charge. Though varying from product to product, the increase was identical for all VOTOB members. Uniform adaptation of the charge ignores differences in each individual member's circumstances. Some VOTOB members were already very close to achieving the required reductions in vapour emissions, while others were not. Furthermore, members of VOTOB employed different techniques to reduce emissions, and did not expend investment costs simultaneously. The charge ignored this. In addition, all VOTOB members retained the proceeds of the charge individually. The Commission therefore maintained that had there been no horizontal fixing of this particular cost element, individual members could have calculated the cost of necessary investment, decided whether to meet it from their own profit or to pass it on to their customers, and, if they decided to pass it on to their customers, determined by how much to increase their prices. This would have been done by the companies independently, having regard to prevailing market conditions and according to their own competitive position. Thirdly, the charge was invoiced to customers as a separate item, suggesting it was a 'charge' imposed by the government. Prior to the Commission's proceeding to a decision, VOTOB agreed to renounce its separate charging system and not to apply the uniformly fixed charge. In the light of these developments the Commission agreed to suspend proceedings.

This case makes clear that the Commission is not *a priori* opposed to the possible passing on to customers of environment-related investment costs, since this makes them more aware of environmental problems and their implications. However, customers should not be barred from challenging price increases and shopping around for the smallest increase. A system whereby members invoiced a total price, stating that it included the additional environmental investment cost, would be acceptable to the Commission. Customers reluctant to accept a higher price would remain in a position to negotiate conditions.

In this regard the WEEE Directive and the private system set up to implement it in the Netherlands provide an interesting example. The WEEE Directive contains a so-called 'old-for-new' obligation, on the basis of which retailers (and ultimately importers and producers) must take back old appliances whenever a consumer buys a new appliance. This means that for the waste products collected initially, constitute so-called historical waste, i.e. products that were marketed before the entry into force of the WEEE Directive. Moreover, it may very well be that the producer of that waste no longer exists, in which case the waste is classified as orphan historical waste. For this type of waste, the WEEE Directive allows a fixed uniform fee which may be mentioned separately on the invoice. A similar system in the Netherlands was initially rejected by the Netherlands Competition Authority, but following the entry into force of the WEEE Directive it was allowed.[57]

3.3.4   Competition Must not be Eliminated

The Commission has to investigate on the one hand to what extent the companies concerned in the agreement still compete with each other (internal competition) and on the other what position they occupy in the relevant market and to what extent the market has been affected by the agreement (external competition). In particular it must be noted that whatever the environmental gains, the agreement must not eliminate competition in terms of product or process differentiation, technological innovation or market entry.

On the latter point the *Spa Monopole/GDB* case is illustrative.[58] Because the agreement hindered access by foreign water producers to the German market, external competition was almost completely excluded. The decision in *Assurpol*[59] and in *BBC Brown Boveri*[60] both imply that the condition that competition is not entirely eliminated is met if the more environmentally friendly products are in competition with more traditional products. Finally, *CECED* shows that environmental cooperation by undertakings representing more than 90% of the industry will still not completely eliminate competition because the undertakings will still be able to compete with regard to other aspects of their products, such as price, quality and service.[61]

3.3.5   Block Exemptions

Article 81(3) EC can also be applied to entire categories of agreements in the form of so-called block exemptions. There exist block exemptions for *inter alia* vertical agreements, research and development agreements and specialisation agreements and know-how licensing.[62] Again, by application of the integration principle, regulations containing these group exemptions should also preferably be interpreted in the light of the environmental objectives of Article 174(1) EC. The decisions in *BBC Brown Boveri* and *KSB/Goulds/Lowara/ITT* show that the environmentally friendly interpretation of block exemption agree-

---

[57] See for further details Vedder (2002).

[58] XXIIIrd Competition Report, point 240.

[59] OJ 1992 L 37/16.

[60] OJ 1988 L 301/68.

[61] Decision 2000/475 *CECED*, OJ 2000 L 187/47, para. 64.

[62] Respectively, Commission Regulation 2790/1999, OJ 1999 L 336/21, Commission Regulation 2659/2000, OJ 2000 L 304/7, Commission Regulation 2658/2000, OJ 2000 L 304/3.

ments does not mean that the scope of the block exemption can be extended on environmental grounds. In these cases the Commission took the environmental benefits into account, but nevertheless considered the block exemption inapplicable because the requirements laid down in the regulation were not met. As a result the Commission applied Article 81(3) EC on an individual basis.

The environmentally friendly interpretation in view of the integration principle should also mean that negative effects are taken into account. However, this cannot result in automatic non-applicability of the block exemption for the simple reason that the requirements for the applicability of these regulations, a market share cap and a so-called black list, do not envisage a balancing of environmental factors. However, the regulations do contain a provision on the basis of which the Commission or a national competition authority may withdraw the block exemption benefit if an agreement or a group of agreement no longer fulfils the criteria of Article 81(3) EC. As a result, the Commission may find that the negative environmental effects negate possible economic or technical advantages so that the first requirement of Article 81(3) EC no longer is met which would justify withdrawal of the block exemption benefit.

4 Article 82 EC[63]

Article 82 EC provides that any abuse by one or more undertakings that occupy a dominant position within the common market or in a substantial part of it is prohibited as incompatible with the common market in so far as it may affect trade between Member States. It lists a number of examples of such abuse: imposing unfair purchase or selling prices or unfair trading conditions, limiting production or markets to the prejudice of consumers. Unlike Article 81 EC, this provision does not explicitly allow for exceptions. Nevertheless the doctrine of the objective justification may save behaviour that *prima facie* resembles abuse. For example, might not an undertaking which has a dominant position, and whose environmental image is important to it, require that its suppliers also act in an environmentally friendly manner, whether in the area of production, distribution or waste disposal? The dominant undertaking might well have an interest in protecting or improving its image. It is normally an abuse of a dominant position for an agreement to contain requirements which are not connected with the subject matter of the contract. Superficially, requiring suppliers to act in an environmentally friendly manner could be regarded as such an abuse. However, under the integration principle the question whether or not there had been an abuse of a dominant position should be answered in the light of the environmental objectives. An undertaking's protecting or improving its environmental image and attempting to achieve this by requiring suppliers to act in a certain manner would then not necessarily have to be regarded as abuse of a dominant position. The older example in which Article

---

[63] Cf. the renumbered Article 102 FEU after the entry into force of the Reform Treaty.

82 EC was referred to was the *Spa Monopole/GDB* case, where the Commission found that, in view of the dominant position of the GDB in the market for mineral water containers, its refusal to grant foreign EC water producers access to its pool of standardised refillable glass bottles and crates, despite the fact that such access was essential in order to be able compete effectively in the mineral water market, constituted an abuse of a dominant position within the meaning of Article 82 EC.[64] Even though environmental issues were at stake, they did not play a decisive role for the Commission. It simply applied its standard rules on the abuse of a dominant position. Much the same happened in the *DSD* case.[65] DSD, *Duales System Deutschland*, is the undertaking set up by the German packaging industry to meet the collection and recycling obligations imposed upon them by the German Packaging Ordinance.

> DSD works with a green dot that is placed on products in return for a fee that producers must pay to DSD and that is differentiated on the basis of the recyclability of the products. This green dot signifies to consumers that they must collect that waste through a separate waste collection system that exists alongside the municipal waste collection (hence dual system). At this moment the DSD system works in such a way that producers are under a *de facto* obligation to mark all of their products with a green dot and pay the fee for this, even if the products will not be returned using DSD's collection infrastructure. The hairdressing supplies association complained about this to the Commission, which resulted in a decision that found DSD to have abused its dominant position on the market for the collection of packaging waste in Germany.

DSD collects nearly all the packaging waste in Germany, has a market share exceeding 90% and was thus found to be dominant. The abuse arose from the fact that DSD required a fee from the hairdressing supplies companies, even if the empty shampoo bottles were taken back through a special system for the collection of shampoo bottles from professional hairdressers since the same bottles were also sold to consumers and thus had a green dot printed on them. Setting up a separate packaging line and distribution network for shampoo without the green dot would entail extra costs. According to the Commission this meant that unfair prices were charged since the shampoo manufacturers would have to pay the fee even for products that would never be collected through the DSD system.[66] In its decision the Commission does not refer to the integration principle or the protection of the environment, even when it investi-

---

[64] XXIIIrd Competition Report, point 240.

[65] Commission Decision 2001/463 *DSD*, OJ 2001 L 166/1.

[66] In addition the Commission considered this amounted to a discriminatory or unfair trading condition and tying which would keep competing undertaking from becoming active on the market for the collection of packaging waste. The appeal by DSD was rejected, see Case T-151/01 *Duales System Deutschland v. Commission* [2001] ECR II-3295.

gates the possible objective justification. The Commission's approach to private environmental monopolies (Article 82 EC) may be contrasted with the Court's approach to environmental public monopolies pursuant to Article 86(2) EC, examined below.

5 The *Useful Effect* Doctrine

5.1 The Position of the Member States

Apart from undertakings, the EC competition rules are also addressed at the Member States. Above it has been noted that in many cases environmental agreements are not completely 'voluntary'. Such agreements may be the result of the threat of legislation, or they may actually be reinforced by legislation. With regard to the precise definition of responsibilities between the undertakings and the Member State the Commission has also noted that measures taken by public authorities may compromise the effect of the competition rules, 'for example by requiring firms to engage in behaviour which restricts competition.'[67]

> VOTOB, for example, took the decision to charge their customers a uniform 'environmental charge' after concluding a covenant with the Dutch Government to improve environmental standards.[68] A further example of state actions that may be relevant under the *useful effect* doctrine is the system which exists in the Netherlands, whereby the minister can extend the applicability of a collective agreement to cover an entire industry. This could also be applied to environmental agreements which include a disposal fee, like the one in the *Wit en Bruingoed* case.[69] Declaring such an agreement generally binding would mean that also companies which were not a party to the original agreement would now have to charge this fixed fee to their customers. In these cases Article 81 EC applies to the underlying agreement between the companies in question, and the useful effect doctrine, consisting of Article 10 read in conjunction with Articles 3(1) sub g, 81 or 82, would apply to the Member State's actions.

According to settled case law, Member States are required not to introduce or maintain in force measures, even of a legislative or regulatory nature, which may deprive the competition rules applicable to undertakings from their useful effect.[70] Such is the case, according to that case law:
· if a Member State requires or favours the adoption of agreements, deci-

---

[67] Commission, XXIInd Competition Report, at point 77.

[68] XXIInd Competition Report, point 179.

[69] See further Vedder (2002) at 24 *et seq.*

[70] Case C-379/92 *Peralta* [1994] ECR I-3453, para. 21.

sions or concerted practices contrary to Article 81 or reinforces their effects, or
· deprives its own legislation of its official character by delegating to private traders responsibility for taking decisions affecting the economic sphere.

An example of the first indent could be a government's extending the application of an environmental agreement to cover an entire industry. An example of the second might be the extensive privatisation of parts of a country's environment policy, for example by allowing the industry in question to set its own emission standards or product standards.

As far as environmental law is concerned, the Court's judgment in *Peralta* can be taken to imply that the sole fact that a government environmental measure has anti-competitive effects will not cause it to be in breach of the useful effect doctrine. The case concerned Italian legislation prohibiting vessels from discharging harmful substances into the sea. The Court came to the conclusion that the useful effect doctrine may not be relied upon as against legislation like the Italian legislation since '[t]hat legislation does not require or foster anti-competitive conduct since the prohibition which it lays down is sufficient in itself. Nor does it reinforce the effects of a pre-existing agreement.'

Any other conclusion would have led to a totally unacceptable result since environmental regulation invariably has anticompetitive effects. When emission standards are adopted by a government, this in fact means it is no longer possible to use an environmentally harmful process. To some degree environmental legislation makes it impossible to exploit competitive advantages at the expense of the environment. These anti-competitive effects can be quite considerable, as was shown in the *TiO2* case.[71] In that case the increase in the cost of production as a result of the environmental standards in question was of the order of 20% of the total costs. Government regulation can thus have a significant effect on competition. The mere fact that this is the case does not, however, make the legislation incompatible with the useful effect doctrine.

Member State actions will only be incompatible with the useful effect doctrine if the underlying environmental agreement or practice is prohibited by Article 81 or 82 EC. This means that the exceptions provided for in Article 81(3) EC and the *Wouters* case are also relevant.[72] Even though this is not as such required by European law, it is wise to notify the Commission of government involvement that is possibly contrary to the useful effect doctrine on the basis of Article 10 EC.

---

[71] Case C-300/89 *Commission v. Council* [1991] ECR I-2867.

[72] See, for example, Case C-67/96 *Albany* [1999] ECR I-5751, where a government measure declaring an agreement generally binding was found not to infringe the useful effect doctrine because the underlying agreement itself was compatible with Article 81 EC.

5.2 The Position of the European Institutions

The European institutions are also indicating that they would like to see undertakings taking more responsibility for the environment. In Chapter 1 reference was made to the subsidiarity principle, which has been regarded as implying a preference for the use of voluntary agreements. The Fifth Environmental Action Programme[73] also indicates a preference for self-regulation by industry and for more indirect steering by public authorities, including the European authorities.

> The best-known example of European action in this field concerns the ozone problem. In resolutions and recommendations the Member States and the industries concerned (organisations, manufacturers and importers) are urged to limit the use of certain ozone-depleting substances and products. A good example is the Council Resolution of 14 October 1988 on the limiting of the use of chlorofluorocarbons and halons.[74] The Council invited the Commission: 'In cooperation with the Member States, to initiate discussions on voluntary agreements at the Community level with all the industries concerned, wherever feasible to substitute chlorofluorocarbons and halons in products, such as aerosols, or in equipment or processes using them, or if such substitution is not feasible, to reduce the use of these substances, so that the total amounts of these substances used will be reduced to the maximum possible extent.' Another example is that the Commission is a party to the ACEA Agreement to reduce carbon dioxide emissions by cars.[75]

The compatibility of the behaviour of the institutions with Article 10 EC taken in conjunction with Articles 3(1) sub g, 81 and 82 EC should be reviewed in this area too. It should not be regarded as permissible for the EC to act in breach of the competition rules.[76] However, here too, applying the integration principle, the competition rules should be interpreted so as to take account of the environmental objectives mentioned in Article 174(1) EC.

6 Article 86 EC[77]

Article 86(1) EC deals with so-called public undertakings (or public monopolies) and provides that in the case of public undertakings and undertakings to which Member States grant special or exclusive rights,

---

[73] OJ 1993 C 138/1.

[74] OJ 1988 C 285/1.

[75] Cf. Bongaerts (1999) and Commission Communication on Implementing the Community Strategy to Reduce Carbon Dioxide Emissions from Cars, COM (98) 495.

[76] See, for example, Case C-341/95 *Bettati* [1998] ECR I-4355, at para. 61.

[77] Cf. the renumbered Article 106 FEU after the entry into force of the Reform Treaty.

Member States shall neither enact nor maintain in force any measure contrary
to the rules contained in the Treaty, in particular to those rules provided for in
Article 12 and Articles 81 to 89 EC. Article 86(2) EC provides that undertakings
entrusted with the operation of services of general economic interest are subject
to the rules of the Treaty, '*in so far as the application of such rules does not obstruct
the performance, in law or in fact, of the particular tasks assigned to them.*'

The importance of these provisions has been greatly enhanced thanks to
the case law of the Court of Justice. From this it is clear that Article 86 EC is
often applied in combination with Article 82 EC (abuse of a dominant position).
Given the complexity of the material, it is impossible to discuss the case law in
detail in this context. In general terms it can be said that Article 86 EC, taken
in combination with Article 82 EC, prohibits a Member State from conferring
special rights on an undertaking where that undertaking would be abusing its
dominant position simply by exercising those rights, or where those rights could
create a situation in which the undertaking would be brought to such an abuse.
The Court of Justice case law in which Article 86 EC played a part in relation to
the environment will now be considered.

6.1   Article 86(1) EC and Environmental Protection

As concerns Article 86(1) in connection with Article 82 EC,
there have been several cases. Most of these involve national monopolies dealing
with waste management that somehow limit the export of waste. The *Inter-
Huiles* case, for example, involved a French system set up pursuant to the Waste
Oils Directive which required collectors of waste oil to deliver their waste oils
to authorised disposal companies.[78] One of the arguments put forward was that
collection and disposal companies could be regarded as undertakings entrusted
with the operation of services of general economic interest. The implicit prohibition on exports was said to be essential in order to fulfil this task, while the
negative effect on inter-state trade would be kept to a minimum.

In *Dusseldorp* the Court was asked whether Article 86 EC, in conjunction
with Article 82 EC, precludes national rules that require undertakings to deliver
their dangerous waste for recovery to a national undertaking on which it has
conferred the exclusive right to incinerate dangerous waste, unless the processing of their waste in another Member State is superior to that performed by
the public undertaking.[79] According to the Court, the grant of exclusive rights
for the incineration of dangerous waste on the territory of a Member State as a
whole must be regarded as conferring on the undertaking concerned a dominant position in a substantial part of the common market. Merely creating a
dominant position is not, in itself, incompatible with Article 82 EC.[80] So far the

---

[78] Case 172/82 *Inter-Huiles* [1983] ECR 555, see also Case C-37/92 *Vanacker* [1993] ECR I-4947.

[79] Case C-203/96 *Dusseldorp* [1998] ECR I-4075.

[80] Cf. the judgment of the Swedish Supreme Administrative Court on 16 June 1999, case no. 1424-1998,
2397-1998 and 2939-1998, RÅ 1999 ref. 76, regarding the cessation of the right to operate the nuclear

Court is applying existing case law and in that sense the judgment can hardly be said to be remarkable. A Member State is only breaching Article 86 EC in conjunction with Article 82 EC if it adopts a measure which enables an undertaking to abuse its dominant position. In this case the Court found the abuse to follow from the fact that AVR Chemie (the public undertaking that was granted the exclusive rights) received waste for recovery that was intended for processing by a third undertaking, even though the quality of processing was comparable with that provided by AVR Chemie. This favouring of the national undertaking resulted in the restriction of outlets, which can be regarded as abuse of a dominant position.[81] The Court's strict approach in *Dusseldorp* may be contrasted with that in *Sydhavnens*. In *Sydhavnens* a regulation by the Municipal Authorities of Copenhagen meant that only one public undertaking could process the building and construction waste generated in that municipality. The Court's approach to Article 86(1) EC in connection with Article 82 EC was much less straightforward than that in *Dusseldorp*.[82]

6.2 Article 86(2) EC and Environmental Protection

In *Inter-Huiles* and *Vanacker* only the Advocates General explicitly addressed the applicability of Article 86(2) EC. Only in the *Almelo* case did the Court shed some light in the relation between Article 86(2) EC and environmental concerns. In that case the Court held that undertakings entrusted with the operation of services of general economic interest may be exempted from the application of the competition rules contained in the Treaty in so far as this is necessary to ensure the performance of particular tasks assigned to them.[83] In that regard, it is necessary to take into consideration the economic conditions in which the undertaking operates, in particular the costs which it has to bear and the legislation, particularly concerning the environment, to which it is subject.[84] Thus in *Almelo* the Court considered that environmental protection is one of the reasons that could justify an exception to the competition rules. In *Sydhavnens Sten & Grus* however the Court decided that the treatment of waste could be regarded as a service of general economic interest in the meaning of Article 86(2) EC.[85] Following *Sydhavnens* environmental protection can thus be

---

power reactor Barsebäck I, which ruled that the EC competition rules do not preclude a closure by the Government of a nuclear power station – a decision dictated by public interests – even if this would lead to the strengthening of a competitor's dominant position on the market. Cf. also Case C-209/98 *Sydhavnens Sten & Grus* [2000] ECR I-3743, paras. 66-68.

[81] Additionally, it also restricts exports contrary to Article 29 EC; see Chapter 6, section 5.2.

[82] Case C-209/98 *Sydhavnens Sten & Grus* [2000] ECR I-3743, paras. 57-65, see further Vedder (2003) at 255 *et seq.*

[83] Case C-393/92 *Gemeente Almelo v. NV Energiebedrijf IJsselmij* [1994] ECR I-1477.

[84] See also Case C-159/94 *Commission v. France* [1997] ECR I-5815, paras. 70-71.

[85] Case C-209/98 *Sydhavnens Sten & Grus* [2000] ECR I-3743, para. 75.

considered to justify an application of Article 86(2) EC without any additional
considerations. Furthermore, the necessity or proportionality of an exception
to the competition rules can be founded upon the profitability of the public
environmental undertaking. In *Sydhavnens* a statutory monopoly was considered
necessary in order for the public undertaking to be able to recoup its investment
in setting up a high capacity waste treatment installation. This high capacity
centre was in turn considered necessary to attain the environmental objective
of a higher percentage of recycling, because it would bring the costs down. It is
interesting to note that the Court refused to accept similar profitability-based
reasoning in *Dusseldorp*.[86]

7   State Aid and Articles 87 and 88 EC[87]

7.1   Why There is Environmental Aid and Why it Distorts Competition

It has already been noted that the polluter pays principle is
one of the fundamentals of European environmental policy. When applied,
this allows the price mechanism to perform its signalling function by translat-
ing into costs the negative effects of a particular product or production process
on the environment. However, when a Member State decides to increase the
level of environmental protection, this will result in increased costs and thus
a deterioration of the position of the national industry. No Member State will
therefore have an incentive to make the first move with the internalisation of
environmental costs, for example in the form of the introduction of an ecotax or
the introduction of more stringent emissions standards. In fact, most national
attempts at implementing the polluter pays principle go hand in hand with a
partial exception for the industries that are particularly polluting and would
thus have to pay considerably more. The decisions of the Commission show that
state aid cannot be given if it conflicts with the polluter pays principle laid down
in Article 174(2) EC.

> Its decision in respect of aid to *Cartiere del Garda*, which will be discussed in
> more detail below, is exemplary.[88] In that case the Commission concluded that
> the proposed aid to Cartiere del Garda does not meet the polluter pays principle
> contained in Article 174(2) EC. Applying this principle, the costs of measures
> required to reduce nuisances and pollution to an acceptable level should be borne
> by the firms whose activities are responsible for them. The general grant of state
> aid simply means that the public and not the polluter pays in the end. State aid
> should be granted only when the objectives considered essential for the environ-

---

[86]   Case C-203/96, *Dusseldorp* [1998] ECR I-4075. See further Vedder (2003) at 272 *et seq.*

[87]   Cf. the renumbered Articles 107-108 FEU after the entry into force of the Reform Treaty.

[88]   OJ 1993 L 273/51.

ment are seriously in conflict with other social or economic objectives also of priority importance or when market forces by themselves are not sufficient to cause people to act in such a way that environmental objectives are attained.

As the primary institution responsible for enforcing the provisions on state aid, the Commission addressed the problem of state aids for environmental protection for the first time in 1974 when it drew up the first environmental aid guidelines.[89] These guidelines were applied, with certain amendments, until the end of 1993. At the end of 1993 the Commission drafted new rules for assessing national aid measures.[90] These were replaced by the 2001 Guidelines on Environmental Aid that are in force at this moment and will be discussed below.[91]

Just as with the other competition provisions, the integration principle does not mean that environmental state aid is not *a priori* exempted from the prohibition of state aids contained in Article 87(1) EC. This is not more than logical given the role that undistorted competition may play in attaining environmental objectives. This view can also be seen in the Commission decision amending German aid schemes for the motor vehicle industry.[92] In that case the German Government decided not to apply the Commission Guidelines on state aid to the motor vehicle industry.[93] One of the arguments for this was that incentives for global environmental protection aid schemes represented a top political priority in Germany, and the EC itself pursues the same objectives according to Article 174 EC. According to the Commission, the development of environmentally friendly and energy-saving vehicles is a standard requirement for the motor industry, partly imposed by European legislation, and should, as a general principle, be financed by the company's own resources. The reduction of motor vehicle pollution and the associated technologies have become a major aspect of competition between manufacturers, and their importance should increase further in the future. The Commission seeks to avoid that competition is distorted through the granting of aid to manufacturers in order to assist them in catching up with existing technologies in this domain.[94]

The most important legal consequence of a measure being a grant of aid within the meaning of Article 87(1) EC is that it has to be notified to the Commission according to Article 88(3) EC. The Commission can then decide whether the proposed aid is compatible with the common market. Until the Commission has taken a final decision in its favour, the Member State may not put its proposed measures into effect pursuant to the so-called stand still clause.

---

[89] The 'old' Guidelines; IVth Competition Report, points 175-182.

[90] The 1994 Guidelines; OJ 1994 C 72/1. Cf. also Case T-150/95 *UK Steel Association* v. *Commission* [1997] ECR II-1433 on environmental aid and the ECSC Treaty.

[91] OJ 2001 C 37/3.

[92] OJ 1990 L 188/55.

[93] OJ 1989 C 123/3.

[94] See also the remarks above on the scope of the prohibition on cartels contained in Article 81(1).

Environmental aid which is granted without the Commission being informed or without its approval is granted unlawfully. Moreover, the standstill clause, contained in the final sentence of Article 88(3) EC is directly effective.[95]

7.2   The Scope of Article 87(1) EC

Article 87(1) EC provides that any aid granted by a Member State which distorts competition by favouring certain undertakings is, in so far as it affects trade between Member States, incompatible with the common market. Under certain circumstances aid will be compatible with the common market or may be considered compatible with the common market, according to Article 87(2) or 87(3) EC. Before considering the question under what circumstances the Commission may consider state aid compatible with the common market, it must be decided when environmental aid has to be regarded as aid within the meaning of the Treaty. The definition in Article 87(1) EC gives some indications, which are discussed below.

7.2.1   Aid Granted Through State Resources

From the case law of the Court it is clear that the term aid must be interpreted broadly. Whenever companies benefit from relief which is funded from public resources, the measure will generally be regarded as aid. Not only *direct* aid in the form of grants etc., but also *indirect* aid is regarded as aid in this sense. Indirect aid may be involved in any case where the state does not receive income it otherwise would, as in the case of preferential tariffs, tax remissions, accelerated depreciation for tax purposes, guarantees, interest subsidies, tax relief, etc. The Commission has also regarded a reduction in the cost price of electricity as aid.[96] The Commission has regarded the following as examples of aid schemes:

- tax relief for companies using a minimum of 50% recycled material as raw material in their production;[97]
- a scheme to promote the recycling of surplus manure;[98]
- subsidies to stimulate investment in wind power;[99]
- a reduction in the waste-collection tax paid to the city of Wiesbaden in return for a commitment to purchase from the city at current market prices, all waste paper collected;[100]
- subsidised loans for effluent treatment, waste management, air pollution control and energy conservation;[101]

---

[95] Case 47/69 *Steinike & Weinlig* [1977] ECR 595.

[96] OJ 1994 C 32/37.

[97] XXIIIrd Competition Report, point 420.

[98] XXIInd Competition Report, point 449; OJ 1991 C 82/3 en OJ 1992 L 170/34.

[99] XXIInd Competition Report, point 449.

[100] XXIInd Competition Report, point 452.

[101] XXIInd Competition Report, point 453.

· interest subsidies on loans for investments for energy savings and the
rational use of energy;[102]
· partial tax relief from CO_2/energy taxes for energy-intensive firms.[103]

As far as the financing of an aid measure is concerned, Article 87(1) EC requires
that the aid be financed from state resources. Even aid which is funded from
levies imposed on the companies in question can be regarded as aid within the
meaning of Article 87(1) EC, as was shown in the case concerning aid to Dutch
manure processors.[104]

The Dutch Government argued that there was no question of aid, as the aid
would be wholly funded by levies paid by the farmers themselves. The fact that
the funds were raised by means of a levy on the production of surplus manure
was no reason for the Commission not to consider the measure an aid measure.
In reaching this decision, the Commission took into account that the levy was
introduced by a regulation of the *Landbouwschap* (Agricultural Board), in other
words as an obligatory measure under public law, and that payment of the levy
could be enforced. More generally, the fact that a subsidy is financed by a parafiscal charge levied on production in a certain sector is not sufficient to divest the
system of its character as aid granted by a Member State within the meaning of
Article 87 EC.[105]

In *PreussenElektra* the limits to this line of reasoning were clarified by the
Court.[106] At stake was a German measure according to which regional electricity distributors were obliged to buy all the renewable energy produced in their
region at a price that was higher than the market price. Despite the fact that
this clearly conferred an economic advantage upon the producers of renewable
energy, as the Court explicitly recognised, it was considered to fall outside the
scope of Article 87(1) EC, because at the end of the day this benefit was paid
by private regional energy distributors and consumers. Thus since no state
resources were involved, Article 87(1) EC did not apply.[107]

7.2.2 Favouring Certain Undertakings

Article 87(1) EC applies only if the measure favours certain
undertakings or products. In other words: there must be an advantage that must
furthermore benefit a selected group of undertakings. These two requirements,

---

[102] OJ 1991 L 156/39.

[103] XXIInd Competition Report, point 451.

[104] Decision 92/316, OJ 1992 L 170/34.

[105] Case 259/85 *France v. Commission* [1987] ECR 4393.

[106] Case C-379/98 *PreussenElektra* [2001] ECR I-2099.

[107] Case C-379/98 *PreussenElektra* [2001] ECR I-2099, paras. 54-60. This line of reasoning appears to also
underlie the *Dutch Car Wrecks* case, press release IP/01/1518, Competition Policy Newsletter 2002/2,
at 87.

favouring and *selectivity*, are closely related and will be treated together in this section.

It can sometimes be difficult to draw the dividing line between 'aid' that favours an undertaking and genuine compensation paid by the government. This was an issue in the *ADBHU* case on the compatibility of the former Articles 13 and 14 (currently Articles 14 and 15) of Directive 75/439 on the disposal of waste oils[108] with Articles 87 and 88 EC.[109] In the preamble to the directive the Council considers that in cases where certain undertakings are required to collect and/or dispose of waste oils, compensation by indemnities of that part of their costs relating thereto and not covered by their earnings should be possible. These indemnities might, *inter alia,* be financed by a charge on new or regenerated oils. Article 13 of the directive read as follows: 'As a reciprocal concession for the obligations imposed on them by the Member States pursuant to Article 5, indemnities may be granted to collection and/or disposal undertakings for the service rendered. Such indemnities must not exceed annual uncovered costs actually recorded by the undertaking taking into account a reasonable profit. The amount of these indemnities must be such as not to cause any significant distortion of competition or to give rise to artificial patterns of trade in products.' Article 14 continued: 'The indemnities may be financed, among other methods, by a charge imposed on products which after use are transformed into waste oils, or on waste oils. The financing of indemnities must be in accordance with the 'polluter pays' principle.' The validity of these articles was disputed before the Court in connection with their possible incompatibility with the provisions of Articles 87 to 89 EC on state aid. It was argued that the financial indemnities should have been regarded as aid. The Court clearly felt otherwise:

> 'In that respect the Commission and the Council, in their observations, rightly argue that the indemnities do not constitute aid within the meaning of Article 92 [now Article 87, authors] et seq of the EEC Treaty, but rather compensation for the services performed by the collection or disposal undertakings.'

Financial indemnities such as those provided for in the Waste Oils Directive, as well as in some other directives, are not to be regarded as aid to the waste disposal companies, but as remuneration for services performed on behalf of the government. A Commission decision which is relevant in this respect is that to approve a Danish scheme to pay firms engaged in the collection of waste oils.[110] The Commission, like the Court in the *ADBHU* case, considered that the payments were straightforward remuneration for services, and not aid.

---

[108] OJ 1975 L 194/31, later amended, see Chapter 8, section 15.3.

[109] Case 240/83 *ADBHU* [1985] ECR 531.

[110] XXIIIrd Competition Report, point 421. See also XXIVth Competition Report, point 388. With respect to a Danish scheme introducing an environmental charge on the sale of tyres to finance collection and disposal of used tyres in an environmentally friendly way, the Commission considered that payment

This reasoning was further elaborated in the *Altmark Trans* case.[111] This case involved the compatibility of a subsidy that would compensate the extra costs arising from the fulfilment of a service of general economic interest pursuant to Article 86(2) EC. According to the Court such a compensatory scheme would not constitute state aid provided that the public service obligations have been clearly defined and the public undertaking is actually charged with providing these services. The compensation must take place in a transparent manner and may not entail any overcompensation. Finally, if public service obligation is not tendered the costs should be established using an objective benchmark.

A related question is whether damages payable in compensation for damage suffered are to be considered aid. This is a type of payment regularly encountered in the field of environmental law. In general a distinction is made between damages which have to be paid for an *unlawful* act, whether by a private polluter or by public authorities, and compensation for a *lawful* act on the part of the public authorities. In terms of European law, the issue of unlawfulness hardly poses a problem. In *Asteris* the Court held that compensation paid on the grounds of liability for an unlawful act by public authorities was not aid within the meaning of Article 87 EC:[112]

> 'State aid, that is to say measures of the public authorities favouring certain undertakings or certain products, is fundamentally different in its legal nature from damages which the competent national authorities may be ordered to pay to individuals in compensation for the damage they have caused to those individuals.'

Nor can payment of damages by private individuals, on the ground of their liability for pollution caused by them unlawfully, be regarded as aid for the simple reason that there is no funding through State resources, as required by Article 87.

More difficult, however, is the case of compensation for *lawful* acts by public authorities, something which occurs in many Member States.[113] Generally this involves a direct contribution from the public authorities to the polluter, often intended to avoid endangering a company's competitive position where it has to meet disproportionately high costs to fulfil new or stricter environmental provisions. Most of these cases hinge on the degree of discretion the public authori-

---

to the collecting companies constituted compensation for the service rendered and therefore did not involve any state aid. See also Case N 638/02, OJ 2003 C82/10, on the compensation of the costs arising from the collection of CFCs and halons.

[111] Case C-280/00 *Altmark Trans* [2003] ECR I-7747, see also Case C-53/00 *Ferring* [2001] ECR I-9067.

[112] Case 106/87 *Asteris* [1988] ECR 5515.

[113] Whether or not Community law also *requires* Member States to pay compensation for damage caused by lawful actions of the state will not be discussed here; Cf. e.g. Case C-237/98 *Dorsch Consult* v. *Council and Commission* [2000] ECR I-4549.

ties have in furnishing compensation. Thus the Commission has decided that an amendment to German legislation providing for a levy on effluent discharges was an improvement from the point of view of undistorted competition, because a discretionary power to waive the levy for economic reasons was abolished.[114] Applied to the problem of compensation for lawful acts by public authorities, this case justifies the conclusion that such compensation should as far as possible be given in accordance with objective criteria and that too much administrative latitude should be avoided.

This ties in rather nicely with the second requirement, namely that a measure must be selective if it is to constitute aid. Aid that is awarded to *every* company is not aid within the meaning of Article 87(1) EC. The benefits must be awarded to specific industries or undertakings and thus contain an element of selective favouring. The financial position of these specific industries is then favoured in comparison with their competitors. A good example of the degree of specificity required was the proposed aid to Dutch manure processing factories. The aid envisaged was to be given to a specific industry and would have distorted competition in various ways. In the first place, foreign manure processing plants, which have to operate without such aid, would be put at a disadvantage. In the second place, the competitive position of the artificial fertilizer industry, which manufactures a competitive product, would be adversely affected. And in the third place, competition between Dutch farmers and their foreign counterparts might be distorted. The aid to manure processing plants would inevitably mean that not all the environmental consequences of intensive animal husbandry in the Netherlands would be charged to the producer, which might be the case abroad. The Commission also acknowledged that the aid measures might very well increase the competitiveness of Dutch factory farms and processed manure.[115] German aid to the chemical company Riedel for the construction of a bromine-recovery plant was held to distort competition in two ways. First, because it would allow Riedel to process its residues more cheaply than other chemical companies and, second, because aid for investment in the recovery plant would give Riedel a competitive advantage over companies which did not receive such state aid.[116]

Ecotaxation can also lead to problems concerning selectivity in two ways. Firstly, ecotaxation schemes often include exceptions or rebates for industries that would face a particularly high tax burden and thus a reduction of competitiveness. These rebates/exceptions may be selective and thus constitute aid.[117] The *Adria-Wien* case contains a good example of this type of measure.[118]

---

[114] XVIth Competition Report, point 261.

[115] Decision 92/316, OJ 1992 L 170/34, at IV.

[116] Decision 1999/671, OJ 1999 L 267/51.

[117] See further, Commission Guidelines on Environmental Aid, OJ 2001 C 37/3, section E.3.2.

[118] Case C-143/99 *Adria-Wien* [2001] ECR I-8365.

At hand was an Austrian energy tax that contained a rebate for undertakings primarily producing goods where the tax would exceed a certain threshold. Undertakings supplying services could not qualify for this rebate no matter how much energy tax they would have to pay. According to the Court the tax rebate constituted 'aid granted through state resources', so selectivity was the most important element. A measure is selective if it favours certain undertaking or productions that are in a comparable position to other undertakings or productions in a similar factual and legal position in the light of the objective the measure. This means that any differentiation in the tax burden must be objectively justified in the light of the objectives of the tax scheme. [119] Thus the Court investigated whether the environmental objectives of the energy tax could justify the rebate for goods producing industries only. As the Court rather dryly noticed: energy consumption by companies supplying services is equally damaging to the environment as energy consumption by undertakings producing goods. [120] As a result the rebate was not objectively justified and thus selective. This conclusion was also borne out by the statement of reasons for the Austrian energy tax, according to which the rebate was intended to preserve the international competitiveness of the Austrian industry. [121]

The second problem concerning selectivity and ecotaxation schemes arises from the fact that any functioning ecotax will make environmentally unfriendly production methods or products more expensive compared to environmentally friendly production methods or products. As a result there may be companies claiming that the ecotaxation confers a selective benefit on the environmentally friendly products or production methods. The *BAA* case provides a textbook example of such a case. [122]

This dealt with the Aggregates Levy, which is a tax imposed on the use of certain aggregates (granulated materials used in construction etc.). As the objective of the Aggregates Levy was to come to a more rational use of virgin aggregates and to encourage the recycling of aggregates, the Levy contained an exemption for recycled aggregates and aggregates that are essentially byproducts. The Court found that the Commission was right to conclude that this exemption could be justified in the light of the environmental objectives of the Levy. [123]

---

[119] Case C-143/99 *Adria-Wien* [2001] ECR I-8365, paras. 41, 42.

[120] Case C-143/99 *Adria-Wien* [2001] ECR I-8365, para. 52.

[121] Case C-143/99 *Adria-Wien* [2001] ECR I-8365, para. 54.

[122] Case T-210/02 *British Aggregates Association (BAA)* [2006] ECR II-2789.

[123] Case T-210/02 *British Aggregates Association (BAA)* [2006] ECR II-2789, paras. 107-109.

7.2.3   Adverse Effect on Trade Between Member States

Only state aid that affects trade between Member States is prohibited. The Court generally gives a wide interpretation to this requirement.[124] Despite this, the Commission has issued a *de minimis* regulation according to which state aid not exceeding €200,000 over a three-year period is outside the scope of Article 87 EC.[125]

7.3   Application of Article 87(2) and (3) EC to Environmental Aid

7.3.1   General Remarks

The second and third paragraphs of Article 87 EC provide for an exhaustive list of grounds on which aid may be considered compatible with the common market. Here, too, the mere fact that protection of the environment is involved will not as such result in compatibility by virtue of the integration principle. This means that it must be examined to what extent the normal grounds for exemption can be used to make aid compatible. In the light of the integration principle such exemptions should be interpreted in an environmentally friendly way.[126]

Finally it should be noted that, in assessing aid by Member States in fields other than that of the environment, the environmental effects of the aid should be taken into account.[127] Equally, aid for projects which entail disproportionate effects for the environment should be avoided.

Member States desiring to grant aid will have to show that the aid does indeed benefit the environment. From its decision on proposed aid to Hoffmann-La Roche it is clear that the Commission will look closely at the objectives of the aid.[128] In that case the Austrian Government indicated that part of the aid was intended for environmental purposes. By this it meant aid for measures to reduce the risk of accidents and combat air and water pollution. The Commission held aid for the latter measures allowable, but regarded the measures to reduce the risk of accidents as a normal obligation for the company. Such measures were not therefore viewed as environmental measures and aid for them would be regarded as general investment aid.

---

[124] See, for example, Case C-280/00 *Altmark Trans* [2003] ECR I-7747, which dealt with an aid measure concerning local public transport from a municipality in the middle of Germany, paras. 77-82.

[125] Regulation 1998/2006, OJ 2006 L 379/5.

[126] See also the remarks made earlier in this chapter on exemption from the prohibition on cartels.

[127] See further Vedder (2003) at 315 *et seq.* and Commission Guidelines on Environmental Aid, OJ 2001 C 37/3, para. 83. These Guidelines are currently being updated.

[128] Decision 98/251, OJ 1998 L 103/28.

7.3.2   Article 87(2) EC

Article 87(2) EC provides for three exemptions which will make aid compatible with the common market. Article 87(2)(b) EC may well be relevant for the environment, as it provides for aid to make good the damage caused by natural disasters or other exceptional occurrences. Flooding caused by the River Maas in the southeast of the Netherlands gave rise to aid approved under this provision.[129]

7.3.3   Article 87(3) EC

Article 87(3) EC contains essentially two grounds for exemptions that are relevant for environmental state aids. Firstly, Article 87(3)(b) EC provides that aid 'to promote the execution of an important project of common European interest' may be considered compatible with the common market. In *Glaverbel* the Court recognised that this provision might be used for environmental purposes.[130] It held 'that a project may not be described as being of common European interest for the purposes of Article 92(3)(b) [now Article 87(3)(b), authors] unless it forms part of a transnational European programme supported jointly by a number of governments of the Member States, or arises from concerted action by a number of Member States to combat a common threat such as environmental pollution.'

In view of the discretion that is inherent in the application of Article 87(3) EC, it should not come as a surprise that the Commission has issued Guidelines on Environmental Aid.[131] The old guidelines, which applied up to 1993, concerned the application of the exemption provided for in Article 87(3)(b) EC. The current guidelines function on the basis of Article 87(3)(c) EC and the exemption provided for in Article 87(3)(b) EC currently applies only to aid 'to promote the execution of important projects of common European interest which are an environmental priority and will often have beneficial effects beyond the frontiers of the Member State or States concerned'.[132] The aid must be necessary for the project to proceed and the project must be specific and well defined, qualitatively important, and must make an exemplary and clearly identifiable contribution to the common European interest. Where these strict criteria are met, the Commission may authorise aid at higher rates than normally allowed pursuant to Article 87(3)(c) EC. The guidelines have a legal effect in that they bind the author (the Commission), on the strength of the principle of legitimate expectations.[133]

---

[129] Cf. XXIVth Competition Report, point 354.

[130] Case 62/87 *Glaverbel* [1988] ECR 1573.

[131] For an overview and discussion of the current Guidelines see Vedder (2003) at 301 *et seq.* and Seinen (2005).

[132] Commission Guidelines on Environmental Aid, OJ 2001 C 37/3, para. 73.

[133] Case C-351/98 *Spain* v. *Commission (Plan Renove)* [2002] ECR I-8031, para. 76.

The current guidelines contain definitions or fundamental concepts such as 'environmental aid' and set out the Commission's policy concerning environmental aid. As such the guidelines distinguish between *investment* aid and *operating* aid.[134]

Investment aid subsidises environmental investments and this type of aid is generally described in terms of a percentage of the eligible costs arising from the environmental investment. The eligible costs must be strictly confined to the extra investment costs necessary to meet environmental objectives.[135] General investment costs not attributable to environmental protection must be excluded. Thus, in the case of new or replacement plant, the cost of the basic investment involved merely to create or replace production capacity without improving its environmental performance is not eligible.[136] In any case aid ostensibly intended for environmental protection measures but which is in fact for general investment is not covered by the guidelines. This is true, for example, of aid for relocating firms to new sites in the same area.[137] The current guidelines only allow for investment aid in these cases where the firm is located in an urban area or a Natura 2000 area.[138]

With regard to investment aid, a distinction must be made between investments necessary to adapt to new environmental standards and investments that will allow the firms to exceed environmental standards. Aid for investment to comply with new European standards can still be authorised up to the level of 15% gross of the eligible costs, but only for small and medium sized undertakings.[139] All other forms of investment aid are allowed up to 30% of the costs, but only if the investment will result in environmental performance that improves on European standards or, if that is stricter,[140] national standards. For investments in energy (energy saving, combined production of heat and power and the promotion of renewables) 40% of the costs may be subsidised. These percentages may be increased with various bonuses.[141]

The rules for investment aid in general also apply to aid for investment to repair past damage to the environment, for example by making polluted indus-

---

[134] Case C-490/00 *Spain* v. *Commission* (*Plan Renove*) [2002] ECR I-8031, para. 77.

[135] See for example Case T-166/01 *Lucchini* [2006] ECR II-2875 on environmental investments in the coal and steel sector.

[136] Commission Guidelines on Environmental Aid, OJ 2001 C 37/3, para. 37.

[137] See, for example, Decision 93/564, OJ 1993 L 273/51 on the relocation of the Cartiere del Garda.

[138] Commission Guidelines on Environmental Aid, OJ 2001 C 37/3, para. 39.

[139] Commission Guidelines on Environmental Aid, OJ 2001 C 37/3, para. 20, 28. Under the old guidelines, such aid was allowed for all firms, OJ 1994 C 72/1, section 3.2.3 A.

[140] In cases of minimum harmonisation where the Member State has decided to enact more stringent measures, see Chapter 3.

[141] For assisted regions, small and medium sized enterprises and firms that supply an entire community, Commission Guidelines on Environmental Aid, OJ 2001 C 37/3, section E.1.4, E.1.5.

trial sites again fit for use.[142] Cleaning up polluted industrial sites at the government's expense must in principle be regarded as aid to the person responsible for causing the pollution. Under the polluter pays principle, that person should pay for the costs of repair himself.[143] However, in cases where the person responsible for the pollution cannot be identified or called to account, aid for rehabilitating such areas may not fall under Article 87(1) EC in that it does not confer a gratuitous financial benefit on *particular* firms or industries. The Commission will examine such cases on their merits. In the *Kiener Deponie Bachmanning* case, the Commission was prepared to allow the clean-up of the landfill with part State funding, but only subject to the condition that everything possible was done to recover the costs from the polluter.[144]

Aid for the provision of *training and consultancy* to small and medium sized enterprises may be granted at rates up to 50% of the eligible costs.[145]

Operating aid which relieves firms of costs resulting from the pollution or nuisance they cause will, in accordance with long-standing policy of the Commission, not normally be approved because they run counter to the polluter pays principle.[146] In the Guidelines the Commission distinguishes between operating aid for waste management and operating aid for energy saving. In principle such aid is limited to the compensation of the extra costs arising from an environmental standard that is either stricter than the European standard or exists in the absence of a European standard. Furthermore the aid must be limited in time to a maximum of five years and be digressive. The Guidelines contain fairly elaborate rules on operating aid in the form of tax reductions and operating aid for renewable energy production.

As far as tax reductions are concerned, the *Adria-Wien* case shows that they may constitute state aid. This does not mean that they cannot be allowed. The Commission explicitly recognises the need to protect the competitiveness of industries subject to ecotaxation where there is no European taxation. The Commission will allow such tax exemptions if the Member State shows that the tax will result in environmental protection, for example because environmental agreements are concluded.[147] For renewable energy production the Commission acknowledges that, because of the high investments costs involved, market entry may be difficult due to the price differences between renewable energy and traditional energy. Member States are therefore allowed to subsidise the higher

---

[142] Commission Guidelines on Environmental Aid, OJ 2001 C 37/3, section E.I.8. See for example XXIVth Competition Report, point 389. The Commission authorised a Dutch scheme for the cleaning-up of polluted industrial sites.

[143] See also Chapter 8, section 8 below on the Environmental Liability Directive.

[144] Decision 1999/272, OJ L 109/51. See on cleaning-up costs also Decision 1999/646, OJ L 260/1.

[145] Commission Guidelines on Environmental Aid, OJ 2001 C 37/3, para. 41 in connection with Article 5(a) of Regulation 70/2001, OJ 2001 L 10/33.

[146] Commission Guidelines on Environmental Aid, OJ 2001 C 37/3, section E.3.

[147] Commission Guidelines on Environmental Aid, OJ 2001 C 37/3, para. 51.

production costs of renewable energy for example through direct subsidies or so-called green certificates. Member States may also choose to subsidise renewable energy production using the *PreussenElektra* method, when they oblige private parties to buy all renewable energy produced.[148]

7.3.4   The Future of the Guidelines

As we saw above, the Commission has recorded a great deal of its experience in guidelines. Regulation 994/98 enables the Commission to issue group exemption regulations applying to certain categories of horizontal state aid.[149] Aid measures covered by such a regulation are compatible with the common market and are not subject to the notification requirements. Article 1(1)(iii) specifically refers to aid in favour of environmental protection as a category of measure that may be exempted. The current Guidelines will expire at the end of 2007 and at this moment the Commission is conducting a review in which the Commission is also interested in the possibilities of a block exemption.[150]

7.4   European Aid for Environmental Protection

Aid for the protection of the environment is not only provided by the Member States. The European institutions also have means of supplying aid. Below follows a brief overview of the main provisions in this respect.

7.4.1   The Structural Funds

In the first place there are the Structural Funds – the European Regional Development Fund (ERDF), the European Social Fund (ESF) and the Cohesion Fund.[151] Under Article 6 EC, the EC's environment policies should be fully integrated into these funds. However, that stage had not yet been reached under Regulation 1260/99,[152] the predecessor of the current regulation. It remains to be seen to what extent the new legislation, Regulation 1083/2006,[153] in particular its Articles 3, 17, 40(f), 47 and 52(c) and the strategic guidelines on

---

[148] See above, section 7.2.1.

[149] Regulation 994/98, OJ 1998 L 142.

[150] The Commission has just published a revised version of the new draft guidelines on the website of DG Comp. In addition a draft block exemption regulation that also covers environmental aid has been published in OJ 2007 C 210/14.

[151] For the period 2007-2013, the European Fisheries Fund (EFF) and the European Agricultural Fund for Rural Development (EAFRD) have been moved to a different heading of the Financial Perspectives.

[152] OJ 1999 L 161.

[153] OJ 2006 L 210/25.

cohesion[154] adopted pursuant to Article 25 of Regulation 1083/2006 will improve in practice the integration of environmental considerations in the structural polices.[155]

7.4.2   Life

The general objective of Regulation 1655/2000 establishing a financial instrument for the environment ('Life') is to contribute to the development and implementation of European environmental policy and legislation by financing all kinds of environmental actions in the Community.[156] Life is the EC's only financial instrument specifically focusing on environmental protection.

Life is now in its third phase. The first phase lasted until 1996 and was concluded with the entry into force of Regulation 1404/96. The changes made in the second phase were designed to produce more concentrated efforts and increase the efficiency and transparency of application procedures and promote joint national action and cooperation. To this end the second phase acknowledged three areas of activity eligible for financial support from Life: Life-Nature, Life-Environment and Life-Third Countries.

Life operates solely on the basis of co-financing. The rates of assistance vary depending on the area of activity supported and are different from those contained in the guidelines on state aid for environmental protection.

The third phase maintains the division into three thematic components: Nature, Environment and Third Countries. For the third phase the connection between individual EU-financed projects has been improved and, in addition, measures are proposed to ensure a better dissemination of the results. With the third phase ending in 2006 the next phase, LIFE+, is currently being discussed.[157] LIFE+ will continue to fund the same type of activities but is conducted along two major themes: LIFE+ Implementation and Governance and LIFE+ Information and Communication. In essence this reflects the fact that environmental protection must be integrated in everyday decision-making and administration.

---

[154] OJ 2006 L 291/11.

[155] See COM (2006) 639 on the relation between the SEA Directive, see Chapter 8, section 3.4 below, and the assessment of the environmental effects under the Community funds.

[156] OJ 2000 L 192/1, as amended by Regulation 1682/2004, OJ 2004 L 308/1. Regulation 1655/2000 was annulled in Case C-378/00 *Commission* v. *EP and Council (LIFE – Comitology)* [2003] ECR I-937, because Article 2 of the Comitology decision was disregarded.

[157] COM (2004) 621 final, on 24 October 2006 the European Parliament voted for amendments as a result of which the proposal is now subject to conciliation (Article 215 (3) EC).

7.4.3   The Cohesion Fund

Another important source of European environmental aid is the Cohesion Fund referred to in Article 161 EC.[158] The Cohesion Fund is a structural instrument that helps Member States to reduce economic and social disparities and to stabilise their economies since 1994. The Cohesion Fund finances up to 85% of eligible expenditure of major projects involving the environment and transport infrastructure. At present Greece, Portugal, Spain, Cyprus, Czech Republic, Estonia, Hungary, Latvia, Lithuania, Malta, Poland, Slovakia and Slovenia qualify for payments from this fund.

The Council Regulation establishing the Cohesion Fund[159] provides that the fund can provide assistance for 'the environment within the priorities assigned to the Community environmental protection policy under the policy and action programme on the environment. In this context, the Fund may also intervene in areas related to sustainable development which clearly present environmental benefits, namely energy efficiency and renewable energy and, in the transport sector outside the trans-European networks, rail, river and sea transport, intermodal transport systems and their interoperability, management of road, sea and air traffic, clean urban transport and public transport.' (Article 2(1)(b)). Interestingly, the 'old' Cohesion Fund Regulation contained Article 8 according to which the projects financed by the Cohesion Fund 'shall be in keeping with the provisions of the Treaties, with the instruments adopted pursuant thereto and with Community policies, including those concerning environmental protection.' A similar provision has been omitted from the current regulation. However, the fact that its objective is to improve cohesion as well as sustainable development (Article 1(1) in connection with the fact that Regulation 1083/2006[160] partly governs the Cohesion fund (Article 1(2), an environmentally unfriendly application of the Cohesion fund seems unlikely. The new Cohesion Fund Regulation entered into force on 1 August 2006.

8   Conclusions

All the cases discussed aobve in the context of Articles 81 and 82 lead to the conclusion that, even though environmental considerations are relevant in the sense that they are taken into account, the Commission has still to take a decision in which environmental reasons are in themselves the *decisive* factor.[161] Integration may well require a more active, more creative attitude on

---

[158] Cf. Coffey & Fergusson (1997). Cf. the renumbered Article 177 FEU after the entry into force of the Reform Treaty.

[159] Regulation 1084/2006, OJ 2006 L 210/79, repealing Regulation 1164/94, OJ 1994 L 130/1.

[160] See above, section 7.4.1.

[161] Gyselen (1993), see also Vedder (2003) at 166.

the Commission's part in this respect. Moreover, protection of the environment can no longer be seen purely as a responsibility of government. This is reflected in the increasing use of environmental agreements as an instrument of environmental protection. These have been acknowledged at the European level, too, and their use is encouraged. In this context the traditional black-and-white approach on which European competition policy and law were founded is becoming increasingly inappropriate. This approach assumed that it was up to public authorities to establish and pursue environmental policy by means of legislation and its application through prohibitions and permits, and up to 'the market' to respond by operating as profitably as possible within these constraints. In this climate, competition policies which allowed only marginal room for environmental considerations were appropriate. However today, where the market is very much expected to act responsibly on its own account, environmental objectives should play a greater part in competition policy than is currently the case. This is a necessary consequence of the integration principle of Article 6 EC.

This may be contrasted with the application of Article 86 and 87 EC in an environmental context. Here we see that the Commission and Court provide ample room for manoeuvre for Member States that want to encourage industry to go beyond the minimum environmental standards. Moreover, Community and Member State subsidies that do not have a specific environmental objective are also scrutinised concerning their environmental impact.

CHAPTER 8

Substantive European Environmental Law

The preceding chapters have dealt with a number of general aspects of European environmental law, mainly in terms of primary European law in its relation with environmental protection. In the following sections an overview will be given of substantive European environmental law as created through legal acts of the Council and the Commission. Relevant case law of the Court of Justice will specifically be discussed. The chapter will begin with a brief discussion of the broad outlines of the EU's policy on the environment as set out in the Environmental Action Programmes that have been adopted over the years. After this, the so-called 'horizontal' environmental legislation is examined. This refers to legislation which, in contrast with sectoral legislation, relates not only to a single sphere of the environment (water, air, noise, soil, radiation etc.) but which examines a given activity from a variety of environmental viewpoints. Finally, sectoral legislation is examined.

1 The Environmental Action Programmes

The European institutions have produced six action programmes on the environment since 1973. These contain priority policy plans for the coming years. The programmes give a good picture of the opinions – at least those held by the EU institutions – on the importance and possible role of a European environment policy, as these have changed with the years.

Thus, in 1973, the first programme[1] spelled out the objectives and principles of environment policy and went on to list a large number of essentially remedial actions that were seen to be necessary at European level. The second programme,[2] in 1977, largely updated and extended the first and elaborated on the ideas contained in it. However, by 1983, when the third programme was adopted,[3] more emphasis was placed on a preventive approach, in other words, an approach requiring economic and social developments to be undertaken in such a way as to avoid the creation of environmental problems. The resources of the environment were recognised as constituting the basis of, but also setting the limits to, further development.

By the time of the fourth programme,[4] it was the view of the Commission that the context had again changed. The Commission had become convinced that, in view of the continuing deterioration of the environment, the establishment of strict standards for environmental protection was no longer merely an option, but had become essential. It had also become convinced that, in view of the growing public demand for improved standards of environmental protection and for environmentally friendly goods, European industry would not be successful unless it increasingly geared itself towards meeting that demand.

---

[1]   OJ 1973 C 112/1.

[2]   OJ 1977 C 139/1.

[3]   OJ 1983 C 46/1.

[4]   OJ 1987 C 328/1.

High standards of environmental protection had thus become an imperative, and an economic imperative at that. On the basis of this perception, the
Commission had designated a number of policy areas as priority areas. This
meant that in establishing its priorities, the Commission would give preference
to measures which would result in an improvement in the functioning of the
common market.

In 1993 the Commission drafted the Fifth Environmental Action
Programme, titled 'Towards Sustainability'. The general approach and strategy
contained in this programme were approved by the Council in a Resolution of 1
February 1993. The Fifth Action Programme represented a departure from its
predecessors in several respects. The central objective was 'sustainable development'. As used in the programme, the word 'sustainable' was intended to reflect
a policy and strategy for continued economic and social development without
detriment to the environment and the natural resources on the quality of which
continued human activity and further development depend. The programme
aimed to achieve such changes in society's patterns of behaviour necessary
for sustainability through the optimum involvement of all sectors of society in
a spirit of shared responsibility, including public administration, public and
private enterprise, and the general public. The emphasis on joint responsibility required a broadening of the range of instruments used in environment
policy. Not only traditional instruments such as prohibitions and permits, but
also market-based instruments (taxes, fiscal incentives) should be employed
and so-called horizontal, supporting instruments such as public information
and education. Thus, in contrast with its predecessors, the Fifth Environmental
Action Programme[5] was much more a strategic programme and much less a
list of concrete measures that ought to be taken in the short term. By Decision
2179/98 of the European Parliament and of the Council the Fifth Environmental Action has been reviewed.[6] This review process has resulted in the adoption of the Sixth Environmental Action Programme.[7] Like its predecessor, this
programme is strategic, but it also recognises four priority areas where action is
necessary. These are: climate change, nature and biodiversity, environment and
health and quality of life and sustainable management of resources and wastes.[8]
As far as the instruments are concerned the Sixth Action Programme envisages ten basic strategies:[9] introducing and amending legislation, improving the
implementation of legislation,[10] integrating environmental concerns into other
policies,[11] using market-based instruments to achieve sustainable development,
involving the industry and social partners to achieve sustainable development,

---

[5]   OJ 1993 C 138/1.

[6]   OJ 1998 L 275/1.

[7]   Decision 1600/2002, OJ 2002 L 242/1, adopted on the basis of Commission proposal COM (2001) 31.

[8]   Decision 1600/2002, OJ 2002 L 242/1, Article 1(4).

[9]   Decision 1600/2002, OJ 2002 L 242/1, Article 3.

[10] See Chapter 4.

[11] See, for example, Chapter 7 on the integration of environmental considerations in competition policy.

making environmental information available for consumers in order to make consumption more sustainable, integrating environmental concerns in the financial sector, creating an environmental liability scheme, improving environmental governance and integrating environmental considerations in land-use planning and management decisions. Unless indicated otherwise, these basic strategies and their further implementation will be discussed in this chapter. In addition the Sixth Environmental Action Programme envisages the adoption of so-called thematic strategies by the Commission and Council and the European Parliament within three years from the adoption of the action programme.[12] Thematic strategies are envisaged in the following areas: soil protection, the protection of the marine environment, sustainable use of pesticides, integrated and coherent policy on air pollution, improvement of the urban environment, sustainable use of resources and waste recycling. Again, these strategies and their implementation will be discussed in this chapter below. Finally the action programme contains provisions on international cooperation, policy making on the basis of the programme and on the monitoring and evaluation. The programme began on 22 July 2002 and will be valid for ten years.[13]

2 The Notification Directive and other Notification Obligations

In the discussion of Articles 176 and 95(4-6) EC in Chapter 3, it became clear that national environmental measures which are more stringent than the European ones generally have to be notified to the Commission. Moreover, directives always contain provisions requiring Member States to notify the Commission of national implementing legislation. However, European environmental law also contains a large number of such provisions apart from the cases just mentioned. In the past national environmental measures had to be notified under the Notification Agreement of 5 March 1973.[14] This requires that the Commission shall be informed as soon as possible of any draft legislative, regulatory or administrative measures and of any international initiative concerning the protection or improvement of the environment which. In practice, although as far as we are aware it has never officially been withdrawn, the Notification Agreement has lost much of its significance since the adoption of Directive 83/189, as amended by Directive 94/10 and now consolidated by Directive 98/34 laying down a procedure for the provision of information in the field of technical standards and regulations, the so-called Notification Directive.[15] Under this directive Member States are required to notify the Commission of legislative

---

[12] Decision 1600/2002, OJ 2002 L 242/1, Article 4.

[13] Decision 1600/2002, OJ 2002 L 242/1, Article 1(3).

[14] OJ 1973 C 9/1.

[15] OJ 1998 L 204/37, as amended by Directive 98/48, OJ 1998 L 217/18. The preamble to this directive contains a reference to the Notification Agreement of 1973 where it speaks of its inadequate time limits.

proposals in the field of technical regulations applying to products. Article 1 defines 'technical regulation' as meaning the following: 'technical specifications and other requirements, including the relevant administrative provisions, the observance of which is compulsory, *de jure* or *de facto,* in the case of marketing or use in a Member State or a major part thereof'. De *facto* technical regulations include voluntary agreements to which a public authority is a contracting party and which provide, in the public interest, for compliance with technical specifications. For example, voluntary agreements whereby product standards are agreed upon between the public authorities and an industry. 'Technical specification' is defined as: a specification contained in a document which lays down the characteristics required of a product such as levels of quality, performance, safety or dimensions, including the requirements applicable to the product as regards the name under which the product is sold, terminology, symbols, testing and test methods, packaging, marking or labelling and conformity assessment procedures. Environmental product specifications will therefore often fall within the scope of application of this directive, and will therefore have to be notified.

Two cases in which the Court of Justice has ruled on the matter in an environmental context are *Bic Benelux* and Case C-279/94.[16] In *Bic Benelux* the Court had to answer the question of to what extent the Notification Directive was applicable to a Belgian law which introduced an environmental tax on disposable razors. In addition the legislation required a marking to be placed on products subject to the environmental tax. Bic, which marketed integral disposable razors in Belgium before the environmental tax arrangements came into force, asked the Belgian *Raad van State* to annul this legislation, on the ground that the law had not been notified to the Commission prior to its adoption. According to the Belgian Government the obligation to mark the razors had to be regarded as an environmental protection measure falling outside the scope of the Notification Directive. The Court disagreed in no uncertain terms, stating that the fact that a national measure was adopted in order to protect the environment does not mean that the measure in question falls outside the scope of the directive. Its final conclusion was that an obligation to affix specific distinctive signs to products which are subject to a tax levied on them on account of the environmental damage which they are deemed to cause, constitutes a technical specification within the meaning of the Notification Directive.

Case C-274/97 concerned Italian legislation on asbestos. More particularly the legislation dealt with the extraction, importation, processing, use, marketing, treatment and disposal in the national territory, as well as the exportation, of asbestos and products containing asbestos, and laid down rules for the cessation of the production and trade, extraction, importation, exportation and use of asbestos and products containing asbestos. It also prohibited the extraction, importation, exportation, marketing and production of asbestos, asbestos prod-

---

[16] Case C-13/96 *Bic Benelux* v. *Belgium* [1997] ECR I-1753 and Case C-279/94 *Commission* v. *Italy* [1997] ECR I-4743.

ucts and products containing asbestos after a period of one year after the date of entry into force of the Italian legislation. The Court ruled as follows: 'Such a provision, in prohibiting the marketing and use of asbestos, constitutes a technical regulation which the Italian Government ought to have notified in accordance with the first subparagraph of Article 8(1) of the directive.'

If national legislation contains provisions of which some are within the scope of the directive, but others are not, the Commission can nevertheless require that it is notified of the legislation as a whole. Only full communication will enable the Commission to evaluate correctly the exact scope of any technical regulations contained in that law.[17]

If the Commission should have any objections to the national regulations, the Member States may be required to postpone their adoption for a certain period (Article 9). Breach of the obligation to notify renders the technical regulations concerned inapplicable, so that they are unenforceable against individuals and individuals may rely on them before the national court, which must decline to apply a national technical regulation which has not been notified in accordance with the directive.[18]

Environmental directives may themselves also contain specific information requirements. One example is Article 3(2) of the 'old' Waste Directive,[19] which provided that the Commission must be informed of draft national rules concerning, *inter alia*, waste prevention, the development of clean technologies, recycling and re-use. The question of whether such a requirement also applied to measures adopted by local and regional authorities has been addressed by the Court of Justice in the *Balsamo* case.[20] In that case the Italian Government had contended that the obligation under Article 3(2) of the directive to inform the Commission related only to 'measures of a certain degree of importance and could not cover provisions whose practical effects are extremely limited, such as those adopted by a small municipality.' The Court rejected this argument:

'It need merely be stated that the directive does not provide for any derogation or limitation regarding the obligation to inform the Commission of the draft rules referred to in Article 3. Consequently, that obligation extends to draft rules drawn

---

[17] Case C-279/94 *Commission v. Italy* [1997] ECR I-4743. However, the mere fact that all the provisions have been notified to the Commission does not prevent the Member State from bringing provisions which do not constitute technical regulations into force immediately, and therefore without waiting for the results of the examination procedure provided for by the directive.

[18] Case C-194/94 *CIA Security* [1996] ECR I-2201. See also Case C-303/04 *Lidl Italia* [2005] ECR I-7865 on an Italian rule holding a prohibition to market non-biodegradable cotton buds.

[19] Directive 75/442, OJ 1975 L 194/47, before its amendment by Directive 91/156, OJ 1991 L 377/48.

[20] Case 380/87 *Balsamo* [1989] ECR 2491. Cf. with respect to the notification requirement of Article 7(3) of the 'old' Waste Directive Case C-209/98 *Sydhavnens Sten & Grus* [2000] ECR I-3743, paras. 96-102, where the same approach was being followed.

up by all authorities in the Member States, including decentralized authorities such as municipalities.'

Thus where the obligation is unconditional, the Member States must also notify the Commission of measures adopted by local and regional authorities. Be that as it may, in the *Balsamo* case the failure to comply with the obligation did not affect the lawfulness of the national rules in question:

> 'Neither the wording nor the purpose of the provision in question provides any support for the view that failure by the Member States to observe their obligation to give prior notice in itself renders unlawful the rules thus adopted. It follows from the foregoing that the abovementioned provision concerns relations between the Member States and the Commission and does not give rise to any right for individuals which might be infringed by a Member State's breach of its obligation to inform the Commission in advance of draft rules.'

This decision does not imply that failure to comply with an obligation to notify the Commission of a measure could *never* affect the enforceability of that measure. The arguments for deciding the local measure was not unlawful in this case had to do with the nature of the notification obligation in question. In this case there was no question of European monitoring, nor did the directive make implementation of the national measures conditional upon the Commission's not having any objections. It is clear from the judgment in the *CIA Security* case[21] that if there is a monitoring procedure, and the Commission is entitled to raise objections, failure to notify does have consequences for the national measures in question.

Other provisions containing specific notification requirements are those relating to the application of safeguard clauses by the Member States. Especially in directives laying down total harmonisation of product standards, Member States are often empowered to depart from the directive in emergencies. Application of such clauses generally requires that the Commission be notified. Incidentally, in Case C-43/90 it was held that, even if a national measure is provisional, there is no obligation to state in so many words that it is.[22] Simple notification is sufficient.

Where the application of such a safeguard clause is delegated to local or regional authorities, the national legislation must contain provisions requiring those authorities to inform the central government of the measures in question, so that it in turn can notify the Commission. This emerged in Case C-237/90, where implementation in Germany of the safeguard powers under Articles 9 and 10 of Directive 80/778 relating to the quality of water intended for human consumption were at issue.[23] This is inherent in the Court's case law on imple-

---

[21] Case C-194/94 *CIA Security* [1996] ECR I-2201.

[22] Case C-43/90 *Commission v. Germany* [1992] ECR I-1909.

[23] Case C-237/90 *Commission v. Germany* [1992] ECR I-5973.

mentation by decentral authorities according to which the central government is ultimately responsible.[24]

Finally, there is Article 10 EC, by which the Member States are required to facilitate the achievement of the EU's tasks. In order to fulfil this task properly the Commission must be fully informed of the measures adopted by Member States for the purpose of implementing decisions of the EU institutions. The practical significance of this became apparent in the Court's judgment in the *Campania* case.[25] Under the Waste Directives, Member States must draw up a report on the measures taken to implement their obligations in respect of waste disposal and send it to the Commission. The Commission had asked the Italian Government for information concerning the quantities produced, the methods employed and the importation of waste into the region of Campania. The Italian Government maintained that it was not obliged to furnish the information requested, because this went beyond the obligation to produce the reports. The Court rejected this argument and held that Italy had failed to meet its obligations under Article 10 EC:

> 'In so far as it concerned the disposal of waste covered by the directive on waste and the directive on toxic and dangerous waste and the competent authority for disposal operations, that request for information came within the scope of the Commission's power to supervision. The inaction on the part of the Italian Government, which thus prevented the Commission from obtaining an accurate picture of conditions in Campania, must be treated as a refusal to cooperate with that institution.'

The Court added that the Italian Government was in any case obliged to explain its position further. This case could be taken to imply an obligation on the Member States to provide information to the Commission, even where there are no explicit provisions, where the information relates to matters within the scope of application of a directive and the information would enable the Commission to exercise its task of monitoring compliance with the directive.[26]

3 Environmental Impact Assessment

Environmental impact assessment was first introduced by the US National Environmental Policy Act 1969.[27] It is a procedural instrument that implements the prevention principle by requiring an assessment of the

---

[24] See Chapter 4, section 2.8, e.g. Case C-87/02 *Commission v. Italy (Lotto Zero)* [2004] ECR I-5975, para. 38.

[25] Case C-33/90 *Commission v. Italy (Campania)* [1991] ECR I-5987.

[26] The Court seems to have confirmed this in Case C-285/96 *Commission v. Italy* [1998] ECR I-5935.

[27] 42 USC 4321-4347.

environmental effects of certain decisions in advance.[28] In the EU environmental assessment is required for certain projects and plans. For *projects* the legal framework consists of the Environmental Impact Assessment (EIA) Directive.[29] Environmental assessment for *plans* and *programmes* is governed by the Strategic Environmental Assessment (SEA) Directive.[30] Below, first the EIA Directive will be discussed

3.1 The Scope of the EIA Directive

Article 2(1) of the EIA Directive is one of the central provisions and requires that, before consent is given, projects likely to have significant effects on the environment by virtue, *inter alia*, of their nature, size or location are made subject to a requirement for development consent[31] and an assessment with regard to their effects. Article 2(1) of the directive results in a very wide scope, that is limited in a number of ways. Article 1(1) states that the directive shall apply to public and private projects which are likely to have significant effects on the environment. For the purposes of the directive, 'project' means the execution of construction works or of other installations or schemes, or other interventions in the natural surroundings and landscape including those involving the extraction of mineral resources. Article 1(4) allows for the Member States to decide that 'projects serving national defence purposes' are outside the scope of the EIA Directive.[32] In the *Bozen* case the Court ruled:

> 'That provision thus excludes from the Directive's scope and, therefore, from the assessment procedure for which it provides, projects intended to safeguard national defence. Such an exclusion introduces an exception to the general rule laid down by the Directive that environmental effects are to be assessed in advance and it must accordingly be interpreted restrictively. Only projects which mainly serve national defence purposes may therefore be excluded from the assessment obligation.
> It follows that the Directive covers projects, such as that at issue in the main proceedings which, as the file shows, has the principal objective of restructuring

---

[28] See on the subject in general Holder (2004) and Moreno (2005). See, concerning the EIA Directive, Case C-392/96 *Commission v. Ireland* [1999] ECR-5901, para. 62.

[29] Directive 85/337 on the assessment of the effects of certain public and private projects on the environment, OJ 1985 L 175/40, as amended by Directive 97/11, OJ 1997 L 73/5 and Directive 2003/35, OJ 2003 L 156/17.

[30] Directive 2001/42 on the assessment of the effects of certain plans and programmes on the environment, OJ 2001 L 197/30.

[31] On the definition of this concept see Case C-290/03 *Barker* [2006] ECR I-3949, paras. 39-41.

[32] These decisions must be taken on a case-by-case basis. Moreover, this may only take place if the Member States consider that applying the EIA Directive would adversely affect the national defence purposes. The fact that this exemption has to take place on a case-by-case basis excludes blanket-decisions exempting all national defence projects from the scope.

an airport in order for it to be capable of commercial use, even though it may also be used for military purposes.'[33]

However, Article 1(5) provides that the directive is not to apply to projects the details of which are adopted by a specific act of national legislation, since the objectives of the directive, including that of supplying information, are achieved through the legislative process. In the *Bozen* case the Court clarified its position.[34] In order to be able to apply the exemption two conditions have to be met. The first requires the details of the project to be adopted by a specific legislative act; under the second, the objectives of the directive, including that of supplying information, must be achieved through the legislative process. With regard to the first condition the Court argued that the legislative act, which grants the developer the right to carry out the project, must be specific and display the same characteristics as the development consent and must lay down the project in detail. It is only by complying with such requirements that the objectives referred to in the second condition can be achieved through the legislative process.

Concerning the temporal scope of the directive there have been a number of cases dealing with the so-called 'pipeline-problem'.[35] This refers to the fact that the projects the EIA Directive refers to can take many years to complete. In the meantime the balance between (economic) progress and environmental protection may have shifted, leading to requests for assessments.[36] As a result there have been questions on the applicability of the EIA Directive to projects that were said to have started before the deadline for implementation of the EIA Directive had passed. The applicability of the EIA Directive hinges on whether or not the application for development consent was lodged before the deadline for implementation, 8 July 1988 for Directive 85/337.

This was ruled in the *Bund Naturschutz* case in response to questions from the *Bayerische Verwaltungsgerichtshof* on the permissibility of national transitional rules, the Court pointed out that:[37]

'there is nothing in the directive which could be construed as authorizing the Member States to exempt projects in respect of which the consent procedures were initiated after the deadline of 3 July 1988 from the obligation to carry out

---

[33] Case C-435/97 *World Wildlife Fund* v. *Autonome Provinz* [1999] ECR I-5613, paras. 65-66.

[34] Case C-435/97 *World Wildlife Fund* v. *Autonome Provinz* [1999] ECR I-5613, paras. 55-63. Cf. for some national case law on Article 1(5): the Danish Supreme Court ruling of 2 December 1998 on the building of the Öresund bridge, *Greenpeace* v. *Minister of Traffic*, EfR. 1999.367 H (referred to by Peter Pagh in *YEEL* (2000) at 474-475 and the Dutch *Raad van State* 16 June 1995 [1995] *M&R* 93 on the *Deltawet Grote Rivieren*, legislation containing rules on the repair of river-dykes.

[35] See for this terminology Case C-201/02 *Wells* [2004] ECR I-723, para. 48.

[36] See, for example, the reverie by Advocate General Mischo in Case C-81/96 *B en W Haarlemmerliede en Spaarnwoude* v. *GS van Noord-Holland* [1998] ECR I-3923, para. 32.

[37] Case C-396/92 *Bund Naturschutz* v. *Bayern* [1994] ECR I-3717.

an environmental impact assessment. On the contrary, all the provisions in the directive were formulated on the basis that it was to be transposed into the legal systems of the Member States by 3 July 1988 at the latest.

Accordingly, regardless whether the directive permits a Member State to introduce transitional rules for consent procedures already initiated and in progress before the deadline of 3 July 1988, the directive in any case precludes the introduction in respect of procedures initiated after that date of rules such as those at issue in the main proceedings by a national law, which, in breach of the directive, transposes it belatedly into the domestic legal system. Such an interpretation would result in an extension of the deadline of 3 July 1988 and would be contrary to the obligations under the directive.'[38]

The Court added to that in the *Großkrotzenburg* case that informal contacts between the competent authority and the developer, even relating to the content and proposal to lodge an application for consent for a project, cannot be treated for the purposes of applying the directive as a definite indication of the date on which the procedure was initiated. The date when the application for consent was *formally* lodged constitutes the sole criterion which may be used.[39]

Following the amendment by Directive 97/11, the EIA Directive makes clear that the EIA Directive in its current form will only apply if a request for development consent is submitted after 14 March 1999 (the deadline for implementation of Directive 97/11).[40]

3.2 Projects Subject to an EIA

Even when a project is within the scope of the directive, an assessment is not always required. The directive distinguishes between so-called Annex I projects which are always made subject to an assessment (Article 4(1)) and Annex II projects where the Member States shall determine through a case-by-case examination, and/or thresholds or criteria set by the Member State whether the project shall be made subject to an assessment (Article 4(2)).

When a case-by-case examination is carried out or thresholds or criteria are set, the relevant selection criteria set out in Annex III shall be taken into account. These include both the characteristics of the project (its size, the accumulation with other projects, the use of natural resources, the production of waste, pollution and nuisances, the risk of accidents), its location (the environmental sensitivity of geographical areas likely to be affected) and the characteristics of the potential impact (the extent of the impact, the transfrontier nature, the magnitude and complexity, the probability and the duration, frequency and reversibility of the impact).

---

[38] Case C-396/92 *Bund Naturschutz* v. *Bayern* [1994] ECR I-3717. Cf. also Case C-301/95 *Commission* v. *Germany* [1998] ECR I-6135.

[39] Case C-431/92 *Commission* v. *Germany (Großkrotzenburg)* [1995] ECR I-2189.

[40] Directive 97/11, OJ 1997 L 73/5, Article 3(3).

Under the 'old' directive the Court set clear limits on the Member States' powers when setting thresholds. Ruling on Belgian legislation which excluded certain whole classes of projects listed in Annex II from the requirement of an impact assessment, the Court held that the criteria and/or the thresholds mentioned in Article 4(2) were designed to facilitate examination of the actual characteristics of any given project in order to determine whether it is subject to the requirement of assessment, not to exempt in advance from that obligation certain whole classes of projects listed in Annex II which may be envisaged as taking place on the territory of a Member State.[41] In the *Kraaijeveld* case the Court confirmed this position and stated it more precisely.[42] The Court acknowledged that Article 4(2) of the directive conferred on Member States a measure of discretion to specify certain types of projects which would be subject to an assessment. However, the limits of that discretion are to be found in the obligation set out in Article 2(1) that projects likely to have significant effects on the environment are to be subject to an impact assessment. The question of whether, in laying down such criteria, the Member State went beyond the limits of its discretion cannot be determined in relation to the characteristics of a single project. It depends on an overall assessment of the characteristics of projects of that nature which could be envisaged in the Member State.

In Case C-392/96 the Court ruled against the way Ireland had made use of its discretion to set thresholds. On the setting of 'absolute thresholds' the Court ruled that 'a Member State which established criteria or thresholds taking account only of the size of projects, without also taking their nature and location into consideration, would exceed the limits of its discretion under Articles 2(1) and 4(2) of the directive'.[43] On the 'cumulative effect' of projects the Court ruled in the same case that the Member States must ensure that the objective of the legislation would not be circumvented by the splitting of projects:

> 'Not taking account of the cumulative effect of projects means in practice that all projects of a certain type may escape the obligation to carry out an assessment when, taken together, they are likely to have significant effects on the environment within the meaning of Article 2(1) of the Directive.'[44]

Annex I projects include crude-oil, thermal power stations and other combustion installations, various nuclear installations, integrated works for the initial smelting of cast-iron and steel, installations for the extraction of asbestos, integrated chemical installations, construction of lines for long-distance railway traffic,[45] construction of motorways,[46] inland waterways and ports, waste disposal

---

[41] Case C-133/94 *Commission v. Belgium* [1996] ECR I-2323. Cf. on the question of the interpretation of the concept of classes of projects, Case C-301/95 *Commission v. Germany* [1998] ECR I-6135, paras. 38-46.

[42] Case C-72/95 *Kraaijeveld* [1996] ECR I-5403.

[43] Case C-392/96 *Commission v. Ireland* [1999] ECR I-5901, para. 65.

[44] Case C-392/96 *Commission v. Ireland* [1999] ECR I-5901, para. 76.

[45] Case C-227/01 *Commission v. Spain* (*Valencia-Tarragona railway*) [2004] ECR I-8253, paras. 48-54.

[46] Case C-87/02 *Commission v. Italy* (*Lotto Zero*) [2004] ECR I-5975, paras. 41-49.

installations, groundwater abstraction or artificial groundwater recharge schemes, waste water treatment plants, extraction of petroleum and natural gas for commercial purposes, dams, pipelines for the transport of gas, oil or chemicals, installations for the intensive rearing of poultry or pigs,[47] quarries and open-cast mining, construction of overhead electrical power lines, and installations for storage of petroleum, petrochemical, or chemical products. Some of these projects are subject to a threshold. Where the threshold is not exceeded the project will generally be covered by Annex II. Annex II also contains a whole list of projects, ranging from reclamation of land from the sea and installations for the slaughter of animals, tourism and leisure projects[48] such as ski-runs, ski lifts and cable-cars to urban development projects.[49]

Annex II also covers any change or extension of projects listed in Annex I or Annex II, already authorised, executed or in the process of being executed, which may have significant adverse effects on the environment (changes or extensions not listed in Annex I).[50] The same applies to projects in Annex I.[51]

The Court's case law already clarified that modifications to projects listed in Annex II are not *a priori* exempted from the directive.[52]

3.3 The EIA Procedure

The directive allows Member States considerable freedom as to the manner in which the assessment should be carried out. Article 5(3) provides that the information to be provided should include at least:

· a description of the project comprising information on the site, design and size of the project;
· a description of the measures envisaged in order to avoid, reduce and, if possible, remedy significant adverse effects;
· the data required to identify and assess the main effects which the project

---

[47] Case C-121/03 *Commission v. Spain (Pig Farms in Baix Ter)* [2005] ECR I-7569, paras. 86-98.

[48] Case C-117/02 *Commission v. Portugal (Hotels in the Sintra-Cascais site of Community importance)* [2004] ECR I-5517. This case shows that the mere fact that a project takes place in a national park does not mean that it will have significant effects on the environment, paras. 80-88.

[49] Case C-332/04, *Commission v. Spain (Cinema in Paterna)* [2006] ECR I-40, paras. 70-88. This case shows that the mere fact that a project is implemented in an urban area is not enough to rule out possible environmental effects, particularly if the cinema is presented to be the second-largest in Europe attracting more than 60,000 people per week. Cf. also the intensity of review to be exercised by national courts the English Court of Appeal 14 February 2003 *Goodman and Hedges v. LB Lewisham and Big Yellow Property Co. Ltd.* [2003] EWCA Civ 140.

[50] See for instance Case C-431/92 *Commission v. Germany* [1995] ECR I-2189.

[51] Annex I, point 22.

[52] Case C-435/97 *World Wildlife Fund v. Autonome Provinz* [1999] ECR I-5613, para. 39: 'the mere fact that the Directive did not expressly refer to modifications to projects included in Annex II, as opposed to modifications to projects included in Annex I, did not justify the conclusion that they were not covered by the Directive'. Cf. also Case C-72/95 *Kraaijeveld* [1996] ECR I-5403, para. 40.

is likely to have on the environment;
· an outline of the main alternatives studied by the developer and an indication of the main reasons for his choice, taking into account the environmental effects;
· a non-technical summary of the information.

Annex IV contains details of the information to be supplied. Besides this the
directive lays down rules that have to be complied with before consent for a
project is given. Consultation of the public is inherent in the EIA-instrument,
and has been reinforced by the amendments to the EIA Directive by Directive
2003/35 on public participation.[53] Member States are required to ensure that
any request for development consent and any information in that connection
is made available to the public within a reasonable time in order to give the
public concerned the opportunity to express an opinion before the development
consent is granted (Article 6(2)). Even though Article 6(2) is silent on this point,
the Court has ruled that Member States may require a reasonable sum for this
information.[54] They must also take the measures necessary to ensure that the
authorities likely to be concerned by the project by reason of their specific environmental responsibilities are given an opportunity to express their opinion on
the information supplied by the developer and on the request for development
consent (Article 6(1)).[55] The logical consequence of these provisions is that the
results of consultations and the information gathered must be taken into consideration in the development consent procedure (Article 8).

According to Article 2(2) the EIA may be integrated into the existing procedures for consent to projects in the Member States. The question to what extent
an *ordinary* environmental authorisation procedure, in other words one that is
not a specific EIA procedure, complies with the directive's requirements was
addressed by the Court in Case C-431/92.[56] The Court seems to have accepted
this as long as all the requirements of the directive have been complied with.[57]
The same rationale – one that hinges on the effectiveness of the EIA Directive – can also be seen in the case law on the time of an EIA in a multi-stage
procedure. Normally, an EIA should be carried out at the earlier stage, but when

---

53   See further section 6.3 below.

54   Case C-216/05 *Commission* v. *Ireland* [2006] ECR I-10787, paras. 42-47, where a fee of €20 or 45 was
     considered reasonable an not to constitute an obstacle to the participation rights.

55   However, according to Article 6(3) the Member States can determine the details for such information
     and consultation; cf. Case C-216/05 *Commission* v. *Ireland* [2006] ECR I-10787, paras. 24-28.

56   Case C-431/92 *Commission* v. *Germany* [1995] ECR I-2189.

57   Confirmed in Case C-435/97 *World Wildlife Fund* v. *Autonome Provinz* [1999] ECR I-5613, para. 52 and
     Case C-278/98 *Linster* [2000] ECR I-6817, paras. 49-58. See for an application at national level of this
     doctrine the judgment of the Swedish Supreme Administrative Court of 16 June 1999, case nos. 1424-
     1998, 2397-1998 and 2939-1998, RÅ 1999 ref. 76, regarding the cessation of the right to operate the
     nuclear power reactor Barsebäck 1.

the actual environmental effects can only be known at the later stage, the EIA should also be conducted at that later stage.[58]

Article 2(3) provides that Member States may, in exceptional cases, exempt a specific project in whole or in part from an EIA. However in that case the Member States shall consider whether another form of assessment would be appropriate and whether the information thus collected should be made available to the public. They must also provide the Commission with the relevant information prior to granting consent.[59]

In case of projects with transboundary effects, the Convention on Environmental Impact Assessment in a Transboundary Context, the so-called Espoo Convention, signed by the EC on 25 February 1991, is relevant. This convention was implemented at the EU level in the form of changes to Article 7 of the EIA Directive.

Where a Member State is aware that a project is likely to have significant transboundary effects or where a Member State likely to be significantly affected so requests, the Member State in whose territory the project is intended to be carried out shall send to the affected Member State as soon as possible and no later than when informing its own public, *inter alia:*

- a description of the project, together with any available information on its possible transboundary impact;
- information on the nature of the decision which may be taken;
- and shall give the other Member State a reasonable time in which to indicate whether it wishes to participate in the EIA procedure.

If a Member State which receives the above information indicates that it intends to participate in the EIA procedure, the Member State in whose territory the project is intended to be carried out shall, if it has not already done so, send to the affected Member State all information to be given pursuant to Article 6(2). The Member States concerned shall also arrange for the information to be made available pursuant to Article 6(3)(a) and (b). They shall ensure that those authorities and the public concerned are given an opportunity, before development consent for the project is granted, to forward their opinion within a reasonable time on the information supplied to the competent authority in the Member State in whose territory the project is intended to be carried out.

Finally, the Member States concerned shall enter into consultations regarding, *inter alia*, the potential transboundary effects of the project and the

---

[58] Case C-201/02 *Wells* [2004] ECR I-723, paras. 42-52 and Case C-508/03 *Commission v. UK* [2006] ECR I-3969, paras. 104-106 and Case C-290/03 *Barker* [2006] ECR I-3949, paras. 46-48.

[59] Irish legislation failed to meet these requirements; Case C-392/96 *Commission v. Ireland* [1999] ECR I-5901, para. 87. According to the Dutch *Raad van State* 16 June 1995 [1995] *M&R* 93, a failure to notify does not affect the legality of the legislation concerned or permits granted on the basis of it. The Commission has published a guidance document concerning this provision on the D-G environment website http://ec.europa.eu/environment/eia/pdf/eia_art2_3.pdf.

measures envisaged to reduce or eliminate such effects and shall agree on a reasonable time frame for the duration of the consultation period.

National legislation transposing the obligations of Article 7 of the directive must contain explicit provisions requiring the authorities to transmit the information to the other Member States.[60]

When a decision to grant or refuse development consent has been taken,[61] Article 9 of the EIA Directive requires the competent authority to inform the public thereof and to make available to the public the following information:

· the content of the decision and any conditions attached thereto;

· having examined the concerns and opinions expressed by the public concerned, the main reasons and considerations on which the decision is based, including information about the public participation process;

· a description of the main measures to avoid, reduce and, if possible, offset the major adverse effects.

Article 10a was introduced by Directive 2003/35 and requires that the Member States grant access to a judicial review procedure for members of the public concerned.[62]

3.4   The Strategic Environmental Assessment Directive

The SEA Directive implements the idea that the environmental effects of certain actions should be identified in advance at an even earlier stage than the EIA Directive.[63] Where the latter requires an EIA for projects, the former applies to the strategic or planning stage that precedes the action project-stage. The integration of environmental concerns at this stage is generally considered to contribute to sustainability.[64] The initial proposal for the SEA Directive dates from 1996,[65] was amended in 1999[66] and resulted in the SEA Directive in 2001.[67] According to Article 13 the SEA Directive had to be implemented before 21 July 2004.[68] The framework of the SEA Directive closely follows that of the EIA Directive.

---

[60] Case C-392/96 *Commission v. Ireland* [1999] ECR I-5901, para. 94. In view of the judgment of the Court in Case C-186/91 *Commission v. Belgium* [1993] ECR I-851, Article 7 contains 'rights for individuals'.

[61] Such a decision must be explicitly taken, so-called tacit authorisation according to which a positive decision as deemed to have been taken after the expiry of a certain time-limit is not compatible with the EIA Directive, Case C-230/00 *Commission v. Belgium* [2001] ECR-4591.

[62] See section 6.3 below and Chapter 5.

[63] See for an appraisal of the SEA Directive in the light of the EIA Directive, Sheate (2003).

[64] Marsden & De Mulder (2005).

[65] COM (1996) 511, OJ 1997 C 128/14.

[66] COM (1999) 73, OJ 1999 C 83/13.

[67] Directive 2001/42, OJ 2001 L 197/30

[68] Several Member States failed to implement the SEA Directive on time: see e.g. infringement Case C-159/06 *Commission v. Finland* [2006] ECR I-114.

3.4.1 The Scope of the SEA Directive

The SEA Directive applies to plans and programmes. Article 2(a) defines this as 'plans and programmes, including those co-financed by the EU, as well as any modifications to them, which are subject to preparation and/or adoption by an authority at national, regional or local level or which are prepared by an authority for adoption, through a legislative procedure by Parliament or Government, and which are required by legislative, regulatory or administrative provisions'. This very wide definition is narrowed down by Article 3(8). On the basis of this provision, plans and programmes the sole purpose of which is to serve national defence or civil emergency and financial or budget plans and programmes are excluded from the scope of the directive.[69]

For co-financed plans and programmes Article 13(9) contains an exception for plans and programmes co-financed under the 2000-2006 programming period for the 'old' Cohesion Fund Regulation 1260/1999 and the 2000-2006 and 2000-2007 programming periods for the European Agricultural Fund for Rural Development Regulation 1257/1999.

Contrary to the EIA Directive, the SEA Directive contains provisions as regards its temporal scope. According to Article 13(3) the obligation to conduct a prior environmental assessment applies only to plans and programmes of which the first formal preparatory act is subsequent to the deadline for implementation (21 July 2004). Furthermore, for plans and programmes initiated before 21 July 2004 (i.e. pipeline plans and programmes), the environmental assessment obligation applies if these plans and programmes are finally approved only after 21 July 2005. For the pipeline plans and programmes, the Member States can decide that the environmental assessment obligation does not apply on a case-by-case basis if they consider this 'not feasible'.[70]

3.4.2 Plans and Programmes Subject to SEA

According to Article 3(1) all plans and programmes likely to have significant environmental effects are subject to the environmental assessment obligation. Article 3(2) further specifies this by making an environmental assessment mandatory for two categories of plans and programmes. Firstly those which are prepared for agriculture, forestry, fisheries, energy, industry, transport, waste management, water management, telecommunications, tourism, town and country planning or land use and which set the framework for future development consent of projects listed in Annexes I and II to Directive 85/337. Secondly the plans and programmes which, in view of the likely effect on

---

[69] This provision can be compared to Article 1(4) of the EIA Directive which will probably result in a narrow interpretation of this exception, see by analogy: Case C-435/97 *World Wildlife Fund* v. *Autonome Provinz* [1999] ECR I-5613, paras. 65-66.

[70] On the basis of the *Kraaieveld* case law of the Court this provision can probably be invoked in order to ascertain whether or not a Member State has exceeded the limits to its discretion set by Article 13(3).

sites, have been determined to require an assessment pursuant to Article 6 or 7 of the Habitats Directive.[71] These categories of plans and programmes are always subject to the environmental assessment obligation unless they involve only minor modifications or small areas at local level (Article 3(3); *de minimis* exception) and the Member States have determined that they are not likely to have significant environmental effects.

Environmental assessment is optional for all other plans and programmes which set the framework for future development consent of projects, insofar as these are likely to have significant environmental effects. (Article 3(4). Article 3(5) requires the Member States to establish a so-called screening mechanism on the basis of which it will be determined whether or not there is a likelihood of significant environmental effects in case of the *de minimis* exception or in their application of the optional environmental assessment. On doing so the Member States have to use the (non-exhaustive) criteria in Annex II. This situation resembles that with regard to Annex II-projects under the EIA Directive and is thus likely to lead to comparable case law. The first indent of point 1 of Annex II, for example, allows the Member States to set quantitative thresholds, similar to the thresholds allowed under Article 4(2) of the EIA Directive.

3.4.3   The SEA Procedure

The SEA procedure is also comparable to the EIA procedure. Basically, an environmental report that will become part of the plan or programme (Article 2(c)) needs to be completed according to Article 5 in connection with Annex I. This report must be completed during the preparation of the plan or programme (Article 4(1) and is subject to consultation (Article 6(1)). The consultation on the basis of the SEA Directive can be transboundary as well (Article 7).[72] The SEA procedure may be integrated into existing procedures or it may take the form of a special procedure to implement the directive (Article 4(2)). As the usefulness of SEA hinges on the quality of the environmental assessment, Article 12(2) constitutes a major step forward compared to the EIA Directive because it requires the Member States to implement some form of quality control for the environmental reports.

Because the plan or programme subject to SEA may also set the framework for future projects subject to EIA, the SEA Directive contains Article 4(3) dealing with so-called 'tiering' of environmental assessment. This addresses the desire to avoid unnecessary duplication of environmental assessments. During the negotiations leading up to the SEA Directive, an amendment was introduced according to which only one environmental assessment (either an SEA or an EIA) would be required. This was rejected, and Article 11(1) explicitly states that the fact that there has been an SEA for a plan does not rule out the

---

[71]   See further section 17.2 of this chapter.

[72]   This implements the Espoo convention and the ECE Protocol on strategic environmental assessment to the Espoo convention (Kiev 2003).

requirement of an EIA for a project implementing that plan. This does, however, highlight the problems arising from a wide definition of plans and programmes in connection with an equally wide definition 'project'.[73] This will probably have to be resolved in the form of an integration or consolidation of the EIA and the SEA Directives.

According to Article 8, the environmental report and results of the (transboundary) consultations have to be taking into account in the preparation of the plan or programme. Indications that SEA is more than just a purely procedural tool[74] can be found in Articles 9 and 10. Article 9 requires the final decision on the plan or programme to be communicated to the authorities, the public concerned and the parties in the (transboundary) consultation. Importantly, it also requires the communication of a statement summarising how the environmental considerations have been integrated, thus presuming a duty to integrate them, rather than a duty to take them into account. Moreover, the decision should also include a monitoring mechanism so that the unforeseen significant environmental effects of the implementation of the plan or programme are identified and remedial action is possible (Article 10). The introduction of a monitoring mechanism is a major step forward compared to the EIA Directive where the introduction of a similar obligation met with strong opposition.[75]

4 The Seveso II Directive

Directive 82/501 on the major-accident hazards of certain industrial activities,[76] better known as the Post-Seveso Directive, provided for measures to protect the public and the environment from the consequences of possible major industrial accidents. The immediate reason for drafting the directive was the dioxin disaster in the Italian town of Seveso. The directive was mainly concerned with the prevention of such accidents.

After a number of amendments the directive has now been replaced by Directive 96/82 on the control of major-accident hazards involving dangerous substances the so-called 'Seveso II Directive'.[77] Directive 96/82 is intended to implement the Convention on the Transboundary Effects of Industrial Accidents.[78]

According to Article 1 the directive aims at the prevention of major accidents which involve dangerous substances, and the limitation of their consequences

---

[73] See further Sheate (2003) at 345.

[74] Lee (2005) at 171.

[75] Sheate (2003) at 346.

[76] OJ 1982 L 230/1, later amended. See on the interpretation of some of its provisions Case C-190/90 *Commission v. Netherlands* [1992] ECR I-3265.

[77] OJ 1997 L 10/13, amended by Directive 2003/105, OJ 2003 L 345/97, in the light of recent industrial accidents.

[78] Decision 98/685 concerning the Convention on the Transboundary Effects of Industrial Accidents, OJ 1998 L 326/1.

for man and the environment, with a view to ensuring high levels of protection throughout the EU in a consistent and effective manner. The directive is applicable to establishments where dangerous substances are present in quantities equal to or in excess of the quantities listed in Annex I. Article 4 states that the directive does not apply to, for instance, military establishments, hazards created by ionizing radiation, the transport of dangerous substances outside establishments, the transport of dangerous substances in pipelines outside establishments, the activities of the extractive industries concerned with exploration for minerals in mines and quarries and waste land-fill sites.

Under the general obligations of the directive, Member States are required to ensure that the operator is obliged to take all measures necessary to prevent major accidents and to limit their consequences for man and the environment (Article 5(1)) and that the operator is required to prove to the competent authority, at any time, that he has taken all the measures necessary as specified in the directive (Article 5(2)).

The operator is also required to send a notification to the competent authority, containing all kinds of information on the establishment (Article 6). He is required to draw up a document setting out his major-accident prevention policy and to ensure that it is properly implemented (Article 7).[79] To avoid dangers caused by the 'domino effect' the competent authority must, using the information received from all operators, identify establishments or groups of establishments where the likelihood and the possibility or consequences of a major accident may be increased because of the location and the proximity of such establishments (Article 8).

The additional requirements of Articles 9, 11 and 13 apply in respect of certain establishments. Member States must require the operator to produce a safety report (Article 9)[80] and draw up an internal emergency plan (Article 11) and must ensure that comprehensive information on safety measures is supplied to the relevant authorities so that they can draw up external safety plans. This also applies in the case of transboundary effects (Article 13).

Article 12 on land-use planning provides an example of application of the integration principle. Member States are required to ensure that the objectives of preventing major accidents and limiting the consequences of such accidents are taken into account in their land-use policies and/or other relevant policies.[81]

As soon as practicable following a major accident, the operator shall be required to send detailed information to the competent authorities (Article 14). Articles 17 and 18 are particularly relevant in terms of the actual application of the directive in the Member States. The first paragraph of Article 17(1) provides that Member States *shall* prohibit the use or bringing into use of any establish-

---

[79] See on the supervision of the implementation Case C-336/97 *Commission v. Italy* [1999] ECR I-3771, paras. 23-25.

[80] The dispensation from this obligation (Article 9(6)(a)) should be subject to the criteria in Decision 98/433, OJ 1998 L 192/19.

[81] See also Chapter 1, section 4.

ment, installation or storage facility, or any part thereof where the measures taken by the operator for the prevention and mitigation of major accidents are *seriously deficient*, while the second paragraph provides that they may prohibit the use or bringing into use of any establishment, installation or storage facility, or any part thereof if the operator has not submitted the notification, reports or other information required by the directive within the specified period. Finally, under Article 18 the Member States are required to organise a system of inspections, or other measures of control appropriate to the type of establishment concerned.

5 The IPPC Directive

Directive 96/61 concerning integrated pollution prevention and control, the so-called IPPC Directive, represents an important step towards a more integrated and horizontal approach.[82] As stated in its preamble, different approaches to controlling emissions into the air, water or soil separately may encourage the shifting of pollution between the various environmental media rather than protecting the environment as a whole. The IPPC Directive establishes a general framework for integrated pollution prevention and control.

5.1 The Scope of the IPPC Directive

The IPPC Directive applies only to installations, defined in Article 2(3), as stationary technical units in which one of the activities listed in Annex I are carried and any other directly associated and technically connected activities. The effect of Annex I is to basically confine the scope of the IPPC Directive to large (defined in terms of production capacity) industrial installations producing, *inter alia*, energy, metals, minerals (cement), chemicals and various other categories such as intensive animal husbandry. The directive applies to all new permits and changes in permits.

The temporal scope of the directive is defined in Articles 4 and 5. Basically all installations in operation before the deadline for implementation of the directive (30 October 1999, Article 2(4) in connection with 5 and 21(2)) are subject to an eight-year transitional period (Article 5(1)). New installations, i.e. those not already in operation before 30 October 1999 must have an integrated permit (Article 4).

---

[82] OJ 1996 L 257/26, as amended by Directive 2003/35, OJ 2003 L 156/17, Directive 2003/87, OJ 2003 L 275/32 and Regulation 166/2006, OJ 2006 L 33/1.

5.2   The Integrated Approach

The integrated approach follows from the fact that the environment is more than the sum of its component parts (air, land, water) together with the realisation that environmental improvements in one area may actually result in environmental deterioration in another area. Installing a more effective filter on a chimney may, for example, result in cleaner air as well as the production of more waste (when the filter cleaned). To ensure that this balance takes account of all areas or sectors of the environment an integrated approach is required. This integrated approach can be seen in the numerous references to 'the environment as a whole'[83] in the directive as well as in the general obligations upon the operator contained in Article 3 of the directive.[84] Member States are required to ensure that installations are operated in such a way that:

- all the appropriate preventive measures are taken against pollution, in particular through application of the best available techniques;
- no significant pollution is caused;
- waste production is avoided in accordance with the Waste Framwork Directive; where waste is produced, it is recovered or, where that is technically and economically impossible, it is disposed of while avoiding or reducing any impact on the environment;
- energy is used efficiently;
- the necessary measures are taken to prevent accidents and limit their consequences;
- the necessary measures are taken upon definitive cessation of activities to avoid any pollution risk and return the site of operation to a satisfactory state.

The integrated approach should be implemented by means of permits. Article 6 requires Member States to take the necessary measures to ensure that an application to the competent authority for a permit includes a description of:

- the installation and its activities;
- the raw and auxiliary materials, other substances and the energy used in or generated by the installation;
- the sources of emissions from the installation;
- the conditions of the site of the installation;
- the nature and quantities of foreseeable emissions from the installation into each medium as well as identification of significant effects of the emissions on the environment;
- the proposed technology and other techniques for preventing or, where this not possible, reducing emissions from the installation;
- where necessary, measures for the prevention and recovery of waste generated by the installation;

---

[83]   See for example Article 1 of the IPPC Directive.

[84]   See for an overview of the difficulties in achieving an integrated approach: Bohne & Dietze (2004).

· further measures planned to comply with the general principles of the basic obligations of the operator as provided for in Article 3;
· measures planned to monitor emissions into the environment.

To ensure an integrated approach to issuing permits, Article 7 requires *substantive* as well as *procedural* integration.[85] As regards the latter, Member States are required to ensure that the procedure for the grant of the permit is *fully coordinated* where more than one competent authority is involved. The substantive integration is to be ascertained by a requirement of full coordination of the conditions of the permit. The permit must contain conditions that guarantee that the installation complies with the IPPC Directive; otherwise the permit must be refused (Article 8).

The most important of these conditions take the form of the requirement in Article 9(3) to include in the permit emission limit values for pollutants likely to be emitted from the installation.[86] The rules on the emissions limits values reflect the difficulty in finding a compromise between the protection of the environment by ensuring good environmental quality standards on the one hand and subsidiarity considerations that result in local (geographical) considerations playing a role on the other.[87] Emission limit values shall be based on 'the best available techniques',[88] without prescribing the use of any technique or specific technology, but taking into account the technical characteristics of the installation concerned, its geographical location and the local environmental conditions. In all circumstances, the conditions of the permit shall contain provisions on the minimisation of long distance or transboundary pollution and ensure a high level of protection for the environment as a whole (Article 9(4)). However, where an environmental quality standard requires stricter conditions than those achievable by the use of the best available techniques, additional measures shall in particular be required in the permit (Article 10). The Council can set European-wide emissions limit values if the setting of emissions limit values on the basis of the best available techniques proves insufficient (Article 18).

Competent authorities must periodically reconsider and, where necessary, update permit conditions (Article 13(1)).

---

[85] Bohne and Dietze (2004) at 199.

[86] Article 9(3) was amended by Directive 2003/87 so as to preclude emissions limit values for greenhouse gasses subject to the emissions trading scheme; see further section 11.4 below.

[87] See recitals 17 and 18 of the preamble. See further: Doppelhammer (2000) at 203.

[88] Often abbreviated as BAT. See for a definition Article 2(11) of the directive: 'the most effective and advanced stage in the development of activities and their methods of operation which indicate the practical suitability of particular techniques for providing in principle the basis for emission limit values designed to prevent and, where that is not practicable, generally to reduce emissions and the impact on the environment as a whole'. Note that the second indent effectively introduces economic/cost considerations. Guidance as to what are best available techniques is provided by so-called BAT Reference Documents (BREFs), drawn up by the European IPPC Bureau in Seville (http://eippcb.jrc.es/), see also Article 16(2).

Finally, the directive contains provisions on compliance (Article 14), access to information and public participation in the permit procedure (Article 15)[89], access to justice (Article 15a),[90] transboundary effects (Article 17) and various transitional provisions, particularly relevant in respect of Directive 76/464 on pollution caused by certain dangerous substances discharged into the aquatic environment of the Community[91] and Directive 84/360 on the combating of air pollution from industrial plants.[92]

6 Environmental Governance and the Aarhus Convention

Throughout the Sixth Environmental Action Programme references to environmental governance can be found. For the purposes of this book environmental governance is equated with:[93]
· access to environmental information;
· public participation in decision-making in environmental matters;
· access to justice in environmental matters.

These three main headings correspond to the so-called three pillars of the UNECE Aarhus Convention, to which the European Community and the Member States are signatories.[94] Below these three pillars and their implementation by the EU as well as the Member States will be discussed

6.1 Access to Environmental Information at Member State Level

The steps announced in the Fourth Environmental Action Programme to improve public access to information[95] resulted in the adoption of Directive 90/313.[96] From 14 February 2005 Directive 90/313 has been replaced with Directive 2003/4, partly with a view to implementing the Aarhus convention.[97] The new directive also consolidates the Court's case law concerning Directive 90/313 and expands the existing access to environmental information

---

[89] Article 15(3), containing the obligation to publish an inventory of all emissions from IPPC-installations was repealed with effect from 24 February 2006 on the basis of Article 21(2) of Regulation 166/2006, OJ 2006 L 33/1, the so-called PRTR Regulation, see further section 6.2 below.

[90] Article 15 was amended and Article 15a was introduced by Directive 2003/35, see further section 6 below.

[91] OJ 1976 L 129/23, later amended.

[92] OJ 1984 L 188/20, later amended.

[93] See for a discussion: Lee (2005) at 113.

[94] Concluded on behalf of the EC by Decision 2005/370, OJ 2005 L 124/1. Cf. Jendroska (2005).

[95] OJ 1987 C 328/1 point 2.6.2.

[96] OJ 1990 L 158/56.

[97] OJ 2003 L 41/26, see COM (2000) 402 for the proposal.

according to the second recital of the preamble. The scope of the directive is confined by essentially two concepts: 'environmental information' and 'public authorities'. Article 2(1) contains a very wide definition of 'environmental information', that encompasses all media and forms and every aspect of the environment.[98] The 'public authority' is similarly widely defined in Article 2(2), to also include bodies without a specific environmental function or objective at all levels of government as well as private entities having public functions or responsibilities.[99] This is further expanded because also environmental information held on behalf of the public authorities should be accessible; Article 2(4) in connection with Article 3(1).

The central provision is Article 3, paragraph 1 of which requires the Member States to make environmental information available upon request without the applicant having to state an interest. This request must be sufficiently precise, because requests that are too general may be refused, provided that the authority has invited the applicant to specify his request (Article 4(1)(c) in connection with Article 3(3)). A similar duty to set up a dialogue with the applicant applies to requests sent to the wrong public authority (Article 4(1)(a)). Finally, Article 3(5) requires the Member States to set up registers and lists of environmental information in order to facilitate access to this information.

The access to environmental information is subject to exceptions listed in Article 4 of the directive. The first paragraph of Article 4 contains a list of exceptions that relate primarily to the internal working of the authority. The exceptions in the second paragraph of Article 4 involve interests of third parties or a more general nature, such as confidentiality of commercial information (Article 4(2)(d)). According to the last paragraph of Article 4(2) whenever one of the exceptions is invoked by an authority a balance must be struck between the public interest served by free access to the information and the interests protected by the exceptions. In all cases the exceptions must be interpreted narrowly.[100] Furthermore, with the exception of the interests listed in paragraph 1 and 2 (b), (c) and (e), there will always be an overriding public interest in disclosure of the information if it relates to emissions into the environment.

---

[98] See, concerning Directive 90/313, Case C-321/96 *Mecklenburg* v. *Kreis Pinneberg* [1998] ECR I-3809, paras. 21 and 22, where the Court ruled that the directive is to be interpreted as covering a statement of views given by a countryside protection authority in development consent proceedings if that statement is capable of influencing the outcome of those proceedings as regards interests pertaining to the protection of the environment.

[99] See, again concerning Directive 90/313, Case C-217/97 *Commission* v. *Germany* [1999] ECR I-5087. The Court made it clear that even authorities, like for instance courts, acting normally in the exercise of their judicial powers and therefore not in principle covered by the directive, may also have responsibilities relating to the environment or be in possession of information on the environment within the meaning of the directive when they act outside their strictly judicial functions. If that is the case they must be regarded as public authorities for the purposes of the directive.

[100] Article 4(2) last paragraph, see also, concerning Directive 90/313, Case C-321/96 *Mecklenburg* v. *Kreis Pinneberg* [1998] ECR I-3809, para. 25.

Emission-related information must thus always be made public. Unfortunately, the term 'emissions' is not further defined. However, in view of the Court's case law concerning Directive 90/313, it seems likely that this concept will receive a wide interpretation, leading to environmental information being as widely available as possible. Particularly in connection with the PRTR Regulation this is interesting.[101] Information held by public authorities shall be supplied in part where it is possible to separate out information that is subject to one of the exceptions in Article 4.[102]

Taken together with the intention of the directive, Article 176 EC would seem to leave the Member States room to restrict the number of grounds for refusing information even further; it seems likely that the more stringent protective measures referred to there are better ensured by greater freedom of information. The wording of Article 4(1) and (2) – 'may provide' – seems to allow for this. That 'Member States *may* provide for a request for such information to be refused' makes it clear that they are not under a duty to maintain confidentiality, but merely have a discretionary power. The directive does not itself provide protection for a person who feels that the authorities have exceeded their competence by, for example, publishing confidential commercial or industrial data, or breaching the confidentiality of his personal data and/or files, assuming these grounds for confidentiality had been transposed in the relevant national legislation.

Article 5(1) prohibits the Member States from imposing any charges for access to the lists referred to in Article 3(5). However, Article 5(2) expressly permits Member States to impose a charge for supplying the information, but goes on to state that such charge may not exceed a reasonable cost. Concerning the nearly identical provision in Directive 90/313, the Court held that in the absence of more details in the directive itself, what constitutes a reasonable cost must be determined in the light of the purpose of the directive:

'any interpretation of what constitutes "reasonable cost" for the purposes of Article 5 of the directive which may have the result that persons are dissuaded from seeking to obtain information or which may restrict their right of access to information must be rejected. Consequently, the term "reasonable" for the purposes of Article 5 of the directive must be understood as meaning that it does not authorise Member States to pass on to those seeking information the entire amount of the costs, in particular indirect ones, actually incurred for the State budget in conducting an information search.'[103]

---

[101] See further below section 6.2.

[102] Article 4(4) of Directive 2003/4. Concerning a similar provision in Directive 90/313, the Court has held that it must be transposed explicitly in national law; Case C-217/97 *Commission v. Germany* [1999] ECR I-5087.

[103] Case C-217/97 *Commission v. Germany* [1999] ECR I-5087.

A person who considers that his request for information has been unreasonably refused or ignored, was inadequately answered, or otherwise not dealt with in accordance with Articles 3,4 or 5 by a public authority, may seek a judicial or administrative review of the decision in accordance with the relevant national legal system (Article 6). Compared to the similar provision in Directive 90/313, the current wording is significantly wider.[104] This will probably mean that judicial review is not limited to the statement of reasons alone and could also involve a review of the reasons invoked.

In addition to a right – freedom of access to information – the directive also provides for a corresponding duty: Member States are required to provide general information to the public on the state of the environment by such means as the periodic publication of descriptive reports (Article 7).

Apart from the provisions of Directive 2003/4, there are many other directives containing information requirements. These may differ markedly from the requirements of the freedom of information directive. Under Directive 67/548[105] (as amended by Directive 92/32[106]) on the packaging and labelling of dangerous preparations, any manufacturer intending to place certain dangerous substances on the market must notify the competent authority. Article 19 provides that if he considers that there is a confidentiality problem, the notifier may indicate the information which he considers to be commercially sensitive and disclosure of which might harm him industrially or commercially, and which he therefore wishes to be kept secret from all persons other than the competent authorities and the Commission. Here there is no question of a discretionary power to maintain confidentiality, but of a duty. The European Eco-label Regulation also requires non-disclosure of certain information.[107] Other such requirements are to be found in Article 16 of Regulation 793/93 on the evaluation and control of the risks of existing substances,[108] Articles 19 and 21 of Regulation 304/2003 concerning the export and import of certain dangerous chemicals,[109] Article 20 of the Seveso II Directive[110] and Article 25 of Directive 2001/18 on the deliberate release of GMOs.[111]

---

[104] Article 4 of Directive 90/313 only speaks of the 'request for information [that] has been unreasonably refused or ignored, or has been inadequately answered by a public authority'.

[105] OJ 1967 L 196/1.

[106] OJ 1992 L 154/15.

[107] Point 3 of Annex IV to Regulation 1980/2000, OJ 2000 L 237/1. Cf. Article 13 of the 'old' Eco-label Regulation, 880/92, OJ 1992 L 99/1.

[108] OJ 1993 L 84/1.

[109] Also referred to as the Prior Informed Consent (PIC) Regulation, OJ 2003 L 63/1, see further section 13.4 of this chapter.

[110] See also Article 13(4) of the Seveso II Directive, see further section 4 above.

[111] OJ 2001 L 106/1.

6.2   Access to Environmental Information at EU Level

As it is a signatory itself, the European Community must also implement the Aarhus convention. It has done so in the form of Regulation 1367/2006 (the Aarhus Regulation).[112] Title II of the Aarhus Regulation concerns access to environmental information and Article 3 declares the general Regulation on access to information held by the EU institutions,[113] applicable. The Aarhus Regulation contains additional provisions on access to environmental information. For example, Article 6(1) of the Aarhus Regulation ensures that information on emissions into the environment shall always be disclosed.[114] Interestingly, the duty to always disclose emissions-related information also applies to intellectual property related information, whereas for environmental information held by the Member States a similar duty does not apply.[115] The EU is also obliged to set up registers and to disseminate environmental information.

Whereas the Member States are not allowed to pass on the complete costs of complying with a request for information, the EU is allowed to do exactly this for copies of more than 20 pages.[116] Finally, concerning review of decisions refusing access to information, Articles 7 and 8 of Regulation 1049/2001 provide for a two-stage administrative procedure and access to the European Ombudsman or a Court.

A very important type of environmental information relates to emissions into the environment. The gathering of this type of information was the subject of the so-called EPER Decision (European Pollutant Emission Register).[117] Because it is a signatory, the European Community had to implement the UNECE Protocol on Pollutant Release and Transfer Registers to the Aarhus Convention. This has taken place in the form of Regulation 166/2006, the Pollutant Release and Transfer Register (PRTR) Regulation.[118] According to Article 5(1) the reporting obligation applies to all releases from installations mentioned in Annex I of pollutants mentioned in Annex II for which a certain threshold is exceeded. The list in Annex I is nearly identical to that in Annex I to the IPPC Directive. In this regard PRTR Regulation hardly goes beyond

---

[112] Regulation 1367/2006 on the application of the provisions of the Aarhus Convention on Access to Information, Public Participation in Decision-making and Access to Justice in Environmental Matters to Community institutions and bodies, OJ 2006 L 264/13.

[113] Regulation 1049/2001 Regarding Public Access to European Parliament, Council and Commission Documents, OJ 2001 L 145/43.

[114] Cf. Article 4(2) last paragraph of Directive 2003/4.

[115] See Article 4(2), last paragraph, of Directive 2003/4 since the duty to always disclose emissions related information does not apply to Article 4(2)(e).

[116] Article 10(1) of Regulation 1049/2001, compare with Article 5(2) of Directive 2003/4, see section 6.1 above.

[117] Decision 2000/479, OJ 2000 L 192/36.

[118] OJ 2006 L 33/1, for a discussion on the compatibility of the EPER Decision with the PRTR Protocol see Lee (2005) at 132.

the EPER Decision it builds upon. In addition to true releases, transfers of hazardous waste are also subject to a reporting obligation. The information thus collected by the national authorities has to be reported to the Commission on the basis of Article 7(2). With assistance from the European Environment Agency, the Commission will then incorporate the information in a European PRTR (Article 5(3)). The PRTR will also include information on releases from diffuse sources, but only insofar as this information has already been reported by the Member States (Article 8). The PRTR shall be freely accessible from the internet (Article 10) and possible exceptions to the free access to the information contained therein or in the Member State report must comply with Article 4 of Directive 2003/4 (Article 11). The PRTR Regulation apparently allows for confidentiality of information on releases. In view of the fact that emissions-related information must always be disclosed, this leads to the question of what the exact relation is between the 'release' within the meaning of Article 2(10) of the PRTR Regulation and 'emissions' as referred to in Article 4(2) of Directive 2003/4. It would seem that the European legislature considers that emissions are not to be equated with, for example, discharging. It appears doubtful whether this narrow concept of emission is tenable. The regulation provides for public participation (Article 12) as well as access to justice (Article 13). Article 15 may just be of greatest practical importance, as it can be construed as containing an obligation on the part of the Member States and the Commission to 'translate' the technical information contained in the PRTR into layman's terms, thus making the information truly accessible.[119]

6.3 Public Participation in Decision-making at Member State Level

Environmental information is interesting if it can be used to influence the decision-making. This requires access to decision-making procedures, in other words public participation. This pillar of the Aarhus Convention is implemented, as far as the Member States are concerned, by Directive 2003/35, the Public Participation Directive.[120] The Public Participation Directive consists of two main parts. Firstly, Article 2 contains provisions for a general public participation procedure. Secondly, Articles 3 & 4 amend the EIA and IPPC Directives in order to improve the public participation as part of those directives.

The scope of the general public participation procedure is defined primarily by Annex I. The following plans and programmes are subject to the public participation requirement:
· waste management plans pursuant to the Waste Framework Directive;
· plans to reduce the environmental impact of batteries and accumulators

---

[119] See on this problem Lee (2005) at 132.

[120] Directive 2003/35 providing for public participation in respect of the drawing up of certain plans and programmes relating to the environment, OJ 2003 L 156/17.

pursuant to Article 6 of the Batteries Directive 91/157;
- programs for vulnerable zones pursuant to Article 5(1) the Nitrates Directive 91/676;
- hazardous waste management plans pursuant to Article 6(1) of the Hazardous Waste Directive 91/689 – Packaging waste management plans pursuant to Article 14 of the Packaging Waste Directive 94/62;
- plans for zones where air quality exceeds the limits pursuant to Article 8(3) of the Ambient Air Quality Directive 96/62.

Article 2(5) excludes all plans and programmes that fall under the SEA Directive[121] as well as those subject to public participation on the basis of the Water Framework Directive. As was said above, the IPPC- and EIA Directives have their own specific provisions on public participation. Provisions on public consultation can also be found in the field of GMO-legislation.[122]

The actual obligation to allow for public participation applies only to natural and legal persons and, but only insofar as national law allows for this, associations or groups of natural and legal persons (Article 2(1)). The first stage of public participation involves informing the public about the proposals and the possibility of participation (Article 2(2)(a)). After this there must be possibility for effective participation. This refers to the stage in the decision-making process when the options are still open. The central obligation according to Article 2(2)(c) is to take due account of the views of the results of the public consultation. Under Article 2(2)(d) the public must be informed of the final decision and public participation process.

The provisions on public participation in the EIA- and IPPC Directive are quite similar, but they have a wider scope in that they also provide for cross-border public participation[123] and provisions on access to justice.[124]

6.4   Public Participation in Decision-making at EU Level

The provisions on public participation in decision-making by the European institutions can be found in Title III of the Aarhus Regulation.[125] Public participation is open to natural or legal persons as well as associations of these and concerns the preparation, modification or review of plans or programmes relating to the environment (Article 9(1)). Article 2(1)(e) gives a wide definition of plans and programmes relating to the environment that is significantly narrowed down by the last paragraph of that provision. According to this financial or budget plans are outside the scope of the Title on public participation. Just as the national authorities, the European institutions and bodies are

---

[121] See above, section 3.4.

[122] Articles 9 and 24 of the GMO Deliberate Release Directive 2001/18, OJ 2001 L 106/1 and

[123] Article 7 of the EIA Directive and Article 17 of the IPPC Directive.

[124] Article 10a of the EIA Directive and Article 15a of the IPPC Directive.

[125] Regulation 1367/2006, OJ 2006 L 264/13.

under a obligation to inform the public of the proposals and the possibility of public participation. Secondly, they have a duty to take due account of the results of the public participation. Finally the public must be informed of the final decision and the public participation. It is interesting to note that the last information obligation is formulated differently for the Member States and the EU. Only the Member States are obliged to inform the public of the public participation *process*,[126] whereas the EU institutions must inform the public of the public participation. This could mean that Member States must only inform the public of the procedure followed (time-limits etc.) and not of the actual impact the public consultation has had.

6.5   Access to Justice at Member State Level

In order to implement the third pillar (access to justice) on the Member State level a directive has been proposed by the Commission.[127] This directive would contain the general provisions on access to justice in addition to the specific rules on access to justice resulting from the public participation in the EIA and IPPC Directives and the specific rules on access to environmental information.[128]

The provisions on access to justice in the EIA Directive and the IPPC Directive are identical.[129] Essentially they require the Member States to grant access to justice for the public concerned insofar as they have a sufficient interest or maintain the impairment of a right. The public concerned is defined as 'the public affected or likely to be affected by, or having an interest in, the taking of a decision on the issuing or the updating of a permit or of permit conditions' The directives state that non-governmental organisations promoting environmental protection and meeting any requirements under national law are considered to be public concerned. It is important to note that national requirements still ultimately determine whether or not an ngo qualifies as public concerned. What constitutes a sufficient interest or impairment of a right is determined by the Member States, again leaving the definition of the exact scope to the Member States. However, in doing so they must act consistently with the objective of giving the public concerned wide access to justice. As far as the actual procedures are concerned, the directive does not exclude the possibility of a preliminary review procedure and confines itself to stating that the procedure must be fair, equitable, timely and not prohibitively expensive.

The proposal for the directive is currently undergoing the first reading and much is still uncertain. Article 4 of the Commission proposal requires the Member States to grant access to justice to all natural and legal persons that have a sufficient interest or maintain the impairment of a right. In addition, so-called qualified entities have a right to judicial review even if they cannot

---

[126] Article 2(2)(d) of Directive 2003/35, OJ 2003 L 156/17.

[127] COM (2003) 624 final, Co-decision procedure COD/2003/246.

[128] The provisions on access to justice in Directive 2003/4 have already discussed above, section 6.1.

[129] Article 10a of the EIA Directive and Article 15a of the IPPC Directive.

show a sufficient interest or the impairment of a right (Article 5). This is subject to the requirement that the qualified entity is acting within its statutory and geographic area of activities. Article 8 contains the requirements for recognition as a qualified entity whereas Article 9 lays down a procedure for this. Access to justice is available only if the natural or legal person or the qualified entity has first submitted a request for internal review (Article 6). Only when this request for internal review is not taken within 12 to 18 weeks or when the decision is insufficient to ensure compliance with environmental law is there a right to start 'environmental proceedings'. This is defined as the administrative or judicial review proceedings in environmental matters, other than proceedings in criminal matters, before a court or other independent body established by law, which is concluded by a binding decision (Article 2(1)(f)).

The European Parliament has approved the proposal, albeit with some rather far-going amendments. For one it considers that criminal procedures should not be excluded from the scope of the concept of environmental proceedings. Furthermore, the qualified entity is controversial since it considered to go beyond what is required by the Aarhus convention and may open up environmental procedures to a very great extent. The future of the proposal is uncertain as it still needs to undergo the first reading in the Council.

6.6   Access to Justice at EU Level

The provisions on access to justice at the EU level can be found in Title IV of the Aarhus Regulation 1367/2006.[130] The system of the Aarhus Regulation follows that proposed by the Commission for access to justice in the Member States.

7   Integrated Product Policy

In each phase of their life cycle, products have an impact on the environment. The manufacture, use and ultimate disposal of a product cause a greater or lesser degree of harm to the environment. Today, a life-cycle approach to environmental product policy is increasingly being adopted. This means that a number of environmental issues must be addressed. These range from the energy efficiency of the production process and distribution, the environmental impact a product will have during its usage by the consumer to the waste the product becomes once it reaches its end of life. This means that a number of pieces of European environmental law can be brought under the heading of integrated product policy (IPP) or life cycle analysis (LCA).[131] This section will deal the Eco-label Regulation, the Eco-audit Regulation and the Ecodesign

---

[130] See on this regulation Chapter 5, section 4.2.

[131] See the Commission Green Paper on Integrated Product Policy, COM (2001) 68 final, follow-up in Communication on Integrated Product Policy – Building on Environmental Life-Cycle Thinking, COM (2003) 302 final.

Directive.[132] An integrated product policy also includes, among others, initiatives to internalise external costs and efforts at greening public procurement.

7.1 The Eco-label Regulation

The Eco-label Regulation links the life-cycle approach to a scheme whereby the reduced environmental impact is visualised through a sign (the flower logo).[133] A system of eco-labels awarded for products with reduced environmental impact is intended to draw the consumers' attention to environmentally friendly options, enabling them to take reasoned decisions when purchasing products. The first objective of the regulation, stated in Article 1, is to promote products which have the potential to reduce negative environmental impacts, as compared with the other products in the same product group, thus contributing to the efficient use of resources and a high level of environmental protection. The Court's judgment in *Energy Star* shows that this link between the actual impact on purchasing decisions and thus trade and creating environmental awareness, environmental protection is not always clear.[134] This case concerns the legal basis for the Council decision approving the EC's accession to the US Energy Star Program. The Council opted for Article 175 EC, whereas the Commission considered Article 133 EC the appropriate legal basis. According to the Court the Energy Star Program encourages the supply of, and demand for, energy-efficient products and therefore promotes energy conservation. Furthermore, the extension of the program to the EC by means of the Energy Star Agreement helps to achieve that objective. Nevertheless the Court held that the fact remains that the Energy Star Agreement itself does not contain new energy-efficiency requirements but merely renders existing standards applicable.[135] The effect on energy conservation is seen as merely an indirect and distant effect, in contrast to the effect on trade in office equipment which is direct and immediate.[136] As a result the Court comes to the conclusion that it is a predominantly commercial policy-instrument. The fact that eco-labelling schemes have only an indirect and uncertain environmental impact compared to a direct impact on trade could be taken more generally – and the Court appears to do so as well – to mean that the Eco-label Regulation should have been based on Article 95 EC.[137] In our opinion this does not reflect the fact that the environmental impact and the effect on consumption and trade are reciprocal in that the effect on trade is

---

[132] The energy efficiency related legislation is addressed below in section 7.3. Waste related legislation is dealt with below in section 15.

[133] Regulation 1980/2000, OJ 2000 L 237/1, repealing Regulation 880/92, OJ 1992 L 99/1, Cf. Kramer (2000A).

[134] Case C-281/01 *Commission v. Council (Energy Star)* [2002] ECR I-12049. Cf. on this also Chapter 2, section 5.

[135] Case C-281/01 *Commission v. Council (Energy Star)* [2002] ECR I-12049, para. 42.

[136] Case C-281/01 *Commission v. Council (Energy Star)* [2002] ECR I-12049, para. 41.

[137] Case C-281/01 *Commission v. Council (Energy Star)* [2002] ECR I-12049, para. 46.

directly related to the environmental impact and vice versa. In that regard a dual legal basis (internal market and environment) would better reflect the nature of eco-labelling.

The eco-label is a voluntary award, not a requirement. In other words, products which meet certain requirements may bear the European eco-label, but are not required to do so. Existing or future national eco-labels are not affected by the regulation and may therefore co-exist (Article 11).

An eco-label can be awarded to products which meet the conditions established for a given product group (Articles 2, 3 and 4). However, the eco-label shall not be awarded to certain products, namely those which have already been classified as dangerous under European legislation or those manufactured by processes which are likely to harm significantly man and/or the environment (Article 2(4)). The decision to establish product groups and the specific ecological criteria for each group will be taken by the Commission (Article 6), assisted by a committee (Article 17) and the European Union Eco-labeling Board (EUEB; Article 13).[138] Up until now ecological criteria have been established by Commission Decision for, *inter alia*, bed mattresses,[139] dish washers,[140] refrigerators[141] and growing media.[142]

Applications for the award of an eco-label must be made to the competent national body designated for the purpose. It decides whether to award a label (Article 7). Every application is subject to the payment of the costs of processing the application (Article 12).[143] The competent body concludes a contract with the applicant covering the terms of use of the label (Article 9). In the meantime, a standard contract has been established by Commission Decision 2000/729.[144]

To avoid eco-label shopping, the regulation provides that the application may be made only in the Member State in which the product is manufactured or first marketed or into which the product is imported from a third country (Article 7(3)). It should be noted that the regulation does not provide for legal protection against decisions concerning the award of eco-labels, though the need will no doubt be felt, particularly by applicants whose request has been refused. Whether the same applies to the improper *award* of an eco-label is less clear. Given the fact that environmental organisations and consumer organisations are expressly named as principal interest groups in Article 15 of the regulation, it seems arguable that these organisations at least should be able to appeal against decisions of a competent authority improperly awarding an eco-label.

---

[138] Set up by Decision 2000/37, OJ 2000 L 293/24. The EUEB consists of representatives of the national certification authorities and representatives from the various branches of the industry, trade unions, traders, retailers, importers, environmental protection groups and consumer organisations.

[139] Decision 98/634, OJ 1998 L 302/31, as amended by Decision 2002/740, OJ 2002 L 236/10.

[140] Decision 98/483, OJ 1998 L 216/12, as amended by Decision 2001/397, OJ 2001 L 139/21.

[141] Decision 96/703, OJ 1996 L 323/34, as amended by Decision 2004/669, OJ 2004 L 306/16.

[142] Decision 2007/64, OJ 2007 L 32/14, 137.

[143] See further Decision 2000/728, OJ 2000 L 293/18.

[144] OJ 2000 L 293/20.

Finally, Article 9(2) of the regulation provides that any false or misleading advertising or the use of any label or logo which leads to confusion with the European eco-label is prohibited. The use of the word 'prohibited' gives rise to the presumption that the regulation contemplates a criminal sanction and that civil or administrative law sanctions by Member States will not suffice.

7.2   The Eco-audit (EMAS) Regulation

Regulation 761/2001 provides for rules allowing voluntary participation by organisations in a European eco-management and audit scheme (EMAS Regulation).[145] This is based on the assumption that organisations have their own responsibility to manage the environmental impact of their activities. The eco-management and audit scheme introduced by the regulation is designed to assess and improve the environmental performance of organisations, and provide information about them to the public. Participation in the old EMAS scheme was open to companies operating a site or sites where an industrial activity is performed. The current EMAS Regulation has significantly expanded the scope and is open to all organisations that have their own functions and administration, irrespective of the public or private ownership, legal form and whether or not it is for profit (Article 2(1)(s) in connection with Article 3(1)). In order to qualify for EMAS the organisation must be willing to continually improve the environmental performance (Annex I (2)(B)(2)) which is defined in Article 2(b) as the process of enhancing, year by year, the measurable results of the environmental management system related to an organisation's management of its significant environmental aspects, based on its environmental policy, objectives and targets. The organisation must furthermore conduct an environmental review, adopt an environmental management system, carry out environmental auditing and prepare an environmental statement (Article 3(2)(a)-(c)). The requirements for the environmental review, the environmental management system, environmental auditing and the environmental statement are set out in Annex I-III.[146] The outcome of this must be verified (Article 3(2)(d)) and be sent to the competent authority of the Member State (Article 3(2)(e) in connection with Article 5).

Article 4 gives more detailed rules for the accreditation of the environmental verification and Article 5 provides for the competent bodies to be set up by the Member States. If the competent national authority is satisfied that an organisation satisfies all the conditions of the regulation, and a validated environmental statement has been received, the organisation is registered and placed on a list of registered sites (Article 6(1) and 6(2)). A fee may be required for registration (Article 16).

---

[145] Regulation 761/2001 allowing voluntary participation by organisations in a Community eco-management and audit scheme (EMAS), OJ 2001 L 114/1, repealing Regulation 1836/93, OJ 1993 L 168/1.

[146] The Commission has provided further guidance in the form of Commission recommendations, OJ 2001 L 247/1 and 2003 L 184/19 and Decision 2001/681, OJ 2001 L 247/24.

The site will be deleted from the register if an organisation fails to submit a validated environmental statement and registration fee or if at any time the competent body concludes that the organisation is no longer complying with all the conditions of the regulation (Article 6(3)). The same applies if a competent body is informed by the competent enforcement authority of a breach of relevant environmental requirements (Article 8(4)). Refusal or suspension shall be lifted if the competent body has received satisfactory assurances from the competent enforcement authority that the breach has been rectified and that satisfactory arrangements are in place to ensure that it does not recur.

Organisations may use the EMAS-logo on letters, environmental statements and other communications (Article 8(2)). The logo may further be used for advertising (Article 8(2)(e)),[147] except for comparative advertising (Article 8(3)(b)). The logo may not be used on products or their packaging (Article 8(3)(a)).[148]

7.3   The Ecodesign Directive

Directive 2005/32 contains the framework for the setting of ecodesign requirements for energy-using products.[149] It is based on Article 95 EC and contains the general framework for setting ecodesign requirements for energy-using products as part of the new approach to harmonisation. Energy-using products is defined as all products dependent on energy (in whatever form) and thus defined in a rather wide sense, excluding only transportation means (Article 1(3)). Ecodesign is defined in Article 2(23) of the directive as 'the integration of environmental aspects into product design with the aim of improving the environmental performance of the [product] throughout its whole life cycle'. As part of the new approach the directive itself does not contain the actual rules with which the products must comply. Instead, it contains the general rules (essential requirements, Article 15 in connection with Annex I and II) for setting ecodesign standards which will then have to take place on the basis of so-called implementing measures.[150] In this regard it is interesting to note that the directive allows for voluntary agreements or self-regulation by the industry as an alternative to Commission implementing measures (Article 17, in connection with Annex VIII). A further element of the new approach is the procedure for assessing conformity of products with the rules established in the implementing measures (Article 8). This assessment can take place through internal design control or through a management system (Article 8(2). The management system of an organisation participating in EMAS shall be presumed to comply

---

[147] The 'old' EMAS Regulation prohibited this, Cf. Regulation 1836/93, Article 10(3).

[148] The Commission may, however, authorise the use on packaging in exceptional cases, see Decision 2006/193, OJ 2006 L 70/63.

[149] OJ 2005 L 191/29.

[150] The Ecodesign Directive regards the following Directives as implementing measures: Directive 92/42 on hot-water boilers, OJ 1992 L 167/17, as amended, Directive 96/57 on freezers and refrigerators, OJ 1996 L 236/36 and Directive 2000/55 on ballasts in fluorescent lighting, OJ 2000 L 279/33.

with the directive if the design function is included in the EMAS. Moreover, products qualifying for the European eco-label are presumed to be in conformity with the directive if the design requirements are part of that eco-label. Given that both the EMAS and the Eco-label Regulation use the life-cycle analysis, the design-function should be included.[151] Any product complying with the ecodesign parameters should benefit from the free movement of goods (Article 6).

8 The Environmental Liability Directive

Another example of a horizontal measure is Directive 2004/35 on environmental liability.[152] It is horizontal because it covers a range of environmental sectors that may be damaged. Moreover, it is the result of protracted negotiations and constitutes a careful compromise.[153] It implements the principle that the polluter should pay, by making the polluter liable for the environmental damage caused.[154] The idea of environmental liability should also have preventive effects in that operators of installations that could potentially damage the environment will now have an incentive to minimise the chances of environmental damage actually occurring. As the directive is based on Article 175 EC, Member States are allowed to adopt more stringent measures, such as the extension of the scope or a stricter liability regime.[155] Given that this would only be detrimental to the national industry (reverse discrimination), this will probably not lead to problems concerning the compatibility with the EC Treaty.

8.1 Scope

The scope of the Environmental Liability Directive is limited in three ways. First, the personal scope is limited to 'operators' of 'occupational activities' (Article 3(1)). Article 2(6) defines operator as 'any natural or legal, private or public person who operates or controls the occupational activity'. Occupational activity is similarly widely defined in Article 2(7) as any activity carried out in the course of an economic activity, a business or an undertaking, irrespectively of its private or public, profit or non-profit character. This definition may be problematic with regard to public entities that are active in the field of

---

[151] Eco-label Regulation 1980/2000, OJ 2000 L 237/1, Art. 3(2) and EMAS Regulation 761/2001, OJ 2001 L 114/1, Art. 3(2)(a) in connection with Annex VI, point 6.3(a).

[152] Directive 2004/35 on environmental liability with regard to the prevention and remedying of environmental damage, OJ 2004 L 143/56, as amended by Directive 2006/21, OJ 2006 L 102/15. Cf. Roller (2005).

[153] The Commission proposal, COM (2002) 17 final, was preceded by white paper, COM (2000) 66 final, and a green paper, COM (93) 47 final.

[154] Recital 2 of the preamble to the directive, see on the polluter pays principle, Chapter 1, section 3.3 above.

[155] On the basis of Article 176 EC and Article 16(2) of the directive.

environmental protection, as they may not be involved in an economic activity.[156] As a result they would be outside the scope of the directive even though their activities may very well result in environmental damage. Another interpretation would risk a divergence of the concept of an undertaking and the notion of economic activity in the directive from that used in EC competition law.

Second the material scope is limited to 'environmental damage'. This is defined in Article 2(1) as damage to protected species and habitats, water damage and land damage. Damage, in turn is defined as a measurable adverse change in a natural resource or a measurable impairment of a natural resource service. The latter concept refers to function that natural resources may have for other natural resources (e.g. migrating birds need a quiet and unpolluted area to rest) or the public. Defining a natural resource service as the function a natural resource may have for the public would appear to be risky, in that the public utility of a natural resource may very well be at odds with the natural utility. Lower groundwater levels, for example, may be devastating to the natural utility, but because the area will also become more accessible, the public utility may actually increase. As regards damage to protected species and habitats, the directive refers to the Habitats and Wild Birds Directives[157] (Article 2(1)(a), in connection with 2(3) and Annex I). The further definition of this type of damage turns on the term conservation status (defined in Article 2(4)). Concerning damage to water the directive refers to the Water Framework Directive.[158] According to Article 2(1)(b) water damage exists if there are significant adverse effects for the ecological, chemical and/or quantitative status and/or ecological potential, unless Article 4(7) of the Water Framework Directive applies.[159] For land damage the directive does not refer to other secondary European law, because this does not exist. The directive defines land damage as land contamination that creates a significant risk of human health being adversely affected. Contrary to the damage to nature and water damage, land damage thus employs an ethnocentric concept of environment, focusing on the risk to humans and not the environment as a whole. Furthermore, it is interesting to note that damage exists when there is a *measurable* adverse effect, whereas water damage and damage to nature damage all require *significant* adverse effects and for land damage simple adverse effects on human health suffice. It remains to be seen whether this choice of words was deliberate and indeed intends to put the bar for damage to nature and water higher than for land damage. Concerning the material scope, regard must also be had to Article 4 of the directive. This excludes liability on the basis of the directive for damage caused by armed conflicts and natural phenomena. Furthermore, the directive does not apply to activities subject to a

---

[156] See, for example, the SEPG in Case C-343/95 *Diego Calì & Figli* v. *SEPG* [1997] ECR I-1547.

[157] See below section 17.

[158] See below section 10.1.

[159] According to Article 4(7) reasons of overriding public interest can justify failure to reach the environmental objectives of the Water Framework Directive, subject to conditions.

special liability regime (Article 4(2) and (4))[160] and it is without prejudice to the right of an operator to limit his liability in accordance with the international conventions on limitation of the liability for maritime claims and inland navigation (Article 4(3)).

Third, the temporal scope is restricted to damage caused by an event taking place after 30 April 2007, the deadline for implementation. For damage caused by an event after 30 April 2007 there is no liability on the basis of the directive if the event derives from an activity that took place and was finished before 30 April 2007 (Article 17 in connection with Article 19(1)). Concerning the second indent it is interesting to note that the directive does not define the causal relation (derives from) between the event and the activity that was finished. The fact that no further qualification, such as directly deriving from, was included appears to indicate that operators may also be liable for environmental damage caused by third parties, for example entering a poorly fenced off abandoned industrial installation. Finally, the directive limits the liability to 30 years following the event that caused the damage.

8.2 Environmental Liability and Preventive and Remedial Action

The actual extent of the environmental liability depends on the liability regime applicable and possible exceptions or justifications available to the person held liable. In this regard, the directive distinguishes between two liability regimes. For so-called Annex III activities, there is strict liability, whereas all other occupational activities are subject to fault liability. The activities in Annex III could be summarised as activities that are inherently dangerous to the environment. They include all installations requiring IPPC-permits, waste management operations and installations dealing with dangerous substances and the use of genetically modified organisms. For non-Annex III activities, liability exists only for damage to protected species and natural habitats. Land damage and water damage will thus not lead to liability on the basis of the directive. Furthermore, the operator must have been at fault or negligent. For liability arising from pollution of a diffuse character, a term not further defined in the directive,[161] the directive requires a causal link between the damage and the activities of the individual operators.

Mere liability will not necessarily protect the environment. For this reason the directive contains provisions on preventive and remedial action. According to Article 5 the operator shall take all the necessary preventive measures where there is an imminent threat of environmental damage occurring. Article 6 on remedial action requires the operator to take all practicable steps to limit or to

---

[160] Referred to in Annex IV. This includes liability for oil spills, transport of dangerous substances and nuclear damage.

[161] It seems likely that the Court will refer to similar definitions provided in its case law concerning other pieces of secondary community law, such as Case C-232/97 *Nederhoff* [1999] ECR I-6385.

prevent further environmental damage (containment action). In addition, the operator is required to take all necessary remedial measures. The difference in wording between Article 5(1) (all *necessary* steps) and Article 6(1)(a) (all *practicable* steps for containment action) appears to indicate a greater degree of freedom on the part of the operator in case of remedial actions. Determining necessity accepts the environmental protection objective whereas practicability involves a balance between the environmental protection objective and the practical (economic) possibilities of the operator and may thus result in a less ambitious environmental objective. The costs for the preventive and remedial actions shall be borne by the operator (Article 8(1)).

8.3   Implementing Environmental Liability

The Commission initially envisaged a system of private liability, where private parties would effectuate the liability. The current directive has opted for a system of public liability, with a competent authority being primarily responsible for making the environmental liability work in practice. Article 11 requires the Member States to designate the competent authority. This competent authority must be informed of environmental damage or the threat of environmental damage by the operator (Article 5(2) and 6(1)). Once it has been informed, the competent authority can request further information from the operator. It may give the operator instructions to prevent or limit the environmental damage and it may require the operator to take the necessary preventive and remedial measures (Article 5(3)(b) and Article 6(2)(c)). Furthermore, the competent authority can itself take the necessary preventive and remedial measures (Article 5(3)(d) and Article 6(2)(e)). It follows from Article 6(3) that the competent authority can only take the remedial measures itself as a means of last resort.[162] Concerning both remedial and preventive measures the directive makes it clear that the primary obligation rests with the operator. Only if the operator does not comply with the instructions and obligations, cannot be identified or is not obliged to bear the costs under the directive will the competent authority be able to take the measures itself.

The competent authority is obliged to recover the costs arising from preventive or remedial measures[163] it has implemented itself (Article 8(2)). However, the competent authority may decide not to recover the costs if this would not be cost-effective or where the operator cannot be identified. In our opinion the criterion of cost-effectiveness is misplaced in this context. In this connection we refer to the fact that public authorities go to great lengths to recover fines (even if the costs of doing so outweigh the actual fine) because not recovering them would diminish the effect of the fine, thus reducing its preventive effect. Since

---

[162] A similar provision does not exist for preventive measures, leading to the conclusion that the competent authority could take these itself also when it is not a measure of last resort.

[163] The directive refers to preventive and remedial *actions*. It is assumed that this is sloppy drafting and that this term can be taken to mean preventive and remedial measures.

the environmental liability should have a similar preventive effect and implements the polluter pays principle, it is our opinion that the costs should always
be recovered.

Article 8(3) contains two further exceptions to the general rule that the
operator shall bear the costs or the preventive or remedial actions. For the first
exception the operator needs to prove that a third party caused the damage
despite the fact that appropriate safety measures were in place. The second
exception requires the operator to prove that the damage resulted from an order
or an instruction coming from a public authority insofar as this order was not
consequent upon an incident caused by the operator. This refers to the scenario
where water used to extinguish a fire pollutes nearby land or water. If the fire
was caused by a natural phenomenon within the meaning of Article 4(1)(b) the
operator will not be liable. If, however, the fire was caused by the operator, the
costs will have to be recovered. In these situations the Member States must take
the appropriate measures to allow the operator to recover the costs.

Article 8(4) contains two exceptions that will result in the operator not
having to bear the costs of remedial actions. This provision differs from Article
8(3) in that it applies only to remedial actions and does not require the operator
to *prove* anything, but simply demands that he *demonstrates* that he was not at
fault or negligent. The operator must further demonstrate that the damage was
caused by an emission or event expressly authorised on the basis of national
laws implementing the directives and regulation in Annex III. This is referred to
as the 'permit defence'. Even though Article 8(4)(a) does not explicitly mention
this, it is to be assumed that the permit defence will only be available for
permits given on the basis of national laws that correctly implement the directives in Annex III. Anything else would only increase the disparities arising
from incorrect implementation. The second exception in Article 8(4) exonerates
the operator from the damage caused by emissions or use of a product when he
demonstrates that this emission or that use was not considered likely to cause
environmental damage according to the state of the scientific and technical
knowledge at that time. This raises the question to what extent the precautionary principle applies to this provision, making it applicable to the operators'
assessment of the state of the scientific and technical knowledge. Recital 20 of
the preamble to the directive speaks of a potential for damage that 'could not
have been known' at the time the emission or event took place. In our opinion
this exception to the general rule that the polluter should pay should be interpreted narrowly in the light of the precautionary principle. This means that even
inconclusive scientific evidence of the potential for environmental damage can
rule out the applicability of Article 8(4)(b).

Given that the directive wants to implement the polluter pays principle, it
may seem surprising that it requires the Member States to encourage the development of financial security instruments with the aim of enabling operators
to use financial guarantees to cover their responsibilities. On second thought,
however, this is all but surprising since the insurance premium may well func-

tion as a very effective risk indicator creating an incentive for the operators to minimise risks and thus premiums.

Article 10 contains a limitation period of five years during which the competent authority can initiate recovery procedures.

Because the directive relies on the competent authority to actually implement the liability there are also rules on the possibilities for natural or legal persons to file requests for action. In a way that closely resembles the provisions on access to justice in the proposal for a directive implementing the Aarhus convention,[164] Article 12 gives natural or legal persons the right to make the competent authority aware of environmental damage or the threat thereof.[165] More importantly, they are also entitled to request the competent authority to take action under the directive (Article 12(1)). On the basis of Article 13 the same natural or legal persons must have access to justice to review the procedural and substantive legality of the decisions, acts or failure to act of the competent authority.

A final consequence of the choice for a public liability system has found its way into Article 16(2) according to which the directive does not prevent the Member States from prohibiting double recovery of costs in case of concurrent action by the competent authority and a person whose property is affected by environmental damage.

9   The European Environment Agency

At the beginning of May 1990, the Council adopted Regulation 1210/90 on the establishment of the European Environment Agency and the European Environment Information and Observation Network.[166] It is the Agency's task to provide the EU and the Member States with objective, reliable and comparable information at the European level enabling them to take the requisite measures to protect the environment, to assess the results of such measures and to ensure that the public is properly informed about the state of the environment. The information in question is scientific and technical information about the present and foreseeable state of the environment (quality, sensitivity, pressures). The regulation designates a number of priority areas of work, with particular emphasis on transfrontier, plurinational and global phenomena. The Agency is also open to countries which are not members of the European Communities. The powers and duties of the Agency were a particular bone of

---

[164] See above section 6.5.

[165] See Joined Cases T-236/04 and T-241/04 *EEB and Stichting Natuur en Milieu* v. *Commission* [2005] ECR II-4945, where the parties relied unsuccessfully on, *inter alia*, this provision to get standing under Article 230(4) EC. Cf. also Chapter 5, section 4.

[166] OJ 1990 L 120/1, as amended by Regulation 933/1999, OJ 1999 L 117/1, Regulation 1641/2003, OJ 2003 L 245/1. Amendment proposed by COM (2005) 190 final as regards the term of office of the executive director.

contention when it was set up. It was decided not to give it powers of inspection of its own in the Member States. Its tasks have been kept limited, leaving open the possibility of deciding on further tasks for the Agency within two years of the entry into force of the regulation, in particular:

· associating in the monitoring of the implementation of European environmental legislation;
· preparing environmental labels and criteria for the award of such labels to environmentally friendly products, technologies, goods, services and programmes which do not waste natural resources;
· promoting environmentally friendly technologies and processes and their use and transfer;
· establishing criteria for assessing the impact on the environment with a view to application and possible revision of the EIA Directive.[167]

Regulation 933/99 amending Regulation 1210/90 has broadened the scope of the Agency, albeit not spectacularly.[168] The main effect of Regulation 1641/2003 has been to make Regulation 1049/2001, on access to environmental information, applicable to the Agency.

10 Legislation on Water Protection

European environmental legislation designed to protect both fresh water and seawater generally aims to prevent pollution at its source whilst also laying down environmental quality standards. Incidentally, it also addresses water quantity issues. As early as 1976 the Council adopted a directive to prevent pollution by products which, in view of their toxicity, persistence and bioaccumulation, constitute a particular and permanent threat to the environment and public health. Since then, European environmental water law has steadily evolved into what has been called two waves.[169]

The first wave started with the 1975 Drinking Water Directive[170] and can be said to have lasted until the adoption of the 1980 Groundwater Directive.[171] This group of water directives protects the European water resources by virtue of the various uses that it may have, such as drinking water, shellfish water or water for freshwater fish. The second wave occurred in 1991 when the Urban Waste Water Directive[172] and the Nitrates Directive[173] were adopted. The adoption of the

---

[167] OJ 1985 L 175/40, later amended.

[168] OJ 1999 L 117/1.

[169] Grimeaud (2001) at 41 and 43.

[170] Directive 75/440, OJ 1975 L 194/26.

[171] Directive 80/68, OJ 1980 L 20/43.

[172] Directive 91/271, OJ 1991 L 135/40.

[173] Directive 91676, OJ 1991 L 375/1.

2000 Framework Directive on Water Protection (hereafter Water Framework Directive)[174] can be characterised as the third wave.

In addition to the legislation mentioned in this paragraph there are many other pieces of European environmental law that relate (indirectly) to the protection of water, such as the EIA Directive, the Habitats Directive and the IPPC Directive.[175]

The transfrontier and international character of water pollution means that European action alone is often not sufficient. The EC is therefore a party to a large number of regional and international conventions on the subject. The most important are:

· the 1974 Paris Convention for the prevention of marine pollution from land-based sources and the 1986 Paris Protocol amending the Convention;[176]
· the 1974 Helsinki Convention on the protection of the environment of the Baltic Sea area (as revised in 1992);[177]
· the 1976 Barcelona Convention for the protection of the Mediterranean Sea against pollution, and various Protocols to the Convention;[178]
· the 1976 Bonn Agreement on the protection of the Rhine against chemical pollution;[179]
· the 1983 Bonn Agreement for cooperation in dealing with pollution of the North Sea by oil and other harmful substances;[180]
· the 1990 Lisbon Accord of Cooperation for the protection of the coasts and waters of the Northeast Atlantic against pollution;[181]
· the Convention on the International Commission for the Protection of the Elbe[182] and
· the United Nations Convention on the Law of the Sea (UNCLOS).[183]

---

[174] Directive 2000/60 establishing a framework for Community action in the field of water policy, OJ 2000 L 327/1.

[175] See above, sections 17.2 and 5 respectively.

[176] OJ 1975 L 194/5 and OJ 1987 L 24/47.

[177] OJ 1994 L 73.

[178] OJ 1977 L 240/3, see, e.g. Case C-239/03 *Commission* v. *France* [2004] ECR I-9325.

[179] OJ 1977 L 240/53.

[180] OJ 1984 L 188/9.

[181] OJ 1994 L 73/20.

[182] OJ 1991 L 321/25.

[183] Decision 98/392 concerning the conclusion by the European Community of the United Nations Convention of 10 December 1982 on the Law of the Sea and the Agreement of 28 July 1994 relating to the implementation of Part XI thereof, OJ 1998 L 179. The decision is based on the combined Articles 37, 133 and 175(1) EC.

10.1 The Water Framework Directive 2000/60[184]

The Water Framework Directive is the result of fairly protracted negotiations and represents a complete overhaul of the water protection legislation of the EC.[185] Contrary to older water protection legislation the Water Framework Directive adopts a more holistic approach to water that is reflected in the river basin approach. This means that all interconnected waters in a river basin are protected by this one instrument. This holistic approach can also been seen in the fact that it replaces most of the fragmented first wave water protection instruments.[186] On the basis of Article 22 the following directives and decisions will be repealed in December 2007:
· Directive 75/440 on water for the abstraction of drinking water;
· Decision 77/795 on the exchange of information concerning water quality;
· Directive 79/869 on measuring and analysis of water for the abstraction of drinking water.

In December 2013 the following directives will be repealed:
· Directive 78/659 on freshwaters for fish;
· Directive 79/923 on shellfish waters;
· Directive 80/68 on groundwater;
· Directive 76/464 on the pollution caused by dangerous substances.[187]

Concerning Directive 76/464 a special transitional regime applies. The provision in that directive enabling the Council to adopt so-called daughter directives has been replaced by Article 16 of the Water Framework Directive with effect from the entry into force of this directive. The remainder of Directive 76/464 continues to apply, but it has in the meantime been replaced with Directive 2006/11 subject to some transitional provisions (Article 22(3)).

As was mentioned above, the Water Framework Directive adopts the river basin approach. This means that water protection measures attach to 'the area of land from which all surface run-off flows through a sequence of streams, rivers and, possibly, lakes into the sea at a single river mouth, estuary or delta' (Article 2(13)). The Member States have to designate river basin districts and competent authorities for the river basins (Article 3(1) and (2)). Moreover, the Member States are under a duty to assign river basins extending to more than one Member State to an international river basin district. In such an international river basin district, the Member States shall ensure the coordination of their

---

[184] Cf. on this directive in general and on the implementation in the Netherlands and Germany in particular, Van Rijswick (2003).

[185] Formally starting with Commission proposal COM (1997) 49, see, however, Grimeaud (2001) at 43.

[186] The Bathing Water Directive 76/160, for example, will not be repealed by the Water Framework Directive, see further section 10.5 below.

[187] This directive has been replaced by Directive 2006/11, see below, section 10.3.

national measures (Article 3(4)).[188] Article 12 provides for a procedure according to which the Commission can help resolve issues between Member States that cannot be resolved between the Member States. Finally, river basins extending into non-Member States are subject to a less strict duty to ensure coordination (Article 3(5)). The last sentence of Article 3(5) appears to indicate that the fact that a river basin extends to non-Member States does not exonerate the Member States for the purposes of this directive. This may be problematic given that it may be difficult to meet the directive's environmental objectives in a downstream Member State where pollution originates in an upstream non-member state. The environmental objectives are laid down in Article 4 of the Water Framework Directive. The directive contains such objectives for surface water (Article 4(1)(a)), groundwater (Article 4(1)(b)) and protected areas (Article 4(1)(c)). Moreover, within the category of surface water there is a separate category for artificial and heavily modified bodies of surface waters. Surface water is defined in Article 2(1) as inland waters, transitional waters and coastal waters. Groundwater is defined as all water which is below the surface of the ground in the saturation zone and in direct contact with the ground (Article 2(2)). Protected areas are defined in Annex IV of the directive as those areas that are designated for the abstraction of drinking water, areas designated for the protection of economically significant aquatic species, bathing waters, nutrient-sensitive areas[189] and areas protected by virtue of European nature protection legislation. An artificial water body is a body created by human activity. Heavily modified bodies of water are those that as a result of human activity are substantially changed in character. Such artificial and heavily modified bodies of water must be designated by the Member State. This designation has to take place using the procedure set out in Annex II on the basis of the following criteria (Article 4(3)):

· The changes to the body of water necessary for achieving good ecological status (as opposed to good ecological potential) would have significant adverse effects on the wider environment, navigation, purposes for which water is stored (e.g. abstraction of drinking water), water management or other equally important sustainable human development activities and
· there is no technically or economically viable alternative to the water body where that alternative is a significantly better environmental option.

All in all the criteria for designating a body of surface water as heavily modified are quite open and leave the Member States considerable leeway in designating waters as such. This has important consequences for the environmental objectives that apply.

For all surface waters, including those that are artificial and heavily modified, a standstill obligation applies according to which the Member States must

---

[188] This can take place through an instruction of national delegations to international commissions, see Case C-32/05 *Commission* v. *Luxembourg* [2006] ECR I-11323, paras. 71-72.

[189] This includes, but is not confined to, vulnerable zones pursuant to the Nitrates Directive and sensitive areas pursuant to the Urban Waste Water Directive,

implement the necessary measures to prevent deterioration (Article 4(1)(a)(i). Similarly, irrespective of the type of surface water, pollution from priority (hazardous) substances is subject to regulation on the basis of Article 16 of the Water Framework Directive, discussed below. For non-artificial and non-heavily modified surface water the Member States must protect, enhance and restore with the aim of achieving *good surface water status* before 2015 (Article 4(1)(ii)). Member States must further take measures with the aim to reduce pollution from priority substances and to cease or phase out emissions, discharges and losses of priority hazardous substances (Article 4(1)(iii)). For artificial and heavily modified waters the Member States must implement measures in order to achieve *good ecological potential* and *good surface water chemical status* by 2015. The surface water status is determined by the ecological and chemical status, and good surface water status requires good ecological status as well as a good chemical status (Article 2(17) and (18)). The precise criteria for determining the ecological and chemical status are laid down in Annex V, though this does not contain any limit values or environmental quality indicators.

Groundwaters are also subject to a standstill obligation (Article 4(1)(b)(i)) and Member States are obliged to take the necessary measures to prevent or limit the input of pollution into groundwater. Furthermore, Member States must protect, enhance and restore all bodies of groundwater and ensure a balance between the abstraction and recharge of groundwater with the aim of achieving *good groundwater status* by 2015 (Article 4(1)(b)(ii)). Again the criteria for determining the groundwater status are laid down in Annex V, without any specific environmental quality values. Article 4(1)(b)(ii) is interesting because it addresses, when it refers to the balance between abstraction and recharge, water quantity aspects. Quantitative water management is of course subject to a special decision-making procedure and a separate legal basis (Article 175(2)(b), second indent, EC), begging the question whether the quantitative aspects are indeed subordinate to the quality aspects so that the Water Framework Directive could indeed be based on Article 175(1) EC.[190] In our opinion the Water Framework Directive clearly has the primary objective of protecting water quality. Finally, the Member States have a duty to reverse significant and sustained upwards trends in groundwater pollution (trend reversal duty, Article 4(1)(b)(iii)).

Finally, the environmental objectives for protected areas are those laid down in the Water Framework Directive or – if these are more stringent – those laid down in the specific pieces of environmental law. For protected areas the 2015 deadlines also applies.

Much of the complexity of the Water Framework Directive is due to the exceptions contained in it. According to Article 4(4) the 2015 deadline may be extended if certain criteria are met. These criteria, laid down in points i to iii of Article 4(4) contain a wide margin of discretion for the Member States. Article 4(4)(a)(ii), for example, allows an extension if the measures needed to be complied with 'would be disproportionately expensive'. Such extensions must be

---

[190] See Case C-36/98 *Spain v. Council* (*Danube Convention*) [2001] ECR I-779.

limited to two further updates of the river basin management plan, i.e. 12 years (Article 4(4)(c) in connection with 13(7)). According to Article 4((4)(c) the extension can be for an indefinite period if the natural conditions are such that the objectives cannot be achieved on time.

Apart from the extension of the 2015 deadline there are further exceptions in Article 4(5), (6) and (7). Article 4(5) allows the Member States to aim for less stringent environmental objectives if achieving these objectives would be infeasible or disproportionately expensive, provided the cumulative conditions in (a) to (d) are met. Interestingly, Article 4(5) refers to 'feasibility' whereas other provisions (such as Article 4(4)(a)(i) and 4(7)(d)) refer to 'technical feasibility' are a reason for an exception. It is possible that, for example, reasons of political feasibility would allow the application of Article 4(5). Article 4(5) only applies to surface waters, not to ground water or protected areas. Article 4(6) contains an exception for temporary deteriorations of the status of water bodies as a result of exceptional and not reasonably foreseeable circumstances, such as floods, droughts or accidents. The application of this exception is subject to the cumulative criteria contained in Article 4(6)(a) to (e). It may be noted that Article 4(6)(e) ensures that these circumstances will not allow for an exception in the future, as the management plans have to be adapted to include them. As a result, they will no longer be unforeseen in the future. The increased probability of flooding as a result of climate change can probably be brought under this heading. Article 4(6) does not apply to protected areas. Finally, Article 4(7) allows an exception from the environmental objectives and the duty to prevent deterioration of the status of a body of water if this is the result of new modifications to the physical characteristics of the surface water or alterations of the groundwater level or new sustainable human development activities. With regard to the latter reason for an exception, it may be noted that the term 'sustainable human development activities' is not defined anywhere. Again application of this exception is subject to four cumulative conditions (Article 4(7)(a) to (d)). As Article 4(7)(c) shows, this provision probably fulfills the same role as Article 6(4) of the Habitats Directive (an exception for overriding public interests), it can therefore be assumed that the Court's interpretation of this provision will be similar.[191] Concerning this provision, it is probable that pipeline-problems[192] will emerge, as the cumulative criteria in Article 4(7) will not apply to alterations and modifications that are not 'new'. It cannot be excluded that Member States will want to classify an alteration as not new. The Court will probably apply its caselaw concerning the pipeline problem in the EIA Directive, meaning that new alterations are those that have formally started after the deadline for implementation (22 December 2003).

Concerning all the exceptions and derogations, the bottom line is laid down in Article 4(8). This provision stipulates the application of Article 4(3) (artificial

---

[191] See, concerning a similar concept in the Wild Birds Directive, Case C-57/89 *Commission v Germany* (*Leybucht*) [1991] ECR I-881.

[192] See section 3 of this chapter, concerning the EIA Directive.

and heavily modified bodies), 4(4) (extension of the deadline), 4(5) (less stringent objectives), 4(6) (derogation for exceptional circumstances) and 4(7) (new
activities and changes). Moreover, Article 4(9) obliges the Member States to take
steps to ensure that the application of Article 4 guarantees at least the same level
of protection as existing European legislation. The complexity of the environmental objectives has resulted in some scholars questioning the possibility to
invoke this directive in a national court. Indeed, the Court has characterised
most of the provisions of the directive as requiring the Member States to take
the necessary measures to ensure that certain (more or less generally) formulated objectives are attained, whilst leaving the Member States some discretion
as to these measures.[193] This probably means that these obligations will not be
directly effective or that the Court's test will be confined to a review whether the
limits to the discretion have been exceeded or not.

Article 5 requires the Member States to review the river basins, the effects
of human activities on those basins and an economic analysis of the water use.
Furthermore, pursuant to Article 6 the Member States must keep a register of
protected sites. For drinking water, Article 7 contains special rules. Article 8
lays down the rules for monitoring the status of surface waters and groundwater
and protected areas. The monitoring programmes must be implemented before
2009 (Article 8(2)). Article 9 contains an implementation of the polluter pays
principle and requires the Member States to ensure that by 2010 water pricing policies contain 'adequate incentives' for efficient water usage. All of this is
part of the principle that the costs of water services should be recovered. 'Water
services' is defined in Article 2(38) as encompassing all services which provide
for households and any other (economic or public) activity abstraction, impound-
ment, storage, treatment and distribution of surface water or groundwater
as well waste-water collection and treatment. In our opinion this definition
includes water quantity management (such as emergency storage of excessive
rainfalls), leading to the question whether the costs arising from this (dyke
reinforcement) should also be recovered. In our opinion the second sentence
of Article 9(1) makes it clear that the idea behind all this is that costs are to
be recovered from the final users of water. As a result costs for water quantity
management, insofar as they are not connected to water use, do not have to be
recovered. Furthermore, the Member States must ensure that water prices are
differentiated for, at least, industry, households and agriculture. In setting up
such a differentiated pricing scheme the Member States may have regard to
the social, environmental and economic effects that the recovery of costs will
have. This provides Member States with a possibility to mitigate the effects of
a straightforward application of the polluter pays principle. A further exception
can be seen in Article 9(4), according to which the duty to set up a differentiated water-pricing scheme does not apply where this would be incompatible with
'established practices'. However, this may not compromise the purposes and the
achievement of the environmental objectives of the Water Framework Directive.

---

[193] Case C-32/05 *Commission v. Luxembourg* [2006] ECR I-11323, para. 43.

Finally, it is worth recalling that, although Article 9(3) states that this directive does not stand in the way of government funding of measures in order to achieve the objectives of the directive, this is without prejudice to Article 87 en 88(3) EC.[194]

Article 10 contains the so-called combined approach for point and diffuse sources. This means that point sources should be subject to emissions controls supplemented with environmental quality standards. In the emission limit values prove insufficient to achieve the environmental quality standards, the emissions limit values should be made more stringent (Article 10(3)). The emission controls should based on the best available techniques (Article 10(2)(a)) or the relevant emission limit values (Article 10(2)(b)) whereas diffuse sources should be subject to the controls set out in the IPPC Directive,[195] the Urban Waste Water Directive,[196] the Nitrates Directive,[197] the so-called Daughter Directives[198] and any other relevant European legislation. Such controls must be in place before 2012, i.e. one year before the Water Framework Directive replaces the last batch of Directives.

Articles 11 to 15 contain the provisions that deal with the procedural side of the Water Framework Directive. On the basis of Article 11 the Member States must implement a programme of measures in order to achieve the environmental objectives of Article 4. A distinction is made between so-called basic measures and supplementary measures (Article 11(2)), with the former certainly being mandatory. An important change compared to the old regime can be found in Article 11(3)(g) and (h), according to which point and diffuse sources of pollution may now also be subject to regulation on the basis of general binding rules, and not necessarily a specific permit. The programme of measures must be established before 2009 and be operational before 2012. Finally, the programme must be reviewed before 2015 and every six years thereafter (Article 11(7) and (8)). Article 13 requires the Member States to draw up river basin management plans before 2009, and to be reviewed by 2015 at the latest and every six years thereafter (Article 13(6) and (7)). In case of river basins covering more than one Member State the Member States are required to coordinate their river basin management plans (Article 13(2)). For river basins covering non-Member States as well, there is a less far-going obligation to 'endeavour to produce' a single river basin management plan (Article 13(3)). Details about the river basin management plans can be found in Annex VII. Article 14 contains rules on public information and consultation in connection with the production and review of river basin management plans. Article 15 requires the Member States to report to the Commission on the river basin management plans and

---

[194] See Chapter 7 above.

[195] See above, section 5.

[196] See below, section 10.8.

[197] See below, section 10.9.

[198] These are the directives adopted pursuant to Article 16 of the Water Framework Directive and those adopted pursuant to Directive 76/464, now replaced by Directive 2006/11, see below, section 10.3.

submit summaries of the analyses conducted pursuant to Article 5 and the monitoring programmes set up under Article 8.

Article 16 is a more substantive provision that replaces Article 6 of Directive 76/464. On the basis of the latter provision the Council, acting on a proposal from the Commission, could set emission limit values for List I substances in the form of so-called Daughter Directives. Thus far this has resulted in five such directives, which can hardly be called a success given that the Commission list was several times longer.[199] Article 16 contains a similar enabling clause, but requires the European Parliament and the Council to adopt the daughter directives to reduce discharges, emissions and losses priority substances and to completely phase out all emissions and discharges of priority hazardous substances (Article 16(1). These measures should be taken on the basis of a Commission proposal. The list of priority (hazardous) substances can be found in Annex X to the Water Framework Directive,[200] and replaces the list in the Commission communication pursuant to Directive 76/464.[201] As a follow up to this list of priority (hazardous) substances, the Commission has proposed a directive on environmental quality standards.[202] Pursuant to Article 16(6) the Commission will propose measures to completely phase out priority hazardous substances within 20 years from the adoption of these measures by the Council and European Parliament. As was mentioned above, the adoption of daughter directives up until today can hardly be considered successful and the lack of action on the basis of Directive 76/464[203] has resulted in a safety net provision in the form of Article 16(8). According to this provision lack of action on the part of the Council and the European Parliament before 2006 will mean that the Member States will become responsible for establishing environmental quality standards themselves. The mandatory language of the provision ('shall adopt') suggests that failure to adopt these standards could trigger an action for failure to act (Article 232 EC) on the part of the Commission.

Article 17 contains a comparable enabling clause for the protection of groundwater. This provision requires the Council and the European Parliament to adopt before December 2002, on the basis of a Commission proposal, specific measures to prevent and control the pollution of groundwater. These

---

[199] Directive 82/176 on mercury discharges (OJ 1982 L 81/29), Directive 83/513 on cadmium discharges (OJ 1983 L 291/1), Directive 84/156 on mercury (OJ 1984 L 74/49), Directive 84/491 on hexachlorocyclohexane discharges (OJ 1984 L 274/11) and the Directive 86/280 on discharges of dangerous substances (OJ 1986 L 181/16), listed in Annex IX to the Water Framework Directive.

[200] On the basis of Article 16(11) of the Water Framework Directive. The list was adopted by the Council and the European Parliament by Decision 2455/2001, OJ 2001 L 331/1.

[201] Communication of 22 June 1982, OJ 1982 C 176/3.

[202] COM (2006) 397 final (2006/0129/COD).

[203] This absence of Daughter Directives effectively means that Black list substances (a term that more or less equates to priority hazardous substances within the meaning of the Water Framework Directive) would only be subject to the much lighter Grey list-regime (the regime for priority substances in the Water Framework Directive).

measures consist of two main components: criteria for the assessment of good groundwater chemical status (Article 17(2)(a)) and criteria for the identification of significant and sustained upward trends and for the definition of starting points for trend reversals in groundwater chemical status (Article 17(2)(b). In a similar vein to the safety net provision in Article 16(8), Article 17(4) makes the Member States individually responsible to define the abovementioned criteria before 2005 in case the EU fails to do so. Interestingly, Article 17(5) adds to this another safety net in that failure to apply Article 17(4) will result in 75% of the current quality standards[204] becoming the norm for trend reversal. However, with the adoption of Directive 2006/118, the criteria mentioned in Article 17(2) have been set, so that recourse to Article 17(4) and (5) is no longer necessary.[205]

Articles 18 and further again contain more procedural rules, concerning reporting, adaptations, comitology etc. Article 22, as was noted above, contains the repeals and transitional provisions.

10.2   The Flood Risk Directive

Directive 2007/60 on the assessment and management of flood risks closely follows the framework approach that can be seen in the Water Framework Directive and complements the latter with measures concerning flood risk management.[206] The objectives of the directive are to reduce the adverse consequences for human health, the environment, cultural heritage and economic activity associated with floods (Article 1). Interestingly, the definition of floods allows the Member States to exclude floods from sewage systems (2(1)). This is problematic given that such sewage overflows are particularly dangerous for human health and the environment.[207] It does so by adopting a four-stage procedure whereby Member States first have to conduct a preliminary flood risk assessment before 22 December 2011 (Article 4). However, Member States may also choose to use flood risk assessments conducted at an earlier stage (Article 13(1)). The preliminary flood risk assessment must use the river basin approach also adopted by the Water Framework Directive (Article 4(1)).

The second stage consists of the identification of those areas where a potential significant flood risk exists or might be considered likely to occur (Article 5(1)).

The third stage is laid down in Article 6(1) and involves the drawing up of flood hazard maps and flood risk maps. The flood hazard maps must distinguish three categories of flood scenarios ((a) low probability or extreme event

---

[204] Laid down in the Groundwater Directive 80/68, see below, section 10.4.

[205] Directive 2006/118, OJ 2006 L 372/19, see below, section 10.4.

[206] OJ 2007 L 288/27.

[207] The Urban Waster Water Directive, however, requires waste water treatment installations to be designed in a way that will limit the pollution of receiving waters due to storm water overflows, insofar as this does not entail excessive costs (Annex I under A).

scenarios; (b) medium probability which is defined as an event with a likely return period equal to or exceeding 100 years and (c) flood with a high probability. For these categories the flood extent, water depth and water flow must be shown on the map. The flood risk maps must reflect the combination of flood risk and potential adverse effects on human health, the environment, cultural heritage and economic activity (Article 5(5) in combination with Article 2(2)). The directive provides that flood risk must be expressed as (a) the number of inhabitants affected; (b) the type of economic activity involved; (c) IPPC installations and protected areas affected and (d) other information considered relevant by the Member States. As the directive is based on Article 175 EC, it must be possible for the Member States to take further elements into account when drawing up their flood risk maps as part of adopting a more stringent approach. However, the directive allows for less stringent measures for coastal waters where adequate protection is in place and for floods from groundwater sources (Articles 5(6) and (7)). Flood risk maps and flood hazard maps must be drawn up before 22 December 2013.

The fourth and final stage requires the Member States to establish flood risk management plans that should contain appropriate objectives and focus on the reduction of potential adverse effects of flooding on human health, the environment, cultural heritage and economic activity. The Member States may decide to include non-structural initiatives and/or the reduction of the likelihood of flooding when they consider this appropriate. Such plans must take into account the costs and benefits, flood extent, flood conveyance routes, flood retainment areas, the environmental objectives of the Water Framework Directive, soil and water managements, land use and spatial planning, nature conservation and navigation and port facilities (Article 7(3)). The aspects to be addressed in such plans are also quite widely set out in the third subparagraph. All in all this provision appears to give the Member States considerable leeway when they draw up such plans. This discretion is exacerbated by the fact that Member States may extend the list of factors taken into account when drawing up flood risk maps. It is also limited in an important way by the solidarity requirement imposed upon the Member States by Article 7(4). According to this provision flood risk management plans shall not include measures which, by their extent and impact, significantly increase flood risks in upstream or downstream countries, unless such measures have been coordinated and agreed upon by the states concerned pursuant to Article 8 of the directive. A more stringent implementation of the flood risk criterion in a downstream state could thus result in less room for manoevre for upstream states. The flood risk management plans should be completed before 22 December 2015. The directive contains provisions on coordination with the Water Framework Directive, public information and consultation (Article 10), comitology (Articles 11 and 12), transitional measures (Article 13) and reporting and review (Articles 14-16). The directive entered into force on 26 November 2007 and must be implemented before 22 November 2009 (Articles 17 and 18).

10.3   Directive 2006/11 on Pollution by Dangerous Substances

Directive 2006/11[208] on pollution caused by certain dangerous substances discharged into the aquatic environment of the Community replaces and codifies Directive 76/464.[209] It applies only to the waters listed in Article 1, which are (a) inland surface water, (b) territorial waters, and (c) internal coastal waters. Article 7 protects waters outside the scope of the directive by requiring the Member States to ensure that these waters are not subjected to increased pollution. Morever, the Member States must ensure that the provisions of the directive are not circumvented.

Central to the directive is the distinction between so called List I substances and List II substances (also referred to as Black and Grey-list substances). Pollution by List I substances must ultimately be completely eliminated by the Member States. Pollution by List II substances must be reduced. List I contains particularly dangerous substances selected mainly on the basis of their toxicity, persistence and bioaccumulation and includes mercury and cadmium and their compounds, carcinogens, persistent mineral oils and hydrocarbons and certain persistent synthetic substances. List II includes certain heavy metals, biocides, cyanides and fluorides.

In order to eliminate the pollution by List I substances, Article 4(a) requires the Member States to ensure that all discharges of these substances require prior authorisation. This authorisation should include emissions standards and may be granted for a limited period only (Article 4(a) and (b)). The term 'discharge' defined in Article 2(d) means the introduction into the waters referred to in Article 1 of any List I or II substances, with the exception of discharges of dredgings, operational discharges from ships in territorial waters and dumping from ships in territorial waters.[210] With respect to pollution from other significant sources, including multiple and diffuse sources, Member States have the obligation to avoid or eliminate them, by means of specific programmes according to Article 5(1) of Directive 86/280.[211] It follows that European law has established two distinct systems for combating pollution of surface water by dangerous substances: first, a system of authorisation, applicable where the pollution derives from an act attributable to a person in the form of a discharge, and, second, a system of specific programmes, applicable where the pollution cannot be attributed to a person because it derives from multiple and diffuse sources.[212]

---

[208] OJ 2006 L 64/52.

[209] OJ 1976 L 129/23, later amended.

[210] See, on the meaning of discharge in the Directive 76/464, Case C-232/97 *Nederhoff* [1999] ECR I-6385, para. 37, concerning the placing by a person in surface water of wooden posts treated with creosote. Cf. also Case C-231/97 *Van Rooij* [1999] ECR I-6355 concerning the emission of contaminated steam which is precipitated on to surface water.

[211] OJ 1986 L 181/16, later amended.

[212] Case C-232/97 *Nederhoff* [1999] ECR I-6385, para. 42.

The greater part of the directive, however, must be regarded as a framework directive. In the 'old' directive, Article 6 required the Council to lay down in implementing directives (so-called 'daughter directives') the limit values which the emission standards must not exceed. Directive 2006/11 no longer contains this obligation, as it has been moved to Article 16 of the Water Framework Directive.[213]

Article 6 now requires the establishment of implementation programmes to reduce pollution by List II substances. To constitute a programme within the meaning of Article 6, the national measures

> 'must embody a comprehensive and coherent approach, covering the entire national territory of each Member State and providing practical and coordinated arrangements for the reduction of pollution caused by any of the substances in List II which is relevant in the particular context of the Member State concerned, in accordance with the quality objectives fixed by those programmes for the waters affected. They differ, therefore, both from general purification programmes and from bundles of ad hoc measures designed to reduce water pollution'.[214]

According to Article 6(3) these programmes must contain quality objectives for water, to be laid down in accordance with Council directives, where these exist. The Council has not adopted any implementing directives containing quality objectives for these substances. In addition, all discharges of such substances require prior authorisation, in which emission standards shall be laid down (Article 6(2)). The laying down by a Member State of limit values for emissions of List II substances does not constitute in itself a more stringent instrument than the implementation programmes and is therefore not sufficient to exempt that Member State from drawing up the implementation programmes.[215] As to the argument that so long as there is no water *pollution* there is no requirement for quality objectives to be laid down, the Court noted that the purpose of the implementation programmes is to reduce water pollution. The requirement to draw up programmes extends therefore to waters affected by discharges, as any discharge will inevitably lead, sooner or later, to pollution of the aquatic environment affected by it.[216] In similar vein, the Court held that there is a duty to set up pollution reduction programmes for all List II substances.[217]

---

[213] See above, section 10.1.

[214] See, concerning Article 6 of Directive 76/464, Case C-207/97 *Commission v. Belgium* [1999] ECR I-275, para. 40. Cf. also Case C-184/97 *Commission v. Germany* [1999] ECR I-7837, Case C-214/96 *Commission v. Spain* [1998] ECR I-7661, Case C-384/97 *Commission v. Greece* [2002] ECR I-3823, Case C-261/98 *Commission v. Portugal* [2000] ECR I-5905 and Case C-282/02 *Commission v. Ireland* [2005] ECR I-4653, para. 38.

[215] Case C-184/97 *Commission v. Germany* [1999] ECR I-7837, paras. 40 and 29.

[216] Case C-184/97 *Commission v. Germany* [1999] ECR I-7837, para. 60.

[217] See, concerning Article 7 of Directive 76/464, Case C-282/02 *Commission v. Ireland* [2005] ECR I-4653, paras. 35-43.

The directive further contains a standstill requirement (Article 8)[218] and a provision expressly allowing Member States to take more stringent measures (Article 9). The possibility to take more stringent measures is understandable given that the directive now has Article 175 EC as a legal basis. However, it appears to be at odds with the fourth recital in the preamble.[219] Article 9 permits Member States to make the authorisation for a discharge subject to additional requirements not provided for in the directive, in order to protect the European aquatic environment against pollution, even if these requirements have the effect of making the grant of authorisation impossible or altogether exceptional.[220] The additional requirements may include the obligation to investigate or choose alternative solutions which have less impact on the environment.

The provisions of Directive 2006/11 will remain applicable to existing installations until the measures required pursuant to Article 5 of the IPPC Directive have been taken by the competent authorities.[221] For new installations the relevant provisions concerning authorisation systems in Directive 2006/11 will not be applied now the IPPC Directive has been brought into effect.[222] The directive, like Directive 76/464, does not contain any provision on the deadline for transposition, but according to the Court this does not rule out the possibility to hold a Member State responsible if transposition did not take place in a reasonable period.[223] Finally, as references to Directive 76/464 have to be construed as references to Directive 2006/11 (Article 13), the latter will be repealed in December 2013 on the basis of Article 22 of the Water Framework Directive.

10.4   Groundwater Protection

The preamble to Directive 76/464[224] had already referred to the adoption of specific European rules on discharges into groundwater. Directive 80/68 provides just those rules.[225] Furthermore, Directive 2006/118, a daughter directive to the Water Framework Directive, contains rules on pollution of groundwater by priority (hazardous) substances. This directive requires Member States to take the necessary measures to *prevent* the discharge into groundwater of certain substances (contained in List I in the Annex to the directive) and to

---

[218] See, concerning Article 9 of Directive 76/464, Case C-282/02 *Commission* v. *Ireland* [2005] ECR I-4653 paras. 88-91, according to which failure to implement a the directive is not a violation of the standstill obligation if there is a deterioration of water quality.

[219] This recital appears to be left over from the 'old' directive that had Articles 100 (now 94) and 235 (now 308) EC as a legal base.

[220] Case C-232/97 *Nederhoff* [1999] ECR I-6385, para. 61.

[221] Article 20(1) of the IPPC Directive. Cf. also Case C-207/97 *Commission* v. *Belgium* [1999] ECR I-275, para. 36.

[222] Article 20(2) of the IPPC Directive.

[223] Case C-282/02 *Commission* v. *Ireland* [2005] ECR I-4653, para. 33.

[224] OJ 1976 L 129/23, later amended.

[225] OJ 1980 L 20/43, later amended.

limit the discharge into groundwater of other substances (contained in List II in the Annex; Article 3). From the judgment in Case 360/87, it is apparent that the national legislation implementing the directive must make the distinction between substances in lists I and II in so many words.[226] The Court held 'the distinction between the two types of substances is mandatory in view of the objective of the directive. It follows that it must be incorporated in national legislation with the requisite precision and clarity in order to meet the requirement of certainty.'

From the case law of the Court it is also clear that the prohibition on direct discharges of List I substances in Article 4(1) 'is general and absolute':

> 'and applies to discharges of substances in list I without distinguishing between the substances themselves and solutions thereof. That article does not empower the competent authorities of the Member States to determine, on a case-by-case basis and having regard to the circumstances, whether or not discharges have a detrimental effect.'[227]
>
> The Court noted that Article 2(b), which provides that the directive shall not apply to discharges of substances in such a small quantity as to exclude any danger to the groundwater, makes no difference in this respect.

The two lists of the Groundwater Directive do not correspond entirely with those of Directive 2006/11. For the purposes of the directive, 'direct discharge' means the introduction into groundwater of substances without percolation through the ground or subsoil (Article 1(2)(b)), while 'indirect discharge' means the introduction into groundwater of substances after percolation through the ground or subsoil (Article 1(2)(c)). Member States must prohibit all direct discharge of substances in list I (Article 4). Any disposal or tipping for the purpose of disposal of these substances which might lead to indirect discharge shall be subject to prior investigation,[228] and depending on the results of that investigation be prohibited or require authorisation. The investigation shall include examination of the hydrogeological conditions of the area concerned, the possible purifying powers of the soil and subsoil and the risk of pollution and alteration of the quality of the groundwater from the discharge (Article 7). It must establish whether the discharge into groundwater is a satisfactory solution from the point of view of the environment. Authorisations may be granted only if all technical precautions have been taken to prevent indirect discharges (Article 4). Member States must take all appropriate measures they deem necessary to prevent any indirect discharge due to other activities. Direct discharge of substances in list II and disposal or tipping for the purpose of disposal of these

---

[226] Case 360/87 *Commission v. Italy* [1991] ECR I-791.

[227] Case C-131/88 *Commission v. Germany* [1991] ECR I-825.

[228] See on this Case C-131/88 *Commission v. Germany* [1991] ECR I-825. In this context Germany referred, *inter alia*, to the general procedures in its law on administrative procedure *(Verwaltungsverfahrensgesetz)*. These provisions were also not sufficiently precise and specific to withstand the scrutiny of the Court.

substances which might lead to indirect discharge must also be made subject to prior investigation (Article 5). Member States may grant an authorisation in the light of that investigation, provided that all the technical precautions for preventing groundwater pollution have been observed. From 16 January 2009 onwards all authorisations pursuant to Articles 4 and 5 of this directive will have to take into account the requirements laid down in Articles 3, 4 and 5, of the Groundwater Daughter Directive.[229] Article 6 of the directive contains provisions on the artificial recharge of groundwater subject to which a special authorisation may be issued for the artificial recharge of groundwater, namely 'if there is no risk of polluting the groundwater'.[230]

Articles 9 to 12 deal with the content of authorisations.[231] A system of 'tacit authorisation' is not allowed. According to Italian legislation a provisional authorisation was deemed to have been granted if the application for grant of authorisation had not been rejected within six months. According to the Court, the directive provides that the refusal, grant or withdrawal of authorisations must take place by way of an express measure in accordance with precise rules of procedure which comply with a number of necessary conditions, conditions which create rights and obligations on the part of individuals. Consequently, tacit authorisation cannot be considered compatible with the requirements of the directive, since such authorisation does not make it possible to carry out prior inquiries, subsequent inquiries or checks.

Article 11 requires Member States to grant authorisations for a limited period, which must be reviewed at least every four years. The grant of authorisations for an indefinite period, even if they can be withdrawn or amended at any time, is incompatible with the directive. And as the Court held in Case C-131/88, the requirement contained in Article 11 is not met where the 'administrative authorities are free to decide whether or not to restrict the period of validity of the authorization'.[232]

Article 13, which requires Member States to monitor compliance with the conditions laid down in each authorisation and the effects of discharges on groundwater, was considered in Case C-360/87.[233] The Italian Government's argument that the fact that failure to observe the conditions laid down in authorisations constitutes a criminal offence automatically entails a duty of surveillance and monitoring on the part of the authorities responsible for investigating offences was not accepted by the Court. From this it appears that the national implementing legisla-

---

[229] Directive 2006/118, Article 7, see below in this section.

[230] This provision must be expressly transposed into national law; Case 291/84 *Commission* v. *Netherlands* [1987] ECR 3483.

[231] Case C-360/87 *Commission* v. *Italy* [1991] ECR I-791. See further Case C-416/02 *Commission* v. *Spain* [2005] ECR I-7487, paras. 106-109, according to which the use of agricultural slurry from farms is not subject to the authorisation regime on the basis of the Groundwater Directive.

[232] Case C-131/88 *Commission* v. *Germany* [1991] ECR I-825.

[233] Case C-360/87 *Commission* v. *Italy* [1991] ECR I-791.

tion must contain explicit and specific instructions to carry out the necessary control and monitoring. For the same reason a German administrative provision requiring individuals to permit monitoring was held not to be sufficient, because it did not 'itself impose an obligation to monitor compliance with the conditions laid down in the authorizations'.[234] The scope of the standstill obligation in Article 18 was considered by the Court in Case 291/84.[235] Article 18 requires that the application of the measures taken pursuant to the directive may on no account lead, either directly or indirectly, to pollution of the water referred to in Article 1 of the directive. The Commission argued that Article 18 must be regarded not only as implying a standstill requirement, but as prohibiting any increase in the pollution of groundwater, even that caused by other substances. The Court rejected the Commission's argument stating that Article 18 refers to 'the measures taken pursuant to this Directive', causing the standstill obligation in turn to be confined to the pollution of groundwater by List I en II substances.

The Groundwater Directive will be repealed in December 2013,[236] but given that the Water Framework Directive already applies, this should not be a problem. As was already mentioned, a daughter directive on the basis of Article 17 of the Water Framework Directive has been adopted. This Groundwater Daughter Directive contains the criteria for the assessment of groundwater chemical status and the criteria for trend reversal. It complements the Water Framework Directive. The criteria for assessing groundwater chemical status are laid down in Article 3 in connection with Annex I. The specific criteria/threshold values have to be established by the Member States before 22 december 2008 (Article 3(5)). The detailed rules for trend reversal can be found in Article 5 in connection with Annex IV. Article 6 implements the duty contained in Article 4(1)(b)(i) of the Water Framework Directive to take measures to prevent inputs into the groundwater of any pollutants. Article 6(3) allows for exemptions from this duty on the grounds listed in points (a) to (f). The Groundwater Daughter Directive must be implemented before 16 January 2009.

10.5   The Protection of Bathing Water

Directive 2006/7 (hereafter the new Bathing Water Directive) lays down rules for the quality of bathing water.[237] It replaces Directive 76/160 (hereafter the current Bathing Water Directive) with effect from 31 December 2014 (Article 17(1)) and complements the Water Framework Directive (Article 1(2)).[238] Many of the core elements of the current Bathing Water Directive have found their way into the new directive.

---

[234] Case C-131/88 Commission v. Germany [1991] ECR I-825.

[235] Case 291/84 Commission v. Netherlands [1987] ECR 3483, para. 21.

[236] Article 22(2) Water Framework Directive, see above, section 10.1.

[237] OJ 2006 L 64/37.

[238] OJ 1976 L 31/1, later amended.

Central to the new Bathing Water Directive is the concept of bathing water. The definition in Article 1(3) is slightly narrower compared to that in the current Bathing Water Directive. In the new definition, bathing water exists if the authority expects a large number of people to bathe therein and has not prohibited bathing or issued a warning against bathing. The current directive does not require any expectations on the part of the authority and simply referred to waters where bathing is not prohibited and traditionally practised by a large number of bathers (Article 1(2)(a)).

Under the current Bathing Water Directive, Member States must ensure that the quality of bathing water conforms to the set limits within ten years (Article 4).[239] However, it does not provide for what should be done if Member States fail to comply with the values set out. Of course the Member States are required to take measures to ensure that the values are achieved, but it is does not require that bathing should be prohibited or restricted if the values are exceeded.[240] Such a prohibition is only required if public health is endangered.

The current directive also contains provisions on sampling (Articles 5 and 6)[241] and a standstill requirement (Article 7). Article 8, finally, indicates in what cases the directive may be waived, for example in the case of exceptional weather or geographical conditions.[242] In no case may exceptions be made which disregard the requirements 'essential for public health protection'.

An important judgment which clarifies certain aspects of the current Bathing Water Directive was given by the Court in the *Blackpool* case.[243] In the first place the Court rejected the United Kingdom's argument that the directive did not provide a precise definition of the term 'bathing water' and that Member States thus had a discretionary power in that respect. The Court ruled that the objectives of the directive could not be achieved:

'if the waters of bathing resorts equipped with facilities such as changing huts, toilets, markers indicating bathing areas, and supervised by lifeguards, could be excluded from the scope of the directive solely because the number of bathers was below a certain threshold. Such facilities and the presence of lifeguards constitute

---

[239] Cf. Case C-198/97 *Commission v. Germany* [1999] ECR I-3257. See further Case C-278/01 *Commission v. Spain*, where the Court imposed a penalty payment for breach of Articles 3 and 4 of the current Bathing Water Directive, [2003] ECR I-14141.

[240] Case C-307/98 *Commission v. Belgium* [2000] ECR I-3933, paras. 59-63.

[241] On sampling, see Case C-198/97 *Commission v. Germany* [1999] ECR I-3257, paras. 44-47. See on this case also Chapter 4, section 4.1.

[242] Cf. Case C-92/96 *Commission v. Spain* [1998] ECR I-505, concerning abnormal drought. However in this case the Spanish Government had not provided any specific evidence, either of the abnormal nature of the alleged drought or of the resultant inability on the part of the authorities to achieve the minimum standard for bathing water imposed by the directive, even by undertaking further efforts.

[243] Case C-56/90 *Commission v. UK* [1993] ECR I-4109. Cf. also Case C-307/98 *Commission v. Belgium* [2000] ECR I-3933.

evidence that the bathing area is frequented by a large number of bathers whose health must be protected.'

If certain areas fulfil these criteria, as was the case with Blackpool and South-port in this case, the water in question is bathing water and the quality standards laid down in the directive apply.

The judgment also clarifies the legal nature of the obligations under the current directive. The UK contended that the directive merely required the Member States to take 'all practicable steps' to comply with its obligations. The Court rejected this argument. More is required:

> 'It follows that the directive requires the Member States to take steps to ensure that certain results are attained, and, apart from those derogations [the ones in Articles 4(3), 5(2) and 8, authors], they cannot rely on particular circumstances to justify a failure to fulfil that obligation.'[244]

In other words, best endeavours are not enough: the directive imposes an obligation to achieve a result. The new Bathing Water Directive contains a similar set of environmental objectives, albeit in a more elaborate framework. The first step the Member States must annually identify all bathing waters and the length of the bathing season (Article 3(1) before the start of the first bathing season after March 2008. In addition the Member States have to ensure that monitoring of the bathing waters takes place in conformity with the directive. On the basis of the results of the monitoring the bathing water quality assessment takes place (Article 4). This assessment will in turn result in a classification of the bathing water as poor, sufficient, good or excellent. This classification takes place on the basis of the microbiological criteria monitoring rules in Annex I and II. The first such classification must take place before the end of the 2015 bathing season (Article 5(2)) and the Member States must ensure that at that time all bathing waters are of at least sufficient quality (Article 5(3)). Article 5(3) also requires the Member States to take the 'realistic and proportionate measures' they consider appropriate to increase the number of bathing waters classified as good or excellent. Article 5(4) contains a derogation allowing the Member States to classify bathing waters as poor without being in breach of the directive. The Member States will then have to alert the public to this status and identify the cause of the pollution and take adequate measures. Classification as poor for five consecutive years will result in a permanent bathing prohibition or a permanent advice against bathing, unless achievement of sufficient status would be infeasible or disproportionately expensive. In sum, the Member States are allowed a derogation on economic grounds. Member States have a duty to monitor and inform the public in cases of cyanobacterial risks (algal bloom, Article 8). Interestingly, Article 9 requires the Member States to ensure visual inspection of bathing waters for pollution such as tarry residue, glass or any other waste and

---

[244] Emphasis added by the authors.

to take adequate management measures. Notwithstanding that the adequacy of measures may be open to discussion, this would appear to be a provision that has direct effect and could form the basis of a claim for damages suffered as a result of, for example, injury sustained because of glass that was in the bathing water. Article 10, on transboundary cooperation, corresponds to Article 4(4) in the current Bathing Water Directive. An important change in the new Bathing Water Directive relates to the information of the public. Under the current directive, there is only a duty to report to the Commission, and the Commission will then publish a report (Article 13). The new Bathing Water Directive, in line with the Aarhus convention, contains more elaborate provisions on public information and consultation (Articles 11 and 12) in addition to the duty to report to the Commission (Article 13). Finally, the deadline for implementation is 24 March 2008 (Article 18(1), and from this date onwards, the new Bathing Water Directive will be applicable, replacing Directive 76/160. As a result, anyone wishing to rely on the Bathing Water Directive will, from the date of implementation onwards, have to rely on the new Bathing Water Directive, even if the current directive is not repealed at that time.

10.6 The Protection of Shellfish Waters and Fresh Water for Fish

There are two directives concerning waters designated by the Member States as needing protection or improvement in order to support shellfish life and growth[245] and freshwater fish life.[246] Both directives codify amendments to earlier directives and follow a nearly identical scheme. The scope of both directives is restricted by the fact that the Member States first have to designate waters as needing protection in order to support freshwater fish life or shellfish life. Concerning the latter, the directive is confined to coastal or brackish waters (Article 1 of Directive 2006/113). By not designating waters, a Member State could easily avoid its obligations. However, in the light of the decisions the Court has given on the basis of the 'old' directives, it would no longer seem possible to uphold such a literal interpretation. In Case 322/86, Italy failed to designate certain waters under the Fresh Water for Fish Directive:[247]

> 'No salmonid or cyprinid waters situated on Italian territory have been designated other than those in the autonomous province of Bolzano. The government has also failed to set, for these waters, specific values for the parameters laid down in Annex 1 of the directive, and to draw up programmes in order to ensure that these parameters conform to the values set. It must therefore be held that by failing to

---

[245] Directive 2006/113, OJ 2006 L 376/14, repealing with effect from 15 January 2007 Directive 79/923, OJ 1979 L 281/47.

[246] Directive 2006/44, OJ 2006 L 264/20, repealing with effect from 14 October 2006 Directive 78/659, OJ 1978 L 222/1.

[247] Case 322/86 Commission v. Italy [1988] ECR 3995.

adopt within the prescribed period the measures necessary in order to comply with Council Directive 78/659/EEC of 18 July 1978 the Italian Republic has failed to fulfil its obligations under the EEC Treaty.'

From this it must be concluded that, although the wording of the directives suggests otherwise, the Member States' power to designate waters under the directives is not unlimited.[248] The Court's judgment does not, however, indicate what the limits are. Perhaps a parallel can be drawn with the Court's case law on the designation of special protection areas under the Wild Birds Directive.[249] This would then result in an obligation to designate those waters that support fish life or shellfish life or could support such life once pollution is reduced to such an extent that these fish or shellfish can grow and be of a high quality edible by man. When waters have been designated the Member States must observe values for certain pollutants or parameters (such as temperature, salinity and heavy metals; Article 3 in connection with Annex I). The directives lay down both I values which Member States are required to observe and G values which they must endeavour to observe (Article 3(2). The Member States then have to set up programmes[250] to ensure that within five years from the designation pollution is reduced so that the fresh waters comply with these values (Article 5). For shellfish waters the Member States have six years (Article 5).

The directives also contain provisions regarding monitoring (Article 6) sampling (Article 7), and a standstill requirement (Article 8). More stringent national measures are allowed on the basis of Article 9 and Article 10 contains rules on cross-border consultation. Furthermore a derogation is possible in the event of exceptional weather or geographical conditions (Article 11). Both directives will be repealed in December 2013.[251]

10.7 The Protection of Drinking Water

The protection of drinking water takes place through two directives. Directive 75/440 concerning the quality of surface water intended for the abstraction of drinking water in the Member States sets forth the quality requirements which surface fresh water used or intended for use in the abstraction of drinking water must meet.[252] Directive 98/83,[253] which covers the area where consumer protection and protection of the environment converge, lays

---

[248] See further Case C-148/05 *Commission* v. *Ireland*, judgment of 14 June 2007, n.y.r. in the ECR, paras. 46-48.

[249] Case C-3/96 *Commission* v. *Netherlands* [1998] ECR I-3031, see further section 17.1 below.

[250] Once again 'specific programmes' are required. General water purification programmes are not sufficient, Case C-298/95 *Commission* v. *Germany* [1996] ECR I-6747, para. 24.

[251] Article 22(2) of the Water Framework Directive, in connection with Article 16, second paragraph, of the Shellfish Water and Freshwater Fish Directive.

[252] OJ 1974 L 194/34, later amended.

[253] OJ 1998 L 330/32, repealing Directive 80/778, OJ 1980 L 229/11.

down product standards which have to be met by water intended for human consumption. As Directive 75/440 will be repealed in December 2007,[254] only limited attention will be devoted to it.[255] For the purposes of the directive, surface water is divided into three categories of limiting values: A1, A2 and A3. These correspond to three different qualities of surface water based on physical, chemical and microbiological characteristics. Surface water having characteristics falling short of quality A3 may not be used for the abstraction of drinking water. Article 4(2) requires Member States to take measures to ensure a continuing improvement in the environment. To this end they must draw up systematic plans of action and timetables. The directive provides for a specific provision on transfrontier pollution. Under Article 4(1) of the directive, each Member State must apply the directive without distinction to national waters and to waters crossing its frontiers. This requirement imposes obligations on states situated downstream where the surface water is polluted upstream. The Court made it clear that the directive imposes an obligation to improve the waters if pollution is caused outside the national frontiers, even where the state in question is not a EU Member State. From December 2007 onwards Article 7 of the Water Framework Directive will constitute the legal framework for the protection of water intended for abstraction of drinking water.

Directive 98/83 lays down product standards which have to be met by water intended for human consumption.[256] Compared to its predecessor, Directive 98/83 shows signs of the influence of the subsidiarity principle when it focuses on compliance with essential quality and health parameters, leaving Member States free to add other parameters if they see fit. Furthermore, the directive seems to have broadened the scope of derogations. This is probably a late response by the Council to the Court's judgments in Case 228/87 and Case C-337/89.[257]

10.8   The Urban Waste Water Directive

Directive 91/271 concerns the collection, treatment and discharge of urban waste water and the treatment and discharge of waste water from certain industrial sectors.[258] Article 3 requires Member States to ensure

---

[254] Article 22(1) of the Water Framework Directive.

[255] An interesting case that deals with several aspects of this directive is Case C-58/89 *Commission* v. *Germany* [1991] ECR I-4983.

[256] See, concerning the 'old' Directive 80/778, Case C-42/89 *Commission* v. *Belgium* [1990] ECR I-2821. The directive does not cover water from private wells. The Court held that it follows from Article 2 of the directive that the directive applies only to water supplied for human consumption and to water used in foodstuffs by a food production undertaking, but not to water from private sources, see further Article 3(2)(b) of Directive 98/83.

[257] Case 228/87 *Pretore di Torino* v. *Persons unknown* [1988] ECR 5099; Case C-337/89 *Commission* v. *UK* [1992] ECR I-6103.

[258] OJ 1991 L 135/40, later amended. Cf. on the relation with the Waste Directive also Case C-252/05 *Thames Water*, judgment of 10 May 2007, n.y.r. in the ECR and section 15 of this chapter *infra*.

that all agglomerations are provided with collecting systems for waste water, and lays down requirements such a system must meet. The period within which such a system must have been implemented is linked to population equivalents and the existence of 'sensitive areas'.[259] Article 4 sets criteria which the treatment of waste water must meet before it may be discharged into the collecting systems. Here, too, the periods by which implementation must have been fulfilled are linked to population equivalents. Discharges from urban waste water treatment plants must satisfy certain requirements.

Article 5 deals with 'sensitive areas', which must be identified by the Member States according to certain criteria. Discharges of urban waste water into these areas are required to undergo more stringent treatment than other discharges. The same applies to discharges into catchment areas of sensitive areas. Article 5(8), in particular, is important. Member States do not have to identify sensitive areas if they implement the treatment for sensitive areas over all their territory.

Article 9 concerns the problem of discharges with transfrontier effects and provides for notification and consultation in such cases. Member States must ensure that pollution caused by discharges does not exceed the limits laid down in the directive. However, the second paragraph of Annex II B provides that Member States must recognize the presence of sensitive areas outside their national jurisdiction. This could imply that the existence of transfrontier effects might result in stricter standards being applied than if there were only national effects.

Article 11 provides that the discharge of industrial waste water into collecting systems and treatment plants is subject to prior regulations and/or specific authorisations. Article 13 similarly provides that biodegradable industrial waste water from certain industrial sectors which is discharged directly into surface waters is subject to prior regulations and/or specific authorisations. The competent authority or body must set requirements appropriate to the nature of the industry concerned.

Article 14 is designed to ensure that sludge arising from waste water treatment is re-used wherever possible. The disposal of such sludge must be made subject to general rules or registration or authorisation before 31 December 1998, and the disposal of sludge to surface waters is prohibited as of that date. Until then, Member States must ensure that the total amount of toxic, persistent or bioaccumulable materials is licensed and progressively reduced.

The directive also requires Member States to carry out monitoring (Article 15) and publish reports (Article 16).

10.9 The Nitrates Directive

It is a fact that modern intensive farming methods are a cause of many environmental problems. One of the consequences of applying live-

---

[259] These will also constitute protected areas under the Water Framework Directive; Cf. Article 4(1)(c) in connection with Annex IV under 1(iv).

stock manure to land is the pollution of water by nitrates. The use of fertilizers containing nitrates is one of the main causes of pollution from diffuse sources affecting Europe's waters. Directive 91/676 aims to reduce water pollution caused or induced by nitrates from agricultural sources.[260]

The Member States are required to have identified the waters which were affected (or could be affected) by nitrate pollution before the end of 1993 (Article 3(1)).[261] The criteria for this are set out in Annex I, which sets the threshold for nitrates at 50 mg/l. According to the Court in the *Standley* case, Member States are not required to determine precisely what proportion of the pollution in the waters is attributable to nitrates of agricultural origin or that the cause of such pollution must be exclusively agricultural.[262] Indeed, in a later case the Court held that a 17% to 19% contribution by Walloon agriculture to nitrogen levels in several basins flowing into the North Sea was 'minor', but by no means insignificant. Any other solution would of course undermine the protection of the North Sea, which is one of the directive's objectives.[263]

Article 3(2) provides that Member States must designate as vulnerable zones all known areas of land in their territories which drain into the waters identified according to paragraph 1.[264] Once these zones have been designated, Member States must establish action programmes consisting of certain mandatory measures (Article 5 in conjunction with Annex III).[265] The limit for the application of livestock manure is, for example, set at 170 kg of nitrate per hectare (Annex III, paragraph 2).[266] There are a number of Commission decisions concerning the possibility of a derogation from this maximum.[267]

Outside the vulnerable zones, the general obligation contained in Article 4 applies. The Member States were supposed to have established a 'code of good agricultural practice', to be implemented by farmers on a voluntary basis, before the end of 1993. The items such a code should cover are contained in Annex II.

The directive provides for a special consultation procedure in the event of transfrontier pollution (Article 3(3))

---

[260] OJ 1991 L 375/1. Cf. on the implementation COM (98) 16 and COM (97) 473.

[261] Case C-258/00 *Commission v. France* [2002] ECR I-5959, paras. 45-54, shows that the Member States cannot restrict the scope of the directive when they consider that other substances than nitrogen trigger eutrophication.

[262] Case C-293/97 *Standley* [1999] ECR I-2603.

[263] Case C-221/03 *Commission v. Belgium* [2005] ECR I-8307, paras. 84-89.

[264] These will also constitute protected areas under the Water Framework Directive, cf. Article 4(1)(c) in connection with Annex IV under 1(iv).

[265] See, on the limits to national action programmes, Case C-322/00 *Commission v. Netherlands* [2003] ECR I-11267.

[266] See, on the way in which the amount of manure should be calculated, Case C-161/00 *Commission v. Germany* [2002] ECR I-2753, paras. 36-47.

[267] For example, Decision 2002/915, OJ 2002 L 319/24 (*Denmark*) Decision 2005/889, OJ 2005 L 324/89 (*Netherlands*) and Decision 2006/189, OJ 2006 L 66/44 (*Austria*).

The directive does not preclude the Member States from applying the provisions of the directive in cases not covered by it.[268]

10.10   The Titanium Dioxide Directive

The manufacture of titanium dioxide (TiO2), a whitener used in paints and toothpaste, among other things, is particularly harmful to the environment. It is responsible for producing a large quantity of highly acidic waste. This waste largely ends up in water as a result of dumping or discharge. For this reason the EU has been actively engaged in imposing specific measures on this particular industry since 1978. Moreover, the cost of waste disposal has a significant impact on the price of the product. From the point of view of the internal market, this is an additional reason for European action.

Directive 78/176 sets general targets for the prevention and reduction of waste produced by the TiO2 industry.[269] Thus the Member States are required in a general sense to take the necessary measures to ensure that waste is disposed of without endangering human health and without harming the environment, and in particular without risk to water, air, soil and plants and animals and without deleteriously affecting beauty spots or the countryside (Article 2). They must also take appropriate measures to encourage the prevention, recycling and processing of waste, the extraction of raw materials and any other process for the reuse of waste (Article 3).

More specific is the obligation to issue authorisations contained in Article 4. The discharge, dumping, storage, tipping and injection of waste must be prohibited unless prior authorisation is issued by the competent authority of the Member State in whose territory the waste is produced. Prior authorisation must also be issued by the competent authority of the Member State in whose territory the waste is discharged, stored, tipped or injected or from whose territory it is discharged or dumped. The authorisation may be granted for a limited period only, though it may be renewed.

Articles 5 (discharge or dumping) and 6 (storage, tipping or injection) lay down the conditions under which authorisations may be granted. These are that:
  · the waste cannot be disposed of by more appropriate means;
  · an assessment carried out in the light of available scientific and technical knowledge shows that there will be no detrimental effect, either immediate or delayed, on underground waters, the soil or the atmosphere;
  · there is no deleterious effect on leisure activities, the extraction of raw materials, plants and animals on regions of special scientific importance or on *other legitimate uses of the environment* in question.

New industrial establishments are also subject to authorisation (Article 11). An authorisation must be preceded by an environmental impact survey. The

---

[268] Case C-293/97 *Standley* [1999] ECR I-2603.
[269] OJ 1978 L 54/19.

authorisation may be granted only to firms which give an undertaking to use only such of the materials, processes and techniques available on the market as are least damaging to the environment.

The directive contains several monitoring requirements (Article 7), which are further specified in Directive 82/883.[270] If the conditions laid down in the authorisation have not been fulfilled, the Member State concerned must take all appropriate steps to remedy the situation and may, if necessary, require the suspension of the discharge, dumping, etc. Member States are required to supply information and prepare reports (Articles 13 and 14). They are expressly permitted to adopt more stringent national regulations (Article 12).

Articles 9 and 10 concern the drawing up of programmes for the reduction and elimination of pollution. These programmes, which were supposed to have been sent to the Commission before 1 July 1980, were to have formed the basis for further legislation by the Council on the matter. However, it was not until December 1992 that the Council was able to introduce the further harmonisation measures announced in Article 9(3) of the directive, when it introduced Directive 92/112.[271] If it had not been for the Court's judgment in the *TiO2* case[272] annulling Directive 89/428[273] because it had been adopted on an inappropriate legal basis, this could have been done three years earlier. It should be added that Directive 92/112 is virtually identical to the directive that was annulled.

Under Article 3, the dumping of any solid waste, strong acid waste, treatment waste, weak acid waste, or neutralised waste is prohibited with effect from 15 June 1993. For the purposes of the directive, dumping means any deliberate disposal of substances and materials by or from ships or aircraft. The discharge of solid waste and strong acid waste, in particular, is prohibited from that date (Article 4). Articles 6 and 7 set emission limit values for other discharges of waste, in particular weak acid waste and neutralised waste. As an alternative to these limit values, Member States may choose to make use of quality objectives (coupled with appropriate limit values), if they are applied in such a way that the effects in terms of protecting the environment and avoiding distortions of competition are equivalent to that of the limit values laid down in the directive (Article 8). In that case the Commission must give its consent (Article 8(2) in conjunction with Article 10 of Directive 78/176). The directive also contains provisions requiring Member States to prevent air pollution (Article 9), to monitor each establishment (Article 10), to take preventive measures and to promote the re-use of waste (Article 11). Member States are permitted to take more stringent national measures, though this is noted in the preamble to the directive rather than in an express provision.

---

[270] OJ 1982 L 378/1.

[271] OJ 1992 L 409/11.

[272] Case C-300/89 *Commission v. Council* [1991] ECR I-2867.

[273] OJ 1989 L 201/56.

10.11 Protection of the Marine Environment

The protection of the marine environment takes place through three sets of rules. Firstly, there are the rules on the prevention of accidents at sea and the remedying of the consequences of such accidents. Secondly, there is the EU's own Thematic Marine Strategy, that will function in a setting formed by international treaties.[274] Thirdly, part of the EU's fisheries policy also pertains to protecting the marine environment.[275]

Concerning the first limb, international policy in respect of the prevention of accidents at sea and the environmental problems connected with them are embodied above all in IMO Resolutions and the SOLAS and MARPOL Conventions.[276] The first European rules are to be found in Directive 79/116 concerning minimum requirements for certain tankers entering or leaving EU ports.[277] However, this directive is replaced by Directive 2002/59 concerning minimum requirements for vessels bound for or leaving EU ports and carrying dangerous or polluted goods.[278] Furthermore, Directive 95/21 contains rules on port state control concerning vessels and the protection of, *inter alia*, pollution prevention.[279] Pursuant to Regulation 1406/2002 the European Maritime Safety Agency has been established.[280] This Agency is (co-)responsible for monitoring many of the maritime safety rules. Following the Erika tanker disaster it has also been given powers in the field of pollution control.[281] Finally in this context it is worth mentioning Council Decision 2007/162 setting up a Civil Protection Financial Instrument that will cover, among others, cooperation in the fields of accidental marine pollution.[282] Concerning deliberate pollution from ships, Directive 2005/35[283] and Framework Decision 2005/667[284] make it an infringement to discharge a polluting substance from a ship in the internal waters, territorial waters, international straits or the exclusive economic zone if this discharge is committed intentionally, recklessly or by serious negligence (Article 4 in connection with Article 3(1) of Directive 2005/35. Moreover, such discharges are considered criminal offences if the conditions of Framework Decision 2005/667 are fulfilled.

---

[274] See above, section 4.

[275] This will not be dealt with here, see for information on this topic: Wolff (2002).

[276] At Community level the Commission's policy is set out in COM (93) 66 final.

[277] OJ 1979 L 33/33.

[278] OJ 2002 L 208/10, repealing Directive 93/75, OJ 1993 L 247/19.

[279] OJ 1995 L 175/1, amended by Directive 2002/84, OJ 2002 L 324/53.

[280] OJ 2002 L 208/1.

[281] Regulation 724/2004, OJ 2004 L 129/1.

[282] OJ 2007 L 71/9. This instrument takes over following the expiry of Decision 2850/2000 setting up a Community framework for cooperation in the field of accidental or deliberate marine pollution, OJ 2000 L 332/1.

[283] OJ 2005 L 255/11.

[284] OJ 2005 L 255/164; see Case C-440/05 *Commission* v. *Council*, where the Commission contends that the measure should have been adopted pursuant to the EC transport provisions.

The EU's Thematic Strategy on the Protection and Conservation of the Marine Environment is the result of the Sixth Environmental Action Programme[285] and envisages a further integration of the abovementioned marine protection initiatives.[286] Moreover, as part of this thematic strategy a Marine Strategy Directive has been proposed by the Commission.[287] This proposal aims to apply the methodology of the Water Framework Directive to the protection of the marine environment. This too is protected in a fragmented way and in need of an integrated protection instrument. As a result, the proposal envisages the designation of marine regions as sub-regions and the development of marine strategies that will have to be coordinated if a marine (sub)region is shared by more than one Member State. The marine strategies will have to include measures necessary to attain good environmental status.[288]

11   Legislation on Air Pollution

European legislation for the prevention of air pollution focuses on the following areas:
- establishing minimum ambient air quality standards and maximum emission standards for certain harmful substances;
- reducing the emissions from certain sources (cars and other motor vehicles, industrial installations);
- protection of the ozone layer.

This legislation was adopted partly to fulfil the European obligations resulting from international treaties concluded by it, for example the 1979 Geneva Convention on Long-range Transboundary Air Pollution and the Protocols of Geneva (1984: monitoring and evaluation), Helsinki (1985: sulphur compounds), Sofia (1988: oxides of nitrogen),[289] and Gothenburg (1999: Acidification, Eutrophication and Ground-Level Ozone),[290] the 1985 Vienna Convention for the Protection of the Ozone Layer and the 1987 Montreal Protocol on Substances which Deplete the Ozone Layer[291] and the 1992 Framework Convention on Climate Change (Rio de Janeiro).[292]

---

[285] See above, section 1 of this chapter.

[286] COM (2005) 504 final.

[287] COM (2005) 505 final.

[288] At the time of writing the Council had reached political consensus on 18 December 2006, Number 16976/06.

[289] OJ 1981 L 171/13; OJ 1986 L 181/2; OJ 1993 L 149/16.

[290] Decision 2003/507, OJ 2003 L 179/1.

[291] OJ 1988 L 297/10 and OJ 1988 L 297/21.

[292] OJ 1994 L 33/13, concluded by Council Decision 94/69, OJ 1994 L 33/11. See also the subsequent Kyoto Protocol, agreed upon in December 1997 and signed by the EC on 29 April 1998. See on 'Kyoto' in general: French (1998). Cf. Communication of the Commission Preparing for Implementation of the

11.1 Ambient Air Quality Directives

In the 1980s the Council adopted three directives laying down minimum air quality standards for various substances.[293] In 1992 the Council adopted a further Directive on ozone in ambient air.[294] These directives have lost much of their significance since the entry into force of Framework Directive 96/62 on ambient air quality assessment and management.[295] The general aim of the Framework Directive is to define the basic principles of a common strategy to (Article 1):

· define and establish objectives for ambient air quality designed to avoid, prevent or reduce harmful effects on human health and the environment as a whole;
· assess the ambient air quality in Member States on the basis of common methods and criteria;
· obtain adequate information on ambient air quality and ensure that it is made available to the public, *inter alia* by means of alert thresholds;
· maintain ambient air quality where it is good and improve it in other cases.

This framework directive does not itself contain any limit values or target values, but Article 4 does provide that the Commission shall submit to the Council proposals for the setting of limit values and, as appropriate, alert thresholds according to a detailed timetable. The pollutants for which limit values must be set include both pollutants which were already covered by legislation and ones that were not (Annex I).

Member States are required to take the necessary measures to ensure compliance with the limit values (Article 7(1)). They are also required to draw up action plans indicating the measures to be taken in the short term where there is a risk of the limit values and/or alert thresholds being exceeded, in order to reduce that risk and to limit the duration of such an occurrence (Article 7(3)).

Furthermore, the directive contains provisions on the assessment of ambient air quality (provisionally or otherwise, Articles 5 and 6 respectively), measures applicable in zones where levels are higher than the limit (Article 8), requirements in zones where the levels are lower than the limit value (standstill; Article 9) and measures applicable in the event of the alert thresholds being exceeded (Article 10). For instance, Article 10 provides that when the alert thresholds are exceeded, Member States must ensure that the necessary steps are taken to inform the public (e.g. by means of radio, television and the press). Finally,

---

Kyoto Protocol, COM (1999) 230 and the Commission Green Paper on Greenhouse Gas Emissions Trading within the EU, COM (2000) 87. See also *YEEL* (2000) at 362-371.

[293] Directive 80/779 (sulphur dioxide), OJ 1980 L 229/30, Directive 82/884 (lead), OJ 1982 L 378/15 and Directive 85/203 (nitrogen oxide), OJ 1985 L 87/1.

[294] Directive 92/72, OJ 1992 L 297/1.

[295] OJ 1996 L 296/55. Cf. Lefevere (1997).

the directive contains a wide range of reporting and information requirements (Article 11).

Pursuant to the Framework Directive four so-called 'daughter directives' have been adopted:

- Directive 1999/30 relating to limit values for sulphur dioxide, nitrogen dioxide and oxides of nitrogen, particulate matter and lead in ambient air;[296]
- Directive 2000/69 relating to limit values for benzene and carbon monoxide in ambient air;[297]
- Directive 2002/3 relating to ozone in ambient air;[298]
- Directive 2004/107 relating to arsenic, cadmium, mercury, nickel and polycyclic aromatic hydrocarbons in ambient air.[299]

The whole package on ambient air quality is finally supplemented by a decision on the exchange of information on air quality.[300] The First and Second Daughter Directives follow a similar scheme in prescribing limit values and alert values for certain pollutants as well as a timetable for attaining these values. The Third and Fourth Daughter Directives are slightly different in that these only contain target values, long-term objectives and alert values. In practice it has proven difficult to attain the limit values for nitrogen dioxide and particulate matter (very fine dust suspended in the air; often referred to as PM10 and PM2.5) and ozone laid down in the first and third daughter directive. For nitrogen dioxide, for example, the limit value distinguishes between the protection of human health and the protection of vegetation.[301] For human health protection the limit value is laid down in the form of an hourly limit value and an annual limit value. For vegetation the limit value is prescribed in the form of an annual limit value. The limit value is complemented by a margin of tolerance that decreases from 50% on 1 January 2001 to 0% on 1 January 2010. In addition to the limit value there is an alert value (set at twice the limit value for more than three consecutive hours).[302] Exceeding the limit values and, where applicable, the margin of tolerance obliges the Member States to draw up a plan to attain the limit value (Article 8(3) of the Framework Directive). This is again different for the Third and Fourth Daughter Directives, because these only require the Member States to draw up plans and programmes to achieve the target value, insofar as these

---

[296] OJ 1999 L 163/41. This directive has replaced Directive 80/779 and Directive 82/884 with effect from 1 January 2005. Directive 85/203 has also been repealed with the exception of Articles 1(1), first indent, and (2), 2, first indent, 3(1), 5, 9, 15 and 16 of Directive 85/203/EEC and Annex I thereto, which will be repealed with effect from 1 January 2010.

[297] OJ 2000 L 313/12.

[298] OJ 2002 L 67/14. This directive repealed Directive 92/72 with effect from 2003.

[299] OJ 2004 L 23/3.

[300] Decision 97/101, OJ 1997 L 35/14, as amended by Decision 2001/752, OJ 2001 L 282/69.

[301] Annex II to Directive 1999/30, table I.

[302] Annex II to Directive 1999/30, under II.

plans are *not disproportionate* (for example, Article 3(3) of Directive 2002/3).
When the alert values are exceeded, the Member States are obliged to immediately take steps, because there is a risk to human health (Article 2(6) of Directive
1999/30). These steps are prescribed in Article 10 of the Framework Directive
and include information of the public.

There are considerable differences concerning the application of these
rules in the various Member States.[303] One of the solutions to the difficulty that
certain Member States face in reaching the air quality objectives is the so-called
balancing of slight reductions in air quality in one area where the air quality
is good with improvements of air quality in other areas with poor air quality.
The standstill provision in Article 9 of the Framework Directive allows such a
balancing method, provided that the limit values are not exceeded as a result of
the reduction in air quality.

In 2005 the Commission submitted a proposal for a directive on ambient
air quality and cleaner air for Europe[304] as part of its thematic strategy on air
pollution.[305] It envisages a repeal of the Framework Directive, the first three
daughter directives and the information exchange decision with a more coherent legal instrument. When sufficient experience has been gathered with the
implementation of Directive 2004/107 (the Fourth Daughter Directive), it may
also be integrated in the new directive. On 25 June 2007, the Council adopted
a common position on a Directive on ambient air quality and cleaner air for
Europe.[306] This new directive will not change the existing air quality standards.
For very fine particulate matter (PM 2.5), the monitoring requirement in Directive 1999/30 will be replaced by a target value and limit value. Other innova-
tions include a possibility to take account of naturally occurring air pollution
(Article 20), whereas this is currently only possible for the substances listed in
the First Daughter Directive.[307] In a similar vein, it also allows for excesses of the
standards for particulate matter as a result of winter-salting or sanding of roads
(Article 21).

11.2   Directives on Emissions into the Air

As was mentioned above, part of European law on air pollu-
tion deals with the sources of air pollution. Here we find Directive 2001/81 on
national emission ceilings that was adopted in part to implement the Gothenburg Protocol to the UNECE Convention on long-range transboundary air
pollution.[308] Furthermore, there are directives covering emissions from various
sources. With regard to the latter a distinction can be made between emissions

---

[303] Cf. Backes et al (2005).

[304] COM (2005) 447.

[305] COM (2005) 446.

[306] OJ 2007 C 263E/1.

[307] Article 3(4) and 5(4) of Directive 1999/30.

[308] OJ 2001 L 309/22.

from industrial plants (e.g. energy generation, waste incineration) and emissions from mobile sources (cars, boats, aircraft).

Overarching emissions ceilings can be found in the Emissions Ceilings Directive. The objective this directive is to limit emissions of acidifying and eutrophying pollutants and ozone precursors in order to protect human health and the environment in the EU (Article 1). The directive covers all emissions resulting from human activity from the territory of the Member States and their exclusive economic zones irrespective of the source. There are, however, exceptions for international maritime traffic and aircraft emissions beyond the landing and take-off cycle (Article 2(a) and (b)). The landing and take-off cycle is defined in Article 3(g) as a 32,9 minute period in which the aircraft approaches, lands, taxies, takes-off and climbs. The preamble to the directive is quite clear when it states that the WHO guideline values are substantially exceeded in all Member States (recital 5), so that complete protection of the environment and human health are not possible at this time for reasons of technical and economic feasibility. As a result the directive contains in Article 5 the following interim objectives to be attained in 2010:

  · for acidification the areas where the critical load is exceeded shall be reduced by 50% compared to the 1990 situation;
  · for ozone the load above the critical level for human health shall be reduced by two-thirds compared to the 1990 situation;
  · for ozone the load above the critical level for crops shall be reduced by one-third compared to the 1990 situation;
  · for ozone there are absolute limits for human health and crops.

This interim objective is to be attained through the national emissions ceilings for sulphur dioxide, nitrogen oxides, volatile organic compounds and ammonia to be found in Annex I (Article 4). Interestingly, Article 5 contains no interim objective for eutrophication, as would be expected on the basis of Article 1. The footnote to Annex I shows that the emissions ceilings are expected to result that is subject to nitrogen deposits in excess of the critical load will be reduced by 'about 30%' compared to 1990. The Member States must draw up national emission reduction programmes (Article 6) and make an inventory of the emissions taking place on their territory (Article 7). These programmes and the inventories must be reported to the Commission and the European Environment Agency (Article 8). This will in turn lead to a Commission report (Article 9). This report may also contain a reconsideration of the scope of the directive (relating to the exclusion of international maritime traffic and flying aircraft) and the possibility of further reductions. Member States may prescribe more stringent national emissions ceilings (Article 4(1) and Article 4(2) contains a standstill provision. Indeed, the Member States will have to go beyond their emissions ceilings prescribed in Annex I if they want to reach the environmental objectives in Article 5. Annex II contains the EU's 15 emissions ceiling designed to attain the interim objectives and these ceilings are consistently lower than the sum of the 15 Member States' national emissions ceilings in Annex I.

The national emissions ceilings are to be attained through reductions of the emissions of various sources. Rules on emissions from industrial plants and can be found in the following directives:

· Directive 84/360 on air pollution from industrial plants;[309]
· Directive 96/61 on integrated pollution prevention and control (IPPC);[310]
· Directive 2001/80 on the limitation of emissions of certain pollutants into the air from large combustion plants;[311]
· Directive 2000/76 on the incineration of waste.[312]

Directive 84/360 on the combating of air pollution from industrial plants used to be an important directive containing general obligations for the prevention of air pollution. However, its importance has been greatly reduced since the entry into force of the IPPC Directive.

Article 3 requires Member States to take the necessary measures to ensure the prior authorisation of certain industrial plants belonging to the categories listed in Annex I. These include the energy industry, the production and processing of metals and minerals, the chemical industry and waste disposal. The required authorisation also applies to a 'substantial alteration' of such plants (Article 3(2)). Article 4 adds that the authorisation may be issued only when:

· all appropriate preventive measures against air pollution have been taken, including the application of the best available technology, provided that the application of such measures does not entail excessive costs;
· the use of plant will not cause significant air pollution;
· none of the emission limit values applicable will be exceeded;
· all the air quality limit values applicable will be taken into account.

The directive also contains provisions on applications for authorisation (Article 6), informing the public (Article 9), consultation in the event of transfrontier pollution (Article 10) and monitoring of compliance (Article 11). It is worth noting the Member States' obligation in Article 12 to follow developments as regards best available technology and the environmental situation. In the light of this examination they shall, if necessary, impose appropriate conditions on plants. It seems, therefore, that the directive requires the conditions to be modified in the light of technological developments and the environmental situation. This is further reflected in Article 13, according to which the Member States shall implement policies and strategies to adapt existing Annex I plants to the best available technology. The Court has held that, although the Member States enjoy a margin of discretion in implementing this provision, it does not allow

---

[309] OJ 1984 L 188/20, later amended.

[310] This directive will not be dealt with here, see section 5 above.

[311] OJ 2001 L 309/1, This directive repeals Directive 88/609, OJ 1988 L 336/1.

[312] OJ 1994 L 365/34.

them to not adapt a plant at all, in view of the environmental situation or the costs involved.[313] Stricter national provisions are allowed.

Directive 84/360 will be repealed on 30 October 2007 by virtue of the IPPC Directive.[314] Its provisions will continue to apply to existing installations until the measures required pursuant to Article 5 of the IPPC Directive have been taken by the competent authorities.[315] The relevant provisions concerning authorisation systems will not apply to new installations now that the IPPC Directive has been brought into effect.[316]

The Large Combustion Plants Directive 2001/80 repeals Directive 88/609[317] and applies to all combustion plants intended for the production of energy having a rated thermal input of 50 MW or more irrespective of the type of fuel used. However, waste and hazardous waste are excluded from the concept of fuel, because there is a separate directive for the incineration of waste (Article 2(6), see below). At the heart of the directive are emission limit values for sulphur dioxide, oxides of nitrogen and dust. These must be included in all licenses for the construction or operation of plants (Article 4 in connection with Annex III to VII) or extensions to existing plants (Article 10). Member States may set more stringent emission limit values than those set out in the directive, or for other pollutants (Article 4(5)). Article 5 contains a derogation from the emission limit value for sulphur dioxide subject to conditions. Compared to the 'old' directive, the Large Combustion Plants Directive is more stringent because such plants will have to be phased out.[318] Furthermore, the directive contains detailed rules on abnormal operating conditions, such as a breakdown of the abatement equipment (Article 7(1)) or problems with the supply of the environmentally friendly fuels (Article 7(2) and (3)). The directive requires Member States to draw up programmes for the reduction of emissions (Article 3), ensure monitoring (Articles 12, 13 and 14) and provides for cross-border information and consultation in accordance with the Environmental Impact Assessment Directive (Article 11).

The Waste Incineration Directive 2000/76 repeals the 'old' Municipal Waste Incinerators Directives[319] and the Hazardous Waste Incineration Plants Directive[320] with effect from 28 December 2005 (Article 18).[321] According to recital

---

[313] Case C-364/03 *Commission v. Greece* [2005] ECR I-6159. This case shows that the Court's analysis of the proportionality of the costs involved is quite far going.

[314] Article 20(3) Directive 96/61, OJ 1996 L 257/26. See on this directive section 5 of this chapter.

[315] Article 20(1) of the IPPC Directive.

[316] Article 20(2) of the IPPC Directive.

[317] OJ 1988 L 336/1, as last amended by Directive 94/66, OJ 1994 L 337/83. The repeal is with effect from 27 november 2002 and includes transitional rules for plants licensed before 27 November 2002 (Article 17).

[318] Article 5(1), second indent requires these plants to be used less after 1 January 2016, cf. Article 5(1) of Directive 88/609.

[319] Directive 89/369, OJ 1989 L 163/32 and Directive 89/429, OJ 1989 L 203/50.

[320] Directive 94/67, OJ 1994 L 365/34.

[321] Article 20 contains transitional provisions.

15 of the preamble, Directive 2000/76 is more stringent than its predecessors. The directive covers incineration as well as co-incineration plants (Article 2(1)), subject to exceptions for plants treating vegetable waste, radioactive waste, animal carcasses and off-shore oil exploration residues that are incinerated on board (Article 2(2)). An incineration plant is one that is dedicated to the thermal treatment of waste (Article 3(4)), whereas a co-incineration plant is one the main purpose of which is the generation of energy and which uses waste as a fuel or in which waste is thermally treated for the purpose of disposal.[322]

Incineration plants may only operate with a permit (Article 4(1) and should contain rules on the emissions limit values, the measurement techniques required to monitor the observance of these values and the types of waste that may be treated. Article 4(9) obliges the competent authority to take action to enforce compliance with the permit conditions. The exact rules to which the plants are subject depend on whether or not they will be treating hazardous waste (Article 3(2)). The rules on, for example, the delivery and reception of waste (Article 5) are stringent for hazardous waste (Article 5(4)), as are the operating conditions (Article 6). This relates to higher temperatures required for the incineration of hazardous wastes (1100°C instead of 850°C) and a higher frequency for measurements (Article 11(7)).

Central to the directive is the obligation to operate the plant in such a way that the emission limit values in Annex V are not exceeded (Article 7(1)). For co-incineration plants the values in Annex II apply, unless more than 40% of the heat release comes from hazardous waste. These values are equally stringent, but take into account that in co-incineration only a fraction of the fuel is made up of waste. Article 8 concerns the discharges of water used for cleaning exhaust gases, and tries to prevent a shift from atmospheric pollution to water pollution by requiring that such emissions must at least comply with the values in Annex IV. There are also rules on the residues resulting from the incineration (Article 8). Article 12 contains special rules on access to information and public participation. Article 13 contains rules on abnormal operating conditions. Finally, it is worth mentioning that the directive applies without prejudice to various other Directives, such as the IPPC Directive, The Directive on Pollution by Dangerous Substances, The Ambient Air Quality Framework Directive and the First Daughter Directive to it (Article 4(4).

Another source of emissions into the atmosphere are motor vehicles, aircraft and maritime traffic. It may be recalled that emissions from maritime traffic and aircraft, other than during the take-off and landing cycle, are excluded from the Emissions Ceiling Directive. The first European measures to limit and prevent air pollution by emissions from motor vehicles date from as early

---

[322] This relates to waste gassification, where waste is gassified and the resulting gases are incinerated in a connected installation. This leads to the interesting question to what extent the gasses resulting from the gassification are still waste, and thus to what extent the installation is to be classified as a (co-)incineration plant or a large combustion plant. Needless to say, the rules applying to the former are more stringent than those applying to the incineration plants.

as 1970. Directive 70/220[323] has been amended and updated many times since then, both in the light of the technical advances in the manufacture of motor vehicles and of new insights into environmental protection. The directive provides that no Member State may refuse type-approval to vehicles whose emissions meet the standards laid down in the annexes to the directive. The most recent amendment was effected by Directive 2003/67.[324] There are similar directives for diesel engines and engines using liquefied natural gas.[325] In an effort to influence consumer decisions involved in purchasing cars the Council and the EP adopted Directive 99/94 relating to the availability of consumer information on fuel economy and CO_2 emissions in respect of the marketing of new passenger cars.[326] The sulphur content of certain liquid fuels was regulated in Directive 75/716, which was replaced on 1 October 1994 by Directive 93/12. From that date Member States were required to prohibit the marketing of diesel fuels in the EU if their sulphur compound content exceeded 0.2% by weight. This percentage was reduced to 0.05% by weight on 1 October 1996 (Article 2(1)). The sulphur content of other gas oils, with the exception of aviation kerosene, was also reduced to 0.2% (Article 2(2)). Article 2(2) of Directive 93/12 provided that lower limits must be set for the sulphur content of gas oil (and new limit values for aviation kerosene) by 1 October 1999 at the latest. However, this is by no means the case. Article 4 of Directive 99/32, recently adopted, relating to a reduction in the sulphur content of certain liquid fuels and amending Directive 93/12 provides for a limit value of 0.1% by mass, but only from 1 January 2008.[327] Until then the limit value remains 0.2% (Article 4). It does seem that the exception for aviation kerosene has been removed. The new directive also provides for limit values for other liquid fuels, such as heavy fuel oils, bunker fuel oils and marine gas oils. For example, Article 3 provides that Member States must ensure that as from 1 January 2003 within their territory heavy fuel oils are not used if their sulphur content exceeds 1.00% by mass. Directive 93/12 has also been amended by Directive 98/70.[328] This directive provides for the gradual elimination of leaded petrol by the year 2000. It requires Member States to prohibit the marketing of leaded petrol within their territory no later than 1 January 2000 (Article 3). New environmental specifications are set out for diesel fuel in an Annex (Article 4). Unlike Directive 99/32, which must have been

---

[323] OJ 1970 L 76/1, amended many times since then.

[324] OJ 2003 L 206/29, Directive 2006/96 only contains amendments necessary for the accession of Romania and Bulgaria.

[325] Directives 72/306, OJ 1972 L 190/1, as amended by Directive 2005/21, OJ 2005 L 61/25 and Directive 2005/55, OJ 2005 L 275/1.

[326] OJ 2000 L 12/16, as amended by Directive 2003/73, OJ 2003 L 186/34.

[327] Directive 99/32 relating to a reduction in the sulphur content of certain liquid fuels and amending Directive 93/12, OJ 1999 L 121/13.

[328] Directive 98/70 relating to the quality of petrol and diesel fuels and amending Directive 93/12; OJ 1998 L 350/58. Cf. also the Auto/Oil Programmes, COM (96) 248 and COM (98) 495. See, most recently, COM (2000) 626 containing a review of the Auto/Oil II programme.

implemented before 1 July 2000, Member States were required to comply with Directive 98/70 not later than 1 July 1999. The most recent step in this process of introducing cleaner fuels can be found in Directive 2003/17, according to which the Member States must ensure before 1 January 2009 that petrol and diesel comply with requirements in the annexes to that directive.

11.3 Protection of the Ozone Layer

Europe's involvement in protecting the ozone layer dates from 1978. In that year the Council adopted a resolution on fluorocarbons in the environment, urging that all appropriate measures should be taken to ensure that the European industry did not increase its production capacity in respect of chlorofluorocarbons.[329]

However, it was not until 1980 that legally binding measures were taken. In Council Decision 80/372 concerning chlorofluorocarbons in the environment,[330] the Member States were required to take all appropriate measures to ensure that industry situated in their territories did not increase its production capacity of certain chlorofluorocarbons.

The current law in respect of the protection of the ozone layer is laid down in Regulation 2037/2000.[331] The regulation was adopted in order to fulfil the obligations under the Vienna Convention for the Protection of the Ozone Layer and the Montreal Protocol on Substances that Deplete the Ozone Layer[332] and under the second amendment of the Montreal Protocol of 25 November 1992 on Substances that Deplete the ozone layer,[333] to which instruments the Member States and the EC are parties. Regulation 2037/2000 is more stringent than its predecessor, Regulation 3093/94, and the Montreal Protocol. This is reflected in the complete cessation of production and consumption of methyl bromide, subject to derogations for critical uses.

The scope of the regulation is determined by Article 1. In paragraph 1 a number of ozone depleting substances, the so-called controlled substances (Article 2, fourth indent), are listed, whereas Article 1(2) declares the regulation applicable to the substances in Annex II (so-called new substances, Article 2, fourteenth indent). However, the new substances are covered only insofar as they are produced, imported, placed on the market and used. Exportation of new substances is therefore not regulated, whereas the exportation of controlled substances is.

Under the regulation, the release for free circulation in the EU of controlled substances is made subject to an import licence, issued by the Commission

---

[329] OJ 1978 C 133/1.

[330] OJ 1980 L 90/45.

[331] OJ 2000 L 244/1, as amended by Regulation 1791/2006, OJ 2006 L 363/1.

[332] Decision 88/540, OJ 1988 L 297/8, which was amended on 29 June 1990; see Council Decision 91/690, OJ 1991 L 377/28; see Council Decision 94/68 of 2 December 1993, OJ 1994 L 33/1.

[333] Decision 94/68, OJ 1994 L 33/1.

(Article 6).[334] Exports of controlled substances also require authorisation by the Commission (Article 12). The importation of controlled substances from a state which is not party to the Protocol of Montreal is prohibited (Article 8), as is the release for free circulation in the EU of products containing chloro-fluoro-carbons or halons imported from such states (Article 9). The Council must adopt rules for imports from such states of products produced from controlled substances but not containing them (Article 10). Exports to states which are not party to the Protocol are also prohibited (Article 11). Only in exceptional cases may the Commission authorize trade with such states (Article 13).

Articles 3, 4 and 5 contain detailed provisions regulating the production, supply and use in the EU of certain ozone-depleting substances. In the light of the Court's judgment in the *Betatti* case these provisions seem compatible with other provisions of European law.[335] Central to these provisions is on the one hand the phasing out or complete cessation of production of ozone depleting substances, and on the other hand the derogations for so-called critical uses (e.g. Annex VII). Concerning methyl bromide, for example, Article 3(2)(ii) requires the Commission, following proposals by the Member States, to decide every year on the critical use of this substance. The Commission will then have to determine the critical use, the quantities that may be used and who may use it.[336]

It is interesting that the regulation contains a system of tradable pollution rights, by allowing manufacturers to move production rights. Article 3(8) allows this for the purpose of rationalisation within a Member State, while Article 3(9) allows this between Member States, and Article 3(10) allows it concerning a state which is a party to the Protocol, but not a Member State. In the last two cases the authorisation of the Commission and the agreement of the states in question are required.

Articles 14 to 17 contain provisions on the recovery of used controlled substances, leakages of controlled substances, as well as provisions on management and reporting. The most interesting provisions are those on inspection (Article 20). When the Commission requests information from an undertaking, it must at the same time forward a copy of the request to the competent authority of the Member State within whose territory the undertaking's head office is situated (Article 20(2)). Article 20(3) provides that the competent authorities must carry out the investigations the Commission considers necessary. This indicates that the Member States have little or no discretion in the matter. Though this article does not actually confer formal powers of investigation on the Commission within the territory of the Member States, it goes a long way towards it, as Article 20(4) provides that, subject to the agreement of the

---

[334] Cf. Case T-336/94 *Efisol* [1996] ECR II-1343.

[335] Case C-341/95 *Gianni Bettati* [1998] ECR I-4355, See further Case T-216/05 *Mebrom*, judgment of 22 May 2007 (appeal pending, Case C-373/07), n.y.r. in the ECR, para. 86, where the CFI finds that the Commission's quota system does not distort competition.

[336] The practical working of the system is set out nicely in T-216/05 *Mebrom*, judgment of 22 May 2007 (appeal pending Case C-373/07), n.y.r. in the ECR, paras. 20-28.

competent authority of the Member State within whose territory the investigations are to be made, the officials of the Commission shall assist the officials of that authority in the performance of their duties. This situation is remarkably similar to that concerning the enforcement of Articles 81 and 82 EC.[337]

11.4   Legislation on Climate Change

The EC is a member to the Kyoto Protocol to the UNFCCC, as are the Member States.[338] This means that the EC as well as the Member States have to reduce emissions of greenhouse gases as agreed in the Kyoto Protocol. For the fifteen old Member States this has resulted in the so-called burden sharing, according to which they have to contribute to a European-wide emissions reduction target of 8%.[339] As the Kyoto Protocol already envisages flexible instruments that will allow a Member State to achieve its emissions reduction in another Member State, a similar trading scheme has also been implemented in the EU. In addition to legislation dealing directly with emissions reductions, the EU has also adopted legislation on energy efficiency as part of its package to meet the 'Kyoto challenge'.

11.4.1   Implementing the Kyoto Protocol in the EU

Decision 2002/358 approves the Kyoto Protocol and contains the so-called burden sharing agreement. The respective emissions limit values for the EU and its Member States are laid down in Commission Decision 2006/944.[340] The data necessary to come to these emissions levels were gathered by national monitoring mechanisms set up pursuant to the Monitoring Mechanism Decision.[341]

The Monitoring Mechanism Decision repeals Decision 93/389[342] and establishes a fourfold framework. Firstly for monitoring anthropogenic greenhouse gas emissions. Secondly for evaluating the progress made by the Member States and the EU. Thirdly for setting up the national and European registries and programmes required by the Kyoto Protocol. Fourthly for ensuring timely, transparent and correct reporting on these issues by the EU and the Member States. Article 2 contains the framework for the national and European programmes. Article 3 contains rules on reporting by the Member States. Reporting should take place concerning the emissions of the greenhouse gases listed in Annex A to the Kyoto Protocol (Article 3(1)(a), but also on emissions of other gases and substances (Article 3(1)(b). Apart from having to report on sources of greenhouse

---

[337] Cf. the rules on inspection laid down in Chapter V of Regulation 1/2003, OJ 2003 L1/1.

[338] Decision 2002/358, OJ 2002 L 130/1. Cf. on the subject in general, Peeters & Deketelaere (2006) and Streck & Freestone (2005).

[339] Cf. recital 10 of the preamble to Decision 2002/358, OJ 2002 L 130/1.

[340] OJ 2006 L 358/87, corrected in OJ 2006 L 367/80.

[341] Decision 280/2004, OJ 2004 L 49/1.

[342] OJ 1993 L 167/31, as amended by Decision 1999/296. OJ 1999 L 117/35.

gases, the Member States must also report on so-called sinks of greenhouse gasses (Article 3(1)(c)). Sinks is the Kyoto Protocol-terminology for anything that removes greenhouse gases from the atmosphere, such as forests. On the basis of these reports the EU shall compile a greenhouse gas inventory (Article 4). The Commission will then annually assess the progress of the Member States and the EU in meeting the Kyoto targets (Article 5(1) and report on this to the Council and the European Parliament (Article 5(2). On the basis of the data gathered and the reports both the EU and the Member States have to report to the UNFCCC Secretariat on so-called demonstrable progress. Because the Kyoto Protocol and the implementation thereof by the EU allow for emissions trading a registry is necessary. Article 6 requires the EU and the Member States to set up such registries that will allow for accurate accounting of the emissions reductions and the trading of emissions. Article 7 contains provisions on the assigned amounts. This corresponds roughly to a quota for greenhouse gases that may be emitted in order to meet the reductions target agreed in the Kyoto Protocol and the burden sharing agreement.[343] The fact that both the EC and its Member States are signatories to the Kyoto Protocol also necessitates a provision on full and effective cooperation between these two in the international negotiations (Article 8). The Monitoring Decision is further implemented by Commission Decision 2005/166.[344]

The Kyoto Protocol recognises that emissions of greenhouse gases contribute to a global environmental problem. This means that the actual place where the emissions reductions take place is not relevant and this in turn opens up possibilities of achieving emissions reductions at places where the costs of doing so are relatively lower. This is called emissions trading and it takes place on an international scale and between the member States. Internationally, emissions trading can take place between a Member State and a developing country through the Clean Development Mechanism (CDM) and between a Member State and a developed third state Joint Implementation (JI).

11.4.2 Emissions Trading

Directive 2003/87 allows emissions trading for greenhouse gases (hereafter the Emissions Trading Directive (ET Directive)).[345] To this end all large industrial plants (Annex I) require a Greenhouse gas emissions permit (Article 4), but only for the greenhouse gas listed in Annex I (carbon dioxide). Currently, the directive does not apply to emissions of other greenhouse gases (see Annex II), though a review could lead to the inclusion of these gases (Article 30(1)). Furthermore, the Commission has presented a proposal for the inclusion of the aviation sector in the ET Directive.[346] The conditions for the application

---

[343] Decision 2002/358, OJ 2002 L 130/1.

[344] OJ 2005 L 55/57.

[345] OJ 2003 L 275/32, as amended by Directive 2004/101, OJ 2004 L 338/18.

[346] COM (2006) 818 final. The proposal is currently awaiting the first reading. As it is the first major amendment to the ET Directive, there are indications that it may be used to improve the ET Directive as

and the contents of the greenhouse gas emissions permits are laid down in Articles 5 and 6. As many of the Annex I installations will also require an IPPC permit, Article 8 provides for coordination with that directive. It may be recalled that the IPPC Directive was amended so as to preclude the inclusion of conditions relating to greenhouse gas emissions.[347] The central provision concerning the greenhouse gas emissions permit can be found in Article 6(2)(b) and (e) and relates to the obligation imposed on the operator to monitor the emissions of greenhouse gases and surrender allowances equal to the total emissions of the installation in the previous calendar year. It is with regard to these allowances that the trading takes place. These allowances are described as allowances to emit one ton of carbon dioxide during a specified period (Article 3(a)). Under the ET Directive the Member States must first allocate the allowances in so-called national allocation plans (NAPs) pursuant to Article 9. The NAPs must be approved by the Commission on the basis of Article 9(3) in accordance with the criteria laid down in Annex III.[348] The total amount of allowances to be allocated must correspond to the Member State's emissions ceiling laid down in Decision 2006/944 and the emissions reductions objective of that Member State.[349] The total amount of available allowances must then be distributed over the Annex I installations pursuant to the NAP. In this regard the ET Directive distinguishes two phases: the start-up phase (January 2005-January 2008) and the operational phase from January 2008 onwards. In the start-up phase at least 95% of the allowances are to be allocated free of charge (grandfathering); in the operational phase at least 90% of the allowances are to be grandfathered. This means that after January 2008 some Member States may chose to auction up to 20% of the allowances. The choice for grandfathering or auctioning and the general allocation is problematic with regard to the correct functioning of the emissions trading system, the need to maintain undistorted competition as well as the possibility of entry on to the market of a Member State. For one, grandfathering does not ensure that a market price is paid for the allowances. Furthermore, over allocation of allowances may mean that a company receives an advantage from the state without having to pay for this, which may constitute state aid. Thirdly, a company wanting to establish a new Annex I installation will need to obtain allowances to cover for its emissions. These could either be unavailable (because the Member State NAP has handed out allowances corresponding to its emissions ceiling) or it may have to buy them on the market whereas the incumbent

---

a whole.

[347] See above, section 5.

[348] See Case T-178/05 *UK* v. *Commission* [2005] ECR II-4807 on some formalities surrounding this decision and Case T-374/04 *Germany* v. *Commission*, judgment of 7 November 2007, n.y.r. in the ECR on the scope of Commission discretion in adopting such a decision and the Court's review of these decisions. Cf. Case T-28/07 *Fels-Werke a.o.* v. *Commission*, judgment of 11 September 2007, n.y.r. in the ECR making it clear that undertakings have no *locus standi* at the CFI in an action for annulment of the decision of the Commission; see also section 3.1 of Chapter 5.

[349] Point 1 of Annex III to the EMT Directive.

companies received the allowances free of charge. This is part of the reason why the Commission has to approve the NAPs and this includes an appraisal on the basis of the Treaty's state aid provisions (Articles 87 and 88 EC) as well as the need to allow for market entry (Points 5 and 6 of Annex III and Article 11(3)).[350]

After the allocation of the allowances on the basis of the NAPs, the actual trading can take place. The idea behind this is that the Member States will gradually reduce the available amount of allowances so as to attain the emissions reduction targets. As a result the allowances will become scarce and, since these are tradable, this means that the price will increase. A company that has reduced its emissions will thus have an excess of allowances that it could sell on the market to companies that have not reduced emissions and thus need to surrender allowances pursuant to their greenhouse gas emissions permit. As the amount of allowances is further reduced, scarcity and price increase leading to a greater incentive to actually reduce emissions. Because the allowances can be traded, the emissions reduction takes place most efficiently, i.e. by the company that can reduce emissions at the lowest costs. Companies can buy allowances from other participants in the EU emissions trading scheme, but they can also use so-called CERs en ERUs. CER stands for Certified Emissions Reduction (Article 3(n)) and ERU refers to an Emissions Reduction Unit (Article 3(m)). CERs and ERUs both represent emissions reductions as a result of the Kyoto protocol's project mechanisms (CDM and JI). The inclusion of CERs and ERUs in the ET is made possible by Directive 2004/101, which introduced, *inter alia*, Article 11a and 11b in the ET Directive.[351] It is interesting to see that the EU has set limits to the use of these CERs and ERUs, resulting in the obligation to achieve a certain amount of the emissions reduction within the EU. This is closely connected with the obligation following from the Kyoto Protocol to ensure that JI and CDM are supplemental to domestic action, as it has been implemented in the Monitoring Mechanism Decision.[352] According to Article 11a(1) the Member States may provide for a maximum percentage per installation. Moreover, CERs and ERUs resulting from nuclear facilities (until 2012) or land use, land use change and forestry activities may not be used in the ET Directive (Article 11a(3). This is in recognition of the fact that these activities may not be sustainable or may even result in the emission of more greenhouse gases. For example, the production of palm oil as a biofuel in tropical areas has resulted in deforestation and a lower groundwater level in these areas which results in a spontaneous decomposition of the peatlands and thus in carbon

---

[350] See Case T-387/04 *EnBW Energie Baden-Württemberg AG* v. *Commission*, Order of 30 April 2007, n.y.r. in the ECR, concerning the legal nature of such a decision. According to the CFI, the Commission decision does not qualify as a state aid decision pursuant to Article 88 EC. Undertakings that consider their competitive position harmed by an approved NAP may institute national proceedings on the basis of a violation of the directly effective standstill obligation in Article 88(3) EC.

[351] This directive links the EU ET with the CDM and JI project mechanisms; OJ 2004 L 228/18.

[352] Article 2(2) of Decision 280/2004, see above in this section.

dioxide emissions. A similar concern with the actual environmental impact of projects can also be seen in Article 11b(6) concerning hydroelectric dams.

The allowances, CERs and ERUs thus generated must be tradable within the EU and internationally (Article 12(1)(a) and (b). The allowances thus traded or generated must be surrendered before 30 April each year to cover for the emissions in the preceding calendar year, after which the allowances are cancelled. If a company fails to surrender sufficient allowances it will have to pay a fine and the name of the company will be made public (Article 16(2)). The amount of the fine varies from €40 per ton in the start-up phase to €100 per ton in the operational phase (Article 16(3)). In addition, the company will have to surrender the missing amount of allowances the next year.

The ET Directive further contains provisions on the competent authorities, the administrator in charge of the allowance administration and verification and monitoring.[353] Somewhat odd is Article 24 on the unilateral inclusion of additional activities and gases. This refers to so-called more stringent measures whereby a Member State could expand the scope of the ET system to installations not listed in Annex I and more greenhouse gases than just carbon dioxide. Such measures are subject to the Commission's approval. This is surprising given that the directive is based on Article 175, which results in the Member States always being able to adopt more stringent measures pursuant to Article 176 EC. The procedure in Article 24 of the ET Directive effectively tries to restrict the Member State's power pursuant to Article 176 along the lines of Article 95(4)-(6) EC.[354] With respect to the question whether the use of Article 176 EC can be restricted or altered by secondary law, such as the ET Directive, we refer to our observations in Chapter 3, section 5 in particular. Finally, the distinction between the start-up and the operational phase is important because the Member States can exclude certain installations (Article 27) and apply for extra allowances in cases of *force majeure* (Article 29) with the Commission only during the start-up phase.

11.4.3   Other Instruments to Combat Climate Change

The ET Directive is by far the most important and high-profile instrument used by the EU to combat climate change. Nonetheless there are

---

[353] Furthermore, it is supplemented by a number of decisions, directives and regulations. Decision 2006/780 was adopted pursuant to Article 11b(7) of the ET Directive and wants to avoid double counting of ERUs, CERs and allowances, OJ 2006 L 316/12. Decision 2004/156 was adopted pursuant to Article 14(1) of the ET Directive and contains guidelines for the monitoring and reporting of greenhouse gas emissions, OJ 2004 L 59/1. Commission Regulation 2216/2004 was adopted pursuant to Article 19(3) of the ET Directive and Article 6(1) of the Monitoring Mechanism Decision and contains the rules for a standardised and secured system of registries allowing for the administration of the trade in allowances, OJ 2004 L 386/1.

[354] See above Chapter 3, sections 5 and 6.

various other instruments that deal with other greenhouse gases and try to improve energy efficiency.

Regulation 842/2006 aims to reduce emissions of fluorinated greenhouse gases.[355] The term fluorinated greenhouse gases covers so-called hydrofluorocarbons (HFCs), perfluorocarbons (PFCs) and Sulphur hexafluoride listed in Annex I to the regulation.[356] All substances already covered by the regulation on the protection of the ozone layer are outside the scope of Regulation 842/2006 (Article 2(1)).[357] In order to reduce these emissions the regulation contains rules on the use, containment, recovery and destruction of these gases as well as rules on the labelling and marketing of these gases and equipment containing these gases. This has resulted in a dual legal basis for this regulation. The bulk of the regulation has been based on Article 175 EC, but the provisions dealing with labelling, control of use and marketing (Articles 7-9) were based on Article 95 EC. Article 3 is directed at the operators of stationary refrigeration, air conditioning, heat pump and fire protection equipment insofar as this equipment contains fluorinated greenhouse gases. It requires them to use all technically available measures that do not entail disproportionate costs to prevent leakage and repair detected leakages as soon as possible (Article 3(1). Moreover, when the equipment contains more than 3 kg of these gases the operators are also required to check their equipment for leakage at certain intervals depending on the amount of gases contained (Article 3(2)). If more than 300 kg of these gases are contained a leakage detection system must be installed (Article 3(3). This means that operators of, for example, air conditioning equipment containing less than 3 kg of fluorinated greenhouse gases, are under the general duty pursuant to Article 3(1) of the regulation to prevent leakage and to repair detected leakages. There is nothing in the regulation to suggest that this excludes final consumers of household air conditioning equipment.[358] Many of these aircos are filled with R-410A. Article 4 contains a duty for the operator of various types of stationary equipment to ensure that the gases contained in them are recovered. Given that the regulation applies without prejudice to the WEEE Directive (Article 1 third paragraph), this should not entail any costs for final consumers.[359] Article 5 contains rules on training and certification of personnel involved in the installation, maintenance etc. of equipment containing fluorinated greenhouse gases. Article 6 lays down reporting obligations for producers, importers and exporters of fluorinated greenhouse gases. Article 7 contains rules on the labeling of equipment containing fluorinated greenhouse gases. Article 8 prohibits certain applications of sulphur hexafluoride, such as

---

[355] OJ 2006 L 161/1.

[356] These groups of chemical substances feature also in Annex II to the ET Directive, and may thus eventually be included in the ET scheme.

[357] See above, section 11.3.

[358] Many of these aircos are filled with R410A, which is a mixture of the HFCs listed in Annex I to the regulation.

[359] Directive 2002/96, see below, section 15.5.

the filling of vehicle tyres. Article 9(1) prohibits the marketing of products and equipment containing fluorinated greenhouse gases. The types of products and equipment, the gases contained in them and the date on which the marketing prohibition enters into force is laid down in Annex II. However, products that are shown to have been manufactured before the date of entry into force may still be marketed (Article 9(2)). Article 9(3) contains what could be called a specialised implementation of the possibility for a derogation pursuant to Article 95(4) EC. More stringent measures that have been adopted before 31 December 2005 may be maintained until 31 December 2012, provided that these measures are notified to the Commission before 4 July 2007 and these measures are compatible with the Treaty. It is interesting to note that, contrary to Article 95(6) EC, no explicit authorisation by the Commission is required for this. It may be wondered whether this is compatible with the Treaty as secondary European law cannot detract from primary European law and the effect of Article 9(3) is to effectively rob the Commission of its powers to ensure that the Treaty is applied (Article 211 EC). Moreover, the test of compatibility with the internal market is arguably less strict than the test required by Article 95(6) EC. The special position of Article 9 is reaffirmed by Article 14, that accidentally is the only provision without a title. This declares the standard Treaty procedures for more stringent measures applicable to the various provisions of the regulation, however, without prejudice to Article 9(3). The marketing prohibition entered into force on 4 July 2006 and the rest of the regulation entered into force on 4 July 2007.

Energy efficiency and energy saving is the focus of many initiatives, such as SAVE: Specific Action for Vigorous Energy Efficiency. More concrete rules can be found in Directive 2006/32 on energy end-use efficiency[360] and Directive 2002/91 on the energy performance of buildings.[361]

Directive 2006/32 replaces Directive 93/76 (Article 17)[362] and aims to enhance cost-effective improvements in energy-efficiency. The directive applies to companies involved in the distribution and sale of energy and final consumers of energy. Member States may, however, exclude small energy companies (Article 2(a) in connection with Article 3(r)). Furthermore, the directive does not apply to companies subject to the ET Directive. It does so by providing for a national indicative energy savings target of 9% to be achieved in 2015 (Article 1(a) in connection with Article 4(1).[363] Annex I contains the detailed rules for calculating the target. Further means to achieve this objective boil down to the creation of a market for the efficient end use of energy (Article 1(a)) and a market for energy services and other energy efficiency improvement measures for final consumers (Article 1(b)). The directive envisages intermediary energy savings targets (Article 4(2) that will be included in the so-called Energy Efficiency

---

[360] OJ 2006 L 114/64.

[361] OJ 2003 L 1/65.

[362] OJ 1993 L 237/28.

[363] This assumes that the directive will be applied from its entry into force (May 2006), if the first year of application is in 2007 (when the first plans must be submitted), the target is to be achieved in 2016.

Action Plans (EEAPs) to be submitted by the Member States to the Commission (Article 14). Furthermore, the public sector is to play an exemplary role (Article 5(1)).[364] The public sector is to fulfil this role in part by greening its public procedures (Article 5(1) and seventh recital of the preamble). The market that the directive aims to create deals with so-called energy services and other energy efficiency improvement measures. These energy services may be provided by energy distributors, distribution system operators and other natural or legal persons. Interestingly, the Member States must refrain from any activities that might impede the creation of a market for energy services (Article 6(1)(b)) and they are under a duty to ensure that there is equal competition on this market (Article 6(3)). This effectively means that the directive contains specialised competition rules addressed at companies as well as the Member States that may have a wider scope than the general competition rules.[365] The market for energy services may also be created by voluntary agreements or a market based scheme involving tradable so-called white certificates (Article 6(2)(b) in connection with Article 3(s)). The directive further contains provisions on the exchange of information, such as best practices (Article 7), and the certification of technical experts (Article 8). Very interesting are the provisions that deal with the financial incentives and tariff structures. According to Article 9(1) the Member States are to repeal or amend legislation that disproportionately impedes or restricts the use of financial instruments for energy saving. This may in effect lead to a greening of all state operated or funded financial instruments, with the exception of measures of a clearly fiscal nature. This exception probably follows from the exception contained in Article 175(2)(a) EC.[366] Article 10 necessitates a similar greening of tariffs and regulations for net-bound energy. Article 11 allows for government funds to subsidise energy efficiency, albeit without prejudice to Articles 87 and 88 EC. These funds should also target higher risk sectors and may not compete with commercially financed energy efficiency improvement measures. It is submitted that anything else would render these funds unacceptable under Article 87 anyhow.[367] On the basis of Article 12 the Member States must ensure the availability of energy audits. Final consumers have an important role to play in the directive, as they will ultimately have to increase energy efficiency. Article 13(1) of the directive envisages the introduction of meters that will adequately show the individual consumer's energy consumption. Moreover, when old meters are replaced such new meters must always be provided, unless this would not be cost-effective in relation to the long term energy savings. Moreover, energy bills should also include information that will enable the consumer to reduce energy consumption (Article 13(2) and (3)). Member States

---

[364] The public sector includes the armed forces, which are in principle subject to the directive, Article 2(c)).

[365] See Chapter 7.

[366] Interestingly, Article 175(2) EC refers to measures of a *primarily* fiscal nature.

[367] See Chapter 7, section 7.3.4 and the draft Guidelines for State Aid for Environmental Protection according to which state aid is allowed only to correct market failures or if it will help to promote sustainable development.

may decide to not apply Articles 6 and 13 for small energy distributors. The directive must be implemented before 17 May 2008.[368]

Directive 2002/91 aims to increase the energy efficiency of buildings. It does so by providing for, *inter alia*, a framework for the calculation of the energy efficiency and by providing for minimum energy efficiency requirements. The minimum energy efficiency requirements are to be set by the Member States and may differentiate between various categories of buildings. The Member States are then to take the necessary measures to ensure that new buildings will meet the minimum requirements. For existing large buildings that have a useful floor area of more than 1000 square meters that undergo a total renovation the Member States must also take the necessary measures to ensure that the minimum requirements are met (Article 6). It is interesting to see how this directive respects the subsidiarity principle by allowing the Member States unlimited discretion in setting the minimum requirements. This may very well result in a distortion of the level playing field, as higher standards will often result in higher building costs. In this connection it is furthermore interesting to see that for large buildings, that are more likely to house activities subject to international competition, the energy efficiency requirements include an obligation to investigate the economic, technical and environmental feasibility of alternative energy systems, such as heat pumps (Article 5, second paragraph). For large buildings the directive fortunately contains a fairly specific definition of what constitutes a 'complete renovation' within the meaning of Article 6 (recital 13), but the requirement to upgrade the building to meet the minimum standards is, however, subject to an (economic, technical and environmental) feasibility test. The directive further provides for rules on the inspection of large boilers and large air conditioning systems (Articles 8 and 9). Most interesting for consumers is probably the mandatory energy performance certificate that will have to be provided with the building when it is constructed, sold or rented out (Article 7). The directive must be implemented before 4 January 2006.

12 Legislation on Noise

European legislation on noise can broadly be divided into two categories. In the first place there are directives harmonising national regulations on anything from motor mowers to vehicles and prescribing maximum permissible noise levels. In the second place there is more recent legislation dealing not so much with the sources of noise, but with the environmental effects of it. The first group of legislation stipulates that products which do not meet the standards may not be marketed. Although primarily focusing on the functioning of the internal market, these directives are a fine example of the application of the prevention and the source principles.[369] There used to be diffe-

---

[368] The reporting obligation should however be implemented before 17 May 2006.

[369] Cf. Van Calster (1997) at 174 and McManus (2005).

rent directives for various categories of products, but these have been replaced by Directive 2000/14 on noise emissions of equipment for use outdoors.[370] This directive may be regarded as implementing total harmonisation. In other words, products which meet the requirements of the directive in question may not be barred from markets for reasons of the noise they produce. There is furthermore legislation on noise emitted by household appliances,[371] motor vehicles[372] and on the protection of workers from the risks related to exposure to noise at work.[373] There are also Directives on noise produced by aircraft. For example, Directive 80/51 on the limitation of noise emissions from subsonic aircraft[374] and Directive 89/629 for the limitation of noise emission from civil subsonic jet aeroplanes.[375] The latter directive requires the Member States to ensure that civil subsonic jet aircraft registered in their territories after 1 November 1990 are only used in their territory or in the territory of other Member States if they have been granted a noise certificate on the basis of certain noise emission standards.

An example of the second group of noise related legislation is Directive 2002/30 which contains rules and procedures for the introduction of noise-related restrictions at airports in the Member States.[376] It constitutes a shift from the old aircraft-based noise regulation described above to an approach where noise is dealt with on the basis of the airport and its environment. Based on Article 80(2) EC, this is a measure aimed at safeguarding the internal market and at the same time protecting people from the harmful effects of noise. It furthermore seeks to promote sustainable airport development. The directive adopts the so-called balanced approach of the ICAO,[377] according to which noise management requires assessment of the following four factors: reduction of airplane noise at source, land-use planning, noise abatement operational procedures and operating restrictions (Article 4(1) in connection with 2(g)). The directive also recognises that the balanced approach may not be sufficient to achieve effective and sustainable noise reduction (recital 11). It therefore allows for more stringent measures, such as more stringent noise standards and actions to take

---

[370] OJ 2000 L 162/1, amended most recently by Directive 2005/88, OJ 2005 L 344/44.

[371] Directive 86/594, OJ 1986 L 344/24, later amended.

[372] Directive 70/157, OJ 1975 L 42/1 amended most recently by Directive 2007/34, OJ 2007 L 155/49.

[373] Directive 2003/10, OJ 2003 L 42/38.

[374] OJ 1980 L 18/26, later amended. See on this directive Case C-389/96 *Aher-Waggon GmbH* [1998] ECR I-4473, where the Court ruled that Article 28 EC does not preclude national legislation which makes the first registration in national territory of aircraft previously registered in another Member State conditional upon compliance with stricter noise standards than those laid down by Directive 80/51, while exempting from those standards aircraft which obtained registration in national territory before that directive was implemented.

[375] OJ 1989 L 363/27, later amended. See also Directive 92/14, OJ 1992 L 76/12, according to which Member States must ensure that aircrafts covered by Directive 89/629 are no longer used unless a noise certificate has been granted (Article 2).

[376] OJ 2002 L 85/40.

[377] International Civil Aviation Organisation, see recital 10 of the preamble.

noisy aircraft out of service.[378] This takes the form of operating restrictions for noisy aircraft, i.e. a limitation of the use of these aircraft. Such operating restrictions must be the result of an environmental assessment (Article 5) and must be notified in advance. Moreover, the aircraft operator must have a right to appeal a decision containing the operating restrictions (Article 12). Article 6 allows for operating restrictions that may entail a restriction of up to 20% of aircraft movements for noisy aircraft. For city airports (Article 2(b) and Annex I) more stringent rules are allowed (Article 6(2)). There is an exemption for noisy aircraft registered in developing countries (Article 8) and an exemption for aircraft operations of an exceptional nature (Article 9), which is drafted in very vague terms. Article 7 restricts the retroactive application of the directive.[379] The directive repeals the so-called Hushkits Regulation, which dealt with the registration and operation of aircraft fitted with noise reduction systems (hushkits).[380]

Just as Directive 2002/30 shifts the focus of legislation away from the regulation of sources to an assessment of the environmental effects of noise, Directive 2002/49 also adopts the environmental approach.[381] Directive 2002/49 can moreover be characterised as a framework directive, along the lines of the Water Framework Directive and the Framework Directive for Ambient Air Quality. The Noise Framework Directive aims to avoid, prevent or reduce the harmful effects, including annoyance, due to exposure to environmental noise (Article 1). To this end the directive envisages firstly the determination of exposure to noise by means of so-called noise mapping (Article 1(a) in connection with Articles 3(r) and 7). The results of this noise inventory (noise maps) and the effects of exposure to noise should be made available to the public (Article 1(b) in connection with Article 9). The directive further requires the adoption of action plans to prevent and reduce environmental noise where necessary and particularly where exposure levels can induce harmful effects on human health. Such action plans must moreover aim to preserve environmental noise quality where it is good (standstill; Article 1(c) in connection with Article 8). Article 1(2) indicates that the directive can also function as a basis for emissions-based European legislation for other sources than those already covered by Directive 2000/14. The directive applies only to environmental noise to which humans are exposed and excludes noise caused by the exposed person himself, noise from domestic activities, created by neighbours, noise at work places,[382] noise inside transport means and noise from military activities (Article 2). Central to the directive is the concept of environmental noise, defined in Article 3(a) as unwanted or harmful outdoor sound created by human activities. Interestingly, this definition includes noise during concerts, as this will – depending on the noise

---

[378] These are referred to as marginally compliant aircraft, Article 2(c).

[379] See on this provision Case C-422/05 *Commission* v. *Belgium*, judgment of 14 June 2007, n.y.r. in the ECR, paras. 40-49.

[380] Regulation 925/1999, OJ 1999 L 115/1.

[381] Directive 2002/49, OJ 2002 L 189/12, hereafter the Noise Framework Directive.

[382] For noise at work places see Directive 2000/13, see above in this section.

levels – be harmful to human health, even if it is wanted, and is not created by that person himself. The result of this could be that noise levels may have to be mitigated at concerts. As may be recalled from the objectives, the first step in the directive is to determine exposure to noise by means of noise mapping. This involves four indicators: Lden (noise during day, evening and night), Lday (noise during day), Levening (noise during the evening) and Lnight (noise during the night). Lden, Lday and Levening indicate annoyance and Lnight indicates sleep disturbance. Using these indicators, the Member States have to produce strategic noise maps before 30 June 2007, which show the exposure to noise in the preceding calendar year (Article 7). Articles 5 and 6 contain the detailed rules for the use of these indicators and the assessment methods. These strategic noise maps will show the environmental noise in major agglomerations of more than 250,000 inhabitants and for all major roads which have more than 6 million vehicle passages per year, major railways with more than 60,000 train passages per year and major airports (more than 50,000 take-offs or landings per year). Such strategic noise maps must be updated at least every five years (Article 7(4)). On the basis of these strategic noise maps action plans must be drawn up. These plans focus on places near major roads, major railways and major airports and agglomerations. Such plans must also aim to protect quiet areas (Article 8(1)(b)). In this regard it may be noted that a quiet area may not necessarily be entirely quiet. From the context it may be inferred that the quiet area referred to in Article 8(1)(b) is actually a quiet area in an agglomeration. This means that quiet is defined on the basis of exposure to noise below a certain limit value (Article 3(l), in contrast to the concept of a quiet area in open country (Article 3(m)). The directive explicitly states that the measures contained in the plans are at the discretion of the Member States, effectively ruling out the direct effect. However, the second obligation arising from Article 8(2)(b) could probably be construed as an enforceable right requiring measures to deal with excesses of the limit values. These limit values can be set by the Member States (Article 3(s)). The Member States are free to set these, but an extrapolation of the Court's jurisprudence on similar provisions in other directives, such as Article 4(2) of the EIA Directive will probably result in a limitation of this discretion in view of the environmental objectives of the Framework Noise Directive. The directive contains various provisions dealing with the information of the public (Article 9) and public consultation (Article 8(7)). There are furthermore provisions on reporting to the Commission and reporting by the Commission to the Council and the European Parliament. On the basis of the Commission reports, additional measures regarding specific sources may be contemplated (Article 11(2)(b)). The directive should have been implemented before 18 July 2004.

13 Legislation on Dangerous Substances

European legislation on dangerous substances underwent a complete overhaul in 2006 with the entry into force of the REACH package. REACH refers to the Registration, Evaluation, Authorisation and Restriction of Chemicals and the package consists of Regulation 1907/2006[383] and Directive 2006/121.[384] As a result of REACH, the old cornerstone of European policy on chemicals, Directive 76/548 on the classification, packaging and labelling of dangerous substances, has been amended.[385] Moreover, several directives and regulations have been replaced or amended in order to create one uniform system for chemicals. Below, we will first analyse the REACH Regulation and then analyse the REACH Directive. Finally we will look at legislation concerning the export and import of chemicals and a specific category of chemicals: pesticides and biocides.

13.1 The REACH Regulation

At more than 800 pages in the Official Journal, the REACH Regulation is an impressive legislative feat. It applies to all substances, which are given a very wide definition (Article 1 in connection with 3(1)). Radioactive substances, substances in customs control, waste and so-called non-isolated intermediates (intermediary chemicals that remain in the installation used for their creation (Article 3(15)(a)) are outside the scope of the REACH Regulation (Article 2(1) and (2)). Moreover, the regulation does not apply to the transport of substances and it applies without prejudice to the specialised regimes for certain substances, such as radioactive substances, medicinal products, chemicals for use in foodstuffs (Article 2(4), (5) and (6)).

Central to the REACH Regulation is the duty for producers and importers to register substances in a database managed by the European Chemicals Agency (ECA) that is established by the regulation (Title X). This registration requirement implements the principal duty laid down in Article 1(3) according to which the producers, importers and downstream users of substances are responsible for ensuring that substances will not adversely affect human health or the environment. Registration is required before a substance can be marketed (Article 5).[386] As a rule, registration is required for substances imported or produced in quantities exceeding one ton per year (Article 6) as well as for articles containing substances above a certain threshold (Article 7). However, the regulation contains a number of exceptions to this rule for polymers, substances covered by specialised regimes and substances considered harmless (Listed in Annex IV).

---

[383] OJ 2006 L 396/1, corrected text to be found in OJ 2007 L 136/3.

[384] OJ 2006 L 396/850.

[385] OJ 1967 L 196/1, amended many times since then. Cf. in general on European chemicals legislation, Pallemaerts (2005).

[386] See also Article 128(1), which contains the free movement clause.

There is an exception for substances used in research and development (Article 9). Finally, there are transitional rules contained in Article 23. The rule is that the registration duty applies from 1 June 2008 onwards. Pursuant to Article 23, however, the entry into force of the registration requirement may be as late as 1 June 2018 depending on the quantities involved and the dangerousness of the substance. These transitional rules apply only to so-called phase-in substances, a term that is defined in Article 3(20) as basically encompassing substances marketed before 1 January 1995.[387] These transitional rules apply only to substances preregistered between 1 June 2008 and 1 December 2008 (Article 28).

The registration involves the submission of a technical dossier including formal details such as the name of the producer or importer and the identity of the substance but also, and most importantly, all physicochemical, toxicological and ecotoxicological information (Article 12). The exact detail and content of this information depends on the quantity of the substance imported or produced and is set out in Annex VII and VIII.

As the information contained in the technical dossier will often be expensive to gather, the regulation provides for various mechanisms to avoid duplication. Firstly, it envisages joint registration (Article 11). Secondly, substances subject to notification and approval as part of specialised regimes, such as plant protection products, are regarded as being registered (Article 15). Thirdly, Title III contains various rules on data sharing and the avoidance of animal tests.[388] On the basis of these provisions there is a duty to inquire prior to registration to see whether there are prior registrations. If this inquiry yields that tests on vertebrate animals have already been conducted less than 12 years ago, the regulation prohibits repetition of these tests (Article 26(3). Furthermore, the regulation envisages a procedure whereby the ECA can require sharing of data subject to payment of a proportionate part of the costs involved in the generation of these data (Article 27). The information contained in the registration should be communicated through the supply chain, and notably downstream (i.e. to the users of the substances; Title IV).

The second step in the REACH system relates to the evaluation of substances. This takes place on the basis of Title VI and can take two forms: dossier and substance evaluation. Dossier evaluation involves the ECA checking to see whether animal tests proposed in a registration are necessary (Article 40). The ECA may also check registrations in so as to ascertain conformity of the technical dossier with Articles 10, 12 and 13 of the REACH Regulation (Article 41). Substance evaluation takes place on the basis of Article 44 and further and

---

[387] It also includes so-called existing substances listed in the European Inventory of Existing Commercial Substances EINECS.

[388] The testing methods themselves have been largely harmonised through the principles of so-called Good Laboratory Practices (GLP), as defined in Directive 2004/10 on the application of the principles of good laboratory practice (GLP) and the verification of their applications for tests on chemical substances (OJ 2004 L 50/44) and Directive 2004/9 on the inspection and verification of GLP (OJ 2004 L 50/28).

involves the ECA and Member State authorities conducting tests themselves. The regulation contains a system for allocating specific evaluations to the various national authorities.

The third step concerns the authorisation of substances (Title VII). This aims to ensure the good functioning of the internal market while at the same time assuring that the risks from substances of very high concern are properly controlled (Article 55). Moreover, such substances are to be replaced by suitable alternative substances or technologies where this is economically and technically viable. Just as with the registration-phase, the manufacturers and importers must actually do the required research. These substances of very high concern are defined in Article 57(a)-(f) as substances that are carcinogenic, mutagenic, toxic for reproduction, (very) persistent, bioaccumulative and toxic or any other substance outside the previous categories for which there it scientific evidence of probably serious effects to human health or the environment, such as substances that have endocrine disrupting properties (so-called Annex XIV-substances). The last category opens up the Annex XIV list, in accordance with the precautionary principle. Article 56(1) contains a general prohibition of marketing so-called Annex XIV-substances, subject to a number of exceptions. Firstly, the prohibition applies only after the sunset-date (Article 58(1)(c)(i). This relates to the procedure whereby the ECA can decide to place a substance in the Annex XIV list. This procedure allows for the continued use of these substances upon application to the ECA (Article 58(1)(c)(ii)) until a decision concerning the authorisation is taken. Secondly, the prohibition does not apply where the use of the substance has been authorised (Article 56(1)(a) and (b). Thirdly, the prohibition is declared inapplicable by Article 58(4) and (5) for a number of categories of substances.

Whereas it is the ECA that decides on placing a substance in the Annex XIV list, it is for the Commission to decide on the authorisations. From this division of responsibilities it could be inferred that it is for the ECA to protect human health and the environment in the light of the precautionary principle, whereas it is for the Commission to balance this with economic arguments and ensure the proper functioning of the internal market. The procedure for an authorisation decision is laid down in Article 60. According to Article 60(2) authorisations may only be granted if the risk to human health or the environment are adequately controlled. A further limit to the authorisation can be found in Article 60(3) according to which certain substances may not be authorised (substances for which no safe threshold may be determined, and substances that have (very) persistent, bioaccumulative and toxic properties). This exception is, however, subject to yet another exception contained in Article 60(4) that allows for an authorisation if it is shown that the socio-economic benefits outweigh the risk to human health or the environment (the balancing test) and if there are no suitable alternative substances or technologies (the alternatives test). It is not entirely certain if it is for the Commission or the applicant to show that the socio-economic benefits outweigh the risks, as it is the Commission that takes the decision whereas Article 60(5(b) refers to the applicant as the person for whom the technical and economic feasibility of alternatives is to be taken into account. The latter provision also appears to further define the suitability-requirement in Article 60(4) as encompassing technical and economic considerations. The inclusion of economic considerations as part of the suitable alternatives test is wrong in our opinion as an economic appraisal is also part of ascertaining the socio-economic benefits, and the alternatives test cannot be seen as part of the balancing test.

The REACH Regulation allows for so-called restrictions (Title VIII) for substances. Such restrictions take the form of placing a substance in Annex XVII by a Commission decision following a proposal by a Member State, the ECA or the Commission itself. The procedure for such decisions is set out in Article 69-73. Restriction decisions are only allowed if there is an unacceptable risk to human health or the environment, which needs to be addressed on a European-wide basis. Such decisions shall take into account the socio-economic impact of the restriction, including the availability of alternatives (Article 68). In contrast to the authorisation decision (Article 60), socio-economic impacts appear to have a smaller role here and cannot outweigh the risks to human health and the environment. The REACH Regulation contains a special application of Article 95(4) EC in the form of Article 67(3), which allows the Member States to maintain in force any more stringent restrictions for Annex XVII substances subject only to the requirement that such restrictions have been notified according to the Treaty. A Commission decision is therefore not necessary.

Titles IX and X contain the rules for the establishment and working of the ECA including provisions on legal protection against decisions taken by the ECA. The following decisions may be appealed (Article 91(1)):

- Article 9 – Conditions for the use of substances in research and development;
- Article 20 – Decisions concerning the completeness of registration of substances;
- Article 27(6) – Decisions on the sharing of information from prior registrations;
- Article 30(2) & (3) – Decisions on the repetition of animal tests and sharing of costs involved;
- Article 51 – Decisions on dossier evaluation.

Such an appeal shall have a suspensive effect (Article 91(2). The requirements for standing under Article 91 basically conform to those used under Article 230 EC. Only the addressee or those who are directly and individually concerned can appeal. Moreover such appeals must be brought within three months of the notification of the decision. Appeals on the basis of Article 91 will be decided by the Board of Appeal of the ECA (Article 93). Decisions of the Board of Appeal and all decisions of the ECA that cannot be appealed on the basis of Article 91 may be appealed before the Court of First Instance or the Court of Justice in accordance with Article 230 EC (Article 94(1)). Failure to act of the ECA may be the subject of proceedings pursuant to Article 232 EC. Concerning the above system of legal protection a number of comments are possible. Firstly, the regulation does not envisage Article 232 EC-proceedings against a failure to act on the part of the Board of Appeal. Secondly, it may be recalled that there is a two-month time limit for appeals pursuant to Article 230 EC, whereas Article 92 contains a three-month period in this regard. Finally, by allowing for appeals in accordance with Article 230 against ECA decisions not mentioned in Article 91 and Commission decisions pursuant to the REACH Regulation, the rules on standing, and particularly those dealing with individual concern, become relevant. From the perspective of the importers and manufacturers much depend on whether these decisions are taken on the basis of substances, or on the basis of applicants. The latter option will greatly increase the possibilities of a manufacturer or importer being individually concerned.[389]

Title XI contains the rules on the classification and labelling of substances. This title basically declares Directive 76/548, as amended by the REACH Directive,[390] applicable. Title XII deals with information and reporting. Article 118 declares Regulation 1049/2001 on access to information applicable to the ECA. However, paragraph 2 restricts the access to this information by declaring, *inter alia*, details on the full composition of a preparation and the precise use of a substance will normally undermine the protection of the commercial interests. This means that information relating to these aspects may be withheld. Interestingly, the word 'normally' in Article 118(2) appears to allow for exceptions to this general duty not to disclose the information. Title XIII and XIV deal with the competent authorities in the Member States and the enforcement of the REACH Regulation. Finally, Title XV contains the transitional and final provisions. Basically, the regulation entered into force on 1 June 2007 and it applies from 1 June 2008 onwards. Since it is based on Article 95 EC, the REACH Regulation contains a free movement clause (Article 128(1). Paragraph 2, however, allows the Member States to maintain or enact national rules on the protection of workers, human health or the environment insofar as these rules are outside the scope of the regulation.[391] Article 129 contains the safeguard clause, allowing for Member State action where there is an urgent risk for human health or the environment. The REACH Regulation replaces the Marketing of Dangerous Substances Directive from 1 june 2009 onwards (Article 139).[392] Commission proposal COM (2007) 355 final intends to amend the REACH Regulation in order to adapt it to the Globally Harmonised System of Classification and Labelling of Chemicals, the so-called GHS.

---

[389] See further Cana (2004) at 107.

[390] See section 13.2 of this chapter.

[391] See, concerning Directive 76/769, Case C-473/98 *Kemikalieninspektionen* v. *Toolex Alpha* [2000] ECR I-5681, para. 30.

[392] Directive 76/769 on the marketing and use of certain dangerous substances and preparations OJ 1976 L 262/201, amended many times since then.

13.2 Directive 76/548 on the Classification, Packaging and Labelling of Dangerous Substances

Directive 76/548 was amended several times. The most important amendments are referred to as the sixth[393] and seventh amendment.[394] On 1 June 2008 it will be amended by the REACH Directive 2006/121. The sixth amendment introduced a system of notification for new chemicals throughout the EU. The directive contained a different regime for existing substances, in other words substances which were already on the market before 18 September 1981.[395] The Commission was required to draw up an inventory of these substances, based on the information provided by the Member States.[396] With the REACH Directive, the distinction between new and existing substances will disappear and as a result the rules on the notification of new substances will be repealed. The directive also contained provisions that applied equally to new and existing substances. For example, the Member States were not allowed, on grounds relating to notification, classification, packaging or labelling, to prohibit, restrict or impede the placing on the market of substances, old or new, which complied with the provisions of the directive.

Finally, the directive provided that Member States might provisionally prohibit the sale of a substance or subject it to special conditions in its territory where it constituted a hazard for man or the environment, even if it did comply with the provisions of the directive. The Member State in question was required to inform the Commission and the other Member States immediately, after which the Commission would consult the Member States and, within six weeks, give its view and take appropriate measures.[397] The directive provided a fine example of total harmonisation.[398] The seventh amendment introduced substantial changes to the sixth amendment and represents a general tightening-up of European policy on dangerous substances. It contains amended provisions on the testing of substances (Article 3[399]) and the classification of substances

---

[393] Directive 79/831, OJ 1979 L 259/10.

[394] Directive 92/32, OJ 1992 L 154/15.

[395] The collection, circulation and accessibility of information on 'existing' substances (substances included in the European Inventory of Existing Commercial Substances, EINECS) and the evaluation of the risks of these substances to man and the environment are the subject of Regulation 793/93 (repealed with effect from 1 June 2008, cf. Article 139 of the REACH Regulation), OJ 1993 L 84/1, on the evaluation and control of the risks of existing substances.

[396] This was published in OJ 1990 C 146.

[397] Case C-43/90 *Commission* v. *Germany* [1992] ECR I-1909. On the application of the safeguard clause in Article 23 the Court ruled that it is clear that when a measure is being notified, it is unnecessary to state in so many words that it is a provisional measure. Simple notification is sufficient.

[398] Case 278/85 *Commission* v. *Denmark* [1987] ECR 4069. See also Chapter 3 for a more exhaustive treatment of this case.

[399] Such tests shall be conducted in accordance with the REACH Regulation, Article 1(3) of the REACH Directive.

according to categories such as 'dangerous for the environment', 'mutagenic', 'carcinogenic' (Article 4). Article 6 requires traders and importers to carry out an investigation of 'existing' dangerous substances, on the basis of which they are required to label and package the substances.

This directive is intended to achieve total harmonisation. Member States may not prohibit, restrict or impede the placing on the market of substances which comply with its requirements, on grounds relating to notification, classification, packaging or labelling within the meaning of the directive (Article 30). Only where a Member State, in the light of new information, has justifiable reasons to consider that a substance, which has been accepted as satisfying the requirements of the directive, nevertheless constitutes a danger for man or the environment, by reason of classification, packaging or labelling which is no longer appropriate, may it take temporary measures to address the situation (Article 31). The Commission must be informed of such action, and if it considers action to be necessary, this may lead to adaptation of the relevant European legislation. However, the directive does not harmonise the conditions under which dangerous substances may be *marketed* or *used,* which are still matters that fall within the purview of national legislation.[400] The directive will be amended to incorporate the GHS.[401]

13.3   Pesticides Legislation

There are several European measures relating to the agricultural, internal market, human health and environmental aspects of the use of pesticides:
· legislation on the marketing of plant protection products;
· legislation on the classification, packaging and labelling of pesticides;
· legislation on maximum residue levels of pesticides;
· legislation concerning the marketing of biocidal products.

13.3.1   Legislation on the Marketing of Plant Protection Products

Directive 91/414 concerning the placing of plant protection products (insecticides, herbicides and fungicides) on the market aims to strike a delicate balance between the demands of the internal market, the need to have a level playing field in the agricultural sector and the need to protect human health and the environment. It harmonises the national procedures for authorising *plant protection products* on the one hand and creates an authorisation for *active substances* at European level on the other. The system thus created can therefore be described as a dual authorisation system.[402] Plant protection prod-

---

[400] Case C-473/98 *Kemikalieninspektionen* v. *Toolex Alpha* [2000] ECR I-5681, para. 29.

[401] COM (2007) 355 final, see above in section 13.1 on the GHS.

[402] Vogelezang-Stoute (1999) at 145.

ucts are not to be placed on the market without first having been authorised by the competent authority.[403]

A plant protection product may not be authorised unless its active substances are listed in Annex I of the directive (Article 4(1)).[404] In addition, having regard to all the normal circumstances under which the product may be used, it must be established that:

· it is sufficiently effective;
· it has no unacceptable effect on plants or plant products;
· it does not cause unnecessary suffering and pain to vertebrates to be controlled;
· it has no harmful effect on human or animal health, directly or indirectly (e.g. through drinking water, food or feed) or on groundwater;
· it has no unacceptable influence on the environment.

It is also worth noting that the directive establishes a link with the residue levels adopted under the MRL Regulation (Article 4(1)(f)).[405]

The Council is required to adopt 'uniform principles'.[406] These principles contain more detailed rules pertaining to the application of the authorisation criteria by the Member States. Following the annulment by the Court of Justice of an earlier version of the principles, new ones are now applicable.[407]

Authorisations may be granted only for a fixed period (of up to ten years; Article 4(4)), and may be reviewed at any time if there are indications that any of the requirements are no longer satisfied (Article 4(5)). An authorisation will be cancelled if it is established that the requirements are no longer satisfied or if false or misleading particulars were supplied by the applicant (Article 4(6)).[408] The authorisation must be modified if it is established that on the basis of developments in scientific and technical knowledge the manner of use and amounts used can be modified.

Article 10 regulates the mutual recognition of national authorisations. Where an application for authorisation is submitted to a Member State for a product already authorised in another Member State, the Member State is bound to authorise the product in its territory, if it contains only substances listed in

---

[403] Cf. Case C-400/96 *Harpegnies* [1998] ECR I-5121.

[404] The procedure to list a substance as an 'active substance' is governed by Article 5 of the directive. See Commission Directives 97/73, OJ 1997 L 353/26 (imazalil); 98/47, OJ 1998 L 191/50 (azoxystrobin); 99/1, OJ 1999 L 21/21 (kresoxym methyl); 99/73, OJ 1999 L 210/13 (spiroxamine); 99/80, OJ 1999 L 210/13 (azimsulfuron). See however Case T-229/04 *Sweden* v. *Commission*, judgment of 11 July 2007, n.y.r. in the ECR, annulling Commission Directive 2003/112, OJ 2003 L 321/32, listing paraquat.

[405] See below, section 13.3.3.

[406] Directive 94/43 OJ 1994 L 227/31, replaced by Directive 97/57, OJ 1997 L 265/87.

[407] Case C-303/94 *EP* v. *Council* [1996] ECR I-2943; Directive 97/57, OJ 1997 L 265/87. Cf. on the annulment the case annotation of Cardonell in [1996] *EELR*, 271-274.

[408] Cf. Case C-326/05P *Industrias Químicas del Vallés* v. *Commission*, judgment of 18 July 2007, n.y.r. in the ECR.

Annex I. That is, to the extent that agricultural, plant health and environmental (including climatic) conditions relevant to the use of the product are comparable in the regions concerned (Article 10(1), second indent). A Member State's specific circumstances may therefore provide a ground for not recognizing authorisations made in another Member State.[409] Other reasons for not authorising a plant-protection product in a Member State's territory are not permitted.

On the issue of parallel imports the Court ruled in *British Agrochemicals* that:

'where a plant protection product covered by marketing authorisation granted in accordance with the provisions of the Directive in one Member State is imported into another Member State as a parallel import of a plant protection product already covered by marketing authorisation in the Member State of importation, the provisions of the Directive on the procedure for the grant of marketing authorisation do not apply'.[410]

Nor may Member States require the repetition of tests and analyses that have already been carried out in connection with authorisation in another Member State. Here too we find the proviso that agricultural, plant health and environmental (including climatic) conditions relevant to the use of the product are comparable in the regions concerned. In addition, the directive contains several transitional measures (Article 8),[411] provisions concerning the application for authorisation (Article 9), several requirements concerning data protection and confidentiality (Article 13 and a quite remarkable Article 14), packaging and labelling (Articles 15 and 16)[412], control (Article 17) and research and development (Article 22).

In connection with the marketing of pesticides it is also important to devote some attention to Directive 79/117 on the prohibition of the marketing of certain pesticides and active substances.[413] Central to this directive is the Annex that

---

[409] Cf. Article 95(4-6) EC and our observations in Chapter 3, section 6.

[410] Case C-100/96 *British Agrochemicals* [1999] ECR I-1499, para. 31. The same applies to a plant protection product imported from an EEA State in which it is already covered by marketing authorisation granted in accordance with the directive, but not to the importation of a plant protection product from a third country.

[411] See Case C-306/98 *Monsanto* [2001] ECR I-3279, para. 39 *et seq.* according to which Article 8(3) does not apply to an application for first authorisation to market a generic plant protection product containing an active substance not listed in Annex I to the directive, which is already on the domestic market two years after notification of that directive. This means that the Member State is not under an obligation to assess such an application in accordance with the requirements laid down in Article 4(1)(b)(i) to (v), and (c) to (f) of Directive 91/414. See further Case C-316/04 *Stichting Zuid-Hollandse Milieufederatie* [2005] ECR I-9759 and Case C-138/05 *Stichting Zuid-Hollandse Milieufederatie* [2006] ECR I-8339.

[412] The reference to Directive 78/631 must be read as a reference to Directive 99/45; see Article 21(3) of Directive 99/45, OJ 1999 L 200/1.

[413] OJ 1977 L 33/36, as amended by Regulation 850/2004, OJ 2004 L 229/5.

contains a list of prohibited substances and – where this is specified – exemptions from the prohibition. The directive does not apply to pesticides intended for exports or for research and development (Article 5). Substances shall be included in the Annex when they, even when used correctly, give rise to or are likely to give rise to harmful effects on human or animal health or unreasonable adverse effects on the environment (Article 6(6)). The imperative wording of this provision and the reference to the likelihood of the effects show that this provision implements the precautionary principle.[414] Article 7 allows the Member States to authorise the marketing of prohibited substances for a maximum of 120 days to combat unforeseen danger to plant production for which there is no alternative means for containment. This provision appears to be at odds with the basic principle underlying Directive 91/414, according to which the protection of human health and the environment should take priority over the improvement of plant production. Directive 79/117 has lost some of its importance with the entry into force of Directive 91/414. However, current practice, according to which the Annex to Directive 79/117 is no longer updated and expanded and the procedures in Directive 91/414 are applied to active substances,[415] is problematic in view of the imperative wording of Article 6(6) of Directive 79/117.

13.3.2   Labelling and Packaging of Pesticides

Directive 99/45 concerning the approximation of the laws, regulations and administrative provisions of the Member States relating to the classification, packaging and labelling of dangerous preparations has changed the law considerably.[416] Directive 99/45 repeals Directive 78/631 which regulated the law prior to it.[417] Based on Article 95 EC, the 'new' directive deals with the classification, packaging and labelling of dangerous preparations, and with certain preparations which may present *hazards*, whether or not they are classified as dangerous within the meaning of the directive. By comparison with the 'old' directive, which focused on danger rather than on environmental aspects, the importance of the latter has been significantly increased (Article 7 taken in conjunction with Annex III). Dangerous preparations have to classified according to the degree and specific nature of the hazards involved and have to packaged and labelled according to their classification (Articles 10-11).

Member States are required to take all necessary measures to ensure that the preparations covered by the directive cannot be placed on the market unless they comply with its provisions (Article 8).

The requirement to provide safety data sheets (Article 14) has been repealed and replaced with effect from 1 June 2007 by the general rules on downstream

---

[414] See further Vogelezang-Stoute (2004) at 172.

[415] Vogelezang-Stoute (2004) at 174.

[416] OJ 1999 L 200/1.

[417] OJ 1978 L 206/13.

information pursuant to the REACH Regulation.[418] The directive contains a free movement clause, by which Member States may not prohibit, restrict or impede the placing on the market of preparations because of their classification, packaging, labelling or safety data sheets if such preparations comply with the provisions laid down in the directive (Article 18). The 'traditional' safeguard clause can be found in Article 19. Where a Member State has detailed evidence that a preparation, although satisfying the provisions of the directive, constitutes a hazard for man or the environment, it may provisionally prohibit the placing on the market of that preparation or subject it to special conditions in its territory. In that case it shall immediately inform the Commission and the other Member States.

13.3.3   Pesticide Residues

There are several directives pertaining to the setting of maximum residue levels (MRL) in agricultural products, such as fruit and vegetables,[419] cereals,[420] foodstuffs of animal origin,[421] and products of vegetable origin), and honey.[422] These directives are being repealed by Regulation 396/2005 because the directives were amended several times and a clarification was considered necessary.[423] The process of repeals depends on the adoption and publication of regulations establishing Annex I – IV pursuant to the MRL Regulation. At this moment Regulation 178/2006 establishing Annex I to the MRL Regulation has been adopted.[424] Annex II (setting MRLs), Annex III (setting temporary MRLs) and Annex IV (substances for which no MRL is considered necessary) have not been adopted yet. This means that only chapters I, IV and VI to X of the MRL Regulation apply with effect from 5 April 2005. The MRL Regulation is based on Articles 37 and 152(4)(b) EC and aims to ensure a high level of consumer protection and harmonised provisions relating to pesticide residues. The MRL Regulation should be seen in the context of the General Food Law[425] and Directive 91/414 on plant protection products.

---

[418] Article 140 of Regulation 1907/2006, see above, section 13.1.

[419] Directive 76/895 relating to the fixing of maximum levels for pesticide residues in and on fruit and vegetables, OJ 1976 L 340/26, frequently amended.

[420] Directive 86/362 on the fixing of maximum levels for pesticide residues in and on cereals, OJ 1986 L 221/37, frequently amended.

[421] Directive 86/363 on the fixing of maximum levels for pesticide residues in and on foodstuffs of animal origin, OJ 1986 L 221/43, later amended.

[422] Directive 90/642 on the fixing of maximum levels for pesticide residues in and on certain products of plant origin, including fruit and vegetables, OJ 1990 L 350/71, frequently amended.

[423] Regulation 396/2005 on maximum residue levels (MRL Regulation), OJ 2006 L 70/1. See also Directive 2002/63 on sampling for the control of pesticide residues, OJ 2002 L 187/30.

[424] Regulation 178/2006, OJ 2006 L 29/3.

[425] Regulation 178/2002, OJ 2002 L 31/1, as amended by Regulation 1642/2003, OJ 2003 L 245/4.

Chapter I of the MRL Regulation contains the general provisions and determines the scope. The MRL Regulation applies to products of plant or animal
origin, whether processed or not, covered by Annex I. It does not apply to products of animal or plant origin that are not intended for food or feed or to products treated before export to third countries (Article 2). Finally, the regulation
applies without prejudice to the Biocides Directive[426] and a directive on undesirable substances in animal feed[427] and the regulation on residues of veterinary
medicines.[428] Article 4(1) enables the Commission to adopt Annex I. It further
envisages the adoption of Annex IV containing plant protection products for
which no MRL needs to be set. To this date Annex IV has not been adopted.
Chapter II, which does not apply yet, contains the procedure for application of
an MRL. This procedure commences with an application to the Member State
which is then forwarded to the European Food Safety Authority (EFSA)[429] and
the Commission along with an evaluation by the Member State. The evaluation
shall take place in accordance with the uniform principles adopted pursuant to
Directive 91/414. The EFSA will then give a reasoned opinion on, in particular,
the risks to consumers and animals (Article 10(1)) within a maximum to six
months from the date of receipt of the application (Article 11). Article 12 contains
the procedure for the assessment of existing MRLs by the EFSA. MRLs are set
by means of a Commission regulation pursuant to Article 14(1). This Regulation may result in the inclusion of a new or modified MRL in Annex II or the
inclusion of a new or modified temporary MRL in Annex III (Article 15). The
Commission may also reject the application for an MRL by means of a decision. Article 16 contains the procedure for setting temporary MRLs. When the
(temporary) MRLs have been set in Annex II and III, Chapter III, which does
not apply yet, contains the rules on the MRLs applicable to products of plant and
animal origin. Article 18(1)(a) dictates that Annex I products must comply with
the MRLs set in Annex II and III. The default obligation is set out in Article
18(1)(b), according to which the residue may not exceed 0.01 mg/kg for Annex I
products for which no MRL is set or for active substances not listed in Annex IV.
Products that comply with the MRLs benefit from a free movement clause (Article 18(2)). Article 18(3) allows for exceeding the MRLs provided that there are
adequate controls to ensure that these products are not immediately consumed.
The provisions of Chapter III do not apply to products produced or imported into
the EU before the date of application of that chapter. Chapter IV requires the
Commission to incorporate the existing MRLs in Annex II (Article 21). MRLs
set pursuant to Directive 91/414 should similarly be incorporated as temporary MRLs in Annex III (Article 22). The level at which these temporary MRLs
should be set is the lowest level that can be achieved in all Member States on the

---

[426] See below, section 13.3.4.

[427] Directive 2002/32, OJ 2002 L 140/10.

[428] Regulation 2377/90, OJ 1990 L 224/1.

[429] The MRL Regulation refers to the authority as defined in Article 22 of Regulation 178/2002, OJ 2002 L
31/1.

basis of good agricultural practice (Article 25). The term good agricultural practice (GAP) is defined in Article 3(2)(a) as the nationally recommended, authorised or registered safe use of plant protection products under actual conditions. This implies a correct application of Directive 91/414. Chapter V, which does not apply yet, contains rules on controls, reports and sanctions. It envisages national controls (Article 26) on the basis of a national control programmes (Article 30) and a European control programme (Article 29). Interestingly, Article 30(3) merely allows for internet publication of the names of the retailers, traders or producers whose products exceeded the MRLs whereas recital 34 is formulated in a more imperative manner. On the basis of the national reports an Annual Report shall be drawn up by the EFSA (Article 32). Chapter VI allows for emergency measures by the Commission or a Member State. Chapter VII contains rules on support measures for harmonised MRLs. Such measures may be fully subsidised by the EU (Article 37(1)). Chapter VIII deals with the coordination of applications for MRLs. Chapter IX contains the procedure for the adoption of the implementing legislation. Chapter X contains the final provisions.

As the chapters on the application for MRLs, the MRLs applicable and the controls of MRLs do not apply, the directives mentioned above are still relevant and therefore deserve mention here. Under Directive 76/895 Member States may not prohibit or impede the putting on the market within their territories of the products covered by the directive if the quantity of these residues does not exceed the maximum quantities laid down (Article 3(1)). However, where they consider it justified, Member States are expressly authorised to allow such products which contain higher quantities of residues (Article 3(2)).[430] Since its amendment by Directive 97/41[431] the directive also applies to products intended for export to third countries (Article 9).

Directive 90/642 complicates the issue in that it provides that products shall not contain pesticide residue levels higher than those specified, in other words, Member States may no longer allow higher residue contents (Article 3(1)). This provision was necessary because the provision of Article 3(2) in the earlier directive had caused barriers to trade which had to be eliminated, with a view to completion of the internal market.

Directive 90/642 does, in principle, apply to exports to third countries (Article 1(3)). It provides expressly that it applies without prejudice to the provisions

---

[430] Case 94/83 *Albert Heijn* [1984] ECR 3263 and Case 54/85 *Mirepoix* [1986] ECR 1067 where the Court ruled that that the Member States are in principle, and of course subject to the rules on the free movement of goods, entitled to set maximum levels for residues of substances which are not yet subject to Community legislation. The Court added that in so far as the relevant Community rules do not cover certain pesticides, Member States may regulate the presence of residues of these pesticides in a way which may vary from one country to another according to climatic conditions, the normal diet of the population and their state of health. See also with respect to Directive 90/642, Joined Cases C-54/94 and C-74/94 *Stanghellini en Cacchiarelli* [1995] ECR I-391.
[431] OJ 1997 L 184/33.

of Directive 76/895 (Article 1(2)(c)), so that the provisions of the earlier directive apply to products which are not covered by the newer one.

As to the relationship between the two directives the Court observed in Joined Cases C-54/94 and C-74/94, *Stanghellini and Cacchiarelli*[432] that it is apparent from Directive 90/642 that it is without prejudice to Directive 76/895 but is intended to replace it progressively as and when the pesticide residues mentioned in Directive 76/895 are included in Directive 90/642 and maximum levels fixed.

13.3.4   Biocides Directive 98/8

Finally mention must be made in this chapter of Directive 98/8 concerning the placing of biocidal products on the market.[433] These are a group of pesticides used primarily by industry and in the home to combat harmful organisms.

The structure of Directive 98/8 is similar to that of Directive 91/414, in particular the system of 'dual authorisation'.[434] On the one hand the directive provides for the establishment at European level of a positive list of active substances which may be used in biocidal products and on the other it contains rules on the authorisation and the placing on the market for use of biocidal products within the Member States. Like Directive 91/414 mutual recognition of authorisations is a key element (Article 4).[435]

Member States are required to ensure that a biocidal product shall not be placed on the market and used in their territory unless it has been authorised (Article 3(1)). However, the directive distinguishes a special category of 'low-risk biocidal products', for which a simpler procedure applies (Article 3(2)). Authorisations shall be granted for a maximum period of 10 years (Article 3(6)).

Article 5 provides that Member States shall authorize a biocidal product only if the active substances it includes are listed in Annex I or IA of the directive and it is established that the biocidal product is sufficiently effective, has no unacceptable effects on the target organisms, such as unacceptable resistance or cross-resistance or unnecessary suffering and pain for vertebrates, and has no unacceptable effects on human or animal health, or on surface water and groundwater, and has no unacceptable effect on the environment. Article 5(2) provides that a biocidal product classified as toxic, very toxic or as a category 1 or 2 carcinogen, or as a category 1 or 2 mutagen or classified as toxic for reproduction category 1 or 2, shall not be authorised for marketing to, or use by the general public.

---

432 Joined Cases C-54/94 and C-74/94 *Stanghellini en Cacchiarelli* [1995] ECR I-391.

433 OJ 1998 L123/1. The directive is based on Article 100a, now Article 95, making it clear that its primary objective is the functioning of the Internal Market. Cf. Wilson (1998).

434 Cf. Vogelezang-Stoute (2004) at 133.

435 See Case C-433/02 *Schreiber* [2004] ECR I-7275, paras. 34-39 on the application of Article 4(1).

During the period for which an authorisation has been granted, it may be reviewed at any time if there are indications that any of the conditions referred to in Article 5 are no longer satisfied (Article 6).

An authorisation shall be cancelled if:
- the active substance is no longer included in Annex I or IA;[436]
- the conditions for obtaining the authorisation are no longer satisfied;
- it is discovered that false or misleading particulars were supplied concerning the facts on the basis of which the authorisation was granted (Article 7).

Application for authorisation shall be made by the person who will be responsible for the first placing on the market of a biocidal product in a particular Member State. Every applicant shall be required to have a permanent office within the EU (Article 8).

Article 10(5) is also interesting. It provides that an entry of an active substance in Annex I, IA or IB may be refused or removed if there is another active substance for the same product type which, in the light of scientific or technical knowledge, presents significantly less risk to health or to the environment. This is known as the 'substitution principle'.

The directive also contains provisions concerning the use of data held by competent authorities for other applicants (Article 12), cooperation in the use of data for second and subsequent applications for authorisation (Article 13), derogation from the requirements (Article 15), transitional measures (Article 16),[437] research and development (Article 17), information exchange (Article 18), confidentiality (Article 19) and the classification, packaging and labelling of biocidal products (Article 20[438]). The 'standard' safeguard clause can be found in Article 32.

13.4   Import and Export of Dangerous Chemicals

For some time now the dangers for man and the environment of the international trade in dangerous chemicals have been the subject of attention within the context of several international organisations, such as the OECD, UNEP and FAO. These organisations have established a procedure of 'prior informed consent' (PIC), which is intended to prevent substances

---

[436] See for the inclusion of an active substance in Annexes I, IA or IB, Articles 10 and 11 of the directive. See further Case C-433/02 *Schreiber* [2004] ECR I-7275 where the Court adopts a precautionary approach to substances and classifies blocks of Cedar wood as biocidal because the cedar oil in them repels insects. Note, however, that this was the result of the fact Annex IA and IB had not been adopted. At this moment only two substances have been included in Annex I, see Directive 2006/140, OJ 2006 L 414/78 and Directive 2000/70 OJ 2000 L 94/23.

[437] See on the transitional rules: Case C-316/04 *Stichting Zuid-Hollandse Milieufederatie* [2005] ECR I-9759.

[438] The reference to Directive 88/379 must be read as a reference to Directive 99/45; see Article 21(3) of Directive 99/45, OJ 1999 L 200/1.

being exported to third countries without the importing country having given its consent. On 11 September 1998 the Rotterdam Convention was signed by the EC.[439] The Rotterdam Convention is implemented by means of Regulation 304/2003.[440] In doing so, Regulation 304/2003 is actually more stringently protective than the Rotterdam Convention.[441]

The main provision in the regulation is a PIC procedure for the export of certain dangerous chemical substances (and preparations) from the EU to third countries. The regulation is more stringent in that it covers not only the substances in the Rotterdam Convention list[442] but also all substances subject to restrictions and bans within the EU.[443] In addition the regulation applies to the classification, packaging and labelling of all chemicals exported.

Article 6 declares a certain PIC procedure applicable to chemicals in the three parts of Annex I. Part 1 chemicals are subject to the export notification procedure laid down in Article 7. Part 2 chemicals fall under Article 7 and the PIC notification procedure in Article 10. Part 3 chemicals are subject to the PIC procedure. The level of detail and specific information to be submitted as part of the procedure also differs for the various parts of Annex I.

Briefly, the export notification procedure in Article 7 involves the following. When a chemical subject to notification is due to be exported from the EU to a third country *for the first time,* the exporter must provide the national authorities with certain information. The authorities must then check the completeness of the information in the light of Annex III and forward the information to the Commission who will then take the necessary measures to ensure that the country of destination receives notification of the intended export (Article 7(1)). The Commission compiles a database of all notifications (Article 7(1) third paragraph. No new notification is required for subsequent exports to a third country, unless there has been a major change to European legislation in respect of the substance in question or the composition of the preparation has been changed (Article 7(3)). The export notification procedure no longer applies when the PIC procedure applies and the importing country has decided to consent or not to consent in the import and this decision has been received by the Commission and forwarded to the Member States (Article 7(5). However, the importing coun-

---

[439] Approved by Decision 2003/106, OJ 2003 L 63/27. This decision has been annulled by the ECJ in Case C-94/03 *Commission* v. *Council* [2006] ECR I-1, because the wrong legal basis (Article 175(1) in connection with 300(3) EC) had been used (Articles 133 and 175(1) in connection with Article 300 EC should have been used).

[440] OJ 2003 L 63/1, as amended by Regulation 777/2006, OJ 2006 L 136/9. Regulation 304/2003 repeals the old PIC Regulation 2455/92, OJ 1992 L 251/13. In Case C-178/03 *Commission* v. *Council and EP* [2006] ECR I-107, the ECJ has annulled Regulation 304/2003 because the wrong legal basis (Article 175(1) EC) had been used (Articles 133 and 175(1) EC should have been used). The effects of that regulation are maintained.

[441] Recital 4 of the Preamble to Regulation 304/2003.

[442] Article 2(1)(a) and Part 3 of Annex I.

[443] Article 2(1)(b) and Part 1 and 2.

try may still require notification, in which case the export notification procedure will also still apply. Finally, the notification requirement may be waived by the importing country.

Article 10 contains a special PIC procedure for chemicals that are severely restricted or banned in the EU. The notification of exports of these chemicals must comply with Annex II (Article 10(2)).

Article 13(6) prohibits the export of chemicals in parts 2 or 3 of Annex I unless explicit consent has been received from the importing country. For part 3 chemicals such consent may also be in the form of a circular by the secretariat of the Rotterdam Convention (Article 16(3)(ii)). Article 14(2) categorically prohibits the export of the chemicals listed in Annex V.

Besides the PIC procedure, the regulation contains two further instruments for the protection of man and the environment outside the EU. Article 13(7) prohibits the export of chemicals later than six months before the expiry date. Moreover exporters are to ensure that the size of containers is optimised to as to minimise the risk of the creation of obsolete stocks. This provision intends to prevent stockpiling of old chemicals in other countries. The second instrument relates to the classification, packaging and labelling of chemicals. Article 16 provides that dangerous chemicals which are intended for export are subject to the measures on packaging and labelling contained in Directives 67/548, 1999/45, 91/414 and 98/8. As far as practicable the information on the label must be given in the language of the country of destination or of the area of intended use (Article 16(4)). Moreover, information on the storage conditions and shelf life should be relevant to the local conditions in the importing country (Article 13(8)).

In fact Article 16 extends the application of the above directives to products intended for third countries. However, it is not clear whether Article 16 must be regarded as having the characteristics of a directive or a regulation. In other words, does it require transposition into national legislation, as the other provisions of the directives in question do, or is it in fact directly applicable? In the latter case exporters are required to act in conformity with its provisions, even without further implementing measures. The special labelling requirements in the regulation, such as Article 13(8) in our view support the conclusion that these rules have the characteristics of a Regulation. This would mean that they apply directly, even if the directives in question had not been implemented.

14   Legislation on Genetically Modified Organisms

The European rules on genetically modified organisms and micro-organisms (GMOs and GMMs) are contained in two directives and thee regulations.

· Directive 90/219 on the contained use;[444]

---

[444] OJ 1990 L 117/1, as amended most recently by Decision 2005/174, OJ 2005 L 59/20.

· Directive 2001/18 on the deliberate release;[445]
· Regulation 1829/2003 on genetically modified food and feed;[446]
· Regulation 1830/2003 on the traceability and labelling;[447]
· Regulation 1946/2003 on transboundary movements.[448]

These five instruments basically form a triptych, where Directive 90/219 contains rules on the contained use, Directive 2001/18 and Regulation 1829/2003 and 1830/2003 deal with the deliberate release of GMOs and Regulation 1946/2003 is concerned with the transboundary movements of GMOs.

GMMs are defined a micro-organisms in which the genetic material has been altered in a way that does not occur naturally (Article 2(b)). Annex I, Part A, contains an indicative list of genetic modification techniques, whereas Annex I, Part B, contains a number of techniques that will not result in genetic modification resulting in the organisms falling outside the scope of the directive. Another central concept is 'contained use' which is defined as any operation in which micro-organisms are genetically modified or in which GMOs are cultured, stored, etc. and for which specific containment measures are used to limit their contact with, and to provide a high level of safety for, the general population and the environment (Article 2(c)). The directive distinguishes between two groups of genetically modified organisms: safe GMMs and all other GMMs.[449] For the so-called safe GGMs Article 3 creates an exception from the application of the directive. This exception, however, is without prejudice to Article 5(1) that contains a general duty for Member States to ensure that appropriate measures are taken to avoid adverse effects on human health or the environment. For all other GMMs the directive applies, including the general obligation laid down in Article 5(1). To meet this obligation, the user is required to carry out an assessment of the contained uses as regards the risks to human health and the environment that these contained uses may incur (Article 5(2)). This assessment shall result in the final classification of the contained uses in four classes. Class 1 consists of activities implying 'no or negligible' risk, Class 2 those implying 'low' risk, Class 3 'moderate' risk and Class 4 'high' risk. Each class corresponds with a given containment level. Where there is doubt as to which class is appropriate for the proposed contained use, the more stringent protective measures shall be applied unless sufficient evidence, in agreement with the competent authority, justifies the application of less stringent measures (Article 5(4)).

Article 6 provides that the user shall apply the general principles and the appropriate containment and other protective measures set out in the directive

---

[445] OJ 2001 L 106/1, as amended by Regulation 1830/2003. This directive repeals Directive 90/220, OJ 1990 L 117/15.

[446] OJ 2003 L 268/1

[447] OJ 2003 L 268/24.

[448] OJ 2003 L 287/1.

[449] Following an amendment by Directive 98/81, OJ 1998 L 330/13.

so as to keep workplace and environmental exposure to any GMMs to the lowest reasonably practicable level, and so that a high level of safety is ensured.

Depending on the class of contained use, various notification requirements apply. Under Article 7, when premises are to be used for contained uses *for the first time*, the user will be required to notify the competent authorities. However, once this has been done, subsequent Class 1 contained use may proceed without further notification (Article 8). Notification must be given of every Class 2 contained use, but if a previous notification has been given and any associated consent requirements have been satisfied, the Class 2 contained use may proceed immediately following the new notification (Article 9(2)). If no previous notification has been given, the Class 2 contained use may not proceed until 45 days after submission of the notification. Finally, a Class 3 or higher class of contained use may not proceed without the prior written consent of the competent authority. The competent authority is required to communicate its decision at the latest 45 days after submission of the new notification in cases where a previous notification has been submitted, or at the latest 90 days after submission of the notification, in other cases. Each specific notification requirement also specifies the information that is required to be given. Article 12(1) requires the user to notify the competent authority of new information or changes in the contained use which could have significant effects on the risks involved. Interestingly, the mandatory nature of this requirement to forward new information is not reflected in the authority's duty to act upon such information as it *may* require modification, suspension or termination of the contained use (Article 12(3). It is submitted that in the light of the directive's objectives such new information must result in a reaction on the part of the authority that protects human health and the environment. Furthermore, the directive contains provisions on consulting the public (Article 13), drawing up emergency plans and furnishing information on safety measures (Articles 14 to 16),[450] ensuring control (Article 17), reporting ((Article 18) and the confidentiality of certain information (Article 19).[451]

Directive 2001/18 defines 'deliberate release' as any intentional introduction into the environment of a GMO, for example by placing it on the market, without such containment measures (Article 2(3)). From this definition and the definition of contained use, set out above in this paragraph, it is clear that Directive 90/219 is primarily concerned with the measures necessary to reduce the potential risks for man and the environment that can arise in working with GMMs, while Directive 2001/18 concerns the use of GMOs for research and development and commercial purposes. This is also reflected in the different

---

[450] See Case C-429/01 *Commission v. France* [2003] ECR I-14355, where the Court finds that the implementation of Article 14(a) requires a legal obligation to determine on a case by case basis whether a emergency action plan is necessary (paragraph 41). Moreover Article 14(b) dictates that such emergency plans must be made available as such, not as part of more general information published (paragraph 59).

[451] See Case C-429/01 *Commission v. France* [2003] ECR I-14355 paras. 74-88 on the implementation of Article 19(2) and (3).

legal basis. Whereas Directive 90/219 is based on Article 130s (now Article 175) EC, Directive 200/18 has been adopted on the basis of Article 95 Directive 2001/18 is not only concerned with the protection of human health and the environment, but also the removal of barriers to trade caused by disparities in national rules, are important aims.

The scope of Directive 2001/18 is defined by the term GMO, which is comparable to that employed by Directive 90/219, with the exception that humans are explicitly excluded (Article 2(2)). Moreover, Article 3(1) excludes certain categories of organisms (resulting from the techniques listed in Annex I B) and Article 2(2)(b) excludes certain techniques (listed in Annex IA, part 2) from the term genetic modification, and thus also from the scope of the directive.[452] Directive 2001/18 contains provisions on the deliberate release of GMOs for research and development purposes (Part B; Articles 5 to 11) and on the placing on the market of products containing GMOs (Part C; Articles 12 to 24). It imposes a general obligation on the Member States to ensure in accordance with the precautionary principle that all appropriate measures are taken to avoid adverse effects on human health and the environment (Article 4(1)).

As far as the deliberate release of GMOs for research and development purposes is concerned, a notification must be submitted to the competent authority, including a technical dossier with information on the dangers for human health or the environment (Article 6). The competent authority may either accept the notification, in which case the release may proceed, or indicate that the release does not fulfil the conditions of the directive and the notification is rejected (Article 6(5)(a) or (b)). Only after express consent is the release allowed, and then only in conformity with any conditions required in the consent (Article 6(8)). Article 7 allows for the introduction by means of a Commission decision of a simplified procedure for the release of GMOs with which sufficient experience has been gathered. Part B further contains rules on the consultation and information of the public (Article 9), reporting obligations (Article 10) and the exchange of information between the authorities and the Commission (Article 11).

Part C similarly envisages notification and consent for the placing on the market of products containing GMOs (Article 13). However, as the placing on the market has an effect on all the Member States, there is a procedure whereby the competent authority must forward the notification to the Commission and the competent authorities of the other Member States. Furthermore, in comparison with Part B additional information must be submitted, including information on the effects on the ecosystems which may be affected by the use of the product and on the packaging and labelling of the product (Article 13(2)). The competent authority must then prepare an assessment report that contains an indication whether the decision is going to be negative (no consent for marketing) or positive (consent for marketing). In case of a negative assessment, the report will be

---

[452] It may be noted that Annex I B is more restrictive compared to the corresponding Annex II, part A, of Directive 90/219.

sent to the notifier alone and the notification will be rejected in a reasoned decision (Article 14(2), first indent) in connection with Article 14(3(b) and Article
15(2)). Positive assessments must be forwarded to the Commission which shall
forward it to the other competent authorities (Article 14(2), second indent). The
other competent authorities and the Commission then have 60 days to raise
reasoned objections. If no such objections are raised in the 60-day period, the
competent authority shall give consent. In case of objections, the authorities and
Commission have an extra 45 days (in total 105 from the date of notification) to
resolve outstanding issues (Article 15(3)). If these issues are resolved, consent is
given.[453] When the issues are not resolved Article 18 provides for a Commission
decision within 120 days. If the Commission has taken a positive decision, the
competent authority that received the original notification will give its written
consent to the notification so that the product in question may be placed on the
market (Article 18(2)). Consent decisions should comply with the requirements
set out in Article 19(3) and may not be given for more than 10 years (Article
15(4). Article 19(3)(e) requires the labelling of the product to clearly state that it
contains genetically modified organisms. Once a product has received written
consent, the principle of mutual recognition laid down in Article 19(1) applies.
Moreover, the product benefits from a free movement clause (Article 22). It
may then be used without further notification throughout the EU, provided the
specific conditions of use and the environments and/or geographical areas stipu-
lated in these conditions are strictly adhered to. A list of all products receiving
final written consent is published in the Official Journal (Article 24(2)).[454] The
directive contains a procedure whereby lighter notification requirements may be
adopted (Article 16) and a renewal procedure (Article 17). This procedure is basically comparable to that set out in Articles 14 and 18. Notable differences are the
shorter time-limits and the fact that the consent maybe given for a longer period
(Article 17(6)). Notification for a renewal of consent does not stand in the way of
continued marketing in accordance with the conditions laid down in the original
consent (Article 17(9)).

---

[453] See on the procedure (Article 13) in the old Directive 90/220, Case C-6/99 *Association Greenpeace
France v. Ministère de l'Agriculture et de la Pêche* [2000] ECR I-1651. According to the Court this procedure is to be interpreted as meaning that, if, after an application for placing a GMO on the market
has been forwarded to the Commission, no Member State has raised an objection, in accordance with
Article 13(2) of that directive, or if the Commission has taken a favourable decision under paragraph (4)
of that provision, the competent authority which forwarded the application, with a favourable opinion,
to the Commission *must* issue the consent in writing, allowing the product to be placed on the market.
However, irregularities at the national level might have an effect on the legality of the Commission's
decision and subsequent decisions at national level implementing the Commission's decision.

[454] See for instance Commission Decision 98/292 concerning the placing on the market of genetically
modified maize (*Zea mays L. line Bt-11*), OJ 1998 L 131/28. Commission Decision 2007/364 concerning
the placing on the market of a carnation (*Dianthus caryophyllus L., line 123.2.38*) genetically modified for
flower colour, OJ 2007 L 138/50.

The free movement clause in the directive rules out more stringent measures. The directive does, however, contain a safeguard clause, by which Member States may provisionally restrict or prohibit the use or sale of such products where they nevertheless have justifiable reasons to consider that a product constitutes a risk to human health or the environment (Article 23).[455] The Commission must immediately be informed of such action and then has 60 days to take a decision on the matter. Member States may also invoke the procedure under Article 95(4) or (5) EC to maintain or introduce more stringent measures. In Decision 2003/653, the Commission rejected Austria's application for a derogation from Directive 2001/18 on the basis of Article 95(5).[456]

The directive further contains a requirement to produce reports (Article 31) and provisions on confidentiality (Article 25) and labelling (Article 26). Article 26a is the result of Regulation 1829/2003 on genetically modified food and feed and requires the Member States to take the necessary measures to avoid the unintentional presence of GMOs in other products.[457]

Regulation 1829/2003 is quite similar to Directive 2001/18 in that it also seeks to protect the environment, human health, animal welfare and consumer interests whilst ensuring the effective functioning of the internal market (Article 1(a)).[458] It must be read in conjunction with sister Regulation 1830/2003 on the traceability and labelling of GMOs[459] and the General Food Law Regulation.[460] Regulation 1829/2003 contains a chapter on genetically modified food (chapter II) and a chapter on genetically modified feed (chapter III). Genetically modified food and feed may not be placed on the market without an authorisation (Article 4(2)(food) and 16(2)(feed)). Such authorisation may only be granted if the applicant shows that the food or feed does not have adverse effects on human health, animal health or the environment, and mislead the consumer. Moreover, the food or feed must not differ from the food or feed it intends to replace to such an extent that this is nutritionally disadvantageous (Article 4(1) in connection with 4(1) and 16(3) in connection with 16(1)). The procedures for the authorisation of GM food and feed are comparable and similar to that laid down in Directive 2001/18. The procedure starts with an application for authorisation with the national competent authority. That competent authority will then inform the European Food Safety Authority (EFSA), which will in turn inform the other Member State's competent authorities and the Commission. The EFSA will then issue an opinion on the authorisation which may be positive or nega-

---

[455] See Case C-6/99 *Association Greenpeace France* v. *Ministère de l'Agriculture et de la Pêche* [2000] ECR I-1651.

[456] OJ 2003 L 230/34. An appeal against this decision was rejected in Joined Cases T-366/03 and T-235/04 *Land Oberösterreich and Republic of Austria* v. *Commission* [2005] ECR II-4005. Upheld by the ECJ in Case C-439/05P and C-454/05P, judgment of 13 September 2007, n.y.r. in the ECR.

[457] Regulation 1829/2003, OJ 2003 L 268/1, Article 43(2).

[458] OJ 2003 L 268/1.

[459] OJ 2003 L 268/24.

[460] Regulation 178/2002, OJ 2002 L 31/1.

tive (Articles 6 and 18). The Commission will then decide on the authorisation (Articles 7 and 19). Interestingly, the regulation explicitly provides that such authorisation shall not lessen the general civil and criminal liability of any food operator in respect of the food concerned (Articles 7(7) and 19(7)), which effectively rules out a permit-defence.[461] The regulation further contains a procedure for the renewal of existing authorisations on the basis of previous legislation (Articles 8 and 20) and renewals of authorisations granted on the basis of the regulation (Articles 11 and 23). Moreover there are provisions on the, supervision of the conditions imposed in the authorisation (Articles 9 and 21), the modification, suspension and revocation of authorisations (Articles 10 and 22). Finally, both chapters contain similar rules on labelling, which boil down to an obligation to clearly state that the food or feed contains or consists of genetically modified organisms (Articles 13 and 25). Such labelling is, however, not required if the presence of GMOs is below a certain threshold (0,9%) and this presence is adventitious or technically unavoidable (Articles 12(2) and 24(2)).[462] According to Articles 12(3) and 24(3) operators must be able to show that they have taken the necessary steps to ensure that the presence was adventitious. This implies that the authorisation should contain rules to minimise the chance of adventitious presence of GMOs (conditions or restrictions for use or handling; Article 7(5) in connection with Article 6(5)(e) and Article 19(5) in connection with Article 18(5)(e)). Chapter IV contains the common provisions on public access (Article 29) and confidentiality (Article 30). Concerning the latter it is interesting to see that it is much more comprehensive as regards the information that will always be public compared to Directive 2001/18.[463] This is odd given that Directive 2001/18 and Regulation 1829/2003 both concern the exposure of humans and the environment to GMOs. The provision on data protection (Article 31) is similarly interesting when compared to the REACH Regulation. It may be recalled that the REACH Regulation contains a procedure for the mandatory sharing of animal test results,[464] whereas Article 31 explicitly provides for the protection of the test data, which may also include results of animal tests. Furthermore, the safeguard procedure in the General Food Law Regulation is declared applicable (Article 34), various regulations are repealed (Article 37) and a number of Regulations and Directives are amended.[465] Finally, the regulation contains information on the application of the Cartagena Protocol (Article 44) and transitional measures (Articles 46 and 47).

The third and final panel in the triptych is formed by Regulation 1946/2003 on the transboundary movements of GMOs.[466] This Regulation implements the

---

[461] See the discussion in section 8 of this chapter.

[462] See, however, Article 47 for transitional rules in this regard.

[463] In fact the list in Article 25(4) of Directive 2001/18 is more like that in Article 19(3) of Directive 90/219 on the contained use.

[464] See above, section 13.1.

[465] Notably Directive 2001/18, see above in this paragraph.

[466] OJ 2003 L 287/1.

Cartagena Protocol on Biosafety[467] by regulating the transboundary movements of GMOs that may have adverse effects on the conservation and sustainable use of biological diversity, also taking into account human health (Article 1). The regulation applies without prejudice to Directive 2001/18. The regulation distinguishes between exports (Chapter II) and unintentional transboundary movements (Chapter III) of GMOs. The former are subdivided into GMOs intended for deliberate release and GMOs intended for direct use as food, feed or for processing. GMOs intended for deliberate release are subject to a prior informed consent (PIC)-procedure, whereby express written consent of the importing country is required (Article 5(1)). The parties to the Cartagena Protocol may agree on a lighter procedure for categories of GMOs which would then be subject to an exception (Article 8). For GMOs intended for direct use as food, feed or for processing the PIC procedure in Article 10 applies. GMOs intended for contained use are not subject to the PIC procedure, provided that the transboundary movements comply with the national standards of the importing country (Article 11(1)). Article 12 lays down the rules for identification and documentation. Chapter III on unintentional transboundary movements is quite short. It only contains a general duty on the part of the Member States to take appropriate measures to prevent unintentional movements (Article 14(1) and a procedure for the information of the public and consultation of the affected or potentially affected Member States. Chapter IV contains the procedure for participation in the international information procedure set up under the Cartagena Protocol (Article 15) as well as provisions on confidentiality (Article 16). The latter rules are comparable to those under Directive 2001/18.

15 Legislation on Waste

European waste law has been described as 'strangely engaging'[468] and has even resulted in a former ECJ judge expressing his amazement at the judicial effort put into defining the concept of 'waste'.[469] Central to European waste law is the Waste Framework Directive.[470] It defines central concepts such as 'waste', contains a general duty to ensure waste is treated in an environmentally friendly fashion and provides for detailed measures concerning specific types of waste.[471] There are a number of directives that deal with specific waste streams and methods of treating waste, such as:

---

[467] Article 1 and recital 3 of the preamble to Regulation 1946/2003. The Cartagena Protocol was concluded on behalf of the Community by Decision 2002/628, OJ 2002 L 201/48, See also Opinion 2/00 [2001] ECR I-9713.

[468] Lee (2000) at 213.

[469] Former judge Kapteyn, as cited by Tieman (2003) at 5.

[470] Directive 2006/12, OJ 2006 L 114/9.

[471] See, on the framework character, Case C-252/05 *Thames Water*, judgment of 10 May 2007, n.y.r. in the ECR, para. 39.

· packaging waste;
· waste electrical and electronic equipment;
· waste incineration;
· landfill of waste.

Finally, there is a regulation on shipments of waste. Below we will first examine the Waste Framework Directive. Then we will look at some of the directives dealing with specific waste streams and methods of waste treatment. Finally, we will look at the Waste Shipments Regulation.

15.1   The Waste Framework Directive

15.1.1   The Concept of Waste

Directive 2006/12, the Waste Framework Directive, codifies and repeals Directive 75/442 and lays down general rules that apply to all categories of waste.[472] Central to this directive and the rest of European waste law is the concept of 'waste'. 'Waste' is defined as any substance or object in the categories set out in Annex I 'which the holder discards or intends or is required to discard' (Article 1(a)). Article 2 excludes a number of categories from the scope of the directive, such as gaseous effluents emitted into the atmosphere (Article 2(1)(a)). This is particularly interesting in connection with the implementation of the Kyoto Protocol, where so-called carbon capture is contemplated. This means that carbon dioxide is filtered out, compressed and possibly sold or (permanently) stored underground, which would make it waste within the meaning of the directive.[473] Article 2(1)(b) contains an exception for categories of waste covered by other legislation.[474] The reference in Article 1(a) to Annex I is not really helpful in determining what is waste. Annex I lists 16 specific categories of waste[475] and concludes with category Q16 referring to 'Any materials, substances

---

[472] Directive 2006/12, OJ 2006 L 114/9. This directive repeals with effect from 17 May 2006 Directive 75/442, OJ 1975 L 194/47 as amended by Directive 91/156, OJ 1991 L 78/32. A further going revision is proposed by Commission proposal COM (2005) 667. This proposal will integrate the Framework Directive with the Hazardous Waste Directive and the Waste Oils Directive. See for a discussion: Pocklington (2006).

[473] Subject to the exception for non-waste by-products, see below in this section.

[474] The directive only refers to other legislation, but the ECJ has made it clear in Case C-114/01 *AvestaPolarit Chrome* [2003] ECR I-8725, that it refers to Community legislation and national legislation implementing the Framework Directive (paras. 44-53). This was confirmed in Cases C-416/02 *Commission v. Spain* [2005] ECR I-7487, para. 99 and C-121/03 *Commission v. Spain* [2005] ECR I-7569, para. 69. Case C-252/05 *Thames Water*, judgment of 10 May 2007, n.y.r. in the ECR, paras. 33, 34 adds to this the requirement that such legislation must contain precise obligations concerning waste management and offer a level of protection at least equivalent to that resulting from the Waste Framework Directive.

[475] Q4, for example, relates to materials spilled including materials contaminated as a result of the mishap. See concerning the classification as waste of leaked hydrocarbons and the contaminated soil Case C-1/03

or products which are not contained in the abovementioned categories.' A literal interpretation of Q16 would thus mean that all substances should be regarded as waste! This is obviously not what is intended. But what then is the exact meaning of 'waste'? The Court of Justice has addressed this point on numerous occasions.[476] First we shall consider the case law of the Court before Directive 75/442 was amended by Directive 91/156. As the definition of waste has not changed with the entry into force of Directive 2006/12, these judgments are still relevant.

In *Vessoso and Zanetti*, the competent Italian court, the Pretura di Asti, referred to the Court for a preliminary ruling on whether the concept of waste was to be understood as excluding substances and objects which are capable of economic reutilisation.[477] The Court held that it was clear from the preambles to the directive and from various of its provisions that a substance of which its holder disposes may constitute waste within the meaning of the directive even when it is capable of economic reutilisation.

The second part of the Pretura's question sought to ascertain whether the concept of waste presumes that a holder disposing of a substance or an object intends to exclude all economic reutilisation of the subject or object by others. The Court observed that the directive referred generally to any substance or object of which the holder disposes, and draws no distinction 'according to the intentions of the holder disposing thereof'. Moreover, the provision specified that waste also includes substances or objects which the holder 'is required to dispose of pursuant to the provisions of national law in force'. The essential aim of the directive, namely the protection of human health and the safeguarding of the environment, would have been jeopardized if the application of the directive was dependent on whether or not the holder intended to exclude all economic reutilisation by others of the substances or objects of which he disposes. The Court concluded that the concept of waste does not presume that the holder disposing of a substance or an object intends to exclude all economic reutilisation of the substance or object by others.[478]

In *Tombesi* the Court ruled that this interpretation is not affected by the amendments of Directive 91/156.[479] The system of supervision and control established by the directive is intended to cover all objects and substances discarded by their owners, even if they have a commercial value and are collected on a commercial

---

Van der Walle [2004] ECR I-7613. See also Case C-252/05 *Thames Water*, judgment of 10 May 2007, n.y.r. in the ECR, on leaked sewage water as waste, para. 28, 29.

[476] See for some Dutch case law Tieman (2003).

[477] Joined Cases C-206 and C-207/88 *Vessoso and Zanetti* [1990] ECR I-1461. Confirmed in Case C-422/92 *Commission* v. *Germany* [1995] ECR I-1097.

[478] To some extent this decision was confirmed in the *Walloon Waste* case where the Court decided that waste, whether or not capable of recycling, was covered by rules on the free movement of goods, Case C-2/90 *Commission* v. *Belgium* [1992] ECR I-4431.

[479] Joined Cases C-304/94, C-330/94, C-342/94 and C-224/95 *Tombesi a.o.* [1997] ECR I-3561, para. 48.

basis for recycling, reclamation or re-use. The objectives of the directive still provide a guiding principle for its interpretation.[480]

However, one major problem remains: it is still not clear what is the correct interpretation of 'to discard'. In *Inter-Environment* the Court acknowledged that that the scope of the term 'waste' turns on the meaning of the term 'discard'.[481] The Court observed:

'It is also clear from the provisions of Directive 75/442, as amended, in particular from Article 4, Articles 8 to 12 and Annexes IIA and IIB, that the term 'discard' covers both disposal and recovery of a substance or object. As the Advocate General has pointed out in paragraphs 58 to 61 of his Opinion, the list of categories of waste in Annex I to Directive 75/442, as amended, and the disposal and recovery operations listed in Annexes IIA and IIB to that directive demonstrate that the concept of waste does not in principle exclude any kind of residue, industrial by-product or other substance arising from production processes. This finding is further supported by the list of waste drawn up by the Commission in Decision 94/3[482].'

The reference to the disposal and recovery operations listed in Annexes IIA and IIB seems to suggest that they are indicative in this respect.[483] However, the mere fact that something undergoes one of the treatments listed in the Annexes do not necessarily mean any substance treated accordingly has to regarded as waste being discarded, as the Court made perfectly clear in *ARCO Chemie*.[484] Nor is it decisive if substances, without any further significant processing, can be used as fuel under environmental sound conditions.[485] Although indicative, this does not necessarily exclude a substance of being waste.

---

[480] Joined Cases C-418/97 and C-419/97 *ARCO Chemie Nederland* [2000] ECR I-4475, para. 37. See, however, on the precise nature of these objectives and how this relates to the Court's jurisprudence Scotford (2007).

[481] Case C-129/96 *Inter-Environnement Wallonie ASBL v. Waals Gewest* [1997] ECR I-7411. Confirmed in Joined Cases C-418/97 and C-419/97 *ARCO Chemie Nederland* [2000] ECR I-4475. Cf. also English High Court 9 November 1998 *Mayer Parry Recycling v. Environment Agency* [1999] Env. L.R. 489 in which Carnwath J stated that the term 'discard' encompasses not only the disposal of waste but also its consignment to a recovery operation.

[482] Footnote by the authors: as required by Article 1(a), the Commission has drawn up a list of wastes, the 'European Waste Catalogue' (EWC). This is however no means an exhaustive list. The current EWC is to be found in Decision 2000/532, OJ 2000 L 226/3, as amended by Decision 2001/537, OJ 2001 L 203/18. According to Case C-194/01 *Commission v. Austria* [2004] ECR I-4579, paras. 44-48) the EWC does not have to be literally transposed in national law.

[483] See on the so-called 'Euro Tombesi Bypass' Van Calster (2000) 165-169.

[484] Joined Cases C-418/97 and C-419/97 *ARCO Chemie Nederland* [2000] ECR I-4475, para. 49. See on the interpretation of some aspects of Annex II A, Joined Cases C-175/98 en C-177/98 *Lirussi and Bizzaro* [1999] ECR I-6881.

[485] Joined Cases C-418/97 and C-419/97 *ARCO Chemie Nederland* [2000] ECR I-4475, para. 72.

Particularly in connection with so-called by-products there has recently been considerable judicial activity.[486] This relates to the fact that the directive contains what has been called two layers of prevention.[487] The first layer tries to prevent waste from being produced in the first place (Article 3(1)(a)). The second (regulatory) layer tries to prevent environmental damage from occurring once waste has been produced (Article 3(1)(b)). The first layer would thus result in a concept of waste that excludes by-products that can be used, so as to avoid the interference that results from the application of waste legislation. The second layer, however, would lead to a very wide concept of waste and thus a wide scope of waste legislation to ensure that such by-products do not harm the environment. This difficulty also ties in rather nicely with the rather thin line that is tread when distinguishing between the recovery (Annex IIB) of waste and normal use of a (secondary) raw material.[488] In *ARCO Chemie* the Court held that the fact that something is a production residue, i.e. a product not in itself sought, is an indication that the holder intends to discard it, thus making it waste.[489] In *Saetti* the Court further clarified when something is a production residue. This case concerned petroleum coke, which is one of the substances resulting from the refining of crude oil, that was used to fire a power plant. The Court held that since the production of the petroleum coke was the result of a technical choice, it was not a production residue.[490] Moreover, even in the absence of a technical choice the Court classified the petroleum cokes as one of the many fuels intended to be produced in the refining process and thus excluded it from the definition of waste if its use a fuel is certain.

In *Palin Granit* and *AvestaPolarit*, the ECJ further refined the distinction between production residues (waste) and non-waste by-products. In *Palin Granit* the basic question was whether the irregularly shaped granite blocks that are produced when quarrying for large granite blocks were to be regarded as waste (a production residue, see Q1 of Annex I) or by-products that the owner does not want to discard but simply stores for sale at a later time. The Court held that the production residues will not constitute waste depending on the degree of likelihood of their reuse without any further processing. Moreover the reuse must be lawful.[491] The likelihood of certainty that a residue will be reused increases if

---

[486] See Commission interpretative communication on waste and by-products, COM (2007) 59 final, where the Commission sets out its interpretation of the Court's case law; see, however, footnote 2 of the communication.

[487] Scotford (2007) at 8.

[488] See the opinion of A-G Jacobs in Joined Cases C-304/94, C-330/94, C-342/94 and C-224/95 *Tombesi a.o.* [1997] ECR I-3561, para. 54.

[489] Joined Cases C-418/97 and C-419/97 *ARCO Chemie Nederland* [2000] ECR I-4475, para. 84.

[490] Order in Case C-235/02 [2004] ECR I-1005, para. 45.

[491] Case C-114/01 *AvestaPolarit Chrome* [2003] ECR I-8725, para. 43. The lawfulness can also follow from national law, see Case C-121/03 *Commission* v. *Spain* [2005] ECR I-7569, para. 65, where the ECJ refers to the Good Agricultural Practice laid down by the Spanish authorities.

there is a financial advantage in doing so.[492] Production residues will therefore not constitute waste if they meet the following four cumulative conditions[493]

· further use of the residues must be certain;
· further use must be allowed by national and European law;
· further use must take place without any further processing;
· this further processing must be an integral part of the production process.

Thus, if the reuse is not certain and will only occur after an indefinite period the leftover stone constitutes waste for the duration of that storage. The rationale behind this is that the directive also seeks to protect the environment from the nuisance arising from the storage of the leftover stone.[494] This exception for non-waste by-products does not apply to consumption residues, unless they are second-hand goods that will certainly be reused in a similar manner without prior processing.[495] From *Palin Granit* it is clear that a substance may constitute waste until it is reused. That brings us to the end of the classification of a substance as waste. The Court has elucidated this point in *Mayer Parry*. This case concerned a scrap metal recycling company that basically sorts, cleans and shreds metal packaging waste and then sells it to steelmakers. Mayer Parry wanted to be officially recognised as reprocessor. This would require its process to be brought under the heading of recycling within the meaning of the Packaging Waste Directive.[496] The Court thus defined recycling as meaning that the reprocessing of packaging waste must enable new material or a new product possessing characteristics comparable to those of the material from which the waste was derived to be obtained.[497] According to the Court the recycling process was only completed when the steelmakers turned the scrap metal into new metal sheets that could be used in the packaging industry etc. Applied to the *Palin Granit* case this means the granite blocks would cease to be waste only when they would actually be used in, for example, dyke reinforcement works.

Whatever the correct interpretation of the concept of waste may be, it should be noted that, as the directive in its present form is based on Article 175 EC, it does not prevent Member States from extending the meaning of waste!

---

[492] Case C-9/00 *Palin Granit* [2002] ECR I-3533, para. 37.

[493] See also cases C-416/02 *Commission v. Spain* [2005] ECR I-7487, para. 88 and C-121/03 *Commission v. Spain* [2005] ECR I-7569, para. 58. For a critical analysis see: Scotford (2007).

[494] Case C-9/00 *Palin Granit* [2002] ECR I-3533, paras. 36-39. See also C-114/01 *AvestaPolarit Chrome* [2003] ECR I-8725, paras. 36-38.

[495] Case C-457/02 *Niselli* [2004] ECR I-10853, paras. 48, 49.

[496] These findings also hold for the Waste Framework Directive, Case C-444/00 *Mayer Parry* [2003] ECR I-6163, para. 93.

[497] Case C-444/00 *Mayer Parry* [2003] ECR I-6163, para. 73.

15.1.2   Obligations for the Member States

Article 3 contains the so-called waste hierarchy and requires Member States to take appropriate measures to encourage:
- the prevention or reduction of waste production and its harmfulness, for instance by the development of clean technologies;
- the recovery of waste by means of recycling, reuse or reclamation or any process with a view to extracting secondary raw materials, or the use of waste as a source of energy.[498]

The waste hierarchy makes waste prevention the first objective, followed by recovery of waste. Disposal of waste should be the last option. The distinction between recovery and disposal of waste has important consequences for the regime applicable to shipments of waste. Moreover, both categories are mutually exclusive.[499] Furthermore, also the distinction between recovery and disposal is fraught with definitional difficulties. What, for example, is the distinction between incineration (D10 or D11 of Annex IIA) and use as a fuel (R1 of Annex IIB)?[500] In *ASA*, the Court stated that the essential characteristic of a waste recovery operation is that its principal objective is that the waste serves a useful purpose in replacing other materials which would have had to be used for that purpose, thereby conserving natural resources.[501] Prior treatment before the waste is put to its useful purpose is not required for the classification as recovery, as is the possibility to reclaim or subsequently reuse the waste. In a later case the Court applied this rule to the distinction between incineration and use as fuel. The Court held that the combustion of waste constitutes a recovery operation where its principal objective is that the waste can fulfil a useful function as a means of generating energy, replacing the use of a source of primary energy which would have had to have been used to fulfil that function.[502] The effect of this has been that most municipal waste incinerators, including some that were designed to produce energy and thus function as recovery installations, were classified as disposal facilities. This in turn means that incineration is put

---

[498] The *Balsamo* case made clear that a provision like Article 3 of the directive does not prohibit a municipal prohibition of the sale of non-biodegradable plastic bags; Case 380/87 *Balsamo* [1989] ECR 2491.

[499] Case C-6/00 *ASA* [2002] ECR I-1961, paras. 62, 63.

[500] E.g. Case C-228/00 *Commission* v. *Germany* [2003] ECR I-1439, paras. 38 and 39 where the Commission and Germany share this difference of opinion.

[501] Case C-6/00 *ASA* [2002] ECR I-1961, para. 69, confirmed in Joined Cases C-307/00 to C-311/00 *Oliehandel Koeweit* [2003] ECR I-1821, para. 87.

[502] Case C-228/00 *Commission* v. *Germany* [2003] ECR I-1439, para. 46. As a result the calorific value of waste was abandoned. Instead the classification turns on the following three criteria: energy generation, combustion should create more energy than is consumed (energy surplus) that should effectively be used and the greater part of the waste must be consumed and the greater part of the energy used.

– in terms of the waste hierarchy – on equal footing with landfilling, which is cheaper but environmentally less advantageous.[503]

Article 4 requires Member States to ensure that waste is recovered or disposed of without endangering human health and without using processes or methods which could harm the environment (water, air, soil, plants and animals) or causing a nuisance through odours or noise or adversely affecting the countryside or places of special interest.[504] The abandonment, dumping or uncontrolled disposal of waste must be prohibited. Article 4 is however not directly effective.[505] In the light of the *Lombardia* case it was not easy to see what status, if any, the objectives of Article 4 might have.[506] However, some clarification on this point has been given by the Court in the Case C-387/97 and the *San Rocco* case.[507] In Case C-387/97 the Court ruled that the obligations flowing from Article 4 were 'independent' of the more specific obligations contained in the directive. And in Case C-365/97 the Court ruled that whether Article 4 of the directive imposes obligations on Member States must be separated from the question of whether the provisions have direct effect and may be relied upon directly by individuals as against the State. The Court went on by stating that whilst Article 4 does not specify the actual content of the measures which must be taken in order to ensure that waste is disposed of without endangering human health and without harming the environment, it is nonetheless true that it is binding on the Member States as to the objective to be achieved, whilst leaving to the Member States a margin of discretion in assessing the need for such measures. If a situation is not in conformity with the objectives laid down in Article 4 and if that situation persists and leads in particular to a significant deterioration in the environment over a protracted period without any action being taken by the competent authorities, it may be an indication that the Member States have exceeded the discretion conferred on them by that provision. Although Article 4 is not directly effective it imposes certain legal obligations on the Member States anyway.

Of great importance are the self-sufficiency and proximity principles embodied in Article 5. Member States are required to establish an integrated and adequate network of disposal installations.[508] The network must enable the EU

---

[503] See in this connection section 15.4 below on the Packaging Waste Directive and section 15.8 on the Landfill Directive.

[504] Cf. on the question of applicability of Article 4 and temporary storage of waste, Joined Cases C-175/98 and C-177/98 *Lirussi and Bizarro* [1999] ECR I-6881, para. 54.

[505] Case C-236/92 *Comitato di coordinamento per la difesa della Cava* v. *Regione Lombardia* [1994] ECR I-485.

[506] Cf. English Court of Appeal 5 May 1998 *Regina* v. *Bolton Metropolitan Council*, ex parte *Kirkman* [1998] *Journal of Planning and Environment Law* 787.

[507] Case C-387/97 *Commission* v. *Greece* [2000] ECR I-5047 and Case C-365/97 *Commission* v. *Italy (San Rocco)* [1999] ECR I-7773. See further Case C-135/05 *Commission* v. *Italy*, judgment of 26 April 2007, n.y.r. in the ECR and Case C-494/01 *Commission* v. *Ireland* [2005] ECR I-3331 in connection with a general and persistent infringement.

[508] See on this provision Joined Cases C-53/02 and C-217/02 *Commune de Braine-le-Château a.o.* [2004] ECR I-3251 and Case C-494/01 *Commission* v. *Ireland* [2005] ECR I-3331, paras. 149-158.

as a whole to become self-sufficient in waste disposal and the Member States to move towards that aim individually (Article 5(1)). The network must also enable waste to be disposed of in one of the nearest appropriate installations (Article 5(2)). The text of Article 5 does not indicate precisely how the two principles should operate together. It may be noted in this connection that Article 5 apparently implies a minor contradiction. Article 5(1) requires Member States to move towards self-sufficiency, whereas in Article 5(2) emphasis is on the proximity principle. Where the nearest waste disposal installations are situated in another country, the two principles clash. In response to questions in the European Parliament, the Commission has observed that the proximity principle should not be applied too strictly or absolutely. It must be interpreted flexibly, taking account of geographical circumstances and the need for specialised installations for certain types of waste. The Commission expressly acknowledged that specific shipments of waste may not be in conformity with the principle of proximity.[509] In the *Dusseldorp* case the Court ruled that the principles of self-sufficiency and proximity could not be applied to waste for recovery.[510] And in its Resolution of 7 May 1990 on waste policy[511] the Council specified that the objective of self-sufficiency in waste disposal does not apply to recycling.

It appears there is also a Declaration of the Council and the Commission on the interpretation of Article 5, which is reportedly attached to the minutes of the directive.[512] It states that the Council and the Commission agree that the reference to the fact that Member States must move towards self-sufficiency individually may not form an impediment to collaboration between the Member States, nor to the possibility of a Member State disposing of its waste in another Member State or disposing of another Member State's waste, if the geographic circumstances and the need for specialised installations for certain types of waste justify it. Though such declarations are not legally binding,[513] this declaration does lend support to the view that the self-sufficiency principle and the proximity principle should not be taken too literally. In any case, the directive has to be interpreted in the light of the Treaty provisions concerning the free movement of goods.[514]

Article 7 requires Member States to draw up waste management plans.[515] Legislation or specific measures amounting only to a series of ad hoc normative interventions that are incapable of constituting an organised and coordi-

---

[509] OJ 1994 C 32/8; cf. also OJ 1993 C 6/37-38.

[510] Case C-203/96 *Dusseldorp* [1998] ECR I-4075, para. 30.

[511] OJ 1990 C 122/2.

[512] Hannequart (1993).

[513] Case 429/85 *Commission* v. *Italy* [1988] ECR 843.

[514] In this regard recital 10 to Directive 2006/12 is particularly interesting. See Further Case 172/82 *Inter-Huiles* [1983] ECR 555. Confirmed in Case C-341/95 *Gianni Bettati* [1998] ECR I-4355. See further Chapter 6 and particularly the remarks made on Case C-203/96 *Dusseldorp* [1998] ECR I-4075.

[515] See on Article 7 (in connection with Article 9) Joined Cases C-53/02 and C-217/02 *Commune de Braine-le-Château a.o.* [2004] ECR I-3251.

nated system for the disposal of waste cannot be regarded as plans under the directive.[516] Movements of waste which are not in accordance with these waste management plans must be prevented (Article 7(4)).[517] Undertakings which carry out waste disposal operations or operations which may lead to recovery of waste must obtain a permit from the competent authority (Articles 9 and 10).[518] Exemptions may be granted in certain cases (Article 11) and subject to conditions,[519] for example for undertakings which carry out their own waste disposal at the place of production (Article 11(1)(a)).

The directive further contains provisions on reporting to the Commission (Article 16), periodic inspections (Article 13),[520] record-keeping by undertakings (Article 14) and on the cost of disposing of waste (Article 15). The latter provides that, in accordance with the polluter pays principle, the cost of disposing of waste must be borne by:

· the holder who has waste handled by a waste collector and/or;
· the previous holders or the producer of the product from which the waste came.

In the *Traen* case, various questions of interpretation arose in criminal actions against three operators of waste-disposal undertakings and a driver.[521] They were charged with infringing the Flemish law by discharging waste in fields without being in possession of a permit. Though the case concerned Directive 75/442 before its amendment by Directive 91/156, the questions addressed are nevertheless still relevant.

The first question was about whom the directive precisely applied to. The Court answered this question in the light of the primary objective of the directive, namely the protection of human health and the environment. This objective would in any event be endangered if the application of measures for the control and supervision of such activities were to be conditional upon distinctions based on criteria such as the company objects of the undertaking, whether the disposal of waste is a main or subsidiary activity or the foreseeable impact on the environment. The Court concluded that any operator engaging in any of the activities referred to in Articles 8 to 12 of Directive 75/442 is subject to the measures provided for in those provisions.

The second question concerned the role and the position of the owner or occupier of the land on which the waste is tipped. Article 8 (currently Article

---

[516] Case C-387/97 *Commission* v. *Greece* [2000] ECR I-5047, para. 76.

[517] See on this provision Case C-209/98 *Sydhavnens* [2000] ECR I-3743, para. 92.

[518] See on these provisions Case C-494/01 *Commission* v. *Ireland* [2005] ECR I-3331, where the Court also links the failure to actually apply and enforce the permit requirement (Articles 9 and 10 of the directive, see para. 118) to an infringement of Article 4 (paras. 169-176).

[519] See on the requirement to fix maximum thresholds Case C-103/02 *Commission* v. *Italy* [2004] ECR I-9127, paras. 26-35.

[520] See on these provisions Case C-494/01 *Commission* v. *Ireland* [2005] ECR I-3331, paras. 190-192.

[521] Joined Cases 372-374/85 *Traen* [1987] ECR 2141.

10) of the directive states that 'any installation or undertaking treating, storing or tipping waste on behalf of third parties must obtain a permit from the competent authority'. The Court ruled that the permit cannot be replaced by the consent of the owner or occupier of the land where the waste is discharged.

As far as the designation by the Member States of the authority competent to issue permits is concerned, the directive does not lay down any restrictive criteria, and the Member States are therefore unrestricted in their choice of such authorities.

The Court's observations on the original Article 10 of the directive are also interesting. The question at issue was whether the Member States enjoyed a discretionary power under this article. The article provided that:

> 'Undertakings transporting, collecting, storing, tipping or treating their own waste and those which collect or transport waste on behalf of third parties shall be subject to supervision by the competent authority referred to in Article 5.'

The Court held that that provision 'does not therefore lay down any particular requirement restricting the freedom of the Member States regarding the way in which they organize the supervision of the activities referred to therein'. That freedom must, however, be exercised having due regard to the objective of the directive, namely the protection of human health and of the environment.[522]

15.2   The Hazardous Waste Directive

Directive 91/689 specifically addresses *hazardous* waste.[523] Where the directive does not depart from the Waste Framework Directive, discussed above, that directive also applies to hazardous waste. The directive applies to all wastes featuring on a list of hazardous waste.[524] These are wastes which have one or more of a number of properties listed in Annex III to the directive ('explosive', 'carcinogenic', 'mutagenic' etc.). In the *Fornasar* case the Court ruled that that the decisive criterion, as regards the definition of 'hazardous waste, is whether the waste displays one or more of the properties listed in Annex III to the directive.[525]

---

[522] See also Case C-270/03 *Commission* v. *Italy* [2005] ECR I-5233, on Article 12 of Directive 75/442.

[523] OJ 1991 L 377/20, as amended by Directive 94/31, OJ 1994 L 168/28.

[524] Council Decision 94/904 establishing a list of hazardous waste pursuant to Article 4(1) of Council Directive 91/689 on hazardous waste, OJ 1994 L 356/14. Cf. de Sadeleer & Sambon (1997). Decision 94/904 has now been replaced by Decision 2000/532, OJ 2000 L 226/3, as amended by Decision 2001/537, OJ 2001 L 203/18.

[525] Case C-318/98 *Fornasar* [2000] ECR I-4785, para. 56.

Apart from wastes which have been placed on the list, Member States may designate any other waste which they consider to display such properties as hazardous waste.[526]

The directive contains numerous additional, more stringent provisions aimed specifically at hazardous waste. For example:
- · it requires that every site where hazardous waste is tipped is recorded and identified (Article 2(1));
- · hazardous waste and non-hazardous waste may, in principle, not be mixed (Article 2(2));
- · mixing may be allowed only subject to certain conditions (Article 2(3));
- · the derogation from the permit requirement referred to in Article 11 of the Waste Framework Directive does not apply to hazardous waste (Article 3);
- · stricter requirements apply to the preservation of records (Article 4);
- · it requires the proper packaging and labelling of hazardous waste (Article 5).

In addition, it requires Member States to draw up plans for the management of hazardous waste, which may either be separate or integrated in their general waste management plans (Article 6).

Article 7 contains a fairly broadly defined safeguard clause: in cases of emergency or grave danger, Member States shall take all necessary steps, including, where appropriate, temporary derogations from this directive, to ensure that hazardous waste is so dealt with as not to constitute a threat to the population or the environment. It may be recalled that the Court held in *Fornasar* that Directive 91/689 allows the Member States to introduce more stringent protective measures, in particular to classify any other waste as hazardous waste.[527] Finally, COM (2005) 667 intends to repeal the Hazardous Waste Directive and integrate it in a new Waste Framework Directive.

15.3 Waste Oils

Because of the environmental hazards involved in the disposal of waste oils, the Council adopted specific rules on the subject in Directive 75/439.[528] This requires Member States to take the necessary measures to ensure that waste oils are collected and disposed of without causing any avoidable damage to man and the environment. In this connection the directive expresses a preference for the processing of waste oils by regeneration rather than by

---

[526] The hazardous waste list does not prevent the Member States from classifying as hazardous waste other than that featuring on the list, Case C-318/98 *Fornasar* [2000] ECR I-4785, para. 51.

[527] Case C-318/98 *Fornasar* [2000] ECR I-4785. In that event, the Member States are bound to notify such cases to the Commission for review in accordance with the procedure laid down in Article 18 of Directive 75/442, now Article 19 of Directive 2006/12.

[528] OJ 1975 L 194/31, as most recently amended by Directive 2000/76, OJ 2000 L 332/91.

combustion (Article 3).[529] The Court has repeatedly held that this priority for regeneration is to be taken seriously. Studies undertaken to examine the feasibility of such regeneration are allowed, provided that they lead to tangible steps.[530] Moreover, problems envisaged with the economic viability of the regeneration do not justify a departure from the priority for regeneration as such problems could be overcome by the Member States objection against shipments of waste oils.[531]

Under Article 4, Member States are required to take the necessary measures to ensure the prohibition of:

· any discharge of waste oils into inland surface water, ground water, territorial sea water and drainage systems;
· any deposit and/or discharge of waste oils harmful to the soil and any uncontrolled discharge of residues resulting from the processing of waste oils;
· any processing of waste oils causing air pollution which exceeds the level prescribed by existing provisions.

Any undertaking which disposes of waste oils is required to obtain a permit, which may only be granted when all appropriate environmental and health protection measures have been taken, including use of the best technology available, where the cost is not excessive (Article 6).[532] Under Article 5(2), Member States allocate zones within which one or more undertakings carry out the collection and/or disposal of waste oils.[533] In the *ADBHU* case the Court ruled that national legislation imposing a system of permits on undertakings which disposed of waste oils and a system of zones within which such undertakings had to operate is not incompatible with European law.[534] However, in the *Inter-Huiles* case the Court ruled that the directive does not automatically authorize the Member States to establish barriers to exports and ruled against French legislation which required that waste oils should be delivered to approved French disposal undertakings.

The directive requires Member States to lay down conditions for the regeneration of waste oils (Article 7) and to take measures to prevent air pollution caused by the combustion of waste oils (Article 8); it prohibits the mixing of waste oils with PCBs and PCTs (Article 10), and requires establishments producing, collecting and/or disposing of more than a given quantity (500 litres) of waste oils per year to keep records (Article 11).

---

[529] See on Member States obligations to take measures necessary to give priority to the processing of waste oils by regeneration, Case C-102/97 *Commission v. Germany* [1999] ECR I-5051.

[530] Case C-424/02 *Commission v UK* [2004] ECR I-7249, para. 25.

[531] Case C-92/03 *Commission v. Portugal* [2005] ECR I-867, paras. 33-36. See section 15.7 below on the shipments of waste.

[532] See on these permits Case C-392/99 *Commission v. Portugal* [2003] ECR I-3373, paras. 77 and further.

[533] Case 172/82 *Inter-Huiles* [1983] ECR 555. See also Chapter 7, sections 6.1 and 6.2. This ruling was confirmed in Case C-37/92 *Vanacker* [1993] ECR I-4947.

[534] Case 240/83 *ADBHU* [1985] ECR 531. See on this case also Chapter 1, section 1.

The financial provisions (Articles 14 and 15) are interesting.[535] As a reciprocal concession for the obligations imposed on them by the Member States pursuant to Article 5, collection and/or disposal undertakings may be granted indemnities for the service rendered. These indemnities may be financed by a charge imposed on products which after use are transformed into waste oils (Article 15).

More stringent protective measures are allowed by virtue of Article 16, whereby the prohibition of the combustion of waste oils is explicitly mentioned. This provision, which was not in the original text but added later, must be regarded as superfluous. The Court had already acknowledged the Member States' power to prohibit the combustion of waste oils in 1985.[536] COM (2005) 667 intends to repeal the Waste Oils Directive and to integrate it into a new Waste Framework Directive. This proposal envisages the abolition of the strict priority for regeneration.

15.4   Packaging and Waste Packaging

Prevention is the important theme of Directive 94/62 on packaging and packaging waste.[537] This directive aims to harmonise national measures concerning the management of packaging and packaging waste in order, on the one hand, to prevent any impact thereof on the environment and, on the other hand, to ensure the functioning of the internal market and to avoid obstacles to trade and distortion and restriction of competition within the EU. In the light of this clearly dual objective,[538] the fact that the Council based the directive solely on Article 100a (now Article 95) of the Treaty seems slightly odd. In view of the judgment in the TiO_2 case, it would have been more logical for it to have been based both on Article 100a (now Article 95) and on Article 130s (now Article 175).[539] The first priority of the directive is the prevention of the production of packaging waste (Article 1(2)). Reusing packaging, recycling and other forms of recovering packaging waste and, hence, reducing the final disposal of such waste are regarded as additional fundamental principles.[540]

The directive covers all packaging placed on the market in the EU and all packaging waste, whether it is used or released at industrial, commercial, office, shop, service, household or any other level, regardless of the material used (Article 2(1)). In addition to the general obligation contained in Article 4, requiring the Member States to take the necessary preventive measures, the directive lays down a number of more concrete requirements. On the subject of

---

[535] See Case 172/82 *Inter-Huiles* [1983] ECR 555, as discussed in Chapter 3 section 2 and 6 and Chapter 7, sections 6.1 and 6.2.

[536] Case 240/83 *ADBHU* [1985] ECR 531.

[537] OJ 1994 L 365, as amended by Directive 2005/20, OJ 2005 L 70/17.

[538] Cf. Case C-463/01 *Commission v. Germany* [2004] ECR I-11705, para. 37.

[539] See Chapter 2, section 4.

[540] See on the legal importance of a such hierarchy of principles Van Calster (2000) at 196-197.

recovery and recycling,[541] it provides that, within five years of the date by which the directive must be implemented, between 50% as a minimum and 65% as a maximum by weight of the packaging waste must be recovered or incinerated with energy recovery[542] and that between 25% as a minimum and 45% as a maximum by weight of the totality of packaging materials contained in packaging waste must be recycled with a minimum of 15% by weight for each packaging material ((Article 6(1)). Member States which have, or will, set programmes going beyond the targets are permitted to pursue those targets on the condition that these measures avoid distortions of the internal market and do not hinder compliance by other Member States with the directive (Article 6(10)). This provision also contains a notification requirement similar to that in Article 95(4-5) EC. Member States are required to inform the Commission of measures going beyond the targets of the directive. The Commission must confirm these measures, after having verified, in cooperation with the Member States, that they are consistent with the conditions just mentioned and do not constitute an arbitrary means of discrimination or a disguised restriction on trade between Member States.[543]

Furthermore, the directive requires Member States to take the necessary measures to ensure that systems are set up to provide for:

· the return and/or collection of used packaging and/or packaging waste from the consumer;
· the reuse or recovery of packaging and/or packaging waste collected (Article 7).[544]

Such systems may take the form of agreements between industry and the Member State authorities, as the directive explicitly envisages implementation by means of such agreements (Article 22(3a)). This means that the competition rules may apply as well as the provisions on the free movement of goods.[545] According to Article 9 Member States must ensure that packaging may be placed on the market only if it complies with all essential requirements defined by the directive. Article 11 contains some specific provisions on concentration levels of heavy materials (lead, cadmium, mercury and hexavalent chromium) present in packaging. Member States must not impede the placing on the market of packaging which satisfies the provisions of the directive (Article 18).

---

[541] The Court has held that there is no hierarchy between these two, Case C-463/01 *Commission v. Germany* [2004] ECR I-11705, para. 40.

[542] The reference to incineration with energy recovery as a means to achieve the recovery targets has been included by Directive 2004/12, OJ 2004 L 47/26, as a response to the Court's strict interpretation of recovery, see section 15.1.2.

[543] See for an application of Article 6(6), the predecessor of Article 6(10), Commission Decision 99/42, OJ 1999 L 14/24 and Decision 2003/82, OJ 2003 L 31/32.

[544] See on the conditions for systems set up pursuant to Article 7, Case C-309/02 *Radlberger* [2004] ECR I-11763, paras. 39-50.

[545] Case C-463/01 *Commission v. Germany* [2004] ECR I-11705, paras. 44-52, see further Chapter 6.

Finally, the directive contains provisions on the marking of packaging (Article 8), on information (Articles 12 and 13), management plans (Article 14) and economic instruments (Article 15).

15.4   End of Life Vehicles

Directive 2000/53 implements the principle of producer responsibility for so-called end of life vehicles.[546] This term broadly refers to automobiles that have become waste (Article 2(2)). Central to the directive is the duty for the Member States to ensure that importers and manufacturers of vehicles are responsible for the collection and reuse and recovery of end of life vehicles. This producer responsibility will also have a preventive effect in that the producers will thus have an incentive to minimise the costs of reuse and recovery by improving the recyclability of their vehicles. Article 4(1)(b) requires an integration of these environmental considerations in the design stage of production. The prevention aspect of the directive further translates into a restriction on the use of certain substances such as heavy metals and a duty on the Member States to encourage the use of recycled materials.

The actual producer responsibility attaches to the collection and reuse and recovery of end of life vehicles. To make the collection system as consumer friendly as possible there is a duty to take back end of life vehicles at least free of charge (Article 5(4), first subparagraph), provided the vehicle is still intact (Article 5(4), third subparagraph). Setting up and financing this system is the responsibility of the economic operators (Article 5(1), first indent, and Article 5(4) second subparagraph). The treatment of the vehicles thus collected is subject to the rules in Article 6. Once collected, the vehicles and their parts should as a priority be reused, then recovered or recycled (Article 7(1) Moreover, the economic operators must attain certain reuse and recovery rates for end of life vehicles (Article 7(2)). The directive further contains provisions on the coding of parts in order to facilitate their reuse and recovery (Article 8) and envisages European legislation on the recyclability and reusability of vehicle parts (Article 7(4) and (5)). Implementation of the directive can take place through agreements between the Member States and the economic operators (Article 10(3). The duty to set up a collection system applies only to vehicles marketed after 1 July 2002 and, from 1 January 2007 onwards, to vehicles marketed before 1 July 2002 (Article 12(2). However, the Member States may opt for an early implementation (Article 12(3)).

15.5   Waste Electrical and Electronic Equipment

The producer responsibility principle has similarly been implemented for electrical and electronic equipment. Although they started out as one proposal, there are now two relevant directives. Directive 2002/95 contains

---

[546] OJ 2000 L 269/34, as most recently amended by Decision 2005/673, OJ 2005 L 254/69.

rules on the restriction of certain hazardous substances (ROHS).[547] The ROHS Directive is based on Article 95 EC and contains predominantly product-related rules according to which from 1 July 2006, new electrical and electronic equipment put on the market does not contain lead, mercury, cadmium, hexavalent chromium, polybrominated biphenyls (PBB) or polybrominated diphenyl ethers (PBDE; Article 4(1)). This basic rule is however subject to exceptions for products and applications listed in the Annex.

Directive 2002/96 contains the actual producer responsibility scheme and is often referred to as the waste electrical and electronic equipment (WEEE) Directive.[548] Like the End of Life Vehicles Directive, the WEEE Directive contains a general duty for the Member States to encourage ecodesign (Article 4). The producer responsibility attaches to the separate collection. The Member States are responsible for ensuring that WEEE is collected separate from other waste streams (Article 5(1). For WEEE from private households, however, there is an additional duty to ensure that such waste may be returned at least free of charge (Article 5(2)(a). One very consumer friendly method of collecting WEEE is the so-called old-for-new obligation laid down in Article 5(2(b), according to which the distributor is required to take back at least free of charge the old appliance whenever a new similar appliance is sold. This old-for-new obligation applies irrespective of the brand and may only be disapplied when the old appliance is incomplete or contaminated with other waste (Article 5(2), last paragraph). The WEEE thus collected should be treated in accordance with the rules laid down in Article 6. Article 7 requires the Member States to ensure that the producers and importers of electrical and electronic equipment set up a system that will guarantee specified minimum levels of reuse, recycling and recovery of the WEEE. As a basic rule, the costs for the collection and treatment of WEEE are to be borne by the importers and producers of the appliances (Articles 8 and 9). They may choose to do so individually or collectively.[549] As a result of the old-for-new obligation and the relatively long lifespan of electrical equipment, the WEEE initially collected will be so-called historical waste, i.e. equipment put on the market before 13 August 2005.[550] Moreover, part of the historical waste will be orphaned waste, i.e. equipment marketed by a manufacturer or importer that may have ceased to be active on the market. For WEEE from private households the financial burden arising from this should be overcome by the obligation for the producers and importers to join a collective system to which all importers and producers contribute proportionately (Article 8(3)). In addition, the directive allows the producers and importers to show these costs separately during a transitional period that will last until 13 February 2011.[551] After the transitional

---

[547] OJ 2002 L 37/19, as most recently amended by Commission Decision 2006/692, OJ 2006 L 238/50.

[548] OJ 2002 L 37/24, as most recently amended by Directive 2003/108, OJ 2003 L 345/106.

[549] Collectively accepting a producer responsibility may result in the applicability of Article 81 or 82 EC.

[550] One year after the deadline for implementing the directive; Article 17(1).

[551] Eight years after the date of entry into force of the WEEE Directive. For a specific category the transitional period is ten years.

period it is no longer allowed to separately show the costs of collection and treatment (Article 8(2), third subparagraph)). For non-private household historical WEEE there are special financial provisions that allow for some of these costs to be borne by the non-private household. Given that the distinction between private households and other users is financially so important, it is surprising to see that the definition of what constitutes a private household is anything but clear. Article 3(k) includes commercial, industrial, institutional and other sources which produce WEEE that is, because of its nature and quantity, similar to that from private households. This allows for Member States to include SMEs and schools in the definition of a private household and thereby free them from all costs arising from the separate collection and treatment of WEEE. Articles 10 and 11 contain provisions on the information to be supplied to the consumer and treatment facilities. Finally, the directive contains provisions dealing with reporting, comitology and implementation. The WEEE Directive also allows for implementation by means of an agreement between the sector concerned and the Member State (Article 17(3)).

15.6   Waste Batteries and Accumulators

Batteries and accumulators often contain dangerous substances such as heavy metals. The European legislature therefore considered it necessary to have product rules and rules concerning their separate collection and safe treatment once these batteries become waste. Directive 2006/66 contains these rules and is based on Article 95 as well as 175 EC.[552] This directive replaces, with effect from 26 September 2006 the old Batteries Directive.[553] The product related rules consist of a ban for batteries and accumulators containing mercury and cadmium above a certain threshold (Article 4(1)(a) and (b)). However, both bans are subject to exceptions. For mercury, the threshold for the ban increases from 0.0005% to 2% for so-called buton cells (Article 4(2)) and for cadmium the prohibition is declared inapplicable for batteries intended for use in emergency and alarm systems, medical equipment and cordless power tools (Article 4(3)). Article 6 contains the free movement clause for batteries meeting the requirements of the directive and corresponding duty the restrict the marketing of all other batteries. The final part of the product rules is contained in Article 21 and deals with the labelling of batteries and accumulators.

The rules on separate collection and safe treatment take the form of a mitigated producer responsibility, in that the Member States have an independent obligation to set up a collection infrastructure in addition to the collection to be undertaken by the producers. In this regard a distinction is made between portable batteries on the one hand and industrial and automotive batteries on the other (recital 8 of the preamble). A portable battery is defined as a sealed battery

---

[552] OJ 2006 L 266/1, corrected in OJ 2006 L 311/58. Hereafter we will only refer to batteries when accumulators are also included.

[553] Directive 91/157, OJ 1991 L 78/38.

that can be hand-carried and is not an automotive or industrial battery (Article 3(3)). Automotive batteries are those used for starting, lighting or ignition in cars (Article 3(5)) and industrial batteries are those designed exclusively for industrial or professional uses (Article 3(6)).[554] The general framework for the collection is laid down in Article 8(1) and requires the collection to be end-user friendly. For portable batteries this means that distributors that supply such batteries are required to take back waste batteries for free (Article 8(1)(b) and (c)). For industrial and automotive batteries a similar duty to take back waste batteries applies (Article 8(3)), albeit without the stipulation that such collection must take place without any costs to the end-user. Only for automotive batteries from private non-commercial vehicles it there a duty take them back for free (Article 8(4), last sentence). Article 16 requires the Member States to ensure that producers pay the separate collection, treatment and recycling.[555] Such costs shall not be shown separately to end-users (Article 16(4)). Interestingly, there is no transitional regime for batteries (Article 16(6), whereas the WEEE and End of Life Vehicles Directives do provide for a such rules in view of historical waste. Finally, it worth mentioning that in accordance with Article 18 Member States may exempt small producers from the financial obligations. Such exemptions have to be approved by the Commission (Article 18(2) and (3)), which appears very sensible in view of the obvious effects that such exemptions may have on the internal market and given that the definition of a small firm is gnomic at best and leaves the Member States considerable room for discretion.

Article 9 provides for the introduction of differentiated taxes by the Member States to promote environmental improvements concerning batteries. Such measures must be notified to the Commission. Articles 10 and 12 contain targets for the collection and treatment and recycling of waste batteries. Concerning the treatment and recycling, the distinction between portable and industrial and automotive batteries is again relevant as the first subparagraph of Article 12(1) allows for the disposal in landfills or in underground storage of portable batteries that contain lead, mercury or cadmium. This disposal – as opposed to recycling – is allowed when no viable end market is available or if this method of phasing out of heavy metals is shown to be preferable over recycling. In determining whether or not disposal is preferable economic, environmental and social impacts have to be taken into account. For industrial and automotive batteries this method of disposal is not allowed (Article 14). In any case the recycling efficiencies contained in Article 12(4) in connection with Annex II, part B will have to be achieved.[556] Article 11 requires the Member States to ensure manufactures design products in a way that will facilitate the removal

---

[554] Recitals 9 and 10 of the preamble contain indicative lists of these categories.

[555] Article 16(2) requires the Member States to ensure that double charging is avoided because the producers will already have to bear these costs on the basis of the WEEE and End of Life Vehicles Directives.

[556] See Article 15(2) on the proof needed to take into account recycling operations that take place after export to non-member state countries.

of waste batteries. This is particularly relevant in connection with the WEEE[557] and the End of Life Vehicles Directives. Article 20 contains rules on information for end-users, Articles 22 to 25 contain the standard provisions on reporting, comitology and penalties. Finally, Articles 26 and 27 contain the rules for the implementation, which could also involve the use of agreements between the Member State and the economic operators concerned.

15.7 Legislation on Transfrontier Shipments of Waste

15.7.1 General Remarks

Regulation 259/93, replacing Directive 84/631[558], on the supervision and control of shipments of waste within, into and out of the EC[559] – the 'old' Basel Regulation – has applied since 6 May 1994. In effect from 12 July 2007 it has been replaced with Regulation 1013/2006, hereafter referred to as the Basel Regulation.[560] The regulation is an extremely complicated piece of legislation. One of the reasons for this is that it serves to implement not only the EU's own objectives in the waste sector, but also several of its international law obligations. In this connection it should be noted that the EC is itself a party to the 1989 Basel Convention on the Control of Transboundary Movements of Hazardous Waste and their Disposal,[561] in addition to the Member States. Moreover, Article 39 of the Lomé IV Convention[562] contains provisions on waste and the EC has approved the Decision of the OECD Council on the control of transfrontier movements of wastes destined for recovery operations.[563] Finally, the conclusion of the EEA Convention[564] and the changing position of the EFTA States in the light of this also influenced the content of the regulation. In view of this complex background, only the main contours of the regulation will be given here.

The Basel Regulation distinguishes between shipments of waste between the Member States and shipments into and out of the EU, i.e. to and from third countries. Concerning the latter a further distinction is made between EFTA countries, OECD Decision-countries and non-OECD Decision countries. A second important distinction relates to the recovery or disposal that the waste

---

[557] See also Article 12(3).

[558] OJ 1984 L 326/31, later amended.

[559] OJ 1993 L 30/1, later amended. The regulation is correctly based on Article 130s (now Article 175) EC; Case C-187/93 *EP v. Council* [1994] ECR I-2857. See also Chapter 1. In addition, several French importers of waste have had their cases declared inadmissible by the Court, Case C-209/94P *Buralux* v. *Council* [1996] ECR I-615.

[560] OJ 2006 L 190/1, see Article 61(1) concerning the repeal of the old Basel Regulation.

[561] OJ 1993 L 39/23.

[562] OJ 1991 L 229.

[563] Recital 5 of the preamble to the Basel Regulation. Notice that this decision has been revised by Decision C(2001) 107 final.

[564] OJ 1994 L 1.

will subjected to following the shipment.[565] Basically, this means that shipments destined for recovery benefit from less restrictions compared to shipments destined for disposal.[566] Finally, it is important to notice that there are categories (lists) of waste to which different regimes apply. Compared to the 'old' Basel Regulation things have become a bit less complex given that the number of lists has been reduced from three to two, as have the number of procedures. The old Basel Regulation had three lists, the so-called green, amber and red list. Generally speaking the categorisation as green, amber or red list waste corresponded with increasing danger to human health and the environment and thus more stringent procedures and rules for shipments. The current Basel Regulation only distinguishes between a green list (Annex III) and an amber list (Annex IV). In addition, there is a list of wastes where the export is prohibited (Annex V). Shipments of green list waste are subject to a general information requirement, whereas shipments of amber list waste are subject to a prior informed consent procedure.

15.7.2   Shipments of Waste between Member States

Title II (Articles 3 to 32) concern shipments of waste between Member States. These are subject to a prior notification and consent (PIC) procedure or a general information requirement. The applicability of the two procedures is set out in Article 3 according to which the PIC procedure applies to all shipments of waste destined for disposal (Article 3(1)(a), shipments of mixed municipal waste (Article 3(5)) and in case of shipments destined for recovery (Article 3(1)(b):
  · wastes listed in Annex IV[567] and IVA;
  · wastes not classified under a single entry in Annex III, IIIB, IV or IVA;
  · mixtures of wastes[568] not classified under a single entry in Annex III, IIIB, IV or IVA.

The general information requirement applies to all shipments in excess of 20 kilograms of waste
  · listed in Annex III or IIIB;
  · that are mixtures not classified under a single entry in Annex III of two or more wastes listed in that Annex provided that the mixing does not impair the environmentally sound recovery and that the mixture is listed in Annex IIIA.

---

[565] See this chapter, section 15.1.2 on the definition of recovery and disposal.

[566] Case C-203/96 *Dusseldorp* [1998] ECR I-4075, para. 33.

[567] This includes wastes listed in Annexes II and VIII to the Basel Convention.

[568] See on the classification of mixtures of wastes under the old Basel Regulation Case C-259/05 *Omni Metal Service*, judgment of 21 June 2007, n.y.r. in the ECR and Case C-192/96 *Beside and Besselsen* [1998] ECR I-4029.

The PIC procedure is set out in Article 4, which deals with the prior notifica-tion,[569] and Article 9, which contains the provisions on the consent required of the authorities of dispatch, transit and destination. The notification is to be submitted to the authority of dispatch (Article 4), which will check it for completeness (Article 4(2))[570] and then forward the notification to the authority of destination.[571]

According to Article 9(1) the authorities of dispatch, destination and – if relevant – transit have 30 days to consent to the shipment (with or without condi-tions (Article 9(1)(a) or (b)) or to raise objections. Tacit consent will be assumed if no objection is raised within this 30-day period.

Article 11 contains the grounds for objections against shipments of waste destined for disposal whereas Article 12 lists the grounds for objections against shipments destined for recovery. Both provisions have the following grounds in common:[572]

- the planned shipment, disposal or recovery would be contrary to national legislation on environmental protection, public order or public health concerning actions taking place in the objecting country (Article 11(1)(b) and 12(1)(b));
- the notifier or consignee has previous convictions for violations of envi-ronmental law (Article 11(1)(c) and 12(1)(d));
- the notifier or treatment facility has repeatedly failed to comply with Arti-cle 15 (on interim recovery and disposal operations) and 16 (on conditions following consent; Article 11(1)(d) and 12(1)(e));
- the planned shipment conflicts with international obligations for the Member States or the EU (Article 11(1)(f) and 12(1)(f);
- the treatment will take place in an IPPC-installation[573] that does not apply the best available techniques (Article 11(1)(h) and 12(1)(i);
- the treatment is not in accordance with binding European environmental protection standards relating to the disposal or recovery (Article 11(1)(j) and 12(1)(j).

---

[569] See, on the person who is the notifier under the old Basel Regulation Case C-215/04 *Pedersen* [2006] ECR I-1465. This case turned on Article 2(1)(g) of the Old Basel Regulation according to which a licensed waste collector may exceptionally be considered the notifier. Article 2(15) of the current Basel Regulation no longer requires this exceptional nature.

[570] From Case C-6/00 *ASA* [2002] ECR I-1961, para. 48, it may be inferred that this check may not result in the authority's *ex officio* reclassification of the objective of the shipment from recovery to disposal. The authority can, however, raise objections against a shipment. In ASA the Court held that this should take place on the basis of the classification error, the current Basel Regulation provides for an objection to the shipment in Article 12(1)(h). See further Case C-472/02 *Siomab* [2004] ECR I-9971, paras. 27 and 28.

[571] The authority of destination will, if necessary, forward the notification to the authority of transit, Article 7(1).

[572] The Member State of transit may only raise the objections under Article 11(1)(b), (c), (d) and (f), Article 11(2) and Article 12(1)(b), (d), (e) and (f), Article 12(2).

[573] See section 5 above.

As was mentioned above, shipments destined for disposal are subject to a stricter regime than shipments destined for recovery. For one, all shipments of mixed municipal waste destined for disposal may be objected to (Article 11(1)(i)). Moreover, the implementation of the principles of proximity, priority for recovery and self-sufficiency may result in systematic objections to all shipments of waste intended for disposal (Article 11(1)(a). Article 11(1)(g) allows for a similar restriction of shipments of waste. This brings us back to the difficulties already identified above in connection with the principle of self-sufficiency and proximity.[574] Taken together these principles have resulted in the Member States setting up waste management structures on a primarily (if not purely) national basis. Moreover, in order to ensure the profitability of the disposal installations that make up such structures, exports of waste will often be minimised as this guarantees optimal use of these facilities.[575] We have already noted that the proximity principle may actually plead for an export of waste if the treatment installation in another Member State is closer than the national installation. Furthermore, a closer reading of the principle of self-sufficiency reveals that it is about self-sufficiency at European and national levels. The Basel Regulation and the Waste Framework Directive are therefore ambiguous with regard to the legality of such predominantly national waste management structures. The requirement in the heading of Article 11(1) that objections must be in accordance with the Treaty, and thus the provisions on the free movement of goods, has not proven helpful in solving this problem either.[576] Finally, Member States may exercise their right pursuant to the Basel Convention to restrict the import of hazardous waste (Article 11(1)(e).

Shipments of waste destined for recovery may meet with the following objections:

· the planned shipment or recovery is not in accordance with the Waste Framework Directive (Article 12(1)(a);[577]
· the planned shipment or recovery is not in accordance with the national standards of the country of dispatch (Article 12(1)(c);
· the ratio of the recoverable and nonrecoverable waste, the estimated value of the materials to be finally recovered or the cost of the recovery and the cost of the disposal of the nonrecoverable fraction do not justify the recovery under economic and environmental considerations (Article 12(1)(g);[578]

---

[574] This chapter, section 15.1.2.

[575] See, for example, Case C-203/96 *Dusseldorp* [1998] ECR I-4075 and Case C-209/98 *Sydhavnens* [2000] ECR I-3743, where the Member States invoked reasons relating to the profitability of waste treatment installations to justify (possible) restrictions of the export of waste.

[576] See Case C-324/99 *DaimlerChrysler* [2001] ECR I-9897.

[577] See, concerning Article 7(4)(a), first indent, of the old Basel Regulation, Case C-227/02 *EU Wood Trading* [2004] ECR I-11957, where the fact that treatment abroad does not meet the environmental standards of the country of dispatch could be raised as an objection to the shipment. This ground for objection is now included in Article 12(1)(c).

[578] See, concerning the identical Article 7(4)(a), fifth indent, of the old Basel Regulation, Case C-113/02 *Commission v. Netherlands* [2004] ECR I-9707, paras. 17-25.

· the waste is shipped for disposal instead of recovery (Article 12(1)(h);
· the waste will not be treated in accordance with waste management
plans drawn up in order to meet binding European recycling or recovery
targets.[579]

The objection listed in Article 12(1)(c) is particularly interesting as it could
allow the Member States the possibility to systematically restrict shipments
of waste destined for recovery in a manner similar to the way shipments for
disposal may be restricted. By setting higher national recovery standards, a
Member State could simply block the export of waste destined for recovery. The
fact that Article 12(1)(c) requires such objections to respect the need to ensure
the proper functioning of the internal market will not resolve this problem as
setting higher standards for recovery operations that take place on the territory
of a Member State will fall outside the scope of the free movement provisions
(as a wholly internal situation). Moreover, European standards on recovery
will invariably constitute minimum harmonisation in view of Article 176 EC.
In this regard, the exceptions listed in (i) and (ii) are probably more effective.
Under (i), a Member State may not object against a shipment if the recovery in
another Member State conforms to a European minimum standard. Moreover,
if the recovery in the other Member State takes place under conditions that are
'broadly equivalent' to those in the state of dispatch the objection cannot be
raised either (ii). Whatever more stringent national recovery standards exist,
they must have been notified (iii).[580] Article 12(1)(c) is furthermore interesting
in connection with Article 12(1)(a). The latter provision closely follows Article
7(4)(a), first indent, of the old Basel Regulation which has been interpreted by
the Court as allowing the Member State of dispatch, in assessing the effects
on health and the environment of the recovery envisaged at the destination,
provided it complies with the principle of proportionality, to rely on the criteria
to which, in order to avoid such effects, the recovery of waste is subject in the
State of dispatch, even where those criteria are stricter than those in force in the
State of destination.[581] It appears that the Court thus allows the Member States
more leeway under Article 12(1)(a), particularly in view of the fact that the Court
also held that the mere fact that national legislation is more stringent does not
necessarily mean that it is disproportionate.[582]

To reduce the administrative burden arising from the PIC procedure, the
possibility of general notifications for more than one shipment is envisaged
(Article 13) as well as the possibility of preconsenting to certain recovery facilities (Article 14).

---

[579] See sections 15.6, 15.5 and 15.4 above concerning such targets with regard to batteries, WEEE and packaging waste.

[580] See section 2.1 above concerning the Notification Directive.

[581] Case C-227/02 *EU Wood Trading* [2004] ECR I-11957, paras. 44-54.

[582] Case C-227/02 *EU Wood Trading* [2004] ECR I-11957, para. 51.

The general information procedure applies to the categories of waste listed in Article 3(2) and (4) and is set out in Article 178. Basically, this procedure requires certain information to accompany the shipment. No prior consent is required. The general requirements applying to all shipments of waste are set out in Articles 19-21 and include a prohibition of mixing waste and a duty to keep information for at least three years after the shipment. Articles 22-25 relate to the duty to take back waste when the shipment or treatment cannot be completed. In this case costs for the take-back shall primarily be borne by the notifier (Article 23(1)(a)).[583] For illegal shipments (Article 2(35))[584] a similar framework applies (Articles 24 and 25). As far as these costs are concerned, the Basel Regulation lays down an obligation to secure a financial guarantee or insurance (Article 6). Chapter 5 contain general administrative rules. Chapter 6 contains specialised rules on shipments within the EU with transit via third countries.

The rules on the shipment of waste do not apply to shipments within a Member State (Article 2(34)). Here the regulation requires only that the Member States establish an appropriate system for the supervision and control of such shipments and that the system takes account of the need for coherence with the European system established by the regulation (Article 33(1)). This allows Member States the necessary freedom to arrange matters as they see fit within their own jurisdiction.

15.7.3   Exports of Waste Out of the EU

As far as exports of waste are concerned, the regulation distinguishes between EFTA countries and non-EFTA countries and between OECD and non-OECD countries. Furthermore the two lists and the distinction between recovery and disposal are relevant.

The basic rule is a prohibition of all exports for disposal (Article 34(1)), with an exception for EFTA countries that are also a party to the Basel Convention (Article 34(2). In case of such exports to EFTA countries Article 35 declares the regime for shipments within the EU applicable, albeit subject to a few procedural changes (set out in Article 35(2) and (3)).

In the following cases exports for recovery to non-OECD decision countries are also prohibited (Article 36(1)):
- hazardous waste (Annex V), including mixtures with non-hazardous wastes;

---

[583] See Case C-389/00 *Commission* v. *Germany* [2003] ECR I-2001, where the Court finds a mandatory contribution to a solidarity fund to constitute a charge of equivalent effect prohibited under Articles 23 and 25 EC.

[584] Cf. Case C-192/96 *Beside* [1998] ECR I-4029, where the Court ruled 'that the Member State of destination may not unilaterally return waste to the Member State of dispatch without prior notification to the latter; the Member State of dispatch may not oppose its return where the Member State of destination produces a duly motivated request to that effect.'

· waste where the country of dispatch has reasons to believe that they will not be managed in an environmentally sound manner (the rules for establishing this are set out in Article 49).

The procedures for exporting waste listed in Annex III or IIIA, green list waste) is laid down in Article 37 and also involves a procedure whereby the Commission requests from the non-OECD country a decision according to which the import will be prohibited, subject to the PIC procedure set out in Article 35 or subject to the general information requirement (Article 18). A list with these decisions is included in a Commission regulation (Article 37(2)).[585]

For exports of green and amber list waste OECD decision countries the provisions for shipments of waste within the EU apply (Article 38(1), again subject to the changes and additions listed in Article 38(2), (3) and (5). This means that the PIC procedure and the general information requirement are applicable with the scope of the PIC procedure being slightly widened.[586] Finally, exports of waste to the Antarctic are prohibited (Article 39), as are exports for disposal in overseas countries (Article 40(1)).

15.7.4 Imports of Waste into the EU

In principle all imports into the EU of waste for disposal are prohibited (Article 41(1)). Exceptions apply to the countries which are parties to the Basel Convention, countries with which the EC and its Member States have concluded agreements and countries subject to war or crisis. Again the regime for intra-EU shipments is declared applicable (Article 42) subject to procedural changes and additions.

Imports of waste destined for recovery are subject to a comparable regime with the exception that such imports will also be allowed from OECD decision countries (Article 43(1)). The same procedure also applies to non-OECD decision countries which are party to the Basel Convention (Article 45). Imports of waste from overseas countries for recovery are subject to the regime applicable to intra-EU shipments.

15.7.5 Transit and other Provisions

The Basel Regulation also contains specific provisions on the transit of waste through the EU for disposal and recovery outside the EU (Articles 47 and 48). Finally, it contains several general provisions dealing with matters such as the general duty on the part of all the parties involved in a shipment to take all steps to ensure that the environment is protected (Article 49),

---

[585] Currently Regulation 801/2007, OJ 2007 L 179/6, repealing Regulation 1547/1999.

[586] For example shipments of waste listed in Annex IIIA and IIIB are subject to the PIC procedure whereas they are subject to the general information requirement as far as intra Community shipments are concerned (Article 38(2)(a) and (b), this paragraph appears to be erroneously numbered as 1).

enforcement (Article 50), reporting and other procedural and organisational issues surrounding the application of the regulation (Articles 51-56). Finally, the regulation repeals the old Basel Regulation with effect from 1 July 2007, albeit subject to transitional rules contained in Article 62. Moreover the regulation envisages transitional rules for certain Member States (Poland, Slovakia, Bulgaria and Romania, Article 63).

15.8   Landfill of Waste

Very broadly formulated environmental objectives can be found in Directive 99/31 on the landfill of waste.[587] According to Article 1 the directive's overall objective is 'to prevent or reduce as far as possible negative effects on the environment, in particular the pollution of surface water, groundwater, soil and air, and on the global environment, including the greenhouse effect, as well as any resulting risk to human health, from landfilling of waste, during the whole life-cycle of the landfill.'

Each landfill shall be classified in one of the following classes:
· landfill for hazardous waste;
· landfill for non-hazardous waste;
· landfill for inert waste.

Member States must take measures to ensure that only waste that has been subject to treatment is landfilled. This provision may not apply to inert waste for which treatment is not technically feasible, nor to any other waste for which such treatment does not contribute to the objectives of the directive, by reducing the quantity of the waste or the hazards to human health or the environment (Article 6(a)). Only hazardous waste that fulfils the criteria set out in Annex II of the directive may be assigned to a hazardous landfill (Article 6(b)).

Article 6 (c) provides that landfill for non-hazardous waste may be used for:
· municipal waste;
· non-hazardous waste of any other origin, which fulfil certain criteria set out in Annex II of the directive;
· stable, non-reactive hazardous wastes (e.g. solidified, vitrified), with leaching behaviour equivalent to those of the non-hazardous mentioned above. However, these hazardous wastes shall not be deposited in cells destined for biodegradable non-hazardous waste.

Inert waste landfill sites shall be used only for inert waste (Article 6(d)). Annex I lists general requirements for all classes of landfills.

The following wastes may not be accepted in landfills, for example, liquid waste, waste which is explosive, corrosive, oxidising, highly flammable or flammable, hospital and other clinical wastes, whole used tyres or any other type of waste which does not fulfil the acceptance criteria set out in Annex II (Article

---

[587] OJ 1999 L 182/1.

5(3)). The dilution of mixture of waste solely in order to meet the waste acceptance criteria is prohibited (Article 5(4)).

In Articles 7-9 the directive introduces a specific permit procedure for all classes of landfill in accordance with the general licensing requirements already set out in the Waste Framework Directive and the general requirements of the IPPC Directive.[588]

Members States are required to take measures to ensure the competent authority does not issue a landfill permit unless it is satisfied that the landfill project complies with all the relevant requirements of the directive, the management of the landfill site will be in the hands of a natural person who is technically competent to manage the site and that professional and technical development and training of landfill operators and staff are provided. They must also ensure that measures are taken to prevent accidents and limit their consequences. Furthermore, they must ensure that adequate provisions, by way of a financial security or any other equivalent have been made by the applicant prior to the commencement of disposal operations to ensure that the obligations (including after-care provisions) arising under the permit issued are discharged and that the closure procedures required by Article 13 are followed. Prior to the commencement of disposal operations, the competent authority is required to inspect the site in order to ensure that it complies with the relevant conditions of the permit. However, this will not reduce in any way the responsibility of the operator under the conditions of the permit.

An interesting reference to the polluter pays principle can be found in Article 10 of the directive. All of the costs involved in the setting up and operation of a landfill site, including the cost of the financial security, and the estimated costs of the closure and after-care of the site for a period of at least 30 years must be covered by the price to be charged by the operator for the disposal of any type of waste in that site. This to ensure that the polluter does indeed pay!

The provisions of Article 13 on closure and after-care are important, because landfills can pose a threat to the environment not only in the short but also in the long term. More particularly, measures must be taken against the pollution of groundwater by leachate infiltration into the soil.

A landfill may only be considered definitely closed after the competent authority has carried out a final on-site inspection, has assessed all the reports submitted by the operator and has communicated to the operator its approval for the closure. This shall not in any way reduce the responsibility of the operator under the conditions of the permit (Article 13(b)). After a landfill has been defi-

---

[588] Landfills receiving more than 10 tonnes per day or with a total capacity exceeding 25,000 tonnes, excluding landfills of inert waste are subject to the provisions of the IPPC Directive (Annex I sub 5.2 of the directive). In respect of the technical characteristics of landfills, Directive 99/31 contains, for those landfills to which the IPPC Directive is applicable, the relevant technical requirements in order to elaborate in concrete terms the general requirements of that directive. The relevant requirements of the IPPC Directive shall be deemed to be fulfilled if the requirements of Directive 99/31 are complied with; Article 1(1) Directive 99/31.

nitely closed, the operator remains responsible for its maintenance, monitoring and control in the after-care phase for as long as may be required by the competent authority. The operator is required to notify the competent authority of any significant adverse environmental effects revealed by the control procedures and must follow the decision of the competent authority on the nature and timing of the corrective measures to be taken (Article 13(c)). For as long as the competent authority considers that a landfill is likely to cause a hazard to the environment and without prejudice to any European or national legislation as regards liability of the waste holder, the operator of the site shall be responsible for monitoring and analysing landfill gas and leachate from the site and the groundwater regime in the vicinity of the site (Article 13(d)).

The directive also aims to achieve a reduction of the amount of biodegradable waste going to landfills (Article 5). National strategies have to be set up, which must ensure that not later than 15 years after the date laid down for transposition, biodegradable municipal waste going to landfills must be reduced to 35% of the total amount (by weight) of biodegradable municipal waste produced in 1995.[589]

Furthermore, the directive lays down detailed rules on waste acceptance procedures (Article 11) and control and monitoring procedures in the operational phase (Article 12).[590] It contains a detailed time-table to ensure that existing landfills will meet the requirements of the directive as soon as possible and within eight years after the transposition deadline at the latest (Article 14).

15.9   Other European Legislation on Waste

One of the few European rules dealing specifically with protection of the soil is contained in Directive 86/278 concerning the use of sewage sludge in agriculture.[591] The core of the directive is a prohibition of the use of sludge where the concentration of certain heavy metals exceeds the limit values laid down in the directive.

The Mining Waste Directive 2006/21 basically requires a permit for mining waste facilities (Article 7).[592] The directive distinguishes between category A (where failure or incorrect operation could give rise to a major incident or where dangerous substances or waste are present above a certain threshold, Annex III) and all other facilities. Such facilities need to draw up waste management plans (Article 5), and plans for major accident hazards (Article 6). Finally, it is worth mentioning the fact that the directive contains a regime for financial guarantees comparable to that found in Landfill Directive (Article 14), albeit subject to a

---

[589] See on national strategies that are more stringent Case C-6/03 *Eiterköpfe* [2005] ECR I-2753.

[590] Decision 2003/33 contains the criteria and procedures for the acceptance of waste at landfills, OJ 2003 L 11/27.

[591] OJ 1986 L 181/6, as amended most recently by Regulation 807/2003, OJ 2003 L 122/36.

[592] OJ 2006 L 102/15.

transitional regime (Article 24). Directive 2006/21 must be implemented before 1 May 2008.

Finally, the Commission has issued a Green Paper on ship dismantling[593] which is interesting in connection with a Commission communication on abandoned offshore oil and gas installations.[594] In both cases the Commission essentially advocates international action to address the problems involved.

16 Legislation Concerning Nuclear Safety

16.1 The Euratom Directive on Basic Safety Standards

Member States are required to have implemented Directive 96/29/Euratom laying down basic safety standards for the protection of the health of workers and the general public against the dangers arising from ionizing radiation before 13 May 2000.[595] By that date the directive replaces the 'old' Euratom directives laying down basic standards of radiation protection.[596]

The new directive applies to all practices which involve a risk from ionizing radiation emanating from an *artificial* source or from a *natural* radiation source in cases where natural radionuclides are or have been processed in view of their radioactive, fissile or fertile properties. It also applies to other work activities which involve the presence of natural radiation sources and lead to a significant increase in the exposure of workers or members of the public which cannot be disregarded from the radiation protection point of view and to any intervention in cases of radiological emergencies or in cases of lasting exposure resulting from the after-effects of a radiological emergency. The directive does not apply to exposure to radon in dwellings or to the natural level of radiation, i.e. to radio-nuclides contained in the human body, to cosmic radiation prevailing at ground level or to aboveground exposure to radionuclides present in the undisturbed earth's crust (Article 2(4)).

Practices covered by the directive must be reported or be made subject to a prior authorisation (Articles 3 and 4).

Member States shall ensure that all new classes or types of practice resulting in exposure to ionizing radiation are justified in advance of being first adopted or first approved by their economic, social or other benefits in relation to the health detriment they may cause (Article 6(1)). Existing classes or types of practice may be reviewed as to justification whenever new and important evidence about their efficacy or consequences is acquired. In addition each Member State shall ensure that:

· in the context of optimisation all exposures shall be kept as low as reason-

---

[593] COM (2007) 269 final.

[594] COM (98) 49 final.

[595] OJ 1996 L 159/1, corrected in OJ 1996 L 314/20.

[596] OJ 1980 L 246/1, later amended.

ably achievable, economic and social factors being taken into account (the 'ALARA' principle);
· the applicable dose limits are not exceeded.

The directive contains several dose limits.[597] For example in Article 9, which lays down a limit on the effective dose for exposed workers of 100 millisieverts in a consecutive five-year period, subject to a maximum effective dose of 50 mSv in any single year.

In addition, the directive contains provisions on, for example, operational protection of exposed workers, apprentices and students, including medical surveillance (Articles 17 to 39), rules on significant increase in exposure due to natural radiation sources (Articles 40 to 42), provisions on the implementation of radiation protection for the population in normal circumstances (Articles 43 to 47) and measures to be taken in the case of radiological emergencies[598] (Articles 48 to 53). In cases of transboundary effects there is a duty to cooperate with other affected Member States and non-Member States alike (Article 50(4)).

16.2   The Regulations on Radioactive Foodstuffs

Following the nuclear accident at Chernobyl on 26 April 1986, the European legislature adopted two measures designed to prevent the marketing of contaminated agricultural products in the EU. Regulation 3955/87 concerned imports of contaminated agricultural products from third countries,[599] while Regulation 3954/87 concerned the placing on the market of contaminated agricultural products within the EU.[600] The regulations both prohibit the release

---

[597] In Case C-376/90, the Court decided that the limit doses laid down in the 'old' directive must be regarded as a form of minimum harmonisation and that Member States are entitled to set stricter limit doses; Case C-376/90 Commission v. Belgium [1992] ECR I-6153. This case law is undoubtedly still valid with respect to Directive 96/29. See also Chapter 3.

[598] See also Directive 89/618 on informing the general public about health protection measures to be applied and steps to be taken in the event of a radiological emergency, OJ 1989 L 357/31. Under this directive, Member States must ensure that the population likely to be affected in the event of a radiological emergency is given certain information. The information must be permanently available to the public. In the event of a radiological emergency, Member States are required to ensure that the population is informed without delay of the facts of the emergency, of the steps to be taken, and of the health protection measures applicable to the specific case. The directive also provides for the information of persons who might be involved in the organisation of emergency assistance in the event of a radiological emergency. Note that this directive and all other Euratom-provisions do not apply to military use of nuclear energy, Case C-65/04 Commission v. UK [2006] ECR I-2239.

[599] OJ 1987 L 371/14. Case C-62/88 EP v. Council [1990] ECR I-1527. In this case the Court held that the fixing of maximum permitted levels of radioactive contamination for agricultural products is within the commercial policy powers of the Council under Article 133 of the Treaty. See also Chapter 2.

[600] OJ 1987 L 371/11. Case C-70/88 EP v. Council [1991] ECR I-4529. See further the discussion of the case in Chapter 2. In this case the Court held that the purpose of the prohibition on trading in products that

for free circulation or placing on the market of agricultural products which exceed the maximum permitted levels of radioactive contamination laid down in the regulations.

As Regulation 3955/87 applied only until 31 March 1991, it was replaced in 1990 by Regulation 737/90.[601] The essence of the new regulation, making the release for free circulation of products subject to their meeting fixed maximum levels, is the same as in Regulation 3955/87.

16.3   The Transboundary Transport of Radioactive Waste

In view of the fact that the Basel Regulation does not cover shipments of radioactive waste,[602] specific legislation was needed to cover such shipments. This was provided by Directive 92/3.[603] The directive distinguishes between shipments of radioactive waste between Member States (Articles 4 to 9) and imports into and exports out of the EU (Articles 10 to 12). Basically, the directive envisages a PIC procedure for shipments of radioactive waste whereby the holder of that waste must apply for authorisation to the competent authorities of the country of origin. The competent authorities must then send the application to the competent authorities of the country of destination and of the countries of transit, if any (Article 4). The directive does not state the grounds that may be raised for objection. However, Article 6(2) does provide that any conditions required may not be more stringent than those laid down for similar shipments within the Member States. Reasons must be given for any refusal to grant approval, or any conditions attaching to approval. Article 6(4) provides for a tacit approval procedure that can, however, be rejected by Member States.

Imports into and exports out of the EU are also subject to a notification procedure. The directive does not set out the grounds on which imports may be refused, but it does contain provisions on exports. Article 11 provides that shipments will not be authorised to the Antarctic area, to ACP states or to a third country which, in the opinion of the competent authorities of the country of origin, does not have the technical, legal or administrative resources to manage the radioactive waste safely. This provision is a clear example of European environmental legislation with an extraterritorial protective objective.

Finally, the directive contains various provisions on the return of radioactive waste to the country of origin (Articles 13 to 16).

---

had been contaminated with radioactivity was to protect the public health. The regulation was therefore correctly based on Article 31 of the Euratom Treaty.

[601] OJ 1990 L 82/1, as most recently amended by Regulation 806/2003, OJ 2003 L 122/1. See also Commission Regulation 1635/2006 laying down detailed rules for the application of Regulation 737/90, OJ 2006 L 306/3.

[602] See Article 1(3)(c) of Regulation 1013/2006, see above, section 15.7.

[603] OJ 1992 L 35/24. Cf. also Council Resolution on radioactive-waste management, OJ 1994 C 379/1.

With effect from 25 December 2008, Directive 92/3 will be replaced by Directive 2006/117/Euratom.[604] This repeal was necessitated by the need to clarify and streamline the procedures and the need to ensure consistency with other provisions of European law[605] and international obligations.[606] Directive 2006/117 maintains the distinction between intra-EU shipments and extra-EU shipments and, albeit in slightly simplified form, the PIC procedure for intra-EU shipments (Articles 6 and 9). Importantly, spent nuclear fuel intended for reprocessing is now also included in the scope of the directive (Article 1(2)).[607] Another important change relates to the inclusion of grounds for a refusal of consent (Article 6(3)). Member States of transit may refuse consent if they consider the transport to be contrary to international, European or national legislation on such transports (Article 6(3)(a)), whereas Member States of destination may additionally invoke relevant legislation on the management of radioactive waste or spent fuel (Article 6(3)(b)). Interestingly, this leaves open the question of whether the legislation relied on by the Member State of destination on the management must originate from the international, European or national level. Similar to Directive 92/3, any conditions attached to the consent may not be more stringent than those laid down for similar shipments within that Member State. It is submitted that this basic non-discrimination rule should not only apply to the conditions attached to consents, but also to the decision whether or not to grant consent. It may furthermore be inferred from this that such consent may be withheld on the basis of national legislation on the management of nuclear waste or spent fuel, provided that this is non-discriminatory, irrespective of whether or not such national legislation is more stringent than international or European[608] legislation.[609]

17 Legislation on the Conservation of Nature[610]

Although the legal competence in the field of nature conservation was initially doubted by many (in view of the lack of any relevance to market integration), a large number of measures have been adopted since 1979 rang-

---

[604] OJ 2006 L 337/21.

[605] Such as Directive 2003/122/Euratom on high-activity sealed radioactive sources, OJ 2003 L 346/57.

[606] See Decision 2005/84/Euratom, OJ 2005 L 30/10 approving the accession of the European Atomic Energy Community to the 'Joint Convention on the Safety of Spent Fuel Management and on the Safety of Radioactive Waste Management'.

[607] See also recital 6 of the preamble.

[608] COM (2004) 526 final contains an amended proposal for a directive on the safe management of spent nuclear fuel and radioactive waste.

[609] See, in connection with a similar problem in the context of shipments of other waste, section 15.7.2 of this chapter.

[610] Cf. in general on the subject De Sadeleer (2005A).

ing from Directive 99/22 relating to the keeping of wild animals in zoos[611] via the Protocol on Protection and Welfare of Animals[612] to Regulation 2158/92 on protection of the Community's forests against fire.[613] European legislation on the conservation of nature is to some extent designed to fulfil obligations resulting from international treaties concluded by the EC, like the 1979 Berne Convention on the Conservation of European Wildlife and Natural Habitats,[614] the 1979 Bonn Convention on the Conservation of Migratory Species of Wild Animals[615], the 1992 Convention on Biological Diversity[616] and the Agreement on the International Dolphin Conservation Programme.[617]

Under the present Treaty the objectives set out in Article 174 EC must be regarded as more than sufficient to enable further measures to protect wildlife, flora and fauna. Nevertheless, these areas above all are likely to feel the impact of the subsidiarity principle, particularly where there is no question of the protection of threatened or transboundary nature values.

17.1 The Wild Birds Directive

17.1.1 The General Scope of the Directive

Directive 79/409 lays down general rules on the conservation of wild birds.[618] According to Article 1, the directive relates to the conservation of all species of naturally occurring birds in the wild state[619] *in the European territory of the Member States.*[620] From the case law of the Court it is clear that it is not sufficient, when a Member State is implementing the directive, for it to confine itself to those species found in its territory.[621] After all, species occurring elsewhere may be transported to that Member State, or kept there or sold,

---

[611] OJ 1999 L 94/24.

[612] Attached to the 'Amsterdam Treaty'.

[613] OJ 1992 L 217/3, as most recently amended by Regulation 308/97, OJ 1997 L 51/11.

[614] OJ 1982 L 38/3.

[615] OJ 1982 L 210/11.

[616] OJ 1993 L 309/1. Cf. also the Cartagena Protocol on Biosafety, adopted by the EC on 29 January 2000 and Commission Communication on a European Community Biodiversity Strategy, COM (98) 42.

[617] Council Decision 1999/337, OJ 1999 L 132/1.

[618] OJ 1979 L 103/1, as amended by Directive 2006/105, OJ 2006 L 363/368.

[619] The directive is not applicable to specimens of birds born and reared in captivity, Case C-149/94 *Vergy* [1996] ECR I-299. Therefore Member States remain competent to regulate trade in those specimens, subject of course to Articles 28-30 EC.

[620] Although the Court held in Case C-202/94 *Van der Feesten* [1996] ECR I-355, para. 18, that the directive also applies to bird *subspecies* which occur naturally in the wild only outside the European territory of the Member States if the species to which they belong or other subspecies of that species occur naturally in the wild within the territory in question.

[621] For example, Case 247/85 *Commission v. Belgium* [1987] ECR 3029 and Case C-149/94 *Vergy* [1996] ECR I-299.

alive or dead. By including in national legislation only those species occurring in their own territory, Member States would fail to provide the protection
required by the directive. The case law shows that Member States not only have
a responsibility to protect species occurring in their own territory, but that their
responsibility extends to the whole territory of the EU. This is borne out by the
Court's regular confirmation that the effective protection of birds is typically a
transfrontier environment problem entailing common responsibilities for the
Member States.[622]

The directive covers the protection, management and control of these species
and lays down rules for their exploitation. The third recital of the preamble
expresses the underlying consideration that effective bird protection is typically
a transfrontier environmental problem entailing common responsibilities for
the Member States. As was noted in Chapter 4, the Court has taken this to imply
a stricter requirement than usual in its assessment of the implementation of the
directive by the Member States.

Article 2 of the directive contains a general obligation for the Member States.
They are required to take the requisite measures to maintain the population
of the species in question at a level which corresponds in particular to ecological, scientific and cultural requirements, while taking account of economic and
recreational requirements. The question that has arisen in respect of Article
2, in particular from the fact that it indicates that bird protection has to be
balanced against other interests, is whether that provision constitutes an independent derogation from the general requirements of the directive. The Court
has consistently stated that it does not.[623]

In order to achieve effective protection, the directive contains measures to
protect the habitats and to limit the hunting of, and trading in, bird species. As
far as the former is concerned, Article 3 provides that Member States must take
the requisite measures to preserve, maintain or re-establish a sufficient diversity and area of habitats for all the species of birds covered by the directive. The
following measures are specifically mentioned:

· creation of protected areas;
· upkeep and management in accordance with the ecological needs of habitats inside and outside the protected zones;
· re-establishment of destroyed biotopes;
· creation of biotopes.

17.1.2   Special Conservation Measures

Special conservation measures must be taken for a number of
species mentioned in Annex I of the directive (Article 4(1)). Member States are

---

[622] Case 262/85 *Commission v. Italy* [1987] ECR 3073.

[623] Case 247/85 *Commission v. Belgium* [1987] ECR 3029; Case C-435/92 *Association pour la protection des
animaux sauvages* [1994] ECR I-67; Case C-44/95 *Royal Society for the Protection of Birds* [1996] ECR
I-3805.

required to classify in particular the most suitable territories in number and size as special protection areas for the conservation of these species. This requirement led to the additional requirement that Member States should take appropriate steps to avoid pollution or deterioration of habitats or any disturbances affecting the birds in these protection areas (Article 4(4)). Moreover it also had some measure of external effect: by virtue of the same provision, Member States are expressly required to strive to avoid pollution or deterioration of habitats outside these protection areas. However, Article 7 of the Habitats Directive provides that any obligations arising under Article 4(4) of the Wild Birds Directive shall be replaced by Article 6(2), (3) and (4) of the Habitats Directive from the date of its implementation. As will appear in the discussion of the Habitats Directive below, the possibilities of derogating from the legal consequences of classifying a special protection area under the Habitats Directive are far wider than under the Wild Birds Directive. In fact, the latter directive contains no express grounds allowing derogation. In the *Leybucht* case the Member States' obligations to classify special protection areas were at issue.[624] The Court acted on the principle that Member States do have a certain discretion in deciding whether or not to designate a given area as a special protection area for birds. However, in the *Marismas de Santoña* case, it transpired that this discretion may be very limited in any particular case, if it exists at all.[625] In that case the area in question was held to constitute one of the most important ecosystems of the Iberian peninsula, where various migratory birds and species threatened with extinction exist. The Court decided that this area should have been classified a special protection area. Further clarification on the margin of discretion available to the Member States was given by the Court in Case C-3/96. The Court made it perfectly clear,[626]

> 'that the Member States' margin of discretion in choosing the most suitable territories for classification as SPAs does not concern the appropriateness of classifying as SPAs the territories which appear the most suitable according to ornithological criteria, but only the application of those criteria for identifying the most suitable territories for conservation of the species listed in Annex I to the Directive.'

In this context it is important to note the relevance of IBA 89 (Inventory of Important Bird Areas in the European Community). In para. 70 of the above-mentioned case the Court attributed a *de facto* binding effect to the IBA 89, albeit that the Member States may produce evidence to the contrary. In view of

---

[624] Case C-57/89 *Commission* v. *Germany* [1991] ECR I-883.

[625] Case C-355/90 *Commission* v. *Spain* [1993] ECR I-4221. Cf. also Case C-166/97 *Commission* v. *France* [1999] ECR I-623, with respect to the French failure to classify a sufficiently large special protection area in the Seine estuary and Case C-96/98 *Commission* v. *France* [1999] ECR I-8531, with respect to the failure to classify a sufficiently large special protection area in the Poitevin Marsh.

[626] Case C-3/96 *Commission* v. *Netherlands* [1998] ECR I-3031, para. 61.

the fact that the Netherlands had failed to do this, the Court applied the IBA 89 as a criterion by which to judge whether the Netherlands had fulfilled its classification obligations under Article 4(1) of the Wild Birds Directive.[627]

This case law must necessarily also affect Member States' freedom to declassify SPAs. As long as the areas fulfil the conditions of Article 4(1), declassification, for instance through a reduction in size, does not seem possible, unless Article 6(2-4) of the Habitats Directive can be applied. Of course, for a complaint of infringement of the directive by reason of the declassification to be upheld, it is necessary, in any event, for the area in question to have been part of a classified SPA, or an area that should have been so classified.[628]

Once an area has been classified as a protection area, or if it should have been, as in the *Marismas de Santoña* case, the obligations to avoid pollution laid down in Article 6(2) of the Habitats Directive apply.[629] Most importantly it requires Member States to take appropriate steps to avoid, *inter alia*, deterioration of habitats in the SPAs classified pursuant to Article 4(1).[630]

In the *Leybucht* case the Court held that Member States are not free to derogate at will from these obligations. They do not have the same discretion under Article 4(4) as they do in choosing which areas to classify. Derogation can be justified only on exceptional grounds, grounds which correspond to a general interest which is superior to the general interest represented by the ecological objective of the directive. The Court stressed that the economical and recreational interests referred to in Article 2 cannot be considered such interests. Nor did the Court regard fishing interests as a sufficiently serious reason. On the other hand, it did regard 'the danger of flooding' and 'the protection of the coast' as constituting sufficiently serious reasons to justify measures which would adversely affect the ecology of the special protection areas, as long as the measures contemplated were confined to a strict minimum and the disturbance arising from the construction work itself did not exceed what was necessary to carry it out.

On the subject of interests which would not be regarded as sufficiently serious to justify such measures, it appeared in the *Leybucht* case that measures which would adversely affect a special protection area were possible, under certain circumstances. There the measures in question would have resulted in

---

[627] See Case C-235/04 Commission v. *Spain*, judgment of 28 June 2007, n.y.r. in the ECR, para. 23-40, where the Court attributes a similar binding effect to the IBA 98, which is an updated version of the IBA 89.

[628] Cf. Case C-96/98 Commission v. *France* [1999] ECR I-8531, paras. 48-56. Simply the rectification of an error in the classification of an SPA does not constitute a declassification.

[629] Cf. also Case C-166/97 Commission v. *France* [1999] ECR I-623, para. 48 and Case C-96/98 *Commission* v. *France* [1999] ECR I-8531, para. 41.

[630] In both its original version and as amended by the Habitats Directive, Case C-96/98 *Commission* v. *France* [1999] ECR I-8531, para. 35. In this case the drying out of wetlands, marine-farming construction and embankment works, thereby disturbing bird life, and the falling of the average population of wintering ducks were accepted as evidence that France failed to take appropriate measures to avoid deterioration of the areas concerned.

the formation of new areas of considerable ecological importance. Such 'offsetting ecological benefits' might justify measures which Article 4(4) would otherwise not allow. This strict approach to Article 4(4) by the Court in the *Leybucht* case was largely confirmed in the *Marismas de Santoña* case.

Whether these judgments are still relevant is extremely doubtful, in view of the fact that, since the expiry of the period for implementation of the Habitats Directive, Article 4(4) of the Wild Birds Directive has been replaced by the derogations in the Habitats Directive.[631] However, in its first judgment since then, in the *Lappel Bank* case, the Court seems to want to maintain a strict approach as far as possible.[632] It confirmed that Article 6(4) of the Habitats Directive only affects measures encroaching upon Special Protection Areas already designated as such. Consequently, under the Habitats Directive, SPAs must be designated only on the basis of the – above all ornithological – criteria of Article 4 of the Birds Directive.

17.1.3   Restrictions on Hunting and Trading

To restrict the hunting of, and trading in, protected species of birds the directive contains three basic provisions. First, it prohibits the deliberate[633] killing or capture of birds, the deliberate destruction of, or damage to, their nests and eggs or removal of their nests (Articles 5 and 6(1)).

Second, it provides for derogations from these general prohibitions in respect of the species referred to in the Annexes. Thus, the sale of species mentioned in Annex III and the hunting of species mentioned in Annex II may be allowed, provided certain conditions and restrictions are observed (Article 6(2) to 6(4) and Article 7). This means that the general prohibitions remain in force for the species not mentioned in the Annexes, or if the conditions and restrictions are not observed. For instance, Article 7(4) provides that Member States must ensure that species to which hunting laws apply are not hunted during the rearing season or during the various stages of reproduction (nor, in the case of migratory species, during their return to their rearing grounds). The Court requires the Member States to lay down that period with particular care:

---

[631] As will appear below, these are much wider than those formulated in the *Leybucht* case. In this respect the Habitats Directive must clearly be regarded as a retrograde step for conservation law.

[632] Case C-44/95 *Royal Society for the Protection of Birds* [1996] ECR I-3805. Confirmed in Case C-209/04 *Commission v. Austria* [2006] ECR I-2755, para. 40. See for national case law applying this doctrine: German *Bundesverwaltungsgericht* 19 May 1998, *NVwZ* 1998, 961 on the planning of the track of the Ostseeautobahn.

[633] Cf. on this Case 412/85 *Commission v. Germany* [1987] ECR 3503. See for an interpretation of 'deliberate' in Article 12 Habitats Directive the English High Court, Queen's Bench Division (Maurice Kay J) 5 November 1999 *Regina v. Secretary of State for Trade and Industry, ex parte Greenpeace* [2000] Env. L.R. 221.

'Protection against hunting activities cannot be confined to the majority of the birds of a given species, as determined by average reproductive cycles and migratory movements. It would be incompatible with the objectives of the directive if, in situations characterized by prolonged dependence of the fledglings of the parents and early migration, part of the population of a given species should fall outside the protection laid down.'[634]

A method by which the closing date for hunting was fixed by reference to the period during which migratory activity was at its peak was considered incompatible with Article 7(4).[635] The same applied to those methods which take into account the moment at which a certain percentage of birds have started to migrate, or those which consist in ascertaining the average date of the commencement of pre-mating migration. More generally the Court reached the following conclusion:

'Methods whose object or effect is to allow a certain percentage of the birds of a species to escape such protection do not comply with that provision.'

A second important question in this judgment was whether the national authorities are empowered by the directive to fix staggered closing dates for hunting which vary according to the species concerned. In principle this is not acceptable, the Court held, unless the Member State concerned can produce scientific evidence that staggering the closing dates does not impede the complete protection of the species of bird in question. As to whether the directive permits the closing of hunting to be fixed at different dates in different parts of the territory of a Member State, the Court noted that this was in itself compatible with the directive. Here, too, the only requirement is that the complete protection of migratory birds is guaranteed.

And third, under Article 9, Member States may derogate from the general prohibitions and the provisions on hunting and trading, if three conditions are met:[636]

· there must be no other satisfactory solution;
· the derogation must be for one of the reasons listed, exhaustively, in Article 9(1)(a) (*inter alia,* to prevent serious damage[637] to crops, livestock, forests, fisheries and water);
· it must specify the details laid down in Article 9(2), designed to ensure

---

[634] Case C-157/89 *Commission* v. *Italy* [1991] ECR I-57.

[635] Case C-435/92 *Association pour la protection des animaux sauvages* v. *Préfet de Maine-et-Loire en Préfet de la Loire-Atlantique* [1994] ECR I-67.

[636] Cf. on the interpretation of Article 9, Case C-10/96 *Ligue Royale Belge pour la Protection des Oiseaux and Société d'Études Ornithologiques AVES* v. *Région Wallonne* [1996] ECR I-6775, Case C-344/03 *Commission* v. *Finland* [2005] ECR I-11033 and Case C-60/05 *WWF Italia* [2006] ECR I-5083.

[637] Cf. the questionable judgment of the Scottish Court of Session *the petition of the RSPB and the Wildfowl and Wetlands Trust* v. *Secretary of State for Scotland* [2000] Env. L.R. 168.

the derogations are kept to what is strictly necessary and to enable control by the Commission. Thus the derogations must, for example, specify the species which are subject to the derogations, the means authorised for capture, and the controls which will be carried out.

The Court has devoted particular attention to the transposition of these derogations (they constitute an exhaustive list) provided for in Article 9 into national law.[638] It requires that the essential elements of Article 9 are transposed completely, clearly and unequivocally into the national rules.[639] This is necessary to ensure that the derogations are applied in a strictly controlled and selective manner. Although the provisions of Article 9 allow a fair degree of derogation from the general protective rules, they must nevertheless be applied precisely and specifically, in order to meet clearly defined conditions and specific situations.

17.1.4   Other Provisions

The directive also contains provisions on research (Article 10), prevention of damage to local flora and fauna by the introduction of exotic species of bird (Article 11), reports (Article 12) and a standstill requirement (Article 13).

Article 14 allows Member States to take stricter protective measures than provided for under the directive. This was what was at issue in the *Red Grouse* case.[640] The case concerned the question whether a Dutch prohibition on the importation of red grouse was justified by the directive, in particular given the fact that red grouse do not normally occur in the Netherlands. Red grouse is one of the species named in Annex III/1 of the directive, which means that certain marketing activities are allowed, provided the birds have been legally killed or captured or otherwise legally acquired. That the birds in question had been legally killed was not disputed. The Dutch Government invoked Article 14, which allows the Member States to adopt stricter protective measures, to justify the prohibition. According to the Court, the power to take stricter protective measures in regards of birds named in Annex III/1 is the exclusive prerogative of the Member States where they normally occur. Apparently there can thus be no question of a common responsibility for those species which are neither threatened with extinction nor migratory!

---

[638] Case 236/85 *Commission v. Netherlands* [1987] ECR 3989.

[639] Case 262/85 *Commission v. Italy* [1987] ECR 3073 and Case C-118/94 *Associazione Italiana per il WWF a.o. v. Regione Veneto* [1996] ECR I-1223.

[640] Case C-169/89 *Gourmetterie v.d. Burg* [1990] ECR I-2143.

17.2   The Habitats Directive

Like the Wild Birds Directive, Directive 92/43 on the conservation of natural habitats and of wild fauna and flora[641] – the Habitats Directive
– provides on the one hand for measures to protect conservation areas (Articles 3
to 11), and on the other for measures to protect species (Articles 12 to 16). It can
be argued that the directive is not only applicable on the territory of the Member
States, but on all areas under their jurisdiction, including the Continental Shelf
and/or any Economic and Exclusive Zone.[642]

Among the measures designed to protect conservation areas, the key
measure is the designation of special areas of conservation (SAC), with a view
to setting up a coherent European ecological network of such areas under the
title Natura 2000 (Article 3(1)). This network is to include the special protection
areas classified by the Member States under the Wild Birds Directive. Annex I
lists the various types of natural habitat of Community interest which require
conservation, while Annex II lists the species of animals and plants whose habitats require protection. The lists designate certain habitat types and species as
priority types and species.

SACs are designated according to a procedure laid down in the directive. The
Member States must propose a list indicating which natural habitat types and
which species occur in their territory that are eligible for protection. A distinction must be made between priority habitats and species and those which do not
have priority. On the basis of these national lists, the Commission is required
to establish a list of sites of Community importance (Article 4(2)). Where the
Commission finds that a national list fails to mention a site, a bilateral consultation procedure must be initiated (Article 5(1)). If the dispute remains unresolved,
the Council, acting on a proposal from the Commission, may decide to place the
site on the list. This decision must, incidentally, be taken unanimously, so that
the Member State in question can prevent the site being regarded as a site of
Community importance against its will. When a site has been adopted as a 'Site
of Community Importance' (SCI), the Member State concerned must designate it as a special area of conservation as soon as possible and within six years
at most (Article 4(4)). The entire procedure can thus take up to 12 years! The
actual designation of a site as a special area of conservation by a Member State
is of only limited importance. This is because the legal consequences of designation take effect as soon as the site is placed on the list by the Commission
(Article 4(5)).[643] Furthermore, the Court made clear that although the protective
measures of Article 6(2-4) are required only as regards sites which are on the
list of sites selected as sites of Community importance adopted by the Commission, this does not mean that the Member States are not to protect sites as soon

---

[641] OJ 1992 L 206/7.

[642] Case C-6/04 *Commission v. UK* [2005] ECR I-9017, para. 119. See also English High Court, Queen's
Bench Division (Maurice Kay J) 5 November 1999 *Regina v. Secretary of State for Trade and Industry*, ex
parte *Greenpeace* [2000] Env. L.R. 221.

[643] Except for the provisions of Article 6(1) which apply only when a SCI has been designated as a SAC.

as they propose them as sites eligible for identification as sites of Community importance on the national list transmitted to the Commission. In that case the Member States are required 'to take protective measures appropriate for the purpose of safeguarding that ecological interest'.[644]

Article 6 sets out the legal consequences of designation as a special area of conservation.[645] In the first place, Member States must establish the necessary conservation measures involving, if need be, appropriate management plans (Article 6(1)). They must also take steps to avoid the deterioration of habitats in the special areas of conservation and to avoid disturbance of the species for which the areas have been designated (Article 6(2)).[646] The Dutch *Raad van State*, applying the *Kraaijeveld* doctrine, argued in the *Buitengebied Texel* case that Article 6(2) of the Habitats Directive has direct effect.[647]

Article 6(3) provides that the competent authorities must agree to any plan or project likely to have a significant effect on the site only after having ascertained that it will not adversely affect the integrity of the site concerned.[648] Only after such an assessment has been carried out and after the opinion of the general public has been obtained may the competent national authorities agree to the plan or project.[649]

This provision is worded in such a way so as to imply that it also applies to projects and plans outside the protected area but having effects within it. In the same way as was true of the Wild Birds Directive, the protective measures appear to have some degree of external effect. Moreover, this provision involves a two-stage assessment of the environmental impact. If it cannot be excluded, on the basis of objective information, that the plan or project will have a significant effect on that site, either individually or in combination with other plans or projects, a second in-depth assessment is required.[650] The scene for this first

---

[644] Case C-117/03 *Dragaggi a.o.* [2005] ECR I-167, paras. 25-29. Cf. also Case C-244/05 *Bund Naturschutz in Bayern a.o.* [2006] ECR I-8445.

[645] Cf. in general the Commission's interpretation guide for Article 6 of the Habitats Directive: Managing Natura 2000 sites; the provisions of Article 6 of the 'Habitats' Directive 92/43/EEC, Brussels, April 2000.

[646] See, on the relation between Article 6(2) and 6(4), Case C-127/02 *Waddenvereniging and Vogelbeschermingsvereniging* [2004] ECR I-7405 (*Waddenzee*), paras. 91-96.

[647] Dutch *Raad van State* 31 March 2000 *Buitengebied Texel* [2000] AB 303. See on the possible direct effect of Article 6 with respect to areas not formally designated as a SAC, Chapter 5, section 2.1.1.

[648] In Case C-127/02 *Waddenvereniging and Vogelbeschermingsvereniging* [2004] ECR I-7405 (*Waddenzee*), para. 38, the Court held that Article 6(2) and 6(3) cannot apply concomitantly. However, the Court does not rule out a safety net-role for Article 6(2); see para. 37. For an application of this safety net role, see Case C-304/05 *Commission v. Italy*, judgment of 20 September 2007, n.y.r. in the ECR, where the Court held that on the one hand Articles 6(3) and 6(4) and on the other hand Article 6(2) were infringed (paras. 91-96).

[649] Cf. Case C-256/98 *Commission v. France* [2000] ECR I-2487.

[650] Case C-127/02 *Waddenvereniging and Vogelbeschermingsvereniging* [2004] ECR I-7405 (*Waddenzee*), para. 45.

assessment is set in the light of the precautionary principle and the high level of protection.[651] In the *Waddenzee* case the Court held that this in-depth assessment in accordance with Article 6(3):

> 'provides for an assessment procedure intended to ensure, by means of a prior examination, that a plan or project which is not directly connected with or necessary to the management of the site concerned but likely to have a significant effect on it is authorised only to the extent that it will not adversely affect the integrity of that site'.[652]

As regards the assessment that should take place, the Court has put the bar quite high indeed.[653] Pursuant to the precautionary principle, national authorities must be *certain* that no negative effects will occur. Concerning the level of certainty the Court has held that 'no reasonable scientific doubt may remain' and that the authorities have to rely on the best scientific knowledge in the field.[654] Importantly, the Court has held that Article 6(3) may be relied upon in a national court.[655]

The requirement of Article 6(3), that any plan or project likely to have a significant effect on a site may be carried out only after 'appropriate assessment' of the implications for the site in view of the site's conservation objectives, deserves special attention. Only after such an assessment has been carried out and after the opinion of the general public has been obtained may the competent national authorities agree to the plan or project.[656]

The only derogations from the requirements of Article 6(2-3) are those in Article 6(4).[657] Recourse to Article 6(4) is only possible after an assessment that

---

[651] Case C-127/02 *Waddenvereniging and Vogelbeschermingsvereniging* [2004] ECR I-7405 (*Waddenzee*), para. 44.

[652] Case C-127/02 *Waddenvereniging and Vogelbeschermingsvereniging* [2004] ECR I-7405 (*Waddenzee*), para. 34. Confirmed in Case C-239/04 *Commission v. Portugal* [2006] ECR I-10183 (*Castro Verde*), para. 19 and Case C-304/05 *Commission v. Italy*, judgment of 20 September 2007, n.y.r. in the ECR, para. 56.

[653] The original proposal basically required an EIA, this was replaced with the requirement that an assessment take place. In Case C-127/02 *Waddenvereniging and Vogelbeschermingsvereniging* [2004] ECR I-7405 (*Waddenzee*), para. 42 the Court equates this terminology with that of the EIA Directive thereby suggesting that an EIA may be the appropriate assessment. It may be noted that the EIA Directive does not necessarily apply to projects by virtue of their location in a protected area, see preamble Directive 97/11 OJ 1997 L 73/5.

[654] For example Case C-304/05 *Commission v. Italy*, judgment of 20 September 2007, n.y.r. in the ECR, para. 59. This case also provides a fine example of how the Court will examine whether or not an assessment complies with these requirements, see paras. 60-70.

[655] Case C-127/02 *Waddenvereniging and Vogelbeschermingsvereniging* [2004] ECR I-7405 (*Waddenzee*), para. 69.

[656] Cf. Case C-256/98 *Commission v. France* [2000] ECR I-2487.

[657] To determine the temporal scope of this provision the Court has adopted an approach that is similar to that developed for the EIA Directive (section 3 above), see Case C-209/04 *Commission v. Austria* [2006]

complies with the framework laid down in Article 6(3).[658] If there are imperative reasons of overriding public interest[659], including those of a social or economic nature, a plan or project may nevertheless be carried out in spite of a negative assessment of the implications for the site. In that case the Member State is required to take all compensatory measures necessary to ensure that the overall coherence of Natura 2000 is protected.[660] According to the Commission the compensation can consist of:

- recreating a habitat on a new or enlarged site, to be incorporated into Natura 2000;
- improving a habitat on part of the site or on another Natura 2000 site, proportional to the loss due to the project;
- in exceptional cases, proposing a new site under the Habitats Directive.[661]

However, where the site hosts a priority habitat or species, the derogations allowed are more limited. The second paragraph of Article 6(4) provides that the only considerations which may be raised are those relating to human health or public safety, or to beneficial consequences of primary importance for the environment. However, 'other imperative reasons of overriding public interest' may also justify derogation, though only after the Commission has given its opinion.

These 'overriding interests' clearly allow Member States more discretion to derogate from the obligations resulting from designation as a special protection area than was allowed by the Court in the *Leybucht* case. There, economic reasons were expressly excluded. As Article 6(2), (3) and (4) of the Habitats Directive expressly replaces any obligations arising under Article 4(4) of the Wild Birds Directive (Article 7), the Council clearly intended to deflect of the Court's case law under the Wild Birds Directive it was not happy with.

It is not clear what the legal consequences are if no compensatory measures can be taken which are capable of protecting the coherence of Natura 2000. The wording of Article 4, and the objective of the directive, suggest that the project could not in that case be carried through.

The Habitats Directive also prohibits the deliberate[662] capture or killing of animal species needing strict protection (listed in Annex IV), the deliberate

---

ECR I-2755, paras. 57, 58.

[658] Case C-304/05 *Commission v. Italy*, judgment of 20 September 2007, n.y.r. in the ECR, para. 83.

[659] The concept of 'imperative reasons of overriding public interest' is not defined in the directive. The Dutch *Raad van State* argued that large-scale house-building plans near Amsterdam could be considered as falling within the concept; Dutch *Raad van State* 11 January 2000 *IJmeer building* [2000] NJB 463 nr. 9.

[660] Cf. the *Leybucht* case, Case C-57/89 *Commission v. Germany* [1991] ECR I-883, though the 'offsetting ecological benefits' there were actually at the same site.

[661] See the Commission's interpretation guide for Article 6 of the Habitats Directive: Managing Natura 2000 sites; the provisions of Article 6 of the 'Habitats' Directive 92/43/EEC, Brussels, April 2000 at 41.

[662] Cf. on the notion of 'deliberate' Case C-221/04 *Commission v. Spain* [2006] ECR I-4515, para.71. Cf. also English High Court, Queen's Bench Division (Maurice Kay J) 5 November 1999 *Regina v. Secretary of*

disturbance of these species, the deliberate destruction or taking of eggs from the wild, or the deterioration or destruction of breeding sites or resting places (Article 12(1)). In principle, the keeping of, or trading in, these species is prohibited (Article 12(2)).

Article 13 provides for the protection of the plant species listed in Annex IV, requiring the prohibition of the deliberate picking, collecting, cutting, uprooting or destruction of such plants in their natural range in the wild (Article 13(1)). Keeping or trading in these species is also, in principle, prohibited.

A slightly less stringent regime applies to animal and plant species listed in Annex V. Taking them in the wild and exploiting them is not necessarily prohibited, but may be made subject to certain control measures. The most important restriction is the prohibition of indiscriminate means capable of causing local disappearance of, or serious disturbance to, populations of such species (Article 15(a)).

The derogations mentioned in Article 16 are clearly more extensive than those in the Wild Birds Directive. Derogation is allowed, among other things:

· in the interest of protecting wild fauna and flora and conserving natural habitats;
· to prevent[663] serious damage, in particular to crops, livestock, forests, fisheries and water and other types of property;
· in the interests of public health and public safety, or for other imperative reasons of overriding public interest, including those of a social or economic nature and beneficial consequences of primary importance for the environment;
· for the purpose of research and education, of repopulating and reintroducing these species and for the breeding operations necessary for these purposes, including the artificial propagation of plants.

Unlike the derogations allowed in the context of the special protection areas, the ones allowed for the protection of species are not stated to be applicable *mutatis mutandis* to the Wild Birds Directive. It must therefore be assumed that, within the scope of the Wild Birds Directive, derogations are possible only from the prohibitions on capture and marketing referred to in Article 9 of that directive.

17.3 The CITES Regulation

On 3 March 1973, the Convention on international trade in endangered species of wild fauna and flora, or CITES, was opened for signature in Washington. The Convention was intended to protect endangered species of wild fauna and flora by regulating international trade in these species. The EC is not as such a party to the Convention, which does not allow for accession by international organisations. The Convention is applied unilaterally by the

---

State for Trade and Industry, ex parte *Greenpeace* [2000] Env. L.R. 221.

[663] Cf. on the issuing of hunting permits on a *preventive* basis Case C-342/05 *Commission* v. *Finland,* judgment of 14 June 2006, n.y.r. in the ECR.

EU, first through Regulation 3626/82[664] and now by Regulation 338/97 on the protection of species of wild fauna and flora by regulating trade therein.[665] The Court has consistently held that the CITES Regulation is to be interpreted in the light of the CITES Convention.[666]

The regulation sets out four different protection regimes. Annex A corresponds to Appendix I of CITES; Annex B to Appendix II; Annex C to Appendix III, while Annex D contains species which are not listed in one of the CITES Appendices. In this respect the regulation actually has a wider scope than CITES.

The import into the EU of Annex A and B species is subject to completion of the necessary checks and the prior presentation, at the border customs office at the point of introduction, of an import *permit* issued by a management authority of the Member State of destination (Article 4(1) and(2)). The import of Annex C and D species is only subject to completion of the necessary checks and the prior presentation, at the border customs office at the point of introduction, of an import *notification* (Article 4(3) and (4)).

The import permit for Annex A and B species may only be issued when the following conditions have been met (Article 4):

· the competent scientific authority has advised that the introduction into the EU would not have a harmful effect on the conservation status of the species or on the extent of the territory occupied by the relevant population of the species;[667]

· the applicant provides documentary evidence (an export permit or a re-export certificate) that the specimens have been obtained in accordance with the legislation on the protection of the species concerned;

· the competent scientific authority is satisfied that the intended accommodation for a live specimen at the place of destination is adequately equipped to conserve and care for it properly;

· the management authority is satisfied that the specimen is not to be used for primarily commercial purposes;

· the management authority is satisfied that there are no other factors relating to the conservation of the species which militate against issuance of the import permit;

· in the case of introduction from the sea, the management authority is

---

[664] OJ 1982 L 384/1, amended many times since then.

[665] OJ 1997 L 61/1, as most recently amended by Regulation 1332/2005, OJ 2005 L 215/1. Implemented by Regulation 865/2006, OJ 2006 L 166/1.

[666] Case C-510/99 *Tridon* [2001] ECR I-7777, para. 25 and Case C-154/02 *Nilsson* [2003] ECR I-12733, para. 39.

[667] Cf. Case C-182/89 *Commission v. France* [1990] ECR I-4337. In that case, under Regulation 3626/82, the French Government contended that the only decisive factor as regards the granting of import permits was the favourable opinion of the national scientific authority in the importing country, which had been obtained in this case. This argument was rejected by the Court. This case law seems still to be valid under the new regulation.

satisfied that any live specimen will be so prepared and shipped as to minimize the risk of injury, damage to health or cruel treatment.

Any permit or certificate issued under the regulation may stipulate conditions and requirements to ensure compliance with its provisions (Article 11(3)).

Permits and certificates issued by the competent authorities of the Member States are valid throughout the EU (Article 11(1)). This does however limit their power to adopt or maintain stricter measures![668] Member States are required to recognize the rejection of applications by the competent authorities of the other Member States, where such rejection is based on the provisions of the regulation. However, this need not apply where the circumstances have significantly changed or where new evidence to support an application has become available (Article 6(4)). The *export or re-export* of Annex A, B and C species also requires a permit, which may be issued only when certain conditions have been met (Article 5). It should be noted that the regulation only applies to trade with third countries and does not affect the free movement of goods within the EU. Finally, the regulation also provides for derogations (Article 7), provisions relating to the control of commercial activities (Article 8),[669] movement of live specimens (Article 9), monitoring of compliance and investigation of infringements (Article 14), and sanctions (Article 16).

17.4   The Seal Pups Directive

Directive 83/129, concerning the importation into Member States of skins of certain seal cubs and products derived therefrom,[670] aims to protect seal cubs living outside the territory of the EU. Under the directive, Member States were required to ensure that the products listed in an Annex were not commercially imported into their territories. The directive was originally to apply from 1 October 1983 to 1 October 1985, but its duration was extended to 1 October 1989 and in 1989 the Council agreed to extend its application indefinitely.[671]

17.5   The Whales Regulation

Regulation 348/81 on common rules for imports of whales or other cetacean products[672] is intended for the conservation of the cetacean species. This calls for measures which will restrict international trade. According to

---

[668] Cf. the much more elaborate provision of Article 15 of the 'old' CITES Regulation 3626/82.

[669] See, on the interpretation of this provision, Case C-510/99 *Tridon* [2001] ECR I-7777 and Case C-154/02, *Nilsson* [2003] ECR I-12733.

[670] OJ 1983 L 91/30.

[671] Directive 89/370, OJ 1989 L 163/37.

[672] OJ 1981 L 39/1, later amended.

the preamble, these should be European-level measures and should at the same time respect the EU's international obligations.

The primary operational part of the regulation is contained in Article 1. From 1 January 1982 the introduction into the EU of the products listed in the Annex is subject to the production of an import licence. However, no such licence will be issued in respect of products to be used for commercial purposes.

17.6 The Leghold Trap Regulation

Regulation 3254/91 is intended to abolish the use of leghold traps to catch and kill certain species of animal.[673] Leghold traps are devices designed to restrain or capture an animal by means of jaws which close tightly upon one or more of the animal's limbs, thereby preventing withdrawal of the limb or limbs from the trap. The animals thus trapped and killed are used to make furs. This inhuman manner of trapping animals must have been prohibited by 1 January 1995 at the latest (Article 2). In addition the regulation prohibits the introduction into the EU of the pelts of the animal species listed in Annex I, unless the Commission has determined that, in the country where the pelts originate:

· there are adequate administrative or legislative provisions in force to prohibit the use of the leghold trap or
· the trapping methods used meet internationally agreed humane trapping standards.

Annex I names the following species, among others: the beaver, otter, wolf, sable, badger, marten, ermine, and even the musk rat.

Implementation of this controversial[674] regulation has been dogged by difficulties.[675] These were largely due to conflicts with the principal fur-exporting countries, in particular Canada, the United States and Russia.[676] Ultimately, in early 1988, the Council approved a Decision concerning the conclusion of an Agreement on international humane trapping standards between the EC, Canada and the Russian Federation.[677] The Leghold Trap Regulation is implemented in the EC by Commission Regulation 35/97.[678] A proposal to amend the Leghold Trap Regulation was withdrawn.[679]

---

[673] OJ 1991 L 308/1.

[674] Cf. Case T-228/95R S. Lehrfreund Ltd. v. Council [1996] ECR II-111.

[675] See Commission Regulation 1771/94, OJ L 1994 184/3.

[676] Cf. Harrems (1998).

[677] Decision 98/142/EG concerning the conclusion of an Agreement on international humane trapping standards between the European Community, Canada and the Russian Federation and of an Agreed Minute between Canada and the European Community concerning the signing of the said Agreement, OJ 1998 L42/40.

[678] OJ 1997 L 8/2.

[679] COM (1995) 737, see OJ 1999 C 235/7.

Bibliography

BACKES & VERSCHUUREN (1998)

C.W. Backes and J. Verschuuren, 'The Precautionary Principle in International, European and Dutch Wildlife Law' [1998] *Colorado Journal of International Environmental Law and Policy* 43-70.

BACKES ET AL. (2005)

C.W. Backes, T. van Niewerburgh and R.B.A. Koelemeijer, 'Transformation of the first Daughter Directive on air quality in several EU Member States and its application in practice' [2005] *EELR* 157-164.

BARENTS (1993)

R. Barents, 'Milieu en interne markt' [1993] *SEW* 5-29.

BETLEM (2005)

G. Betlem, 'Environmental Liability and Private Enforcement – Lessons from the European Court of Justice and European Mining Laws' [2005] 4 *YEEL* 117-148

BÄR & KRAEMER (1998)

S. Bär and R.A. Kraemer, 'European Environmental Policy after Amsterdam' [1998] *JEL* 315-330.

BOHNE & DIETZE (2004)

E. Bohne and D. Dietze, 'Pollution Prevention and Control in Europe Revisted' [2004] *EELR* 198-217.

BONGAERTS (1999)

J. Bongaerts, 'Carbon Dioxide Emmissions and Cars: An Environmental Agreement at EU level' [1999] *EELR* 101-104.

VAN CALSTER (1997)

G. van Calster, 'EC Noise Legislation and Policy' [1997] *EELR* 174-181.

VAN CALSTER (2000)

G. van Calster, 'The Legal Framework for the Regulation of Waste in the European Community' [2000] 1 *YEEL* 161-224.

VAN CALSTER & DEKETELAERE (1998)

G. van Calster and K. Deketelaere, 'Amsterdam, the Intergovernmental Conference and Greening the EU Treaty' [1998] *EELR* 13-25.

CANA (2004)

R. Cana, 'Registration, Evaluation, Authorisations and Restrictions of Chemicals: An Analysis' [2004] *EELR* 99-109.

COFFEY & FERGUSSON (1997)

C. Coffey and M. Fergusson, 'European Community Funding for Sustainable Development: the Role of the Cohesion Fund' [1997] *RECIEL* 77-85.

COMTE (2005)

F. Comte, 'European Environmental Criminal Law: the Latest Developments' [2005] 4 *YEEL* 209-245.

COMTE & KRÄMER (2004)

F. Comte & L. Krämer (eds), *Environmental Crime in Europe; Rules of Sanctions* (Groningen 2004).

DAVIES (2004)

P.G.G. Davies, *European Union Environmental Law; An Introduction to Key Selected Issues* (Aldershot 2004).

DE SADELEER (2005)

N. de Sadeleer, *Environmental Principles: From Political Slogans to Legal Rules* (Oxford 2005).

DE SADELEER (2005A)

N. de Sadeleer, 'EC Law and Biodiversity' in: R. Macrory (ed.), *Reflections on 30 Years of EU Environmental Law; A High Level of Protection?* (Groningen 2005) 351-370.

DE SADELEER (2006)

N. de Sadeleer, 'The Precautionary Principle in EC Health and Environmental Law' [2006] *European Law Journal* 139-172.

DHONDT (2005)

N. Dhondt, 'Integration of Environmental Protection into the EC Energy Policy' [2005] 4 *YEEL* 247-302.

DOPPELHAMMER (2000)

M. Doppelhammer, 'More Difficult than Finding the Way Round Chinatown? – The IPPC Directive and its Implementation' [2000] *EELR* 199-206, 246-252.

FAURE (1998)

M. Faure, 'Harmonisation of Environmental Law and Market Integration: Harmonising for the Wrong Reasons?' [1998] *EELR* 169-175.

FRENCH (1998)

D. French, '1997 Kyoto Protocol to the 1992 UN framework Convention on Climate Change' [1998] *JEL* 227-239.

FRENZ (1999)

W. Frenz, 'Freiwillige Selbstverpflichtungen/Umweltverein-barungen zur Reduzierung des Energieverbrauchs im Kontext des Gemeinschaftsrecht' [1999] *EuR* 27-48.

GRIMEAUD (2001)

D. Grimeaud, 'Reforming EU Water Law: Towards Sustainability' [2001] *EELR* 41-51.

GYSELEN (1993)

L. Gyselen, 'The emerging interface between competition policy and environmental policy in the EEC', IBA Conference papers (London 1993).

HANNEQUART (1993)

J.P. Hannequart, *Het Europees recht inzake afvalstoffen* (Brussel 1993).

HARREMS (1998)

N. Harrems, 'The Leghold Trap Regulation and Potential Pitfalls During the Dutch Presidency of the EU' [1998] *EELR* 7-12.

HEYVAERT (2006)

V. Heyvaert, 'Guidance without constraint: assessing the impact of the precautionary principle on the European Community's chemicals policy' [2006] 6 *YEEL* 27-60.

HILSON (2005)

C. Hilson, 'The Role of Discretion in EC Law on Non-Contractual Liability' [2005] *CMLRev.* 677-695.

HOLDER (1996)

J. Holder, 'Case law analysis. A dead end for direct effect?: prospects for enforcement of European Community environmental law by individuals. Comitato di Coordinamento per la Difesa della Cava and Others v Regione Lombardia and Others' [1996] *JEL* 313-335.

HOLDER (2004)

J. Holder, *Environmental Assessment* (Oxford 2004).

JANS (2006)

J.H. Jans, 'Did Baron von Munchausen ever visit Århus? Some Critical Remarks on the Proposal For A Regulation on the Application of the Provisions of the Aarhus Convention to EC Institutions and Bodies' in: R. Macrory (ed.), *Reflections on 30 Years of EU Environmental Law; A High Level of Protection?* (Groningen 2005) 475-490.

JANS ET AL. (2007)

J.H. Jans, R. de Lange, S. Prechal and R.J.G.M. Widdershoven, *Europeanisation of Public Law* (Groningen 2007).

JANS & DE JONG (2002)

J.H. Jans and M. de Jong, 'Somewhere between Direct Effect and Rewe/Comet; some remarks on Dutch public law, procedural defects and the EIA Directive' in: K.H. Ladeur (ed.) *The Europeanisation of Administrative Law: Transforming National Decision-Making Procedures* (Aldershot 2002) 68-93.

JARVIS (1997)

M. Jarvis, *Application of EC Law on the Free Movement of Goods by the National Courts of Member States* (Oxford 1997).

JENDROSKA (2005)

J. Jendroska, 'Public Information and Participation in EC Environmental Law; Origins, Milestones and Trends' in: R. Macrory (ed.), *Reflections on 30 Years of EU Environmental Law; A High Level of Protection?* (Groningen 2005) 63-84.

JONES & SUFRIN (2004)

B. Jones and A. Sufrin, *EC Competition Law* (Oxford 2004).

KOCH & ZIEHM (2005)

H.-J. Koch & C. Ziehm, 'Marine Safety and Protection of the Marine Environment' in: R. Macrory (ed.), *Reflections on 30 Years of EU Environmental Law; A High Level of Protection?* (Groningen 2005) 309-324.

KRÄMER (1993)

L. Krämer, 'Environmental Protection and Article 30 EEC Treaty'
[1993] CMLRev. 111-143.

KRÄMER (1993)

L. Krämer, European Environmental Law Casebook (London 1993).

KRÄMER (2007)

L. Krämer, EC Environmental Law (London 2007).

KRÄMER (2003A)

L. Krämer, 'Vertraulichkeit und Öffentlichkeit Europäisches
Vorverfahren und Zugang zu Informationen', in: L. Krämer (ed.),
Recht und Um-Welt; Essays in Honour of Prof. Dr. Gerd Winter
(Groningen 2003) 153-170.

KRÄMER (2006)

Case note Environmental Crime; L. Krämer [2006] JEL 277-288.

LADEUR & PRELLE (2002)

K.-H. Ladeur and R. Prelle, 'Administrative Court monitoring
of procedural errors in environmental impact assessments – a
European-law and comparative-law view' in: K.H. Ladeur (ed.) The
Europeanisation of Administrative Law: Transforming National Decision-
Making Procedures (Aldershot 2002).

LAVRANOS (2002)

N. Lavranos, 'Multilateral Environmental Agreements: Who Makes the
Binding Decisions?' [2002] EELR 44-50.

LAVRANOS (2006)

N. Lavranos, 'The MOX Plant Judgment of the ECJ: How Exclusive is
the Jurisdiction of the ECJ?' [2006] EELR 291-296.

LEE (2005)

M. Lee, EU Environmental Law: Challenges, Change and Decision-
Making (Oxford 2005).

MACRORY (2004)

R. Macrory (ed.), Principles of European Environmental Law (Groningen
2004).

MACRORY (2005)

R. Macrory (ed.), Reflections on 30 Years of EU Environmental Law; A
High Level of Protection? (Groningen 2005).

MACRORY (2005A)

R. Macrory, 'The Enforcement of EU Environmental Law; Some
Proposals for Reform', in: R. Macrory (ed.), Reflections on 30 Years of
EU Environmental Law; A High Level of Protection? (Groningen 2005)
385-395.

MACRORY & TURNER (2002)

R. Macrory, S. Turner, 'Participatory Rights, Transboundary
Environmental Governance and EC Law' [2002] CMLRev. 489-522

MAHMOUDI (2005)

S. Mahmoudi, 'Integration of Environmental Considerations into Transport', in: R. Macrory (ed.), *Reflections on 30 Years of EU Environmental Law; A High Level of Protection?* (Groningen 2005) 185-196.

MARÍN DURÁN & MORGERA (2006)

G. Marín Durán & E. Morgera, 'Towards Environmental Integration in EC External Relations? A Comparative Analysis of Selected Association Agreements' [2006] 6 *YEEL* 179-210.

MARR & SCHWEMER (2003)

S. Marr and A. Schwemer, 'The Precautionary Principle in German Environmental Law' [2003] 3 *YEEL* 125-148.

MARSDEN & DE MULDER (2005)

S. Marsden and J. de Mulder, 'Strategic Environmental Asssessment and Sustainability in Europe – How Bright is the Future?' [2005] *RECIEL* 50-62.

MCMANUS (2005)

F. McManus, 'European Noise Law' in: R. Macrory (ed.), *Reflections on 30 Years of EU Environmental Law; A High Level of Protection?* (Groningen 2005) 373-382.

MONTINI (2005)

M. Montini, 'International Trade and Environmental Protection; The Treatment of National Measures Introducing Trade Restrictions on Environmental Grounds under WTO Law', in: R. Macrory (ed.), *Reflections on 30 Years of EU Environmental Law; A High Level of Protection?* (Groningen 2005) 531-552.

MORENO (2005)

A-M. Moreno, 'Environmental Impact Assessment in EC Law; A Critical Appraisal' in:, R. Macrory (ed.), *Reflections on 30 Years of EU Environmental Law; A High Level of Protection?* (Groningen 2005) 43-60.

MORTELMANS (2002)

K.J.M. Mortelmans, 'The Relationship Between the Treaty Rules and Community Measures for the Establishment and Functioning of the Internal Market – Towards a Concordance Rule' [2002] *CMLRev.* 1303-1346.

NOTARO (2000)

N. Notaro, 'European Community Waste Movements: the Copenhagen Waste Case' [2000] *EELR* 304-312.

OLIVER (1999)

P. Oliver, 'Some Further Reflections on the Scope of Articles 28-30' [1999] *CMLRev.* 783-806.

PAGH (2005)

P. Pagh, 'The Battle on Environmental Policy Competences; Challenging the Stricter Approach: Stricter Might Lead to Weaker

Protection', in: R. Macrory (ed.), *Reflections on 30 Years of EU Environmental Law; A High Level of Protection?* (Groningen 2005) 3-16.

PALLEMAERTS (2005)

M. Pallemaerts, 'EC Chemicals Legislation: A Horizontal Perspective' in: R. Macrory (ed.), *Reflections on 30 Years of EU Environmental Law; A High Level of Protection?* (Groningen 2005) 199-230.

PEETERS & DEKETELAERE (2006)

M. Peeters, K. Deketelaere (eds.), *EU Climate Change Policy; The Challenge of New Regulatory Initiatives* (Cheltenham 2006).

PRECHAL (2005)

S. Prechal, *Directives in European Community Law* (Oxford 2005).

PRECHAL & HANCHER (2002)

S. Prechal and L. Hancher, 'Individual Environmental Rights: Conceptual Pollution in EU Environmental Law' [2002] 2 *YEEL* 89 *et seq.*

POCKLINGTON (2006)

D. Pocklington, 'The Significance of the Proposed Changes to the Waste Framework Directive' [2006] *EELR* 75-87.

PONS (2001)

J.F. Pons, *European Competition Policy for the Recycling Markets*, speech delivered at the Pro Europe International Congres 2001, to be found on http://ec.europa.eu/comm/competition/speeches/text/sp2001_015_en.pdf.

REVESZ (2000)

R.L. Revesz, 'Environmental Regulation in Federal Systems' [2000] 1 *YEEL* 1-35.

RODI (2006)

M. Rodi, 'Motorway Tolls and Sustainable Transport Policy' [2006] 6 *YEEL* 1-26.

ROLLER (2005)

G. Roller, 'Liability' in: R. Macrory (ed.), *Reflections on 30 Years of EU Environmental Law; A High Level of Protection?* (Groningen 2005) 129-140.

SCOTFORD (2007)

E. Scotford, 'Trash or Treasure: Policy Tensions in EC Waste Regulation' [2007] *JEL* 1-22.

SCOTT (2000)

J. Scott, 'Flexibility in the Implementation of EC Environmental Law' [2000] 1 *YEEL* 37-60.

SCHRAUWEN (2006)

Case note penalty payments; Annette Schrauwen [2006] *JEL* 289-299.

SEINEN (2005)

A.T. Seinen, 'Staatssteun voor milieubescherming: uitzonderingen op het verbod' [2005] *M&R* 66-71.

SEVENSTER (1992)

H.G. Sevenster, *Milieubeleid en Gemeenschapsrecht* (Leiden 1992).

SEVENSTER (2000)

H.G. Sevenster, 'The Environmental Guarantee After Amsterdam: Does the Emperor Have New Clothes?' [2000] 1 *YEEL* 291-310.

SHEATE (2003)

W.R. Sheate, 'The EC Directive on Strategic Environmental Assessment: A Much-Needed Boost for Environmental Integration' [2003] *EELR* 331-347.

SOMSEN (2003)

H. Somsen, 'Current Issues of Implementation, Compliance and Enforcement of EC Environmental Law; A Critical Analysis', in: L. Krämer (ed.), *Recht und Um-Welt; Essays in Honour of Prof. Dr. Gerd Winter* (Groningen 2003) 415-428.

STRECK & FREESTONE (2005)

C. Streck and D. Freestone, 'The EU and Climate Change' in: R. Macrory (ed.), *Reflections on 30 Years of EU Environmental Law; A High Level of Protection?* (Groningen 2005) 87-106.

TEMMINK (2000)

H. Temmink, 'From Danish Bottles to Danish Bees: The Dynamics of Free Movement of Goods and Environmental Protection – a Case Law Analysis' [2000] 1 *YEEL* 61-102.

TIEMAN (2003)

J.R.C. Tieman, *Naar een nuttige toepassing van het begrip afvalstof : over de betekenis en toepassing van kernbegrippen van internationaal, Europees en Nederlands afvalstoffenrecht* (Deventer 2003).

TROUWBORST (2006)

A. Trouwborst, *Precautionary Rights and Duties of States* (Leiden/Boston 2006).

VANDEKERCKHOVE (1994)

K. Vandekerckhove, 'The Polluter Pays Principle in the European Community' [1993] *YEL* 201-262.

VANDAMME (2005)

T.A.J.A. Vandamme, *The Invalid Directive; The Legal Authority of a Union Act Requiring Domestic Law Making* (Groningen 2005).

VAN RIJSWICK (2003)

H.F.M.W. van Rijswick, *The Water Framework Directive; Implementation into German and Dutch Law* (Utrecht 2003).

VEDDER (2002)

H.H.B. Vedder, *Competition Law, Environmental Policy and Producer Resposibility* (Groningen 2002).

VEDDER (2003)

H.H.B. Vedder, *Competition Law and Environmental Protection in Europe – Towards Sustainability?* (Groningen 2003).

VERSCHUUREN (2000)

J. Verschuuren, 'EC Environmental Law and Self-Regulation in het Member States: in Search of a Legislative Framework' [2000] 1 *YEEL* 103-121.

VERSCHUUREN (2005)

J. Verschuuren, 'Shellfish for Fishermen or for Birds? Article 6 Habitats Directive and the Precautionary Principle 17' [2005] *JEL* 265-283.

VOGELEZANG-STOUTE (1999)

E.M. Vogelezang-Stoute, 'European Community Legislation on the Marketing and Use of Pesticides' [1999] *RECIEL* 144-151.

VOGELEZANG-STOUTE (2004)

E.M. Vogelezang-Stoute, *Bestrijdingsmiddelenrecht* (Deventer 2004).

WÄGENBAUER & WAINWRIGHT (1997)

R. Wägenbauer and R. Wainwright, 'European Community Energy and Environment Policy' [1996] *YEL* 59-86.

WARD (2000)

A. Ward, 'Judicial Review of Environmental Misconduct in the European Community: Problems, Prospects and Strategies' [2000] 1 *YEEL* 137-159.

WENNERÅS (2004)

P. Wennerås, 'State Liability for Decisions of Courts of Last Instance in Environmental Cases' [2004] *JEL* 329-340.

WENNERÅS (2006)

P. Wennerås, 'A New Dawn for Commission under Articles 226 and 228 EC: General and Persistent (GAP) Infringements, Lump Sums and Penalty Payments' [2006] *CMLRev.* 31-62.

WENNERÅS (2007)

P. Wennerås, *The Enforcement of EC Environmental Law* (Oxford 2007).

WILLIAMS (2005)

R. Williams, 'Community Development Cooperation Law, Sustainable Development and the Convention on Europe: From Dislocation to Consistency?' [2005] 4 *YEEL* 303-375.

WIERS (2002)

J. Wiers, *Trade and Environment in the EC and the WTO; A Legal Analysis* (Groningen 2002).

WILSON (1998)

G. Wilson, 'The Biocidal Products Directive' [1998] *EELR* 204-206.

WINTER (1996)

G. Winter, 'Subsidiarität und Deregulierung im Gemeinschaftsrecht' [1996] *EuR* 247-269.

WINTER (1998)

G. Winter, 'Die Sperrwirkung von Gemeinschaftssekundärrecht für einzelstaatliche Regelungen des Binnenmarkts mit besonderer Berücksichtigung von Art. 130t EGV' [1998] *DöV* 377-381.

WINTER (1999)

G. Winter, 'Individualrechtsschutz im deutschen Umweltrecht unter dem Einfluß des Gemeinschaftsrechts' [1999] *NVwZ* 467-475.

WINTER (2000)

G. Winter, 'Die Steuerung grenzüberschreitender Abfallströme' [2000] *DVBl.* 657-669.

WINTER (2004)

G. Winter, 'The Legal Nature of Environmental Principles in International, EC and German Law', in: R. Macrory (ed.) *Principles of European Environmental Law* (Groningen 2004) 10-28.

WINTER (2005)

G. Winter, 'Matching Tasks and Competences in the EC Multi-level Environmental Administration', in: R. Macrory (ed.), *Reflections on 30 Years of EU Environmental Law; A High Level of Protection?* (Groningen 2005) 399-414.

WHISH (2003)

R. Whish, *Competition Law* (London 2003).

WOLFF (2002)

N. Wolff, *Fisheries and the Environment: Public International and European Community Law Aspects* (Baden-Baden 2002).

Table of Cases

European Court on Human Rights

National Case Law

Index